T0211006

Lecture Notes in Computer Science 12795

More information about this subseries at http://www.springer.com/series/7409

Matthias Rauterberg (Ed.)

Culture and Computing

Design Thinking and Cultural Computing

9th International Conference, C&C 2021
Held as Part of the 23rd HCI International Conference, HCII 2021
Virtual Event, July 24–29, 2021
Proceedings, Part II

 Springer

Editor
Matthias Rauterberg
Eindhoven University of Technology
Eindhoven, The Netherlands

ISSN 0302-9743   ISSN 1611-3349   (electronic)
Lecture Notes in Computer Science
ISBN 978-3-030-77430-1   ISBN 978-3-030-77431-8   (eBook)
https://doi.org/10.1007/978-3-030-77431-8

LNCS Sublibrary: SL3 – Information Systems and Applications, incl. Internet/Web, and HCI

This Springer imprint is published by the registered company Springer Nature Switzerland AG
The registered company address is: Gewerbestrasse 11, 6330 Cham, Switzerland

Foreword

Human-Computer Interaction (HCI) is acquiring an ever-increasing scientific and industrial importance, and having more impact on people's everyday life, as an ever-growing number of human activities are progressively moving from the physical to the digital world. This process, which has been ongoing for some time now, has been dramatically accelerated by the COVID-19 pandemic. The HCI International (HCII) conference series, held yearly, aims to respond to the compelling need to advance the exchange of knowledge and research and development efforts on the human aspects of design and use of computing systems.

The 23rd International Conference on Human-Computer Interaction, HCI International 2021 (HCII 2021), was planned to be held at the Washington Hilton Hotel, Washington DC, USA, during July 24–29, 2021. Due to the COVID-19 pandemic and with everyone's health and safety in mind, HCII 2021 was organized and run as a virtual conference. It incorporated the 21 thematic areas and affiliated conferences listed on the following page.

A total of 5222 individuals from academia, research institutes, industry, and governmental agencies from 81 countries submitted contributions, and 1276 papers and 241 posters were included in the proceedings to appear just before the start of the conference. The contributions thoroughly cover the entire field of HCI, addressing major advances in knowledge and effective use of computers in a variety of application areas. These papers provide academics, researchers, engineers, scientists, practitioners, and students with state-of-the-art information on the most recent advances in HCI. The volumes constituting the set of proceedings to appear before the start of the conference are listed in the following pages.

The HCI International (HCII) conference also offers the option of 'Late Breaking Work' which applies both for papers and posters, and the corresponding volume(s) of the proceedings will appear after the conference. Full papers will be included in the 'HCII 2021 - Late Breaking Papers' volumes of the proceedings to be published in the Springer LNCS series, while 'Poster Extended Abstracts' will be included as short research papers in the 'HCII 2021 - Late Breaking Posters' volumes to be published in the Springer CCIS series.

The present volume contains papers submitted and presented in the context of the 9th International Conference on Culture and Computing (C&C 2021) affiliated conference to HCII 2021. I would like to thank the Chair, Matthias Rauterberg, for his invaluable contribution in its organization and the preparation of the Proceedings, as well as the members of the program board for their contributions and support. This year, the C&C affiliated conference has focused on topics related to ICT for cultural heritage and art, visitors' experiences in digital culture, Design Thinking in cultural contexts, and applications in Cultural Computing in Digital Humanities and New Media.

I would also like to thank the Program Board Chairs and the members of the Program Boards of all thematic areas and affiliated conferences for their contribution towards the highest scientific quality and overall success of the HCI International 2021 conference.

This conference would not have been possible without the continuous and unwavering support and advice of Gavriel Salvendy, founder, General Chair Emeritus, and Scientific Advisor. For his outstanding efforts, I would like to express my appreciation to Abbas Moallem, Communications Chair and Editor of HCI International News.

July 2021   Constantine Stephanidis

HCI International 2021 Thematic Areas and Affiliated Conferences

Thematic Areas

- HCI: Human-Computer Interaction
- HIMI: Human Interface and the Management of Information

Affiliated Conferences

- EPCE: 18th International Conference on Engineering Psychology and Cognitive Ergonomics
- UAHCI: 15th International Conference on Universal Access in Human-Computer Interaction
- VAMR: 13th International Conference on Virtual, Augmented and Mixed Reality
- CCD: 13th International Conference on Cross-Cultural Design
- SCSM: 13th International Conference on Social Computing and Social Media
- AC: 15th International Conference on Augmented Cognition
- DHM: 12th International Conference on Digital Human Modeling and Applications in Health, Safety, Ergonomics and Risk Management
- DUXU: 10th International Conference on Design, User Experience, and Usability
- DAPI: 9th International Conference on Distributed, Ambient and Pervasive Interactions
- HCIBGO: 8th International Conference on HCI in Business, Government and Organizations
- LCT: 8th International Conference on Learning and Collaboration Technologies
- ITAP: 7th International Conference on Human Aspects of IT for the Aged Population
- HCI-CPT: 3rd International Conference on HCI for Cybersecurity, Privacy and Trust
- HCI-Games: 3rd International Conference on HCI in Games
- MobiTAS: 3rd International Conference on HCI in Mobility, Transport and Automotive Systems
- AIS: 3rd International Conference on Adaptive Instructional Systems
- C&C: 9th International Conference on Culture and Computing
- MOBILE: 2nd International Conference on Design, Operation and Evaluation of Mobile Communications
- AI-HCI: 2nd International Conference on Artificial Intelligence in HCI

List of Conference Proceedings Volumes Appearing Before the Conference

1. LNCS 12762, Human-Computer Interaction: Theory, Methods and Tools (Part I), edited by Masaaki Kurosu
2. LNCS 12763, Human-Computer Interaction: Interaction Techniques and Novel Applications (Part II), edited by Masaaki Kurosu
3. LNCS 12764, Human-Computer Interaction: Design and User Experience Case Studies (Part III), edited by Masaaki Kurosu
4. LNCS 12765, Human Interface and the Management of Information: Information Presentation and Visualization (Part I), edited by Sakae Yamamoto and Hirohiko Mori
5. LNCS 12766, Human Interface and the Management of Information: Information-rich and Intelligent Environments (Part II), edited by Sakae Yamamoto and Hirohiko Mori
6. LNAI 12767, Engineering Psychology and Cognitive Ergonomics, edited by Don Harris and Wen-Chin Li
7. LNCS 12768, Universal Access in Human-Computer Interaction: Design Methods and User Experience (Part I), edited by Margherita Antona and Constantine Stephanidis
8. LNCS 12769, Universal Access in Human-Computer Interaction: Access to Media, Learning and Assistive Environments (Part II), edited by Margherita Antona and Constantine Stephanidis
9. LNCS 12770, Virtual, Augmented and Mixed Reality, edited by Jessie Y. C. Chen and Gino Fragomeni
10. LNCS 12771, Cross-Cultural Design: Experience and Product Design Across Cultures (Part I), edited by P. L. Patrick Rau
11. LNCS 12772, Cross-Cultural Design: Applications in Arts, Learning, Well-being, and Social Development (Part II), edited by P. L. Patrick Rau
12. LNCS 12773, Cross-Cultural Design: Applications in Cultural Heritage, Tourism, Autonomous Vehicles, and Intelligent Agents (Part III), edited by P. L. Patrick Rau
13. LNCS 12774, Social Computing and Social Media: Experience Design and Social Network Analysis (Part I), edited by Gabriele Meiselwitz
14. LNCS 12775, Social Computing and Social Media: Applications in Marketing, Learning, and Health (Part II), edited by Gabriele Meiselwitz
15. LNAI 12776, Augmented Cognition, edited by Dylan D. Schmorrow and Cali M. Fidopiastis
16. LNCS 12777, Digital Human Modeling and Applications in Health, Safety, Ergonomics and Risk Management: Human Body, Motion and Behavior (Part I), edited by Vincent G. Duffy
17. LNCS 12778, Digital Human Modeling and Applications in Health, Safety, Ergonomics and Risk Management: AI, Product and Service (Part II), edited by Vincent G. Duffy

18. LNCS 12779, Design, User Experience, and Usability: UX Research and Design (Part I), edited by Marcelo Soares, Elizabeth Rosenzweig, and Aaron Marcus
19. LNCS 12780, Design, User Experience, and Usability: Design for Diversity, Well-being, and Social Development (Part II), edited by Marcelo M. Soares, Elizabeth Rosenzweig, and Aaron Marcus
20. LNCS 12781, Design, User Experience, and Usability: Design for Contemporary Technological Environments (Part III), edited by Marcelo M. Soares, Elizabeth Rosenzweig, and Aaron Marcus
21. LNCS 12782, Distributed, Ambient and Pervasive Interactions, edited by Norbert Streitz and Shin'ichi Konomi
22. LNCS 12783, HCI in Business, Government and Organizations, edited by Fiona Fui-Hoon Nah and Keng Siau
23. LNCS 12784, Learning and Collaboration Technologies: New Challenges and Learning Experiences (Part I), edited by Panayiotis Zaphiris and Andri Ioannou
24. LNCS 12785, Learning and Collaboration Technologies: Games and Virtual Environments for Learning (Part II), edited by Panayiotis Zaphiris and Andri Ioannou
25. LNCS 12786, Human Aspects of IT for the Aged Population: Technology Design and Acceptance (Part I), edited by Qin Gao and Jia Zhou
26. LNCS 12787, Human Aspects of IT for the Aged Population: Supporting Everyday Life Activities (Part II), edited by Qin Gao and Jia Zhou
27. LNCS 12788, HCI for Cybersecurity, Privacy and Trust, edited by Abbas Moallem
28. LNCS 12789, HCI in Games: Experience Design and Game Mechanics (Part I), edited by Xiaowen Fang
29. LNCS 12790, HCI in Games: Serious and Immersive Games (Part II), edited by Xiaowen Fang
30. LNCS 12791, HCI in Mobility, Transport and Automotive Systems, edited by Heidi Krömker
31. LNCS 12792, Adaptive Instructional Systems: Design and Evaluation (Part I), edited by Robert A. Sottilare and Jessica Schwarz
32. LNCS 12793, Adaptive Instructional Systems: Adaptation Strategies and Methods (Part II), edited by Robert A. Sottilare and Jessica Schwarz
33. LNCS 12794, Culture and Computing: Interactive Cultural Heritage and Arts (Part I), edited by Matthias Rauterberg
34. LNCS 12795, Culture and Computing: Design Thinking and Cultural Computing (Part II), edited by Matthias Rauterberg
35. LNCS 12796, Design, Operation and Evaluation of Mobile Communications, edited by Gavriel Salvendy and June Wei
36. LNAI 12797, Artificial Intelligence in HCI, edited by Helmut Degen and Stavroula Ntoa
37. CCIS 1419, HCI International 2021 Posters - Part I, edited by Constantine Stephanidis, Margherita Antona, and Stavroula Ntoa

http://2021.hci.international/proceedings

9th International Conference on Culture and Computing (C&C 2021)

Program Board Chair: **Matthias Rauterberg**, *Eindhoven University of Technology, Netherlands*

- Juan Barcelo, Spain
- Melodee Beals, UK
- Emmanuel G. Blanchard, Canada
- Jean-Pierre Briot, France
- Erik Champion, Australia
- Torkil Clemmensen, Denmark
- Fabiana Lopes Da Cunha, Brazil
- Jean-Gabriel Ganascia, France
- Halina Gottlieb, Sweden
- D. Fox Harrell, USA
- Susan Hazan, Israel
- Rüdiger Heimgärtner, Germany
- Yiyuan Huang, China
- Isto Huvila, Sweden
- Toru Ishida, Japan
- Katerina Kabassi, Greece
- Sagini Keengwe, USA
- Gertraud Koch, Germany
- Marcia Langton, Australia
- Susan Liggett, UK
- Donghui Lin, Japan
- Lev Manovich, USA
- Yohei Murakami, Japan
- Ryohei Nakatsu, Japan
- Jong-Il Park, Korea
- Robert Parthesius, UAE
- Dilip A. Patel, India
- Claus Pias, Germany
- Antonio Rodà, Italy
- Kasper Rodil, Denmark
- Pertti Saariluoma, Finland
- Hooman Samani, UK
- Vibeke Sorensen, Singapore
- William Swartout, USA
- Daniel Thalmann, Switzerland
- Claudia Trillo, UK
- Frans Vogelaar, Germany
- Michael Walsh, Singapore
- Jianjiang Wang, China
- Lin Zhang, China

The full list with the Program Board Chairs and the members of the Program Boards of all thematic areas and affiliated conferences is available online at:

http://www.hci.international/board-members-2021.php

HCI International 2022

The 24th International Conference on Human-Computer Interaction, HCI International 2022, will be held jointly with the affiliated conferences at the Gothia Towers Hotel and Swedish Exhibition & Congress Centre, Gothenburg, Sweden, June 26 – July 1, 2022. It will cover a broad spectrum of themes related to Human-Computer Interaction, including theoretical issues, methods, tools, processes, and case studies in HCI design, as well as novel interaction techniques, interfaces, and applications. The proceedings will be published by Springer. More information will be available on the conference website: http://2022.hci.international/:

General Chair
Prof. Constantine Stephanidis
University of Crete and ICS-FORTH
Heraklion, Crete, Greece
Email: general_chair@hcii2022.org

http://2022.hci.international/

Contents – Part II

Digital Humanities, New Media and Culture

Perspectives on Cultural Computing

Contents – Part I

Technology and Art

Visitors' Experiences in Digital Culture

Design Thinking in Cultural Contexts

Digital Literacy-Based User Experience Design for Medication-Allergy Patients Care

Sunghee Ahn[1]([✉]) and Min-Gyu Kang[2]

[1] School of Design Convergence, Hongik University, Sejong, South Korea
sahn2002@hongik.ac.kr
[2] Department of Internal Medicine, Chungbuk National University Hospital,
Cheongju, South Korea

Abstract. Digital literacy is not based solely on an understanding of technology, but is highly influenced by social and cultural context. This study focused on developing mobile applications for medication allergy care for respiratory-related patients in daily life, which is based on inclusiveness and digital literacy.

With COVID-19, there are growing needs to share the role of primary care hospitals, with, for example GPs, and self-care symptom records applications, in order to supplement the saturated medical service of general hospitals. The mobile application of 'medication-allergy record for respiratory-related patients' which is developed in this study considers cultural digital literacy and provides the solutions to the local people's needs. For these objectives this study has conducted field research and analyzed the influential factors and needs in digital interaction, by interviewing 120 outpatients of respiratory and allergic internal medicine department in general hospital in Cheongju. Based on this, the direction of the mobile application has developed new information architecture and relevant wire-frames.

This study will contribute to the future direction of non-face communication in health-care service by suggesting a self-data-producing digital health care service by bridging the personal culture and user-centered technology.

Keywords: UX design · Digital literacy · Digital health-care service

1 Introduction

1.1 Research Hypothesis

The potential lack of digital literacy in older citizens is considered in this paper in the context of social inclusiveness, and that by being aware of the challenges older citizens are facing in modern society we can consider more clearly the role which digital literacy, and its relation to learning, may play in addressing their predicament. Because of the particular uncertainties of the role of our seniors in society, digital literacy can be of great value as a means of social involvement and assertion. Gaining command of digital literacy senior citizens can retain a hold on the shape of their lives in an era of increasing uncertainty. In a society where intergenerational uncertainty is probably greater than

© Springer Nature Switzerland AG 2021
M. Rauterberg (Ed.): HCII 2021, LNCS 12795, pp. 3–16, 2021.
https://doi.org/10.1007/978-3-030-77431-8_1

it has ever been, it can also offer the possibility of a bridge of understanding across generations.

With above notion, this paper presents an alternative digital healthcare service application of asthma related allergy control based on social inclusiveness, designed for senior generations who could easily be excluded by the rapid change of current digital technology environment.

1.2 Research Process

The research process of this paper follows user experience study model influenced and revised from design thinking's double diamond model which originally from British Design Council. Since it was a collaborative research between UX design field and medical practice filed, the research has two perspectives. In this paper only covers HCI perspective remaining medical and biological fields. Research process and steps are shown in the diagram below (Fig. 1).

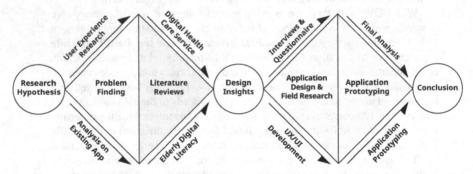

Fig. 1. Research process

2 Digital Literacy and Social Inclusiveness

2.1 Digital Literacy

Health literacy is complex meaning which came from understanding of health information in order to make judgments and take decisions in daily life concerning healthcare, disease prevention and quality of life [1]. The notion of literacy is important in enabling skills to be placed within a context of meaning and social action. Bélisle (2006) describes the evolution of literacy concepts in terms of three models. The functional model views literacy as the mastery of simple cognitive and practical skills, and ranges from the simple view of literacy as the mechanical skills of reading and writing to a more developed approach (evinced by e.g. UNESCO 2006) regarding literacy as the skills required to function effectively within the community. The intellectual empowerment model argues that: Literacy not only provides means and skills to deal with written texts and numbers within specific cultural and ideological contexts, but it brings a profound enrichment and eventually entails a transformation of human thinking capacities [2]. This intellectual empowerment happens whenever mankind endows itself with new cognitive tools, such as writing, or with new technical instruments, such as those that digital technology has made possible [3].

Society is infused with the digital, and the understanding of the COVID-19 pandemic relationship with digital usage is essential. It is necessary to deal with the digital when a person engages with society via digitized information or data. Therefore, the level of digital literacy is highly related to health literacy as well as media literacy. Digital literacy is also, for everybody, a means of engagement between the individual and society through which actions are guided, social patterns develop and change, and the social order evolves. In viewing literacy within the context of a digitally-infused society as, at one level functional, at another socially engaged, and at a third as transformative, we can see it as a powerful tool for the individual and the group to understand their own relationship to the digital, that is, to be aware of the role of the digital in their own development, and to control it, that is, to place the digital at the disposal of their own goals and visions [4]. The term digital literacy was popularized by Glister in his book, Digital Literacy. He emphasizes that the differences between digital information media and conversational print media and there are some more definitions on the term in the media communication and education side arguments. In the digital healthcare fields, inclusive perspective of digital literacy needs to be discussed and considered in user experience point of view.

2.2 Digital Literacy of Elderly Generation

Technology has not changed the notion of what learning is, but it has opened up more avenues in thinking how it can be done. To develop the strategy and design direction for elderly digitally, design should focus on the elderly's digital usage, the areas in which digital activity is socially meaningful and contribute directly to the development of meaning and identity. Therefore, HCI is no more only technological matter covers. It covers various convergence systems and areas in human society.

The number of people over the age over 65 continues to increase, and accordingly, medical expenses for the age group are also increasing in Korea. According to the '2018 National Senior Statistics' (Korea National Statistical Office 2018), the over 65 years group exceeded 14% of the population, and Korea has thus entered the aged society status, not by the UN. The core value provided by digital technological products in the field of monitoring/management is to help users manage and improve their own health, based on measurement of body information, ultimately preventing diseases. In the past, factors such as people's diet and exercise habits have been regarded as secondary for disease treatment, but the recent expansion of the monitoring/management field allows users to manage their own health independently, and will provide input when using medical institutions in the future. It can have medical value in which allows the use of data that monitors daily lifestyle habits.

2.3 Digital Health Care in Asthma Medicine Allergy Care

Since 2014, the healthcare monitoring market has grown quantitatively as global conglomerates such as Apple and Samsung competed by releasing smart watches such as Apple Watch and Gear, respectively.

Asthma is a chronic disease and may occurs in any age. However, compare to other age group, over age 65 group have highest death rate in Korea. Asthma and Chronic Obstructive Pulmonary Disease (COPD) are not curable but their symptoms can be controlled through quality health care. Digital technology can allow patients participate these daily-base control process and collect consistent self-generated-patients data, such as allergy report, medicine records and etc. Among chronic diseases, asthma, which is a respiratory disease, is one of the representative chronic diseases experienced by Americans [5]. Asthma patients repeatedly experience symptoms such as wheezing, shortness of breath, and coughing, but because it is not easy to cure, 'management' is a symptom [6]. Therefore it is very necessary to get better [7]. Since asthma mainly affects children and the elderly, it is not easy to use a device such as a spirometer even when visiting a hospital for treatment [8], and due to the perception of long-term asthma patients.

3 User Test of Existing Application

3.1 User Experience Analysis on Drug Allergy Alert App.

For gaining user needs and finding problems, this research conducted UX field research, user interviews about the experience on existing application, called 'Drug Allegy Alert' which developed for internal usage of Chungbuk national university hospital by one of author of this paper. The previous development was more focused on hospital and organization side so the satisfaction rate founded as low.

With above needs, this research brought the application as a user test material before starts designing this research's allergy application.

One step before the expert user experience test, this research analyzed the general users interview result which was conducted with hospital visited patients. User test consist as two stages, one is about general user test with the existing application and users were all age rages of adult and the other test was for senior citizens only (Table 1).

Table 1. Drug allergy alert app. user experience

1. Intro Page	2. Registration Page	3. Title/Login	4. Main Page
-This screen appears when running the app and represents the overall identity. -When the users enter the login page, then automatically disappears.	-Used once when using the app for the first time. - Users can choose the favorite hospital by their location.	-The screen that appears when the intro page disappears. -If users check automatic login, the main page appears without through the page.	-When logging in, the drug safety card page provides information on drug allergies registered by patients. -Users can click the 'Check Action Plan' button.
5. Action Plan	**6. Search for drug**	**7. 'Search' Button**	**8. QR Code Scan**
-When users click the 'Check Action Plan' button, a pop up rise containing information related to drug allergy.	-When clicking the 'Search Drug Allergy' button at the top, two types of buttons appear.('Search' and 'QR code'.)	-A search box appears where users can search by selecting the drug name or drug number.	-Connected to a camera that can take QR barcodes on hospital prescriptions.

3.2 Interaction Heuristics

Down below Table 2 is extracted heuristics from user interviews on user experience.

Solution part is the answer about the test users unsatisfied experience, which link with the re-designed application of following Sect. 4.

Table 2. Drug allergy alert app. 10 heuristics

No	10 heuristics	User needs (interviews)	App solution
1	Visibility of system status	- Button UI is not recognizable	- Import sound or haptics to improve digital literacy
		- The lack of visual feedback that conveys the user location can cause confusion in positioning and moving	- Need to clearly communicate. (Build intuitive visual feedback such as highlighting on the labels)
2	Interaction between system and the real world	- There are too much English or foreign text in the information	- Do localize completely. (or link with on line translation app)
		- The contraindicated drugs and drugs that can be taken are the same blue color, so users cannot distinguish	- Make a gap between positive and negative by color - Make simple color communication
		- When users press the 'Action Plan' button, it is difficult to understand the word without understanding the terminology of the medical drugs	- Need explanation of the medical terminology - This is future challenge area
		- 'Action Plan' is not a word frequently used so users' understanding level of this word is low	- Needs to enhance understanding of the 'Action Plan' or change to familiar words that we know
3	User control and freedom (recover-ability)	- Users can not enjoy using the app because it is only focused on the drug allergy search function	- Need to add other features besides searching drug information
		- Despite of many error situation of ID and password stage, there is no function to immediately cancel the typing of the wrong password	- By adding a typing cancel function to the text field, when error occurs, it can be easily erased at once and entered again from the beginning
4	Consistency and standards	- The inconsistent text button colors do not intuitively convey the nature of the button's function	- Conversely, red color metaphors can be used through consistent colors

(*continued*)

Table 2. (*continued*)

No	10 heuristics	User needs (interviews)	App solution
		- The item naming of the Drug Safety Card is mixed in Korean and English, which hinders uniformity	- Clearly convey information the item is the same item to users by unifying the item naming of the Drug Safety Card in Korean
		- The roundness of the button corners is inconsistent, which hinders the unity of the buttons in the entire service	- The roundness and style of the button corners are designed to give unity and deliver the functions clearly
5	Error prevention	- There are no measures to prevent typing errors, such as the absence of a 'place holder' in every text field	- Reduce errors by guiding the user in the 'place holder' of the text field.)
		- In the registration process, even if the user don't want, the sign-up button moved which may cause problems in the future	- Precautionary measures are needed, such as activating a button that can move to the next step, only when the input conditions requested
		- When the 'Logout' button is executed, it proceeds without warning or confirmation	- Prevent user mistakes through pop-ups such as warning or confirmation when 'log out'
6	Recognition rather than recall (intuitive)	- 'Action Plan' is not a word often used by users of the target service in reality, so searching or learning is required to understand the service	- Minimizes the user's additional actions by delivering guides and additional explanations to enhance understanding of the 'Action Plan'
7	Flexibility and efficiency of usage	- At least two user actions (button taps) are required to use the 'Search' and 'QR Code' functions but it is an unnecessary process in terms of usability	- When entering the search screen for drug allergy, users can select 'Search' and "QR Code" immediately, reducing unnecessary user actions
		- Typing a difficult and unfamiliar drug name requires a lot of effort from the user and causes a lot of mistakes	- By adding an auto-complete function to the search box, users can easily and quickly search

(*continued*)

Table 2. (*continued*)

No	10 heuristics	User needs (interviews)	App solution
		- The phone numbers of the Chungbuk Regional Drug Safety Center and Chungbuk National University Allergy Internal Medicine are delivered via text at the bottom of the main homepage. However, connection is not easy	- On the service screen, when you select a number, you can connect to the phone immediately, minimizing user behavior. At this time, a confirmation pop-up before connection is displayed to prevent user mistakes
8	Aesthetic and minimalist design (key information)	- The 'logout' button located at the top of the Drug Safety Card screen is relatively insignificant information that is not related to the Drug Safety Card	- Hide the logout feature or move to another location to highlight key information. Then user can be hard to find
9	Help and error recovery	- When entering personal information such as ID, password, during the sign-up process, if the input conditions are not satisfied, the user cannot recognize the error by himself because there is no feedback received	- Using visual feedback (such as green color or smile character), which is a metaphor of affirmation - Conversely, if the condition is not satisfied, real-time visual feedback is provided with warning metaphor so that it can be recognized and recovered
10	Link or documentation	- When scanning a QR code, a text guide of 'Please put the bar code in the square' is provided, but this may not be used if users do not know the bar code or QR code	- When scanning a QR code, the illustration is actively used to clearly guide the QR code and barcode visually - Need to educate by digital literacy levels

4   Digital Literacy-Based User Experience Design

4.1   Key Interaction Elements of the UX Strategy

Based on action research including the analysis form user interviews and literature reviews this paper developed key interaction elements of user experience strategy based on inclusive digital literacy.

• Patient-centered Care and Self-generate Data

In patient-centered care, a person's specific health needs and desired health outcomes are the driving force behind all health care decisions and quality measurements [9].

Patients partner with health care providers, and health care providers treat patients from a clinical perspective as well as an emotional, mental, social and financial perspective.

- GUI Guideline based in Elderly Digital Literacy

Down below table is the GUI guideline based on senior Citizen's digital literacy which adopted in this research (Table 3).

Table 3. Items for GUI design development

Item	Traits
Typography	- Use a single font and Sans serif for readability - Mainly use a text input font size of at least 14 to 16 pt
UI Color	- Apply a contrast ratio of 4.5:1 or higher and use color contrast
Button	- Expand the touch range of the button in consideration of the size of an adult's finger and the senior's motor control ability - Keep the diagonal length of the touch button at least 9.6 mm
Icon and character	- Display of icons as a character to remember easily - Focus on familiar images and minimize details
Graphic UI	- Simple form to convey meaning clearly - Reduce steps when deliver self-generate record (user data)
Warning & notification	- Provides step-by-step buttons for clear recognition
Tab bar	- Separated into top and bottom according to the information hierarchy - Sorted from left to right according to the order of use

(Revised from Ref. G.Lee and S.Ahn, HCI Korea, 2021)

5 User Experience and Interface Design

5.1 Typography and Color Branding

In order to facilitate information transfer to the seniors, a single font was used, a sans serif, with a clean finish. Type size is 16 pt, which is larger than 10–13 pt, which is more generally used in applications, was used, the smallest font was 13 pt, and the largest title was 25 pt for readability. In addition, for elements that require emphasis, such as numbers or numerical expressions other than letters, 35 pt and 40 pt were used to control the strength and weakness of information.

One of physical changes of elderly people can be a reduced visual reaction to color contrast, or color recognition. Color branding of GUI Kit in this research rather focused on the color contrast than color selection to enhance readability in cognitive interaction. The composition of the color branding selected through non-checking is 4 main colors, 14 contrast combinations, 2 gradient colors for graphics, background colors such as white and 3 text colors. Figure 2 and 3 shows the component of color based on contrast. Innovation point here is the color branding based on contrast.

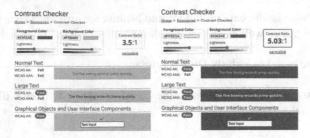

Fig. 2. WebAIM color contrast check

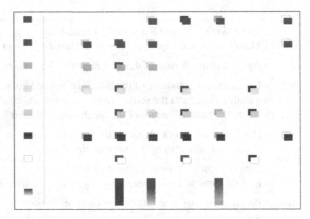

Fig. 3. The overall structure of a smart farm system

5.2 Self-generate Data Visualization

Below shows the personal allergy symptom data record which was generated and recorded by application users. It checks and records the user's medication information and allergic symptoms that appear, and collects data over a long period of time to ensure personalized medical information.

A graphic for self-recording pages of allergy medication time and symptoms was designed. In the case of a graphic showing step-by-step numbers and symptom records, not only the numbers are displayed, but an intuitive graph-type graphic to grasp the flow of the situation at a glance by comparing the front and rear, left and right (Fig. 4).

Reflecting the characteristics of the user experience developed in this research, a application page for recording symptoms by the user as shown in above figure and a page for registering and displaying self-information by statistically digitizing the recorded results were designed.

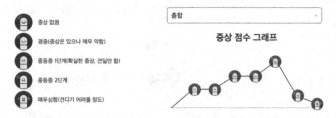

Fig. 4. User-centered numerical comparison graphic

5.3 Alert (SOS) System

To prevent the user from turning off the alarm involuntarily when the alarm goes off, the user's awareness is enhanced by providing a button with two items, close and detail view, as shown in figure down below (Fig. 5).

Fig. 5. Alert Pop-Up

5.4 Service Flowchart

The application developed in this research kept the previous allergy app's flowchart since the unsatisfied user interaction elements were mainly located in interface and visual experience part. However detailed were changes and attached, which helps users belong to senior citizen groups and other inclusive groups in digital literacy (Fig. 6).

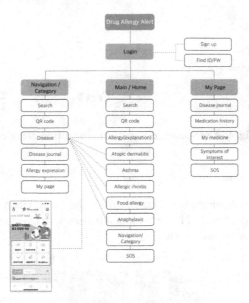

Fig. 6. App. service flowchart

5.5 Wireframe Design

Based on service flowchart and the user analysis from field research, this research developed and finalized wire-frame of application. One of features of wireframe is simple structure and less layers to consider the digital literacy. Since the application is focused on user experience, graphic parts are not fully covered except the graphic interface part which related with the user needs area from user test process (Figs. 7 and 8).

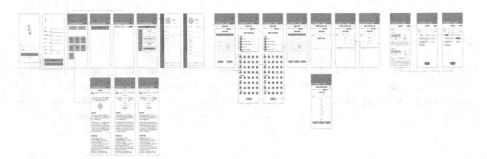

Fig. 7. Wireframe design of digital literacy-based medicine allergy app

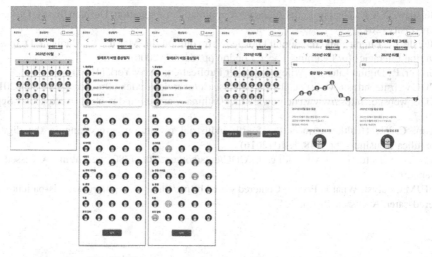

Fig. 8. User-generate data process in the wire-frame

6 Conclusions

Equitable access to digital infrastructure has never been more important than now. Despite the increased demand for digital technologies in response to the COVID-19 crisis, there is a risk that the rapid application of these technologies during the current emergency will broaden the digital divide in the society. Although the existence of a digital divide is not new, the current health and social crisis adds a new dimension of urgency to address its presence.

In Korea, telemedicine is not allowed yet. Digital telemedicine services do not currently exist. Since telemedicine service that provide medical information, such as diagnosis and prescription, is prohibited by the law, certain scope of areas permitted by regulations, such as providing information on disease or judgment on recommend to visit the hospital can be provided. At this point digital literacy can serve as an opportunity to improve the quality of services meanwhile by developing socially considered user experience, as well as age based social alienation which should not occur.

Considering digital literacy with social inclusiveness and Combining digital healthcare with chronic disease such as COPD, this paper brings up social perspective of HCI and convergence.

Acknowledgments. This research was supported by National Research Foundation of Korea (NRF) grant funded by the Korea government Ministry of Science and ICT (No. 2020R1F1A1069087).

References

1. Sørensen, K., et al.: Health literacy and public health: a systematic review and integration of definitions and models. BMC Public Health, 3 (2012)

2. Belshaw, D.A.J.: What is digital literacy? A pragmatic investigation. Durham theses, Durham University (2012)
3. Belisle, C.: Literacy and the digital knowledge revolution. In: Martin, A., Madigan, D. (eds.) Digital Literacies for Learning. Facet, London pp. 51–67 (2006)
4. Gilster, P.: Digital Literacy. Wiley Computer Publications, New York (1997)
5. CDC website. https://www.cdc.gov/chronicdisease/overview/index.htm. Accessed 6 Sept 2017
6. CDC website. https://www.cdc.gov/features/asthmaawareness/index.html. Accessed 6 Sept 2017
7. Kim, C.-W.: Healthcare meet the fourth industrial revolution: everything in the digital healthcare business, pp. 148. KIIP (2016)
8. KDCA website. http://www.nih.go.kr/CDC/cms/content/80/14380_view.html. Accessed 6 Sept 2017
9. NEJM Catalyst, What Is Patient-Centered Care? https://catalyst.nejm.org/what-is-patient-centered-care/. Accessed 25 Apr 2017

Advancing Inclusive Service Design: Defining, Evaluating and Creating Universally Designed Services

Miriam E. N. Begnum[1,2(✉)] and Oda Lintho Bue[3]

[1] Department of Design, Norwegian Labour and Welfare Administration, Fyrstikkalléen 1, 0661 Oslo, Norway
miriam@begnum.no
[2] Department of Design, NTNU, Teknologiveien 22, 2815 Gjøvik, Norway
[3] Department of Innovation and Digitalization, Ullensaker Municipality, 2051 Jessheim, Norway

Abstract. Service Design (SD) may be viewed as the merge of digital, intangible and physical touchpoints to form holistic user experiences. It is a fast-growing discipline; however, universal design (UD) awareness is lacking. At some point during their life, most people will experience a mental or physical condition that limits their capacity to perform certain tasks. As such, service designers should be able to address the needs of all users, contribute to social inclusion and facilitate maximized independent living abilities. This article explores how UD can be ensured in SD. The contributions are: 1) A working definition of a Universally Designed Service, 2) Generating and piloting two new SD methods to assess the UD of services in accordance with the working definition, and 3) Generating and piloting two new SD methods to promote inclusive user need insights and synthesis and consideration of both edge-case and mainstream needs in the design process. By demonstrating four inclusive service design methods and the usefulness of the proposed definition, this paper advances efforts to define, evaluate and create universally designed services.

Keywords: Inclusive core persona · Empathic modelling · Empathic Service Safari · Touchpoint Accessibility Assessment · Universal design service evaluation

1 Introduction

Universal design (UD) is the design of products and environments to be usable to all, to the greatest extent possible [1]. National and international legislation have continuously strengthened UD regulations over the last decades, aiming to ensure citizens receive opportunities to access and use digitalized services [2]. However, persons with disabilities are collectively argued to be the largest group experiencing discrimination in society [3]. Non-disabled users are also in danger of digital exclusion, such as elderly over 80 years of age, first-generation non-western immigrants and persons with low digital competence [4].

© Springer Nature Switzerland AG 2021
M. Rauterberg (Ed.): HCII 2021, LNCS 12795, pp. 17–35, 2021.
https://doi.org/10.1007/978-3-030-77431-8_2

The service design (SD) discipline is key for value creation in digital societies [5, 6]. Service designers are described as shaping future societies [7, 8], and impacting the shape and form of digitalized services [9]. Though service design is a rapidly growing industry, focus is still on the accessibility of specific touchpoints – reflecting the sector-specific legislation – and not of the holistic service experience. As such, service chains could still have barriers in crucial parts (e.g., a summons letter) if service designers launch cross-platform services without UD awareness, making the overall user service journey inaccessible.

The topic of ensuring universally designed services is gaining traction, and a first definition of UD in SD has been proposed [10]. However, service design networks and literature are still lacking methods, success case examples and frameworks for how to create and evaluate universally designed services. This article reports on empirical and applied work done to advance the field of universal service design, asking:

1. Could merging existing SD methods and inclusive design methods be a viable strategy towards building a methodological framework advancing UD of services?
2. How can the proposed definition be applied in practice; can new methods be generated and applied to evaluate whether a service is universally designed in accordance with the definition?

2   Background

The work in this article builds on the findings from Bue and Begnum [10], where a literature survey combined with a series of exploratory semi-structured in-depth interviews documented 7 current challenges:

1. **Awareness**: Inclusive aspects are not completely absent, with several articles mention catering to users with special needs and several service designers enthusiastic, however UD is not integrated into professional practice at the time of the study.
2. **Knowledge**: Current UD expertise in the SD discipline seems low.
3. **Education**: No informants was taught UD related to their SD education. UD does not appear systematically taught in relation to SD.
4. **Definition**: Neither informants nor literature provided any opinions on what UD in SD should entail. All informants asked for a definition of UD in SD.
5. **Methodology**: Marginalized users and edge-case scenarios do not receive focus, and practice lack systematic accessibility assessments (checkpoints) as well as methods for holistic UD service evaluations.
6. **Legislation**: UD regulations cover specific touchpoints only, not service journeys.
7. **Responsibility**: UD responsibility in SD projects is established in relation to digital touchpoints, with service providers legally responsible for accessibility; typically delegated to developers and UI designers. There is no overall responsibility for ensuring finalized services are universally designed overall.

Norway represents a region where the service design profession is rapidly increasing [6, 11] and also where UD legislation is among the firmest. Norway is one of the few countries that have a dedicated governmental body responsible for supervising UD of IT legislation and fining offences [12], as well as equal UD of ICT regulations for public and private sectors. As such, these findings related to the Norwegian sample of service designers was worrying. Combined with the lack of methodology for inclusive service design in the international body of research, Bue and Begnum [10] conclude established UD competence is lacking in the SD discipline Six action points are proposed to advance UD in SD:

1. Create a definition of UD in SD,
2. Legislate inclusive service chains, not only accessible touchpoints,
3. Give service designers the responsibility for UD across a service chain,
4. Integrate UD into SD methodology – providing the tools to ensure UD across a service experience and promote focus on UD from the start,
5. Increase the involvement of marginalized user group, and
6. Include UD focus within SD education.

Finally, they suggest following definition of a universally designed service: "*A service is universally designed when its costumer journeys are usable to all people, to the greatest extent possible, without the need for adaptation or specialized design apart from choosing preferred touchpoints*".

2.1 Inclusive Design Methodology

Inclusive design is a methodological approach to designing for diverse user needs, utilized in order to create universally designed solutions, as well as to create specialized design [13]. Within inclusive design, empathy-building artifacts, assistive technologies (AT) or theatrical techniques are commonly used to gather insights into what edge case users are experiencing [14].

2.2 Service Design Methodology

SD is still a young discipline, and lack an established definition [15], thus some view SD as a UX mindset of balancing technological opportunities, business relevance and human needs [16]. More commonly, SD is regarded as a separate design discipline based on its specialized co-creative and hands-on methods for service mapping, using specific techniques such as service safaris, (user or process) journey charts, touchpoints matrixes, service ecology maps, service blueprints etc. These "SD-techniques" aids the designer in creating new, consistent or improved services experiences.

SD typically follows a "double-diamond" process, in line with Design Thinking – and not the ISO human-centered design model [17]. Still, SD is highly user-centred. Further, SD emphasizes insight visualizations, and typically construct "boundary objects" to facilitate cross-silo communication [16]. Overall, service designers employ a flexible methodology, fitting constructivism as well as critical thinking.

3 Research Approach

Based on empirical insights into the challenges and potential initiatives for promoting universal design in service design, this article applies generative research to test the proposed definition and mitigating the lack of methodological knowledge on how to create and evaluate a universally designed service. The research approach of the study is first exploratory and qualitative [18, 19], and second generative [20].

Generative research denotes the phase between exploratory and evaluating research phases. In the generative phase, concepts and early prototypes are created [20]. Overall, the study is aiming at extending knowledge with applied research to improve practice within a specific discipline [19]. As this iterative work is still in its early phase, we do not (yet) label this a design-based research methodology [21].

3.1 Prioritizing Initiatives to Promote UD in SD

As this study continues the work from Bue and Begnum [10], our first step was to prioritize the six proposed action points. These were prioritized based on a) impact, and b) feasibility, through applying the "idea portfolio" technique [22]. All of the action points are believed to have *impact* and promote UD of SD, however **defining** UD for SD, adding SD to UD **legislation** and integrating UD into SD **methodology** seemed critical first steps. As these have a high impact, they were placed in the upper-most part of the "ide portfolio" matrix, see Fig. 1 to the right.

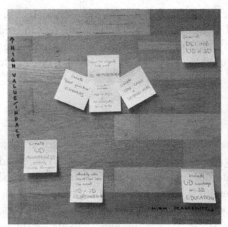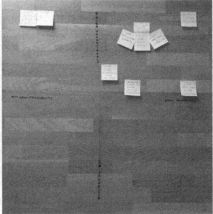

Fig. 1. Idea portfolio prioritization matrix

Not all initiatives are regarded as equally *feasible*, however. In particular, adding SD into UD legislation is considered a long-term goal. In order to propose legislations, more knowledge and research is needed. Thus, this action point is placed to the left in the matrix, see Fig. 1 right side. The two initiatives regarded as having the highest feasibility is a definition (a first proposal already published) and including UD perspectives in SD education (at the time, the first author was planning to teach SD).

Combining feasibility and impact in the matrix, the two prioritized action points are 1) continuing the work on developing a definition of a universally designed service, and 2) create UD-integrated service design methodology, see Fig. 1 left side.

3.2 Empirical Settings to Inform Generative Design

Since the general UD knowledge and awareness in the industry sample was low [10], the idea was to introduce UD perspectives by re-designing established SD methods. New methods are generated by merging established SD methods with well-known techniques from UD, Inclusive Design and Empathic Design to create new methods integrating UD expertise in the SD profession.

Existing SD methods were mapped out using different online and curriculum sources, as well as drawing on the methods reported on from literature. They were categorized as methods supporting Insight, Analysis, Ideation and Validation (including prototyping techniques). These four categories were created based on the double diamond process model associated with service design methodology, see Fig. 2.

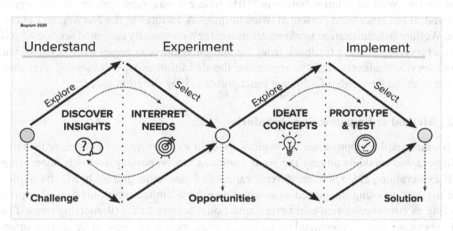

Fig. 2. Double diamond process model, based on IDEO.org

Generative research is typically informed by empirical methods and insights [20]. Empirical settings for introducing and getting feedback on our UD in SD definition and methods was established through A) recruiting the students of a SD course as piloting pioneers and B) setting up industry lectures and workshops on the topic. Six lectures (including three academic presentations) and two workshops were conducted overall. These settings were used to present and discuss the definition, collecting UD of SD best-practice experiences and examples from the participants, and as testbeds for piloting generated methods and receiving feedback.

The SD course was a 7, 5 ECTS course for 2nd year Interaction Design bachelor students at the Norwegian University of Science and Technology [23]. The service case was a museum experience for young persons, provided by the Norwegian National Museum. In the industry workshops, the service case was a child healthcare service from Ullensaker municipality, provided by the Department of Innovation and digitalization.

4   Results

4.1   A Working Definition

The definition was presented in its 1st version at NordDesign 2018 [10], in a 2nd version at Girl Geek Dinner Oslo (GGDO), November 14th 2018 [24], in a 3rd version at the 3 min industry-blog focused on societal digitalization and innovations in technology, design and media [25] as well as in academic seminar hosted by Oslo Metropolitan University. Both academics and industry professionals showed an interesting in learning more about UD of SD, and proposed minor changes to the definition, which was accommodated into a final 4th version:

> *"A service is universally designed when its costumer journey is usable to all people (to the greatest extent possible and without the need for adaptation or specialized design), by selecting suitable touchpoints".*

The 4th version was next discussed in a service design workshop at the Norwegian Labour and Welfare Administration in 2019, where it was translated into a Norwegian version. It has since been presented twice in industry lectures as the Norwegian Labour and Welfare Administration working definition for a universally designed service – both times receiving positive feedback from the audience. Some changes were debated, but most service designers seem to appreciate the definition as-is, commenting that they agree with the flexibility of allowing touchpoints suiting different users.

4.2   Method 1: Empathic Service Safaris

Self-ethnographic approaches are widely used in explorative SD phases, with auto-ethnographic methods among the most common, encompassing methods supporting self-exploration [22]. There are several variants of auto-ethnography in SD. Examples are mystery working (disguised as an employee for a limited time), mystery shopping (acting as customers, often evaluative), traditional service safari (immersing oneself in an experience – often combined with ethnographic methods), explorative service safari (collecting good and bad service experiences – often from competitors) and diary studies (longitudinal studies of self-experiences). To advance UD when discovering insights, an inclusive auto-ethnographic method was generated. Among the auto-ethnographic approaches, we selected a service safari for this purpose, as these approaches are aimed at creating insights through contextual bottom-up experiences.

A service safari method was combined with empathic modeling in the **Empathic Service Safari**. Through empathic modeling, you attempt to experience services the way another individual would [26]. Empathic modeling is commonly used in universal and inclusive design by simulating a capability loss in order to experience and gathering insights, as a complementing approach to recruiting and getting to know edge-case users [14]. In the Empathic Service Safari capability loss simulations are added to the safari approach.

The method was piloted in the SD course, where students worked on creating new museum experiences for young audiences in collaboration with the Norwegian National Museum. Six student group each selected one edge-case user aspect: deaf/loss of hearing, paraplegia/wheelchair user, walking impairment/crutch user, fatigue/ME and two groups focused on visual impairments. Four of these student groups piloted the method (Fig. 3).

Fig. 3. Photo of student groups conducting Empathic Service Safari

Further, the method was piloted at two different museums – using two service safari variations. In the National Museum of Architecture, an open, exploratory version of the Empathic Service Safari (little structure) was conducted. At the Astrup Fearnley Museum of modern arts, more traditional safari was applied (structured user service experience from entrance to exit, including a museum guided tour).

The group modeling *paraplegia* used a borrowed wheelchair throughout the empathic service safari, simulating a disability caused by e.g., a spinal cord injury. Through the Empathic Service Safari, they noted they experience many of the emotions a wheelchair user would, related to irritation, dissatisfaction and frustrations, receiving looks and comments, and the need for extra time and extensive aid. However, they also noted they could not experience all a person with e.g., CP might have, such as spasticity (perhaps fatigue and pain), speech impairments and related stigmas.

The group modeling a *walking impairment* used crutches as a walking aid throughout the traditional safari. During and after the immersive traditional Empathic Service Safari, the group expressed tiredness, muscle strain, discomfort, frustrations, difficulties maintaining engagement due to fatigue, and relief when finding somewhere to rest – e.g., a chair or a raised, carpeted floor.

The final two groups modeled *visual impairments* using a blind fold/closed eyes and Cambridge simulation glasses respectively [27]. The Cambridge Simulation glasses are simulating a 0.74 logMAR – well below the Snellen visus 6/18 (0, 33) 0.5 logMAR ICD-10 benchmark for a *moderate* visual impairment. In the safaris, these two groups did not consistently use the empathic modeling, and insights were more on the practical level and not as empathic as they could have been. Our observation was they tested sporadically, but not immersing themselves in the empathic experience. The degree of immersion discipline and realism seemed to strongly affect the quality of bodily modeled experiences and emotional insights – both for the person embodying a disability, and for peers aiding and observing.

Based on this observation, one of the groups focused on vision conducted two additional auto-ethnographies utilizing empathic modeling; a) exploratory Empathic Service Safari navigating the university campus using the Cambridge glasses, going up and down stairs and moving between campus buildings, and b) empathic modeling while being trained in key mobility and navigation issues by the Norwegian Association of the Blind and Partially Sighted (NABP). At NABP, a range of glasses modeling different types of visual impairments, including cataracts and tunnel vision were used while experiencing the effect of tactile surface guiding lines and warning studs, banisters, door designs, signs and way-finding design, braille, color contrast and contrasting stripes on walls, the ground, external corners of walls and stairs etc. This empathic-modeled training was reported as extremely educational and insightful, and highly effective for increasing in-depth understanding of the effect of capability loss.

Students used empathic insights in the following months, developing personas, specifying value propositions, service ideation and prototyping, indicating the usefulness of the Empathic Service Safari. The piloting of the Empathic Service Safari method confirms how empathic modeling can improve edge-user sensitivity during self-ethnographic SD methods – and that realistic modeling and disciplined immersion is key (you cannot stop using the crutches when they hurt, if the service experience is not ended – you cannot leave the wheelchair even when it is stuck in the snow on the way to the museum – you cannot remove the glasses even if you feel scared).

4.3   Method 2: Inclusive Core Persona

Personas are widely used Stickdorn, Hormess [22]; representing an archetype of the targeted group of people – a specific, fictional person created from real insights (e.g. from interviews with 2–4 users). Empirical insights ensure personas are not "idealized users" and add rich descriptions. If the target user group is heterogeneous, one may develop a range of personas. Stickdorn et al. [22] calls this "core personas" and recommends

3–7 personas used company-wide for planning, designing, developing and marketing solutions.

An early focus on users with disabilities is a characteristic of UD-successful ICT-projects [28]. Edge-case users (also called extreme users) are persons in a user group that face specific challenges, for example a severe disability or a complex situation. Edge-case design points to specialized design to specific and non-typical needs or context of use [29]. In UD and inclusive design, a recommendation is starting with edge-case needs – and then moving towards universal design solutions. The idea is that if a design fit the edges of user needs, the design will also fit the average. UD is often linked to innovation as tapping into edge-case needs trigger innovations [30].

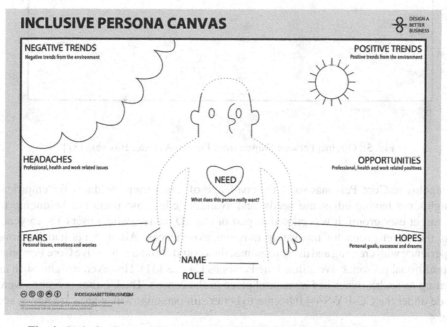

Fig. 4. Inclusive Persona Canvas, Begnum (2019) based on Persona Canvas [31]

In order to advance UD when interpreting and analyzing needs, the idea of creating personas based on edge-case users' needs was generated. Service designers in Bue and Begnum [10] point out how checklists or cards could aid them in remembering to include edge-case needs and know which specific edge-cases to focus on. From this, creating a range of personas representing edge-case users was considered. However, the number of personas needed for this approach seemed too extensive. Instead, a method was generated for aiding service designers in persona-development integrating UD: 1) Create core personas as usual. 2) Add edge-case needs to core personas based on insights from edge-case users, iteratively or in parallel. Using this approach, relevant insights on edge-case needs are merged into core personas. This method was called **Inclusive Core Personas** (Fig. 4).

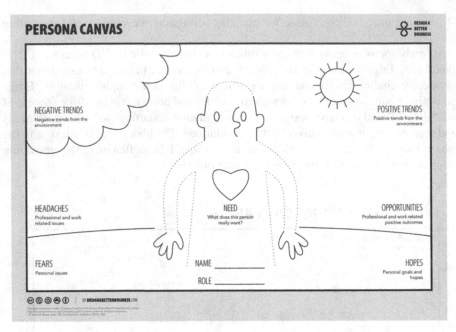

Fig. 5. Original Persona Canvas from Design A Better Business [31]

Inclusive Core Personas solve the challenge of target users available for empirical insights not having edge-case needs, and available edge-case users not belonging to the target user group. It was piloted as part of the SD course, where users 18–25 years was the target group for innovating museum experiences. All students had previous experience with creating and using personas, thus could compare Inclusive Core Personas to traditional personas. We utilized the Personas Canvas [31]. However, insights such as relating to health issues had no natural place in the canvas. Thus, minor revisions were made under the CC-BY-SA 4.0 license to better suit personas with edge-case needs, see Fig. 4.

One student group identified two informants within the desired target user group having edge-case needs and could build personas directly. The other five groups utilized the Inclusive Core Persona approach above to iteratively add edge-case needs to a traditional persona based on a young person. Four groups did this without issues and gave positive feedback, of which three groups had one informant each with desired edge-case *and* target representativeness; this may have aided their confidence when merging additional insights and added descriptions.

The last group reported increased uncertainty about assumptions made compared to personas derived from non-merged insights. This was not a problem for the student group focusing on walking impairments, which built their Inclusive Core Persona on a person using crutches periodically and contextually due to Multiple Sclerosis (MS) symptoms, including foot drop and pain, merged with younger persons in the target audience. Overall, the method appears constructive as an alternative to traditional personas, though there is a risk of assuming – as with the original persona method.

4.4   Method 3: Touchpoint Accessibility Assessment

Service designers commonly use some method to map out a service and all its touchpoints [10]. Empirical findings indicated a lack of checkpoints addressed edge-case needs. In order to support UD in the analysis, ideation and prototyping phase of services, one such touchpoint and interaction mapping method was merged with accessibility evaluations.

A touchpoints matrix overviews interaction between costumers and service mediated by channels, such as social media channels, telecom channels, web channels and physical channels. The method is credited to Gianluca Brugnoli [33]. His matrix lists touchpoints vertically and user intentions horizontally. Through a re-design of the touchpoint matrix, we generated the **Touchpoint Accessibility Assessment** (Fig. 6).

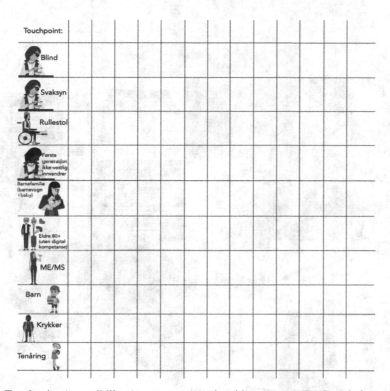

Fig. 6. Touchpoint Accessibility Assessment (matrix with user examples from industry lecture)

Accessibility refers to a physical, practical, technical access to usage, and is an important premise for UD. UD also encompasses the general usability and fit, e.g., the usefulness, user experience and desirability of a product [32]. Accessibility evaluations are typically conducted as expert assessments based on accessibility guidelines. The type of guidelines used to assess depend on what is being assessed – i.e., the type of touchpoint.

The **Touchpoint UD Assessment** method advances UD in the analysis and ideation of service touchpoints, using the following approach: 1) list touchpoints horizontally in the matrix, 2) list edge-case users vertically in the matrix, 3) check for each touchpoint if it is accessible and usable for the edge-case users, and 4) note any usability and accessibility issues (and ideas for improvement). The Touchpoint UD Assessment method was piloted in two iterations: first at the GGDO industry workshop [25] and secondly by the student groups in the SD course (see Fig. 7).

Fig. 7. Touchpoint Accessibility Assessment in industry workshop

In the industry workshop, the method was piloted using expert assessments in groups of 2–3 experts, that were designers and product developers from industry. They were supplied with real physical evidence from a child healthcare service, such as a summons letter, a child health card, pamphlets, and pictures of signs, rooms and spaces. participants assessed. Usability and accessibility assessments were completed using desk research, mainly focused on users using a wheelchair, crutches, with pelvis/back pain, hearing impairment, fatigue, visual impairments, non-digital users and first-generation non-western immigrants. Guidance on edge-case needs for which to assess was provided. Empathetic modelling was used for simulating loss of vision [34]. To further aid the assessment, different types of accessibility and UD guidelines were provided befitting the physical evidence provided [25, 35, 36].

For the student groups, a similar approach was used. Here, the student groups had gathered insights into their chose edge-case needs in previous design phases, and they shared these insights with each other both on-demand during the assessment and in the form of inclusive core personas developed for the museum service experience. The added evidence gathered through auto-ethnography, direct user interviews and observations and desk research on user needs appeared to positively contribute to the ease and confidence of the touchpoint assessment.

Workshop participants experimented with different ways to 'score' touchpoints and note down accessibility and usability challenges. Some simply ticked ok/not ok, while other used a scale. Scoring touchpoints 0–3 worked well (0 = not usable, 3 = excellent), thus students also adopted this approach. Most also wrote notes – either directly in/on the matrix, on post-it notes that they adhered to the matrix, or in notebooks. Both workshop participants and students organically used the insights on UD challenges to ideate on-the-spot on how touchpoints could be re-designed, exchanged for inclusive alternatives or added to complement the existing touchpoints.

4.5   Method 4: Service UD Evaluation

To enable service designers to evaluate UD of a service in line with our proposed definition, a second method was needed. To advance UD in service evaluation, a **Service UD Evaluation** was based on journey mapping, which is a type of service walkthrough (see Fig. 8 and Fig. 9).

Phases: Touchpoints:	Hear about		Find		Use		Leave	

Fig. 8. Service UD evaluation (empty matrix)

We found a service walkthrough fitting for UD evaluation, as it is a holistic and formative approach to service evaluation, identifies critical steps and problem areas, and

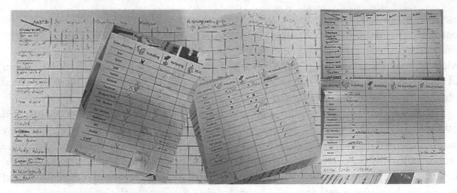

Fig. 9. Service UD evaluation (matrixes from pilot settings)

facilitates both current and future-state evaluations [22, 37]. Service walkthroughs are in essence an enactment of a service journey [22]. They either rely on system mapping (e.g., service blueprints), journey mapping (common approach) or mixed mapping. Service blueprints map interactions between users and services in a comprehensive manner [16], but are more system-focused. Journey mapping is experience centered; following a user through a service, either focused on detailed parts or the overall journey [22]. Blomkvist and Arvola [37] describe service walkthroughs as a blend of pluralistic walkthrough, experience prototyping, and bodystorming. We argue that empathic modeling (empathic design) should be part of this blend.

In the industry workshop, the Service UD evaluation method was used directly after the UD Touchpoint Assessment method had been applied, using a desktop walkthrough approach, where designers remain at "their desk" [22] and physical evidence were used as props. The service walkthrough was conducted for *each* user group in question; empathically evaluating whether users from each group could find and be able to select at least *one* suitable (accessible) touchpoint in each service phase (and as such could complete the service journey). As the definition of a universally designed service proposes, if all users have suitable touchpoints in all phases, the service is universally designed. If not, touchpoints need to be added or re-designed.

In the SD course, the students evaluated the service experience both with and without their changes. The walkthroughs were a bit more playful, using bodystorming and role-playing as needed to evaluate touchpoints. The Service UD Evaluation enabled the students to validate and reflect on the UD of existing services and new service prototypes. All student groups came to the conclusion that with the original design, the National Museum did not offer a universally designed museum service, as persons with visual impairments are unable to fully experience the art exhibited. The students were divided on the subject of inclusiveness for wheelchair users, depending on how strictly one assesses navigation and access touchpoints accessibility (such as getting to, in and out of buildings without assistance). With the changes to the museum service as prototyped by the student groups, the service would be universally designed.

5   Discussion

Though it is positive that accessibility regulations on service environments and touch-points are continuously being strengthened [2], legislation must move beyond a focus on specific touchpoints, and towards a focus on holistic service journey experiences and possibilities. The SD discipline could be a driving force in this regard.

5.1   Merging SD and UD Methods to Build a Methodological Framework

This paper asks if merging existing SD and inclusive design methods could be a viable strategy towards building a methodological framework for advancing UD in the field. In user-centered design, approaches are commonly mixed, for example adding user sensitive design to inclusive design, or mixing empathic design and edge-case design. Embedding inclusive design and empathic design strategies into existing user-centered design and development methodologies could as such be a viable approach to creating an inclusive service design practice.

In order to test this theory, established SD methods were merged with techniques from UD, inclusive design and empathic design to generate new methods. As such, the work draws on the flexibility and user-centered strengths of the current SD methodology. In order to facilitate the ability to gather insights and sensitivity on how edge-case users would experience services, the Empathic Service Safari and Inclusive Core Personas methods were created. In order to advance UD in the assessment, ideation and evalua-tion of services, the Touchpoint Accessibility Assessment and UD Service Evaluation methods were generated.

In the Empathic Service Safari, service designers bodily and emotionally experience some of edge-case user needs in an immersive and contextual manner. This is done by integrating empathic modeling into auto-ethnographic experiences.

Inclusive Core Personas integrate edge-case needs into traditional personas, which introduces UD aspects from the start. Though the Inclusive Core Persona method inher-its the challenges with validity and representability of the original persona method, it inspired students to contact edge-case users directly and use interviews and direct user contact to gather user insights. This part of the method was highly successful – and should encourage all designers to talk to and observe users with edge-case needs, even if they are outside the target user group for a service.

Further, the students utilized the Inclusive Core Personas when piloting the UD Touchpoint Assessment and UD Service Evaluation methods. Though these methods were successful as an expert inspection desktop walkthrough with empathic modeling, inviting edge-case or proxy users into co-creative or pluralistic workshop could also be way to increase the validity of the results as well as gather deeper insights into edge-case and mainstream needs.

As such, the four methods complement each other, and all have the potential to impact service designers' degree of contact and empathy with edge-case users – and contribute to the knowledge needed to design more inclusive services. Our conclusion is the merging of inclusive design, UD and empathic design methods with SD techniques is a promising approach for building a new methodology.

5.2 Applying the Working Definition to Evaluate the UD of a Service

Secondly, this paper asks whether the proposed definition of a universally designed service [10] can be applied in practice, to assess and evaluate the inclusiveness of services. The paper tests whether defining a *universally designed service* based on SD perspectives, by developing services where *all* potential users can use at least *one* touchpoint at each stage of their user journey, appears effective.

UN discusses the need to align, mix and integrate service channels, including offline service channels to be more inclusive and usable [38]. The *universally designed service* definition builds on this idea. It makes little sense to ensure high UD quality in some service touchpoints, if edge-case user encounters inaccessible touchpoints later on – and thus are unable to complete the user journey and utilize the service.

Note that the initial *universally designed service* definition was iterated on, to empha- size the *choice* of a user to *select* a fitting touchpoint. The assumption in this final working definition is that the available touchpoints for the user to choose from are of equivalent quality.

The proposed definition is applied in practice by generating and applying two meth- ods supporting its validation: Touchpoint Accessibility Assessment and UD Service Evaluation. If this or a similar a definition is to be regulated, service providers need to be able to validate whether services are legal or not. By successfully piloting these two new inclusive service design methods in different settings and for different services, the paper demonstrates how service designers can be enabled to assess and verify whether touchpoints, phases, processes and steps in costumer journeys or system maps fit both mainstream and edge-case users in the target population.

In addition, the pilots showed how the definition and supporting methods aided in the re-design of existing services, in order to improve on their inclusiveness. The methods also supported the assessment of the universal design of imagined services.

6 Conclusion

This paper pilots how a working definition of a universally designed service can be applied to evaluate services – and demonstrates that the definition can be used to indicate whether existing as well as prototyped services are inclusive to all users. The definition is as follows: *"A service is universally designed when its costumer journey is usable to all people (to the greatest extent possible and without the need for adaptation or specialized design), by selecting suitable touchpoints".*

In addition, the paper shows merging existing inclusive/universal design methods with service design techniques is a viable approach for building an inclusive service design methodology. Four new inclusive service design methods are generated and piloted, supporting different phases of the service design process: The methods are: *Empathic Service Safari, Inclusive Core Persona, Touchpoint Accessibility Assessment* and *Service UD Evaluation.* The first two aim to improve the consideration of edge-case user needs and show potential towards increasing service designers' degree of contact and empathy with edge-case users. The final two assess the inclusiveness of touch- points and user journeys, in accordance with the working definition. Their successful demonstrations indicate service designers, with their holistic and cross-sector service viewpoint, can help overview universal design perspectives and create services that are usable for as many citizens as possible – without having the direct responsibility for all touchpoints. The proposed definition and four generated inclusive SD methods provide a basis for further work in this area. In conclusion, the paper contributes towards defining what universal design of services entails and empowering service designers to create more inclusive services.

Acknowledgements. We thank all industry collaborators, the GGDO workshop participants, Ullensaker municipality, the Norwegian National Museum, service designers at Norwegian Labour and Welfare Administration, the eInclusion group at the Norwegian Computing Centre and finally, we thank and dedicate this paper to our pioneering service design students at NTNU Bch Interaction Design: André T. Lønvik, Angelika C. D. Kristiansen, Anja Nilssen, Bjørnar E. Bolneset, Brage Arntzen, Christian Ringlund, Christopher M. M. Cox, Emil Perry, Emily L. Tolleshaug, Fredrik Veland, Jan Johan E. Johansen, Jørgen Kjelgård, Kay A. Smådal, Lili L. Nguyen, Lisa F. Larsen, Ola N. Ellevold, Olav Z. Neprud, Oskar K. Skåden, Philip Hodne, Synne E. S. Leiknes, Thea C. Romsås, Tobias H. Jacobsen and Trym L. L. O. Røen.

References

1. Law, C., et al.: A systematic examination of universal design resources: part 1, heuristic evaluation. Int J. **7**, 31–54 (2008). https://doi.org/10.1007/s10209-007-0100-1
2. EU, Amendments by the European Parliament to the Commission proposal Directive (EU) 2019/... of the European Parliament and of the Council of ... on the accessibility requirements for products and services (EAA - European Accessibility Act), E. Commission, Editor. Europarl (2019). http://www.europarl.europa.eu/doceo/document/A-8-2017-0188-AM-363-363_EN.pdf?redirect
3. Åmås, K.O.: Funksjonshemmede møter fordommer (2018)
4. Slettemeås, D.: IKT-bruk i befolkningen og barrierer for digital inkludering, En kunnskapsoppsummering (ICT-use in the population and barriers to digital inclusion) (2014). SIFO - Statens Institutt for Forbruksforskning. http://www.bufetat.no/PageFiles/10967/IKT-bruk%20i%20befolkningen%20og%20barrierer%20for%20digital%20inkludering.pdf
5. Norlie, A., Nordvik, A.: Tjenestedesign: kan bruk av tjenestedesign være hensiktsmessig for å frembringe god kundeopplevelse? NHH Norwegian School of Economics (2012)
6. Tveit, S.R.: Service innovation in a design perspective: a case study of the AT-ONE method. NMBU Norwegian University of Life Sciences, Ås (2011)
7. Kuk, G., Janssen, M.: Assembling infrastructures and business models for service design and innovation. Inf. Syst. J. **23**, 445–469 (2013). https://doi.org/10.1111/j.1365-2575.2012.00418.x
8. Steen, M., Manschot, M., Koning, N.: Benefits of co-design in service design projects. Int. J. Des. **5** (2011)
9. Scott, M., Delone, W., Golden, W.: Measuring eGovernment success: a public value approach. Eur. J. Inf. Syst. **25**, 187–208 (2016). https://doi.org/10.1057/ejis.2015.11
10. Bue, O.L., Begnum, M.E.N.: Towards inclusive service design in the digital society: current practices and future recommendations. In: NordDesign 2018. NordDESIGN series, Linköping, Sweden (2018)
11. AHO. Norge på topp i tjenestedesign (Norway is on top in the field of service design) (2016). Summary of Service Design Network, Service Design Impact Report: Public Sector 2016. Accessed 5 Jan 2021

12. DigDir: Tilsynet for universell utforming av ikt, Information in English (2020). Accessed 5 Jan 2021
13. Keates, S., et al.: Towards a practical inclusive design apprach. In: CUU 2000, Arlington, VA, USA. ACM (2000)
14. Battarbee, K., Suri, J.F., Howard, S.G.: Empathy on the Edge. Scaling and Sustaining a Human-Centered Approach in the Evolving Practice of Design. IDEO (2015). p. 14. http://5a5f89b8e10a225a44ac-ccbed124c38c4f7a3066210c073e7d55.r9.cf1.rackcdn.com/files/pdfs/news/Empathy_on_the_Edge.pdf
15. Stickdorn, M., Schneider, J.: This is Service Design Thinking. Wily, Hoboken (2011)
16. Stickdorn, M., et al.: This is Service Design Doing. O'Reilly Media, Sebastopol (2018)
17. ISO: ISO 9241-210:2010 Ergonomics of human-system interaction – Part 210: Human-centred design for interactive systems. ISO (2010). www.iso.org
18. Marshall, C., Rossman, G.B.: Designing Qualitative Research, 5th edn., p. 321. Sage, Los Angeles (2011)
19. Merriam, S.B.: Qualitative Research, A Guide to Design and Implementation, 2nd edn. Jossey-Bass, San Francisco. A Wiley Imprint. Wiley, Hoboken (2009)
20. Hanington, B., Martin, B.: Universal Methods of Design: 100 Ways to Research Complex Problems, Develop Innovative Ideas, and Design Effective Solutions. Rockport, Beverly (2012)
21. Leedy, P.D., Ormrod, J.E.: Practical Research Planning and Design, 10 edn. Pearson Education Limited, Essex (2014)
22. Stickdorn, M., et al.: This is Service Design Methods: A Companion to This is Service Design Doing, 1st edn., p. 240. O'Reilly, Canada (2018)
23. NTNU. Bachelorprogram 3-årig, Gjøvik: Interaksjonsdesign (2021). Accessed 7 Jan 2021
24. Begnum, M.E.N., Lintho Bue, O.: Lyntalk: "Inkluderende Tjenestedesign: Hvordan sikre universell utforming?" in Girl Geek Dinner Oslo - Tjenestedesign til folket! YouTube (2018). https://www.youtube.com/watch?v=_WSbRNpvbvs&feature=youtu.be&t=2193. p. 10 minutes
25. Begnum, M.E.N.: Inclusive Service Design—for edge-case and mainstream users. In: Lindeberg, A., Støren, H. (eds.) Medium (2018). https://3min.io/inclusive-service-design-for-edge-case-and-mainstream-users-3942ec9f2bd4
26. McDonagh, D.C., Formosa, D.: Designing for everyone, one person at a time. In: Kohlbacher, F., Herstatt, C. (eds.) The Silver Market Phenomenon, pp. 91–100. Springer, Heidelberg (2011). https://doi.org/10.1007/978-3-642-14338-0_7
27. Begnum, M.E.N.: Universal Service Design through Empathic Service Safaris. Inclusive Design Toolkit news bulletin (2019)
28. Harder, S.K., Begnum, M.: Ensuring Universal Design in ICT-Solutions - Towards Identifying Critical Success Factors. NTNU Norwegian University of Science and Technology (2017)
29. Begnum, M.E.N.: Universal design of ICT: a historical journey from specialized adaptations towards designing for diversity. In: Antona, M., Stephanidis, C. (eds.) HCII 2020. LNCS, vol. 12188, pp. 3–18. Springer, Cham (2020). https://doi.org/10.1007/978-3-030-49282-3_1
30. Fuglerud, K.S., Sloan, D.: The link between inclusive design and innovation: some key elements. In: Kurosu, M. (ed.) HCI 2013. LNCS, vol. 8004, pp. 41–50. Springer, Heidelberg (2013). https://doi.org/10.1007/978-3-642-39232-0_5
31. designabetterbusiness.com. Persona Canvas (2019)
32. Begnum, M.E.N.: Facilitating and advancing universal design of ICT. In: Institutt for datateknologi og informatikk. NTNU Open, NTNU, Gjøvik (2019)
33. Brugnoli, G.: Connecting the dots of user experience. J. Inf. Archit. 1(1), 6–15 (2009)
34. University of Cambridge: Inclusive Design Toolkit, Cambridge Simulation Glasses (2017). Accessed 7 Jan 2021

35. NDA: Customer Communications Toolkit for the Public Service - A Universal Design App-roach, I. Department of Public Expenditure and Reform, Editor, Centre for Excellence in Universal Design (CEUD) at the National Disability Authority (NDA). http://publicservice. universaldesign.ie/media/NDA_Universal_Design_Public_Service_Toolkit.pdf
36. Connell, B.R., et al.: The principles of universal design, Version 2.0 - 4/1/97 (1997). Accessed 9 May 2018
37. Blomkvist, J., Arvola, M.: Pausing or not? Examining the service walkthrough technique. In: BCS-HCI 2014 Proceedings of the 28th International BCS Human Computer Interaction Conference on HCI 2014 - Sand, Sea and Sky - Holiday HCI, Southport, UK. ACM (2014)
38. Mebuke, T.: Archetype development in narrative (diachronic study). In: 6th International Conference on Consciousness, Theatre, Literature and the Arts (CTLA), St Francis College, Brooklyn Heights, New York. Cambridge Scholars Publishing (2015)

Civic Community Archiving with the Platform for Experimental Collaborative Ethnography: Double Binds and Design Challenges

Kim Fortun[1] [iD], Mike Fortun[1][(✉)] [iD], Angela Hitomi Skye Crandall Okune[1] [iD],
Tim Schütz[1] [iD], and Shan-Ya Su[2]

[1] Department of Anthropology, University of California, Irvine, CA 92697, USA
fortunm@uci.edu
[2] School of Law, University of California Berkeley, Berkeley, CA 94720, USA

Abstract. Community archives serve an array of purposes and types of communities (fan clubs, scientists in particular disciplines, ethnic neighborhoods). We discuss here *civic* community archives; civic archives, like "civic science," have expressly progressive political aims, question established order, and contribute to inclusive knowledge production and prosperity. Designing civic archives involves many types of analysis and poses many design challenges. In this paper, we share an analytic framework developed to guide the design of civic community archives, drawing on both cultural theory and our experience designing archives for different kinds of communities, with different purposes, within larger ethnographic projects. We question how to characterize "the community" in community archive projects, and the stakeholders in such projects. We ask what should be recollected in community archives and for what purposes. We also ask how, by design, community archives can connect diverse users, analog and digital components (including human and technological), and complicated pasts to creative futures. Throughout, we call out the double-binds of civic community archiving, delineating risks and possible pathologies as well as generative potential. We approach the work as cultural anthropologists and ethnographers involved in building the Platform for Experimental Collaborative Ethnography (https://github.com/PECE-project/pece-distro), open source digital infrastructure for sharing and collaborative analysis of ethnographic data.

Keywords: Ethnography · Cultural heritage · Civic community archiving · Digital infrastructure

1 Introduction

Ethnographers can study ways peoples produce, use, share, and preserve knowledge, sometimes integrating digital tools into their methods. Ethnographers have used Facebook to support interactions among and engagement with the people they study to supplement face-to-face interactions, for example, considering this a type of "expanded ethnography" that is not only observant but also productive of exchanges that lend

© Springer Nature Switzerland AG 2021
M. Rauterberg (Ed.): HCII 2021, LNCS 12795, pp. 36–55, 2021.
https://doi.org/10.1007/978-3-030-77431-8_3

insight into the identities, relationships and processes the ethnographer seeks to understand (Piacenti et al. 2014; Baker 2013; Beneito-Montagut 2011). In turn, ethnographers can also design digital tools and spaces for the people they study, moving from observation, analysis, and interpretation to technology development intended to scaffold and extend the knowledge practices with which they are concerned. The work described here is in the latter vein, leveraging the Platform for Experimental Collaborative Ethnography (PECE), open source software that supports collaborative preservation, curation, analysis and interpretation of qualitative data. Using PECE, the authors have built a suite of digital archives supporting different types of communities in their efforts to understand and address shared problems. The approach integrates emic and etic perspectives, working both with community members' understanding of the knowledge infrastructure they need and with ethnographic and theoretical understanding of their political, social and discursive contexts. It also depends on technical skill, creativity and criticism.

Community archives serve an array of purposes and types of communities (fan clubs, scientists in particular disciplines, and ethnic neighborhoods, for example) (Flinn 2019; Nelson 2016; SAADA 2018). We are particularly interested in *civic* community archives; civic archives, like "civic science," have expressly progressive political aims, questioning established order, contributing to inclusive knowledge production and prosperity (Fortun and Fortun 2005). Designing civic archives involves many types of analysis and poses many design challenges. Most importantly, civic community archives need to be customized to address particular power dynamics and associated social and discursive formations: they need to be designed to *push back* against business as usual (Fortun et al. 2016). Understanding the context of civic community archives is thus critical; their designs need to be "appropriate," meshing with their particular contexts rather than complying with universal standards (Fortun 2004a, b).

Our conception of civic community archives draws extensively on social, literary, psychoanalytic and pedagogical theory, recognizing the importance of many interlaced dynamics both within and in the surrounds of digital systems (Koch 2017). In our work on community archives, John Dewey's *The Public and Its Problems* is a particularly important reference. Dewey argues that democracy depends on the formation of publics with shared concern about social problems, but that powerful market and state forces often subdue the formation of these publics and, in turn, their criticisms. Publics thus need to be prompted to form, leveraging diverse modes of communication, producing signs and symbols through which people can see themselves in context. Dewey explains that as "symbols are related to one another, the important relations of a course of events are recorded and are preserved as meanings. Recollection and foresight are possible; the new medium facilitates calculation, planning, and a new kind of action which intervenes in what happens to direct its course in the interest of what is foreseen and desired (Dewey 1927: 330–331). We envision civic community archives as having the potential to prompt publics into existence in this fashion.

Our work on civic community archives also extends from work in the "literary turn" in history and cultural anthropology. Hayden White's *Metahistory* is illustrative, drawing out how the structure (not only the prose content) of historical and philosophical texts carries their meaning (1973). White describes, for example, how the structure of Ranke's and Hegel's texts are integrative and organicist (with synecdoche as the dominant trope), have the structure of a comedy, and encode a conservative ideology. This way of thinking about texts has continued to be important in experimental ethnography (Fischer 2018; Trouillot 1995; Clifford and Marcus 1986). It has also guided the way we think about digital design and the structure of civic community archives. Digital systems, too, encode ideology and produce meaning through their structure as well as their content. As a result digital systems, like texts, constitute their readers/users as subjects. This is why we see the technical design of digital systems as so generative and significant: such design sets up users in ways at least as powerful as the content they move through.

In what follows, we describe how we have moved from ethnographic research on knowledge, memory and data systems into the design of digital research infrastructure (PECE) to support collaboration among ethnographers. This, in turn, enabled us to move into the development of civic community archives. We describe the design goals, structure and function of PECE, noting how, in many ways, PECE is deliberately out-of-joint with HCI principles (cf. Ambielli 2018). We briefly describe the research we do to support PECE development, and the analytic framework we have developed to guide the design of PECE-supported civic community archives. We then describe two civic community archives now under construction, and the double binds and design challenges they have posed. We close with a description of the process we are planning to vet and refine the community archives we are developing, extending the para-site approach developed at University of California Irvine's Center for Ethnography (Marcus 2013). We envision the parasite events planned as a form of in-process, collaborative peer review particularly suitable for scholar projects that interlace ethnography and design.

2 Memory Making as Cultural and Political Praxis

2.1 Ethnographic Studies of Thought Styles, Memory, Evidence, and Trading Zones

As ethnographers, we specialize in the study of knowledge practices, infrastructures, innovation, and politics. Our ethnographic research then guides our work in what we term design anthropology, moving from what we have learned as ethnographers to the design and development of knowledge infrastructure responsive to the challenges and aspirations of the places and people we study. In this, our ethnography "loops," becoming a guide to collaborative and creative praxis (Fortun 2012).

As ethnographers, we document and analyze the "thought-styles" of different communities, including disciplinarily diverse scientific communities, environmental activists and community organizers. Our focus is on the discursive formations and narratives through which people collectively make sense of and act in their worlds (Fleck 1981 [1935]). We want to understand what is remembered, how the past is narrativized and to what effect. We observe the kinds of data that people consider useful, meaningful and persuasive. What counts as data worth collecting, what goals and ends shape its production, and what analytic perspectives guide its interpretation are some of our concerns as ethnographers of knowledge. Ethnography of knowledge includes the ethnography of data, evidence and memory.

As conceptualized by historian of science and molecular biologist Ludwig Fleck, "thought styles" are far from monolithic or homogeneous; indeed, their ability to generate shared perceptions as well as new thinking and creative solutions depends on different members of a scientific "thought collective" belonging to multiple thought collectives, and on the mixing of the different abilities, insights, and interests of a more "esoteric" circle of experts and professionals with those of a more "exoteric" circle of people with more "generalized" knowledge, including lay persons. Extending from this, we also study how people, ideas, data and memories circulate, and how such circulation drives cultural and social change. In this, we often focus our observations on what historian of science Galison (1997) has called "trading zones," where people with different skills and knowledge come together for collaborative work. Scientists can work across "vast global differences," Galison demonstrates, to "hammer out a local coordination" similar to the way groups that speak different natural languages establish contact languages to enable interaction. Galison's concept of "trading zones" has been taken up in multiple areas, to orient both scholarly analysis and practical work (Fincher and Petre 2004; Gorman 2002; Gorman et al. 2009). In our research, we approach digital systems as trading zones, analysing who they bring together and who they exclude, what is foregrounded and what is occluded or missing. We also analyze the political effects of digital systems and data infrastructure, drawing out connections to social vulnerability, inequality and multiple forms of injustice.

2.2 From Ethnography to Design and Capacity Building

As described above, our ethnographic research has examined how data infrastructure subtends both social vulnerability and capacity to recognize and address such vulnerability. Stemming from this, we have become increasingly invested in understanding and helping build what we have come to think of as public knowledge infrastructure and "data capacity" (including technical infrastructure, public data resources, analytic and visualization capabilities, and supporting educational programs and fields of expertise).[1] Data capacity powerfully shapes how societies anticipate, characterize, and deal with collective problems. Given the tangles of problems contemporary societies face – and need to work on together – building public data capacity with both local relevance and global scope is a high priority. This will be far from straightforward, depending on inventive project designs linking researchers across disciplines, generations, and geographies; linking research to education at all levels; and building new connections between universities, civil society organizations (including cultural institutions), governments, international organizations and businesses. These have become key long-term aims of our work.

Over the last two years, we've developed multiple projects that experiment with ways to build data capacity and public knowledge infrastructure. As previously noted, this work extends from and is guided by what we have learned through ethnographic research: our work in design anthropology translates our findings as ethnographers of knowledge. All of our digital design projects "loop" in this way (Fortun 2012), carrying forward what we have learned in other ethnographic projects.

---

[1] We recognize that "capacity" has become a widely circulated developmental "buzzword" (Cornwall 2007) which carries negative valences amongst many communities who have been frequent subjects of development interventions. We use it to signal the continued importance of building up individual and collective abilities to work together on a tangle of late industrial issues.

Here we describe our work to develop civic community archives, which builds on earlier work to develop digital research infrastructure (PECE) for collaborative ethnography. We first developed PECE for our own research, but always with an eye toward making it more widely usable; it is now freely available (and customizable) as a GitHub download (https://pece-project.github.io/drupal-pece/).

3   The Platform for Experimental Collaborative Ethnography

3.1   PECE Software and Research

PECE is open source (Drupal-based) software supporting virtual research environments for cultural anthropologists, historians, cultural heritage scholars, and other researchers working with diverse data (including extensive unstructured data), largely through interpretive methods. Various, thematically-focused PECE instances provide space to archive and curate data, facilitate collaborative analysis of data, and enable diverse modes of visualization, scholarly communication, and peer review.

In the last decade, PECE software has become widely used, with customizable digital infrastructure supporting the workflows, data types and interpretive modalities in what we call the "empirical humanities." There are now many instances of PECE supporting diverse research communities. (An instance is a distinct copy of the software, with distinct content.) Work on the following instances of PECE informs on-going software development:

> https://theasthmafiles.org/ | http://housingenergy.info/ | https://disaster-sts-net work.org/ | http://centerforethnography.org/ | https://stsinfrastructures.org/ | https://www.researchdatashare.org/ | https://worldpece.org/ |

The worldpece.org instance of PECE houses research supporting PECE development examining, for example, data management and peer review practices in different disciplines, and the theoretical underpinnings of diverse digital humanities projects (Fortun et al. 2020; Poirier et al. 2019; Fortun et al. 2017). An important thread of PECE research especially relevant to the development of civic community archives examines how data infrastructure projects – like California's Cradle-to Career Data System – can be designed to meet the needs of diverse stakeholders. Another thread of PECE research examines how community archives can be designed to support community memory, knowledge production and strategies for dealing with problems like climate change (Almeida and Hoyer 2019; Buchanan and Bastian 2015; Caswell 2017; Caswell et al. 2016). PECE development has also been guided by the PECE Design Group's engagement with the Research Data Alliance, where we have served as co-chairs of the Digital Practices in History and Ethnography Interest Group since 2013.

The worldpece.org instance of PECE also houses tutorials supporting PECE platform administration, project design and use (which are used in workshops like this one for Learning PECE). The PECE user community has included students (as young as middle school through dissertation research) and researchers in multiple counties.

3.2   PECE Architecture and Functionality

PECE is usefully thought of as a triptych, providing shared digital space for archiving, collaborative analysis, and creative expression. Integrating these functions into one platform makes PECE unique, and also imposed a number of design demands which we elaborate below. Overarching all of these was a commitment to build not simply a Drupal-based website that combined these three features, but a Drupal distribution that enables anyone or any organization to download the source code from GitHub and install a new instance of the platform with all of the innovations we have developed, which they can then tailor to their own projects. Every design decision we made, therefore, was done with these larger communities in mind, knowing that both the features and the drawbacks of our platform would carry over to future users.

In the first space of the triptych, for example, users archive and curate data "artifacts," primarily documents, images, audio and video recordings. Because our collaborative ethnographic projects include researchers from many different parts of the world, using technologies of varying kinds and quality, we decided not to build in standards (of recording quality, for example) that many archives require. We also designed all interfaces so that they could render on mobile devices, allowing users to upload photos or recordings directly from a mobile phone while in the field, wherever that might be. And because we wanted to create open archives which anyone could access and to which anyone could contribute, we had to allow (unlike many if not most archives in libraries and institutions) for ongoing registration of new users; spam control and a site administrator always on call became required features.

PECE employs a modified version of Dublin Core metadata for its content. Content in many digital humanities projects is often drawn from materials already catalogued by libraries; because ethnographers and community groups are constantly producing new data, they have to provide this kind of metadata themselves. One effect of this is that PECE as yet does not allow for batch uploads (of a large number of photographs, for example), and requires users to enter metadata, including licensing information, to each artifact. Every user takes some curatorial responsibility. PECE can also assign Archival Research Keys ARKs) as needed, a persistent identifier that makes data always findable while crediting a contributor.

By design, PECE encourages open data sharing when appropriate, partly by allowing researchers to archive data in a way that makes it easy to open access to the data at different points in the research process. But since most ethnographers also produce and work with sensitive materials, content uploaded to a PECE instance can be designated "private" (accessible only to one or more people listed as contributors), as fully public, or as restricted to either a select group or to all registered users of a platform. This allows users to comply with ethics review requirements while still digitally archiving data in a manner ready for sharing when appropriate, and also to change these permissions at any time, opening up previously private material or taking material out of public circulation while still preserving it. Users can also set an expiration date for data content, after which the data content is removed from the platform. Researchers can remove their data from a PECE instance at any time.

PECE as TRIPTYCH		
ARCHIVING	**ANALYZING**	**COMMUNICATION**
bibliographies | pdfs | word documents | images | audio & video recordings | web urls	data sets | news articles | maps | policies | government reports | organizations | scientific studies	text artifacts | timelines | photo essays | collage essays | video | audio | virtual tours

A PECE design innovation is the support it provides for collaborative analysis (the second space of the triptych), by people both within and across different communities. Platforms similar to PECE like Omeka (https://omeka.org/) and Mukurtu (https://mukurtu.org/) excel at exhibiting their archived materials (Mukurtu's "Traditional Knowledge License" also adds nuanced protections to its cultural heritage content), but like almost all archival content, their primary and even exclusive function is to preserve. Data remains inviolate, true to its original form and intent. PECE analytic structures keep archives "feverish" (Derrida 1998) and alive, adding new kinds of metadata in the form of open-ended interpretations to every data object. Data is in effect constantly re-made through the accrual of interpretations that activate new meanings in the initial artifact. PECE analytic structures supporting this can be co-produced with community members, archived and made accessible across communities. This can result in a lively, generative space for both local and trans-local community knowledge production.

3.3 PECE Projects

PECE instances are thematically focused and are designed to host multiple projects that can build on and borrow from each other. The Disaster-STS Network instance of PECE (https://disaster-sts-network.org), for example, includes kindred projects such as the Quotidian Anthropocene project and the Beyond Environmental Injustice project (which includes case studies of environmental injustice in over 20 California counties, produced by undergraduate students at UC Irvine).

Visualizing Toxic Subjects (http://centerforethnography.org/content/visualizing-toxic-subjects-project-page/essay) is a collaborative project (on the UC Irvine Center for Ethnography instance) in which participants collect, narrate, share and analyze ethnographic visualizations, reinventing the use of visual materials in the conduct and expression of ethnography. Participants built digital photo essays and a gallery exhibit of images that convey toxicity in its many forms and guises – environmental, political, media, and others. The project began fall 2018, moved through multiple phases of digital collaboration, then to a gallery show in May 2019.

STS Infrastructures is another instance of PECE, established to provide a digital archive, collaboration, and publishing space for Science and Technology Studies (STS), an international research community focused on the social dimensions of science and technology. "STS Across Borders," a special exhibit for the 2018 annual meetings of the Society for Social Studies of Science (4S), was the first major project run on the platform. "Innovating STS" was a special exhibit for the 2019 annual 4S meeting. STS Infrastructures now hosts an array of projects, including the Transnational STS Working Group, annual workshop materials for the student section of 4S, and oral histories of STS researchers.

3.4   PECE, Writing Culture, and HCI

PECE was first developed to support the practical needs of collaborative ethnographic projects involving geographically distributed researchers working in the so-called "literary turn" of cultural anthropology that began in the mid-1980s. A central feature of the "literary turn," sometimes also called the "postmodern turn," is a shift from a representational "thought style" in which faithful reproduction and observer neutrality were essential terms, to a style in which the performative effects of language, genre, and form became central concerns and objects of analysis in themselves (Marcus and Fischer 1986; Clifford and Marcus 1986).

Mauthner and Gardos (2015) describe a parallel shift in archival theory and practice, as these moved from treating "records and artifacts as representations of reality" to foregrounding how archived data and the memories they embody are "made and remade through multiple practices including data generation, data curation, and data analysis." So although the design and development of PECE was not informed at first by work in HCI or archival sciences, we have since learned much from their research and principles, though aware that, in many ways, we have designed against the HCI or archival grain. Efficient information retrieval is rarely a main goal, for example, nor a match between the systems we are building and "the real world." In most cases, our archives are built to be assertively counter-hegemonic. Our archives are also, often, "rogue" – building from Abigail deKosnik explication of rogue archives as "largely run by people that do not have training or expertise in library and information studies," as "nominally barrier-less to access," housing "content that has never been, and would never likely be, contained in a traditional memory institution, are "identity- and culture-generating," and become "intertextual sites of…community performance, inspiration, [and] reaffirmation" (Watson 2020; De Kosnik 2016).

Many of the design principles that guided our development of PECE were also informed by concepts, theories, and practices of feminist anthropology and feminist science and technology studies (STS). It was only later that we came to appreciate that this scholarship also contributed to feminist approaches in HCI. Bardzell (CHI 2010: 1307) has shown how feminist HCI research and design works to advance many of the same values and goals as we have in developing PECE: valuing pluralism in epistemology and interpretation over universalism; encouraging and incorporating both participatory methods and the participation of marginalized voices; and ensuring that digital technologies like PECE are "self-disclosing," always foregrounding how software and interface design create a certain kind of user-subject, and thus should introduce a "critical distance between users and interactions".

Kindred perspectives have been developed in critical heritage studies. Archivist and scholar Leisa Gibbons, for example, has developed the Mediated Recordkeeping Model (MRkM) as "a tool that can be used to map multiple, simultaneous realities from different points of view," building community capacity to co-create cultural heritage materials and archives (Gibbons 2018: 905). This is highly resonant with the aspirations of PECE and many PECE projects and archives.

4 Designing PECE-Supported Civic Archives

In this section we share an analytic framework that we've developed to guide the design of civic community archives, drawing on both cultural theory and our experience designing archives for different kinds of communities, with different purposes, within larger ethnographic projects. We'll question how to characterize "the community" in community archive projects, and the stakeholders in such projects. We'll ask what should be recollected in community archives and for what purposes. We'll also ask how, by design, community archives can connect diverse users, analog and digital components (including human and technological), and complicated pasts to creative futures.

In moving to construct archives expressly designed for publics beyond our own research groups, we have developed a new set of shared questions that help us envision the purposes, form, functions, risks and potential of these archives. Questions we ask (technically supported by a PECE Analytic Structure) include:

PECE ANALYTIC
DESIGNING CIVIC COMMUNITY ARCHIVES

This World PECE Analytic was develop to guide collaborative conceptualization and design of PECE-supported civic community archives. The questions will be added to worldpece.org as a PECE analytic structure that poses questions that can be addressed across different civic community archiving projects.

1. What was the original purpose of this archive and how has its purpose shifted over time? What social discursive ecologies are the archive situated within?
2. What is the archive designed to remember?
3. What exclusions, inequalities and injustices (procedural, media, economic, imperial, etc.) is this archive designed against?
4. Who are the stakeholders in this archive? What differences of interests and perspective are likely to be in play? What publics/networks/communities does or could the archive interface with?
5. Who are likely and hoped for users of this archive?
6. Does this archive aspire to *create* a public (following John Dewey's arguments about the need to provoke publics into existence)?
7. What types of data does the archive include and why? How is data presented and how are users encouraged to interact with the data?
8. What practices and tasks are the archive designed to support? Are workflows meant to be linear and efficient or exploratory and experiential?
9. What forms of participation (Kelty) does this archive aspire to -- and actually -- support? Where in the archive's architecture and workflows is participation supported and encouraged?
10. How does this archive connect users? What kinds of collaboration does this archive support and encourage?
11. How does this archive leverage the various genre forms PECE supports?
12. What are the affects of engaging with this archive?
13. How is the archive enabled, or constrained, by PECE's design logics?
14. How is the archive discoverable and accessible? If there are restricted spaces, how do users gain entry?
15. How has this archive been connected to events and practices beyond the digital domain?
16. Where is this (PECE-supported) archive hosted and what technical services and infrastructure does it depend on? What software and other technologies beyond PECE does it incorporate or interface with?
17. What labor (voluntary and paid) and financial support does this archive depend on?

5 PECE Civic Archives in Construction

Currently, there are many PECE-supported civic community archives in development. One archive (being built on http://theasthmafiles.org) is designed to support a neighborhood organization that is running a community air monitoring system. One purpose of this archive is to preserve, interpret, and share a growing body of evidence that the neighborhood is subject to severe, disproportionate pollution. Another purpose is to convey how the organization has come to focus on environmental injustice after working for many years on other problems; while environmental injustice in their neighborhood isn't new, its emergence as a *public* problem (in John Dewey's sense) is. PECE timelines and photo essays will be used to convey this history, allowing the neighborhood organization to share their development with neighborhood residents, city planners and funders.

Another PECE-supported community archive project (built on http://disaster-sts-network.org/) is designed to support a transnational, interdisciplinary community of experts working to address radiation health hazards, working across problem areas (uranium mining, bomb test sites, nuclear power plants and nuclear medicine) usually dealt with separately. This archive will, in part, be a portal to other archives (with oral histories, virtual tours of nuclear power plants, government documents obtained through freedom-of-information requests, etc.), providing space for collaborative analysis and interpretation of material in these archives. In this archive, links to items in other archives will be added as PECE artifacts that are then annotated with analytic structures developed specifically for the project. The "community" in this archive isn't local but needs to think in concert about many different localities around the world dealing with radiation hazards.

Each PECE-supported civic community archive has a particular purpose, delineated through ethnographic research. These archives preserve different kinds of data, and use PECE affordances in different ways. Their users are very diverse, and can't be addressed in universalist terms. A key challenge ahead is to learn how to learn across these diverse civic archiving projects, not looking for standard protocols but for creative insight into ways digital archives work (and often fail) as trading zones and animators of civic action. We provide more extensive description of two additional civic community archives below.

5.1 Research Data Share (Nairobi, Kenya)

Research Data Share is a digital workspace and archive established to support a community of practitioners concerned about the kinds of data (especially qualitative data) and data practices needed to (re)animate critical civic engagement in Nairobi. By drawing people into the practical work of building an archive (and deciding what should be preserved and shared), it seeks to recollect the vibrancy of Nairobi's public sphere in the 1960s and 1970s, when there was active and creative visioning of an Africa for and by Africans. In 1972, for example, the trio of Ngugi wa Thiong'o, Henry Owuor Anyumba and Taban lo Liyong famously proposed abolishing the English Department at the University of Nairobi to make space for literary forms and aesthetics rooted in Kenya rather than outside (Musila 2019; Gikandi and Mwangi 2007). Paradoxically, the civic vibrancy of the earlier period has now been largely eclipsed, despite both putatively democratic governance and Nairobi's recent rise as "Silicon Savannah" (Stroisch 2018; Bright 2015). As a major tech hub today, Nairobi is dotted with start-up spaces and is teeming with (idealized) tech entrepreneurs. It also produces large quantities of qualitative data, much of it for commercial purposes (to guide development of app-based banking services, for example, and to understand "tech culture" itself). Meanwhile, many people (both tech entrepreneurs and people living in the city's massive, under- resourced informal settlements) feel over-researched, without reciprocal benefit. And the halls of the university are quiet. Students have become tightly focused on upwardly mobile job opportunities and there is limited visioning of what Nairobi and Kenya could become on its own terms.

Research Data Share (RDS) was established (as its own PECE instance) in late 2018 by anthropologist Angela Okune as an elicitation device for understanding the diverse "thought-styles" of Nairobi-based researchers producing and working with qualitative data. From the start, RDS was also used to share the project's own data, modeling what open data in qualitative research can look like, inviting commentary. Okune's research included engagements with different kinds of Nairobi-based organizations (of different sizes, with different histories, international connections and ambitions, sometimes commercial) that produce qualitative data about Kenyans. In some cases, there was interest in PECE simply because it provides an organizational structure for storing, re-finding and commenting on qualitative data. Others were looking to lower their research costs (by reusing other people's data rather than collecting their own). Still others were (or became) concerned about the postcoloniality of research in Kenya and with ways to reach beyond knowledge imperialism (Okune 2020).

Okune learned about these sentiments through traditional ethnographic interviews and also by working with people side-by-side in RDS. Okune also organized a public event - "Archiving Kenya's Past and Futures" – at McMillan Library, one of the oldest libraries in Kenya. This event was designed to create interest in both RDS and a gamut of questions about the kind of knowledge infrastructure needed in Kenya at this stage. The event drew in librarians, academic researchers and people in government agencies charged with catalysing research. It resulted in the formation of the Research Data KE Working Group, which has sustained the dialogue using RDS as virtual workspace.

Work on RDS has rotated around PECE's support for open-ended annotation. In most cases, Okune uploads artifacts – her own interview recordings and data analysis, found material (news articles, social media posts) focused on issues like open access in Africa and the COVID-19 pandemic, proceedings of RDS hosted events – and invites annotation using PECE's analytic structures. All members of the groups have the permissions needed to upload artifacts but this often seems overly laborious, especially since dialogue about the artifacts often begins on a WhatsApp channel before moving to RDS. Here, PECE's design has been both catalyzing and constraining. Since PECE does not allow bulk uploads, each artifact added must be justified with commentary. This means that every artifact has an interpretive supplement from the start but this can be challenging in a fast-paced research environment like Nairobi, where "time is money".

RDS provides a space to learn about the evidence practices and data cultures in play in Nairobi's hyper-lively qualitative research domain, drawing out many factors that influence these (age; whether a researcher is Kenyan, or not; location in a private form, perspectives on multinational corporate involvement, etc.). RDS is also designed to *engender* a public (in John Dewey's sense), prompting sustained collective engagement with issues that market forces easily eclipse.

5.2 Recollecting Multinational Petrochemical Companies (Taiwan, USA, Vietnam)

The Formosa Plastics Global Archive[2] is designed to support a transnational network of people concerned about the operations of Formosa Plastics Corporation, a vertically-integrated Taiwanese petrochemical company. Formosa Plastics is one of the largest chemical companies in the world, with facilities in Taiwan, China, Vietnam, and the United States. Formosa has a damaging record of explosions, routine pollution, and "mafia-like" behavior with environmental activists and other critics (Democracy Now 2020; PRI 2020). Formosa Plastics also has its own museum, located on the grounds of Chang Gung Formosa Plastics University, near Taipei. Chang Gung University grew out of a hospital set up by Formosa in 1976 "to make a meaningful contribution to Taiwan's society." Today, the university uses "the successful management model of Formosa Plastics Corporation and its resources" to build students' management knowledge (https://www.cgu.edu.tw/p/404-1000-17343.php?Lang=en).

The Formosa Plastics Museum has six floors, with exhibits celebrating the founder and spirit of the Formosa Plastics Group (complete with dioramas and wax figures) and a miniature replica of Formosa's 6th Sixth Naphtha Cracking Plant. The fifth floor has an Earth Conservation Theatre. The sixth floor conveys how Formosa has given back to society through investment in education, hospitals, and cultural heritage projects.

Formosa Plastics continues to expand, extending production capacity at existing sites and with plans for a new multi-billion dollar chemical manufacturing complex in St. James Parish, Louisiana, an area already known as "Cancer Alley." Lawsuits have been filed and activists have been mobilized to challenge approval of the project by Louisiana's Department of Environmental Quality. Arguments against approval refer to Formosa Plastics' long history of misconduct, to the area's already exceptionally high pollution burden, and to the history and present challenges of nearby African American communities. They also note massive local property tax exemptions, approved by the Louisiana Board of Commerce. Formosa Plastics and Louisiana state agencies continue to insist that the new complex will bring jobs and other economic benefits (Mosbrucker 2020).

Opposition to Formosa Plastics has, in some cases, been successful. In 2019, for example, a lawsuit filed by people living near Formosa's facility in Port Comfort, Texas resulted in a US $50 million settlement. The lead plaintiff, former shrimp boat captain Diane Wilson, has been watching and resisting Formosa since the early 1990s. The records Wilson has kept (including leaked company audits, interviews with workers, and years of news clippings) fill a large barn. In recent years, traveling by kayak, Wilson and others have been on nurdle patrol, tracking Formosa's plastic pollution discharge to local waterways. The recent legal settlement included funds to support this work to assess compliance with a court order for "zero discharge." Weekly water monitoring reports produced by Wilson and collaborators include photographs and textual descriptions of plastic pellet pollution at water discharge outlets from the Formosa plant. Wilson also donates plastic pellets to the citizen science initiative Nurdle Patrol at the University of Texas at Austin.

---

[2] The archive name remains preliminary and may be changed for strategic or legal reasons.

The PECE-supported Formosa Plastics Archive (at disaster-sts-network.org) grew out of ethnographic research to understand the data infrastructure available and used (by activists, scientists, government regulators and corporations) to characterize environmental health hazards, especially in highly polluted communities, many situated on the fencelines of high risk industrial facilities. This has been an important focus of ethnographic research at least since the 1980s, when the Union Carbide chemical plant disaster in Bhopal, India provoked environmental "right-to-know" legislation around the world (Fortun 2004). Since then, it has become clear that environmental politics always involves data politics. Political antagonism often revolves around what date is produced, used, considered credible, and dismissed. *How* data is represented and narrativized is also contested.

Awareness of ways environmental and data politics are entwined has catalyzed intensive data collection practices among environmental activists, often accumulated over decades of work. The data is heterogeneous, unstructured and usually informally organized. Often, the person who collected the data needs to be interviewed to learn about its provenance and relevance. There is an overwhelming amount of material to sort through, and many ways of thinking about what should be prioritized for sharing. Some of the material is relevant in lawsuits seeking damages or in efforts to slow Formosa Plastics' expansions. In these cases, timing the publication of data needs to be strategic; to manage this, the Formosa Plastics Global Archive uses PECE's capacity to preserve and work with data in digital spaces restricted to a delimited group until ready for release.

The Formosa Plastics Global Archive also includes a set of courtroom sketches drawn by sociologist Paul Jobin supporting plaintiffs in a case. These sketches powerfully recall both the dynamics of the legal case and are an inspiring example of collaboration between academic researchers and communities impacted by pollution. In working with these data, we learned that court illustrations are a recognized data type and that we can learn from on-going curation of these at places like the U.S. Library of Congress.[3]

Environmental data sharing has strategic importance in especially complex ways when dealing with multinational corporations. Data collected in one place can have both informational and tactical value in other places (helping people understand the special processes and hazards of ethylene oxide (EtO) production, for example, as well as ways it has been governed; news that the US has committed to massive reduction in EtO emissions suggest that much improved environmental protection is technically possible elsewhere as well). The Formosa Plastics Global Archive is designed to support data sharing of this sort. It is also designed to prompt people in different Formosa locations to see themselves as part of a shared community-of-practice. Like the Nairobi-centered PECE archive (RDS), the Formosa Plastics Global Archive is designed to *engender* a public that doesn't yet see itself in collective terms. The archive is meant to activate not represent social relations.

Anthropologists Tim Schütz and Shan-Ya Su have taken the lead designing and developing the Formosa Plastics Global Archive, working across sites in Taiwan and the

---

[3] See the Wikipedia entry on the courtroom sketch as a data type (https://en.wikipedia.org/wiki/Courtroom_sketch), and "Drawing Justice: The Art of Courtroom Illustrations archive at the US Library of Congress (https://www.loc.gov/exhibitions/drawing-justice-courtroom-illustrations/about-this-exhibition/).

United States, moving between academia, courtrooms, personal data collections (like Diane Wilson's barn) and cultural institutions (like the Formosa Plastics Museum). They are curators, intensely attuned to the overlapping contexts in which the archive they are building will operate, working against both corporate greenwashing and the isolation of geographically distributed communities impacted by Formosa Plastics' operations.

The Formosa Plastics Global Archive is multi-lingual, and tells many stories at once. Weaving these stories together is a challenge, narratively and technically. One strategy so far – built out under the title Sugar Plantations, Chemical Plants, Covid-19 – literally walks people to Formosa, through a virtual tour of Louisiana's Cancer Alley, stopping at the Sunshine Bridge on the Mississippi River near the proposed site of the new Formosa Plastics complex. At the Sunshine Bridge stop, visitors are invited into the Formosa Plastics Global Archive, which opens up pathways to many other places where Formosa operates. The virtual tour makes use of many PECE functions and genres, especially the shadow-box-like PECE essay. The tour is designed to mimic physical-world walking tours, inspired especially by the "toxic tours" run by environmental activists in many settings. Rendered virtually, the tour collects diverse representations of Cancer Alley (put together over many years) that are especially powerful in tandem (helping people zoom into the deep history and complex landscape of Cancer Alley). The tour also encourages visitors to zoom out, seeing Formosa Plastics' global reach. Efficient, goal-oriented movement through the tour and larger archive is not the design goal; users are meant to explore and experience the material, coming away transformed.

6   Double Binds and Design Challenges

Ethnographic projects are usually replete with double binds and design challenges, especially when critically engaged with the forms of their own articulation (Fortun et al. 2017). Double binds are not simply the result of competing choices or difficult decisions; a double binding situations are the product of at least two incompatible, contradictory statements or demands that can neither be avoided nor resolved (Bateson 2000, Visser 2003). In what follows, we describe a few double binds that we've encountered thus far in PECE-supported civic community archiving projects.

First, there are double binds in naming: names establish and represent a singular stable identity, but every identity is a multiplicity and set of relationalities, already and inevitably unstable. This double bind is particularly powerful in digital knowledge infrastructure, which runs on an ontology of stable names literally coded into the system and has no space for plural and ambivalent meaning. Even basic terms like "archives," "data set," "community," and "civic" have different meanings and valences in different contexts, and to different user communities.[4] This divergence is of course exacerbated when translating between languages. In some contexts, for example, "civic" data is understood narrowly as government data. In many contexts in the Global South, both "civic" and "capacity building" are widely perceived as owned (and tainted) by their association with development projects. In our work on civic community archives, we

---

[4] In translating a description of the Quotidian Anthropocene Archive project into Turkish, for example, we were asked if "data collection" is equivalent to "data set," with the translator oscillating between "veri seti" (data set) and "veri toplama".

work to keep such pluralism and ambivalence in view rather than subsumed beneath the same name.

Another double bind PECE has to negotiate is that between signal and noise, figure and ground, controlled meaning and unruly excess. One way to think about archives, and virtually all digital knowledge infrastructure, is as a machine for ordering and transmitting signals, authorized meanings extracted and isolated from a sea of noise. Archives *must* do this; only ordered, authorized objects can be findable and thus meet the first FAIR principle of data sharing (to be findable, accessible, interoperable, and reusable). We have worked hard to make PECE do this, to make its archival data meaningful, discoverable signal. But as ethnographers, we also work hard to always attend to and present what is marginalized as noise, to keep in our analytic workflows what the hegemonic system considers to be unauthorized or meaningless. PECE encourages community archivists to collect more data than they think they need, to continually put noise into the signalling system, things for which there is currently no ordered space and which do not as yet make sense. Following poet and scholar Fred Moten, we think of this as creating "fugitive spaces" in our archives: spaces on the edges of memory, where objects are both inside a system and outside it, at the limit of established sense and counter-hegemonic norms. (Wallace 2018).

PECE also works the signal-noise double bind in the way it allows researchers to publish archival data along with analytic text, most notably in the "PECE Essay." Most archives present their contents as solitary units of cultural heritage, isolated in their curation. In the PECE Essay users can juxtapose multiple text and image artifacts along with analytic texts, including data that may seem out of place, not making sense. The limits to such juxtaposition of both authorized and fugitive elements are easy to imagine; it's all too easy to overwhelm hard-won and carefully crafted signal with a noisy excess intended to keep it in question or open to other interpretation. There are no easy, immediate, or cost-free solutions to double binds – but we may learn something by remaining in them.

7   Deutero-Learning, Para-Sites and PECE-Supported Civic Community Archiving

Anthropologist and communication theorist Gregory Bateson conceptualized deutero-learning as learning not only how to do something (correcting for errors that would make your bicycle topple, for example) or how to re-think your approach and premises, but learning how to learn from particular operations about one's context and its particular dynamics and complexities. In shorthand, deutero-learning is often described as "learning to learn." It happens through repetition, comparison, reflection and abstraction.

Ethnographers can study practices, infrastructures, and capacities for deutero-learning in the communities they work with. They also need to cultivate their own capacity for deutero-learning, especially when working in an experimental vein that links ethnography to digital design in the manner we describe here. In this way they "learn to learn' how to scaffold the memory practices of diverse communities, tracking between praxis and theory and back, and between different examples of the ways ethnographic insight can be translated into digital system design. A key challenge in this work is to understand variation between contexts, and how the design of digital systems and archives can help communities speak directly and strategically to a particular context - pushing back against very particular hegemonies. Universal standards can get in the way. At the same time, however, critical distance and continued reflection are needed; without these, it can be difficult to see what *isn't* being represented in an archive and its narratives.[5] It also can be difficult to see when and where archives contribute to the reproduction and retrenchment of staid discourses and sign-systems rather than unsettling them and making way for alternatives. Comparative, reflective consideration of civic community archives side-by-side thus has special value, helping ethnographers learn how to learn how to design and build better digital systems, attuned to different contexts. Such deutero-learning by ethnographers also creates valuable opportunities to build new collaborations with HCI researchers, librarians and archivists.

Going forward, we will activate this kind of comparative reflection and deutero learning through work on "para-sites" of the sort developed by the University of California Irvine's Center for Ethnography in the late 2000s (Marcus 2013). Para-sites are events designed by an ethnographer (or group of ethnographers) to bring together differently positioned people to reflect on a project's findings thus far – not seeking to correct or even elaborate those findings but to characterize and strategize their discursive context. Para-sites are a way to get ethnographic projects unstuck, through creative collaboration. Para-sites are spaces for working out what late-stage ethnographic projects can and need to become, leveraging the insights they have already produced to surface and bring into relief the discursive inertia, interpretive gaps, and semiotic risks in the problem-domain they are situated in. Double binds can be identified and worked through (though never solved, of course). Phenomena of concern that can't be articulated in available idioms are somehow drawn out, as are effaced memories. The risks of particular ways of characterizing people, problems and future possibilities are unraveled. In the parasites events we plan to hold, we will add a second layer, working also to characterize and strategize the kind of digital knowledge infrastructure and practice that can effectively move the discursive context the ethnographic project both works within and has delineated. This process can draw out a project's discursive context, as well as possibilities for looping back into that context through digitally-infrastructured community memory and knowledge practices. The diversity that needs to be drawn into these para-sites is thus redoubled, including creative technical as well hermeneutic capacities.

The para-sites will run in a series, encouraging engagements across different projects. PECE-supported digital workspace for each para-site will scaffold interactions before, during, and after each para-site event. In turn, these digital workspaces will also function as memory archives and sources for creative recollection. This will further animate critical reflection in our civic community archiving efforts, situating us deeply within particular projects but with memory of other projects on hand. The para-sites and their archives will thus become our own community archive, enabling our own deutero-learning, helping us move ethnography itself.

---

[5] Lauren Klein, for example, has worked with an archive focused on Thomas Jefferson and the enslaved people he owned, showing how creative modes of handling and displaying data can bring archival absences and silences to the surface and into memory (Klein 2013).

References

Almeida, N., Hoyer, J.: The living archive in the Anthropocene. J. Crit. Libr. Inf. Stud. **2**(3), 1–38 (2019)

Ambielli, B.: 15 Principles for Human Centered Design. Bambielli's Blog, 6 August 2018. https://bambielli.com/posts/2018-08-06-fifteen-principles-for-human-centered-design/

Bardzell, S.: Feminist HCI: taking stock and outlining an agenda for design. In: Proceedings of the 28th International Conference on Human Factors in Computing Systems - CHI 2010, Atlanta, Georgia, USA, p. 1301. ACM Press (2010). https://doi.org/10.1145/1753326.1753521

Baker, S.: Conceptualising the use of Facebook in ethnographic research: as tool, as data and as context. Ethnography Educ. **8**(2), 131–145 (2013). https://doi.org/10.1080/17457823.2013.792504

Bateson, G.: Steps to an Ecology of Mind: Collected Essays in Anthropology, Psychiatry, Evolution, and Epistemology. University of Chicago Press (2000). [1972]

Beneito-Montagut, R.: Ethnography goes online: towards a user-centred methodology to research interpersonal communication on the internet. Qual. Res. **11**(6), 716–735 (2011). https://doi.org/10.1177/1468794111413368

Bright, J.: The Rise of Silicon Savannah and Africa's Tech Movement, TechCrunch, 23 July (2015). https://techcrunch.com/2015/07/23/the-rise-of-silicon-savannah-and-africas-tech-movement/

Buchanan, A., Bastian, M.: Activating the archive: rethinking the role of traditional archives for local activist projects. Arch. Sci. **15**, 429–451 (2015)

Caswell, M.: Teaching to dismantle white supremacy in archives. Libr. Q. **87**(3), 222–235 (2017)

Caswell, M., Cifor, M., Ramirez, M.H.: "To suddenly discover yourself existing": uncovering the impact of community archives. Am. Arch. **79**(1), 56–81 (2016)

Clifford, J., Marcus, G.: Writing Culture: The Poetics and Politics of Ethnography. University of Chicago Press, Chicago (1986)

Cornwall, A.: Buzzwords and fuzzwords: deconstructing development discourse. Dev. Pract. **17**(4/5), 471–484 (2007)

De Kosnik, A.: Rogue Archives: Digital Cultural Memory and Media Fandom. MIT Press, Cambridge (2016)

Democracy Now! Louisiana Activists Face 15 Years for "Terrorizing" Oil Lobbyist with Box of Plastic Pollution. Democracy Now! 29 June 2020. https://www.democracynow.org/2020/6/29/louisiana_formosa_plastics_cancer_alley

Derrida, J.: Archive Fever: A Freudian Impression. University of Chicago Press, Chicago (1998)

Dewey, J.: The Public and Its Problems. Swallow Press, Athens (1927)

Fincher, S., Petre, M. (eds.) Computer Science Education Research. Taylor and Francis, Milton Park (2004)

Fischer, M.M.J.: Anthropology in the Meantime: Experimental Ethnography, Theory, and Method for the Twenty-First Century. Duke University Press, Durham (2018)

Fleck, L.: Genesis and Development of a Scientific Fact. University of Chicago Press, Chicago (1981). Edited by Thaddeus J. Trenn and Robert K. Merton. Translated by Frederick Bradley

Flinn, A.: Rogue archives: digital cultural memory and media fandom and The year's work in the oddball archive. Arch. Rec. **40**(1), 112–116 (2019). https://doi.org/10.1080/23257962.2019.1567318

Fortun, K.: Environmental information systems and appropriate technology. Des. Issues **20**(3), 54–65 (2004a)

Fortun, K.: From bhopal to the informating of environmental health: risk communication in historical perspective. In: Mitman, G., Murphy, M., Sellers, C. (eds.) Landscapes of Exposure: Knowledge and Illness in Modern Environments, special issue of OSIRIS 19/1, pp. 283–296 (2004b)

Fortun, K.: Ethnography in late industrialism. Cult. Anthropol. **27**(3), 446–464 (2012). https://doi.org/10.1111/j.1548-1360.2012.01153.x

Fortun, K., Fortun, M.: Scientific imaginaries and ethical plateaus in contemporary U.S. toxicology. Am. Anthropol. **107**(1), 43–54 (2005)

Fortun, K., Poirier, L., Morgan, A., Costelloe-Kuehn, B., Fortun, M.: Pushback: critical data designers and pollution politics. Big Data Soc. **3**(2) (2016). https://doi.org/10.1177/2053951716668903

Fortun, M., Fortun, K., Marcus, G.: Computers in/and Anthropology: The Poetics and Politics of Digitization. Routledge Companion to Digital Ethnography. Routledge, London (2017)

Fortun, M., Poirier, L., Morgan, A., Callahan, B., Fortun, K.: What's so funny about PECE, TAF and data sharing. In: Boyer, D., Marcus, G. (eds.) Collaborative Anthropology Today: A Collection of Exceptions. Cornell University Press, Ithaca (2020)

Galison, P.: Image & Logic: A Material Culture of Microphysics. The University of Chicago Press, Chicago (1997)

Gibbons, L.: Use of personal reflexive modelling in challenging conceptualisations of cultural heritage. Int. J. Herit. Stud. **24**(8), 904–17 (2018). https://doi.org/10.1080/13527258.2017.1381142

Gikandi, S., Mwangi, E.: The Columbia Guide to East African Literature in English since 1945. Columbia University Press, New York (2007)

Gorman, M.E.: Levels of expertise and trading zones: a framework for multidisciplinary collaboration. Soc. Stud. Sci. **32**(5/6), 933–38 (2002)

Gorman, M.E., Werhane, P.H., Swami, N.: Moral imagination, trading zones, and the role of the ethicist in nanotechnology. NanoEthics **3**(3), 185–95 (2009). https://doi.org/10.1007/s11569-009-0069-8

Klein, L.F.: The image of absence: archival silence, data visualization, and James Hemings. Am. Lit. **85**(4), 661–88 (2013). https://doi.org/10.1215/00029831-2367310

Koch, G.: Digitisation: Theories and Concepts of Empirical Research. Routledge, London (2017)

Marcus, G., Fischer, M.M.J.: Anthropology as Cultural Critique: An Experimental Moment in the Human Sciences. University of Chicago Press (1986)

Mauthner, N.S., Gárdos, J.: Archival practices and the making of 'memories'. New Rev. Inf. Netw. **20**(1–2), 155–69 (2015). https://doi.org/10.1080/13614576.2015.1114825

Mosbrucker, K.: Major Formosa plastics plant in St. James may cost $12 billion, rating agency estimates. The Advocate. Baton Rouge, Louisiana (2020). https://www.theadvocate.com/baton_rouge/news/business/article_2b6e6294-3ee9-11eb-9ade-f77bb74ae6f1.html

Musila, G.A.: East and Central Africa. J. Commonwealth Lit. **54**(4), 593–605 (2019). https://doi.org/10.1177/0021989419877046

Nelson, A.: Voices from the Past - The Niels Bohr Library & Archives Oral History Collection: The history of the American Institute of Physics. Sigma Pi Sigma Physics Honor Society (2016). https://www.sigmapisigma.org/sigmapisigma/radiations/fall/2016/voices-past-niels-bohr-library-archives-oral-history-collection

Marcus, G.: Experimental forms for the expression of norms in the ethnography of the contemporary. Hau **3**(2) (2013). https://www.journals.uchicago.edu/doi/pdfplus/10.14318/hau3.2.011

Okune, A.: Open ethnographic archiving as feminist, decolonizing practice. Catal. Fem. Theory Technosci. **6**(2) (2020). https://doi.org/10.28968/cftt.v6i2.33041

Piacenti, D., Rivas, L., Garrett, J.: Facebook ethnography: the poststructural ontology of transnational (Im) migration research. Int. J. Qual. Methods **13**, 224–236 (2014). https://doi.org/10.1177/160940691401300110

Poirier, L., Fortun, K., Costelloe-Kuehn, B., Fortun, M.: Data infrastructures and data ideologies: the (use) case of cultural anthropology. In: Crowder, J., Fortun, M., Poirier, L., Vesarra, R. (eds.) Anthropology of Data. Palgrave (2019)

Public Radio International (PRI): From Louisiana to Taiwan, environmental activists stand up to a major plastics company. The World from PRX, July 9 2020. https://www.pri.org/stories/2020-07-09/louisiana-taiwan-environmental-activists-stand-major-plastics-company

South Asian American Digital Archive (SAADA): South Asian American Digital Archive (SAADA). http://www.saada.org/. Accessed 8 Jan 2021

Stroisch, J.: The techies turning Kenya into a silicon Savannah: the country is home to a \$1 billion tech scene. Wired (2018). https://www.wired.com/story/kenya-silicon-savannah-photo-gallery/

Trouillot, M.-R.: Silencing the Past: Power and the Production of History. Beacon Press, Boston (1995)

Visser, M.: Gregory Bateson on deutero-learning and double bind: a brief conceptual history. J. Hist. Behav. Sci. **39**(3), 269–78 (2003). https://doi.org/10.1002/jhbs.10112

Wallace, D.: Fred Moten's radical critique of the present. New Yorker (2018). https://www.newyorker.com/culture/persons-of-interest/fred-motens-radical-critique-of-the-present

Watson, B.M.: Rogue performances: a review of Abigail De Kosnik's rogue archives: digital cultural memory and media fandom. Digit. Humanit. Q. **14**(1) (2020). http://www.digitalhumanities.org/dhq/vol/14/1/000446/000446.html

White, H.: Metahistory: The Historical Imagination in Nineteenth-Century Europe. Johns Hopkins University Press, Baltimore (1973)

What Could Safety Research Contribute to Technology Design?

Jaana Hallamaa(✉)

University of Helsinki, 00014 Helsinki, Finland
jaana.hallamaa@helsinki.fi

Abstract. There is already evidence of several mishaps, accidents, and even major catastrophes in which AI technologies have played a part. Among them are traditional types of organizational accidents but also complex misadventures where the effects of the use of AI technology intertwine with human action in the context of intricate socio-technical settings. The origins of problems range from making errors during a planned course of action to accidents due to unintended and unpredictable outcomes of the use of AI. A variety of ethical principles for the use and design of AI have been formulated to remedy the ills. The article sums up the main concepts of the AI ethical codes and discusses their role in attempts to prevent AI-induced problems. According to recent empirical studies, the impact of ethics principles is weak in terms of real-life AI design and use. As an alternative, the article suggests the findings of safety research as a source for a practice-oriented approach to tackle the problems. A century-long study of safety provides both conceptual models and practical tools for the prevention of accidents and creating the means to improve safety. The article introduces the main findings of this line of research and suggests how the Normal Accident Theory, High Reliability Organizations studies, and Just Culture approach could contribute to a safer AI design.

Keywords: AI-Ethics · Organizational accidents · Safety culture · High Reliability Organizations · Normal Accident Theory · Just culture

1 Introduction

Human life is a constant struggle against adversities of various sorts. Normal happenings are often harmful to human endeavors, whether they come in the form of biological decay, illness, or as natural catastrophes. Human-induced accidents add to the number of challenges.

Technological development combined with scientific knowledge has made it possible to control natural processes and direct them to further human purposes. Standardized modeling and the ability to apply great amounts of energy together with mechanized work processes have widened the possibilities and accelerated the speed of affecting the natural world to serve human purposes.[1]

---

[1] Inkster [43], 1–17.

© Springer Nature Switzerland AG 2021
M. Rauterberg (Ed.): HCII 2021, LNCS 12795, pp. 56–79, 2021.
https://doi.org/10.1007/978-3-030-77431-8_4

This development has its costs and side-effects. Along with the hoped-for outcomes of human action, also unwanted consequences have grown in impact and effect. When the forces harnessed to serve industrial production get out of human control, the effects are often devastating [48].

With the ubiquitous use of AI in all walks of life, the possibilities of adversities grow further. The problems are also likely to become more complex, it will be more difficult to make sense of them, and their effects are going to be harder to curb or mitigate. AI applications form intricate systems where different software solutions are designed to carry out some detailed task of the complex whole. Strategic and vital functions of societies rely on machinery controlled and run by AI [7].

2 Attempts to Direct AI Design and Use Through Ethics

2.1 Between High Hopes, Real Worries, and Gloomy Dystopias

The rapid rise of the price of shares in technology firms such as Tesla, the rising value of the virtual currency Bitcoin, [35, 88] and the multimillionaires who have made their money by designing popular video games [47] are only a few examples of the high hopes attached to AI. Social media companies Facebook, TikTok, and Twitter have become global political influencers through their services [12]. Amazon reigns over a far greater part of the globe than the British Empire at its largest and it exercises strong control over logistics chains, workers' rights, and environmental restrictions [5].

High hopes concerning the possibilities of AI live also among national governments and multinational humanitarian organizations. Their strategies give AI the role of a savior of the economy, and a multipurpose agent that solves a variety of problems, ranging from the climate change crisis to elderly care [29, 56]. AI-regulated systems already run the supply of energy, lighting, and water and take care of maintenance and delivery services [56]. In the future, autonomous and adaptive robots and AI systems will handle tasks that are hazardous to human actors or so complicated that it is safer to leave performing them to robots programmed to carry through the tasks with great precision [50]. No one would try to manage complicated calculations, data collection, and data management operations without the help of AI. Machine learning will create even more opportunities for making human life easier with AI-run procedures.

Along with the many advantages that AI has offered, there are a growing number of worries. A fine-tuned modern society is extremely dependent on AI systems and their smooth functioning. Hackers who have taken over a database or a control center have been able to paralyze the functions of big organizations, preventing them from running their services [57].

Some decades ago, a skilled technician could fix a mechanical machine, but with AI components, systems become black boxes, the functions of which are incomprehensible. The cause of their malfunctioning becomes impossible to understand. Solving any problem may take more time and resources than the maintenance and repair of the most complicated mechanical machinery.

There have been hopes that social media would democratize and make societies equal by opening up for everyone a channel to express their opinions and share their views with others. The variety of social platforms has made it easier to form international pressure groups and recruit people to join movements for social and political change. Members of small minorities have been able to create communities with people who share rare characteristics and identities. It has become harder for repressive regimes to silence their opponents and oppress minority groups in secret [13, 49].

The web supplies a platform for other types of sociality, too. Encryption techniques secure anonymity for illegal transactions, give cover to networks of abusers, and support the worldwide gray economy [54]. Social bonding through internet arenas strengthens the adopted opinions and creates enclaves of like-minded people. Rumors, lies, and conspiracy theories spread as quickly as – and often even quicker than – any verified piece of news, research report, or meticulously composed political analysis. The possibility of staying anonymous and publishing one's message instantly has enforced forms of hate speech and lent them more volume. Social media have become a platform for harassment, revenge, and ostracizing, even for preteens. While the dark net conceals clandestine activities, ordinary users of social applications may find that the internet is a merciless community. It is difficult or impossible to eradicate posts from the platforms. The internet preserves signs of thoughtless and cruel behavior indefinitely [1, 10, 11, 16, 17, 23, 31].

As there seems to be no end to the gloomy prospects the misuse of AI offers, writers have described a variety of dystopias under the reign of the new type of technology. The prediction is that in the not so far-away future, humans will be mere subordinates of AI-regulated systems, no longer in control of the machinery, and unable to direct their own lives and destinies.[2]

Most people – whatever their role in terms of the design and use of AI – do not give way to catastrophe thinking but rely on the principle summarized in the Latin proverb 'abusus non tollit usum': misuse of something is not a valid argument against its proper use [2]. AI is no different from other human inventions: it has good and bad uses, and along with its favorable effects the users must consider the harms and ills connected to its use.

AI systems know no geographical boundaries. The various applications are, for the most part, outcomes of commercial activity. No global institution has powers of legislation and law enforcement over them. There have been some attempts to curb the unfavorable effects. The European Union has used its mandate to protect the privacy of citizens of member states, setting the model for international legal standards concerning AI.

Even nationally, legislating against new types of crimes or for the protection of customers from the ills of recently developed technologies is a slow process, and the legal conceptualization seldom captures the nuances of the real-life complexity [71, 77, 85]. Legal restrictions may create barriers to design and development, which is an often-used argument not to adopt them as they may slow down profitable ventures and weaken the position of a nation state in the harsh international competition [72]. National entities are often far too weak to do anything that diverges from the policies of their associates because of the interdependencies of trade, manufacturing chains and international co-operation [75].

---

[2] Coeckelbergh [15], 75–76.

Along with the development that has led the nation states to lose many of their powers of self-rule to the AI giants, the public has experienced a similar destiny. In theory, each one of us has a choice whether or not to use virtual services, to converse with bots, or to join a social media community. As there are often no other viable options available, consenting to the conditions of the AI services is the only possibility, unless one decides to decline to use a certain platform, or service, become a member in a group, or accept an offer that is only obtainable via the internet [46, 71]. One's ability to act as a citizen and consumer depends on the conditions set by artificial intelligence and the producers and providers of AI systems.

2.2 Morally Relevant Themes and Ethical Approaches

The need to tackle the existing and forthcoming problems has taken form as efforts to formulate ethical codes. The hope is that designing and using artificial intelligence in an ethically responsible way will prevent and mitigate the existing ills and even prevent future harms.

Different actors – from transnational companies and national strategists to professionals and citizen activists – have their own approaches to AI ethics. Not everyone has welcomed the ethical involvement: especially the mega-companies' eagerness in the field has evoked suspicions. How can we interpret the moral engagement and formulations of ethical guidelines as part of the companies' public relations activities, when they continue to resist attempts to set legally binding restrictions on their economic activity? Commitment to ethical codes translates as an attempt to instrumentalize moral considerations for marketing purposes and whitewash the company brand in the eyes of their customers. The existence of double standards has become visible in silencing the criticism from the companies' workers concerning unethical practices while at the same time keeping up moral appearances towards the public [33, 83].

Hagendorff [30] cites the association Partnership on AI (2018) that brought together the giants Amazon, Apple, Baidu, Facebook, Google, IBM, and Intel as an example of such instrumentalizing of ethics for commercial purposes. According to his interpretation, companies can highlight their membership of morally praiseworthy associations as a defense against demands to commit themselves to legal regulations that would restrict their business activities. Self-regulation offers far wider opportunities to interpret commercially profitable solutions as ethically sound than the demands of specific legislation.

The boom in AI ethics has motivated Hagendorff to ask what their effect on AI developers actually is.[3] He has analyzed 22 recent formulations of comprehensive AI ethics guidelines to offer an overview of the themes that have received attention as ethically relevant questions. The criterion behind the selection was the authors' intention to comprehensively map and categorize normative claims applicable to AI ethics.[4] I will rely on Hagendorff's compilation to summarize the issues identified as morally problematic and the means to tackle them.

---

[3] Hagendorff [30], 101.
[4] Hagendorff [30], 102.

2.3 Overview of Ethical Principles for AI

According to Hagendorff's statistics,[5] four fifths of the 22 AI ethics documents list the importance of accountability, protection of privacy, and fairness as issues needing ethical attention. These three themes also seem to provide the minimal requirements for an ethically sound AI system. Hagendorff points out that the prioritized status of these principles is striking, as there are already technically applicable solutions to secure accountability, privacy, and fairness [30]. Even commercially developed and distributed tools to mitigate data bias and secure fairness in machine learning have long been available: Google, Microsoft, and Facebook have issued several toolkits to cope with such problems, e.g., AI Fairness 360, What-If Tool, Facets, fairlearn.py, and Fairness Flow [3].

Among the most frequently listed ethical values of the AI ethics documents, there are several other characteristics, such as explainability, justice, robustness, and safety that can already be managed in AI design. It is possible to give them a mathematical operationalization and thereby transfer them into the technical design of the AI application or system. Only two of the 22 explored documents contain information concerning the technical explanations or guidelines for implementation of the ethical principles.[6] This is surprising as most of the guidelines mention that there are already technical solutions for many of the listed problems.

In the light of the ethical documents, the view to morally problematic features of AI development is narrow. As accountability, the protection of privacy, and securing of fairness get attention in most of the documents, there is little talk about aspects that concern giving care and nurture, offering help, securing welfare, and taking social and ecological responsibility. Hagendorff interprets this as a sign that in AI ethics, technical artefacts are primarily regarded as isolated entities, the functioning of which technical experts optimize by designing technical solutions to problems occurring that are technical in nature. This approach is understandable, as most of the groups that have published AI ethics codes have a background in computer sciences or technology development.[7] This may also explain why the guidelines concentrate on practice related problems instead of dealing with issues such as machine consciousness and the agency of robots that incite philosophical interest or excite the imagination of the public.

The fact that AI solutions are part of socio-technical systems receives little attention in the AI ethics codes. Only a few – the Montréal Declaration for Responsible Development of Artificial Intelligence 2018 [81] and the AI Now 2019 Report [4] – discuss democratic control, governance, and political deliberation of AI systems. Their approach displays a wider scope of interest in issues relating to the conditions of good life and social justice.[8] Concentration on a narrow view of ethics may also explain why the role of AI in spreading propaganda, deepfakes, and fake news, using bots instead of human staff, microtargeting to direct the electorate, and forging election results does not receive any attention in the documents.

---

[5] Hagendorff [30], 102–103.
[6] Hagendorff [30], 102–103; The European Commission's High Level Expert Group.
[7] Hagendorff [30], 103–104.
[8] Hagendorff [30], 105.

The absence of central social and political issues may stem from the current social makeup of the community of AI developers and other actors in the field. Globally, AI designers form a rather small group, the members of which are predominantly white men. Their view of what is relevant determines the purposes of use and the lines along which they design and optimize AI systems, without there being a conscious bias or an intention to discriminate or exclude.[9]

A social issue that does not receive attention as a relevant ethical feature is the public–private interface of research and development.[10] Large parts of the academic AI research even now come from private companies and corporate partners; the number of corporate-affiliated AI papers has grown significantly in recent years. Governments, too, instead of securing funding for independent research, are tempted to concentrate on supporting applied science as the most profitable way to boost the national economy [75]. This is no wonder as venture capital firms actively look for promising AI startups in the hope of profit-making and patenting new inventions. The estimation is that the global AI market is worth more than 7 billion dollars [9, 27].

Against the economic prospects, the perspective that there is too close a connection between business and academia – traditionally provoking suspicion and even alarm – does not weigh much. Still, commercial interests and the requirements of the freedom of academic research often conflict and in a public–private partnership the paying party often has an upper hand in deciding the direction of action and the criteria of a favorable outcome.

Along with the variety of AI ethics guidelines, members of the research community and other concerned parties have published declarations that express the wish and need to develop and use AI for the good of humankind. AI4people [25] and AI for Good [3] are expressions of the intent and demand to develop AI to serve all human beings. Such intentions clearly take only second place in considerations as the world's leading nations try to beat each other in the competition concerning financially successful AI development and market shares.[11]

Technological companies may take part in the discussion of ethics just to further their economic interests, but most people who invest their intellectual capacities and creativity in the endeavor want their work to have some positive impact. It would be frustrating to formulate ethical standards without them having any practical effect.

McNamara et al. [52] have studied the impact of ethical guidelines for software engineers' ethical decision-making. The – depressing – outcome of the study is that guidelines or ethical codes have almost no effect on the engineers' work and the decisions made by those who had familiarized themselves with such standards did not differ in any way from the deliberative choices of their colleagues who had not acquainted themselves with ethical codes.[12]

---

[9] Hagendorff [30], 105.
[10] Hagendorff [30], 106.
[11] Hagendorff [30], 107.
[12] Hagendorff [30], 108.

2.4 Why Ethics Does Not Play a Role

Hagendorff[13] discusses the reasons why ethics does not seem to have any impact on AI design. The instrumental logic of economic enterprises runs contrary to both value-based and principle-based ethical thinking. The education of engineers and AI developers does not focus on ethical issues, and organizational structures do not encourage employees to take up moral concerns. The development and commercial utilization of systems based on machine learning attract the interest of investors [70] while ethical considerations are often regarded only as a fraction of the public relations management.[14]

Each field of expertise has its own approach to reality that has formed according to its specific tasks and uses during its history. Going through any professional training takes years and gaining seniority in one's specialty adds to the time needed to become a professional. It is no wonder that a list of ethical principles has an insignificant effect in a frantically changing field where designers work under constant pressure. It seems that, without a sanctioning mechanism, ethics is doomed to continue to play an unimportant role.[15]

Another problem, familiar from another, more established field of applied ethics, is the gap between ethical principles and practical work. In medical ethics, there are both bottom-up and top-down attempts to bring theoretical ethical considerations and problems of practical work closer to each other. The four principles of biomedical ethics – nonmaleficence, beneficence, autonomy, and justice – appear as central values in AI ethics, too. There is, however, no standard solution for bringing the theoretical and the practical nearer to each other.[16]

Trustworthy AI [22], one of the few documents in Hagendorff's survey that explicitly address the technical level of AI development, serves as an example of the difficulties. It is an ambitious attempt to deal with a variety of ethical values and embed them into central principles. An analysis of the structure of the document shows that it presents seven levels of ethical standards to back up morally trustworthy AI.

First, there are the guiding principles of lawfulness, ethicality, robustness. The foundation of ethicality is based on the grand European moral tradition of respect for fundamental human rights, a framework of democracy, and the rule of law. From human rights, the document then deduces the ethical principles of respect for human dignity, freedom of the individual, equality, non-discrimination and solidarity, and protection of citizens' rights. The general ethical principles serve as a basis for principles of AI ethics defined as respect for human autonomy, prevention of harm, fairness, and explicability.

The document sums up the distinguishing features of AI design and AI systems in a list of seven requirements, namely human agency and oversight, technical robustness and safety, privacy and data governance, transparency, diversity, non-discrimination and fairness, environmental and societal well-being, and accountability. To bridge the gap between theory and practice, the document formulates both technical and non-technical methods for implementing the seven requirements. They cover all stages of an AI system's life cycle and should be applied during the process according to the dynamism of

---

[13] Hagendorff [30], 108–109.

[14] Boddington 2017, 56.

[15] Hagendorff [30], 108–109.

[16] Coeckelbergh [15], 157.

evolving AI systems.[17] The document sums up its ethics in a Trustworthy AI assessment list that contains questions for each of the seven requirements mentioned.[18]

Trustworthy AI is a theoretically ambitious effort, and it strives to offer practical help, but even the assessment list, the purpose of which is to help the designers in their work, remains very abstract. In the end, it is difficult to say what, for example, considering societal and environmental wellbeing means, when it involves that designers of AI should keep in mind the value 'Society and democracy' by answering the question: "Did you assess the broader societal impact of the AI system's use beyond the individual (end-)user, such as potentially indirectly affected stakeholders?"[19]

2.5 Suggestions for Improvement

The discrepancy between ethical principles and the reality of AI design has given an impetus to look for effective means to curb the ills and regulate the activities. Hagendorff suggests the application of virtue ethics as a remedy: it could change the individual actors' mindsets in AI design.[20] Educating virtues in families, schools, and communities as well as in companies, and cultivating a moral character would then increase the likelihood of ethical decision-making practices in organizations developing and deploying AI applications. It would involve every individual in society in generating a favorable motivation to adopt and habituate moral practices. The process of cultivating virtue ethics would eventually influence technology development and use in a positive manner.

Emphasis on the individual would stress the meaning of subjective moral responsibility even in professional settings. Moving in this direction would be in line with Floridi's [24] insistence that every actor whose actions have been causally relevant in bringing about some consequence of collective action must be held morally accountable for the outcomes.

Virtue ethics has experienced a Renaissance since the 1980s, especially after Alasdair MacIntyre published his renowned work After Virtue in 1981 [51]. There is, however, little evidence that the boom has had any effect on morality on any institutional – or even private – level. [26] Moreover, social psychological research gives grounds for not counting on cultivating moral virtues to improve behavior. There is evidence that using character traits as an explanation for morally praiseworthy behavior is just a fundamental attribution error. Situational factors offer a much more reliable source for explaining and understanding people's actions [20, 34, 38].

Coeckelbergh[21] suggests several ways to combat the prevailing problems. In his view, choosing the right remedy for each ill must start with finding an answer to six questions. Before fixing the course of action, one must form an understanding of why and when measures are needed, what the right level of intervention is, and who should involve themselves in the action. The answers will serve as background knowledge that will help to figure out the nature, extent, and the urgency of the problem at hand.

---

[17] Trustworthy AI [22], 20.
[18] Trustworthy AI [22], 25–31.
[19] Trustworthy AI [22], 31.
[20] Hagendorff [30], 112–113.
[21] Coeckelbergh [15], 145–165.

Citizens' initiatives and professional recommendations resemble ethical principles and general strategies, as they formulate suggestions for the discretion and use of decision makers. Policy proposals go a step further in the sense that they add normative weight to their suggestions by proposing changes in legislation [76]. The AI Now Report serves as an example: instead of a trust-based voluntary commitment to ethical guidelines and self-governance, it calls for novel approaches to governance [4]. Such documents are a way of clarifying the meaning of central values in society.

As Hagendorff's analysis shows, privacy is seen as a central value in AI design. The General Data Protection Regulation (GDPR) [65] is an example of how values translate into practice through legislation. The GDPR defines what data privacy involves for the citizens living in the EU countries [65].

The idea that designers could program ethics into the AI code has become popular as a means to avoid at least part of the ethical problems of AI. Such programming would make machines ethical in the sense that they could make ethical decisions by virtue of their algorithms. Although there are technical solutions to combat many morally relevant issues, the prospect of being able to design a moral machine does not seem to be realizable [37]. We need something else.

In listing measures to tackle ethical problems connected with AI, Coeckelbergh remarks in passing that AI developers could learn something from the aircraft industry, "which is highly regulated and has tough safety certification processes and visible processes of accident investigation". "Could similar regulatory and safety infrastructures be installed for AI?" he then asks, without developing the line of thought further.[22]

Coeckleburgh has adopted the idea of borrowing insights from the aircraft industry and aviation from Winfield and Jirotka [89], who have suggested that there should be a built-in device for recording data concerning the behavior of the system in robots and autonomous AI systems. It would record the functions of the machine and its data would serve analysts in a manner analogous to the utilization of the recordings of a black box in an aircraft cockpit after an accident. The ethical black box would help to establish what went wrong should the system not work in a hoped-for way.

In the following, I will suggest that there is much more in the aircraft industry and aviation safety that can be used to clarify and improve the problems of AI design and use. Although safety has been an object of intensive study for more than a century and the results of the work have had a great practical impact in different fields, it is a neglected source in the present context, save for some attempts, such as Sammarco's study [74].

3   Organizational Safety Research and Its Findings

3.1   The Idea of Improving Safety

Historically, accidents were acts of God and the human contribution was to submit oneself to fate [8]. Advances in the natural sciences paved the way for an understanding of physical phenomena as chains of cause and effect. Experimentation as a reliable means to acquire knowledge and the advancing skills to build mechanical machines showed the relationship between human beings and nature in a new light. Nature is not a spirit realm

---

[22] Coeckelbergh [15], 162.

run by mystical forces but an intricate system that follows mathematizable regularities. By detecting the rules that govern physical reality, it is possible to harness its powers for human purposes [90].

Connecting scientific knowledge and engineering skills to market capitalist endeavors to make profit through mass production were the driving forces behind industrialization. Designing and building machinery to replace the human workforce essentially involved breaking down each process to its constituents and engineering the manufacturing process in a way that made each stage of production plannable and controllable. If the outcome did not match the plan, the system did not run ideally. Disruptions in the process, failures to reach the goals, and unfavorable outcomes were signs of imperfect planning and poor execution, not acts of God or strokes of fate.

The development of the insurance industry also played its part in changing the view on accidents. Technologies, the functioning and effects of which people could not understand, made the public cautious for the dangers looming for those who were daring enough to use the inventions. Insurers, who looked for new fields of activity, started to offer coverage for losses caused by new types of accidents [60].

Attempts to minimize investor risk accentuated the need to investigate whether the loss that insured customers had suffered was real and should be covered.[23] Even more urgent became the necessity to trace down the origins of mishaps and failures that led to great human and economic losses. From the end of the 19th century, industrial and, later, organizational accidents have been an object of systematic study.[24]

The growing ability to control and direct physical nature has paradoxically increased the possibility of devastating, human-induced accidents. The concentration of energy sources, densely inhabited residential areas, and accumulation of power increase the risks and probability of accidents with wide-ranging effects [65]. The changing focus of interest in safety studies displays how researchers have conceptualized accidents and their causes.[25]

3.2 Linear Accident Models

Hollnagel [41] [26] has divided the conceptual changes in understanding the nature of accidents into four phases. First, researchers concentrated on technical matters and the aim was to improve machinery to make its functions more precise and regular. Along with the development of more reliably working technology for mass production, the interest gradually shifted to the part played by the human agent and the machine–human interaction.

The wish to establish the conditions of a smoothly working assembly line turned the focus to the individual, who worked as a cog in the machinery. Attempts to explain failures and accidents concentrated on finding the weak link in the production chain. The domino-effect served as the central metaphor for conceptualizing how accidents take place. The faulty execution of an individual worker was like a leaning domino

---

[23] Clarke [14], 7.

[24] Reiman & Oedewald [66], 39.

[25] Reiman & Oedewald [66], 39–48.

[26] See also Reiman & Oedewald [66], 39–47.

block in a line of blocks. The falling of a single block starts a chain reaction that brings down all the subsequent blocks in the row. Preventing accidents was like removing the unstable block to keep the row erect: the task was to find and remove the individual whose poor execution made the whole system unsafe.[27]

The domino model directed the understanding of accidents for decades mainly because its presenter, Herbert William Heinrich, was a respected pioneer in the field. The findings of his groundbreaking work from 1931 [36] set the foundations for further studies for more than three decades, and signs of its basic concepts are still traceable in practical safety instructions.

Another long-lived concept of Heinrich's research was what has become known as the pyramid model [44]. According to Heinrich, there is a standard ratio in the severity of occupational health incidents. From every 330 incidents, 300 are near misses, 29 are minor accidents and only one leads to a major injury. Heinrich claimed that the minor and major accidents were connected in the sense that major accidents could be prevented by concentrating on eradicating the minor accidents.[28]

Heinrich backed up the metaphors of the domino effect and the incident pyramid by presenting another standard ratio according to which 10% of occupational accidents were due to mechanical causes, 88% were the result of failures of individual workers at the sharp end of the process, and 2% could not be reasonably avoided. It has taken a long time to challenge Heinrich's findings. Manuele[29] finds them both faulty – there is no scientifically sound evidence to support them – and harmful. They have dominated the research of accidents and have led safety research astray for decades.

Heinrich's long-lasting legacy also shows something more general of the nature of research. Heinrich's analysis concerns the human tendency to attribute the cause of negative events to single agents, as far as that singling out does not concern oneself. This tendency, known as the fundamental attribution error (FAE), is often detectable in ex post facto accident reports.[30] Locating the domino that was the first to fall is often only a human construction based on the wisdom of hindsight. The complexity of many accidents has since created mounting criticism of the search for faulty executions of individual workers.

After the Second World War, the problems detected in the human–machine interface led to more active study of human perception, and cognition. The results of the study helped to design dashboards and instrument panels adjusted to human capacities and human attentiveness to prevent failures due to misreading and misinterpretation.[31]

Conceptualizing the causes leading to accidents in a wider manner was possible when researchers combined the search for technical and human causes of accidents. One of the most well-known and widely used models in this line of approach is the Probabilistic Risk Assessment (PRA) tool that was first developed in the 1960s and 1970s. The approach understands risk as any feasible detrimental outcome of an activity or action subject to hazards. Risk is a combination of the severity of the adverse consequences that the

---

[27] Reiman & Oedewald [66], 40.

[28] Manuele [55], 236.

[29] Manuele [55], 234–256.

[30] Hogg & Vaughan [38], 641; Dekker [18], xxii–xxiii, 65.

[31] Reiman & Oedewald [66], 40.

activity or action can potentially bring forth, and the probability of the occurrence of each negative consequence [79].

PRA studies require special technical analysis, but also the examination of human factors that contribute to the severity and probability of risks. Researchers have developed different tools for the purpose, e.g., human reliability analysis (HRA) and dependent-failure or common-cause analysis (CCF) [79].

3.3 Focus on Human–Machine Interface

The investigation of the Three Mile Island nuclear accident in 1979 accentuated the critical nature of human–machine interaction. James Reason was the leading researcher, whose studies consolidated human error as one of the central concepts of safety research. Reason defined human error as an occasion in which a planned sequence of mental or physical activities fails to achieve its intended outcome. He differentiated errors as slips and lapses, and the more severe mistakes, in which the focus of his work lies.[32]

Reason's analysis makes use of a skill–rule–knowledge classification of human per-formance as the basis for a division of errors as skill-based slips and lapses, and rule-based and knowledge-based mistakes. According to his general error-modeling system (GEMS), basic human errors often occur as actions that deviate from the agent's inten-tion due to storage memory failures or less than perfect execution of the task. In other cases, actions may run as planned but the error lies in the design of the action due to either a rule-based – applying a wrong rule to the case – or knowledge-based – not understanding the requirements of the situation – mistake.[33]

Reason's findings on the causes of accidents are often summed up as the Swiss Cheese model, where the slices of Swiss cheese represent successive layers of defenses, barriers, and safeguards in a system designed to secure the functions necessary for carrying out its primary task. The round holes in the slices stand for the active failures, and latent conditions that make the system vulnerable. Latent conditions have a similar role[34] in the system to that of resident pathogens in an organism: they are normally dormant and become active only in certain circumstances.[35] Likewise, latent conditions start to play a role in connection with an unexpected occurrence or a human mistake. When several such factors suddenly coincide, their aggregate harmful effects can be devastating.

Reason's model has been criticized because his conception of an accident is linear. Such a model is based on a mistaken assumption that events follow a linear sequence of actions and their consequences. The safety measures Reason recommends are also linear. In his view, building different sorts of safety barriers will improve organizational robustness. According to his critics, however, the safeguards put in place, may make the system more vulnerable to accidents. Adding regulations, checks and procedures tends to make the system more complicated, its operation slower and clumsier, and its

---

[32] Reason [61], 9.

[33] Reason [61], 53.

[34] Reason [64], 2–3; Reason [61], 17.

[35] Reason [61], 197.

functioning less easy to understand. Instead of preventing accidents, such steps may lead to an increased number of mistakes and thereby to further mishaps.[36]

The safety measures applied in the London Underground after the King's Cross Underground station fire in 1987 have been used as an example of the double nature of increased safety measures. The investigation report of the fatal accident included many recommendations to improve safety. To prevent future fires, they were all applied without assessing their probable effects by conducting a cost–benefit analysis. The outcome of implementing the regulations was an ill-functioning traffic service without any real improvement in safety.[37]

3.4 The Impact of Organizational Factors

The severity and complexity of a nuclear plant accident – that was according to many experts theoretically impossible – became tangible during and after the Chernobyl catastrophe in 1986. Investigation of the factors that led to the accident revealed that placing the blame on individual workers at the sharp end of action, and the hapless circumstances did not grasp the essential elements behind the chain of events. The problems were deeply embedded in the organizational culture and the ways of acting it presupposed of the employees.[38]

The working procedures and the daily routines of the plant contributed to what happened. The power plant operators had to tackle perpetual conflicts concerning their duties in their daily work. The equipment was faulty, the system continuously set off false alarms, and the operational indicators conflicted with each other. The experience and competence of the workers were inadequate due to their poor training. On top of everything, taking care of the daily duties and running the nuclear station was not possible without violating several norms the employees were supposed to follow as they carried out their tasks. It was clear that tracking down the causes of the accident to individuals on shift did not give a correct view of the factors that had led the power plant on the course of events that ended in disaster.[39]

The nature of several severe manmade disasters during the last decades of the century was evidence that focusing on individual actors distorted the view on the causes of accidents and hence was an insufficient basis for attempts to prevent accidents and improve safety. Towards the end of the millennium, the linear accident models were replaced by a more varied systems analysis. The research expanded to cover organizational factors, the resourcing of different tasks, training of workers, updating of regulations and standards, and assessing risks. Researchers pointed out that communication between an organization's diverse levels and departments often plays a decisive role in achieving the aims. Methods to motivate organizations to learn from failures now received attention. Fostering an open atmosphere that would encourage people, irrespective of their rank

---

[36] Perrow 1999 [58], 11.

[37] Maidment 1997 [53], 71.

[38] Reason [63], 77; Reiman & Oedewald [66], 35.

[39] Reason [63], 49–50.

and status, to talk about and pay attention to shortcomings, defects, faults, and weaknesses was accentuated as an important tool to improve safety, along with encouraging everyone to use their own experience to suggest ways to develop the common work.[40]

Both the domino-effect and the Swiss Cheese model assume that the key to safety lies in avoiding mistakes. This way of thinking places the cause of unsafety in the hands of humans who make mistakes and err. The systems approach changes the focus of attention to the many interactions within the socio-technical system that is at the core of any complex organization.

The sociologist Charles Perrow suggests that, instead of the exceptional, researchers should put the everyday normalcy of organizations in the focus in attempts to understand accidents and their causes. Perrow's Normal Accident Theory [58] stresses the fact that possible failures and accidents are constantly present in the structure and normal workings of each organization. To better understand the challenges of organizational safety, Perrow differentiates between normal accidents – that occur as part of the workings of the system – and system accidents that are severe but unexceptional occurrences in the life of the organization.[41]

Perrow's message is that human beings must learn to live with high-risk systems. This involves a better and wider realization of risks in which diverse types of rationality – absolute, economic, and social – have a role. Much can be done to improve the safety of systems, but in the end, humans must learn to live with risk. Most people wish to do their work well and most organizations are committed to doing their best; accidents still happen. Instead of concentrating on accident prevention, organizations should invest their resources in developing their normal, everyday functions. High-risk systems do not emerge and function in isolation but are part of the economic, political, social, and cultural systems with which they constantly interact. High-risk systems are human constructs run by humans; human beings can change them, and the conditions under which they operate.[42]

Erik Hollnagel is another renowned researcher, who has pointed out that the attempts to understand the causes of accidents and to prevent them are just one side of the coin. Like Perrow, Hollnagel stresses that any kind of action involves a risk. Concentrating on risk-avoidance would lead to inaction, which would be absurd. In Hollnagel's view, all goal-oriented action involves a constant struggle against the pressure of scarce resources. Actors always face a choice between the requirements of efficiency and thoroughness as they try to optimize their way towards their goal. Making compromises equals taking risks. To minimize their effect, Hollnagel has introduced what he calls the ETTO (Efficiency–Thoroughness Trade-Off) principle [40].

Hollnagel claims that the predominant explanations from psychologists and engineers have attributed performance failures to the mismatch between demand and capacity but have neglected the fundamental fact that everything takes time and doing things takes place in time. Limited capacity is not an isolated quality of the system but displays a common human inability to be fast – or effective – enough in terms of the time available for performing the task at hand. In any situation, time sets the limits for considering the

---

[40] Reiman & Oedewald [66], 44.
[41] Perrow [58], 5.
[42] Perrow [58], 321–350.

goal and resources, planning the course of action, and executing the actions for the preferred goal. Because of this basic discrepancy, safety cannot be attained by eliminating risks. Instead, other measures, among them the ETTO principles, must be developed and applied.[43]

During the past decades, researchers have widened the systemic approach. The interest has shifted from chasing down the causes of accidents to what makes an organization and a system work safely. What is safety? How does it appear? Do safe organizations have something in common? Along with attempts to understand the theoretical and conceptual nature of safety and its constituents, there is a strong emphasis on real life applications: understanding what safety is must translate into making the daily work and actions of existing people safer [69].

Perrow's Normal Accident Theory (NAT) is one of the theories that have been used as a basis for developing tools for improving the safety of organizations. Another influential strand of research, which started to form at the same time as Perrow first published his book in 1984, was the HRO approach. It started as a study of organizations known for their reliable performance despite the constant pressure and rapidly changing circumstances their employees face. The work is known as the High Reliability Organizations approach or High Reliability Theory (HRT) [68, 78, 86, 87].

The HRO study has concentrated on identifying features that are common to the operations of high performing organizations and to the way in which their employees and leaders work and co-operate, such as in aviation, and at nuclear power plant stations. The study of risk management has inspired the creation of practice-oriented tools, such as the checklist [28] and the HRO Safety Culture approach [21, 42]. Since the 1980s, the practical risk management tools have been applied to new fields of high reliability performance, such as medical practice and banking [28].

The five HRO principles are the most well-known outcome of the HRO approach [80]. They sum up the attitude and practices common to high reliability organizations, but they also function as guidelines that help organizations strengthen the reliability of their functions. The principles consist of short maxims and concise explanations of their meaning. In practice, the aim of the principles is to help each organization concentrate on the most fundamental thing, the primary task, even in the middle of exceptional and adverse circumstances. As part of its standard procedures, the whole organization should focus on making full use of everyone's experience and expertise. Everyone should commit oneself to constant learning, staying curious towards one's own and each other's work. The prevailing attitude to direct the organization should be a willingness to use mistakes and failures as a social resource for constant development.

The differences between Perrow's NAT and the HRT led Sagan [73] to compare the two. Sagan's analysis shows that the systems approach as such is not enough to lead to unanimity concerning the central conceptions of organizational safety. In NAT, accidents are a normal part of a system's life cycle, but the HRT claims that good leadership and organizational planning are effective methods for preventing them.

NAT regards safety as just one factor among many others that any organization must weigh in its work, but according to the HRT it is the most important goal to keep in mind in an organization. The attitude of NAT towards safety layers that form back-up

---

[43] Hollnagel [40], 25, 28.

systems is critical: system-redundancy may become counter-effective because added safety measures complicate both the structure of the organization and the work itself. They may also prompt a temptation to risk-taking as shared responsibility tends to decrease the individual sense of responsibility. In the HRT, redundancy created through back-ups is a central feature of organizational safety.

NAT claims that organizations have a constant need to centralize their functions to effectuate decision-making processes. For HRT, the complexity of the system requires a decentralized organization. NAT encourages multiplicity: in democratic societies, people are unwilling to comply with unifying systems and authoritarian leadership. In HRT, creating and fostering a unified reliability culture is a means to further unified reactions at the sharp end of the organization.

NAT takes the unprecedented nature of system accidents as proof of why it is impossible to foresee them and to be prepared for them. HRT recommends continuous training, going through the operations and arranging simulations to create and maintain reliable operations [73].

Sagan's analysis provoked an academic debate around the two approaches. Shrivastava et al. [78] claim to have solved the conflict between the two theories by using open systems theory. The most important thing the debate has revealed is that neither of the approaches provides a theory concerning what turns safe courses of events into accidents. They are also insufficient as descriptions of safety. The HRO theorists who replied to Sagan's criticism claimed to have presented the necessary, although not necessarily sufficient, conditions of safety.[44]

3.5   The Systems Approach to Accidents

During the 2000s, the systems approach has been used to answer the question as to what accidents and safety are as parts of dynamic systems. This has paved the way to concepts that grasp the constant change that is continually going on in organizations and their nature as complex adaptive systems (CAS) [39]. For such entities, a solid structure or a set of commonly approved principles are not helpful, as it has become part of the functions of such organizations to adapt to the ever-changing circumstances and demands coming from outside and within the system.[45]

The ability of a complex system to adapt itself is called resilience. Resilient organizations adjust their normal activities so that, as they perform their primary task, they also keep an eye on the safety indicators and can thereby avoid risks they are not able to manage as part of their normal routines. A resilient organization keeps its course even amid disruptions, trouble, and distress. Dysfunctions of machinery and absence of keyworkers do not derail them from doing what they are meant to do and committing to their primary task.[46]

The significance of the concept of resilience becomes obvious in an approach named Resilience Engineering. It takes as its starting point Erik Hollnagel's distinction between

---

[44] Reiman & Oedewald [66], 241–242.
[45] Reiman & Oedewald [66], 246.
[46] Dekker [18], 45.

Safety-I and Safety-II [41, 82]. Safety-I refers to the models that concentrate on the lack of safety, while the focus of Safety-II is the presence of safety.

Humans typically do not pay attention to what they think is normal. Thus, when the system usually runs successfully, people habituate to it and do not take any notice of the reasons for the positive outcome. Hollnagel uses the distinction between how people really do their work – Work-As-Done – and the theoretically ideal way to do the work – the Work-As-Imagined. In research that relies on the linear conceptions of Safety-I, the theoretical normal establishes the point of reference against which the causes of accidents are constructed. This is a faulty conception, in Hollnagel's opinion, since the viewpoint on events – before or after something has happened – strongly affects the analysis concerning chains of causality. The emphasis should be on the trivial normality and the chains of causes that keep things running favorably. Conceptions of Safety-I apply to simple systems, but its linear explanations are inadequate for making sense of what takes place in complex systems. To understand them, we need a new model, Safety-II [41].

According to Safety-II, the work in complex systems cannot be specified in detail. The difference between Work-As-Done and Work-As-Imagined becomes impossible to explain, as even the experts are often unable to understand why parts of the systems run correctly or what the cause of their malfunctioning is. The relation between cause and effect may be non-linear. Outputs emerge rather than being products of a controllable process. Performance adjustment and performance variability become important characteristics as means for identifying which kinds of adjustments any prevailing situation calls for [41].

Being able to meaningfully strive for the set goals in a complex system under constant change requires both reactive and proactive measures. Safety-II defines safety as a dynamic non-event that cannot be observed or measured precisely. Instead, it emerges in actions and procedures that realize the tasks and functions of the system. This type of safety makes a system resilient [41].

Hollnagel's model has been actively put into use in the Resilience Engineering Association, the central task of which is to promote it and develop it further. The development is visible in the various definitions of resilience the association has published during the 2010s [67].

In 2019, Hollnagel widened the perspective of what resilience involves to the organization's ability to make use of change as a favorable opportunity. According to Hollnagel: "A system is resilient if it can adjust its functioning prior to, during, or following events (changes, disturbances, and opportunities), and thereby sustain required operations under both expected and unexpected conditions" [67].

Along with the multi-factorial cultural, social, and systemic approaches to risks, accidents and their causes, and safety, there is a reemerging need to focus on the human-induced nature of organizational accidents. Adopting too wide a perspective may lead to losing focus and not being able to deal with anything anymore. Dekker and Breakey [19] make use of James Reason's suggestion of a Just Culture strategy as a remedy.[47] Its aim is to preserve the approved methods of accident investigation and incorporate the study of organizational culture into it. Theoretical thinking on what this would involve

---

[47] Reason [62], 195–196.

has been used to create a practical "just culture" reporting environment for successful implementation of safety regulations [45].

The Just Culture concept emphasizes the importance of a blame-free approach to functional anomalies in creating a working environment where people willingly report safety-related issues instead of trying to hide them. Without such reporting, it is difficult to improve the prevailing practices and boost organizational resilience. The ex-post-facto investigation of accidents has supplied vital information concerning the causes of accidents and offered a basis to improve safety in many fields. The Just Culture concept aims at preserving the traditional blame-free approaches to accident investigation as a guarantee to support people's willingness to keep reporting safety-related issues. At the same time, it protects the possibility for managerial interventions to sustain moral integrity and safety within the organization [19].

Dekker & Breakey formulate a set of concepts of justice to safeguard a sound culture in terms of reporting and responsibility. Substantive justice prescribes the conditions for the fairness and legitimacy of regulations, rules, and procedures. Procedural justice regulates processes for determining rule-breaches, offers protections for the accused, and governs who should make such determinations. Finally, restorative justice consists of measures aiming at restoring the status of the individual involved and healing relationships and injuries of victims and the wider community when the organization has had a part in or has committed an ethical breach. Applying Just Culture approaches provides a foundation for a multi-faceted just safety culture, that encourages the reporting of problems and mismanagement, engagement in the common endeavor, and improving safety [19].

The century of safety studies reflects the changes that human societies and their technological systems have undergone since the beginning of the 1900s. The emphasis given to varied factors displays their changing importance in reconstructions of the causes of accidents and the conceptions of what constitutes safety.

The variety of approaches also shows that there is no consensus on what safety is and what the best method to prevent accidents from happening could be. Still, the practice-oriented nature of the work has produced many considerable benefits and applicable methods to prevent and mitigate harms. The history of aviation is the most brilliant example of its successes: air travel used to be the most dangerous means of transport, but now it is the form of travel with the fewest fatalities [84].

Accidents will happen in the future, too. Some of them are likely to cause extensive damage to both people and the environment. Some accidents will be difficult to detect as they come about slowly and have widespread effects. The trade-offs between profit-making and the protection of priceless values will go on with varying results. It will not become easier to measure the desired benefits against the expected harms. Even the best planning will not be able to predict what will happen. With the use of AI, the socio-technical systems will become even more complex and the need to find practical tools to control the drawbacks of technology will grow. In the face of such challenges, it is wise to use the extensive work of safety researchers as a resource.

4 What Could Safety Research Contribute to the Ethics of AI Design?

Even a brief overview of the history of safety research shows that there are a variety of feasible approaches and practical methods for dealing with a variety of problems related to technology and its uses. By combining the findings of safety research with the approach known as human-centered design, it would not be difficult to prepare toolkits for better dealing with many of the problems of AI systems [6, 32].

There is a relevant connection to ethics in most of the problems central to safety research. Still, the ethics of technology plays a minor role in the writings concerning safety and in efforts to improve it. This lack does not make safety studies unethical or amoral, though. On the contrary, the field of research is typically committed to finding practical solutions to real problems by trying to understand what leads to errors, accidents, and damage. It is justified to say that the approach of safety studies has been ethically sound.

Both the conceptual and the practical development of safety studies provide ample resources for more ethical design and use of AI. Like the first phase of safety studies, current AI design ethics conceptualizes problems according to a linear model. The locus of mitigating ills and preventing harms in the present AI ethical codes are the designers, and their ways of thought. There are also attempts to widen the view to the organizational level and to regard AI systems in relation to the surrounding societies. None of the current AI ethics models, however, deals with ethical aspects as problems emerging from the systemic totality. To understand the challenges better, we need theoretical conceptualizations of AI as an integral part of the complex adaptive systems from which new types of ethical and other issues emerge. Without such an overall view, it is not possible to tackle the difficult problems that require global co-operation, new types of consumer awareness, and more fine-tuned means of regulation.

AI ethics could become more relevant as a discussion partner in terms of the industry by adopting the reality-based practice-orientation of safety studies. Acknowledging that mistakes happen, errors are made, and accidents occur has not led human inventors to fatalism but persistent endeavors to try to improve machine-assisted human action. A shift of focus from questions formulated as ethical conflicts to seeing them as practical problems could be welcome in relation to the many worries we currently face with the design and use of AI.

It is difficult to direct the work of AI designers to fulfill moral ideals and follow abstract ethical principles when their current tasks concern programming a function to an application. The practice-oriented approaches that safety research offers make it possible to formulate quandaries and difficulties related to the practical problems at hand and to real world situations. Many of the central ethical problems formulated in relation to AI can be translated into questions concerning safety. A hands-on discussion of the hoped-for solutions and unwanted outcomes would help to give the discourse a less theoretical flavor and give impetus to finding applicable answers to the problems.

Safety studies also make visible that the conflict between financial and other values is real but that it is possible to overcome it by translating the costs of neglecting safety into economic losses. Neglecting safety will – at least eventually – cost more than investment in it. With the help of safety studies, the same correlation could be established between financial interests and ethically sound AI design.

Safety studies have a close connection to the technology studies and the substance knowledge concerning each branch or field of activity in which the technical applications are used. The experience of those who know the technology as its users has played an important role in the discussion concerning what safety is and how to promote it.

As investigations of severe organizational accidents have revealed the complexity of factors that lead to catastrophes, safety studies have lent resources even from the humanities and social sciences. The practice-oriented approach in which different theoretical approaches serve a common practical end has been a basis for developing a variety of ways to assess how the interplay between means, goals, and resources has an impact on safety and proneness to accidents in organizations and complex adaptive systems. Making use of the same types of approaches could help to bridge the gap between theory and practice in AI ethics, too, and to support the design of morally sustainable AI systems.

Acknowledgment. This paper is part of the ETAIROS (https://etairos.fi/en/front-page/) funded by The Strategic Research Council (SRC) within the Academy of Finland.

References

1. A walk on the dark side. The Economist (2007)
2. Abusus non tollit usum (s.a.). https://www.merriam-webster.com/dictionary/abusus%20non%20tollit%20usum
3. AI for Good Global Summit 2017. ITU News (2017). https://www.itu.int/en/ITU-T/AI/Pages/201706-default.aspx
4. AI Now: 2019 Report. AI Now Institute, New York University (2019). https://www.google.com/url?sa=t&rct=j&q=&esrc=s&source=web&cd=&ved=2ahUKEwiix8_MmcvuAhVFl4sKHVuLDWsQFjAAegQIAxAC&url=https%3A%2F%2Fainowinstitute.org%2FAI_Now_2019_Report.pdf&usg=AOvVaw2hwdlsKFcce1B1wW0ucWRL
5. Alimahomed-Wilson, J., Reese, E.: The Cost of Free Shipping: Amazon in the Global Economy. Pluto Press, London (2020)
6. Auernhammer, J.: Human-centered AI: the role of human-centered design research in the development of AI. In: Boess, S., Cheung, M., Cain, R. (eds.) Synergy - DRS International Conference 2020, 11–14 August (2020). https://doi.org/10.21606/drs.2020.282
7. Bayern, M.: How AI is spreading everywhere with the rise of smart machines. TechRepublic, Innovation (2018). https://www.techrepublic.com/article/how-ai-is-spreading-everywhere-with-the-rise-of-smart-machines/
8. Bernstein, P.: Against the Gods: The Remarkable Story of Risk. Wiley, Hoboken (1998)
9. Blumberg, D.: What AI startups need to achieve before VCs will invest. Extra Crunch (2019). https://techcrunch.com/2019/11/13/what-ai-startups-need-to-achieve-before-vcs-will-invest/
10. Bradshaw, S., Howard, P.N.: Challenging truth and trust. A global inventory of organized social media manipulation. Computational Propaganda Research Project. Oxford Internet Institute. University of Oxford, Oxford (2018). http://comprop.oii.ox.ac.uk/wp-content/uploads/sites/93/2018/07/ct2018.pdf
11. Carback, J.T.: Cybersex trafficking: toward a more effective prosecutorial response. Crim. Law Bull. **54**(1), 64–183 (2018)

12. Chaffey, D.: Global social media research summary August 2020. Smart Insights (2020). https://www.smartinsights.com/social-media-marketing/social-media-strategy/new-global-social-media-research/
13. Chui, M., Harrysson, M., Manyika, J., Roberts, R., Chung, R., Nel, P., et al.: Applying artificial intelligence for social good. Discussion Paper. McKinsey Global Institute (2018). https://www.mckinsey.com/featured-insights/artificial-intelligence/applying-artificial-intelligence-for-social-good
14. Clarke, M.: Insurance fraud. Br. J. Criminol. **29** (1), 1–20 (1989). https://www.jstor.org/stable/23638129?seq=8#metadata_info_tab_contents
15. Coeckelbergh, M.: AI Ethics. The MIT Press Essential Knowledge Series. The MIT Press, Cambridge (2020)
16. Combating cyber crime: Department of Homeland Security (2012)
17. Cyber crime: Federal Bureau of Investigation (2017)
18. Dekker, S.: The Field Guide to Understanding 'Human Error', 3rd edn. CRC Press, Boca Raton (2014)
19. Dekker, S.W.A., Breakey, H.: 'Just culture:' improving safety by achieving substantive, procedural and restorative justice. Saf. Sci. **85**, 187–193 (2016)
20. Doris, J.: Lack of Character. Personality and Moral Behavior. Cambridge University Press, Cambridge (2002)
21. Enya, A., Dempsey, S., Pillay, M.: High reliability organisation (HRO) principles of collective mindfulness: an opportunity to improve construction safety management. In: Arezes, P.M.F.M. (ed.) AHFE 2018. AISC, vol. 791, pp. 3–13. Springer, Cham (2019). https://doi.org/10.1007/978-3-319-94589-7_1
22. Ethics guidelines for trustworthy AI. High-Level Expert Group on Artificial Intelligence. European Commission, Brussels (2019). https://ec.europa.eu/digital-single-market/en/news/ethics-guidelines-trustworthy-ai
23. Feinberg, T.: Whether it happens at school or off-campus, cyberbullying disrupts and affects all aspects of students' lives (2008). http://docplayer.net/17558112-Whether-it-happens-at-school-or-off-campus-cyberbullying-disrupts-and-affects-all-aspects-of-students-lives.html
24. Floridi, L.: Faultless responsibility: on the nature and allocation of moral responsibility for distributed moral actions. Philos. Trans. Ser. Math. Phys. Eng. Sci. **374**(2083), 1–13 (2016)
25. Floridi, L., Cowls, J., Beltrametti, M., Chatila, R., Chazerand, P., Dignum, V., et al.: AI4People: an ethical framework for a good AI society: opportunities, risks, principles, and recommendations. Minds Mach. **28**(4), 689–707 (2018)
26. Fossheim, H.: Virtue ethics and everyday strategies. Revue Internationale de Philosophie **267**(1), 65–82 (2014). https://doi.org/10.3917/rip.267.0065
27. Fresneau, V.: 10 promising European deeptech startups leading us into the future. EU-Startups (2020). https://www.eu-startups.com/2020/05/10-promising-deeptech-startups/
28. Gawande, A.: The Checklist Manifesto: How to Get Things Right. Profile Books, London (2011)
29. Grace, K., Salvatier, J., Dafoe, A., Zhang, B., Evans, O.: Viewpoint: when will AI exceed human performance? Evidence from AI experts. J. Artif. Intell. Res. **62**, 729–754 (2018)
30. Hagendorff, T.: The ethics of AI ethics: an evaluation of guidelines. Minds Mach. **30**, 99–120 (2020). https://doi.org/10.1007/s11023-020-09517-8
31. Halder, D., Jaishankar, K.: Cyber Crime and the Victimization of Women: Laws, Rights, and Regulations. IGI Global, Hershey (2011)
32. Hanington, B.: Methods in making: a perspective on the state of human research in design. Des. Issues **19**(4) 9–18 (2003). Massachusetts Institute of Technology. http://scholar.google.fi/scholar_url?url=https://www.ida.liu.se/divisions/hcs/ixs/material/servicedesignGbg10/2%2520Additional%2520readings/humancentereddesign.pdf&hl=fi&sa=X&ei=iXYaYP

TGCY-Ny9YP3o6D2AY&scisig=AAGBfm0uqeu6IdfPOI3kEXfH1CUmKFZKEA&nossl=
1&oi=scholarr
33. Hao, K.: In 2020, let's stop AI ethics-washing and actually do something. MIT Technol. Rev.
(2019). https://www.technologyreview.com/2019/12/27/57/ai-ethics-washing-time-to-act/
34. Harman, G.: Moral philosophy meets social psychology: virtue ethics and the fundamental
attribution error. In: Proceedings of the Aristotelian Society, vol. 99, pp. 315–356 (1998–1999)
35. Harper, J.: Tesla: Soaring share price creates army of 'Teslanaires'. BBC News (2020). https://
www.bbc.com/news/business-55391571
36. Heinrich, H.W.: Industrial Accident Prevention. McGraw-Hill, New York (1931)
37. Hibbard, B.: Ethical Artificial Intelligence (2015). https://arxiv.org/abs/1411.1373
38. Hogg, M.A., Vaughan, G.M.: Social Psychology, 5th edn. Pearson Education Limited, Harlow
(2008)
39. Holland, J. H.: Complex adaptive systems. Daedalus **121**(1), 17–30 (1992). A New Era in
Computation. https://www.jstor.org.stable/20025416
40. Hollnagel, E.: The ETTO Principle: Efficiency-Thoroughness Trade-off: Why Things That
Go Right Sometimes Go Wrong. Ashgate, Farnham (2009)
41. Hollnagel, E.: Safety-I and Safety-II: The Past and Future of Safety Management. CRC Press,
Boca Raton (2014)
42. HRO Safety Culture Definition: United States Nuclear Regulatory Commission and United
States Government Accountability Office (2010)
43. Inkster, I.: Science and Technology in History: An Approach to Industrial Development.
Macmillan Educational, New Brunswick (1991)
44. Johnson, A.: Examining the foundation. Saf. Health Mag. (2011). https://www.safetyandhea
lthmagazine.com/articles/print/6368-examining-the-foundation
45. Just Culture. Skybrary. https://www.skybrary.aero/index.php/Just_Culture
46. Kibby, M.: The impact of AI on human intelligence: can we live without it?
AmeInfo (2020). https://www.ameinfo.com/industry/tech-and-mobility/the-impact-of-ai-on-
human-intelligence
47. Knapp, A.: Six billionaires who made their fortunes from videogames. Forbes
(2017). https://www.forbes.com/sites/alexknapp/2017/03/21/six-billionaires-who-made-for
tunes-from-videogames/
48. Kranzberg, M.: Technology and history: "Kranzberg's laws". Technol. Cult. **27**(3), 544–560
(1986). https://doi.org/10.2307/3105385
49. Krupiv, T.: A vulnerability analysis: theorising the impact of artificial intelligence decision-
making processes on individuals, society and human diversity from a social justice perspective.
Comput. Law Secur. Rev. **38** (2020). https://doi.org/10.1016/j.clsr.2020.105429
50. Lin, P., Abney, K., Jenkins, R. (eds.): Robot ethics 2.0: From autonomous cars to artificial
intelligence. Oxford Scholarship Online (2017)
51. MacIntyre, A.: After Virtue: A Study in Moral Theory. University of Notre Dame Press, Notre
Dame (1981)
52. McNamara, A., Smith, J., Murphy-Hill, E.: Does ACM's code of ethics change ethical decision making in software development? In: Leavens, G.T., Garcia, A., Păsăreanu C.S. (eds.)
Proceedings of the 2018 26th ACM joint meeting on European Software Engineering Conference and Symposium on the Foundations of Software Engineering—ESEC/FSE 2018,
pp. 1–7. ACM Press, New York (2018)
53. Maidment, D.: The effect of the accident inquiry process within the railway industry. In: Hale,
A., Wilpert, B., Freitag, M. (eds.) After the Event. From Accident to Organisational Learning,
Pergamon, Oxford, pp. 61–76 (1997)
54. Mann, D., Sutton, M.: Netcrime. Br. J. Criminol. **38**(2) 201–229 (2011). CiteSeerX
10.1.1.133.3861

55. Manuele, P.A.: On the Practice of Safety, 4th edn. Wiley, Hoboken (2013)
56. Marr, B.: Artificial Intelligence in Practice: How 50 Successful Companies used AI and Machine Learning to Solve Problems. Wiley, Chichester (2019)
57. Osoba, O.A., Welser IV, W.: The risks of artificial intelligence to security and the future of work. Perspective. Expert insights Timely Policy Issue. https://www.google.com/url?sa=t&rct=j&q=&esrc=s&source=web&cd=&ved=2ahUKEwigjOPD68ruAhXsiIsKHQ98CIUQFjALegQIJRAC&url=https%3A%2F%2Fwww.rand.org%2Fcontent%2Fdam%2Frand%2Fpubs%2Fperspectives%2FPE200%2FPE237%2FRAND_PE237.pdf&usg=AOvVaw2RDrXdeOZjnxJrVoXqV0pk
58. Perrow, C.: Normal Accidents: Living with High-Risk Technologies. Princeton University Press, Princeton (1999)
59. Perrow, C.: The Next Catastrophe: Reducing Our Vulnerabilities to Natural, Industrial, and Terrorist Disasters. Princeton University Press, Princeton (2007)
60. Railway Passengers Assurance Company Ltd. http://www.aviva.com/about-us/heritage/companies/railway-passengers-assurance-company/
61. Reason, J.: Human Error. Cambridge University Press, Cambridge (1990)
62. Reason, J.: Managing the Risks of Organizational Accidents. Routledge, London and New York (1997)
63. Reason, J.: The Human Contribution. Unsafe Acts, Accidents and Heroic Recoveries. Routledge, New York (2008)
64. Reason, J.: Organizational Accidents Revisited. Ashgate, Farnham (2016)
65. Regulation (EU) 2016/679 of the European Parliament and of the Council of 27 April 2016 on the protection of natural persons with regard to the processing of personal data and on the free movement of such data, and repealing Directive 95/46/EC (General Data Protection Regulation) (2016). http://data.europa.eu/eli/reg/2016/679/oj
66. Reiman, T., Oedewald, P.: Turvallisuuskriittiset organisaatiot: Onnettomuudet, kulttuuri ja johtaminen. (Safety-Critical Organizations: Accidents, Culture, and Leadership) Edita, Helsinki (2008)
67. Resilience Engineering (2019). https://www.resilience-engineering-association.org/blog/2019/11/09/what-is-resilience-engineering/
68. Roberts, K.H.: New challenges in organizational research: high reliability organizations. Organ. Environ. 3(2), 111–125 (1989). https://doi.org/10.1177/108602668900300202
69. Robertson, K., Black, K., Grand-Clement, S., Hall, A.: Human and Organisational Factors in Major Accident Prevention: A Snapshot of the Academic Landscape. RAND Corporation, Santa Monica (2016). https://www.google.com/url?sa=t&rct=j&q=&esrc=s&source=web&cd=&ved=2ahUKEwiipdWKqMvuAhVwAxAIHaWZD00QFjATegQIChAC&url=https%3A%2F%2Fwww.rand.org%2Fcontent%2Fdam%2Frand%2Fpubs%2Fresearch_reports%2FRR1500%2FRR1512%2FRAND_RR1512.pdf&usg=AOvVaw27bcYG_JDYDOKlcAn5bSe1
70. Rosenberg, S.: Why AI is still waiting for its ethics transplant. Wired (2017). https://www.wired.com/story/why-ai-is-still-waiting-for-its-ethics-transplant/
71. Rossi, B.: Has AI become something we cannot live without? Information Age (2016). https://www.information-age.com/has-ai-become-something-we-cant-live-without-123461456/
72. Russell, C.: A case for not regulating the development of artificial intelligence. Towards Data Science (2019). https://towardsdatascience.com/a-case-for-not-regulating-the-development-of-artificial-intelligence-f3d23db2e8cd
73. Sagan, S.D.: The Limits of Safety. Organizations, Accidents, and Nuclear Weapons. Princeton University Press, Princeton (1993)
74. Sammarco, J.J.: Operationalizing normal accident theory for safety-related computer systems. Saf. Sci. 43(9), 697–714 (2005). https://doi.org/10.1016/j.ssci.2005.03.001

75. Saran, S., Natrajan, N., Srikumar, M.: In Pursuit of Autonomy: AI and National Strategies. Observer Research Foundation, New Delhi (2018)
76. Scherer, M.U.: Regulating artificial intelligence systems: risks, challenges, competencies, and strategies. Harv. J. Law Technol. **29**(2) (2016). https://doi.org/10.2139/ssrn.2609777
77. Schmeltzer, R.: The complex nature of regulating AI. SearchEnterpriseAI. TechTarget (2019). https://searchenterpriseai.techtarget.com/feature/The-complex-nature-of-regulating-AI
78. Shrivastava, S., Sonpar, K., Pazzaglia, F.: Normal accident theory versus high reliability theory: a resolution and call for an open systems view of accidents. Hum. Relat. **62**(9), 1357–1390 (2009). https://doi.org/10.1177/0018726709339117
79. Stametalatos, M.: Probabilistic Risk Assessment: What is It and Why Is It Worth Performing It? (2000). http://www.hq.nasa.gov/office/codecq/qnews/prs.pdf
80. Stultz, J.: High Reliability Organization Toolkit. Manage Operations (2018). https://web.mhanet.com/media-library/high-reliability-organization-toolkit/
81. The Montréal Declaration for a Responsible Development of Artificial Intelligence. Inven_T, University of Montreal's Technosocial Innovation Centre (2018). https://www.montrealdeclaration-responsibleai.com/
82. Vanderhaegen, F., Hollnagel, E.: Safety-I and Safety-II, the past and future of safety management. Cognit. Technol. Work **17**(3), 461–464 (2015). https://doi.org/10.1007/s10111-015-0345-z
83. Wagner, B.: Ethics as an escape from regulation. From "ethicswashing" to ethics-shopping? Repositorium für die Medienwissenschaft (2018). https://doi.org/10.25969/mediarep/13281
84. Why Air Travel is The Safest Mode of Transportation? Sheffield School of Aeronautics. https://www.sheffield.com/air-travel-safest-mode-transportation
85. Why is regulating artificial intelligence so tricky? The Startup (2020). https://medium.com/swlh/why-is-regulating-artificial-intelligence-so-tricky-f202c967c2b4
86. Weick, K.E., Sutcliffe, K.M.: Managing the Unexpected: Assuring High Performance in an Age of Complexity. Jossey Bass, San Francisco (2001)
87. Weick, K.E., Sutcliffe, K.M.: Managing the Unexpected: Sustained Performance in a Complex World, 3rd edn. Wiley, Hoboken (2015)
88. Winck, B.: 3 reasons why bitcoin has doubled in less than a month – and why experts think it won't repeat its 2012 crash. Businessinsider (2021). https://markets.businessinsider.com/currencies/news/bitcoin-price-btc-performance-explanation-cryptocurrency-market-crash-token-investing-2021-1-1029945005
89. Winfield, A.F.T., Jirotka, M.: The case for an ethical black box. In: Gao, Y., Fallah, S., Jin, Y., Lekakou, C. (eds.) TAROS 2017. LNCS (LNAI), vol. 10454, pp. 262–273. Springer, Cham (2017). https://doi.org/10.1007/978-3-319-64107-2_21
90. Wootton, D.: The Invention of Science: A New History of the Scientific Revolution. Penguin, Random House, London (2016)

User Interface Design of Virtual Conferencing Tools – Towards a Method for Considering Cultural Impact – Exemplified by Zoom

Olga Lange[1](✉) and Rüdiger Heimgärtner[2](✉)

[1] Fern-Universität in Hagen, Stuttgart, Germany
olga.lange@posteo.de
[2] Intercultural User Interface Consulting (IUIC), Berlin, Germany
ruediger.heimgaertner@iuic.de

Abstract. For designing user interfaces, it is essential to know the influence of the task complexity and its impact in the intercultural context. First, a model for task complexity evaluation will be presented in this paper. This method considers a task to be completed at the UI. In the second step, cultural interaction indicators and their characteristics are considered regarding the complexity level of a task. The matching of task evaluation characteristics, HCI dimensions and cultural dimensions/variables allows aligning the development of different UIs for different cultural environments. Consequently, the relationship model between culture and HCI will be proposed and discussed for five intended cultural environments (China, Germany, India, Poland, and Russia).

Keywords: User interface design · Task complexity · China · Germany · India · Poland · Russia · Culture · Cultural dimensions · UI · HCI · Process flow · Zoom · Lecturing · Teaching · IUID

1 Introduction and Related Work

In times of Covid-19, lecturers at many universities switched to use virtual conferencing tools for teaching. In times of globalization, many universities have students from different cultures that are using virtual conferences tools. Hence, it is reasonable to investigate how user interface design of virtual conferencing tools needs to be enhanced to consider the cultural background of the users applying such tools. Therefore, in this paper, an approach towards a method for considering the cultural impact in designing the user interface of virtual conferencing tools will be indicated.

1.1 Task Complexity

In the design of user interfaces, it is mandatory to analyze the related user tasks for better implementation of applications. Therefore, the task complexity as an inherent UI characteristic needs to be classified [1].

© Springer Nature Switzerland AG 2021
M. Rauterberg (Ed.): HCII 2021, LNCS 12795, pp. 80–94, 2021.
https://doi.org/10.1007/978-3-030-77431-8_5

The first core concept according to [2] is based on three generally valid components of a task - event, action, and information flow. Wood presents three analytical dimensions of task complexity. The first dimension, the *components complexity*, is a direct function of identified events and information flow numbers. *Coordinate complexity*, as a second dimension, focuses on the relationship between task inputs and task events. The third dimension describes the *dynamic complexity* by the means of task inputs and task events.

The second fundamental concept according to [3] focuses on basic frameworks and a typology of task complexity. The following four characteristics describe the source of complexity - multiple paths, multiple outcomes, conflicting independence among paths, and associated characteristics. Depending on the evaluated combination of characteristics the analyzed task will be classified as *simple task*, *decision task*, *judgement task*, *problem task* or *fuzzy task*.

[4] extended the basic core concepts by [2] and [3] presented above with the new assumption of four dimensions of task complexity. Those four dimensions are:

- the separability of the task from behavior and context;
- the degree of analysis;
- the nature of complexity and
- the functional form.

The concepts presented above according to [2] and [3] provide a fundamental view of complexity as one of the most important characteristics of a task. The extended concept according to [4] adds task requirements to these concepts that have changed over time.

However, a basis for aligning the considered task along the elementary process steps at the human-computer interface is missing. Therefore, [5] elaborated the measurement methodology for the classification of task complexity added as requirement to the process steps. Table 1 presents the basics of this measurement methodology for the classification of the task complexity:

"low complexity" (1) happens

- with 0–5 variable steps ($n <= 5$) in the process execution,
- with more than 50% process steps at the user-SW interface.

"medium complexity" (2) arises

- with 6–8 variable steps ($5 < n < 9$) in the process execution and
- with more than 50% process steps at the user-SW interface.

"high complexity" (3) comes along

- with 9 and more variable steps ($n > = 9$) in the process execution and
- with more than 50% process steps at the user SW interface.

Table 1. Basics of the measurement methodology for task complexity classification according to [5].

Complexity classification	Measuring values	Process requirements
Low (1)	$n <= 5 > 50\%$	1. *Number of process steps, n*
Medium (2)	$5 < n < 9 > 50\%$	2. *Share of process steps on the human - computer interface, %*
High (3)	$n > = 9 > 50\%$	

1.2 Determining the Task Complexity

The task analysis is the first step in the task complexity evaluation. Therefore, the task will be described by the detailed process steps of the task execution exemplified by a sample virtual conference call using Zoom.

Figure 1 shows an example of a process flow diagram for the task "Virtual conference call participation" during a sample session with the tool "Zoom". Splitting the process steps into the user, software and user-software process levels allows a detailed examination of the task flow with all steps in the software user interface. The detailed analysis of the process steps gives a basis for the evaluation of the complexity of the task "participate at a virtual conference call". The planned use of this method will provide a breakdown by the use case of lecturing students as a model for student training. The investigated task includes nine process steps:

1. Opening the tool.
2. The SW starts the tool.
3. Entering the conference.
4. Sharing the desktop.
5. Presenting your work.
6. Gathering feedback on your work (verbally)
7. Gathering feedback on your work (using chat, whiteboard, etc.).
8. Leaving the conference.
9. Closing the tool.

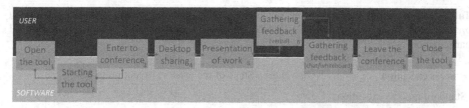

Fig. 1. Process flow diagram for the task "Virtual conference call participation".

As a preparatory work, all process steps of the process flow diagram are determined and evaluated in Table 2 according to the rules given below:

1. All process steps from the process flow diagram are classified as start process-, node process-, and end process steps.
2. Start and end process steps remain constant for all process executions.
3. Node process steps define the variable process steps in the task execution that have branches with different decision possibilities.
4. The order of the node process steps is the same as for all process executions.
5. All process steps for the task must be executed exactly once.

The results from the analyzed process steps contained in the task "Virtual conference call participation" indicated in Table 2 point to five node process steps (variable process steps), which serve for the determination of the parameter "Number of variable process steps, n" with n = 5. Any sequence of executions without knowledge of the standard process can be calculated according to the faculty in the considered target group of beginners and occasional users. According to formulas n! = 1*2*3*...n with n = 5, 5! = 1*2*3*4*5 the calculated value is 120 possible process executions in the investigated task "Virtual conference call participation". The 120 possible sequences can be executed by the completion of this task. A consideration of the process step determination for the parameter "*Share of process steps on the level USER-SOFTWARE-interface, %*" shows that 78% of the process steps take place at the Zoom UI. This means that an improvement may be necessary to execute the task easily.

1.3 Deriving UI Assistance and UI Elements

The task complexity is assigned to user assistance as usual, expected/foresighted, and foresighted/intelligent (self-learning) assistance [5]. According to the results presented in the Tables 1 and 2 above (5 variable process steps and 78% share of process steps regarding the UI), a medium task complexity was derived from the analyzed task "Virtual conference call participation" requiring e.g., online help, mouse control and expected and foresighted assistance (indicated bold in Table 3).

Table 2. Determination of measuring values *Number of variable process steps, n* and *Share of process steps on the level USER-SOFTWARE-interface, %* for the task "Virtual conference call participation".

Process execution	Value	1	2	3	4^1	5^2	6^3	7^4	8^5	9
Standard process execution		1	2	3	4^1	5^2	6^3	7^4	8^5	9
Process steps		*start-*			*node-*					*end-*
Number of process steps, n	**5**					1*2*3*4*5				
Steps on process level *USER*	1							x		
Steps on process level *USER-SOFTWARE-interface*	7	x		x	x	x		x	x	x
Steps on process level *SOFTWARE*	1		x							
Share of process steps on the process level USER-SOFTWARE-interface, %	**78%** **(7)**	x		x	x	x		x	x	x

Table 3. Implemented selection of user support concepts in interaction and at the interface assigned to the classification of complexity [5].

Task complexity	Concepts		User assistance
	Interaction	Interface	
Low	Online support	Keyboard input, mouse control	Usual assistance
Medium	**Online help, semantic system evaluation, database-based support, navigation**	**Keyboard input, mouse control, touch/multi-touch operation, display devices**	**Expected and foresighted assistance**
High	Combination of online help, semantic system evaluation, database-based support, navigation	Combination of keyboard input, mouse control, touch/multi-touch operation, vision devices	Foresighted and intelligent (self-learning) assistance

2   Culture and UI Design

Intercultural user interface design (IUID) is a prerequisite for improving the intercultural usability of software, which in turn is a prerequisite for global sales opportunities. Using methods of intercultural usability engineering, further design guidelines for IUID can be iteratively derived from the results of the tests with potential users from all over the world and their feedback. Hence, the perception and consideration of the customs and requirements of other cultures by developers of intercultural user interfaces is one of the main tasks within intercultural user interface design. Differences between cultures can be found by analyzing critical interaction situations between people [6]. [7] made this method available for cultural differences in Human-Machine Interaction (HMI): critical interaction situations that arise due to problematic functionality of user interfaces must be analyzed. [8] found that e.g., Hofstedes "Individualism Index" (cf. [9]) is related to user satisfaction and usability of the product and has a significant influence on intercultural usability. [10] proposed the "Method for Culture-Oriented Design" (MCD), which integrates the factors of new concepts of culture-oriented HCI design and the knowledge of cultural differences into existing concepts of HCI design. Relevant cultural variables for intercultural HCI design must be determined analytically based on literature and requirement studies. Their values represent culture-dependent variations that occur at all levels of HCI localization (surface, functionality, interaction) and that can be used for IUID. Similarly, for culture-oriented design, [11] considered a simplified version of a culture-centered HCI design process while focusing on social and cultural aspects to cover the value of the user's cultural context. Further methods apply user interface characteristics [12] or cultural markers [13]. To make cultural dimensions available for user interface design, [12] developed characteristic factors for user interfaces and gave examples that can influence user interface design (such as different colors or behaviors). Cultural markers have been determined by empirical studies (e.g., [13–15]), which are specific for a certain culture and preferably used within this specific culture (such as flags). Other approaches, e.g., by [16] or [17], are based on semiotic theory. In semiotic engineering, HCI is seen "as a two-tiered communicative process: one is the designer-to-user communication and the other is the user-system interaction. [..] HCI can only be achieved if both levels of communication are successfully achieved." [18]: 55.

One of the most promising methods for preserving cultural differences in HCI is the observation and analysis of user interaction with the system (cf. [19]). The results of observations of cultural variables and their manifestations serve as a basis for IUID guidelines (e.g., cultural interaction indicators (cf. [19]), a culture dependent HCI model (cf. [20]), cultural adaptation of user interfaces (cf. [21]) as well as for culturally aware systems (cf. [22]).

Based on feedback from tutorials and workshops on IUID and the revised summary of the state of research on IUID in [23], the author reviewed the synopsis of well documented IUID methods to create a reasonable toolbox for IUID, consisting of a IUID method-mix, which will be used in this paper to relate HMI to culture.

2.1 UI Design for Different Cultural Contexts

A hybrid approach integrating a combined use of the following concepts ("IUID Method-Mix" for short) to derive cultural HCI indicators relevant for the formulation of recommendations for IUID can be used:

- HCI dimensions,
- Cultural dimensions,
- Intercultural variables,
- User interface characteristics,

- The culture dependent HCI model,
- The method of culture-oriented design.

The characteristics of cultural dimensions influence the user experience and provide orientation for the usability engineering process. Differences between cultures can be found by analyzing critical interaction situations between people (cf. [6]) expressed by cultural dimensions (cf. [9]) that serve to describe and compare cultural systems (cf. [24]).

Using the "Method for Culture-Oriented Design" [10], relevant cultural variables for intercultural HMI design can be determined analytically based on literature research and requirement studies. Their values represent culture-dependent variations that occur at all levels of HMI localization (surface, functionality, and interaction) describing the differences in HMI design with respect to the preferences of users from different cultures. "Visible" intercultural variables are immediately perceptible at any given time (font, color, window size, navigation, etc.). In contrast, "invisible" (or "hidden") intercultural variables are only recognizable over a certain period of time (interaction speed, information display duration, dialogue display frequency, use of the navigation bar, etc.).

The "Method for Culture-Oriented Design" (MCD) integrates the factors of culture-oriented HMI design and the knowledge of cultural differences into existing concepts of HMI design [25]. The hypotheses identified in the phase of theoretical analysis will be empirically tested in the next phase with students from different cultures. Finally, the results will be related to the Zoom use case resp. application and how they are used in different cultures by integrating them in the system.

The user interface characteristics "Metaphor", "Mental Model", "Navigation", "Interaction" and "Presentation" (cf. [12]) are linked to five of Hofstede's cultural dimensions (cf. [9, 10]). User interface characteristics can be used in conjunction with empirical surveys on their characteristics for the corresponding cultural target context to derive recommendations for the development of intercultural user interfaces.

According to the classification of means of user support (as indicated in Table 3 before), interaction types/means of control and information management of the UI are to be considered (such as keyboard, mouse, touch screen). This is done by applying the user interface characteristics such as metaphor, mental model, interaction, navigation, and presentation as the most important classes of UI elements by looking at the application or imagining which UI elements are or must be present for the respective use cases (tasks). Such aspects concern layout (order), interaction frequency, information presentation (text, font, IME editor, written language…), input control, etc. These aspects can also be related to HMI dimensions, which in turn can be related to cultural dimensions, thus establishing the connection between culture and HMI. For the selected use case "virtual conferencing tool" regarding the first two tasks "open the tool" and "entering the conference", the following UI elements can be identified according to the user interface characteristics:

- Mental model: switch, link, keyboard input,
- Navigation: navigate to the start button or the link to start the application, navigate to the search bar,

- Interaction: mouse control, move mouse, press left mouse button, touch/multi-touch operation (display devices: iPad, mobile devices, screens), enter text (e.g., Zoom or conference number/meeting ID), typing speed, task duration,
- Presentation: size of start button or link and text size or search window/input fields, font, font size,
- Metaphor: user assistance/virtual agent/agent driven/guided assistance/desktop metaphor.

HMI dimensions describe the behavior of a user (i.e., the HMI style) with an interactive information processing system [20]. HMI dimensions and those of their values useful for HMI design are operationalized by means of interaction indicators representing HMI metrics.

Cultural interaction indicators (CII) represent the correlation of the user's interaction behavior and his culture as well as the correlation of HMI dimensions such as information speed (speed of dissemination and frequency of occurrence of information), information density (number and distance of information units) or information order (sequence of occurrence and arrangement of information) to culturally different basic patterns of behavior [19].

HMI dimensions consistently represented on the basis of cultural variables can be called "(Inter-)Cultural HMI Dimensions", which express the culturally influenced HMI style of the user in the respective cultural context, i.e., how the user interacts with the system. Using the method of the culture-oriented HMI design (MCD, see [10]), cultural differences are identified based on cultural dimensions and cultural variables are derived for the project. With this knowledge of cultural differences and affected aspects of the HMI system, further effects on the HMI design have been determined and supported by hypothesis-driven data transmission using user interface characteristics (see [12]) and HMI dimensions (see [19]). Thereby, recommendations for intercultural UI/UX design and intercultural usability engineering can be obtained (e.g., via cultural interaction indicators and a corresponding model of culture-dependent HMI (cf. [20]).

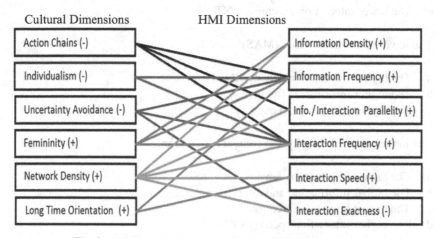

Fig. 2. Relationship between cultural and HMI dimensions.

2.2 Connecting HCI to Culture

The aim is to find the actual connection between the interaction indicators and their (postulated cultural) causes represented by the relationship between cultural and HCI dimensions (and their variables respectively). To solve this, a structural equation model for the relationship between HCI and cultural dimensions has been generated (cf. [19]). The connections between cultural, information related, and interaction related dimensions were modeled using cultural interaction indicators. Results found applying this approach (cf. [19]) led to the conviction that it is justified and useful to use cultural interaction indicators for intercultural HCI research to obtain a reasonable explanatory model for culturally influenced HCI (cf. [20]).

The model contains the following rules expressing the connection between the values of the cultural dimensions and the values of the HCI dimensions, thereby determining the denotation level for culture and HCI (cf. for details [20]):

1) The lower action chain orientation:

   a) The higher information frequency (IN-F).
   b) The higher information parallelism (IN-P) and interaction parallelism (INT-P).
   c) The higher interaction frequency (INT-F).

2) The lower individualism index (IDV):

   a) The higher information frequency.
   b) The higher interaction frequency.

3) The lower uncertainty avoidance index (UAI):

   a) The higher information frequency.
   b) The higher interaction frequency.
   c) The lower interaction exactness (INT-E).

4) The lower masculinity index (MAS):

   a) The higher information density (IN-D).
   b) The higher information frequency.
   c) The higher interaction frequency.

5) The higher network density and context orientation:

   a) The higher information density.
   b) The higher information and interaction parallelism.
   c) The higher interaction frequency.
   d) The higher interaction speed (INT-S).
   e) The lower interaction exactness.

6) The higher long-term orientation index (LTO):

   a) The higher information frequency.
   b) The higher interaction speeds.

7) And vice versa for all six rules (i.e., for Rule 1: the higher action chain orientation, the lower information/interaction frequency and parallelism).

According to the changed values of the cultural dimensions on the left side of the model (antecedents in the production rules in Fig. 2), the values of the HCI dimensions change on the right side of the model (consequences in the production rules in Fig. 2). Therefore, this model does not depend on nations or countries but can be used to cover every cultural group (with at least 20 members, if using Hofstede's Values Survey Module (VSM) (cf. [26] to determine the cultural characteristics of the group).

The explanatory model is based on some of the best classifying cultural interaction indicators, indicating that the expressions of the HCI dimensions depend on the cultural imprint of the users, which can be described by the expressions of cultural dimensions: the higher the relationship orientation (collectivism), the higher the information density, information speed, information frequency, interaction frequency and interaction speed (and vice versa). This supports the assumption that further connections between cultural dimensions, HCI dimensions and cultural interaction indicators can be modeled and explained using structural equation models as a basis for the application of the IUID method-mix supplying the rationale for creating the IUID toolbox (cf. [27]).

In addition, this approach integrates the concepts above to derive design recommendation for the designated cultural context before conducting extensive empirical studies in order to estimate the labor expenditure in advance.

The procedure of applying this approach is as follows: First, the application, main uses cases and the desired target cultures are chosen. Depending on the use case, the respective UI elements (e.g., layout, buttons, text fields) must be determined and mapped to the category of the cultural variables (direct, indirect, visible, hidden) as well as to the user interface characteristics (presentation, interaction, navigation, mental model, and metaphor). Using this information, the time and space related HMI dimensions concerned must be analyzed (such as information density or interaction frequency). Via the rules and the variables in the explanatory model for culturally influenced HMI, the detected HMI dimensions can be related to the cultural dimensions to obtain the related cultural interaction indicators. Design recommendations for intercultural user interfaces can be derived as well (cf. [19]). For example, the higher the density of an information network (e.g., as in China compared to Germany according to [24]), the stronger the values of the HMI dimensions (such as information density and interaction frequency according [20]), as shown in Fig. 2.

2.3 Evaluating Six Cultural Environments

Using Hofstede's figures, the cultural differences of the five countries China, Germany, India, Poland, and Russia become obvious and are related to the UI characteristics via the HMI dimensions according to the approach indicated before.

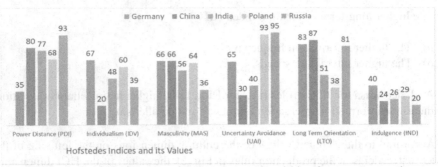

https://www.hofstede-insights.com/country-comparison/china,france,germany,the-usa/. last accessed: 06.02.2021

Fig. 3. Peculiarities of Hofstede's Cultural Dimensions for five countries.

Thereby, based on the use case "Virtual conference call participation", in the following, some hypotheses regarding the different operation of the system by the users from these countries can be derived. Intercultural variables and user interface characteristics based on HCI dimensions are connected and mapped to cultural dimensions via the cultural HCI model to obtain the hypotheses for the empirical study. Therefore, the IUID

Table 4. Results of the application of the IUID method mix.

Application(s)/Country	Zoom
Use Case(s)/Task(s)	Virtual conference call participation/opening tool and joining conference
Cultural dimension(s)	Uncertainty avoidance (from virtual agent)/ PDI (G vs. R)/INV (G vs. C)/MAS (R vs. all)/UAI (CI vs. PR)/LTO (IP vs. RGC)/IND (G vs. all)
User interface characteristic(s)/UI elements	**Mental model:** button, link, keyboard input **Navigation:** navigate to the start button or the link to start the application, navigate to search bar **Interaction:** mouse control, move mouse, press left mouse button, touch/multi-touch operation (display devices: iPad, mobile phone, screens), entering data (e.g., conference number/meeting-ID), speed of entering characters, task duration **Presentation:** size of start button or link and text size and searching window/input fields, font, font size **Metaphor:** user assistance/virtual agent/agent driven/guided assistance/using desktop metaphor
Intercultural variable(s)	direct, visible, hidden
HCI Indicator(s)	Mouse click speed, mouse move speed, number of error clicks, click accuracy, number of interactions per second (e.g., input of chars per second), number of screens resizes (zooming), number of function initiations (e.g., mute, microphone on, video on-off, number of view changes (e.g. tile or speaker view, participant view, etc.)
HCI Dimension(s)	Interaction frequency and exactness, information size and density
Culture Dependent HCI Model	INV (G high 67) ==> IF + INF low vs. C low 20 ==> IF + INF high)/PDI (G low vs. R high)
Cultural HCI Indicator(s) (indicating the hypotheses to be tested in the studies)	C: many mouse clicks, fast mouse movements/low interaction accuracy (e.g., buttons are not clicked in the middle) G: stronger use of function/high interaction accuracy

method mix is used for this purpose to derive hypotheses for the different countries to be tested in empirical studies at universities in the respective countries. Finally, IUID recommendations for the respective cultures regarding the confirmed hypotheses can be derived. Table 4 shows the output of using the IUID toolbox (i.e., the results obtained by systematically applying the IUID method mix as indicated above).

3 Towards Recommendations for Intercultural UI Design

3.1 Cultural Interaction Indicators

Cultural interaction indicators emerge when the hypotheses are culturally validated, i.e., when the IUID recommendations/design rules are culturally sensitive and have a different value for each culture (e.g., number of incorrect interaction steps or number of information units per minute). These variables can then be expressed concretely as indicators (e.g., number of images per page, or mouse clicks per minute).

The relationship between cultural dimensions and HCI dimensions comes into play by following the rules of the explanatory model expressing the connection between the values of the cultural dimensions and the values of the HCI dimensions (cf. Figure 2). With the right combination of cultural HCI indicators it is possible to get HCI differences that are purely culturally imprinted (cf. [19]). Therefore, the cultural differences found in HCI are quantitatively measurable by a computer system using special combinations of cultural HCI indicators represented by cultural HCI patterns (cf. HCI styles) depending on the culturally imprinted behavior of the user with an interactive system. This means that the analysis (recognition and classification) of cultural HCI patterns and cultural differences in HCI can be achieved purely quantitatively (cf. [19]) - a handful of cultural HCI indicators is enough for this purpose, which also serves for culturally adaptive and aware systems (cf. [22]) because the fact that cultural HCI patterns representing the cultural differences in HCI and the derived cultural HCI indicators are sufficiently statistically discriminating to detect them and to relate the users to a certain cultural imprint (cf. [19]).

3.2 Hypotheses

According to the results of the application of the IUID method mix as derived in Sect. 2 and shown in Table 4, some hypotheses on IUID recommendations for the five countries can be derived. The hypotheses (CIIs) represent the postulated relationship between HCI indicators and their expression for each culture. These CIIs will be evaluated in planned empirical studies with students from different countries.

In the following, the possible range of hypotheses can be derived from the highest cultural distances according to Fig. 3:

The most significant cultural distance regarding individualism is between China and Germany. The lower the individualism index the higher the information frequency (e.g., number of messages in chat within a session) and interaction frequency (e.g., speed of entering chars, number of touch/multi-touch operations, number of actions of participants, number of breakout sessions, number of reactions and comments) and vice versa.

The most significant cultural distance regarding uncertainty avoidance is between China (India) and Russia. The lower the uncertainty avoidance index the higher the information frequency and interaction frequency (e.g., number of mouse clicks, number of used functions within a session) and the lower the interaction exactness and vice versa. The higher the uncertainty avoidance index the lower the probability of recording the session and providing real pictures or switching the video on. The lower the uncertainty avoidance index the higher the expectancy of foresighted assistance (e.g., message about muted micro if you want to speak).

The most significant cultural distance regarding long term orientation is between Poland and China. The higher the long-term orientation index the higher the information frequency and the interaction speed (e.g., speed of mouse moves, speed of entering characters, number of initiating functions within a certain time period) and vice versa.

4 Discussion

For presented elaboration of methods for considering cultural impact, we analyzed the task complexity, UI assistance and UI elements. The presented hypotheses describe the possible user needs regarding the different operation of the virtual conference system Zoom by intercultural variables between HCI and culture. In a study by Norwegian colleagues, the active participation in chats of the conferencing tool Slack was investigated. They found that cultural differences as well as the language level of the participants play a major role in chat activities (cf. [28]). Similarly, we want to do an empirical study to check the perception and performance of using virtual conferencing tools in the cultural context. Therefore, we will have to figure out how these systems are used for learning in environments of teaching. In addition, we must verify if the test setting is appropriate to validate the suggested hypotheses that still must be elaborated in detail for the study. Finally, it should be investigated if this concept is also valid for other learning environments (e.g., school, language institute, higher education or seminars and competence training).

5 Conclusion

For the design of user interfaces, it is essential to know the task complexity influence and its impact in intercultural context. Hypotheses for using the virtual conferencing tool Zoom have been derived from the relationship model between culture and HCI, proposed and discussed for five cultural environments (China, Germany, India, Poland, and Russia). The next step is to conduct an empirical study to validate these hypotheses in the educational context via study projects at universities. Then, a check on the basis of the study results is to show whether the suggested approach and methods are suitable or must be readjusted (and if the presented methods are appropriate for this purpose and the found cultural differences are important to take them into account in using virtual conferencing tools in the cultural context. Implication for virtual conferencing tools based on the results of the planned study should lead to intercultural user interface design recommendations as well as to the adaptation of the tasks in the tool to the cultural requirements. Finally, the results from the study could be used in the future to adapt the development of the tools and their features according to cultural contexts.

Acknowledgements. We would like to thank the German UPA and the members of the German UPA working group "Interculturality" for supporting this project.

References

1. Herczeg, M.: SW-Ergonomie. Theorien, Modelle und Kriterien für gebrauchstaugliche interaktive Computersysteme. 3. Aufl. Oldenbourg Verlag, München (2009)
2. Wood, R.W.: Task complexity: definition of the construct. Organ. Behav. Hum. Decis. Process. **37**(1), 60–82 (1986). https://doi.org/10.1007/978-3-322-88802-0_86
3. Campbell, D.J.: Task complexity. a review and analysis. Acad. Manage. Rev. **13**(1), 40–52 (1988)
4. Hærem, T., Pentland, B.T., Miller, K.D.: Task complexity: extending a core concept. Acad. Manage. Rev. **40**(3), 446–460 (2015). https://doi.org/10.5465/amr.2013.0350
5. Lange, O.: Methodik zur Gestaltung und Evaluierung der Software-Gebrauchstauglichkeit bei der ersten oder bei seltener Anwendung. Fraunhofer Verlag, Stuttgart (2019)
6. Thomas, A., Kinast, E.-U., Schroll-Machl, S.: Handbook of Intercultural Communication and Cooperation. Basics and Areas of Application. Vandenhoeck & Ruprecht, Göttingen (2010)
7. Honold, P.: Interkulturelles usability engineering: Eine Untersuchung zu kulturellen Einflüssen auf die Gestaltung und Nutzung technischer Produkte (Als Ms. gedr. ed. vol. 647). VDI Verl, Düsseldorf (2000)
8. Vöhringer-Kuhnt, T.: The influence of culture on usability. (M.A. master thesis), Freie Universität Berlin (2002)
9. Hofstede, G.H., Hofstede, G.J., Minkov, M.: Cultures and Organizations: Software of the Mind, 3rd edn. McGraw-Hill, Maidenhead (2010)
10. Röse, K.: Methodik zur Gestaltung interkultureller Mensch-Maschine-Systeme in der Produktionstechnik, vol. 5. Univ, Kaiserslautern (2002)
11. Shen, S.-T., Woolley, M., Prior, S.: Towards culture-centred design. Interact. Comput. **18**(4), 820–852 (2006). https://doi.org/10.1016/j.intcom.2005.11.014
12. Marcus, A.: Cross-cultural user-experience design. In: Barker-Plummer, D., Cox, R., Swoboda, N. (eds.) Diagrams 2006. LNCS (LNAI), vol. 4045, pp. 16–24. Springer, Heidelberg (2006). https://doi.org/10.1007/11783183_4
13. Badre, A., Barber, W.: Culturabilty: the merging of culture and usabilty. In: Proceedings of the 4th Conference on Human Factors and the Web. Basking Ridge, USA (1998)
14. Dormann, C.: Cultural representations in web design: differences in emotions and values. In: McEwan, T., Benyon, D., Gulliksen, J. (eds.) People and Computers XIX - The Bigger Picture, pp. 285–299, London (2006)
15. Sun, H.: Building a culturally competent corporate web site: an exploratory study of cultural markers in multilingual web design. In: Paper presented at the Proceedings of SIGDOC, New York (2001)
16. Castro, S., Luciana, C., Leitão, C., Souza, C.: Semiotic engineering and culture. In: de Castro Salgado, L.C., Leitão, C. F., De Souza, C.S. (eds.). A Journey Through Cultures, pp. 19–42. Springer, London (2013). http://doi.org/10.1007/978-1-4471-4114-3_2
17. Pereira, R., Baranauskas, M.C.C., Liu, K.: The value of values for HCI: an informed discussion beyond philosophy. In: Paper presented at the Proceedings of the 14th Brazilian Symposium on Human Factors in Computing Systems, Salvador, Brazil (2015)
18. Souza, C.S.D., Barbosa, S.D.J., Prates, R.O.: A semiotic engineering approach to HCI. In: Paper presented at the CHI 2001 Extended Abstracts on Human Factors in Computing Systems, Seattle, Washington (2001)

19. Heimgärtner, R.: Cultural Differences in Human-Computer Interaction – Towards Culturally Adaptive Human-Machine Interaction (Paperback B: Einband - flex.(Paperback) ed. Vol. 1): Oldenbourg Verlag (2012)
20. Heimgärtner, R.: Reflections on a model of culturally influenced human computer interaction to cover cultural contexts in HCI design. Int. J. Hum. Comput. Interact. (2013)
21. Heimgärtner, R., Holzinger, A., Adams, R.: From cultural to individual adaptive end-user interfaces: helping people with special needs. In: Miesenberger, K., Klaus, J., Zagler, W., Karshmer, A. (eds.) ICCHP 2008. LNCS, vol. 5105, pp. 82–89. Springer, Heidelberg (2008). https://doi.org/10.1007/978-3-540-70540-6_11
22. Heimgärtner, R.: Culturally-Aware HCI Systems. In: Faucher, C. (ed.) Advances in Culturally-Aware Intelligent Systems and in Cross-Cultural Psychological Studies, pp. 11–37. Springer International Publishing, Cham (2018)
23. Heimgärtner, R.: Intercultural user interface design. In: Blashki, K., Isaias, P. (eds.) Emerging Research and Trends in Interactivity and the Human-Computer Interface (2014)
24. Hall, E.T., Hall, M.R.: Understanding Cultural Differences: Germans, French and Americans. Intercultural Press, Boston (2009)
25. Röse, K.: The development of culture-oriented human machine systems: specification, analysis and integration of relevant intercultural variables. In: Michael, K. (ed.) Cultural Ergonomics, vol. 4, pp. 61–103. Emerald Group Publishing Limited (2004)
26. Hofstede, G.: VSM94: Values Survey Module 1994 Manual. IRIC, Tilberg (1994)
27. Heimgärtner, R.: IUID method-mix: towards a systematic approach for intercultural user interface design (IUID). J. Comput. Commun. 07, 162–194 (2019). https://doi.org/10.4236/jcc.2019.77015
28. Stray, V., Moe N.B., Noroozi, M.: Slack me if you can! using enterprise social networking tools in virtual agile teams. In: CM/IEEE 14th International Conference on Global Software Engineering (ICGSE), pp. 11–121 (2019)

Infrastructuring for Collective Heritage Knowledge Production

Sanna Marttila[1](✉) and Andrea Botero[2]

[1] IT University of Copenhagen, Copenhagen, Denmark
sanma@itu.dk
[2] Aalto University, Espoo, Finland
andrea.botero@aalto.fi

Abstract. We look at relational processes of engagement, negotiation and articulation of digital heritage knowledge production. By looking at creative reuse and remix of digital cultural heritage we focus on how those processes manifest at the intersection of established cultural institutions and people outside of these institutions. Two experimental arrangements are described that seek to understand how Human-Computer Interaction and design interventions might contribute to new forms of heritage knowledge production and collective memory-making by mobilizing infrastructuring interventions to question knowledge production, politics and ownership. We conclude by proposing that HCI can contribute to infrastructuring for collective knowledge production by supporting arrangements that open access to digital cultural heritage, open heritage knowledge and its practices, and reimagine authorship and ownership of contributions to heritage.

Keywords: Design · Digital cultural heritage · Heritage knowledge production · Infrastructuring · Remix

1 Introduction

The UNESCO Charter on the Preservation of Cultural Heritage (2003) defines digital cultural heritage as "resources of information and creative expression are increasingly produced, distributed, accessed and maintained in digital form, creating a new legacy – the digital heritage". This charter recognized how emerging technologies have been rapidly changing how people engage and experience their history and heritage. Importantly, the charter also hints at ways in which these new forms of engagement and interaction also enable people to produce heritage knowledge in myriad, sometimes unidentified, ways. These ways range from enriching, annotating and preserving existing historical records, producing and pooling shared resources of heritage, and also creating and sharing cultural narratives. In this sense it is important to remember that heritage is not in itself a given, or a legacy waiting to be discovered and recognized. How and what becomes considered heritage is rather the product of particular processes of construction and production (Kirshenblatt-Gimblett 1995) that both rely on infrastructures, and become infrastructures in themselves (Marttila 2018). Because of their infrastructural qualities

© Springer Nature Switzerland AG 2021
M. Rauterberg (Ed.): HCII 2021, LNCS 12795, pp. 95–112, 2021.
https://doi.org/10.1007/978-3-030-77431-8_6

(Star 1999) these processes are subject to the dynamics of particular forms of social practices that Kuutma (2009) links to knowledge production, heritage politics, and also to questions of ownership. All these pose important challenges for design approaches engaging with this domain. As more and more conservation and digitization initiatives build more encompassing infrastructures for archiving and providing access to cultural heritage in digital forms; rethinking how heritage knowledge production processes can become more collaborative is urgent (Marttila and Botero 2017, Ciolfi 2013, Stuedahl and Mörtberg 2012).

In the past decades HCI (Human-Computer Interaction) has already made a range of knowledge contributions to the digital cultural heritage domain. In her literature review Ciolfi (2013) traces work linking heritage institutions and digital technologies to three key areas of interest: the first one, an interest in the social interaction, engagement, and experience of visitors to heritage collections. The second one relates to the design and development of technologies in relation to cultural heritage, including how this technology use could enhance and mediate visits to the existing heritage sites or institutions. And the third one deals more with the design and creation of interactive installations, artistic objects and performances that, in themselves, form "a heritage artefact". So far, the largest body of work in HCI in relation to digital heritage relates to technology, in particular novel interactive systems, standards and services that support cultural heritage sites or physical organizations (see e.g. Ficarra et al. 2012, Ciolfi and McLoughlin 2012). The issue of how social practices are linked to heritage knowledge production and their (digital) infrastructuring processes is still under-studied within the HCI literature. In addition, as pointed out by Avram et al. (2020) a focus on long-term perspective in cultural heritage work in HCI remains uncommon.

There is an emerging body of knowledge that has applied participatory design tools and techniques to engage audiences and communities in participatory practices within cultural heritage institutions (e.g. Salgado and Botero 2008, Dindler et al. 2010, Bossen et al. 2012, Stuedahl and Lowe 2013), to experiment with for example social media production (e.g. Giaccardi 2012, Stuedahl and Smørdal 2015), in designing exhibitions, encounters and experiences with digital cultural heritage (e.g. Salgado 2009, Avram and Maye 2016, Ciolfi et al. 2016). As opportunities are opening for more on-going and sustained relationships between heritage institutions and the communities they serve (Ciolfi et al. 2016), the need for more horizontal design approaches and strategies for digital cultural heritage become more topical. Therefore, there is also a need for larger inquiry on how digital cultural heritage, and its associated infrastructures could be concerned not only with preservation and access to digital cultural heritage, but also on their potential role as catalyst or barriers for the construction of shared cultural resources and heritage knowledge (Marttila and Botero 2017, Stuedahl and Mörtberg 2012).

In this paper we are interested in some of these relational processes of engagement, negotiation and articulation of digital cultural heritage and heritage knowledge production, and therefore of collective remembering and value. By focusing on how these relational processes manifest at the intersection of established cultural institutions and people outside of these institutions we will take a look at how creative re-use of digital cultural heritage might contribute to new forms of heritage knowledge production and participatory memory-making processes. We arrive at this discussion with the particular angle of what might be the role of design-oriented forms of human computer interaction (HCI) in these processes, and the things we should consider when designing for and contributing to infrastructures for digital heritage. We share the interest in understanding better the types of "connectivities" that need to be established between cultural institutions and people outside of these institutions; as Koch (2021) points in her introductory article to our panel. For bringing between these two entities, in our earlier work (Marttila 2018, Marttila and Botero 2017) we have suggested two key infrastructuring strategies for digital cultural heritage: gateways and in-between infrastructures. Thus, for our exploration of these questions we are drawing insights from two experimental arrangements that deal with creative reuse of digital cultural heritage[1] in which these strategies were further developed. Both experiments invited people – in this case professional artists, designers and practitioners - to explicitly remix digital cultural heritage materials without copyright restrictions that are provided by particular European heritage institutions. The first arrangement involved setting up an experimental exhibition of remix pieces from an emerging open collection of digital visual art, at a large national museum in Denmark (*Mix it Up! Open culture exhibition* 2015). The second one involved exploring visual sampling and image searching strategies of European digital cultural heritage that are part of public domain, in two sites: at workshops with professional design practitioners (*Culture Cam workshops* 2015) and at a creative jam in a FabLab (*Culture Jam Helsinki* 2015).

In the following we trace some of the conceptual themes and tensions that informed these explorations to lay the ground to consider them particular ways of "participatory infrastructuring" (Karasti 2014); teasing some of the frictions existing in digital cultural heritage to experiment with collaborative knowledge production from within. We proceed to describe the objectives, settings and interventive aspirations of each experimental arrangement and conclude with a reflection on the possibilities that participatory oriented HCI and design has for infrastructuring processes aimed at opening heritage and its knowledge practices.

2 Frictions in Digital Cultural Heritage

The notion of digital cultural heritage mobilized in this work is threefold: First, digital cultural heritage understood as digital artefacts and materials that are implemented in digital technologies, and secondly as interactions, relationships and boundaries created and performed in the digital domain (cf. Cameron and Kenderdine 2007). Thirdly, digital cultural heritage is understood as a cultural practice, an on-going dynamic and relational process of engagement, of negotiation and articulation of identity, values and cultural and social meanings, practiced by citizens and institutions (Smith 2006). In this paper we focus especially on the interconnections, gaps and crossings between digital cultural heritage, either digitized or born-digital assets, and various forms of digital cultural production by individuals and groups within and outside of official institutional settings. We also approach the notion of heritage knowledge using two lenses, first, as a practice of preserving, producing, sharing and disseminating knowledge and creating cultural narratives

---

[1] Both interventions have been carried out as part of the Europeana Creative project https://pro. europeana.eu/project/europeana-creative-project.

about heritage, second, as a practice of documenting, sharing and developing creative practice and "craft knowledge" (Stuedahl and Mörtberg 2012). We address heritage knowledge both from professional and from non-professional perspective, including individuals, groups, institutions, and other heritage stakeholders.

The interventions we worked with payed special attention to digital cultural heritage in the public domain (PD). Intellectual Property (IP) issues and other policy frameworks such as PD have had a signifying role in defining the relationship, and level of access, to digital cultural heritage. Perhaps the most known part of IP is copyright law[2]. Copyrights grant exclusive rights and control to an author or creator of original works and their use, access and distribution. As a historical conception and social agreement copyright regime has fundamentally shaped both understanding of the originality of creations, and also how the notion of authorship and ownership in Western societies (cf. Boyle 2008). Well known counter narratives and arguments for access and appropriation surely exists, e.g., Hyde (2010) makes a plea for our common culture, emphasizing how knowledge is common to all and should be safeguarded from purely commercial interests. Similarly, other authors such as Lessig (2004) and Boyle (2008) argue that IP regimes hinder creativity and democratic innovation. In this framework, PD comprises knowledge and information (in the form of for example books, pictures and audiovisual works) that no longer have copyright protection and therefore can be used without restriction, by everyone (Europeana 2010). Historically, PD has provided a balance to the copyrights assigned to creators, for example in Eurore 70 years after the death of an author their works are assigned to PD. In the case of digital cultural heritage, cultural works under PD have been deemed essential to collective memory and to the emerging knowledge base of societies. However, access to digitized public domain cultural heritage has not always actualize in the practices of many digital cultural heritage infrastructures and their hosting institutions (Wallace and Matas 2021). For example, in the last decades many of these institutions have used digitization process to revert copyrights of works that in their analogue form have already been in the PD (see e.g., Europeana 2010). In practice copyrights of digital cultural heritage have also placed tight constraints on both the selection of heritage and on its use (Marttila and Hyyppä 2014). More over the politics of creating access to digital cultural heritage and heritage knowledge have revolved around giving recognition and attribution to the original authors as well as the hosting art and culture institutions for their efforts.

As we already mentioned, the production and designation of culture and of heritage is highly complex, contested and political endeavor (Kirshenblatt-Gimblett 1995, Ahmad Ahmad 2006, Dalbello 2009, Cameron 2010, Silverman et al. 2017). Bourdieu (1983/1993) described well how individuals, groups and institutions are constantly shaping and competing over the power to create meaning and value of cultural works, and to control or influence what is considered art and culture. Bourdieu's notion of 'field of cultural production' combines aspects of social conditions, circulation and consumption of cultural materials and their relations. This field is occupied by various actors competing for the resources, positions, symbolic power and capital (e.g. authority, recognition,

---

[2] We refer here to the European copyright legislation and policies. When discussing works which the copyrights are expired, waived, or fall under the declaration of not-known-copyrights (orphan works) we apply the short-hand public domain (PD).

legitimacy) that the field has to offer. This cultural capital is unevenly distributed among different groups and individuals. Some individuals and institutions, according to Bourdieu, have more accumulated capital and can use this to determine, for example, what is considered art and what is designated as heritage. These accumulations and imbalances separate and create tensions between the actors involved creating friction.

In digital cultural heritage this friction is multifaceted, and sometimes has been increased by digitalization processes. Currently, the friction manifests at least in two important ways:

First, if we agree that cultural heritage is collaboratively made and constructed, Kuutma reminds us that it also "needs to be imagined" (Kuutma 2009, 7). Heritage becomes *real* when someone labels and designates it as such. Achieving the status of heritage entails a process of knowledge production that remains highly professionalized. Despite the long-standing efforts to increase access to digital cultural heritage, today only a small fraction of the digital holdings in Europe are being made available to the wider public by art and cultural institutions (Stroeker and Vogels 2014). Moreover, even if the designation of cultural heritage resources is often considered as of public interest, often only official institutional heritage knowledge processes and mechanisms direct the selection of heritage assets (e.g. objects, intangible culture) to be reproduced as digital cultural heritage, with little or no input from other heritage stakeholders. Furthermore, the maintenance and enrichment of these digitized cultural collections is often guided by rigorously defined best practices, policies and standards that is result of centralized expertise. This has resulted in a situation in which in application fields like digital heritage oriented HCI there is limited amount of discussion regarding the convergence and co-existence of institutional cultural heritage practices and the production and appropriation practices of their publics (see Marttila 2018, Koch 2021). This lack of discussion, plays a role in cultural heritage institutions' continuous struggle with forming fruitful relationships with their audiences and with understanding their emerging digital engagements. More importantly, it is also one of the main factors in perpetuating the practices that continue to limit, and sometimes deny, larger involvement in governance processes of digital cultural heritage materials. This is problematic as heritage is designated in the name of the public, collected for their benefit, and (typically) managed and maintained at the public's expense (Bourdieu 1983).

Secondly, if heritage is about belonging, identifying and managing, these processes are mediated by selection, exclusion and ownership (Kuutma 2009) In digital cultural heritage this is reflected by the strong emphasis that has been given to the practical technological and legal issues and challenges hindering digitalization. Aspects related to preservation, management and documentation, technical interoperability, and the development of shared schemas, standards and formats, have received a lot of attention both in academic discourse and in practical work. Large efforts have been invested in designing digitization processes and forming interoperable digital collections with shared data standards and formats (see e.g. Ioannides et al. 2016, Hemsley et al. 2017).

In many cases, however, the existing legal frameworks and lack of rights prevents cultural heritage institutions from using technology platforms and available tools that could allow making their digitized collections available. Again, issues of ownership and authorship frame what becomes imaginable. In cases where digital cultural heritage materials have been made accessible online, they are often released under restrictive terms of use (Bellini et al. 2014, Estermann et al. 2015, Estermann 2015) and the scope for their circulation and collaborative reuse is often limited (Terras 2014, Marttila and Hyyppä 2014a). As argued by many scholars (Tsolis et al. 2011, Anderson 2013), intellectual property rights and other rights issues such as privacy are important factors preventing open access to and use of digital cultural heritage materials. Some of these limitations have practical reasons: the legal regulations and terms of use of digital cultural heritage materials vary greatly, and there is a need for harmonizing the rights and exceptions to copyrights (e.g. non-commercial use, educational use). In addition, often many cultural heritage institutions do not hold the rights to their assets in the digital collections, or institutions do not have enough resources to conduct the process of clearing those rights. Sometimes also other actors than heritage institutions have a stake and claim for digitalized heritage, such as minority groups, indigenous people and other communities. Commentators also point out that many cultural heritage institutions fear a loss of authority and control over their collections curatorial process, which remain quite traditional and opaque to certain extent. This is coupled with institution's hesitation of releasing digital cultural materials under more open terms, due to fear of losing a source of future revenue (Tsolis et al. 2011, Verwayen et al. 2011).

As we have seen, the digital cultural heritage infrastructures that have been built in the past decades have a fundamental role in the configuration of these frictions. To move forward we propose the notion of infrastructuring as a relevant conceptual and practical device that can help to analyze how design can contribute to bridge gaps and shape shared digital cultural resources (Marttila and Botero 2017, Marttila 2018). We build on work around infrastructures (Star 1999) that brought to the fore the importance to focus on relational and contextual aspects of information infrastructures, considering people and their situated actions; when involved in infrastructural development rather than giving priority to individual technology systems or artefacts. The idea of understanding aspects of design as infrastructuring (Karasti 2014) shifts then the focus of design from a particular information artefact or a single project outcome to the conditions surrounding infrastructures (Pipek and Wulf 2009). Doing infrastructuring work is a continuous effort—before, after and during use and infrastructural development—of constructing, facilitating and maintaining complex socio-material-technical conditions, configurations and relations, while forming alliances and aligning interests and concerns (Karasti and Syrjänen 2004, Lyle et al. 2018). Our approach proposes first, probing an infrastructure's installed base to better identify infrastructural challenges and to orientate infrastructuring activities aimed at building future infrastructures, fostering infrastructural change during the design and development process (Marttila 2018). Second, it proposes stimulating and simulating design and use through gateways – here considered as a passage connecting and giving access to otherwise incompatible parts – and in-between infrastructures to identify and locate incompatible socio-technical infrastructures and practices. This process gives direction and orientation to design experiments and to the arrangements necessary to bridge them. These strategies are also a useful tool to consider when designing new configurations, as they can aid future practices and arrangements between heterogeneous systems and actors and their practices before an infrastructure or its future practices have been settled (Marttila and Botero 2017).

Previous infrastructures provide an installed base, a foundation to a new one, and at the same time provide direction for designers and other participants for the participatory infrastructuring efforts needed. Designed gateways, such as prototypes and experiments, allow infrastructuring processes to happen by enabling experimentation before the final decisions on infrastructural development have been settled.

3 Infrastructuring Explorations for Bridging a Gap

The following infrastructuring interventions have been approached in the spirit of inventive methods (Lury and Wakeford 2012) and design research. We draw from elements of action research and from ethnographically informed qualitative research to structure our design involvement bringing to them particular designs, and actively intervening in the processes we are observing. The first author of the current paper has participated with an active role in all of the experiments, while the second author has participated only in specific instances. Our data includes: Participant observation and field notes from design meetings and planning workshops where the teams in charge of the events and the prototype development planned and defined concept and production details and also from the events themselves. We also draw from documentation (images, texts descriptions and sketches) of the resulting remixed artefacts and works and participants answers to online feedback questionnaires in the events. Drawing on these materials, we crafted textual narratives of the events that have then been analyzed and compared by both authors, using an inductive, qualitative analysis approach (Miles and Huberman 1994).

Staging Digital Cultural Heritage at Mix it up! Open Culture Exhibition

This experimental pop-up exhibition was carried out through a collaboration between the Statens Museum for Kunst (SMK) or Danish National Gallery, and Aalto University School of Arts, Design and Architecture, and the Europeana Creative project[3]. SMKs holds an art collection that spans 700 years of art history, presenting works from Denmark, Europe, and the rest of the world. At the time of this intervention a good portion of the pieces in the collection were in the public domain, free from copyrights to be reutilized. That made them good candidates to be reused and remixed in new cultural forms. SMK's had initiated efforts to freely release digital copies of the artworks in their SMK Open initiative platform[4] without copyright restrictions, however according to the curator in charge, the awareness of the open collections among the public was limited, and its value inside the institution also far from clear (Sanderhoff 2015). The experiment was set up as an infrastructuring activity with the intention to collect concrete examples of what sorts results and new value could be expected from more explicit reuse interventions into the collection and create conditions for a dialogue between curators, audiences and other professionals outside the heritage domain so that they will not happen in the abstract.

The basis of the Mix it Up! Open culture exhibition[5] was an invitation issued to a group of artists, designers and practitioners to explore and experiment with a selection

---

[3] https://pro.europeana.eu/project/europeana-creative-project.

[4] https://open.smk.dk/.

[5] https://www.smk.dk/en/exhibition/mix-it-up/.

of the high-resolution images of artworks from the SMK's open collection in the public domain. Participants were encouraged to send proposals for derivative creative works that could rethink, remix and redesign items from the open collections. The medium, and the approach to new creations was left up to the individual artists. A curatorial team was assembled, including members of SMK and the collaborators in the project, as well as invited experts. The curatorial team was in charge of reviewing the early concept proposals and provided feedback to the artists prior to the production phase. Altogether 13 artists and designers completed the process and created new artworks. The remixes took different forms including e.g. a digital rendering of Danish Golden Age paintings mashed up and projected onto the ceiling of the museum, new ceramic bowls with patterns from paintings, a deconstructed painting turned into an electromechanical machine installation and also sportswear clothing featuring prints of a 19th century landscape painting. The participating designers and artists retained intellectual ownership for their creative works. However, as prerequisite for participation in the exhibition, participants agreed to release documentation of their works under a Creative Commons attribution share-alike license (CC BY-SA).

The interpretations and appropriations were featured at SMK in the form of a weekend pop-up exhibition in late May 2015. No separate space was allocated to the exhibition, instead, the new creations were shown in the gallery side by side to the original artworks which had inspired them giving the spectators, and artists, the chance to reflect on the connections between the two (see Fig. 1). Participating artists enjoyed this rare opportunity to exhibit their creations next to original works; *"It was a very strong symbiotic experience to be in so close dialogue with the original work. It added a fresh dimension to the permanent collections."* (an artist). Being able to see them as part of a bigger whole: *"It was very important to have the visual and conceptual bridge between the two artworks, as it established a historical link. The two artworks sort of became one new artwork together as the commentary between them went both ways, talking about our understanding of our society and our understanding of previous societies."* (an artist).

Fig. 1. (left) Free? A laser cut light-and-shadow installation by Neea Laakso is displayed at Mix it up! exhibition SMK side-by side the original work of C.W. Eckersberg's 'Bella and Hanna. The Eldest Daughters of M.L. Nathanson' (1820) that provided components for her installation. (right) details of the laser cuts (Photo credit: Neea Laakso).

"It made a nice contrast between the more traditional technique and new. Also, the original painting maybe opened up more - hopefully - to the audience". (an artist)

The exhibition was part of the larger SMK Fridays event, which is a monthly evening event that caters for a young urban audience. The event brought over 6000 visitors to the exhibition and associated activities. From the feedback responses we learnt that indeed most of the visitors were unaware of the museum's open collections. Also, many felt that as an institution, the museum was still very traditional, *"You know, sometimes art can feel a bit inaccessible. [And] when it is just set free like this, then people can do with it what they want. I think that's pretty nice."* (feedback from a visitor).

Participating curators also provided feedback. They found the intervention interesting at the conceptual level and they found themselves *"positively surprised by the commitment and investment by the artists and designers"* which was not something they saw clearly in the beginning. They also considered that the decision-making process was *"too rushed and unclear"* and would have preferred a tighter integration with the curatorial *"workflows of SMK"*. Their established process for selection of pieces versus the more rapid response and risk-taking attitude of the experiment were sometimes in tension.

Some of the remixes presented bold questions to the collection, opening up meanings and new interpretations of them. For example, in the installation Free? (Fig. 1), the painting selected by the artist for remix features two sisters with a caged bird. This has been interpreted as a symbol of the lives of young women at the time, who were, like the bird, trapped inside their family and by society's expectations of them. In her laser cut installation, Neea Laakso set the bird free from the cage (using elements from another painting), offering a sharp comment on the topic of freedom. She said this in her artist statement: *Today we have a lot of freedom, yet still many of us feel trapped within thoughts, beliefs, expectations, habits etc. The question is how to let go of all that?*

Guided tours and artists talks were also organized through the weekend in the exhibition. In them creators shed further light on their works and experiences with digital heritage with those visiting the galleries, and with the other artists. One of the authors reflected: *"I have been creating collages using international museum collections for something like 20–25 years already (…) But I have only share them with my friends and family, knowing that if I were to present them publicly, I could face legal retribution. Now I am, for the first time, allowed to share my perspective."* (an artist). We learned that participating artists' intentions with their remixes varied, yet often they addressed history and present time. Some of the authors aimed specifically to explore and communicate cultural heritage and knowledge: *"I wanted to show how there was similarities and differences regarding the position and role of the artist (and citizen) in the 400-year gap between the two artworks."* (an artist). *"The two artworks sort of became one new artwork together as the commentary between them went both ways, talking about our understanding of our society and our understanding of previous societies."* (an artist). Some authors focused exploring the creative practice itself, one of the authors even stated that *"a piece of artwork is never complete"*. In addition, some of the designers and artists also carefully documented their process step-by-step with images and videos online for the public, offering resources for others[6] (See Fig. 2).

---

[6] http://katihyyppa.com/as-light-goes-by/.

Fig. 2. Sample of the documentation of "As Light Goes by" an electromechanical installation by Kati Hyyppä at display in the Mix it Up! Exhibition. The work was inspired by Vilhelm Hammershøi's painting "Interior in Strandgade, Sunlight on the Floor" (1901). (Photo credit: Kati Hyyppä, CC BY)

The questionnaire that was carried out after the Mix it up! exhibition revealed that the majority of authors were not familiar with the SMK's open collection nor other similar initiatives prior to the exhibition. Similarly, only few of them had previous knowledge about the Creative Commons (CC) licensing framework and tool or had used the licenses themselves for their creations. Some authors had not even considered this kind of interpretative practice before participating in the exhibition.

Visual Sampling, Visual Explorations and Remixing at Culture Cam Workshops and A Culture Jam

The second arrangement also involves staging an event; however, we also included an experimental prototype built to act as a gateway to an existing digital heritage infrastructure. Culture Cam[7] prototype is a search tool for a non-text based visual search interface to European digital cultural heritage (See Fig. 3). It was developed by the design collective Spild af Tid (SAT)[8] in collaboration with designers, developers and researchers at Aalto University school of Arts and Design[9] and the Austrian Institute of Technology[10]. The basic idea behind Culture Cam was to experiment with a digital similarity search tool to make it easy and intuitive to browse digital heritage content by other means than text-based search (Gordea et al. 2016). Culture Cam uses content from Europeana[11], a digital infrastructure created by the European Union that provided – at the time of the arrangement – access to digitalized heritage collections of more than 3,000 institutions across Europe. This application interface aims at creating an alternative entry point to

---

[7] https://pro.europeana.eu/data/culturecam.

[8] https://www.spildaftid.dk/.

[9] https://www.aalto.fi/en/department-of-media.

[10] https://www.ait.ac.at/en/.

[11] https://www.europeana.eu/.

Europeana that would support playful exploration of digital heritage and encourage creative reuse. For the first prototype a pre-selected subset of images was handpicked from the Europeana collection. Unlike in many curated collections of digital cultural heritage, images in Culture Cam dataset were selected solely by their visual quality – both content and resolution – and by terms of use. The searchable corpus consists only of images under the public domain and Creative Commons Zero license (CC0) meaning that all their copyrights are waived or expired.

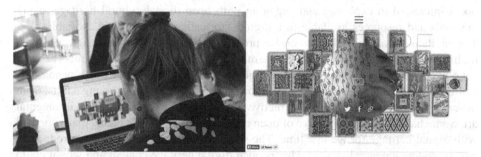

Fig. 3. (left) A group of creative professionals uses Culture Cam to explore the public domain content of Europeana. (right) A pattern is shown to Culture Cam webcam, the visual search result provides a selection of similar items in the public domain (Photo credit: the Europeana Creative project)

This combination of features had the ambition to encourage experimentation with the content, in visual creative terms, as all items included could be re-used legally. The corpus was also curated to filter items that would not be so interesting visually or that lacked quality that could hinder possibilities to manipulate it further (e.g. low resolution that hinders sampling or good quality printing). The application works so that a user "scans" an object in front of the computer's webcam or mobile phone camera, and the tool captures and analyses the picture of the given object. It then provides a search result displaying items similar in colour, shape and pattern from the sub collection from Europana's PD collection. The resulting search provides the searcher a possibility to compare items at a glance, and find similarities which might be too complex to describe in words. Also, as the interaction is mostly done via a webcam, it can be used without typing search words or specific language skills. Moreover, search results also allow diving deeper into each record´s metadata, to learn more about the pieces, their history, current location and time.

We used Culture Cam as a central element in the two arrangements. First, we brought the first stable prototypes of Culture Cam to two co-creation workshops held at professional design and artists working spaces and studios. We searched for graphic designers, illustrators, textile and fashion designers who are used to, and need to, perform visual searches for their work and had sophisticated practices around that. We also considered them experienced in reusing and remixing digital culture professionally. Each of these sessions had 6–7 participants an included a short introduction to our project and to the theme of digital cultural heritage. After that we asked them to helped us map their everyday professional visual search and sampling practices, both with open questions and specific tasks. We then gave an overview of the prototype and a series of specific tasks. They were also free to explore the tool and its collection and provided detail feedback on some of the functionality as well. Broadly we wanted to discuss the place of digital cultural heritage in their work and learn about challenges and possibilities they saw on reusing digital heritage images. We also wanted to understand – if and how – a tool like Culture Cam could be useful for their own (highly visual) practices.

After this first experiences, we also organized an open creative culture jam[12] that welcomed a broader sample of creative tinkerers: DIY practitioners, designers and developers interested in exploring and engaging with open digital cultural heritage, using the tools and resources available in a digital fabrication laboratory (AaltoFabLab)[13]. The invitation was opened to co-create prototypes (for artworks or design artefacts, mobile/web application mockups, ready-made physical products, 3D printed or laser cut objects) that would re-use digital heritage content made available by Europeana. The Culture Jam Helsinki session gathered a group on enthusiast, mainly young adults, from different backgrounds including interactive media, furniture design and environmental art. Some had previous knowledge of open cultural heritage, while others experimented with digital heritage for the first time. The session was organized with an introductory part providing a general view of what is open digital heritage content and why it could be important for creative practices and series of group discussions on themes related to the topic. After that pairs were formed to discuss initial ideas for new creative works. Pair had the opportunity to use a new iteration of the Culture Cam application to search Europeana, find inspiration and relevant material to download and manipulate further. Various experiments were carried out using sampled content and the equipment and facilities available in the FabLab. They included a line of jewelry inspired by images of paleolithic objects such as shells and bones. Natural shapes also inspired others to create 3D printed loudspeakers in the form of seashells. Vintage printed graphic patterns were turned into diary-style books and another team cut vinyl stickers using ornaments from the British Library collection. As in the case with the previous exhibition creators retained intellectual ownership of what they had created during the Culture Jam, but they were asked that pictures and other recorded formats of the results were shared with a Creative Commons license (CC BY-SA) for documentation purposes and for sharing the experience with others.

When doing searchers for material people used Culture Cam as well as other open repositories for digital cultural heritage. Participants also searched expertise advice outside from the events and institutional settings, e.g. during the Culture Jam questions were posted on Twitter to seek guidance on existing 3D models of cultural heritage objects to save time. When using Culture Cam participants often used pattern from their cloths and from their surroundings, they also used sample printed images and objects they have brought with them or found in the surroundings. Like with the case of other image similarity tools Culture Cam retrieved unexpected search results that lead to further explorations. While getting lost in one of her searches one of the designers commented *"It is interesting to think how this kind of historical material changes views, as [the] material has not been easily reachable before…all the information about the images, the*

---

[12] https://pro.europeana.eu/event/creative-culture-jam-helsinki.
[13] https://fablab.aalto.fi/.

times that they were made etc. Is really interesting and brings added value to the work. (a practitioner). The experience was compared to browsing in a workshop or toolbox full of materials and inspiration that could provide a broader context to situate their work more collectively. Most of the participants found the process of search by visual intuition rewarding way to approach digital visual heritage to learn more about it and could see themselves using it more *"Nowadays I mostly browse and sample items in Pinterest, this [points at the search results] made me wonder from what, and from whom, I am building from there? Probably quite limited and very USA centered?"* (a practitioner). Participants also reflected on how the visual sampling and search processes they did compared to what they do in normal circumstances, bringing to the fore questions of authorship, ownership and aesthetics decisions *"For example, a project of mine [points at a vintage illustration in her moodboard]: I found an old image of a pointing hand and wanted to use it but couldn't find who had made it, even though [I] spent a lot of time trying. It most likely was so old that the copyright had already expired, but [I] couldn't be sure. So, in the end [a friend] drew something similar which I used. I did not use the original source, even though I liked better how it "felt".* (a practitioner).

Using Culture Cam has also influence on designers' heritage knowledge. Some designers noted that when performing the similarity search using a picture their own designs and illustrations, the search tool's results enabled them to locate their own work in a continuum and historical context of previous creations. In one hand the similarity search tool increased designers' knowledge about earlier creations and authors, and on the other hand, inspired their future work and sometimes even so-called raw material – a starting point – for their new creations.

While working on the remixes many questions also aroused in relation to authorship and ownership of heritage. Discussions rose on practical issues of creative reuse such as giving credit to the sources one was using even if digital heritage under PD does not require it, or how they would hope in the future their own interpretation could be credited and appropriated. In addition, question of collective authorship came to foreground. To give a practical example, it is a favored practice jams and hackathons that individuals or groups continue the work somebody else had started in another context. From the legal viewpoint these efforts have collective authorship but public 'ownership' as anyone with needed capabilities and skills could enhance these creations or utilize them for their own varying purposes if the chosen license agreement was respected. Rewards or gain of such of work, such as prices after events, were questioned by the participants as the chosen 'winner' was only representing one individual in a chain of creators over a long period of time.

4   Towards Collective Heritage Knowledge Production?

A central contention of the two experiments we presented here is the intention to bridge aspects of the gap that exists between established cultural institutions and people outside of these institutions when it comes to processes of heritage knowledge production. Each of the arrangements described explored particular tensions between on one side the official institutional digital cultural heritage collections, systems and practices that have been built to accumulate, govern and make digital cultural heritage materials accessible

– and on the other side the social practices and tools through which individuals and communities create and share, or would like to create and share digital cultural works. Through this work we have identified at least three tensions that revolve around issues on 1) opening access to digital cultural heritage, 2) heritage knowledge and its practices, and 3) authorship and ownership of contributions to heritage.

In our experimental arrangements the side of official institutional digital cultural heritage collections are represented by an established national museum (Statens Museum for Kunst, SMK) with its nascent open digital collection, and by a Pan-European digital heritage infrastructure (Europeana). Albeit being already invested in opening up processes, the experiences setting up these experimental arrangements point out that they can still get paralyzed by preservation, celebration and protection of the past, and less moved by the processes of transformation in which they are but one of the actors. The setting up of the arrangements included provision to initiate processes that could provide concrete examples (remixes) of what people could do with the collections in a controlled environment, by for example concentrating on works in the public domain. The results were also displayed and staged. Particular decisions involved setting the pieces together with their original sources, making open calls and releasing documentation with a sharing license to increase the possibility of generating conversations about what could be possible. The experiences confirmed the idea that also in digital cultural heritage only "setting things free" is not enough and that supporting the learning processes of all (institutions and people) demand careful orchestration and alignment of motivations, practices and sometimes new tools; in other words, "artful infrastructuring" (Karasti and Syrjänen 2004).

The non-institutional side – citizens – is represented in both cases by professional and non-professional creative practitioners, designers and artists. Our intention to engage with this group was deliberate. While they are not representative of all citizens, creative practitioners, by virtue of their personal interests and professional demands, are professional users of cultural products and cultural heritage consuming, circulating and recreating it. Unlike professional cultural heritage stakeholders, heritage is not a foreground preoccupation for them. However, heritage does sit as a background infrastructural resource, albeit one they do not frequently question. They too are contributing to reinterpret heritage and create "future" heritage in invisible ways both for themselves, and for the institutions. Their contributions too, like that of institutional actors are embedded in ambivalent temporal entanglements (Kuuma 2009) that require enquiry from heritage knowledge production process, heritage politics, and ownership points of view. By using them as proxy we hoped to help everyone involved to understand and imagine what it will take to develop more collaborative arrangements in heritage knowledge production.

First and foremost, the key value in creating gateways such as Culture Cam and in-between infrastructural arrangements such as the Mix it up! exhibition, lies in the possibilities they offer for rehearsing, enacting and negotiating together possible future scenarios. For example, questions revolving around ownership and rights – both copyrights and moral rights – to use previous creations can be made through actual heritage-making in real-life, in co-created and supportive environment. These kinds of rehearsals and 'learning-by-doing' collaborations between heritage institutions, practitioners and other actors can be staged in settings that nurture participants possible future practices, collective arrangements and creative activities (Stuedahl and Mörtberg 2012, Marttila 2018). Importantly, these arrangements can offer a possibility to on one hand to rehearse future conditions, and on the other hand to experiment in public with and through the digital heritage artefacts. Presenting new creations in public – in situ at the event or online through various technology platforms – also opened-up the heritage knowledge production process to a dialogue, for evaluation and assessment.

There are many challenges for HCI in supporting and facilitating open creative reuse of digital cultural heritage. We concentrated on strategic interventions in the form of experimental events and a prototype, together with resources in the public domain, in one hand to make experimentation easier to control, and on the other hand, to advocate for freely accessible culture and knowledge, however that created also constrains for participating authors and practitioners. For example, even though Europeana provides access to 10 s of millions digitized objects available for legal creative reuse, finding high-resolution and suitable content was still found difficult and time-consuming. This hopefully becomes easier as filtering content through various technical and IP related attributes advances. Other examples are pointing to new future heritage practices that are not currently well accommodated by infrastructures for digital heritage. Accessing and appropriating open digital heritage for creative reuse is not only an issue of technical barriers, it becomes also a question of finding more multidimensional and fluid understandings of authorship that question the idea stemming from copyright law. In seek for alternatives, people will configure fluid forms of participation and new modes of creation that rely also on social agreements mediated by technology platforms and open knowledge resources online.

Our experiences also point out to a lack of acknowledgment of various forms of creative reuse in infrastructural development for digital cultural heritage. In most cases individuals engaged in production of heritage knowledge make so called micro-contributions, (e.g., provide feedback to APIs, test technology prototypes, annotate, tag or enrich digital artefacts, write strings of code and so forth) In doing so they are building upon the work of previous authors. These outcomes are partial, yet sometimes important contributions for the infrastructural development. However, they are not often recognized and utilized by official institutions with centralized expertise.

Sharing creative practices and experiences available online, not only open the heritage knowledge production for wider participation but can enable others to learn new skills and perhaps reuse some of the elements produced. When some of the authors documented their creative process step-by-step with images and videos online for public; this guidance supports not only novel heritage knowledge production linked to original heritage artefacts; it also built resources about the practice of creative reuse that is an essential part of a *living* heritage and *future* heritage. Collectively produced and accumulated heritage knowledge (e.g., documentation of good practices, standards, tools) acts as a resource for individuals and institutions alike through online platforms (see also Botero and Saad-Sulonen 2018). These pooled resources then can become sites for varying participatory heritage knowledge activities useful for both professionals and non-professionals. Although, we noticed that if these resources are not interwoven with existing practices or linked to original, and are not updated regularly by its users, they lose their nature of being common knowledge resources. Open and common resources can frame and organize the creative re-use activities, and can enable the emergence of novel cultural heritage practices and future heritage.

Creating access to and opening heritage and its institutional practices is a complex issue. Even more as the notions of authorship, ownership, access and open have various dimensions in scholarly discussions and in practitioners accounts (Anderson et al. 2013, Boyle 2008, Estermann et al. 2014, Hyde 2010). In the past decade there has been an increased interest in opening collections of digital cultural heritage. There are more examples of cultural institutions making a statement and releasing their holdings with a view to support learning and creativity for more people. However, what is an open collection and what kind of value it offers to society is far from clear, also in our experiments. Nonetheless the need for supporting various actors to work towards more shared arrangements where digital cultural heritage knowledge production could be more collectively maintained, enriched and cared for, continue to exist.

Acknowledgements. We want to thank former colleagues from the Europeana Creative project and all participants that contributed to the experiments. Special thanks to Merete Sanderhoff and SMK for hosting the Mix it up! Exhibition; also to Neea and Kati's work for inspiring these reflections. We acknowledge funding from the European Union grant number #325120 and the Academy of Finland grant number #34374270.

References

Ahmad, Y.: The scope and definitions of heritage: from tangible to intangible. Int. J. Herit. Stud. **12**(3), 292–300 (2006)

Anderson, D.: Preserving Europe's digital cultural heritage: a legal perspective. New Rev. Inf. Netw. **18**(1), 16–39 (2013)

Avram, G., Ciolfi, L., Maye, L.: Creating tangible interactions with cultural heritage: lessons learned from a large scale, long term. Co-design Proj. **16**(3), 251–266 (2020)

Avram, G., Maye, L. Co-designing encounters with digital cultural heritage. In: Proceedings of the 2016 ACM Conference Companion Publication on Designing Interactive Systems, pp. 17–20. ACM (2016)

Botero, A., Saad-Sulonen, J.: Challenges and opportunities of documentation practices of self-organised urban initiatives. In: Participatory Design Theory, pp. 230–246. Routledge (2018)

Bellini, F., Passani, A., Spagnoli, F., Crombie, D., Ioannidis, G.: MAXICULTURE: assessing the impact of EU projects in the digital cultural heritage domain. In: Ioannides, M., Magnenat-Thalmann, N., Fink, E., Žarnić, R., Yen, A.-Y., Quak, E. (eds.) EuroMed 2014. LNCS, vol. 8740, pp. 364–373. Springer, Cham (2014). https://doi.org/10.1007/978-3-319-13695-0_35

Bossen, C., Dindler, C., Iversen, O.S.: Impediments to user gains: experiences from a critical participatory design project. In: Proceedings of the 12th PARTICIPATORY DESIGN CONFERENCE: Research Papers, vol. 1, pp. 31–40. ACM (2012)

Boyle, J.: The Public Domain: Enclosing the Commons of the Mind. Yale University PressNew, Haven & London (2008)

Bourdieu, P.: The field of cultural production, or: the economic world reversed. Poetics **12**(4–5), 311–356 (1983)

Cameron, F.: Museum collections, documentation, and shifting knowledge paradigms. Mus. Digit. Age, 80–95 (2010)

Cameron, F., Kenderdine, S.: Theorizing Digital Cultural Heritage: A Critical Discourse (2007)

Ciolfi, L.: The collaborative work of heritage: open challenges for CSCW. In: Bertelsen, O., Ciolfi, L., Grasso, M., Papadopoulos, G. (eds.) ECSCW 2013: Proceedings of the 13TH European Conference on Computer Supported Cooperative Work, 21–25 September 2013, Paphos, Cyprus, pp. 83–101. Springer, Cham (2013). https://doi.org/10.1007/978-1-4471-5346-7_5

Ciolfi, L., et al.: Articulating co-design in museums: Reflections on two participatory processes. In: Proceedings of the 19th ACM Conference On Computer- Supported Cooperative Work & Social Computing, pp. 13–25. ACM (2016)

Ciolfi, L., McLoughlin, M.: Designing for meaningful visitor engagement at a living history museum. In: Proceedings of the 7th Nordic Conference On Human-Computer Interaction: Making Sense Through Design, pp. 69–78. ACM (2012)

Dalbello, M.: Cultural dimensions of digital library development, Part II: The cultures of innovation in five European national libraries (narratives of development). Libr. Quart. **79**(1), 1–72 (2009)

Dindler, C., Iversen, O.S., Smith, R., Veerasawmy, R.: Participatory design at the museum: inquiring into children's everyday engagement in cultural heritage. In: Proceedings of the 22nd Conference of the Computer-Human Interaction Special Interest Group of Australia on Computer-Human Interaction, pp. 72–79. ACM (2010)

Europeana, The Europeana Public Domain Charter. Europeana, 1, (2010). https://pro.europeana.eu/files/Europeana_Professional/Publications/Public%20Domain%20Charter%20-%20EN.pdf

Estermann, B.: Data file and documentation, public use: OpenGLAM benchmark survey 2014–2015. Bern University of Applied Sciences, in cooperation with Open Knowledge's OpenGLAM Working Group (2015). https://outreach.wikimedia.org/wiki/GLAM/OpenGLAM_Benchmark_Survey

Estermann, B., et al.: Questionnaire of the OpenGLAM benchmark survey 2014–2015 (Version 2, Spring 2015). Bern University of Applied Sciences, in cooperation with Open Knowledge's OpenGLAM Working Group. 2015) (2015). http://survey.openglam.ch/questionnaire_en_v2_EUR.pdfEstermann

Cipolla Ficarra, F.V.: Human-computer interaction, tourism and cultural heritage. In: Cipolla Ficarra, F.V., de Castro Lozano, C., Nicol, E., Kratky, A., Cipolla-Ficarra, M. (eds.) HCITOCH 2010. LNCS, vol. 6529, pp. 39–50. Springer, Heidelberg (2011). https://doi.org/10.1007/978-3-642-18348-5_5

Giaccardi, E.: Heritage and Social Media: Understanding Heritage in a Participatory Culture. Routledge (2012)

Gordea, S., Vignoli, M., Marttila, S.: CultureCam: an interactive search tool for small image galleries. In: Ioannides, M., et al. (eds.) EuroMed 2016. LNCS, vol. 10058, pp. 309–321. Springer, Cham (2016). https://doi.org/10.1007/978-3-319-48496-9_25

Hemsley, J., Cappellini, V., Stanke, G · Digital Applications for Cultural and Heritage Institutions. Routledge, London (2017)

Hyde, L.: Common as Air: Revolution, Art, and Ownership. Farrar, Straus and Giroux (2010)

Ioannides, M.: Digital heritage. progress in cultural heritage: documentation, preservation, and protection. In: EuroMed 2016 6th International Conference, EuroMed 2016, Nicosia, Cyprus, October 31 – November 5, 2016, Proceedings, Part I Nicosia Cyprus 2016. Lecture Notes in Computer Science LNCS, vol. 10058. Springer, Cham (2016). http://doi.org/10.1007/978-3-319-48496-9

Karasti, H.: Infrastructuring in participatory design. In: Proceedings of the 13th Participatory Design ConferenceK, vol. 1, pp. 141–150. ACM (2014)

Karasti, H., Syrjänen, A.-L.: Artful infrastructuring in two cases of community PD. In: Proceedings of the 8th Conference on Participatory Design: Artful Integration: Interweaving Media, Materials and Practices, vol. 1, pp. 20–30 (2004)

Kirshenblatt-Gimblett, B.: Theorizing Heritage. Ethnomusicology **39**(3), 367–380 (1995)

Koch, G.: Opening up digital memory making at the panel: digital memory modalities - inquiring the role of hci for participatory memory practices. In: 23rd International Conference on Human-Computer Interaction (2021)

Kuutma, K.: Cultural heritage: an introduction to entanglements of knowledge, politics and property. J. Ethnol. Folkloristics 3(2), 5–12 (2009)

Lessig, L.: The future of ideas: the fate of the commons in a connected world. Vintage (2002)

Lury, C., Wakeford, N. (eds.): Inventive Methods: The Happening of the Social (Hardback) - Routledge, CRESC. Routledge (2012)

Lyle, P., Sciannamblo, M., Teli, M.: Fostering Commonfare. infrastructuring autonomous social collaboration. In: Proceedings of the 2018 CHI Conference on Human Factors In Computing Systems, pp. 452:1–452:12 (2018)

Marttila, S.: Infrastructuring for Cultural Commons. Aalto University (2018)

Marttila, S., Botero, A.: Infrastructuring for cultural commons. Comput. Support. Cooperat. Work (CSCW) 26(1–2), 97–133 (2017)

Marttila, S., Hyyppä, K.: Practices and challenges in creative re-use of audiovisual media. In: Proceedings of the CUMULUS Conference, (in May 2014), pp. 301–315 (2014a)

Miles, M.B., Huberman, A.M.: Qualitative Data Analysis: An Expanded Sourcebook. Sage (1994)

Pipek, V., Wulf, V.: Infrastructuring: towards an integral perspective on the design and use of information technology. J. Assoc. Inf. Syst. 10(5), 447–473 (2009)

Salgado, M.: Designing for an Open Museum, an exploration on content creation in the museum (Doctoral dissertation). Helsinki, Finland (2009)

Salgado, M., Botero, A.: Opening exhibitions: the visually impaired and the design of probes packages. In: Proceedings of the 10th Participatory Design Conference 2008, pp. 150–153. Indiana University (2008)

Sanderhoff, M.: Set art free, and the rest will follow! Europeana Pro, 06 Dec 2015. https://pro.eur opeana.eu/post/set-art-free-and-the-rest-will-follow. Accessed 12 Feb 2021

Silverman, H., Waterton, E., Watson, S. (eds.): Heritage in Action Making the Past in the Present. Springer, Cham (2017). https://doi.org/10.1007/978-3-319-42870-3

Smith, L.: Uses of Heritage. Routledge (2006)

Star, S.L.: The ethnography of infrastructure. Am. Behav. Sci. 43(3), 377–391 (1999). https://doi.org/10.1177/00027649921955326

Stroeker, N., Vogels, R.: Survey report on digitisation in European cultural heritage institutions 2014. (ENUMERATE Thematic Network January 2014) (2014)

Stuedahl, D., Mörtberg, C.: Heritage knowledge, social media, and the sustainability of the intangible. In: Heritage and Social Media: Understanding Heritage in a Participatory Culture, pp. 106–125 (2012)

Stuedahl, D., Lowe, S.: Design experiments with social media and museum content in the context of the distributed museum. Nordes (2013)

Stuedahl, D., Smørdal, O.: Matters of becoming, experimental zones for making museums public with social media. CoDesign 11(3–4), 193–207 (2015)

Terras, M.: Opening access to collections: the making and using of open digitised cultural content. Online Inf. Rev. 39(5), 733–752 (2014)

Tsolis, D., Sioutas, S., Xenos, M.N., Styliaras, G.: Copyright and IPR management for cultural heritage digital content in peer-to-peer networks. J. Cult. Herit. 12(4), 466–475 (2011)

UNESCO. Charter on the Preservation of Digital Heritage, 15 October 2003

Verwayen, H., Arnoldus, M., Kaufman, P.B.: The problem of the yellow milkmaid. A business model perspective on open metadata. Den Haag: Europeana (2011)

Wallace, A., Matas, A.: Keeping digitized works in the public domain: how the copyright directive makes it a reality, Europeana Pro, 21 Jan 2021. https://pro.europeana.eu/post/keeping-digitised-works-in-the-public-domain-how-the-copyright-directive-makes-it-a-reality. Accessed 12 Jan 2021

Core Concepts Linking Exhibit Design and the Visitor Experience in Science Centers: An Early Framework

Jose Ocampo-Agudelo[1]($\boxtimes$) (iD) and Jorge Maya[2] (iD)

[1] Innovation and Development, Parque Explora, Medellin, Colombia
jose.ocampo@parqueexplora.org
[2] Product Design Engineering, Eafit University, Medellin, Colombia

Abstract. Understanding the visitor experience is critical for exhibit designers. Interactive exhibits should engage visitors into meaningful and compelling science learning conversations. However, exhibit design is a complex endeavor, particularly because many factors are interrelated and because of its subjective and dynamic nature. A body of research has addressed this subject from different perspectives over the last two decades. Nonetheless, most of the conceptual and practical contributions have used an under-articulated conceptualization of the visitor experience. This paper attempts to clarify experience in interactive exhibits based on a systematic empirical and theoretical research on the topic. Building on a literature review-based framework, we conducted a card sorting technique to sixteen expert exhibit designers. The seven core concepts that emerged represent a general expert mental model and serve to provide a holistic and articulated perspective of experiential exhibit design. This work can serve as a future reference to develop methods and tools for the design of experience-centered exhibits.

Keywords: Exhibit design · Visitor experience · Science museum

1 Introduction

Interactive exhibits are at the heart of any contemporary science center and museum (SCM) experience. Certainly, they are a vital component in sustaining the institutional image and expanding its popularity [1]. These devices are best seen as tools that enable visitors to actively engage on an intellectual, physical, social, and emotional level [2] and offer opportunities for visitors to actively learn through experience [3].

Increasingly, the field of exhibit design has gained considerable interest in the visitor learning experience [1] as a way of connecting the museum and the visitor agendas in meaningful ways [4]. However, exhibit design has not been widely examined as a field of practice, nor models of its principles and processes are fully developed [5]. In addition, most of the conceptual and practical contributions have used an under-articulated and underdeveloped conceptualization of the visitor experience [6]. Consequently, the fragmentation across diverse knowledge domains has slowed the consolidation of both

© Springer Nature Switzerland AG 2021
M. Rauterberg (Ed.): HCII 2021, LNCS 12795, pp. 113–130, 2021.
https://doi.org/10.1007/978-3-030-77431-8_7

theory and practice [5]. Therefore, exhibit designers are limited to make informed decisions that might enhance those experiences [1, 7]. The consequences of this are evident when visitors find unattractive, boring, frustrating, and confusing exhibits; and therefore, SCM might lose the opportunity to fulfil their institutional purposes and mission.

This paper aims to derive a theoretical foundation on exhibit experience design based on a systematic empirical and theoretical research. To do so, we first reviewed and analyzed previous related research. Next, we conducted an exploratory study aiming to investigate how expert exhibit designers' mental models relate to the visitor experience. Then, based on the core concepts that emerged in the study, we developed a framework using existing related literature. Finally, we conclude with a summary of the results and implications for future work.

2 Related Work

2.1 The Visitor Experience with Interactive Exhibits

Over the past 20 years, several models, frameworks, and theoretical approaches have described the visitor experience with interactive museum exhibits from different perspectives. These include contributions from psychology, museum studies, informal science education, human factors, human computer interaction and other disciplines. Ocampo-Agudelo and Maya [8] grouped these approaches as *exhibit-lens, visitor-lens, process-lens,* and *outcome-lens.*

Visitor-lens approaches are primarily focused on the entry narrative of the visitor as a key factor in understanding motivation, engagement and learning from an informal learning experience [9]. *Exhibit-lens* approaches provide guidelines and explore design attributes and issues that need to be considered when designing or evaluating interactive exhibits. For example, Dancstep and Sindorf [10] identified several design attributes for engaging girls at STEM exhibits. The *Process-lens* approaches help to understand what visitors do and feel while interacting with exhibits. Contributions in this perspective are related to attention [11] or engagement [12–14]. Finally, the *Outcome-lens* explores what visitors take away from the learning experience [9, 15, 16].

Each one of these approaches has helped to understand the richness and nuances of the visitor learning experience when interacting with museum exhibits but also has made clear that designing and shaping experiences of others is a uniquely challenging and multifaceted effort [8]. According to Beghetto [17, p. 4] "exhibit designers are, in a fundamental way, charged with this complex and seemingly untenable task".

2.2 Expertise in Exhibit Design

We follow Perry [2] in using the term exhibit designer very broadly to include all people involved in the decision-making process for developing exhibits. This includes all professionals who are members of a larger team involved in the design and development of an exhibit. In most organizations today, exhibit design is a multidisciplinary effort that involves curators, designers, educators, technicians and, increasingly, evaluators and audiences themselves [18, 19].

According to Mclean [19, p. 99], exhibit design *"requires passion, intuition, scholarship, and expertise of a wide range of people, and more professionals are becoming multilingual (or fluent) in the languages of environmental psychology, aesthetics, learning theory, conceptual and spatial design, and interpretation. They are 'expert generalists,' able to synthesize the variety of disciplines that inform exhibit development process"*. Exhibit design practitioners come from a variety of academic and professional backgrounds, but their expertise in exhibit development is almost always acquired through actual on the job experiences.

Young [20] examined the way science center exhibition developers build their professional expertise. That work revealed that the development of expertise comes primarily from the accumulation of experience through daily practice with little help from explicitly theoretical or discipline-wide methodological frameworks. Similarly, Roppola [21] argued that exhibit design is mostly directed by tacit experience and professional know-how, with limited explicit or formalized disciplinary knowledge, especially about how design decisions are related to the visitor experience.

The work of exhibit design is fundamentally product, deliverable and deadline driven. Exhibit designers and their teams are constantly producing exhibits. For this reason, experienced exhibit designers are solution focused, they move quickly from identifying a problem to framing and proposing a possible solution. Experienced exhibit designers fit the description of experts [22] who can recognize underlying principles, rather than focusing on the surface features of problems. Experts identify patterns in complex arrangements that allow them to respond spontaneously in ways that novices could not. Harteis and Billet [23] argued that experts act intuitively to come to an effective solution that may not be explicit or capable of reasoned justification. Therefore, although experts know their disciplines thoroughly, this does not guarantee that they are able to teach others. Furthermore, experts have acquired knowledge that affects how they organize, represent, and interpret information in their environment and eventually will shape how they solve problems [24].

Thus, experienced designers are experts, who work out solutions using implicit knowledge based on their experience, education, formal and informal mentoring they may have received, and other sources of knowledge. They are not operating based on formalized theories or universally accepted specific or explicit methodologies. Nevertheless, there are underlying concepts which we hypothesize may be shared across the field. The purpose of this work is to begin to make these core concepts explicit, and to test them to help develop a more explicit model of successful exhibit design that is visitor focused.

2.3 Expert Mental Models

To make explicit the knowledge and principles that expert exhibit designers use; we rely on the concept of expert mental models. Mental models are organized knowledge structures that allow people to interact, describe, explain, and predict events in their environment [25]. Rouse and Morris define [26, p. 159] mental models as *"mechanisms whereby humans can generate descriptions of system purpose and form, explanations of system functioning and observed system states, and predictions of future system states"*. Experts form abstractions based on semantic characteristics, central to the domain of their expertise [27]. Toker and Moseley [28] pointed out that expert mental models are cohesive and interrelated. Moreover, they argue that experts are focused on deep structures and underlying principles or theories behind the components and their relations to the same problem.

3 Methodology

This work builds on Ocampo-Agudelo and Maya [8] previous research that proposed an exhibit experience framework based on a thematic analysis of the literature. We aim to validate whether the proposed framework and its concepts describe and align with expert exhibit designers' mental models [29]. We looked for a method which would allow us to search for convergence among multiple and different sources of information to form themes or categories in a study [30]. We hoped to offset researcher biases, evaluate the major findings of the theming process to ensure the credibility and consistency of the interpretation [31].

With this study, we aim to investigate how expert exhibit designers understand and relate to the visitor experience through analyzing their mental models. Since expert mental models are generally implicit resulting from knowledge representations of experts [32], they need to make it explicit using simple methods. Therefore, by reviewing and relating different models of expert exhibit designers, it is possible to generate a general expert mental model. Card sorting, a recognized technique for mental model elicitation, was selected for this research.

3.1 Card Sorting

There are several knowledge elicitation techniques available e.g., interviews, brain-storming, focus groups or observation. However, card sorting has several distinctive advantages, particularly for exhibit designers, who general work in the visual and tactile realms more than in the world of words and speech. According to Fincher and Tenen-berg [27], it is simple to administrate; the categorization task places no special cognitive loads on research subjects, such as time pressure or memory limitations, and therefore is appropriate for a wide range of domain expertise. In addition, they argue that card sorting can be effective in eliciting semi-tacit understanding about objects in the world and the relationships to one another, something that traditional interviews and questionnaires fail to access.

Card sorting is a categorization task where the process includes asking participants to sort items into meaningful groups based on relatedness. We chose a common sorting technique known as open card sort where items are grouped by the participant who then name each group. This method elicits the categories in the mind of the participant, rather than categories in the mind of the researcher.

Content Selection. Ocampo-Agudelo and Maya [8] proposed a literature review derived framework of interactive exhibit experiences in SCMs. The authors identified 7 themes and 17 subthemes that describe the experiential qualities of science museum exhibits (see Table 1).

Table 1. Themes and sub-themes of the visitor experience with interactive museum exhibits (Source: Ocampo-Agudelo and Maya, 2017)

Themes	Subthemes
The visitor	Interests/motivations - Prior experience/prior knowledge
The physical context	Environmental conditions - Exhibit location
The social context	Crowd conditions - Social mediation - Group composition
The interactive exhibit	Content and information - Media and technology - Interactivity
The engagement process	Engagement cycle - Affective response - Behavioral response
The learning experience	Learning outcomes - Learning attributes
The science museum purpose	Educational purpose - design intention

To empirically validate this framework in a card sorting process, the 17 preliminary subthemes were divided into 29 items to have enough overlap for creating groups, as suggested by Spencer [33]. For example, interactivity was divided into social, physical, and mental. As a result, a list of 29 elements along with a short description was obtained (see Table 2). Then, all the items and descriptions were translated into Spanish by the first author and then checked and discussed with the second author to guarantee the accuracy and connotations of the translation.

Participants and Setting. This study was conducted at a single institution, which features a highly educated and professionalized staff (see Table 3). Participant experts were recruited from Parque Explora, a science and technology center located in Medellin, Colombia. Exhibit design at this institution is done by museum professionals from two departments, Innovation and Development (IDE) and Content and Education (CON). Participants were purposefully selected based on their role and experience in the design and development of science museum exhibits.

A sample selection protocol indicated by Tullis and Wood [34] was followed. Sixteen exhibit designers participated in the card sort. 9 (56%) of participants worked at IDE, and 7 (44%) worked at CON department; all participants had an undergraduate education; 37% had a completed or were currently enrolled in a masters or postgraduate program. Most of the participants were under age 35 (n = 12), while the remainder were between 36 and 43 (n = 4); on average participants had over 7 years of experience. 31% of participants reported an experience between 3–5 years, 56% between 5 to 10 years and 13% above 10. Table 3 provides an overview of the participants.

Procedure. The card sorting procedure followed a protocol that started by introducing the activity and handing out the cards and materials. Then each expert sorted the cards into categories and subcategories and labelled them individually with respect to his or her experience, knowledge, and intuition. They were allowed to ask as many questions as necessary to ensure they understood the procedure. At the end of the session, a debriefing process was taken to gather any additional feedback the participant might have and gain further insight into why an item was sorted into a certain category. Participants were

Table 2. List of categories with the description that was provided to exhibit designers participating in the card sorting study.

Item	Name	Description
I1	Interests and motivations	The set of interests and previous motivations that the visitor brings to the museum, and that have a great influence in the visitor's experience
I2	Prior experience/Prior knowledge	The set of prior knowledge and experiences of the visitors. People construct concepts through their previous knowledge, and with these interpret each learning situation
I3	Environmental conditions	The set of physical conditions of the environment that affect the visitor's engagement and experience with the interactive exhibit, such as temperature, sound, color, and lighting
I4	Exhibition configuration	Visitors need to navigate freely through space and at the same time feel oriented and secure. When visitors feel disoriented, it directly affects their ability to engage with the interactive exhibit
I5	Exhibit location	The location of the interactive device in space influences the visitor's involvement; for example, exhibits that are placed near the entrance to an exhibition attract the attention of more visitors
I6	Crowd conditions	Museums are highly social spaces where people gather, share, and participate in different activities and experiences. Crowd conditions or crowd size are important factors in the quality and quantity of visitor's engagement. For instance, if the exhibition is crowded, then visitors will most likely spend less time interacting with exhibits
I7	Social mediation	Social mediation is the social interaction facilitated by museum staff, often referred as explainers or volunteers. Explainers welcome, facilitate and encourage visitors to be actively engaged in activities
I8	Group composition	The group composition of the visit influences the nature and quality of the learning experience. Most visitors go to museums in social groups consisting of family and friends. All social groups in museums interact with each other in a way reinforcing shared beliefs, interpreting information, for meaning making
I9	Educational content	All the concepts, principal laws, stories, or ideas that constitute the core of the desired learning
I10	Instructional content	The information needed to manipulate and operate the exhibit
I11	Media and technology	The technology, whether analogue, digital, low, or hi-tech, is the medium for communicating content and information. The technology employed can afford certain types of interactivity
I12	Social interactivity	All the various ways in which the exhibit stimulates visitors to engage with one another socially
I13	Mental interactivity	All cognitive and intellectual processes that are triggered by the exhibit
I14	Physical interactivity	All the various ways in which the exhibit encourages visitors to interact with their body and their senses
I15	Engagement cycle	The engagement cycle describes the temporal nature of the interaction at different stages: attraction, initial engagement, deep engagement, and disengagement. An engaging exhibit must attract and hold the attention of the visitor, have a clear and attractive entry point, and encourage prolonged interaction
I16	Pleasure and enjoyment	The feeling of pleasure, enjoyment, and fun when interacting with an exhibit
I17	Curiosity and interest	When visitors find the interactive exhibit interesting or their curiosity has been stimulated while interacting with it
I18	Confidence and competence	When interacting with exhibits visitors can have a sense of confidence and competence. On the contrary, visitors could feel frustrated or insecure
I19	Involvement	The visitor is concentrated, absorbed, or immersed in the activity
I20	Personal relevance	Feelings of personal relevance when interacting with the interactive exhibit. The more relevant the device, the greater its interest in interacting with it
I21	Relatedness	The sense of connection to other people while interacting with the exhibit
I22	Behavioral response	The behavioral response consists of all the actions performed by the visitor when interacting with exhibits such as questioning, observing, reasoning, playing, predicting, or manipulating that are often referred as learning behaviors or inquiry behaviors
I23	Learning attributes	Learning in science museums is different from learning in any other setting because of the unique and informal nature of the museum context. Evaluating the learning experience in science museums needs not only to focus on cognitive gains but also the conditions and the engagement that leads to learning. Therefore, learning is characterized by the following attributes: active process, self-directed, autotelic, dialogical, holistic, contextual, subjective, dynamic, and unique

(*continued*)

Table 2. *(continued)*

Item	Name	Description
I24	Meaning	Visitors construct meaning while experiencing the interactive exhibit. These include all the patterns, connections, and relationships that each visitor constructs to make sense of the world. Meaning is related also to knowledge and understanding
I25	Attitudes and motivations	Visitors develop attitudes and motivations while experiencing exhibits. This outcome is related to emotions and feelings that are elicited by the exhibit or the social and physical context. The exhibit experience also motivates and encourages visitors to explore further even beyond the museum visit
I26	Skills	Visitors develop skills while experiencing interactive exhibits. Skills can be physical, social, mental, or emotional. Visitors can develop skills in observing, hypothesizing, or experimenting. They can develop skills related to teamwork. They can manage frustration and failure. They can know how to do something on a practical level
I27	Identity	Visitors develop their own identity while experiencing exhibits. Although the meaning is related to how everyone makes sense of the world, identity means that visitors can also learn about themselves, who they are and how they perceive their place in the world
I28	Educational purpose	The underlying assumptions of designers and educators about the nature of learning in science museums referred to as pedagogies. It is now widely understood within the science museum community that learning is a complex, contextual, participatory, experiential, and visitor-centered process that involves more than just acquisition of facts and concepts. For that reason, contemporary science museums are increasingly adopting a more socio-cultural and constructivist view of learning
I29	Design Intention	Science museums are public institutions that are intentionally designed for learning about science and the physical and natural world. Therefore, every museum exhibit reflects the intended communicative goals and expectations of designers and educators

Table 3. Professional description of expert participants.

#	ID	Years of experience	Background	Role
1	CON1	8	Bioengineer	Head of museology
2	CON2	4	Bachelor of Mathematics and Physics	Mediation Coordinator
3	CON3	8	Biologist	Head of Science Communication
4	CON4	4	Physical engineer	Science Communicator
5	CON5	5	Bachelor in Natural Sciences and Environmental Education	Science Communicator
6	CON6	3	Chemical engineer	Science Communicator
7	CON7	15	Science Communication	Director of Content and Education
8	IDE1	6	Industrial designer	Senior Designer
9	IDE2	6	Industrial designer	Senior Designer
10	IDE3	6	Architect	Senior Designer
11	IDE4	11	Industrial designer	Director of Innovation and development
12	IDE5	8	Industrial designer	Head of Design
13	IDE6	6	Graphic designer	Senior Graphic Designer
14	IDE7	6	Industrial designer	Senior Designer
15	IDE8	3	Graphic designer	Senior Graphic Designer
16	IDE9	8	Industrial designer	Production Coordinator

asked to explain briefly to the researcher the way they sorted the items. This information was helpful to better understand which categories and labels instantly made sense and which ones were potentially unclear. Field notes were taken by the researcher during and after the debriefing process.

Data Collection and Analysis. Card sorting data can be analyzed using both qualitative and quantitative methods. For example, qualitative analysis is focused on understanding the categories participants create as well as the relationships between those categories. Quantitative analysis methods include cluster analysis, item-to-item, and participant agreement. In the current study, we used both approaches to interpret the results. The resulting groupings were analyzed using Syncaps, a card sorting software.

4 Card Sorting Results

4.1 Level of Agreement Between Items

The item-by-item matrix shows the number of times, as a percentage, participants have grouped each individual card with each other card in the set. The matrix offers useful insight into the strength of the relationship between each pair of individual items [35]. The bottom row of the matrix shows a *relative alignment*. Here, darker cells represent items that are consistently grouped while lighter cells indicate less agreement between participants (See Fig. 2).

Items such as *exhibit location (I5), educational purpose (I28),* and *prior experience and knowledge (I2)* evidenced the strongest connections. Whereas *personal relevance (I20)* and *confidence and competence (I18)* showed the lowest connections among participants. Based on the relative alignment results, we grouped items into two categories, strong and weak item-to-item connections respectively. Strong connections were found on items that were mainly related to the museum context, (e.g., *instructional content, media, and technology, design intention,* or *exhibition configuration*), but on the other hand, weak connections were primarily related to the visitor context (e.g., *personal relevance, involvement, skills, pleasure,* and *enjoyment*). One of the reasons why we found weak connections was that exhibit designers often connected these visitor-related items together with museum-related items indicating how a certain design decision about the exhibit (i.e., choosing appropriate technology or media) was influencing the visitor experience (i.e., visitors' feelings of competence or pleasure). For instance, IDE2 paired *confidence and competence* along with *design intention* and *media and technology.* The participant referred to these items as "exhibition development".

4.2 Dendrogram Analysis

Cluster analysis is a statistical procedure which can be used to analyze similarities and differences in the way participants categorize sets of domain items. The results are visualized in a hierarchical tree diagram or dendrogram (see Fig. 3). The dendrogram represents an average of the groups or categories produced by each of the card sort participants. In this paper, we refer to this as the *average sort* that represents a *general expert mental model*. It begins at the right with the list of items that were presented to participants for sorting. Then, branching lines are drawn between items, based on the degree to which participants grouped the items together. Items that are the most frequently grouped together are positioned next to each other vertically, with a line linking them to indicate the connection. The ordering of the clusters is based on the

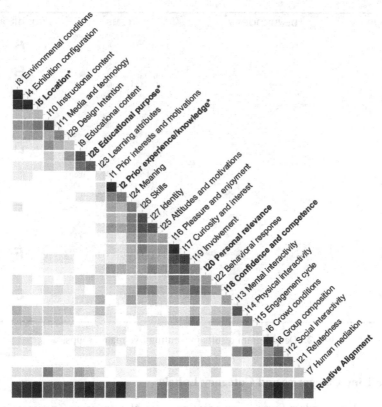

Fig. 1. Item-by-item matrix. The higher correlations, illustrated by the darker colors, indicate stronger item-to-item relationships.

frequency of pairings made by the experts. For example, *environmental conditions, exhibition configuration,* and *location* were strongly linked (Fig. 1).

Then, we created top-level and second-level categories. The clustering data obtained from the exhibit designers allowed sorting the 29 original items into five top-level preliminary categories or groups (see Fig. 2). We started to make sense of the data by reviewing the item correlations as well as the number of items per group. Group 1 was related to the physical environment and interactive exhibit. Group 2 contained items related to education and learning theories. Group 3 was related to the visitor psychological aspects such as feelings, capabilities, or behavior. Group 4 was related to the dynamics of the visitor interaction with the exhibit. Finally, Group 5 was related to the social aspects that are involved in the museum experience. After having a broad understanding of the groups, we decided to create a more fine-grained classification and characterization. We paid attention to the size of the categories, especially to Group 1 and 3 that were the largest. We also considered the numbers of groups created by participants (varied between 5 to 10, with an average of eight groups). We ended up with seven subgroups or second-level categories (subgroups A to G). We decided to keep these two categorizations for further analysis and discussion.

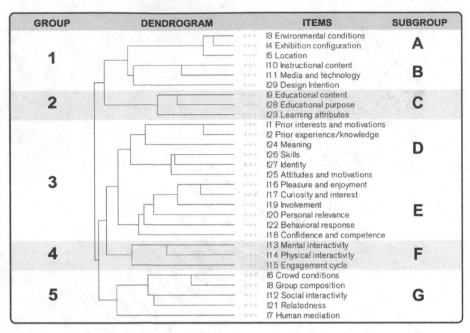

Fig. 2. Dendrogram results presenting five main groups.

4.3 Finalizing Categories and Category Labels

Thus far, we have made a first pass at creating a set of categories for our conceptual framework. We have looked at how experts have grouped items using tools such as item-by-item matrix and dendrogram. To finalize the categories as well as the category labels we evaluated, interpreted, and adjusted the results in relation to related literature to a better conceptual coherence of the content structure. We believe that without such modifications, the results could potentially lead to conceptual incoherence by overlooking its theoretical implications. For example, Ocampo-Agudelo and Maya's [8] considered *the visitor*, *the engagement process*, and *the learning outcome* as separated elements. Our card sorting findings suggest that these elements could be assembled into the *personal* group since they all relate to the visitor's feelings, behaviors, and capabilities.

The card sorting technique allowed us to group and to name the conceptual building blocks of the content. Since this technique is centered on data reduction, it revealed the most meaningful and salient concepts. The resulting categories and labels can be found in Table 4.

5   DEX Framework

Influenced by related literature as well as the card sorting results, we suggest adopting a framework that emphasizes on the following building blocks that exhibit designers should address:

Table 4. Card sorting categorization results.

Group label	Subgroup label	Items
Physical	Place	I3, I4, I5
	Exhibit	I10, I11, I29
Educational	Purpose	I9, I23, I28
Personal	Learning	I1, I2, I24, I25, I26, I27
	Engagement	I15, I16, I17, I18, I19, I20, I21, I22
Relational	Interaction	I12, I13, I14
Social	People	I6, I7, I8

- **The Physical** building block is associated with the interactive exhibit but also considers the environment in which the exhibit is located, e.g., an exhibition or gallery.
- **The Educational** building block incorporates the underlying assumptions, purposes, and pedagogical ideas that help to materialize an educational purpose in form of an interactive exhibit.
- **The Personal** building block includes visitor´s feelings, behaviors, and learning that emerge through interacting with exhibits and the environment.
- **The Relational** building block corresponds to the quality of the relationship that takes place between the visitor and the exhibit through interaction.
- **The Social** building block indicates the social conditions that influence the visitor interaction and engagement with exhibits.

The visitor experience can be understood as the dynamic interplay among these five overlapping building blocks; however, we believe that we need to move towards a more fine-grained conceptualization and categorization of visitors' exhibit experiences in a way that is meaningful for exhibit designers. Hence, based on the card sorting results, these building blocks where then divided into seven interrelated elements as *purpose, exhibit, engagement, interaction, place, people,* and *learning*. While the five building blocks are a broad categorization, the seven elements are the core of the Experiential Exhibit Design framework (hereafter 'DEX'). Following this, we describe each element and illustrate how they are related to exhibit design and visitor experience (see Fig. 3).

Purpose: the element of purpose incorporates the theoretical perspectives that encompass institutional beliefs about how people learn [36]. Learning in science museums is different from learning in any other setting (e.g., school, library) because of the unique and informal nature of the museum context [37]. Museum professionals are increasingly adopting a socio-cultural, ecological, and constructivist view of learning [9, 38–40]. These institutional beliefs are embodied in every exhibit. For example, Witcomb [41] related interactive exhibits with educational theories proposed by Hein [36], such as didactic-expository, stimulus-response, discovery, and constructivist exhibits. She illustrated how every museum exhibit, whether tacit or implicit, reflects educational

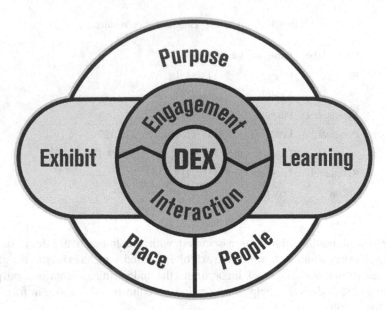

Fig. 3. DEX is an Experiential Exhibit Design framework for SCMs.

assumptions of exhibit designers. Consequently, the educational purpose would eventually shape the way the interactive exhibit is materialized, how the educational content is approached, and ultimately will influence how learning is experienced [17, 42].

Exhibit: interactive exhibits are considered resources through which people individually and collectively engage in learning experiences. Hennes [43, p. 25] argues that *"exhibits aren't actually experiences–rather they are platforms for experiences"*. Interactive exhibits come in many different formats i.e., computers, whole-body and tabletop activities, simulations, or multimedia components [44], and different interactive exhibits engender very different forms of visitor interactions [45]. For example, Dancstep and Sindorf [10] identified interactive design features such as open-ended and multi-sided as key exhibit attributes that foster girls' engagement. Borun and colleagues [46] found that multi-sided, multi-outcome and multi-modal were successful exhibit characteristics for increasing family engagement and active learning.

Engagement: engagement is the heart of the whole exhibit experience and becomes a primary tool for both developing exhibits and evaluating their success [14]. Several studies suggest that the level to which each visitor is engaged by an exhibit is a direct indicator of the learning taking place [9, 13, 47]. Exhibits incorporate certain interactive features that offer opportunities for visitors to imagine, create, observe, or collaborate. When interacting with exhibits, these features trigger a cycle that includes visitor's affective responses such as pleasure or confidence, and behavioral responses such as persistence and time on task. Engagement is a dynamic concept embedded in interaction, and therefore can be identified as a process that has a beginning, middle, and end. Barriault and Pearson [47] refer to this as *levels of engagement* to capture the progression in a visitor's learning experience. An engaging exhibit is the one that attracts and holds the attention of the visitor, have a clear and attractive entry point, and encourage prolonged interaction [12, 48]. Disengagement can occur for intrinsic reasons (i.e., task completion, fatigue, negative affect) or extrinsic reasons (i.e., distractions, agenda).

Interaction: according to Hein [36], there can be no learning if there is no interaction. Learning requires mental, physical, or social engagement by the learner [49]. From this perspective, action is fundamental to a learning experience. Without taking an action, the possibility for subsequent engagement does not exist [50]. From the interaction perspective, DEX focus the attention on the quality of the relationships that exhibit features afford. For example, a multi-sided exhibit is an exhibit feature that facilitates social interaction. We refer to such features as *interactive affordances*. Ideas about affordances build on ecological perspectives on learning that focuses on features of different environments that afford certain learning-related activities [51]. Consequently, interactive affordances describe the type of interactions and learning-related behaviors that the interactive exhibit facilitates. For example, Perry [2] has argued that a successful exhibit experience that leads to learning include six factors: curiosity, confidence, challenge, control, play and communication.

Place: learning always occurs when interacting with the physical environment [37]. This includes the architecture as well as the general atmosphere or ambiance of the exhibition environment. There are several environmental conditions that influence the way people engage and experience exhibits, for example: temperature, light, color, or sound conditions. Visitors also need to navigate freely through space while feeling oriented and secure. When visitors feel disoriented, it affects their ability to engage with exhibits [39]. Moreover, the location of the exhibit influences the degree and quality of visitor engagement; for example, Adams, Luke, and Moussouri [42] found that exhibits that are placed near the entrance to an exhibition attract the attention of more visitors.

People: sociocultural theories emphasize that learning emerges in the interplay between visitors acting in social contexts and the mediators, such as exhibits or explainers, that are afforded by culture, the museum environment and history [36]. Recognizing the relevance of the social interaction component in exhibit design allows us to make better sense of variations in the visitor behavior [39]. For example, the *crowd conditions* are important factors in the quality and quantity of visitor engagement [42]. When the exhibition is crowded, visitors will most likely spend less time interacting with exhibits. *Social mediation* is the social interaction facilitated by museum staff, often referred as explainers or volunteers. Explainers are the human and direct interface with the public who welcome, facilitate, and encourage visitors to be actively engaged in exhibit-related activities [52]. Finally, the *group composition* of the visit influences the nature and quality of the learning experience. Most visitors go to museums in social groups consisting of family and friends. Sociocultural perspectives on visitor learning recognize that individual meaning is mediated among and between communities of interpretation or practice [53]. Learning is a bidirectional and dynamic cultural process. Thus, in addition to developing culturally valued skills, knowledge and identities, individuals also influence the cultural systems they participate in [9].

Learning: learning is conceived as an active, contextual, participatory, experiential, and visitor-centered process that involves more than just acquisition of facts and concepts. From this perspective, the learning experience is generally voluntary, non-sequential and highly reactive to what the setting and exhibit affords [37]. Most of the previous research on learning in museums has focused primarily on what visitor's take away from the experience in terms of learning outcomes. However, learning can be best conceived as a multidimensional and continuous process that requires engagement [38, 54]. From this perspective, every learning experience *"both takes up something from those which have gone before and modifies in some way the quality of those which come after"* [55, p. 35]. Accordingly, visitors will bring to the learning situation a set of *skills*, *motivations*, *prior knowledge*, *experience*, *interests*, *attitudes*, *values*, and *identity*. Through interacting and actively engaging with exhibits these set of personal characteristics could be transformed in some way. Thus, the learning process *"is not a simple addition of items in some sort of mental data bank but a process of transformation of schemas"* [36, p. 22].

6 Implications for Exhibit Design

As addressed before in this article, there is a limited disciplinary knowledge to help exhibit designers to understand, analyze, communicate, and design for the visitor experience. One of the main contributions of DEX framework is the holistic perspective that it offers for studying and designing exhibits that foster engaging learning experiences.

The relationship between the different experiential elements is not always directly observable. Historically, exhibit designers have designed for the visitor experience rather intuitively. Yet, experience and research show that in many cases, expert exhibit designers are not always capable of communicating their understanding. Additionally, because many museum professionals (i.e., designers, educators, or content specialists) might have different mental models, they will most likely not have the same understanding. Therefore, DEX framework can help to support the communication and comprehension of relevant issues about the visitor experience among team members by formalizing this knowledge into a more tangible and clear way.

Furthermore, according to Cross [22], a successful design behavior is based on adequate 'problem scoping' rather to an extensive problem analysis. Thus, DEX framework can help exhibit designers in understanding and scoping problems and opportunities by explicitly considering key elements (e.g., engagement, learning, interaction) related to the visitor experience. In that manner, DEX framework could support exhibit designers to establish connections between different roles within the design team and to think about the implications of design choices over the visitor experience in a more structured way.

7 Conclusions, Limitations, and Future Work

Understanding the visitor experience is critical for exhibit designers. Interactive exhibits should engage visitors into meaningful and compelling science learning conversations. However, it is a complex endeavor, particularly because many factors are interrelated and because of its subjective and dynamic nature. A body of research has addressed this subject from different perspectives over the last two decades. Nonetheless, most of the conceptual and practical contributions have used an under-articulated conceptualization of the visitor experience.

This research attempted to identify core concepts related to the visitor experience with interactive exhibits in SCMs based on a systematic empirical and theoretical research on the topic. Building on a previous thematic analysis of the literature, we conducted a card sorting technique to sixteen expert exhibit designers. As a result, we consolidated a conceptual framework, named DEX, that integrates *purpose, exhibit, engagement, interaction, place, people,* and *learning.*

DEX represents a multidisciplinary and complex phenomenon that will always be dynamic and may be reviewed according to new insights, literature, and visitor studies. The current findings were based on a selected sample of exhibit designers at a single science museum. Given the exploratory nature of this research, we argue that more research is needed to determine the extent to which the findings from this study are applicable and relevant to other exhibit designers and SCMs around the world.

The visitor experience, like any other complex system, can be only partially understood and only partially influenced [39] Even though, we believe that the exhibit designers' intuition, experience, and skills could be enriched by the already simplified and cumulated disciplinary knowledge available in DEX.

This work makes part of an ongoing long-term research project that aims to develop design methods and tools to help exhibit designers to make more informed decisions when designing or evaluating the experiential qualities of an interactive exhibit, particularly in the beginning stages of concept development and prototype design as advocated by Adams [42]. The presented framework might also be useful and inspiring for other cultural and educational institutions that are committed to creating engaging and meaningful experiences for people.

References

1. Falk, J.H., Scott, C., Dierking, L., Rennie, L., Jones, M.C.: Interactives and visitor learning. Curator Museum J. **47**(2), 171–198 (2004). https://doi.org/10.1111/j.2151-6952.2004.tb00116.x
2. Perry, D.: What Makes Learning Fun? Principles for the Design of Intrinsically Motivating Museum Exhibits. Rowman Altamira, Lanham (2012)
3. Ansbacher, T.: Experience, inquiry, and making meaning. Exhibitionist **18**(2), 22–26 (1999). https://doi.org/10.1111/j.2151-6952.2002.tb00052.x
4. Macdonald, S.: Interconnecting: museum visiting and exhibition design. CoDesign **3**(S1), 149–162 (2007). https://doi.org/10.1080/15710880701311502
5. Roberts, T.: Interpretation design: an integrative, interdisciplinary practice. Museum Soc. **12**(3), 191–209 (2014)
6. McCarthy, J., Ciolfi, L.: Place as dialogue: understanding and supporting the museum experience. Int. J. Herit. Stud. **14**(3), 247–267 (2008). https://doi.org/10.1080/135272508019 53736
7. Pekarik, A., Button, K., Doering, Z., Sharbaugh, A., Sutton, J.: Developing Interactive Exhibitions at the Smithsonian. Smithsonian Institution, Washington, DC (2002)

8. Ocampo-Agudelo, J., Maya, J.: Experiential qualities of science museum exhibits: a thematic analysis. In: Proceedings of the 21st International Conference on Engineering Design (ICED17), Vancouver, Canada (2017)
9. Bell, P., Lewenstein, B., Shouse, A.W., Feder, M.A.: Learning Science in Informal Environments: People, Places, and Pursuits. The National Academy Press, Washington, DC (2009). https://doi.org/10.17226/12190
10. Dancstep, T., Sindorf, L.: Exhibit Designs for Girls' Engagement: A Guide to the EDGE Design Attributes. The Exploratorium, San Francisco (2016)
11. Bitgood, S.: An Attention-Value Model of Museum Visitors. Center for Advancement of Informal Science Education, Washington, DC (2010)
12. Humphrey, T., Gutwill, J. (eds.): Fostering Active Prolonged Engagement. The Exploratorium, San Francisco (2005)
13. Haywood, N., Cairns, P.: Engagement with an interactive museum exhibit. In: People and Computers XIX–The Bigger Picture, pp. 113–129 (2006). https://doi.org/10.1007/1-84628-249-7_8
14. Ansbacher, T.: On making exhibits engaging and interesting. Curator Museum J. 45(3), 167–173 (2002). https://doi.org/10.1111/j.2151-6952.2002.tb00052.x
15. Ansbacher, T.: What are we learning? Outcomes of the museum experience. Inf. Learn. Rev. 53(1), 4–7 (2002)
16. Allen, S., et al.: Framework for evaluating impacts of informal science education projects. In: Report from a National Science Foundation Workshop. The National Science Foundation, Division of Research on Learning in Formal and Informal Settings (2008)
17. Beghetto, R.A.: The exhibit as planned versus the exhibit as experienced. Curator Museum J. 57(1), 1–4 (2014). https://doi.org/10.1111/cura.12047
18. Lake-Hammond, A., Waite, N.: Exhibition design: bridging the knowledge gap. Des. J. 13(1), 77–98 (2010). https://doi.org/10.2752/146069210X12580336766400
19. McLean, K.: Museum exhibitions and the dynamics of dialogue. Daedalus 128(3), 83–107 (1999)
20. Young, D.L.: A phenomenological investigation of science center exhibition developers' expertise development. The University of North Carolina at Chapel Hill (2012)
21. Roppola, T.: Designing for the Museum Visitor Experience. Routledge, London (2013)
22. Cross, N.: Expertise in design: an overview. Des. Stud. 25(5), 427–441 (2004). https://doi.org/10.1016/j.destud.2004.06.002
23. Harteis, C., Billett, S.: Intuitive expertise: theories and empirical evidence. Edu. Res. Rev. 9, 145–157 (2013). https://doi.org/10.1016/j.edurev.2013.02.001
24. National Research Council. How people learn: Brain, mind, experience, and school: Expanded edition. National Academies Press (2000)
25. Mathieu, J.E., Heffner, T.S., Goodwin, G.F., Salas, E., Cannon-Bowers, J.A.: The influence of shared mental models on team process and performance. J. Appl. Psychol. 85(2), 273 (2000). https://doi.org/10.1037/0021-9010.85.2.273
26. Rouse, W.B., Morris, N.M.: On looking into the black box: prospects and limits in the search for mental models. Psychol. Bull. 100(3), 349–363 (1986). https://doi.org/10.1037/0033-2909.100.3.349
27. Fincher, S., Tenenberg, J.: Making sense of card sorting data. Expert Syst. 22(3), 89–93 (2005). https://doi.org/10.1111/j.1468-0394.2005.00299.x
28. Toker, S., Moseley, J.L.: The mental model comparison of expert and novice performance improvement practitioners. Perform. Improv. Quart. 26(3), 7–32 (2013). https://doi.org/10.1002/piq.21152
29. Jabareen, Y.: Building a conceptual framework: philosophy, definitions, and procedure. Int. J. Qual. Methods 8(4), 49–62 (2009). https://doi.org/10.1177/160940690900800406

30. Creswell, J.W., Miller, D.L.: Determining validity in qualitative inquiry. Theor. Pract. **39**(3), 124–130 (2000). https://doi.org/10.1207/s15430421tip3903_2

31. Jonsen, K., Jehn, K.A.: Using triangulation to validate themes in qualitative studies. Qual. Res. Organ. Manage. Int. J. **4**(2), 123–150 (2009). https://doi.org/10.1108/17465640910978391

32. Bedwell, W.L., Pavlas, D., Heyne, K., Lazzara, E.H., Salas, E.: Toward a taxonomy linking game attributes to learning an empirical study. Simul. Gaming **43**(6), 729–760 (2012). https://doi.org/10.1177/1046878112439444

33. Spencer, D.: Card Sorting: Designing Usable Categories. Rosenfeld Media, New York (2009)

34. Tullis, T., Wood, L.: How many users are enough for a card-sorting study? In: Proceedings UPA 2004 (2004)

35. Righi, C., James, J., Beasley, M., Day, D.L., Fox, J.E., Gieber, J., Howe, C., Ruby, L.: Card sort analysis best practices. J. Usabil. Stud. **8**(3), 69–89 (2013)

36. Hein, G.E.: Learning in the Museum. Routledge, London (2002)

37. Falk, J., Storksdieck, M.: Using the contextual model of learning to understand visitor learning from a science center exhibition. Sci. Educ. **89**(5), 744–778 (2005). https://doi.org/10.1002/sce.20078

38. Hein, G.E.: Museum education. a companion to museum studies. In: Macdonald, S. (ed.) pp. 340–352 (2006). https://doi.org/10.1002/9780470996836.ch20

39. Falk, J.H., Dierking, L.D.: Museum Experience Revisited. Left Coast Press (2012)

40. Allen, S.: Designs for learning: Studying science museum exhibits that do more than entertain. Sci. Educ. **88**(S1), S17–S33 (2004). https://doi.org/10.1002/sce.20016

41. Witcomb, A.: Interactivity: thinking beyond. A companion to museum studies. In: Macdonald, S. (ed.) vol. 39, pp. 353–361 (2006). https://doi.org/10.1002/9780470996836.ch21

42. Adams, M., Luke, J., Moussouri, T.: Interactivity: Moving beyond terminology. Curator: The Museum Journal, vol. 47, n° 2, pp. 155–170 (2004). https://doi.org/10.1111/j.2151-6952.2004.tb00115.x

43. Hennes, T.: Rethinking the visitor experience: Transforming obstacle into purpose. Curator Museum J. **45**(2), 109–121 (2002). https://doi.org/10.1111/j.2151-6952.2002.tb01185.x

44. Falk, J.H., Scott, C., Dierking, L., Rennie, L., Jones, M.C.: Interactives and visitor learning. Curator Museum J. **47**(2), 171–198 (2004). https://doi.org/10.1111/j.2151-6952.2004.tb00116.x

45. Heath, C., Vom Lehn, D.: Configuring 'interactivity' enhancing engagement in science centres and museums. Soc. Stud. Sci. **38**(1), 63–91 (2008). https://doi.org/10.1177/0306312707084152

46. Borun, M., Chambers, M.B., Dritsas, J., Johnson, J.I.: Enhancing family learning through exhibits. Curator Museum J. **40**(4), 279–295 (1997). https://doi.org/10.1111/j.2151-6952.1997.tb01313.x

47. Barriault, C., Pearson, D.: Assessing exhibits for learning in science centers: a practical tool. Visit. Stud. **13**(1), 90–106 (2010). https://doi.org/10.1080/10645571003618824

48. Hein, G.E.: John Dewey's "Wholly Original Philosophy" and its significance for museums. Curator Museum J. **49**(2), 181–203 (2006). https://doi.org/10.1111/j.2151-6952.2006.tb00211.x

49. Rennie, L.J., Johnston, D.J.: The nature of learning and its implications for research on learning from museums. Sci. Educ. **88**(S1), S4–S16 (2004). https://doi.org/10.1002/sce.20017

50. Whitton, N., Moseley, A.: Deconstructing engagement rethinking involvement in learning. Simul. Gaming **45**(4–5), 433–449 (2014). https://doi.org/10.1177/1046878114554755

51. Bevan, B., et al.: Making Science Matter: Collaborations Between Informal Science Education Organizations and Schools. Center for Advancement of Informal Science Education, Washington, DC (2010)

52. Kamolpattana, S., Chen, G., Sonchaeng, P., Wilkinson, C., Willey, N., Bultitude, K.: Thai visitors' expectations and experiences of explainer interaction within a science museum context. Publ. Underst. Sci. **24**(1), 69–85 (2015). https://doi.org/10.1177/0963662514525560
53. Hooper-Greenhill, E.: Developing a Scheme for Finding Evidence of the Outcomes and Impact of Learning in Museums, Archives and Libraries: the Conceptual Framework. Research Centre for Museums and Galleries, Leicester, Uk (2002)
54. Falk, J.H., Dierking, L.D., Adams, M.: Living in a learning society: museums and free-choice learning. A companion to museum studies. In: Macdonald, S. (ed.) pp. 323–339 (2006)
55. Dewey, J.: Experience and Education, 1997th edn. Touchstone, New York (1938)

Socio-emotional Experience in Human Technology Interaction Design – A Fashion Framework Proposal

Rebekah Rousi[1,2(✉)] [ID] and Hanna-Kaisa Alanen[1] [ID]

[1] Faculty of Information Technology, University of Jyväskylä, PO Box 35, 40014 Jyväskylä, Finland
rebekah.rousi@jyu.fi
[2] Gofore Plc, Kalevantie 2, 33100 Tampere, Finland

Abstract. Technology designers and developers can be understood as social experience (SE) mediators. In user experience (UX), notions of SE have served to identify and define the factors contributing to human-technology interaction (HTI). Three dominant perspectives have been promoted in UX discourse: 1) SE of brand, brand value and consumer culture; 2) technology design as mediator of human-to-human interactions; and 3) meaning generation through action and interaction between actors. Symbolic interactionalism understands meaning as occurring through dialogue, in the construction of the social self, promoting self-reflection as a social construction. This theorisation of social experience is valuable in the context of HTI as it allows for greater insight into the immaterial dimensions of technology integration in human societies. The purpose of this paper is to break down the factors contributing to social emotional experience of technology through illustrating how it operates according to fashion – temporality and spatiality in culture. This is a theoretical paper that presents a review of social experience, social emotional and collective emotion based literature in light of fashion and design. The result is a presentation of a proposed fashion framework of social emotions in technology interaction design (FASHEM). Based on symbolic interactionism, FASHEM helps break down emotional technology experience into a matrix of self, other, design, and semiotic interactions.

Keywords: Social experience · Emotions · Fashion · Human-technology interaction · Symbolic interactionism · Culture · Cognition

1 Introduction

"Fashion speaks a tension between the crowd and the individual at every stage in the development of the nineteenth and twentieth century metropolis."

([1], p.11).

Collective emotions (CEs) are phenomena that have been examined in great detail in the fields of cultural and social psychology (see e.g., [2, 3]), sociology, cultural studies

© Springer Nature Switzerland AG 2021
M. Rauterberg (Ed.): HCII 2021, LNCS 12795, pp. 131–150, 2021.
https://doi.org/10.1007/978-3-030-77431-8_8

and politics, particularly in relation to political propaganda [4], the role of the arts and design in facilitating this propaganda [5], and indeed the links between fashion, politics and technology [6]. While any form of cultural production may be considered technology, as it is intentionally created by human beings for a purpose, what is often known as technology (from the times of industrialization and beyond) encompassing artefacts and systems such as machinery and information technology (IT) can be understood as part and parcel of cultural circumstances. Technology (machinery and IT especially) has been used as symbolic vehicles in various cultural movements such as last century's Bauhaus, a modern movement that offered a new cultural exchange and vision for the era [7]. Bauhaus has just been revived as a symbolic signifier by The President of the European Commission, Ursula Von Der Leyen, under the program called *The New European Bauhaus*. It metaphorically represents a creative and interdisciplinary initiative, convening a space of encounter to design future ways of living, situated at the crossroads between art, culture, social inclusion, science and technology, and which reflects the principles and objectives of current sustainable development as well collective co-creation in the operating environment of the 2020s [8].

Design culture that, according to Guy Julier [9] encompasses designers, production, and consumption, is a culturally specific practice, driven almost entirely by strategies of differentiation. It may be understood as the relationship between the process of value, of creation and circulation and of practice, where the designer's role is in the generation of value. And not just commercial but also social, cultural, environmental, political and symbolic value. Value generation occurs in an expanded field of activity whereby cultural information is filtered through a range of platforms and moments. Non-material elements, such as existing knowledge networks, legislation, political pressure, economic fluctuations and fiscal policies, are also contextual factors on which these draw. That is, culture formulates, formats, channels, circulates, contains and retrieves information. Design, therefore, is more than just the creation of visual artefacts to be used or 'read'. It is also about the structuring of systems of encounter within the visual and material world [9], where technology designers and developers can also be understood as social experience (SE) mediators.

1.1 Fashion and Collective Emotions

Fashion, in turn, can be understood as a general concept that reflects society and culture. Therefore, thinking through fashion can deepen the understanding of human social life, that is, circulating sociocultural dynamics, tangible and intangible systems of value signification, as well as individual and collective agents [10] relevant to human-technology interaction (HTI) development practices. Although fashion is most commonly associated with commodities that signify modernity, desirability, and a particular lifestyle (see e.g.,[11, 12]), it can also be treated as a cultural form of life that applies virtually to the human experience in its entirety and rooted in the very nature of the human being as such [13] (introduction) – indeed, life provides a solid concept for interaction processes and therefore anticipating cultural and life form changes is essential when designing for the future [14]. Fashion also brings with it the dimension of temporality (see e.g., [15, 16]) (often referred to as *Zeitgeist,* "the spirit of the era") as well as the dynamics of collective behavior and mutual adaptation (see e.g., [15, 17]) Thus, in addition to objects, the concept of fashion also refers to the way in which certain forms of culture are disseminated, valued and experienced at a given point in time [18]. Hardly any area of contemporary social life is not subject to fashion [17].

When considering the connections between design, technology, culture, and the human mind(s), it is helpful to understand these connections through collective cognition and emotions. CEs in particular, are a way of explaining how, in relation to cultural production – design and technological discourse – people generate particular emotional reactions and experiences. Design objects alone, without matching mental contents, or previously learned knowledge of the designs held by people who encounter them, possess no meaning [19, 20]. People of the same culture often share mental representations and underlying patterns of thought [14]. Apperception is the term used for describing how people process the information represented in design, whereby the information available in the forms and characteristics present in the artefacts and systems are integrated and associated with already mentally stored, or previously learned knowledge [21]. This covers all aspects of the construction of information contents in mental representations [22]. That is, interpretative processes that occur through informational assimilation and integration are what enable design to exist and operate. It is once an individual possesses knowledge that matches and recognizes the encountered phenomena (i.e., actualized design product), that it maintains the power to signify or mean something [23].

1.2 Design, Culture and Social Experience

Given the cultural, or higher level nature of these designs – people needing to learn about design in order to associate it with e.g., values, actions or functions – it should be understood that design cognition and experience is always dependent on social processes [24, 25]. For example, Van Rompay [26] raises the issue of the ability to *metaphorize* due to the fact that people who interact with products often make implicit comparisons, not only with products in different categories, but also with products and other phenomena (such as other people). This process occurs in order to learn about one object by combining the knowledge of it with another. In addition, he reminds us of the role of *conventions* that are learned through interacting within a culture and that help to readily associate objects with specific socio-cultural values and purposes [26].

Expressiveness of a specific form is enabled through learned responses and associations shared by a group. Certain formal qualities may thus symbolize ideas imbued with emotions [27]. We learn about designed products (i.e., real world objects, systems, services, processes etc.) through other people, and similarly to them, we also learn about the qualities of its experience [28]. Thus, an element of this *social experience* (SE) is CEs. CEs are always dependent on the interplay between actions, emotions and context within the frames of societal discourse [29]. "Collective emotions… play a pivotal role both in shaping the individual and societal responses to conflicting events (i.e., collective and group-based emotions) and in contributing to the evolution of a social context that maintains the collective emotions that have developed" [29] (p. 442). According to the review of Van Kleef and Fischer [30], CEs are qualitatively different from the experience of individual emotions, thus underlining the importance of studying emotional phenomena at the group level. For example, they provide additional insight into ways in which similarity and identification shape emotional experiences in groups [30].

Oftentimes CEs are discussed on a relatively general level. Yet, from this general definition we can understand CEs as emotions that are experienced by numerous people in a similar way within particular societies [31]. Saying this, while the emotions experienced may resemble one another, there may be many different reasons for why individuals experience phenomena in a certain way. That is, expressed emotions may seem similar if not identical, but the qualities of the experiences, or elements and memories through which the emotions are derived may differ radically from one person to the next. Saying this, emotions provide a key 'spiritual' and/or cognitive, experiential link from one person to another. Group emotions, or group-based emotions, serve to connect different individuals within a group [32]. Group membership in itself, and what it reflects in terms of values and actions, is a hub for emotions, and emotional experience through identification. When group membership becomes a salient part of the self, one begins to feel emotions on behalf of the group rather than simply as an individual [30].

2   Collective and Group Emotions in Culture and Social Contexts

Both CEs and group emotions are ways of describing how individuals experience emotions through social, cultural, and other collective events and discourse. These collective experiences may be difficult to separate from solely individual or subjective experiences [33]. This is where culture itself enters the picture, as the relationship between culture and psychology has been a keen area of study for centuries. A cultural approach involves the assumption that emotions are constructed by the process of culture [34]. Emotion theorists have sought the universality of emotions in different cultures. For example, Mesquita, Frijda and Scherer [35] point out that hedonic experiences and making contacts with others, among others, share this universality. However, Mesquita and Ellsworth [36] specify that what is culturally universal is a link between appraisal patterns and emotions, rather than emotions *per se*. Such dimensions may include, for example, *novelty*, *pleasantness*, *control certainty*, *agency*, and *compatibility* with personal or social values. Cultural psychology can be understood as the scholarship of the ways in which cognitive and affective (bodily emotional processes) as well as behavioural ways of being are formed through cultural constructs and socially manifested meanings [37]. This is extremely important to consider when attempting to surpass the limitations of cognitive and behavioural psychology as it is culture and social practice that aids in explaining higher order associative practices and intentionality.

According to Back, cultural activity is, firstly, a product of social norms, the state of technology and the need for self-expression, and secondly, it is a product of creativity and structure, where creativity can be translated into a recognized work. In this way, cultural activity is partly determined by social and psychological factors and is partly free objects of creativity [38]. From a fashion perspective, this is related to the seminal concept for describing its function, that is identity which is also linked to self-realization and chosen life forms that are social in nature [11]. From this perspective, we may begin to understand that cultural context plays a key role in informing emotions [29]. Power & Dalgleish admit, one of the important characteristics of emotion is its role in communication with others [39]. People have unique social experiences that they bring with them to social interactions, and these past experiences (along with expectations and emotions) become part of any social context [40]. Lazarus reminds that to understand what is happening regarding emotions in immediate social encounters, "one must keep in mind that each participant is reacting to cues or signals from the others" [41] (p. 379). That is, social emotions require the development of mutuality and must be created in the minds of more than one individual by implicit or explicit agreement. Therefore, social interaction requires mental processes that enable the construction and implementation of common plans. These processes crucially depend on the fact that each actor has a "self-model" [42].

A social psychological approach to culture leads to focus placed upon the dynamics of collective behavior, as people fit their lines of action together and in the process, *create* culture, especially in the context of small groups. This "culture-in-the-making" approach draws heavily from a symbolic-interactionist perspective and focuses on how people communicate to develop shared understandings. In this perspective culture may be viewed as a "structure of feelings," and the emotions and values linked to shared understandings are grounded in the social contexts in which they are developed and experienced [40]. This is also how fashion often begins, and what Blumer refers to in the collective process, when requirements assessment forms the basis for acceptance or rejection. In Blumer's words, fashion "represents an organic sensitivity to objects of social experience" (p. 284) [43]. Mesquita, Boiger, and De Leersnyder's model of "cultural mandates" (including norms, ideals, or goals) shows that emotions have social functions: they help individuals to achieve certain social goals. The model is based on how people appear to construct their experience of a given emotion within *a particular situation* in ways that match the cultural mandate [44].

2.1 Cultural Symbolism and Social Context

Humans create their own worlds and distinguish among artefacts according to their significance [45] as well as how these respond to concerns based on the symbolic characteristics and experiential benefits beyond interaction [26]. Symbolic life, the existence and dynamics of signifying elements (signs, symbols, forms that stand for and refer to something outside themselves) [19, 20], is generated, instilled and maintained through culture and cultural practice [46, 47]. Symbols permeated through culture are both tangible, as seen within the technological design landscape, as well as intangible, i.e., the meanings, actions and values we associate with these technological designs. Technology embodies rules, habits or routines, practice, as well as narratives, concepts, myths and even art (intentionality converted into expression) [48]. While Geertz [46] and Keesing [47] would argue that these are relatively stable, we on the other hand acknowledge the ephemerality of culture. Culture is always in flux [49]. It is the changes within culture that derive from evolving social, political, economic, environmental etc. conditions that can additionally arguably seen within the expressions of fashion [50].

Based on the above mentioned relationship between culture, cognition, psychology and emotions, the role of social context in affecting emotions is imperative. It is through social processes that the symbolic (and arguably behavioural) world gains its ground, and thus, emotions are highly dependent on social context as it frames and attributes particular meanings to various signifying elements in varying compositions. If we could imagine information in its raw form as collections of tangible objects (building blocks or atoms; assemblages) for instance, we could understand social context as the multisensory, embodied, discursive scaffolding that frames, structures and organises information. This structure provided by social context operates in terms of meaning – what the information signifies, describes and means within action-communication situations, and the valence (positive-negative) or weighting (passive-active - arousal) of this information in terms of emotional value [51]. Ashmore, Deaux and McLaughlin Volpe [52] described the connections between emotions and social context as a "general and continuing multi-layered and interwoven set of material realities, social structures, and shared belief system that surround any situation" (p. 103). In fact, Ashmore and colleagues argue that social contexts are the main source or generator of individually experienced thoughts, feelings and actions. They also however, argue that through removing physical contexts and concentrating on social ones, it is possible to distinguish the roots and degrees of temporality via which specific emotions are experienced.

We argue that social contexts cannot be neatly separated from physical contexts. In fact, there are social dimensions to every physical context and social conditions for every physical aspect, particularly when considering design and technology [53]. To illustrate, the physical element or physicalized embodiment of a design object denotes temporality through style, size, scale, functionality, and how it connects with social cultural discourse [9]. Time provides an immaterial yet ever present physical frame, or series of capsules (design could be interpreted as these series of time capsules) through which cognition, emotions and experience evolve, especially when considering human-made artefacts and systems. For example, according to Saariluoma and Oulasvirta [54], the critical question in experience analysis is how one essentially perceives the meaning of "being in the world" in interaction. Such an approach draws attention, not only to the constructive relationship between human experience and intentions, but also to its material-socio-cultural-historical circumstances [54]. This is also what Forlizzi recalls: designers must pay attention to the ebbs and flows of time and the phrasing of interactions [55]. For example, the importance of presence and its implications is important to understand in creating any physical environment, but in experiencing virtual reality (VR), its necessity has been particularly emphasized [56]. Nature on the other hand, despite its regeneration, can be interpreted in Western cultures in particular, as more static and constant [57].

2.2 Emotional Culture

Structural socio-politics, situations, events and changing or depending of available infor-mation strongly influence collective emotional climates [52]. These contexts along with their contextual cues, help guide emotional orientations. Another concept that can be linked to this collective and social way of understanding emotional experience is that of emotional culture. Emotional culture consists of the combination of culture, social context and the overall emotional value attributed to the repertoire. An emotional cul-ture instils immaterial, value-based and emotional rules of practice that are anchored by meaning for various members and groups in society. For instance, to look at the com-municated emotional culture of modern tech companies – i.e., that of Google, Gofore and Facebook – strategic design moves hand-in-hand with the ethos (philosophy), vision and ambition of the companies. Attached to ambition and aspiration alone, and housed within the design of both the marketing and communication material, user interfaces, as well as the internal organisational design, from wallpaper to professional titles, specific emotional qualities are projected and fostered within the organisational groups (creating frames) [58].

Organisational culture in itself is a composite of fashion [59]. Traditional top-down operation models with steep hierarchies and multi-layers of bureaucracy are no longer in fashion. Instead, more collaborative, horizontal-style companies in which each expert employee feels empowered by their own ability to influence is more the rage [60]. This mode of sensibility is conveyed additionally through the brand image as well as through the products and services that are created and promoted by the companies, whereby communication (e.g., marketing, styling, packaging, events and the milieu) with the audience, plays a significant role, as does the generated use culture – how people understand not only the product use, but also the social dynamics that exist around the products [61]. In this way, we can understand the SE of contemporary tech products as a fashion phenomenon that is permeated from the core of organisational ideology outwards to the grassroots of society – how we see the design objects we consume, and how we see ourselves with the designs and through these in relation to other people. To say this and when fashion is rejected from material and treated, in accordance with Kawamura, as a symbolic tool that exists in people's minds and beliefs [15], fashion can be seen as an embodiment of sociocultural climate.

3 Symbolic Interactionism and Its Function in Social Experience

On this note, we move towards symbolic interactionism (SI). According to SI, meaning occurs through dialogue [43]. In fact, something so seemingly singular as an individual's identity, subjective experience and sense of self is argued as manifesting and being the product of continual processes of interactions that occur through symbolism. SI puts a label on the semiotic logic of both human-technology interactive processes, and human-human interactive processes – explaining the continuum of experience as a reciprocal, cyclical and concurrent network of symbols and their attribution of meaning (interpretation) [62]. As George Herbert Mead emphasizes, "[m]an lives in a world of meaning" (p. 382) [62], and fashion is undeniably a phenomenon of symbolic meanings. According to Matteucci and Marino, "[f]ashion thus attests the existence of a reality in which what is essentially required is not the capacity of interpreting differently a certain "given," but rather the ability of perceptually moving within an aesthetically thick space" (p. 56) [13]. Thus, meanings are often connotative and reflect the communication of socio-cultural values [26]. In this respect, to understand meaning making in interaction, one has to go beyond objects.

Shott [63] examined the relationship between emotion and social life. She argued that SI is apt for the analysis of the processing, experiencing, construction and expression of emotions, particularly in light of the social nature of emotions. In fact, not only did Shott highlight the social contingency of emotions, she also posited that emotions play a major role in social control and order. Shott draws on Schachter's [64] definition of emotion as a physiological (affective) state of arousal experienced and defined (interpreted) by an individual as being emotionally induced. Here, emotions are understood as comprising two distinct parts, that of psycho-physiological processing of information on an affective level and the cognition, or cognitive labelling of these affects. The mental and linguistic (cognitive-linguistic) acts of labelling emotions can be seen to strongly rely on social and cultural principles that aid in the definition of cognitive-affective interpretation. It was Clifford Geertz [65] who once said that, "[n]ot only ideas, but emotions too, are cultural artifacts" (p. 81). To go even deeper into this discussion we may note that social arrangements prescribe "feeling rules" [66] – the types of feelings or emotions that are socially allowed to be experienced (publicly, or admittedly) and expressed. This may also be conveyed into the realms of designed artefacts and technology and the emotions that are expected to be experienced in relation to creations or 'creative intensities' – i.e., *satisfaction* [67] when talking about information technology use, *excitement, desire*, and *passion* [68, 69] when talking about artistic, creative wearables. Even within these small examples there is a dichotomy established between the *me* or *I* (human) and its closeness to what is worn, and what is intentionally creative, to the *technology* – human versus technology, even in social emotional discourse [70].

3.1 The Self and Self-representation in Social Emotional Experience

In fact, in relation to the self and self-representation, Psychologist and Philosopher William James [71] distinguished between the '*I* self' and the '*me* self'. Whereby, the 'I self' was understood as being the information people are aware of regarding themselves in relation to the world. The 'me self' comprised the ways in which an individual subjectively experiences themselves through for instance, self-concepts, self-views, self-image and self-schema. When comparing this insight to popular semiotic views presented by Charles Sander Peirce [23] and Ferdinand de Saussure [72] for instance, we can see that the phenomenological 'I self' is pragmatic, and uses information presented in the external world as a means of catalyst for interpretation and comparison in the internal mental world. The 'me self' resembles de Saussure's views on semiotics in that here, everything is mentally bound – there is no understanding *really* of the external or so-called material world, as everything we know occurs mentally. The signified and signifier cannot be removed from the interpretation as such. In SI however, there is a synthesis of these views existing on the social, discursive and interpretive levels. Thus, to inject the self once again into the discussion, we may draw on Ulric Neisser's [73] understanding of self-representation and self in that the way that one represents the self also affects the experience of self. Neisser uses terms such as 'ecological self' to express how the self exists in networks of systems, and the 'interpersonal self' as the ways in which the self exists as a verbal and non-verbal social construction that manifests through interaction with others.

Both the ecological self and the interpersonal self are interesting to gauge from the perspective of HTI design and development processes. This enables the application of SI to analyse the SE of technology experience through the lens of fashion. These days the ecological self for instance, manifests through multidimensional and complex systems, both atomically (physically) and digitally. Our environments and contexts are both natural and physically constructed. We may live in an airtight eco-smart home that is electronically dependent, in the middle of the forest. Already these juxtaposed material conditions interact with our social ideologies and values in such a way that specific cognitive-affective states glaze over our sense of state, belonging and identity according to how we see our so-called eco-friendly home contributing to environmental sustainability, and how we identify with the nature we are surrounded by. Then, when considering the hyper-textual, hyper-contextual environments we are a part of and interact with through online information every day, our sense of self, self-representation and emotional states emerging through social and symbolic interactions, the domain of social emotions becomes ever more complicated (Fig. 1).

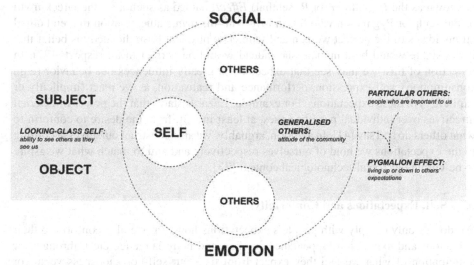

Fig. 1. Fashion, technology and symbolic interactionism in social emotional experience (Adapted from [74] & [43])

Yet, this interpersonal self exists as a part of these highly complex systems. It is through social systems and order that we have arrived upon this social-technological complexity [75]. Our systemic existence is contingent on the societal developments of our environment. This existence is manifested and defined through interpersonal relations and interactions that are either confirmed, reinforced or rejected by emotions – positive and excited emotions for example, versus negative and repellent emotions. We define ourselves in relation to others and how we connect through these social emotional processes. Symbolic interactionism is one way of viewing these complex and dynamic relationships that determine emotional experience through social processes in relation to the self. SI is based on the argument that humans possess a sense of self that renders them conscious of their own actions and being in relation to others []. The self can be seen as both a subject and an object. The self as subject, is a being with agency. This view on the self is one of a person who can choose for themselves – they can choose what to consume, how to express themselves in relation to what and who they would like to be. The self as object exists when we observe and are aware of ourselves and the way we behave. In this scenario our identity and sense of self, combined with self-concept provide a basis for social meanings that are highly dependent on the culture we live in and the reactions of others [74].

Others in any given instance, comprise those who we do not know or who are not particularly significant to us from the perspective of our concept of self, as well as the particular others, who are important to us. While all others (individuals) have the ability to influence our emotions, it is quite strongly the particular or significant others who play key roles in shaping them [76]. As emotions are highly contingent on expectations (they are a way of preparing the mind and body for action/interaction), we also find ourselves either living up to, or living down to the expectations others have for us. This is known as the *Pygmalion* (or Rosenthal) *Effect*, named as such after the Greek myth of the sculptor Pygmalion who fell in love with his own statue creation that embodied all his ideals of the perfect women and wife. The physical form dictated his belief that if the statue would be a human, she indeed would be perfect in all respects [77]. In reflection of this, we may see that expectations greatly influences our behavior (e.g., consumption), self-expression, performance and realisation, as we react (implicitly or explicitly) to these expectations. For example, Lazarus states that the power of external directives over individual persons arises, at least in part, from the desire to conform to what others do and say [41]. In addition, arguably, we also construct ourselves according to the expectations we hold of ourselves respectively and aim to match what we aspire to be within our social-technological context [73].

3.2 Self, Expectations and Conformity

We do not only comply with people's expectations however, we also conform to their behaviour and expression (appearance, spoken and body language etc.), through our anticipation of what we feel they expect from us – our self-consciousness versus or in light of our self-schemata. Humans, as social-emotional beings, are propelled into conformity that has been scientific demonstrated on numerous occasions in experiments such as the Asch conformity task [78]. In the Asch conformity task [79] an individual participant takes part in a group situation, believing that the other members of the group are also there as participants. The other group members however are confederates planted in the situation. The group members are shown a line and then are required to choose a line (1 out of 3) that matches the presented line. As the experiment progresses, the confederate group members unanimously choose the wrong line. Even in Asch's original experiments, approximately 30% of the participants chose the wrong line in conformance with the rest of the group. Similar patterns can be seen in the elevator experiment, for instance, conducted by *Candid Camera* in the 1960s that showed people in an elevator turn and adjust their bodies according to where other elevator travellers were facing [80]. These are very much social technological examples of how humans operate in relation to one another. Here, we argue that this conformity and adjust of behaviour also operates on emotional and experiential levels.

It was Hildred Geertz [81] who argued that cultural systems possess patterned ideas about particular forms of interpersonal relationships and their associated cognitive-affective states. Geertz additionally mentioned that these represent a small portion out of a spectrum of social emotional experiences, operating in a somewhat stereotypical fashion – that is, we take the social-cultural idea of what emotions are expected in relation to what context and which people and often allow this to shape our own emotional experience of subsequent phenomena. This process is known as emotional socialisation

[63] or even emotional specialisation [81] when considering the cognitive-affective process versus the expressive or representational one – how intensely one will show their deep emotions.

3.3 Feeling Rules

The ideas of Geertz [81] link to Goffman's [82] research on impression management. Impression management concentrates on rules and principles that function within differing forms of social interaction. Goffman argued that people manage and control their outward emotion strategically. While this is valuable information from the perspective of measuring emotional experience through face gestures for instance, the explicit processes of social emotional experience on a cognitive-affective level were relatively un-dealt with in his work. Emotional psychology scholars [83, 84] proposed the term "emotion work" to describe the way in which emotions operate in social situations. Hoschild [66] expanded on this with his coined term "feeling rules" that served to emphasise the fact that people not only regulate their externally expressed emotions, but they also attempt to feel and experience the emotions that they expect *should be felt* in certain social situations. This is due to there being a dual layer of emotion guessing, or emotion matching – that which we feel we should be feeling in relation to the user through the lens of empathy, and then naturally, the emotion and situation of the user with which we are attempting to emphasise.

Not only is there the tension between what should be felt and displayed with what perhaps may, if ever, come naturally as in primary emotional processes or basic emotions [19, 69] – that is, instant cognitive-affective reactions that are directly triggered by stimuli such as fear, disgust, excitement etc. – but these "feeling rules" also influence how we genuinely feel. Whether this be a question related to, "if we say it often enough we start believing it," or regarding the emotional quality of these overlapping processes (e.g., stress of trying to cover the feeling of disappointment), remains to be seen and is highly dependent on context [85]. In fact, feeling rules are engrained in our social fabric that strongly define how we imprint encounters, which in turn affects our emotions.

4   Emotional Appraisal Towards a Social Model of Experience

From this perspective we may also observe a multi-levelled appraisal process. Appraisal theory in its basic understanding can be described as the argument that emotions and emotional states arise through continual information processing (cognitive-affective processes) in which humans (or animals) evaluate phenomena against their core concern – wellbeing and survival [86, 87]. Personal meaning, which is what arouses emotions, is the product of appraisal. Although emotions are responses to events that are important to the individual [88], and as previously discussed, the person-environment relationships that arouse emotions most often take place with other people. However, two individuals that construe situations quite similarly and agree on the facts, may still react through very different emotions. This is influenced, for example, by personality variables as well as the reality through which they have appraised the adaptational significance of facts. Personal meanings are nonetheless relational – they have to do with how relationships affect our well-being [88, 89]. Whether this be social or cultural wellbeing, or direct physical safety, our emotions and the cognitive-affective – mental representational level and physiological level of experiencing them - can be seen as an in-built and highly evolved mechanism to adjust our actions to maximise our chances of self-preservation. From this perspective, it is arguably apparent that social interactions, hierarchies and processes are key components to this self-preservation and its associated cognitive-affective evaluation process [86, 89].

Lazarus prioritizes three appraisal components in which culture has a major impact on acquired and considered goals. These are goal relevance, goal congruence or incongruence, and type of ego-involvement. Relevance of an important goal means the potential for strong emotions. Although individuals differ, Lazarus argues that culture influences the values, goals, and main hierarchies that members acquire and express, including their identities [41]. Smith and Mackie [90] indicate that it is possible to conceptualize and explore emotions based on people's social group membership which may become part of a person's "social identity" - an extended version of the self. Authors reassure that when a significant group identity becomes salient, people think of themselves and fellow in-group members as "we" (p. 349). Moreover, like any emotional reaction, the authors recall that group-based emotions may change when the appraisals that generate them also alter. In the case of group-based emotions it is especially likely that social influence from other in-group members may directly influence an individual's perception and appraisal of a situation [90]. Thus, it is possible that appraisal itself may be partly mediated by social interaction. For example, evaluations of personal relevance may develop over the course of conversations with others during which appraised conclusions are negotiated dynamically between interactants rather than formulated completely in either individual mental system [2]. Overall, Mesquita and Ellsworth explain in more detail of the universality of the emotion: "if people from different cultures appraise a situation in the same way, they will experience the same emotions. If they experience a different emotion, it is because they have appraised the situation differently, and appraisal theories allow us to specify (at least roughly) what this difference in appraisal is likely to be" [36] (p. 233).

Manstead and Fischer [91] refer to the appraisal of others' reactions to the emotional event as *social appraisal*. Appraisals of other persons can have a large impact on the course of an individual's process of appraisal. Here, the authors propose a *reappraisal* (the term used by Lazarus [41]) to refer to ongoing evaluation that differs from appraisal only in the sense that it comes later. One basis for this point of view is that the self is almost always entailed in emotion. That is, what is appraised is not the event *per se*, but the event-in-relation-to-self, and the event that is appraised is also very likely to be appraised in relation to the reactions of others. The latter is constitutive of the emotion process, in the sense that it can influence both the perception of coping potential and the way in which the appraisal process unfolds over time [91]. Mesquita, Boiger, and De Leersnyder [44] use the expression "doing emotions" to describe the active process of meaning making that is consequential for the way in which individuals navigate their social environment, and thus also constantly reappraising emotions. Authors highlight that the process also involves selective attention and meaning making [44]. Indeed, John Dewey has portrayed the complexity of the process of experience by drawing from it a stormy ocean in which waves collide, or ripple forward [92]. In general, an idea that the emotional experience is a process, has been widely shared among so-called appraisal theorists.

4.1 Motivation, Emotions and Technological Experience

Motivation has been recognised as a key basis for emotional appraisal [93]. Oatley, Kelter and Jenkins [34] raise three different social motivations: attachment, affiliation, and assertion. In design processes where human positive emotions are most often the subject of consideration, the first two in particular are central. Affiliation draws individuals together; typical positive emotions associated with affiliation are affection, warmth, and liking. Similar to Abraham Maslow [94] with his hierarchy of motivation and needs, Ellsworth and Scherer [93] identify the motivational basis of emotions as encompassing needs, goals and values. They focus on the goals of survival, maintaining positive social relationships, the enjoyment of pleasurable experiences, and even goals embedded in mundane acts such as fetching a cup of coffee. Ellsworth and Scherer go on to emphasise differences between cultures that are shuttled through varying content and elements in social dimensions such as identity, values, justice and norms. These differences, however subtle or exacerbated, cause alterations in the characteristics of goals and priorities. Moreover, in addition to the collective vision of norms, values and justice, there is also the recognition of the importance of self, the social identity and dynamics of self, as well as the conceptualisation of the other. These points strongly correlate with Blumer's [43] theory of symbolic interactionism, as well as many other studies related to self and self-representation [71, 73]. The basic principle of this insight is that social species such as human beings rely on other similar beings for their survival. This is where technology, its design, and the fashions that manifest and are manifested by technology design is so important. Technology, the material and systemic realisation of thought, norms, action and ideologies are the *boundary objects* that aid to bridge individuals. They are concrete touchpoints that connect people and their behaviour. Technology assists social organisation equally as much as social organisation can be considered technology in and of itself. Mass symbolic expressions that take place through technology fashion can be seen as the embodiments of norms (shared rules), status (brand and quality), appropriate and inappropriate behaviour as well as prerogatives (privilege) [9].

Emotions can be seen as a mode of regulation. It is the experience of emotions – i.e., the enthusiasm of a colour (handbag), logic (intuitive user interface) or the experience of an enlarged (celebrity) *self* through vlogging (influencing) – that serves to regulate and conform behaviour to the norms of the context and times. Therefore, the dimensions of value relevance, external standard compatibility, legitimacy and authenticity are also considered a part of appraisal criteria through which we cognitively and affectively evaluate phenomena. We appraise other people and external phenomena equally as much as we evaluate ourselves [95]. The self is appraised in light of a self-ideal, salient social identity or self-concept [96]. This dimension comes close to William James' description of the *me self* [71]. This is also where an understanding of internalised or implicit ethics come into play, as often the reflective evaluation of self is contingent upon a comparison of the individual's being and behaviour in light of their self-ideal and internalised moral code – what they believe to be either right/good or wrong/evil.

In respect to the way in which culture influences this process we can see that culture influences self-concept differentiation [97, 98]. Self-significance is greatly reliant on the social environment's "feeling rules" – how the self can be emphasised in relation to the collective [99, 100]. Emotional reactions and the ways in which emotional experience influences the composition of these reactions are strongly connected to emotional regulation, representation of self, and how this regulation aids in maintaining social coherence [101]. Additionally, appraisals of events and phenomena are very likely to differ from one culture to the next, depending on the role they play within the respective societies. Yet, while the content and semantic value of this content differs across cultures, there are universals that can be observed in relation to appraisal patterns and resulting emotional experiences. Just like technology and its design fashions, cultures and societies are continuously evolving human products – thought, feelings and action move through trends – from the seemingly new or novel to states of mundane and then outdated [41]. These time and situation specific factors are vital to the processing of emotions in light of any phenomena, none the least technology design and its fashions.

4.2   Fashion Framework of Social Emotions in Technology Interaction Design – A Proposal (FASHEM)

Based on the matters mentioned above, we feel the need for the introduction of a model that can serve as a framework for more precisely understanding the socio-emotional experience of human-driven technology design. As established above, technology is cultural and social [95]. Design and the ways in which fashions socially manifest can be seen to both represent and generate the compositions of emotional experience. For these reasons we propose a framework for understanding fashion as a paradigm in the social emotional experience of technology. Our model incorporates a SI approach to the induction and sustainment of social emotions experienced in relation to technology by embracing its existence in a specific (hyper-contextual) environment, at a specific time, in a particular culture. This is where fashion reflects sociocultural phenomena and movements that affect human life forms and manifest as material and/or immaterial signifiers.

The proposed model comprises three distinct dimensions: 1) the context – cultural context, environment, situation etc.; 2) the human dimension – what people are doing within these contexts; and 3) Symbolic Interaction (SI) processes. These components of social emotional experience are constantly acting and are interacting on various levels. The elements in the model are presented in a simplified form. It should be noted that in reality the various elements overlap with varying intensity depending on context-intentionality relations. In the first phase of the Fashion Framework of Social Emotions in Technology Interaction Design (FASHEM) we concentrate on the dynamic interactions occurring on the intrapersonal and interpersonal communication. These take a stance, firstly, in the socio-emotional characters through 'individual me' (self-schemata; self-concept; *I self*) and 'contextual me' (ecological self; *me self*) in intra and inter-personal interactions. Secondly, Level 2 (SYMBOLIC-SEMIOTIC TECHNOLOGY–FASHION [TEF]) refers to how this interaction and emotional experience of interaction takes place in relation to technology design and its properties. As we argue, technology is designed, consumed and exists in fashion paradigms – societal, industrial, scientific

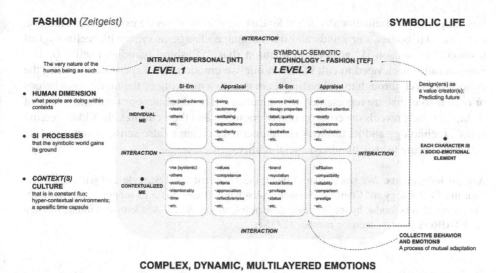

Fig. 2. Fashion framework of social emotions in technology interaction design [FASHEM]

etc. These trends exist through temporality and symbolic discourse – associating and assimilating the perceived phenomena with previously learned knowledge. Finally, the framework guides the discovery of accurate socio-emotional characters so that they can be incorporated as part of the emerging technology interaction design. Each character is a socio-emotional element (presented in the model in a most simplified form) (Fig. 2).

Through this social-cultural approach to emotions and their appraisal we also understand that emotions are complex – for as Ortony and Turner [87] pose, "What's basic about basic emotions?" They not only can conflict and contradict one another – to feel happy to be sad, or, as in the case of "feeling rules" to know that one needs to feel and express grief at a funeral, because hysterical laughter upon remembering a funny incident would not be acceptable at such an event – but they exist on levels. Our emotions are both generated through and operate in relation to collective behaviour and shared group sentiment (socially constructed ways of expressing emotion). We can understand the designer's and design team's work as that of value creator, or indeed 'value collector' – carefully studying and understanding values (cultural, social, personal) and how they operate through the symbolic properties of design, then attempting to channel these through output (product, service and system design).

When understanding these dynamics on a collective level, we may see that technology provides a pivot, node or symbol upon which numerous intra and interpersonal emotional, experiential and interactional processes can anchor. While they are not fixed in any way from an interpretational perspective, they do provide a set point through which these processes manifest and can be shared, or communicated, from one individual to the next. For this reason, the experience of technological design is never *not* a social emotional process. Nor, can technology in its various forms and logics, ever be separated from fashion. Technology and its support of repetitive action as well as transference of values is always collectively consumed and expressed. Yet, as with culture, is constantly evolving.

It is temporally and situationally dependent, as are the emotions we experience in relation to them. Our bodies, our minds and our language change in sync with technological fashions [1]. Wilson [1] goes on to mention that, "[f]ashion parodies itself" (p. 10). Ephemerality is elevated to cult in which intense emotions are experienced among the collectives. Yet, through this elevation there is also a mocking of the moral foundations or pretensions that are represented within culture. The timeliness or temporary state of fashion in itself reveals the construction of societies and their cultures. Just like "feeling rules", technology and its fashions simultaneously create a false sense of reality while actually serving to structure lived social reality.

Acknowledgements. We would like to thank the University of Jyväskylä and particularly the Learning Technology and Cognitive Science research unit (LEACS) for its support in this research. This research was funded by the Strategic Research Council (SRC), Academy of Finland through the ETAIROS project (decision number 327354).

References

1. Wilson, W.: Adorned in Dreams – Fashion and Modernity. Virago Press, London (1985)
2. Parkinson, B.: Emotions are social. Bri. J. Psychol. **87**(4), 663–683 (1996)
3. Von Scheve, C., Ismer, S.: Towards a theory of collective emotions. Emot. Rev. **5**(4), 406–413 (2013)
4. Jasper, J. M.: Emotions, sociology, and protest. In: Collective Emotions, pp. 341–355 (2014)
5. Clark, T.: Art and Propaganda in The Twentieth Century: The Political Image in the Age of Mass Culture. Harry N. Abrams, New York (1997)
6. Jansens, F.: Suit of power: fashion, politics, and hegemonic masculinity in Australia. Aust. J. Polit. Sci. **54**(2), 202–218 (2019)
7. Riley, N., Bayer, P. (eds.): The elements of design: A practical encyclopedia of the decorative arts from the Renaissance to the present. Free Press, Mumbai (2003)
8. European Union: The New European Bauhaus (2021). https://europa.eu/new-european-bauhaus/index_en. Accessed 28 January 2021
9. Julier, G.: The Culture of Design. Sage, London (2014)
10. Rocamora, A.: Thinking through fashion: an introduction. In: Thinking Through Fashion – A Guide to Key Theorists, pp. 1–27. Bloomsburg, London (2016)
11. Svendsen, L.: Fashion: A Philosophy. Reaktion, London (2006)
12. Breward, C., Evans, C.: Fashion and Modernity. Berg Publishers, London (2005)
13. Matteucci, G., Marino, S. (eds.): Philosophical Perspectives on Fashion. Bloomsbury Publishing, London (2016)
14. Saariluoma, P., Cañas, J.J., Leikas, J.: Designing for Life: A Human Perspective on Technology Development. Palgrave MacMillan, London (2016)
15. Kawamura, Y.: Fashion-ology: An Introduction to Fashion Studies. Berg, Oxford (2005)
16. Rocamora, A., Smelik, A. (eds.): Thinking Through Fashion: A Guide to Key Theorists. Bloomsbury Publishing, London (2015)
17. Aspers, P., Godard, F.: Sociology of fashion: order and change. Ann. Rev. Soc. **39**, 172–192 (2013)
18. Crane, D., Bovone, L.: Approaches to material culture: the sociology of fashion and clothing. Poetics. **34**, 319–333 (2006)
19. Rousi, R.: From cute to content: user experience from a cognitive semiotic perspective. Jyväskylä studies in computing, 171. University of Jyväskylä, Jyväskylä (2013)

20. Saariluoma, P., Rousi, R.: Symbolic interactions: towards a cognitive scientific theory of meaning in human technology interaction. J. Adv. Humanit. **3**, 310–324 (2015)
21. Saariluoma, P.: Apperception, content-based psychology and design. In: Lindemann, U. (eds.) Human Behaviour in Design, pp. 72–78. Springer, Berlin (2003). https://doi.org/10.1007/978-3-662-07811-2_8
22. Saariluoma, P.: Foundational Analysis: Presuppositions in Experimental Psychology, vol. 2. Psychology Press, Hove (1997)
23. Peirce, C.S.: The Writings of Charles S. Peirce: A Chronological Edition, vol. 8, pp. 1890–1892. Indiana University, Bloomington (2009)
24. Oatley, K.: Social construction in emotions. In: Handbook of Emotions, pp. 341–352. The Guilford Press, New York (1993)
25. Campbell, K., Gibson, S., Gramlich, C.: On conversation and design: a socially constructed practice. Technol. Pedag. Educ. **14**(1), 9–24 (2005)
26. Van Rompay, T. J.: Product expression: bridging the gap between the symbolic and the concrete. In: Product Experience, pp. 333–351. Elsevier, Amsterdam (2008)
27. Fiore, A.M.: Understanding Aesthetics for the Merchandising and Design Professional. A&C Black, London (2010)
28. Hastrup, K., Hervik, P. (eds.): Social Experience and Anthropological Knowledge. Routledge, London (2003)
29. Bar-Tal, D., Halperin, E., De Rivera, J.: Collective emotions in conflict situations: societal implications. J. Soc. Issues **63**(2), 441–460 (2007)
30. Van Kleef, G.A., Fischer, A.H.: Emotional collectives: how groups shape emotions and emotions shape groups. Cogn. Emot. **30**(1), 3–19 (2016)
31. Stephan, W.G., Stephan, C.W.: An integrated threat theory of prejudice. In: Reducing Prejudice and Discrimination, pp. 225–246. Erlbaum, Hillsdale (2000)
32. Smith, E.R.: Social identity and social emotions: toward new conceptualization of prejudice. In: Affect, Cognition and Stereotyping: Interactive Processes in Group Perception, pp. 297–315. Academic Press, San Diego (1993)
33. McDowell, J.: Subjective, intersubjective, objective. Philos. Phenomenol. Res. **67**(3), 675–681 (2003)
34. Oatley, K., Keltner, D., Jenkins, J.M.: Understanding Emotions. Blackwell Publishing, Oxford (2006)
35. Mesquita, B., Frijda, N.H., Scherer, K.R.: Culture and emotion. In: Handbook of Cross-Cultural Psychology, vol. 2, pp. 255–297. Guilford Press, New York (1997)
36. Mesquita, B., Ellsworth, P.C.: The role of culture in appraisal. In: Appraisal Processes in Emotion: Theory, Methods, Research, pp. 233–48. Oxford University Press, Oxford (2001)
37. Valsiner, J.: Cultural psychology. In: The Encyclopedia of Cross-Cultural Psychology, pp. 319–327. Wiley, New Jersey (2013)
38. Back, K.W.: Modernism and fashion: a social psychological interpretation. In: The Psychology of Fashion, pp. 3–14. Lexington Books, Lexington (1985)
39. Power, M.J., Dalgleish, T.: Cognition and Emotion: From Order to Disorder, 2nd edn. Psychology Press, Hove (2008)
40. Kaiser, S.B.: The Social Psychology of Clothing: Symbolic Appearances in Context. Fairchild, New York (1997)
41. Lazarus, R.: Emotion and Adaptation. Oxford University Press, Oxford (1991)
42. Oatley, K., Johnson-Laird, P.N.: Towards a cognitive theory of emotions. Cognit. Emot. **1**(1), 29–50 (1987)
43. Blumer, H.: Fashion: from class differentiation to collective selection. Sociol. Q. **10**(3), 275–291 (1969)

44. Mesquita, B., Boiger, M., De Leersnyder, J.: Doing emotions: the role of culture in everyday emotions. Eur. Rev. Soc. Psychol. **28**(1), 95–133 (2017). https://doi.org/10.1080/10463283. 2017.1329107

45. Krippendorff, K., Butter, R.: Semantics: meanings and contexts of artifacts. In: Product Experience, pp. 353–376. Elsevier, Amsterdam (2008)

46. Geertz, C.: Ethnic conflict: three alternative terms. Common Knowl. **2**(3), 54–65 (1993)

47. Keesing, R.M.: Theories of culture. Annu. Rev. Anthropol. **3**, 73–97 (1974)

48. Crilly, N., Good, D., Matravers, D., Clarkson, P.J.: Design as communication: exploring the validity and utility of relating intention to interpretation. Des. Stud. **29**(5), 425–457 (2008)

49. Naylor, L.L.: Culture and Change: An Introduction. Greenwood Publishing Group, Westport (1996)

50. Edwards, T.: Fashion in Focus: Concepts. Practices and Politics. Routledge, London (2010)

51. Russell, J.A.: Emotion, core affect, and psychological construction. Cognit. Emot. **23**(7), 1259–1283 (2009)

52. Ashmore, R.D., Deaux, K., McLaughlin-Volpe, T.: An organizing framework for collective identity: articulation and significance of multidimensionality. Psychol. Bull. **130**(1), 80–114 (2004)

53. Wigelius, H., Väätäjä, H.: Dimensions of context affecting user experience in mobile work. In: Gross, T. et al. (eds.) IFIP Conference on Human-Computer Interaction, vol. 5727, pp. 604–617. Springer, Heidelberg (2009). https://doi.org/10.1007/978-3-642-03658-3_65

54. Saariluoma, P., Oulasvirta, A.: User psychology: re-assessing the boundaries of a discipline. Psychology **1**(05), 317–328 (2010)

55. Forlizzi, J.: The product ecology: understanding social product use and supporting design culture. Int. J. Des. **2**(1), 1–10 (2008)

56. Huang, M. P., Alessi, N. E.: Presence as an emotional experience. Stud. Health Technol. Inform. 148–153 (1999)

57. Coates, P.: Nature: Western Attitudes Since Ancient Times. Wiley , Hoboken (2013)

58. Dorst, K.: The core of 'design thinking' and its application. Des. Stud. **32**(6), 521–532 (2011)

59. Stensaker, B.: Culture and fashion in reform implementation: perceptions and adaptation of management reforms in higher education. J. High. Educ. Policy Manag. **20**(2), 129–138 (1998)

60. Christopher, M., Lowson, R., Peck, H.: Creating agile supply chains in the fashion industry. Int. J. Retail Distrib. Manag. **32**(8), 367–376 (2004)

61. Da Silva, O., Crilly, N., Hekkert, P.: Intentions and the aesthetics of artifacts. In: Proceedings of IAEA, pp. 148–152 (2014)

62. Mead, G.H.: The nature of aesthetic experience. Int. J. Ethics **36**(4), 382–393 (1926)

63. Shott, S.: Emotion and social life: a symbolic interactionist analysis. Am. J. Sociol. **84**(6), 1317–1334 (1979)

64. Schachter, S.: Emotion, Obesity and Crime. Academic Press, New York (1971)

65. Geertz, C.: Local knowledge and its limits: some, obiter dicta. Yale J. Crit. **5**(2), 129–135 (1992)

66. Hochschild, A.R.: Emotion work, feeling rules, and social structure. Am. J. Sociol. **85**(3), 551–575 (1979)

67. Nielsen, J.: Iterative user-interface design. Computer **26**(11), 32–41 (1993)

68. Beaudry, A., Pinsonneault, A.: The other side of acceptance: studying the direct and indirect effects of emotions on information technology use. MIS Q. **34**(4), 689–710 (2010)

69. Hekkert, P.: Design aesthetics: principles of pleasure in design. Psychol. Sci. **48**(2), 157 (2006)

70. Keirl, S.: 'Seeing' and 'interpreting'the human-technology phenomenon. In: Williams, P., Jones, A., Buntting, C. (eds) The Future of Technology Education, pp. 13–34. Springer, Singapore (2015). https://doi.org/10.1007/978-981-287-170-1_2

71. James, W.: The Principles of Psychology. Henry Holt and Company, New York (1890). https://www.gutenberg.org/files/57628/57628-h/57628-h.htm. Accessed 02 Feburary 2021
72. De Saussure, F.: Course in General Linguistics. Columbia University Press, New York (2011)
73. Neisser, U.: Five kinds of self-knowledge. Philos. Psychol. 1(1), 35–59 (1988)
74. Beasley, P.: Symbolic interaction theory – a fashion case study (2015). https://paulbeasl eydesign.wordpress.com/2015/02/26/symbolic-interaction-theory-a-fashion-case-study/. Accessed 28 January 2021
75. Rzevski, G.: Complexity as the defining feature of the 21st century. Int. J. Des. Nat. Ecodyn. 10(3), 191–198 (2015)
76. LaRossa, R., Reitzes, D.C.: Symbolic interactionism and family studies. In: Boss, P., Doherty, W.J., LaRossa, R., Schumm, W.R., Steinmetz, S.K. (eds) Sourcebook of Family Theories and Methods, pp. 135–166. Springer, Boston (2009). https://doi.org/10.1007/978-0-387-857 64-0_6
77. Raudenbush, S.W.: Magnitude of teacher expectancy effects on pupil IQ as a function of the credibility of expectancy induction: a synthesis of findings from 18 experiments. J. Educ. Psychol. 76, 85–97 (1984)
78. Walker, M.B., Andrade, M.G.: Conformity in the Asch task as a function of age. J. Soc. Psychol. 136(3), 367–372 (1996)
79. Asch, S.E.: Studies of independence and conformity. a minority of one against a unanimous majority. Psychological Monographs, 70(9, Whole No. 416) (1956)
80. Candid Camera. Human behaviour experiment in lift antics. https://www.youtube.com/watch?v=XZDLbbfT9_Q. Accessed 10 February 2021
81. Geertz, H.: The vocabulary of emotion - a study of Javanese socialization processes. Psychiatry - Interpers. Biol. Process. 22(3), 225–237 (1959)
82. Goffman, E.: The Presentation of Self in Everyday Life. Doubleday, New York (1959)
83. Ekman, P., Friesen, W.: The repertoire of non-verbal behaviour: categories, origins, usage and coding. Semiotica 1(1), 48–98 (1969)
84. Ekman, P.: Biological and cultural contributions to body and facial movement. In: Anthropology of the Body, pp. 34–84. Academic Press, San Diego (1977)
85. Wetherell, M.: Feeling rules, atmospheres and affective practice: some reflections on the analysis of emotional episodes. In: Privilege, Agency and Affect, pp. 221–239. Palgrave Macmillan, London (2013)
86. Frijda, N.H.: The laws of emotion. Am. Psychol. 43(5), 349–358 (1988)
87. Ortony, A., Turner, T.J.: What's basic about basic emotions? Psychol. Rev. 97(3), 315–331 (1990)
88. Lazarus, R.S., Lazarus, B.N.: Passion and Reason: Making Sense of Our Emotions. Oxford University Press, New York (1996)
89. Smith, C. A., & Lazarus, R.S.: Emotion and adaptation. In: Handbook of Personality. Theory and Research, pp. 609–637. Guildford, New York (1990)
90. Smith, E.R., Mackie, D.M.: Dynamics of group-based emotions: insights from intergroup emotions theory. Emot. Rev. 7(4), 349–354 (2015)
91. Manstead, A.S., Fischer, A.H.: Social appraisal. In: Appraisal Processes in Emotion: Theory, Methods, Research, pp. 221–232 (2001)
92. Dewey, J.: Art as Experience. Penguin, London (2005)
93. Ellsworth, P.C., Scherer, K.R.: Appraisal processes in emotion. In: Handbook of Affective Sciences, pp. 572–595 (2003)
94. Maslow, A.H.: A theory of human motivation. Psychol. Rev. 50(4), 370–396 (1943)
95. Stanfill, M.: The interface as discourse: the production of norms through web design. New Media Soc. 17(7), 1059–1074 (2015)
96. Tangney, J.P., Fischer, J. (eds.): Self-Conscious Emotions: The Psychology of Shame, Guilt, Embarrassment, and Pride. Guilford Press, New York (1995)

97. Markus, H.R., Kitayama, S.: Models of agency: sociocultural diversity in the construction of action. In: Nebraska Symposium on Motivation. Cross-Cultural Differences in Perspectives on the Self, vol. 49, pp. 18–74. University of Nebraska Press, Lincoln (2003)

98. Frijda, N.H.: The Emotions. Cambridge University Press, Cambridge (1986)

99. Hochschild, A.: The Managed Heart: Commercialisation of Human Feeling. University of California Press, Berkley (1983)

100. Gordon, S.: The sociology of sentiments and emotion. In: Social Psychology: Sociological Perspectives, pp. 562–592. Basic Books, New York (1981)

101. Frijda, N.: Emotion experience. Cognit. Emot. **19**(4), 473–497 (2005)

Human Research in Technology Design

Pertti Saariluoma(✉)

Jyväskylä University, 40014 Jyväskylä, Finland
ps@jyu.fi

Abstract. Modern technology design processes in intelligent societies are differ-ent from the classic electromechanical technology design processes. Future tech-nology design must be based as much on human research as on natural scientific thinking. Today one can find technologies such as social media applications which are created with minimal technical effort. Thus, understanding the human dimen-sion of technologies is becoming much more important today than in the time of electromechanical technologies. The change in focus motivates to pay attention to the foundational differences between natural science and human research in tech-nology design. The differences between the two traditions have been discussed over the last century, but today the differences between human research and natural science get new forms in designing intelligent technologies.

Keywords: Designing · Human research · Natural science

1 Introduction

Human research is becoming increasingly more important in technology design. Design-ing traditional electromechanical technologies is based on natural scientific and math-ematical thinking [1]. Over the years scientific design and engineering has reached its present forms. However, information technology is different in many respects from the traditional electromechanical technologies because its essence is in intelligent infor-mation processes [2, 3]. Solving problems of intelligence on the basis of mere natural scientific thinking is no longer optimal, and the foundations of the design processes must be rethought.

The invention of the Turing machine meant a revolution from electromechanical thinking to intelligent technologies and it also gave the basic model for intelligent tech-nologies [4, 5]. Turing's mathematical model showed how human thinking can be used in designing intelligent machines. Later, the discussion was expanded into can machines think like people [4–7], and it became evident that machines can capture some aspects of human thinking and for this reason they can carry out intelligence demanding tasks.

Intelligent technologies take part in human work processes. Intelligent machines can be used to free people to other tasks, and they can improve human performance in existing tasks. Information technology has greatly changed work processes in offices since the early 1950's. However, in the future, development will be even more dramatic as the intellectual complexity of machine run tasks shall essentially increase [3].

M. Rauterberg (Ed.): HCII 2021, LNCS 12795, pp. 151–161, 2021.
https://doi.org/10.1007/978-3-030-77431-8_9

Expertise on people and understanding their actions and their lives are presuppositions for constructing a intelligent information society. It will be essential to construct technical systems which can take care of intelligence demanding tasks. Designing such systems, however, requires understanding the action of new systems, what they are supposed to carry out, and how they are should do what they do. As the intelligent processes normally require human information processing, it is evident that human research is a necessary component in designing intelligent technologies.

Designing future intelligent technologies shall thus be linked much more intensively to human research than was necessary in the times of electromechanical technologies. However, human research is meta-scientifically different from traditional natural scientific design thinking and thus it is good to consider that the foundational problems of adding human research into future design thinking requires specific meta-scientific analysis.

Foundationally, integration of human research-based design thinking with traditional natural scientific technology design has its roots deep in the last century European philosophy. The traditional has been divided into Continental and Anglo-Saxon (American and Scandinavian) thinking [7, 8]. The same difference can also be found in the differences between logical empiricism and positivism on the one hand, and phenomenology, existentialism and critical philosophy on the other. Behind the division one can also see the differences between natural sciences and human sociocultural inspired research traditions.

The two traditions, i.e., natural science and human research, have lived separate lives for a century. The difference was already present in Kant's famous remark about heaven above his head and moral law inside himself [9]. However, the new design culture required for developing intelligent technologies and intelligent society should find ways to unify the two ways of thinking. Therefore, it will be essential to find out how the two traditions can be unified in future design processes.

2   Design Thinking

Design processes can be studied as human thinking [10, 11]. When designing, designers try to create something new. Thinking is the mental process which creates these new pieces of information. Thought processes are typical and unique to the human mind and they have been studied in concepts of different research disciplines from psychology to logic and philosophy.

Psychologically, design thinking is based on the contents of information in the minds of the designers. Thoughts are in forms of mental representations. The information in representations is in the form of concepts, emotional schemas, pictures, propositions, stories, and tacit or subconscious intuitive information [11, 12]. Designing people have vast external memories of information from private notes, press articles and television documentaries, to books, company databases and the internet. Human research and scientific knowledge also belong to the pool of knowledge individual designers and design groups use in developing new technologies.

Understanding design processes requires analysis of the information required for the analysis of concrete design thinking. The power of human thinking can be found in its selectivity and power to manipulate information. People concentrate on issues they see relevant for their design goals. In order to be able to mentally represent the things, they have to have information about these issues. The analysis of mentally represented information enables researchers to reflectively think design processes.

The selectivity of human thinking has two sides. On the one hand, people can focus on important issues. They can find relevant topics and they are able to integrate all the necessary knowledge to reach the design goals. However, selectivity can also fixate people in illusionary mental contents [13]. There are situations in which people simply do not see the relevant issues and their meaning. For hundreds of years, people looked how masts of ships rose firstly from the horizon, but they did not understand that the phenomenon was a sign of the earth's form [14].

One explanation for concentrating on irrelevant issues in design thinking is the lack of knowledge. It is easy to believe in credos instead of being aware of research knowledge. The difference is clear, research always presents valid and tested reasons for why some solutions should work. If no one in a design group has a certain relevant piece of information, this often leads to design errors. This is why it is essential to form the teams of designers such that the group has the relevant skills.

The challenge with human research as a component of technical design thinking is, on its deepest level, the meta-scientific difference between human research and natural science [7, 15, 16]. When natural science argumentation is based on causal laws in human research, it is important to understand human intentions. Causal explanation, for example, presupposes that explaining phenomenon emerges before the phenomenon to be explained, while in intentional explaining, the future goal explains what happens now [17]. These differences in the meta-scientific position makes it necessary to consider the foundations of human research applied in design discourse and processes.

A critical difference between science and human research is the notion of meaning, or mental contents. In socio-cultural and parts of psychological research, the information content of thoughts is relevant. The human mind creates mental representations of the external world. In design, the representational contents entail such issues as information contents of design tasks, design problems, concepts, propositions, elements of technologies, and possible solution models. Researchers interested in design thinking should be able to explicate the mental contents of design processes [9, 11]. This can be done, for example, by means of focusing on major research documents in the field such as textbooks and documentary analysis. Here, a philosophical discourse is applied to investigate No fact or theory in research can have an infinitely long chain of supporting argumentation. It is always necessary to stop argumentation at some stage, and for this reason all scientific ideas have their presuppositions or hidden assumptions [11] Hidden assumptions may be explicit or implicit, theoretical or intuitive, but they exist, and there is no single idea in research which does not entail tacit assumptions. We must accept that no percept, no inference or argumentative chain can be free of assumptions, presumptions, or intuitions. Everything cannot be doubted and accepting something without doubt means accepting its certainty on the ground of suppositions.

It is hard to accept that science is always built on preconditions. Social pressures towards the scientific community, scientific self-image, and the need to differentiate scientific knowledge from lay-thinking, pseudoscience, and charlatanism obviously motivates researchers to separate science from all common sense and intuition. Unfortunately, the acceptance of a strict separation would be incorrect and fatal for the practical application of scientific knowledge, scientific self-correction, and hence, it would slow down scientific progress.

Ernst Nagel [18], for Example, Wrote:

"[F]inally, should the formula (i.e., the scientific practice, P. S.) be read as claiming that the practice of scientific method effectively eliminates every form of personal bias or source of error, which might otherwise impair the outcome of the inquiry, and more generally that it assures the truth of every conclusion reached by inquiries employing the method. But no such assurances can in fact be given."

A reason for unwillingness to acknowledge the necessity of preconditions is that the necessity of tacit assumption apparently threatens the credibility of science. If scientific ideas lay on assumption, it is easy to claim that everything in science is wrong. However, the truth of preconditions cannot be resolved on the grounds that they are preconditions. It is possible to have correct assumptions, which eventually prove to be true. In principle, preconditions can be correct or incorrect [11]. The problem is that no one knows if the preconditions are true or false. It is incorrect to think that preconditions are automatically wrong. One cannot say that scientific knowledge or human research is false. If one could, all the scientific knowledge would be false. Actually, all knowledge would be without values. However, scientific ideas form huge coherent webs of information and they are valid because their claims have the best argumentative support [11].

Tacit assumptions are also normal in design thinking, because today design relies on science. Design concepts and solutions entail their presuppositions. Even big companies can fall as a consequence of having adopted mistaken assumptions about markets or technologies. Nokia mobile phones underestimated the importance of the graphic user interface and swiftly lost its dominant market position. It assumed that it would not be so important to develop smartphones, but the markets proved the company had had incorrect intuitions.

Human research is not less intuitive than science. However, these two fields of learning are very different and for this reason the underlying systems of intuitions are very different. Nokia's misconception could have been solved if only the company had paid attention to how human text-related verbal memory and pictorial memory function. This is commonplace knowledge among memory researchers [19], but the company was so technology driven that no-one paid attention to this piece of human research knowledge, even though graphic user interfaces were everyday design solutions in computers. This example illustrates how important it is to get human research as a part of design discourses, and therefore it makes sense to further investigate design to meta-science of design thinking based on human research.

All conceptual, theoretical, and methodological ideas must meet in facts. Facts form "the centre of gravity" in modern research and design thinking. Indeed, in facts, thoughts meet reality. Facts have dual commitments. On the one hand they depend on the conceptual structure of the experiment, given concepts and design models or philosophical observations. Especially, it is important to see how human research facts can be integrated to support the design solutions.

Design solutions must be justified. Designers should have good reason for why the solution should work [11]. The reasons must be based on scientific research as research is the best guarantee for the validity of used knowledge. Validity is important as false assumption and false information, in actual products, cause harms and accidents of different types. Good examples are the space shuttle Challenger, Chernobyl, Bhopal, and the Boeing 727 MAX. Actually, errors of different types in design thinking are based on using invalid information in design decisions.

The complexity of modern technologies makes it understandable that relativity small lapses of attention thinking can have catastrophic consequences. The passenger ship "Estonia", which sank in 1994 taking the lives of over 800 people, is a good example [20]. It began to sink twenty years before the actual accident because designers had made seriously mistaken solutions. The complexity of modern work life is an important cause for accumulating failures with devastating final outcomes.

3 Explaining

Explaining is the method of connecting individual phenomena in both research and design with researched knowledge. In the nineteen sixties, the basic models of explaining in science were developed and they still have their role in design thinking. Nevertheless, the discussion in the sixties was more concerned on the nature of scientific knowledge rather than the role of science in design practices.

The modern conception of explaining relies on the strictly logical use of regularities and invariances. The best-known individual schema for the logic of explanation was developed by Hempel [21]. According to this covering law model, explanation is based on covering laws and individual phenomena can be explained as examples of the covering law. Thus, the explanation for a broken pipeline in winter could be the law that the volume of frozen water is larger than the volume of liquid water. Thus, icy water breaks unprotected pipelines.

The covering law model is logically consistent, and it can be used in several different types of explanatory problems. With inessential variations, the model can also be used in predicting, i.e., in explaining future and past events. Thus, we can thus know that all unprotected pipelines full of water will break in the future as they have done in the past.

However, the covering law model has problems within human research. It is seldom applied in practical psychology. Explaining and prediction in human research uses intuitive practices related to the covering law model. Researchers make their explanatory conclusions on the grounds of general principles and particular occurrences. It seems clear that Hempel's logical schema expresses something essential about the intuitions of researchers in explaining. The tacit logic of explaining is certainly very close to the covering law model because the model would be very counter-intuitive it had never reached its position.

In spite of the undeniable success, Hempel's classic theory of explanation has also met with numerous problems. Especially difficult has been explaining human action. It is very unclear how far the covering law model can be applied to social and historical phenomena. The model has acquired even less success among humanistic researchers. Dray showed its implausibility in historical explanation [22]. If historians should explain Royal succession in Britain, how could they use causal laws? They could find numerous particular occurrences such as how the parliament feels. However, there are no general causal laws of the form: Each time parliament feels itself threatened, it wants to make changes to the settlement rules of the crown. Historical events are often singular and therefore, it would make much sense to think that there are covering laws in historical issues.

History is not the only critical research field for traditional thinking. The challenge of other fields of humanistic research may be even more problematic. In thinking laws and ethics, the covering laws model is inadequate, because causal explanation does not have any real relevance in these fields of learning. Causal analysis does not tell us why van Gogh used colours as he did. Causal analysis is impotent even when verb valences or systems of laws are considered. Causal analysis is by and large irrelevant in humanistic research. Instead, attention in explaining should be improved by moving the focus of explanations from causal laws to human research and analysis of intentions.

4   Analysis of Actions in Human Research

Human research has a different topic, structure and methodology from traditional natural science inspired research. Human research, also often referred to as human science or Geisteswissenschaften [23, 24] is research targeted to understand cultural, ethical, legal and historical phenomena. It essentially refers to understanding why people act as they act or how they should act to reach their goals, and in the end, the best possible quality of life [25, 26]. Important intellectual movements in this respect were phenomenology, hermeneutics, and existentialism. Also, humanists and psychological researchers have developed the analysis in this field.

The core of understanding is in deep encoding of how people experience and act in different situations. This means answers to the question why people act as they act. The questions in human research are often idiosyncratic. Why the Norwegian royal family escaped from their country during the war or why British royals kept themselves in Britain? In a larger perspective, researchers can look for explanations for social phenomena as well. For example, why people follow sport events and are ready to pay to watch them? Thus, understanding means explication of the the meanings and motivations people have for acting in some particular manner.

Classical analyses of actions have been externalist or behaviourist. This means that actions have been described on an external level. However, in modern human research, the notion of action should be studied in internal and representational terms. Decisive in analysing action is mental contents or information contents of human mental representations [6, 27, 28]. The explanation of actions requires understanding how people represent and experience situations, and why they represent it in the way they do represent them. In short, this can be called mental contents. Thus, it makes sense to redesign the analysis of understanding on modern concepts.

Understanding – saying why it makes sense to have a specific kind of action on the grounds of mental content. Napoleon mistakenly assumed that he could win the war against Russia as he had won practically all wars. He did not understand how different the circumstances in Russia were compared to central Europe or Egypt [29]. In a way, Napoleon made an induction error by thinking that the past success can safeguard future success irrespective of the prevailing circumstances [30]. Thus, understanding means understanding of the relevant actors' mental contents in a particular case.

The analysis of mental contents can be based on qualitative methods developed at the end of the previous century [31, 32]. The methods from protocol to documentary analysis can be used to explicate the mental contents of individuals and group mental representations. Thus, the classical analysis of understanding, and the analysis of actions can be given a new form on the grounds of qualitative, cognitive, and emotional psychology.

Human research has its role in modern technology design because it can make it understandable. People organise their actions around technologies. Numerous people will act similarly and use the same technology for similar purposes. Surgeons in different operation rooms apply minimally invasive surgery technologies. They share the same form of life in the way they act [26]. Understanding the structure of the form of life enables a researcher to improve the technical artefacts and work models typical for this particular form of life. The analysis of thought models and other representational content elements typical to this, or to any social form of life, is essential in designing and developing new technologies. Thus, modern analysis of understanding gets an important role in innovating new technologies.

Technologies have always been for people to use and for this reason human research has its role in technology development. The differences between natural scientific and human research are difficult to overcome. If human research is applied in natural scientific issues, it does not provide sufficient analytical power to discuss substance. However, natural science is equally impotent in solving issues relevant in the human dimension of technology. This is why it is essential to think how the two world views can be unified in the practice of design thinking.

5   Explanatory Discourses and Frameworks

Design problems differ from scientific problems. The designer's task is to construct artefacts, information structures or technologies to help users reach a given goal in their life. For example, when designing any technology, the artefact helps people reach their practical goals without causing risks and satisfies the users' needs in their lives [1]. This is why design problems commonly arise from the recognition of a need that people wish to satisfy.

The logical connection between science and design is built on the notion of truth. Deontological propositions can be considered to have a truth value if there is a possible world in which they are true. Only impossible propositions are false in a deontological sense. This rather obscure claim simply means that designed technologies can work if they can be realized, and they can be realized if the principles upon which they are built are true when the technology is used.

In contemporary engineering, basic sciences such as mathematics, physics and chemistry provide conceptual and empirical tools that make design possible [1]. History has shown that science is a prerequisite of modern innovations. Einstein, for example, under-stood the intimate connection between matter and energy. He also realised that it was possible to create a chain reaction when newly freed electrons meet new nuclei. This theoretical phenomenon was later applied by Fermi in nuclear power stations and Oppen-heimer's group in creating the atom bomb. Here, basic natural science created tools for very complicated engineering thinking and applications. In the same way, social sciences can create important visions for political and social thinking.

Human visual and pictorial memory is superior compared to human verbal memory [19]. This simple psychological fact explains why graphic user interfaces are in general better than alphanumeric. It is easier for people to remember interaction relevant issues. Chemistry does not have the power of expression to help in solving such issues. It is thus necessary to organise the design discourse. In that, a good conceptual tool is the explanatory framework [33].

Explanation should be based on science and scientific principles (Fig. 1). When designing for life, it is essential to search for explanatory solutions. The main challenge is to unify design problems, scientific truths, and explanatory grounds in a sense-making manner. In practice, design is not one single discourse but depending on the design problem, different types of discourses come into focus. Natural sciences are required in solving such technical problems as consumption of power or weight of the product. Human research is essential in usability, user experience, and organisational issues.

One method of keeping things in good order is to organise a different discourse to separate explanatory frameworks. This is the way to unify design questions with relevant knowledge to generate argumentatively grounded solutions.

Problem * Relevant knowledge => Solutions

Fig. 1. Explanatory framework

In this model of general explanatory framework (Fig. 1), a designer binds the inter-action problem and relevant scientific knowledge to each other and generates a solution [26, 31]. Each design thought sequence of this type can be seen as a separate explanatory framework, but scientifically grounded design processes are generally characterised by this schema.

Each explanatory framework activates its own discourse. Surgical equipment is used in an operating theatre. It is one discourse to create sufficient lighting, another to make the required screens so well organised that operating doctors can get all the knowledge they need without effort. A third problem is to develop collaborations between the operating personnel so smooth that the operating people can effectively work to save the patients. Solving the problems requires its own design discourse with different research knowledge.

Each design discourse must be linked with scientific information. Problems must be solved, whether designers have scientific knowledge or not. If they do not have the relevant framework knowledge to make proper design solutions, they have to use their intuitions. The have to think a support for the solutions on the grounds of their common-sense knowledge. This may be due to the facts that the knowledge does not exist, or because designers do not have the required knowledge. Ideally, all design problems should be solved on the grounds of the best human research or scientific knowledge that exists.

6 Human Research and Natural Science in Technology Design

Explanatory frameworks provide a meta-scientific model how one can organise the different scientific and human research discourses relevant in solving different problems. Technologies are combinations of human actions and tools to reach the goals of these actions. For this reason, each technology must concentrate on both people and the technical artefacts they use. Design groups must organise themselves following the problem they have to solve and the discourse they have to organise for solving the particular problem.

Natural science provides knowledge about natural phenomena. These phenomena include chemical, physical, and biological phenomena. Typical examples of the first kind are fire, combustion, or chemical reactions. Physical phenomena can be friction, thermodynamics, or the behaviour of planets. Finally, biology is about living organisms' birth, death, growth, or phenomena typical to population ecology. All of these natural scientific phenomena can be used in solving design problems of their kind in developing new technologies.

Natural sciences have their own principles and methods. They use observation and experimentation of collecting well founded facts. Natural scientific phenomena are determined and regular [32]. Therefore, it has become possible to find very strongly founded and regular principles, called laws, typical for natural scientific phenomena.

The task of engineering is to organise a physical object in a purposeful manner following the natural laws [1]. Thus, design means organising things in the way that they can serve for the given human purposes. This goal is as valid with bridges and buildings as well as with modern AI technical artefacts. Often mathematical knowledge is required in developing engineering solutions of different types and for this reason this field of research is seen as a natural science.

The predictability of natural science helps in technology design, as it makes it easier to use this information in supporting design decisions. It is not necessary to rely on only trial and error and traditional type thinking. It is possible to use mathematical and physical knowledge, for example, to be sure that constructions do not collapse. Thus, the laws of nature support the design of physical products.

However, human research is different. The laws of physics and chemistry very seldom provide important information for supporting design decisions. For example, the position of a technical artefact in human life must be analysed in concepts of human research. There is no law of physics that could inform us about the ethical consequences of social media or AI applications in governance. Physics, chemistry, or biology do not have concepts or laws to analyse and design issues relevant for human individuals and social action.

In most of the electromechanical technology human factors are easy and common-sense issues. People walk on the street, and to analyse this action sufficiently accurately for engineering design is not difficult. However, the complexity of technologies has increased, and it is no longer possible to solve design problems intuitively. Cockpits of fighter airplanes, for example, were already so complex that it was necessary to develop a new research area called human factors [26]. This area later became usability, and serious work in it required in-depth human research knowledge. When ICT-consumer electronics got into the mass production state, it became necessary to apply human research into issues of how people feel about these products, and finally, with the development of intelligent technologies, it has become essential to start thinking about the holistic and social issues such as ethics and the required social actions to regulate the human side of human technology interaction.

A sign of transformation from electromechanical technologies to human research relevant technologies is the service industry. Knowledge of platforms and other basic information, but the creative technology development problems are human problems. The human dimension is the moving part, as it is possible to build on one single platform and it is possible to build an unlimited number of services for human actions.

Technology design is thus no longer a discussion on technical artefact and physics. It is essential to also study human capacity and willingness to use technical artefacts, and especially, the functions of new technologies in human life [26]. Ethics is no longer a less essential an issue than electronics in design discussions. Consequently, the focus of philosophical thinking will move from natural scientific and positivist discourse to psychosocial and "Geistewissenschaftliche" or human research-oriented discourses.

Today, two major traditions inside scientific research, natural science and Geisteswissenschaft should be unified. Natural science analyses natural phenomena and Geisteswissenschaft focusses on mental and cultural systems. Sociohistorical and psychological approaches to what happens in the human mind, and consequently in actions and their systems, provides a natural scientific thinking completing research direction to mind.

The term Geist or spirit may appear strange today. However, if we think of the vast cognitive research which has penetrated into all the major domains of human research, it is clear that the word Geist is today expressed in such concepts as information, representation and cognition [6, 35]. to get a conception of modern cognitively oriented human research). One can thus take the issues and the ideas of Geisteswissenschaft under scrutiny inside modern cognitive science and cognitive research.

The long dispute between logical empiricism and positivism with human research can be understood by analysing the foundational intuitions of the two traditions. Causal natural science and intentional and understanding human research look at technology and technology design from different perspectives. Very roughly, one can argue that the first is effective in providing support for artefact design, while the latter opens the human dimension of technologies in all of its complexities. Thus, in future technology design it is possible to see the two directions as complementary rather than controversial.

References

1. Pahl, G., Beitz, W., Feldhusen, J., Grote, K.H.: Engineering Design: A Systematic Approach. Springer, Berlin (2007). https://doi.org/10.1007/978-1-84628-319-2
2. Fukuda, K.: Science, technology and innovation ecosystem transformation towards society 5.0. Int. J. Prod. Econ. **220**, 3–14 (2020)
3. Tegmark, M.: Life 3.0. Penguin Books, Harmondsworth (2017)
4. Turing, A. M.: On computable numbers, with an application to the entscheidungs problem. Proc. London Math. Soc. 42, 230–265 (1936–1937)
5. Turing, A.M.: Computing machinery and intelligence. Mind **59**, 433–460 (1950)
6. Newell, A., Simon, H.A.: Human Problem Solving. Prentice-Hall, Engelwood Cliffs (1972)
7. Radnitsky, G.: Contemporary schools of metascience. Akademieförlaget, Göteborg (1971)
8. Kant, I.: Kritik der reinen Vernunft. [The critique of pure reason]. Felix Meiner, Hamburg (1781/1976)
9. Cross, N.: Designerly ways of knowing. Des. Stud. **3**, 221–227 (1982)
10. Simon, H.A.: The Sciences of Artificial. MIT Press, Cambridge (1969)
11. Saariluoma, P.: Foundational Analysis: Presuppositions in Experimental Psychology. Routledge, London (1997)
12. Bunge, M.: Intuition in science. Greenwood, Westport (1962)
13. Duncker, K.: On problem-solving. Psychol. Monogr. 58 (1945)
14. Hanson, N.R.: Patterns of Discovery. Cambridge University Press, Cambridge (1956)
15. Brentano, F.: Psychologie vom empirischen Standpunkt. Felix Meiner, Hamburg (1874/1955)
16. Stegmueller, W.: Hauptströmungen der Gegenwartsphilosphie. Kröner, Stuttgart (1969)
17. Von Wright, G.H.: Explanation and understanding. Routledge, London (1971)
18. Nagel, E.: The Structure of Science. Harcourt, New York (1961)
19. Baddeley, A.: Working Memory, Thought, and Action. Oxford University Press, Oxford (2007)
20. Loppuraportti [Final report] MV Estonia. Edita, Helsinki (2000)
21. Hempel, C.: Aspects of Scientific Explanation. Free Press, New York (1965)
22. Dray, W.: Laws and Explanations in History. Oxford University Press, Oxford (1957)
23. Dilthey, W.: Der Aufbau der Geschitlichen Welt in de Geisteswissenschaften. Surkamp, Frankfurth am Main (1990)
24. Weber, M.: Gesammelte Aufsätze zur Wissenschaftlehre. Mohr, Tuebingen (1988)
25. Habermas, J.: Diskursethik. Surkamp, Frankfurt am Main (2009)
26. Saariluoma, P., Cañas, J., Leikas, J.: Designing for Life. Macmillan, London (2016)
27. Allport, D. A.: Patterns and actions: cognitive mechanisms are content specific. In Claxton, G. (ed.) Cognitive Psychology: New Directions, pp. 26–64. Routledge and Kegan Paul, London (1980)
28. Fodor, J.: A Theory of Mental Contents. MIT-Press, Cambridge, Mass (1990)
29. Caulaincourt, A. A.: With Napoleon in Russia. Pickle partners, Auckland (1935/2016)
30. Saariluoma, P.: Ajattelu työelämässä [Thinking in work life]. Wsoy, Porvoo (2002)
31. Ericsson, K.A., Simon, H.A.: Protocol Analysis. MIT Press, Cambridge (1984)
32. Patton, M.: Qualitative Evaluation and Research Methods. Sage, Newbury (1990)
33. Saariluoma, P.: Explanatory frameworks for interaction design. In: Pirhonen, A., Saariluoma, P., Isomäki, H., Roast, C. (eds.) Future Interaction Design, pp. 67–83. Springer, London (2005). https://doi.org/10.1007/1-84628-089-3_5
34. Bunge, M.: Scientific research I-II. Springer, New York (1967). https://doi.org/10.1007/978-3-642-48138-3
35. Bechtel, W., Graham, G. (eds.): A Companion to Cognitive Science. Basil Blackwell, Oxford (1999)

Research on the Public Design Innovation Method Based on the Sharing Concept of Cultural Computing

Xin Zhang and Jieming Hu[✉]

Donghua University, West Yan-an Road 1882, Shanghai 200051, People's Republic of China
hjm@dhu.edu.cn

Abstract. Cultural computing requires not only the technical guidance at the elite level, but also the effective participation of the public, and the new development of cultural computing under the concept of sharing. The public can participate in the co-creation and sharing process of cultural computing quickly and with low threshold. Based on a large number of design projects and open design platform of research in the early stage, the author of this paper proposes an effective path for the public to participate in design innovation in the context of cultural computing, so as to solve the technical gap between the public and cultural computing. This paper proposes the concept of "public design innovation" based on the concept of cultural computing sharing, and believes that "public design innovation" has three basic characteristics: openness, decentralization and living growth. The public is both a user and a creator and contributor of cultural computing, and in the process of using various open design platforms, they can effectively use them in tandem to form a cultural computing "skill tree" that meets their own design needs. In this process, it is necessary to create a basic cognition and skill organization structure for cultural computing, and apply their "skill tree" to different application scenarios of cultural computing. The author builds a framework model for serving individual design innovation of the public from three levels: the occurrence layer, the condition layer and the activity layer of design idea realization, and uses a modular approach to effectively connect various platform skills to realize the rapid prototype transformation needs of individual design innovation, and illustrates the specific application methods with public design innovation cases.

Keywords: Cultural computing · Shared concept · Public design innovation

1 The Trend of Sharing and Co-creation in Cultural Computing

1.1 Cultural Computing Needs to Serve the Public

With the rapid development of global democratic design process, design sharing and co-creation have become an important development trend. Cultural computing, based on artificial intelligence and Internet technologies, iterates the process of design creativity. On the one hand, the continuous improvement of computer technology makes

© Springer Nature Switzerland AG 2021
M. Rauterberg (Ed.): HCII 2021, LNCS 12795, pp. 162–174, 2021.
https://doi.org/10.1007/978-3-030-77431-8_10

the prototype realization process of creative design faster, greatly shortening the creative production time; on the other hand, the improvement of technology provides more realization paths for the realization of creativity and richer output results. The impact of the Internet economy has also allowed more users to enjoy the benefits of cultural computing, and the output can quickly enter the "long tail" market, the United States and guest sports promoters Chris Anderson about this aspect of the theoretical analysis in his book "the long tail theory" (Anderson 2004) in detail, in short, it means that as smart technologies become more widespread and accessible, niche products designed and made by the public will take a very significant share of the market, a share that rivals the market for products created by the mainstream elite. This also shows from another perspective, in the future, the masses will need personalized design and experience, and cultural computing is in line with this trend. Culture calculation first is based on the results of the computer technology and social cultural depth integration, and is used to promote the spread of excavation, culture and prosperity, the concept of the earlier by Japanese scholars Tosa son is proposed (Tosa 2004), and through experiments such as ZENetic system to illustrate the accuracy of calculation in promoting cultural exchanges to explain and spread widely, but also to discover and excellent culture heritage. The combination of computer technology and cultural field can effectively reveal the law of local cultural development and form a visual form of communication. Therefore, it can be seen that the essence of cultural computing is based on public service.

Cultural computing is closely related to art and design. Naoko Tosa's practice of cultural computing covers ink art, media art, interactive installations, product design, etc. (Tosa 2016), which enables a lot of art and design to be communicated to the public in a convenient, scientific and effective way. The extraction of cultural genes, the quantification of cultural characteristics, and the structural quantification of cultural data are often difficult to communicate to the public in a simple and interesting form, especially for the understanding of cultures with large spatial and temporal spans in the conventional state is a slow process that accumulates over time, and cross-cultural communication is even more difficult due to the existence of cultural metacognitive barriers. Cultural computing uses computer technology to try to explain some of the laws of culture and improve the public understanding of culture, especially through the visual and artistic means to more intuitively translate some abstract and difficult cultural connotations. In particular, cultural computing for visual analysis is often very intuitive and effective, because more than 80% of the information acquired by human beings comes from visual perception. Visualized presentation of complex content can effectively enhance the cultural wisdom behind the data (Yinghai et al. 2015).

1.2 Cultural Computing Requires Public Participation in Co-creation

Cultural computing requires not only the technical guidance at the elite level, but also the effective participation of the public, and the new development of cultural computing under the concept of sharing. The public can participate in the co-creation and sharing process of cultural computing quickly and with low threshold. The popularization of technology reduces the difficulty of public participation in design innovation under the background of cultural computing, and solves the technical gap between the public and cultural computing. Many technologies and concepts related to cultural computing began to appear in the form of open source platform, which made the main body of design innovation no longer dominated by elite designers. The formation of open source software and hardware also enabled the public to participate in the process of design innovation and became a new mainstream force. In 2016, the Chinese Academy of Engineering released the "Roadmap of China's Innovation Design", one of the results of the major project of "Innovation Design Development Strategy Research", which pointed out that "user participation in innovation design has become possible, and innovation design is undergoing a process of grassroots, popularization and democratization. This indicates that cultural computing requires public participation in the process of connecting technology and culture, and the innovation process of cultural computing is a process of public co-creation. Only based on the continuous participation of the public can more direct personalized innovation results or indirect user experience information be generated, so as to enrich and interpret the diversity of contents in the cultural computing vision, and promote the methods and results of cultural computing to be continuously accurate. Therefore, it is particularly important to explore the public design innovation method based on the shared concept of cultural computing.

In addition, the operating experience of design from software to hardware is becoming more and more accessible and inexpensive, which also lays the foundation for the popularization and development of cultural computing in the field of public innovation design. On the one hand, more ordinary individuals in the society can directly participate in the design, and the thinking and skills of traditional design are no longer exclusive to the designer community, and the "professionalism" of the traditional designer community has been differentiated and reduced. New technology innovations, on the other hand, even brought a large number of traditional design jobs out, where can be quantified, calculable, modular, repetitive, only by memory and practice can master the design will be replaced by artificial intelligence, such as Ali Intelligent Design Lab developed the "deer class" system, which has nearly 100 million increasingly high design quality of the poster production every day, and in 2018, "deer class" system can even reach the market senior designer level. On the other hand, the content replaced by technology can also be more quickly fed back to the public, so that the public can more effectively participate in the decision-making process of design. The 2018 Design Artificial Intelligence Report released by Tongji Tezan predicted that 70% of designers in the industry would be eliminated in the near future. Public participation to create the design process is becoming increasingly generalized, such as "teamlab: the world of water particles in oil tank" immersion in the exhibition, just because of the diversity of public participation makes the content of the exhibition has been generated, the scene of the visual culture has been deduced, the role of cultural calculation under the participation of the public continues to exert effect, leave the public participation in the innovation process, cultural content calculation will become meaningless. At present, based on the calculation of the horizon, from the joint decision making of urban public space transformation to the real-time feedback of product user experience, from the content generation of immersive exhibition public participation to the public participation of various open source platforms making the data platform more sensitive and perfect, from the personalized creative prototype realization of number system to the creative matching marketing process of online information precision, all these are the inevitable trends of public participation in design innovation based on the cultural computing vision. These are the inevitable trends of public participation in design innovation based on cultural computing.

1.3 The Concept of "public Design Innovation" Based on the Shared Concept of Cultural Computing is Proposed

How can the public with zero design skills but creative design needs quickly achieve innovative design in a short period of time? The biggest difference between public participation in design innovation and design innovation by a team of designers is that the latter has received the professional training and mastered the thinking and skills of design innovation, while the design wisdom hidden in the latter is limited, design innovation can be set to the greatest extent of public participation in the intelligence, the different knowledge background and work background, the different background of experience through design innovation activity together. In public collective community, for example, based on the family as the unit of the public in design innovation still has great potential, the community is closer to the end of the consumer groups, more is to design innovative application scenario, as Chris Anderson think products to build the digital revolution is not only the optimization of manufacturing, but also more importantly will be extended to the general public.[1] To stimulate the enthusiasm of the public design innovation and improve the design participation ability,we need to help the public to solve basic technical barriers, therefore, cultural sharing of computing is extremely important.Not all cultural computing today is shared, especially some cultural computing projects that provide professional support for large companies are often not open to the public and enter the closed-loop design applications of small groups of companies, which causes the disadvantage that companies or technology providers need to spend a lot of human, material and financial resources to make these cultural computing platforms with some intelligence smarter and more flexible, and the result is often a disappointment. While some open culture calculation share the project into the benign cycle of development, through a large number of users experience unceasingly, culture data constantly enrich the basis of the calculation, the degree of intelligence and sharing more and more high, the current various computing based on the culture background of search engine promotion of intelligence is a typical case, through the record of a large number of Internet users daily shopping preferences to generate some users might like stereospecific commodity information, and even users buy goods online pay close attention to the length of time, and so on, all feedback to the culture as the user parameter to the platform, Similar information is provided to consumers with directed feedback. For another example, many current video apps, such as Douyin, Kuaishou and WeChat Short Video, also measure the public's preferences through the screening of content and viewing time of each video by the client, which serves as the data basis for continuously providing personalized content. Search engine only a simple of the calculation of the application, because in the process of the public, although also participate in the construction of the content, but the design innovation of participation is not high, the moment a lot in terms of culture as the core of open source design platform requires the public to participate

---

[1] Chris Anderson, Translated by Xiao Xiao, Maker -- New Industrial Revolution [M], CITIC Publishing House, 2015.

in together, let the culture process of calculation is more accurate and fast, such as to the public can make an outfit design one-stop platform "cool" and "imagination", etc., the detailed analysis in the case analysis of below will be focused on. Therefore, "public design innovation" based on the shared concept of cultural computing is an important trend in the development of cultural computing, and also an important way to link cultural computing and the public. The shared concept of cultural computing can be closely related to public innovation in art painting, graphic design, packaging design and environmental design.

2   Public Design System Framework and Innovative Methods Based on Cultural Computing Sharing

2.1   The Basic Characteristics and Structure of the Framework Model

The public design system based on the sharing of cultural computing has three basic characteristics: openness, decentralization and growth of living state. The public is not only the user of cultural computing, but also the creator and contributor of cultural computing. Openness is the basis of cultural computing sharing. The computing process for different cultures can be freely used by the public. The open source process can generate more application scenarios and basic data, so as to make the functions of cultural computing more powerful and sensitive. In addition to ensuring openness to users, openness also needs to ensure the involvement of business, entertainment and education, and fully release the vitality of innovative elements such as information, talent, technology and capital. The innovation process of public participation in cultural computing requires the integration of some other dimensions to ensure the interest and interaction of the system, which can be more conducive to improving public participation. Culture in the process of calculation for the public service to ensure the decentralization, the system is usually distributed, more nodes and grid, everyone is fair because only the public participation, to ensure that cultural calculation process and the result is equal opportunity for every public and true, when the interests of the privileged, the calculation result of culture will unavoidably produce a tendency to change, and this change is not the result of the widespread public will, is calculated against culture Shared purpose, because the real results after interference has not made public by privileged access. Calculated culture sharing of public design system with the public need to continue to participate in and living condition, the process of going through vision, resource integration, carrier construction and iterative update four basic process, and the four process is often the cycle, can continue to make the system level. In addition, the live state growth of the system is also reflected in the system itself, which has a better self-correction and adjustment function, when the system errors, can be timely self-repair, and continue to ensure the normal operation of the system.

According to the law of the realization of design creativity, the framework model of public design innovation serving the sharing of cultural computing can be set up from the occurrence, condition and activity levels of cultural computing. System layer is the demand of design innovation in public sources, system need to build on the public management correctly express demand information collector, access to the public facing the pain points, problems and requirements, etc., because the public is not professional stylist, therefore in the process of use logical expression demand exist certain obstacles, culture work computing needs, by text, data, and a variety of structural problems, to get each participating culture calculation of real design requirements of the public individual, and translating cultural computing language, recognition and understanding by the computer. System layer to construct the conditions of some effective subsystem module to ensure that information from happening layer by effective treatment, such as the establishment of physical or virtual innovation space system for public activities provide effective carrier, establishing evaluation system to ensure that every link of the process of public design innovation is feasible, establish an effective tool for system to ensure that public participation in the process of design innovation implementation skills conditions, establish effective communication system to ensure that public participation in the process of design innovation can get timely guidance and obtain the real-time communication, team to participate in the possibility of, etc. System is to build a series of process of the thematic activities, procedural activities, targeted and practical activities, etc., let the information and conditions of the layer of support through activity layer series, pertinence and system of activities to respond, such as through culture, for different public design innovation needs to provide the corresponding content, layer conditions also need to be equipped with corresponding effective support to jointly promote the implementation of innovative activities. (Fig. 1).

2.2 System Framework of Cultural Computing Technology Tool Support[2]

Public design innovation based on cultural computing sharing needs to realize the need for rapid prototype transformation of individual design innovation by effectively linking various platform skills through modular means. Therefore, how to categorize various technical tools modularly according to the needs of public design innovation is an important research issue to be studied. Culture Shared computing based public design system is inseparable from the support of technical tool, and because of the rich variety of technical tools and the rapid iteration of tools, we need to use the system classification method to culture to the public effectively classified computing tools, which can enhance the public know about these tools technology rapidly, and also facilitate the establishment of skill perceptions that meet their own needs on this basis. People are inventing new design tools, improving the production and transformation efficiency of designs, and thus changing the way of life. Therefore, the new tools invented also shape people. With the development of digital manufacturing technology, customized and personalized production can be popularized and applied in public innovation activities. Chris Anderson called these convenient digital manufacturing tool systems such as 3D printing "four desktop factories", including 3D printers that can print more and more things in the future. This is digital manufacturing. Typical representatives of "addition" tools, CNC machines and laser cutting machines are typical representatives of digital manufacturing "subtraction" tools, 3D scanners realize the capture of realistic three-dimensional objects.[3] Of course,

---

[2] The classification methods and some academic views on public design innovation tools in this section are derived from the author's book < *The Field of Design Maker Education* > published by Zhejiang People's Fine Arts Publishing House in 2020.

[3] Chris Anderson. Maker -- New Industrial Revolution [M]. Beijing: CITIC Press, 2015:105–112.

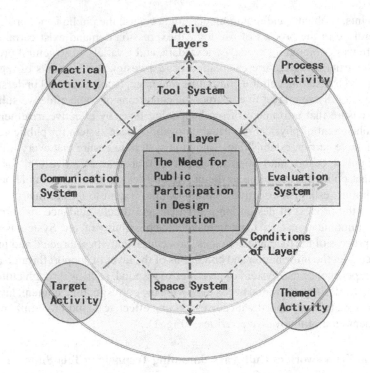

Fig. 1. Framework model of public design innovation based on cultural computing sharing (Picture source: drawn by the author)

the technical tools for public participation in cultural computing can explore various combinations and classification forms according to their own development needs and application scenarios. Professor Neil Gershenfeld, the founder of MIT's Fablab Number System Workshop, once proposed that the core technical capabilities that should be available in the creation of (almost) all things include 2D and 3D design and scanning, additive manufacturing and subtractive manufacturing, circuit creation and Embedding and programming of links, calculations.[4] The configuration system of this public design innovation tool has a strong scientific basis and reference value, and is undergoing the public design innovation practice test of the global Fablab network distribution, and is creating a large number of individualizations in accordance with the needs of regional culture and life around the world Design works. The technical tool support for public participation in cultural computing can be divided into three subsystems: hardware tools, software tools, and thinking tools, and the three systems can be used in conjunction with each other. The hardware tool system is dominated by digital manufacturing tools and open source hardware tools. Digital manufacturing tools rely on computer and Internet technology to analyze and process creative information in digital form, and then output and transform it into creative physical products or virtual products. The most common

---

[4] Neil Gershenfeld. Design Reality [M]. Ding Junfeng et al., translated. Beijing: CITIC Press, 2019:170–171.

and convenient digital manufacturing tool is the 3D printer. According to the different transformation forms of creative prototypes, we can categorize digital manufacturing tools into subtractive category tools and additive category tools. The subtractive tool is to gradually reduce the unnecessary parts of the raw materials by engraving, cutting, hollowing, grinding, cutting and other forms of the physical object. Additive category tools are the process of increasing materials from less to more through continuous stacking, stacking, and pasting. Open source hardware means that it has strong compatibility and versatility. Everyone can use and modify the programming code on the computer so that these hardware can be recombined according to each person's creative needs. For example, the Arduino circuit board and various electronic components are open source hardware. Creatives can realize different creative functions by entering visual programming codes on the Arduino circuit board and then connecting different components to the board as needed. In addition, the commonly used virtual experience devices such as VR glasses can also be regarded as an open source hardware device, which can be connected to different computing devices, and can be used in conjunction with VR handheld controllers and other related devices to output simulated experience information. You can also enter feedback information from the experiencer. The software tool system can be divided into creative expression tools, graphic design tools, programming tools and so on. Creative expression tools are tools for visualizing creativity in the process of public innovation practice, helping the public to share and publicize designs. For example, various H5 generation platforms such as "Yi Qi Xiu" and "MAKA" can quickly publicize and share their creative ideas on WeChat and other public platforms based on the large number of templates provided by the software. Graphic design tools mainly refer to software that can quickly generate various visual graphics, such as the rapid generation software "Tu Biao Show" for chart data visualization. You only need to select the required chart type on the online platform, and then modify the data, you can quickly Realize data visualization, and can quickly generate sharing reports. Programming tools are also tools that the public needs in the current innovative design process. Some high-level programming software such as C language is difficult for the general public to grasp. Therefore, some graphical visualization programming languages such as Scratch, Arduino, etc. can help the public quickly realize various Programming operation and use in conjunction with open source hardware. (Fig. 2) The process of public participation in design innovation requires many corresponding design makers' thinking tools to form a systematic "toolbox". The design maker thinking tool here is actually a lot of design practice strategies and methods, such as the mind mapping method, user portrait method, SWOT analysis, business model diagram and other methods in the design analysis process, in the design creative decision-making and evaluation stage You can use sentiment measurement, goal weighting method.[5] Of course, each method needs to be used in conjunction with the specific problem situation. It can be used alone or in a combination of multiple methods. Each method has its advantages and disadvantages. You should pay attention to the process of combining multiple methods. The principle of maximizing strengths and avoiding weaknesses. (Xin 2020).

---

[5] Relevant methods are compiled and cited from the School of Industrial Design and Engineering, Delft University, Annemiek van Boeijen. Design methods and strategies: Delft Design Guide [M]. Hubei: Huazhong University of Science and Technology Press, 2017: 21–157.

Fig. 2. Creative practice using open source software and hardware (Photo source: self-shot by the research team)[6]

2.3   The Implementation Path and Operation Method of Public Design Innovation

The public design innovation based on cultural computing needs effective implementation path and operation method to ensure the reliability of the results. The implementation path of public participation in design innovation needs to conform to the basic process of design innovation, which involves the introduction of design thinking. The process of design thinking is relatively complex, and for professional designers, it is the design experience and method acquired through long-term training. The Institute of Design at Stanford has published "An Introduction to Design Thinking Process", which points out the five steps of Design Thinking.Since the public is not a professional designer and does not have enough time and energy to get training in design thinking, but we can use five steps of design thinking to make design easier. This design thinking process can be simplified as five innovation design process, namely the present usually discussed "empathy - definition - innovation - prototype – test" five steps, the five widely agreed to be the process can be calculated by culture help obtain more effectively enforced, "empathy" is actually in the process of design pays attention to empathy to understand and find the problem, can interact through immersive experience culture computation method for the public to quickly get empathy, to realize the realistic problems and the demand of self "empathy", speed up the understanding process of empathy. "Definition" is a problem to analyze correctly and objectively, to form effective associated design interests and needs, this is also the design and analysis process, this process also can use culture to simplify the calculation, such as user's portrait and mind mapping in the process of traditional design, etc., can be calculated by culture method and fast access, save a lot of time. "Innovation" is the process of creative design, the process

---

[6] The author of this picture was published in the book < *The Field of Design Maker Education* >, published by Zhejiang People's Fine Arts Publishing House.

is often the most difficult and culture calculation in the advantages of this process is to provide a lot of effective reference, reference this mass type template can provide the public with the personalization process effectively, the mass template according to the demand of the public in the process of different creative mode, tens of millions of and with the constant use of the public more incremental template, this process with the growth of the system, the output of the creative result also tend to infinite close to the original personalized design. "Prototype" is the link to realize the public design and creative production. The aforementioned cultural computing tools and technical support can realize this link quickly. Open source software and hardware enable the public to realize their own prototype transformation process freely. "Test" is a creative design field condition by the simulation and experiment process, this link can be calculated through cultural form of virtual display, simulation and testing data, such as the production of logo design once, can immediately through cultural computing applications in a variety of different objects to see rendering effects, in order to judge whether the public of their own design logo meet their own needs, this is the most simple and convenient rapid test process, compared with the actual production of previous test process, this model is more likely to be accepted and recognized. But it needs to be explained that the traditional model still has a need to exist, for professional designers, more need to refine the process, rather than simplify all the details of the process conducive to in-depth design.

In the process of using various open design platforms, the public also needs to master effective operation methods. One of the most important points is to effectively connect various cultural computing platforms to form a cultural computing "skill tree" that meets their own design needs. In this process, we need to create a basic cognitive and skill organization structure for cultural computing, and apply our "skill tree" to different cultural computing application scenarios.

3   The Practice of Public Design Case Based on Cultural Computing Sharing

3.1   Graphic Design Applications in the Shared Concept of Cultural Computing

In the field of graphic design, open source applications based on the concept of cultural sharing are contributing to public design innovation. Has the size of the computing systems such as "ban" system and "on line", "ban" system is a research and development of China's alibaba group, a graphic design system based on artificial intelligence, through artificial intelligence algorithm and culture in the training of the large amounts of data calculation of design scenario, solve the centerline of the taobao shopping platform for businesses of all kinds of banner and poster design. China's annual Double 11 shopping festival will generate a large number of graphic design needs, every year before November 11, millions of stores on Taobao platform need a variety of activity posters and banner, each year requires a lot of human, material and financial resources to solve, and "Luban" system is for a variety of online stores for the public design The system, which started to be used internally in 2016, allows the public to generate nearly 1,000 posters and other graphic designs of various styles and types every day by setting the themes and elements they need, and the quality level of poster design has even closer to the level of senior designer. Three important technical problems are mainly solved in the graphic design related to a large number of annotated data, in order to solve the data structure, network and standardization; Through the analysis of design aesthetics, some general design rules are found to solve the uncertainty of design. Explore effective algorithmic models to make the process of public participation more convenient and the results more high-quality. Therefore, Ali Artificial Intelligence Lab proposed four parts, namely design framework, element center, actuator and evaluation network, to promote machine learning (Sheng 2017). "Moonline" system is a graphic design intelligent system developed by Tezign Company. The field it faces is mainly some graphic publicity design of real estate companies. A large number of graphic design schemes can be generated through simple theme element selection, and this result has passed the Turing test. In addition, there are a lot of the apps can quickly implement plane innovation design of the public, such as stroke and style characteristics of Prisma master of art by learning, after calculation, culture style public images on the migration as required by the various art master brush effect and stylized images, Tailor, brands and logos FOUNDRY can automatically generate a LOGO design combined with artificial intelligence technology, the public can be a LOGO design in a few minutes fast. Open source tools such as Prezi and Xmind can help the public to map illustrated and progressive transformation logic relationships, the divergent thinking in the process of the method, clear and convenient to set up image, keywords and color expression and memory links between the mind, to help the public in the form of a graphical visualization of complex process and data analysis of plane design.

3.2 Space Design Applications in the Shared Concept of Cultural Computing

Traditional space design is often a more complex process, from preliminary research to space design, from space graphic design to elevation design, from design drawings to construction drawings and so on all need complex process. Calculate current culture concept is gradually into the process of space design, especially the design platform system based on artificial intelligence, can rapid design skills zero basis of public indoor space design, complete virtual reconstruction scheme for their living space, and displayed in the form of AR and VR, and the results of this design is in the form of design material to share with more people with related requirements, to enrich the cultural content. Traditional space design professional software is very difficult to master, such as production softwares 3 dmax, Rhino, Sketch Up, etc., the space design of professionals often require months or even a year of training to learning, in 2020 in one of the courses, I shared 3D platforms such as "KuJiaLe", "ChangXiangJia" and "ZhuZuo" which are easy for the public to learn and master quickly, so that many people with no design foundation can complete a set of space design in tens of minutes. The public can complete a set of space design within tens of minutes. Such as "cool knorr" system is based on the concept of "wysiwyg" panoramic fast indoor space design platform, can realize the cloud design rendering, such as design of cloud and BIM technology communion, and in the form of AR and VR for rapid design experience, the system has a lot of design templates, from condole top, floor, door to wait hard outfit to furniture, adorn article, such as soft outfit, all the facilitation of classification, through a simple drag, move, turn and can realize the rapid design. The process of innovation can be carried out in three different forms: web version, APP and client, so that the public can participate in innovation at any time and anywhere according to their own convenience. "Imagination" and "cool knorr" have similar features, but also has its special advantages, such as modular can quickly achieve a key interior space layout design, and quickly to automatically generate series of complete sets of construction drawings, according to design automatically generate budget sheet, you can even according to the needs of design directly to generate a list of suppliers, etc. "Build" is based on the mobile side one can create virtual space, science fiction creation in architectural space, landscape, landscape design content such as APP, can be used in home decoration, office scene, scene of science and technology, business scenario, the public can use the system for space interaction parent-child games, can be fast building of architectural space, also can build public online shop design, will own personalized virtual design for online retail, etc., the virtual space of aesthetic experience through the form of cultural calculation, and the Oriental aesthetics of architectural space is focused, Very beneficial to the public space design innovation. In addition, the "virtual exhibition curation experiment platform" led by universities can help the public to design exhibition space quickly in an online format,, and can automatically generate exhibition curation reports according to the needs of exhibition, which speeds up the process of exhibition space design and exhibition curation. There are many other platforms for public participation in the concept of cultural computing sharing, and these platforms can also be used in tandem and extended in function, which is actually a manifestation of the "long tail effect" of many niche and convenient software that can compete with mainstream professional software, making up for the long learning period and difficulty of mastering professional design software, and helping the public quickly realize design, that is to say, to help the public implement design innovation in a short period of time.

Acknowledgement. Zhang Xin is the first author and Hu Jieming is the corresponding author of this paper. This paper is supported by the "Prosperity Plan Pre-research Project of Donghua University", the project title of which is "Multiple Evolution and System Construction of Open Design Maker Co-creation Field".

References

Tosa, N.: Intercultural Computing: An Artist's Journey. Springer, London (2016). https://doi.org/10.1007/978-1-4471-6512-5
Haiying, Z., Hong, P., Hong, C.: Chinese cultural gene online service platform. Comput. Syst. Appl. **12**, 52–57 (2015)
van Boeijen, A.: School of Industrial Design and Engineering, University of Delft. Design Methods and Strategies: Delft Design Guide, pp. 21–157. Huazhong University of Science and Technology Press, Hubei (2017)
Anderson, C.: Makers -- New Industrial Revolution, pp. 105–112. CITIC Press, Beijing (2015)
Gershenfeld, N.: Design Reality, pp. 170–171. CITIC Press, Beijing (2019). Translated by Ding, J.
Xin, Z.: The Field of Design Maker Education. Zhejiang People's Fine Arts Publishing House, Hangzhou (2020)
Hatch, M.R.: Maker Platform Revolution. China Machine Press, Beijing (2019). Translated by Meng, Y.

Gushenfeld, N.: Intelligent Manufacturing: A New Digital Revolution. Tongji University Press, Shanghai (2016). Translated by Ding, J.

Hatch, M.: Maker Movement. China Machine Press, Beijing (2015). Translated by Ning, Y.

Chinese Academy of Engineering Innovative Design Development Strategy Research Project Team. China's Innovative Design Roadmap. China Science and Technology Press, Beijing (2016)

Digital Humanities, New Media and Culture

The Ontology of Mixed Reality Agents Memorializing the Dead and Dying

Joshua A. Fisher[✉] [iD]

Department of Interactive Arts and Media, Columbia College Chicago, 600 S Michigan Ave,
Chicago, IL 60605, USA
Jofisher@colum.edu

Abstract. Beginning with the 2009 publication of Michael Massimi's *Dying, Death, and Mortality: Towards Thanatosensitivity in HCI*, researchers have been exploring how to design UX and UI for end-of-life systems and memorials. This work has resulted in the design of interactive posthumous personhoods memorializing those who have lived by utilizing the data the deceased produced while they were alive. HCI designers and researchers have implemented Natural Language Processing (NLP) to create interactive posthumous personhoods in the form of chatbots. Over the last five years, Mixed Reality (MR) has been integrated by practitioners to create posthumous personhoods that they claim offer a greater fidelity with the departed when they were alive than previous technologies. How MR intersects with those previous technologies, cultural, personal heritage, and memorialization to achieve this greater fidelity requires further exploration if the media is to be used to elevate the evidentiary status of these posthumous personhoods. Insights from HCI end-of-life literature, death and dying studies, and interactive non-fiction are used to explore the ontology of these interactive posthumous personhoods to discover what MR is doing. This paper elucidates connected ethical, ontological, and thanatological issues that the HCI field needs to address as this alternative practice of mourning and memorialization becomes a mainstream practice. The paper argues that MR increases the social and spatial presence of an MR posthumous personhood's identity and subjectivity with greater fidelity than previous technologies, and that this supports an audience's active creation of belief in the agent as being evidentiary of a posthumous personhood.

Keywords: Augmented reality · Mixed reality · Human Computer Interaction · Thanatology · End-of-life studies · Death and dying · Interactive non-fiction

1 Introduction

Over the last decade, the Human Computer Interaction (HCI) and cultural heritage communities have aligned to explore issues around the design and development of digital memorialization [1–4]. Concurrently, immersive media scholars have been researching the emerging medias' affordances for similar experiences [5–8]. Memorials, a subject heavily explored by cultural heritage scholars [9–11], have been taken up by the HCI

© Springer Nature Switzerland AG 2021
M. Rauterberg (Ed.): HCII 2021, LNCS 12795, pp. 177–196, 2021.
https://doi.org/10.1007/978-3-030-77431-8_11

community [3] to develop and design user experiences for end-of-life (EoL) processes and the act of death and dying [12, 13] [1].

A subset of these emerging media memorials rely on Mixed Reality (MR)[2] technologies to give spatial form to their interactive non-fiction experiences [5, 6, 14]. Beyond the inclusion of the emerging technology, these memorials are a new generation of chatbots designed specifically to maintain an interactive record of someone's life after they have passed. This form of chat-based interaction has been claimed to confer personhood onto the posthumous agent [15, 16]. James Meese and his colleagues claim that the social presence enabled by such posthumous chatbots on social networks constitutes a personhood through relational ontologies [15]. Similar clams have been made about video of composited posthumous performers and celebrities such as Tupac and Elvis [17, 18]. This paper builds upon Meese's observation that, "digital resources are being used to create different forms of posthumous personhood" by interrogating the integration of MR.

MR's use for memorialization follows the pattern of rituals around death and dying evolving with a society's circumstances [1, 19, 20], and its use can be expected to continue as it is expanded to general audiences. Understanding how MR impacts the ontology of these agents—what they are and how they operate—is critical to understanding how the media impact the evidentiary status of these posthumous personhoods.

For the purposes of this paper, these agents are referred to as Mixed Reality Interactive Agent Memorials (MR IAM). A relational ontology, wherein the relations between different entities give rise to the MR IAM as a posthumous personhood is achieved by enabling the tenets of posthumous personhood discussed by Meese—agency, subjectivity, and identity—to move beyond the biological body. These relations connect emerging media technologies, cultural and personal heritages, government entities, technology, and death workers. Beyond the person memorialized, these relations include a constellation of researchers, biographers, emerging media practitioners, institutions, production studios and technologies. Additionally, the MR IAM requires a user or group of users to interact with it and to identify[3] the agent as representative of an individual who has lived. Within the assemblage of technologies, histories, and institutions, not one of these individual aspects elevates the agent to the status of personhood. Instead, it is the connections between the individual entities, and the result of those connections, that becomes the ontology of the posthumous personhood for the MR IAM. It is the connections between NLP and MR in the ontology that enables the MR IAM of Holocaust survivor Aaron Elster to slouch in his chair, in a way that appears to take up space, as he answers a

---

[1] Wendy Moncur, a professor of Digital Living at the University of Dundee has broken down these processes into one, the conduct of the funeral; two, the burial disposition (how the physical body is handled); three, the identification of the deceased [55, 56]. Technology and emerging media touch these processes in different ways.

[2] I adopt Milgram's original definition of Mixed Reality as, "one in which real world and virtual world objects are presented together within a single display, that is, anywhere between the extrema of the [reality-virtuality] continuum." [57] In 2019, a longitudinal study of papers on Mixed Reality was unable to meaningfully move beyond this general definition [58].

[3] I use the term "identify" in the manner of Kenneth Burke, in that a group of individuals are persuaded by the fidelity of a representation because it aligns with their expectations of what that representation should be and how it acts [59, 60].

question from the audience. Neither NLP nor MR alone is enough to confer posthumous personhood. It is their connections with one another that enables a greater fidelity of agency, subjectivity, and identity between a posthumous personhood and the person they were when alive.

This paper, then, informs the claim that these MR IAMs are evidentiary of their posthumous personhood by exploring their relational ontology and interrogating MR's place and impact within the assemblage. Specifically, this paper looks at the relations between:

- The corpus of data from which an MR IAM intuits answers to the questions users and participants ask and how this contributes to the perception of personhood.
- How those answers are sourced, by whom, and in what situations in order to demonstrate that the personhood is co-constructed rather than autobiographical.
- How a Natural Language Processing (NLP) algorithm is implemented to retrieve these answers and how that impacts one's perception of an MR IAM.
- How MR is used to render a representation, with its accompanying body language and countenance, that responds as part of a conversation.

I argue that the use of MR increases the likelihood that those speaking with an MR IAM will identify the media artifact as a person who has lived, and that such an identification supports a participant's active creation of belief in the MR IAM as evidentiary of a posthumous personhood.

There are two core tactics used by designers to achieve this identification. The first tactic, as discussed by scholars researching non-MR posthumous chatbots, is the chatbot's capacity to maintain a conversation [3, 16, 21]. This achieves the tenets of agency, identity, and subjectivity as proposed by Meese as being central to posthumous personhoods. The second tactic that achieves this identification is the spatial-visual illusion that an MR IAM fills space in the same manner as a living person. That their gestures and body language also fill space like a living human. Their spatiality makes their digital corporeality identifiable with a non-digital individual. Contributing to this spatial presence are the gestures and body language recorded and programmed into the MR IAM as it converses—filling the space in the same manner as a storyteller might. This affordance of MR achieves a greater fidelity of the identity and subjectivity for the posthumous personhood than previous technologies by more accurately representing an individual's persona. I claim that by building upon a foundation of technologies for chat interactions, MR provides a posthumous persona with spatial corporeality that supports the active creation of belief in the MR IAM as someone who once lived, making their representation accepted as a more authoritative posthumous personhood.

1.1 Case Studies of Existing Mixed Reality Interactive Agent Memorials

To understand what MR does in the relational ontology of the posthumous personhood to establish the evidentiary status of the agent as a person who has lived, this paper examines cultural heritage examples of MR IAMs representing Holocaust survivors[4]. The USC Creative Institute's Shoah Foundation created the most famous MR IAM of Pinchas Gutter, seen in Fig. 1. The MR IAMs at the Illinois Holocaust Museum in Skokie, Illinois are explored along with their contemporaries at the National Holocaust Center and Museum in the UK and the Learning with Digital Testimonies project at the Leibniz Supercomputing Centre of the Bavarian Academy of Science and Humanities in Garching, Germany. Each site is in conversation with the USC Shoah Foundation and shares some technology [22]. However, they have different design goals and processes for creating the MR IAMs [23–25]. Inevitably, their different assemblages of technologies and groups, as well as processes, provide unique insights.

Fig. 1. The Pinchas Gutter MR IAM. The photo was taken by the USC Shoah Foundation.

These case studies were chosen for a few reasons. First, the motivation of these projects—to create a record and maintain the history of the Holocaust before its survivors have passed on—addresses a critical knowledge that must be preserved [26]. Second, due

---

[4] As a person of Jewish heritage, I am cognizant of the problematic nature of critiquing representations of the Holocaust, whether they are interactive or not. This issue has been discussed at length by survivors and scholars and is outside the scope of this paper. USC's Shoah Foundation is at the forefront of this work. However, I would like to underscore that I am not critiquing the history shared by these MR IAMs but exploring the use of MR in the design and development of an interactive posthumous personhood to share its history after these survivors have passed on.

to the emerging nature of the practice and the critical importance of the history, most MR IAMs exist in a museum space [23, 27]. Third, unlike generalized examples, designs for MR IAMs that represent Holocaust survivors need to exercise greater sensitivity due to the intergenerational trauma of the Holocaust [8, 23]. Given the above, understanding the ontological nature of an MR IAM is critical to understanding how MR helps to establish their evidentiary status as persons who have lived. Future versions of MR IAMs can draw from these insights to assert the evidentiary status of posthumous individuals.

1.2 Methodology and Structure

The paper is structured to provide readers with insight into the ontological issues surrounding the design and development of interactive posthumous personhoods that use MR. Unlike previous work which has addressed either the technical [28, 29] or the ethical [23, 30, 31], this work seeks to combine both in order to holistically inform future implementations. An approach that accounts for both the theoretical and applied work is critical to the design of these MR IAM because of the artifact's goal. If the goal is to create an MR IAM that is evidentiary of a person who has lived, a theoretical understanding of personhood is required. Without such an understanding, it is difficult to know if the goal has been achieved. The paper provides this theoretical background before moving to the case studies.

As previously discussed, the case studies provide a number of technical and ethnographic insights into the design and developments of MR IAMs. These insights are then connected to the theoretical discussion. In addition to the review of case studies, on-site interviews and observations occurred at the Illinois Holocaust Museum in Skokie, Illinois before the onset of the COVID-19 pandemic. As might be expected, the pandemic made observing and interviewing at the site impossible. This meant that fewer interviews and observations took place than planned, but the data from those interviews is still presented. Over the course of the month of January 2020, 8 h of observation occurred across four separate days. Conversations between the MR IAMs at the museum, the audience, and docents were observed from the back of the agent's exhibition space.

Over the course of the same period, eight individuals who worked at the museum in Skokie were interviewed in a semi-structured format. All interviews were designed to elicit how and in what ways MR helped to establish the evidentiary status of the posthumous personhood. Individuals were interviewed for 30 min to an hour within either their office or within the exhibition site itself. Of these eight individuals, four were docents, three were involved in curation and maintenance of the MR IAM technologies, and one was the director of exhibitions. Their answers were recorded and transcribed the same day. Limited though they may be, the insights provided by the interviews and observations align with case studies' results and build upon them.

2 Thanatology in Human Computer Interaction

A thanatological approach to Human Computer Interaction (HCI) was proposed in 2009 to recognize the growing connection between technologies, the data we produce, and the processes of mortality [3, 13]. With the birth of the internet, the number humans able to produce and archive large amounts of easily accessible and mutable data for future generations became possible[5]. Consider the practice of life logging, collection of biometric data, and consumer data we each develop over the course of a year. As the scale of life on the internet exponentially increased so too did the amount of data. Over time, some—if not many—of those data creators have passed on, leaving in their wake a scatterplot of their life. In 2018, 8000 Facebook users died daily [16]. Each of their social feeds can be considered a separate historical text that documents not only their life, but their death and posthumous existence on the network [10]. The opportunity to comment on the profile of the deceased, or to send them messages, made it possible to interact with this data[6] [20]. Computational media lend thanatography, a literary record of one's dying, interactivity.

3   Digital Thanatography as an Interactive Non-fiction

The posthumous life of a social network user's posts, messages, and information is made interactive through social mourning on a Facebook wall, posthumous tweets, and automated messages [3]. The impact of this posthumous activity on the perception of an individual's personhood can be found in analog examples. The life of Anne Frank would be unknown if it weren't for the publication of her diary by her father [32]. Similarly, Irène Némirovsky's portrayal of life in France during the Nazi occupation of Paris would have been lost. Irène's daughter published her historical work, and it became a best seller in 2004 [33]. In both instances, our understanding of the individual comes from their journals, their recorded testimony. Yet, we know that there are problematic issues with these accounts. Anne Frank herself editorialized her diary after a Dutch radio program inspired her to create the historical artifact. Choices she made were undone by her father [32]. In the case of Némirovsky, her daughter Denise had to transcribe her mother's "indecipherable" handwriting to produce a publishable account. While work and data live on posthumously, the context in which they are produced, and the audience for which they are meant, are collapsed to make them accessible through contemporary structures

---

[5] The creation of this data on social networks such as Facebook and Twitter prompted them to develop rules governing the stewardship of data upon a user's death [2]. In 2014, Facebook enabled users to choose a "Legacy Contact" who could manage their user data [61]. Facebook does not allow a user to act through a deceased person's profile. Twitter does allow this.

[6] EoL literature in HCI has been grappling with posthumous personhood by looking primarily at social networks. There are numerous examples on Twitter, Facebook, and others that have kept accounts active and online even after people have passed. This can look like a user's scheduled posts occurring regularly after they pass, birthday messages, and other forms of automated or generated content. This ongoing interaction with those that have died is an extension of existing human behaviors of mourning from a variety of different cultures [19]. In this contemporary moment, instead of prayer or totems, "digital codes and computational texts are key sites for posthumous personhood." [15] After famous movie critic Roger Ebert passed, his wife Chaz Ebert maintained his twitter account—only occasionally inserting her own voice by signing a Tweet "–Chaz" [62]. Others rely on a data-centric approach. Deadsoci.al will send out pre-recorded messages for users after they pass [63]. Others, such as LivesOn [64], analyze a user's Twitter Feed to discover a user's syntax as well as their likes and dislikes. The service will then algorithmically continue tweeting for a user after they have died.

for audiences [34]. Our digital records are no different. They are modified and presented in new forms so that they can be accessible and understood.

In his initial proposal for HCI and EoL, Michael Massimi recognized these digital forms as Foucault's 'technology of the self' [13, 35, 36]. As Massimi paraphrases Foucault in the initial proposal for HCI EoL studies, "Writing so as not to die...is a task undoubtedly as old as the word" [3]. Interactivity and computation expand the "technology of the self" by scaffolding the intentions of a living person beyond their death. For the MR IAMs discussed, this intention is to engage with the living as a digital and interactive form in the manner they would have in life after they have died. As Meese recognizes, this ability to act after dying, this agency, is a tenet of a posthumous personhood [15].

Key to this conception of Foucault's statement for MR IAM's is that the "technology of the self" moves well beyond the word. MR affords the capacity to inscribe the tenor of the voice, movement of the eyes, the countenance, and the choreography of the body with all its textures, colors, and shapes. For some MR IAM, even the rhythm of their breath continues posthumously. These details comprise the, "technology of the self" for an MR IAM and they are all inscribed. Each constituent part, volumetrically captured and inscribed through immersive media, is a member of the MR IAM's relational ontology. Regarding Meese's observations about posthumous personhood, they also provide more fidelity to the subjectivity and identity of the living individual. Yet, if we are to take any lessons from the revisions to Anne Frank and Irène Némirovsky's biographical accounts, and how they impacted the general perception of them as individuals, we are forced to ask how these inscription technologies and their resulting MR IAMs differ from their original persons.

Critically, practitioners who use immersive media do not create perfect recreations of reality [37, 38]. They do not create perfect recreations of individuals. Immersive media practitioners produce media actualities, situated perspectives on reality, that become both reflections and vessels for the active creation of belief. They reflect this belief by realizing a new standard for visual, spatial, and interactive fidelity with reality [37]. This new standard for fidelity with a representation of reality makes them identifiable with their original subjects to a greater degree than previous forms. In turn, the mediated subject becomes a more effective vessel for the active creation of belief [39]. Conversations with the subject, in this instance a posthumous individual, enforces the active creation of belief in the MR IAM as a representation that achieves fidelity with a person who has died

3.1 From Interactive Non-fiction to Interactive Posthumous Persona

How an individual speaks, carries themselves, and conducts their appearance is connected to their persona. Representing that persona through an MR IAM is integral to establishing the fidelity of the artifact as representing an individual that has lived. An MR IAM is a perennial extension of a living or deceased individual's personhood[7]. In agreement with Meese and other HCI EoL researchers, this paper engages with Daniel Dennett's definition of a personhood. Dennett's definition requires that persons be rational beings capable of verbal communication and consciousness [15, 40]. For an MR IAM, the database of information is an analogy for their memory; the capacity to converse is an analogy for the interface, ostensibly a conversational interface [41]. MR extends the opportunity to identify this interface as a persona due to how their body and gestures are spatially represented and socially viewed.

However, given that the interface is constructed by a team of practitioners, an institution, and a design team, the persona is never autobiographical. These MR IAMs are co-constructed actualities that result in an interactive non-fiction [42]. For example, the group from the National Holocaust Museum in the UK hired a local studio, scholars, and family members to help develop their MR IAMs [28]. Each of these individuals and technologies shaped the resulting persona[8]. The team from USC used an even larger team and had a soundstage to do their work.

The number of entities—technological, institutional, cultural, and otherwise—increases the number of relations and results in unique relational ontologies. The assemblage of these ontologies results in a death aesthetic[9] [43]. This aesthetic is negotiated by a living person and an institution, commercial or otherwise, and the afforded technologies used to create an MR IAM before said individual passes. Each aesthetic results in a co-constructed persona with which users can interact. This persona, a role that is co-developed and co-designed, is supported by the MR IAM's personhood, which is ontologically derived. Accordingly, different death aesthetics may color the same individual as distinctly different posthumous personas. Their underlying personhood, how the subject is understood to be a person, is afforded through the relational ontology that extends their agency, subjectivity, and identity beyond their physical body.

The MR IAMs at the Holocaust museums represent singular negotiated personas. They have chosen a death aesthetic for their identity as a Holocaust survivor and testifier.

---

[7] The distinction between person and personhood is etymological. The conception of a "persona" comes from Latin and was a concept for a, "fundamental entity". The concept of a person came from this foundation. The original idea of persona never referred to a physical, human confined to a biological shell. In Rome, personhood could be lost if one became a slave to the enemy but regained once emancipated and returned home. A persona is then the subjective recognition of a role played by an individual whereas personhood denotes the subject as a person.

[8] In parallel, the identities and personas seen on social media platforms are the, "performative construction of individual and collective entities" [20, 65].

[9] EoL HCI scholars have compared these kinds of aesthetics to different forms of physical memorialization from grave stones, mausoleums, to 1920s death photography and totems [3]. We might extend this understanding to different forms of interactive death aesthetics. These aesthetics include pedagogical ones, such as the MR IAMs at Holocaust museums, to a performance death aesthetic, such as the MR IAM of Tupac [66].

This is in line with the survivors' intention to be an educational resource[10]. This aesthetic frames the individual as a witness and survivor. It is an aesthetic that does not seek to make the deceased appear younger, as if they had just experienced their trauma, nor does it seek to represent them in mid-life. Still, they exist not as an autobiographical account, but as a co-constructed media actuality of an individual at a particular moment in time reflecting on their history [42]. Eva Schloss records the following statement for future audiences, "I'm actually a recording. I can't answer that question." [44]. Schloss' statement highlights the limits of the persona presented by her MR IAM. The MR IAM of Schloss cannot speak to the entirety of her life or her manifold identities. The MR IAM represents just a singular, critical, part of the person she was when she was alive.

3.2 Establishing the Persona in an MR IAM

Previously, I have explored how an MR IAM is not an autobiographical, interactive representation of a person. Instead, it is a co-constructed media actuality of an interactive persona. This persona is a visual dialogic interface made spatial through MR. The persona is developed to carry forward the intentions of a living individual after they pass as an interactive posthumous personhood. To actualize this intention to have a conversation, the persona needs to have testimony, be recognized as a witness, and respond to individual speakers. The first two are achieved in pre-production when evidentiary material is gathered.

For each of the Holocaust MR IAM sites, the process of pre-production proceeded similarly. All of the sites relied on a process that is guided by a pedagogical death aesthetic. Second, they developed a question bank that best suited the goals of that aesthetic. They then recorded a live individual answering these questions. As mentioned before, although each of these examples relies on the same pedagogical death aesthetic, their utilization of distinctive technologies and processes results in subtly different MR IAM experiences.

The first step, then, is to develop a bank of questions that can be used during the interview to get compelling answers from the survivor. The goal is to get answers that both provide insight into who the person is, their personal history, and their knowledge of the Holocaust. NHM in the UK first created a timeline of events in the person's life. They then asked educators, those who knew the person, children, Holocaust scholars, and designers to look at the timeline and generate questions. They developed a list of 600 that could be asked of any survivor. Another 500 were specific to a singular survivor named Steve Frank.

Frank was filmed at the Pollen Studio in York where the questions were asked over a 5-day period. It began with a half day of recorded testimony that was used to generate questions. After that, the team from NHM-UK spent 4.5 days recording the answers to

---

[10] Without exception, those represented at the Holocaust museums have their other personas explored through a film that plays before the interactive experience. However, Minhua Ma, who worked on the MR IAMs at the National Holocaust Museum in the UK, noted that the presence of the survivor within the MR IAM is directly related to the fullness of their testimony and the openness of the subject domain [28]. Ma recognized that the person presented by an MR IAM is directly related to the quantity, diversity, and quality of the recorded media.

questions. They coached the survivor on how on how to comport himself and look at the stereo-pair camera [28]. To maintain "authenticity" [28], the collected data was not processed in any way other than to normalize the image. However, although they do not modify the image, coaching ostensibly influences the witness and may cause a departure from their usual mode of conversation.

In comparison, the MR IAMs developed by the Shoah Foundation and USC Institute for Creative Technologies had a question bank of over 2000 prompts. These prompts were developed from an internal list that was vetted by Holocaust experts as well as specialists in trauma and the preservation of testimony [23]. Questions were gathered from an audience who had seen a film about the survivor and from the survivor's family. A second elicitation script was also developed to get different versions of stories and to increase the presence of the survivor in the MR IAM [23]. By enabling a compelling conversation of depth, the developers provide more opportunities to get immersed in the conversation and for the active creation of belief.

In comparison to the NHM-UK, the Shoah Foundation project utilized a highly sophisticated setup on a sound stage. Survivors were filmed in a geodesic dome with "Panasonic X900MK cameras, spaced every 6 degrees over a 180-degree arc. The cameras were chosen as they recorded HD footage with 3 sensors at 60fps" [23]. Filming was done for 6 h a day for 4 days[11].

For the German project, 1000 questions were developed through observation of museum goers at the English-speaking projects, the existing pool of those projects' questions, interviews with pupils, and specialists in history, education, Jewish history, and didactics [27]. Survivors, both located in the UK, were filmed in York at the same Pollen Studio over five days in sessions of 30–45 min. Three sessions occurred in the morning and four to five occurred after lunch. Follow-up questions were developed between the days to create a richer narrative. Unlike the other two projects, the entire process of pre-production was filmed by the German team to provide transparency for future audiences.

Additionally, the German team's questions were guided by the Beutelsbach consensus. The consensus is an approach to teaching subjects related to politics and conflict. No other projects' questions were guided by such a national or social edict. It is the clearest example of how a national policy can enter into the memorialization of an individual through an MR IAM thereby allowing the state to influence the representation of the posthumous persona.

How a question bank is constructed, what questions it contains, how and where those questions are asked, and answers recorded all impact the knowledge that is co-created. At one level, the questions become the borders of the non-fiction account presented to the audience. They become the markers of knowledge. The Shoah Foundation's effort to ask questions in different ways to get different versions of a story is an example of stretching or expanding these borders. In this way, they add depth to the non-fiction. The German team's use of previous questions sketches perhaps an even clearer boundary of knowledge presented by these MR IAMs.

---

[11] Survivors who were unable to make it to California are able to be filmed in their home with a mobile-rig that contains four to ten cameras [27].

At another level, the answers derived from the question bank sketch the persona, already colored by the aesthetic, and separate it from the living person. One of the MR IAMs, Aaron Elster, discusses in the opening video that precedes his appearance on stage, that he never spoke about his experience during the Holocaust with his family [45]. He did not start to testify until he had retired and had grandchildren. We will likely never know *that* Aaron, the one who chose not to or could not speak about what occurred. The MR IAM does not represent that persona. While it is valuable background information, the persona of Aaron that did not or could not share testimony does not serve the purposes of the Holocaust Museum. It is only one aspect of his life, one persona among many, that is the witness.

The kinds of questions that are asked, under what conditions, and how they are recorded will all influence the co-produced persona. Each piece of technology and scaffolded processes excise the chosen persona out of the manifold identities of the individual. If a particular death aesthetic is being applied, this will further shape that persona to a particular context. And, in the case of the German example, if the state influence is present, that persona may be further distanced from the individual.

4 Conversational Capacity's Influence on the Posthumous Persona

In Massimi's initial proposal, he asks researchers to consider whether we can design personal intelligent agents that permit a person to, "undertake actions past their death?" The MR IAMs discussed in this paper answer this question in the affirmative. If the intention is to converse and educate others after the person has passed, then the MR IAMs capably carry forward this action. Even at a time delay, this is an ethical extension of the individual's wish [31]. The MR IAM maintains their progenitor's intention to educate others about the Holocaust through conversation [22, 23, 27, 28].

Jennifer Huberman, a professor of sociology that studies death and dying, wrote that online memorials were shifting from sites of commemoration to conversation [46]. She provides examples on Facebook of mourners asking questions of the deceased or discussing memories. Facebook's ecosystem, corporate and digital, provides a singular form of one-way communication and engagement with the deceased [41].

In comparison, for the MR IAMs discussed, how this conversation is meant to progress is co-constructed with an individual before they pass. In the documentary *116 Cameras*, which covers the creation of an MR IAM, Eva Schloss expresses disappointment in not being able to use her hands when she speaks [44]. She laments that she cannot talk in a way tied to her identity and culture. She says, "To speak with your hands is so Jewish". [44] This gesture others may take for granted, the folding of one's hands while making a point for example, is bound up in how the self is presented, how a person conducts their body. Since an MR IAM carries forward a person's intention to speak with others after they have passed, the style in which they converse, so tied to identity and who they are, must also be carried onward to effectively achieve an evidentiary posthumous personhood.

4.1 Natural Language Processing and an MR IAM's Conversational Capacity

Up to this point, how the corpus of data is collected and shaped to be presented as a posthumous personhood's persona has been discussed. How the conversation occurs between that persona and a user requires attention. In Sandra Gaudenzi's seminal dissertation on the living documentary, she discusses the helpful term autopoiesis for understanding how technologies like natural language processing co-create the conversational memorials [47]. Autopoiesis is a biological terms she (and other media scholars) applies to interactive non-fiction to describe its mechanism for, "maintain[ing its] particular form despite material inflow and outflow, through self-regulation and self- reference." [47] Because interactive non-fiction is a computational text that responds to user interactivity it adapts and changes. This transformational power is what sets interactive non-fiction apart from linear non-fiction [48].

For the MR IAMs, this autopoietic process is facilitated by a dialogue between the docent, museum goers, natural language processing algorithm, the database of answers, and a remote service team [22]. The ability to freely converse with an MR IAM will impact how that personhood is perceived. How the MR IAM answers or is unable to answer questions will influence an audience's perception of their persona. In Fig. 2 is a diagram of how this autopoietic relationship is carried out at the National Holocaust Museum in the UK and at the Illinois Holocaust Museum.

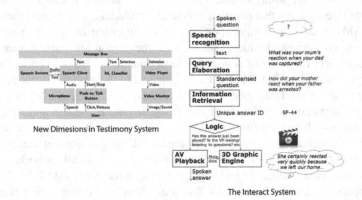

Fig. 2. Two autopoietic processes for conversation with an MR IAM. The New Dimensions for Testimony system on the right [23] and the Interact system at the Holocaust Museum in the UK on the left [28]. These different systems may access the same database of recorded information, but based on their structure, present different personas for the same posthumous personhood.

In an analysis of conversations of MR IAM at the Illinois Holocaust Museum, docent-led interactions resulted in a higher number of appropriate answers as compared to free conversation without a docent [30]. Questions asked by the audience resulted in behavior that seemed appropriate, but only in the sense that the MR IAM responded by saying it did not know an answer [30]. This was considered a preferred response [29]. Considering that an MR IAM for general use would not have a docent present, it is worth questioning the value of non-docent led interactions that result in the agent avoiding a direct response.

This discrepancy demonstrates the limits of the presented MR IAM persona and its reliance on the pre-recorded answers and the NLP algorithms. Further, the inability to ask more personal questions (without the aid of a docent) impedes the active creation of belief in the individual and is a limit to the extension of a posthumous personhood's agency and identity.

Since the mode in which we converse is deeply connected to how one's identity is perceived—whether one is perceived as attentive or aloof or otherwise—the NLP impacts a user's capacity to actively create belief in the MR IAM as an evidentiary representation of a posthumous personhood. If an MR IAM cannot converse in a way parallel to that of its progenitor, it lacks fidelity with the reality of that person before they passed. Since the audience member cannot, or likely does not, know the individual before they passed, they cannot judge this fidelity. They do not know whether the MR IAM is listening in the same way the individual did when they were alive. In turn, the active creation of belief in the MR IAM can mean actively creating belief in a persona that is further removed from the originating individual. Different autopoietic systems will present persona's with different capacities for conversation and influence the extension of a posthumous personhood's agency and identity. An inefficient system may damage the evidentiary status of the MR IAM and negatively influence the perception of its posthumous personhood.

5   Spatializing the Posthumous Presence

I have now established how an MR IAM's persona is developed. A piece of someone, a persona, is constructed through the inscription of answers to very specific questions. The questions and answers are shaped by a particular death aesthetic that results in a persona situated to a particular context. An NLP algorithm then moderates the conversation between this persona and an audience. The effectiveness of this NLP algorithm impacts the audience's capacity to actively create belief in the MR IAM as a posthumous personhood as it influences the agency, identity, and subjectivity of the deceased individual.

It is now possible to discuss how presenting this persona in MR impacts the perception of the MR IAM and their perceived personhood. As a reminder, the presented persona is only possible due to the ontological relations that enable the posthumous personhood to exist. MR affords this personhood a greater fidelity of social, spatial, and visual presence than non-immersive media. According to the case studies' project designers: the MR IAMs use MR to overcome the uncanny valley [28], manifest spatial presence [23], and establish the human scale of the conversational agent [27]. The researchers in the UK and Munich also clearly state that the use of the technology is meant to generate interest [27] and to achieve a satisfying interaction with the agents [28].

In their evaluations, none of the researchers evaluated how the MR visualization and spatialization impacted how the agents were perceived. However, a thesis written on these agents in 2018 by Sydney Hazel Lawall Dratel recorded this statement by a participant:

> From an education perspective it has been wonderful to see because it really has felt like a real-time interaction with a survivor…This is a really nice way of giving

people who can't meet in person with a survivor the opportunity to actually have a conversation and not just sit and hear something that was pre-recorded [25].

Additionally, a docent at the same site stated, "One of the things that visitors respond to is authenticity, and it does feel very authentic to sit and have a conversation and be able to ask a question and have it answered." [25]. Surprisingly, in my interviews with docents at the Illinois Holocaust Museum, the spatial nature of the agents rarely came up. Only two of the four docents brought it up and when they did, they connected it to their attempts to perceive the MR IAM as human. Allan, who had worked at the museum since the installation opened, said, "as if I am working with a live person to tell a story." [22] Carol, a docent for 7 years, said the MR increased her appreciation of the reality of the Holocaust [17].

These statements, limited though they may be, address what MR is actually facilitating. All four of the interviewees state that MR lends a "real-time interaction" that allows for an "actual conversation" that feels, "very authentic" as if they are conversing with a "live person". Yet, as discussed, they are not speaking with a live person and, in contrast to what has been quoted, all of the answers are indeed pre-recorded as testimony. Void the visual and spatial presence, real-time interactions and the conversation could be facilitated by an interactive non-fiction chatbot as well. Given this caveat, it is not the mere act of conversation that differentiates the MR IAM from the chatbot, but the quality of that conversation.

By quality, I am referring to the subjective individual experience of the conversation with the MR IAM. The MR IAM is both spatially and socially present in the same physical environment as those with which it converses. This sense of corporeal presence, a critical affordance of MR, gives the agent the illusion of substance in physical space [49]. While this presence is not manifested in a physical and corporeal manner, as it would be for a living person, MR affords the illusion of this for the posthumous persona. In the famous MR example of a Snoop Dogg performance with a posthumous Tupac, it was the latter's body movements and apparent reaction to Snoop that established the social and spatial presence of Tupac for the audience [17]. Similarly, the MR IAM agent sits on a stage, appears to have depth, and though their gestures are limited, leans toward and away from the audience in apparent reaction to them. These actions situate the MR IAM as present with the audience. In this way, MR extends the fidelity of the posthumous personhood's identity through their spatialized body language and their social engagement with the audience.

This social and spatial presence is enforced through the expanded technologies of the self. The MR IAMs discussed all rely on video evidence and its myth of authenticity [50]. USC's New Dimensions in Testimony group intentionally avoided the use of digital doubles so that the veracity of the MR IAM wouldn't be doubted [51]. Further, they never edited or modified recordings of the survivors as they spoke [23]. This meant volumetric recordings of the subjects maintained their pregnant pauses or tangents [23]. In comparison, the group from the UK developed CGI representations of survivors to fill in the blanks between questions, what they refer to as "passive engagements". The same method was used for the Munich project [27]. These different uses of visual evidence result in MR IAMs that have different spatial presences. In turn, the identity and subjectivity of the posthumous personhoods are extended in different ways. For USC, the identity and subjectivity of the posthumous personhood are hewn to the integrity of their process and volumetric capture technologies. For the UK and German projects, the inscribed volumetric material is a resource for the fabrication of the posthumous personhood's identity and subjectivity. The latter is a construction and presents a persona that is a revision of the originating personhood.

One thing that MR provides, then, is a 3D model rendered from the visual evidence of a subject's body and body language, which through the technology, is given spatial and social presence that has fidelity with a living person. The affordance of spatial presence is fundamentally different from other forms of memorialization—gravesites, statues, and mausoleums—because it moves in a human-like manner. Social presence is achieved by the conversational nature of engaging with the MR IAM and its specialized gestures toward an audience. This correlated presence makes it easier for an audience to identify the MR IAM, not as a fictional person, but as evidence of a person who has lived.

The MR interface is a vehicle, a container, for an audience's active creation of belief. This engagement, this conversation with the spatial, visual, and interactive manifestation of a persona facilitates the active creation of belief in the MR IAM as a witness. While a chatbot or flat interface can certainly facilitate a conversation, MR's affordance of spatial presence increases its social presence [52] through conversation. When the MR IAM Eva Schloss gestures in the direction of the audience or when Aaron Elster's MR IAM slouches to one side while considering an answer, the response immerses the user deeper into the conversation. Just like any good conversationalist, these witnesses use gestures like oral storytellers to immerse those they are speaking with into their history. These same gestures, through the technology of the self, are actualized through MR. As a user exercises their agency by asking questions, the MR IAM provides (to the best of its NLP capacity) more information, thereby facilitating the active creation of belief in their historical presence and testimony.

My observations from the Illinois Holocaust Museum and those made by the designers at the UK museum support this statement. During each of my observations, children were more apt to ask questions directly to the agent. They were also more likely to ask follow-up questions. Further, they were the more frequent question askers. Adults, on the other hand, asked the docent directly. The docent then asked the question of the MR IAM. To my mind, this difference implies that the spatial presence and gestures afforded by the MR technology made the MR IAM identifiable as a person in the eyes of children. Further, that the increased frequency in question-asking displays an effort to actively create this belief in the MR IAM as a historical person and not a media artifact.

6   The Ontology of Mixed Reality Interactive Agents Memorials

In this paper, I have sought to deconstruct the ontology of the MR IAM to figure out how MR influences the perception of the MR IAM's personhood. I have discussed that what is presented by an MR IAM is not autobiographical. It is an aspect of a person, their situated knowledge, that becomes an interactive non-fiction in the form of a persona.

The recorded movements, gestures, and their mode of conversation are all co-constructed and programmed into this persona for the MR IAM. Involved in this process, beyond the subject, is a diverse set of actors from family and friends to institutions and potentially the state. These co-creators take the non-fiction material, the testimony of the subject, and form it to a death aesthetic that, in terms of an MR IAM, is meant to establish the evidentiary status of the posthumous personhood.

MR does not directly impact the content of the MR IAM's spoken speech, but it does enable the inscription of a person's body language, a form of communication deeply situated with an individual's identity. MR extends this spatial communicative capacity, and in turn a person's identity, beyond their biological body after they have passed. This provides agents with a spatial and social presence that has greater fidelity with the identity of the person when they were alive than previous technologies. The spatial presence of the MR IAM represents a new visual, spatial, and interactive standard for the posthumous person. Different inscription technologies and their capacities to record movement, textures, and audio result in posthumous personhoods of varying fidelity with their progenitor's identity, subjectivity, and agency.

As a computational artifact, the MR IAM then becomes the vehicle through which speakers converse with a posthumous personhood's persona. The more expansive the question bank, the deeper the conversation can go, and the more opportunities there are for the active creation of belief in the persona. This creation of belief happens on two levels, first in identifying the MR IAM as a persona that has fidelity with an identity and subjectivity enacted by a person who has lived. Second, in actively believing the MR IAM is evidentiary of a posthumous personhood. The process is autopoietic and is maintained through the MR IAM's conversation with an audience. MR facilitates this active creation of belief in the persona, both through volumetrically captured non-fiction material and an effective dialogic interface that establishes its spatial and social presence, elevating the evidentiary status of a persona and expanding the identity and subjectivity of a posthumous personhood.

7   Conclusion

This paper has established how MR technologies enhance the subjectivity and identity of a persona and establish its evidentiary status as a posthumous personhood. Extracting the influence of a single technology in the MR IAM's relational ontology is a productive practice in understanding how interactive non-fiction artifacts establish their historical authority for users. These kinds of claims have political and cultural consequences. This observation is especially important when an interactive non-fiction artifact represents a historical personage. A recent patent filed by Microsoft [53] that relies on emails and social media posts to construct a posthumous personhood in the form a chatbot fails to address these ontological concerns. It fails to consider the performative nature of these social media posts [54]. The technology, which allows for the creation of multiple personas—which they call themes—of a posthumous personhood, creates posthumous chatbots that cannot achieve a higher fidelity of identity or subjectivity with their progenitor because of their fractional construction. A user's Facebook and Twitter posts are not accurate representations of their personality, they are a constructed performance with the platforms. If we do not look closely at how these personas are being created by industry, how practitioners use emerging media to establish the evidentiary status of their posthumous personhood, we risk losing the very history we strive to save.

Acknowledgements. I am deeply indebted to my friend and colleague Dr. Anna Weisling for her attentive notes on this paper. I would also like to acknowledge the kindness and hospitality shown to me by the docents and staff at the Illinois Holocaust Museum.

References

1. Graham, C., Arnold, M., Kohn, T., Gibbs, M.R.: Gravesites and websites: a comparison of memorialisation. Vis. Stud. **30**, 37–53 (2015). https://doi.org/10.1080/1472586X.2015. 996395
2. Van Der, N.E., et al.: Death and the Internet (2017)
3. Massimi, M., Charise, A.: Dying, death, and mortality: Towards thanatosensitivity In: Proceedings of the HCI Conference on Human Factors in Computing Systems, pp. 2459–2468 (2009). https://doi.org/10.1145/1520340.1520.349
4. Odom, W., Uriu, D., Kirk, D., Banks, R., Wakkary, R.: Experiences in designing technologies for honoring deceased loved ones. Des. Issues **34**, 54–66 (2018). https://doi.org/10.1162/ DESI
5. Handayani, B., Tinggi, S., Bali, P.: Virtual Dark Tourism : The Role of Sound Branding and Augmented Reality for Death Sites. vol. 2, p 1–17 (2018). https://doi.org/10.4018/IJCMHS. 2018070101
6. Dow, S., Lee, J., Oezbek, C., MacIntyre, B., Bolter, J.D., Gandy, M.: Exploring spatial narratives and mixed reality experiences in Oakland Cemetery. In: ACE'05 Proceedings of the 2005 ACM SIGCHI International Conference on Advances in Computer Entertainment Technology, pp. 51–60 (2005). https://doi.org/10.1145/1178477.1178484
7. Fisher, J.A., Schoemann, S.: Toward an ethics of interactive storytelling at dark tourism sites in virtual reality. In: International Conference on Interactive Digital Storytelling, pp. 577–590 (2018)
8. Fisher, J.A., David Bolter, J.: Ethical considerations for AR experiences at dark tourism sites. Adjun. In: Proceedings of the 2018 International Symposium on Mixed and Augmented Reality, ISMAR-Adjunct 2018, pp. 365–369 (2018). https://doi.org/10.1109/ISMAR-Adjunct.2018.00106
9. Getty, E., Cobb, J., Gabeler, M., Nelson, C., Weng, E., Hancock, J.T.: I said your name in an empty room: Grieving and continuing bonds on Facebook. In: Proceedings of the Conference on Human Factors in Computing Systems, pp. 997–1000 (2011). https://doi.org/10.1145/197 8942.1979091
10. Brubaker, J.R., Hayes, G.R., Dourish, P.: Beyond the grave: Facebook as a site for the expansion of death and mourning. Inf. Soc. **29**, 152–163 (2013). https://doi.org/10.1080/01972243. 2013.777300
11. Gould, H., Kohn, T., Gibbs, M.: Uploading the ancestors: experiments with digital Buddhist altars in contemporary Japan. Death Stud. **43**, 456–465 (2019). https://doi.org/10.1080/074 81187.2018.1544948
12. Walter, T., Hourizi, R., Moncur, W., Pitsillides, S.: Does the internet change how we die and mourn? Overview and analysis. Omega J. Death Dying **64**, 275–302 (2011). https://doi.org/ 10.2190/OM.64.4.a
13. Massimi, M., Odom, W., Banks, R., Kirk, D.: Matters of life and death: locating the end of life in lifespan-oriented HCI research. In: Proceedings of the Conference on Human Factors in Computing Systems, pp. 987–996 (2011). https://doi.org/10.1145/1978942.1979090
14. Engberg, M.: Augmented And Mixed Reality Design For Contested And Challenging Histories

15. Meese, J., Nansen, B., Kohn, T., Arnold, M., Gibbs, M.: Posthumous personhood and the affor-dances of digital media. Mortality **20**, 408–420 (2015). https://doi.org/10.1080/13576275. 2015.1083724
16. Bassett, D.: Death and Anti-Death, vol. 16: 200 Years After Frankenstein, p. 16 (2018)
17. Brunt, S.D.: Performing beyond the grave: the posthumous duet. In: Strong, C., Lebrun, B. (eds.) Death and the Rock Star, pp. 165–173. Ashgate Publishing Ltd, Burlington (2015)
18. Bode, L.: No longer themselves framing digitally enabled posthumous "Performance". Soc. Cine. Media Stud. **49**, 46–70 (2010)
19. Gibbs, M., Mori, J., Arnold, M., Kohn, T.: Tombstones, uncanny monuments and epic quests: memorials in world of warcraft. Game Stud. **12**, 2 (2012)
20. Lehner, N.: The work of the digital undead: digital capitalism and the suspension of com-municative death. Continuum (N. Y). **33**, 475–488 (2019). https://doi.org/10.1080/10304312. 2019.1627289
21. Gibson, M., Watkins, R.: The futures of grief. TEXT (2018). https://doi.org/10.1057/palgrave. jors.2601268
22. Fisher, J.A.: Interview Transcripts at the Illinois Holocaust Museum (2020)
23. Traum, D.: New dimensions in testimony: digitally preserving a holocaust survivor's interac-tive storytelling. Lect. Notes Comput. Sci. (including Subser. Lect. Notes Artif. Intell. Lect. Notes Bioinformatics). **9445**, 269–281 (2015). https://doi.org/10.1007/978-3-319-27036-4_26
24. Ballis, A., Barricelli, M., Gloe, M.: Interactive digital 3-D certificates and Holocaust Education - Development, Presentation and research, pp. 1–26 (2020)
25. Dratel, S.H.L.: "An Immersive Journey:" Analyzing the Use of Survivor Testimony in Holocaust Museums (2018). https://doi.org/10.1017/CBO9781107415324.004
26. Monteiro, J., Morais, C., Carvalhais, M.: Interactive Storytelling for the Maintenance of Cultural Identity: The Potential of Affinity Spaces for the Exchange and Continuity of Inter-generational Cultural Knowledge. Lect. Notes Comput. Sci. (including Subser. Lect. Notes Artif. Intell. Lect. Notes Bioinformatics). vol. 10690 LNCS, pp. 299–302 (2017). https://doi. org/10.1007/978-3-319-71027-3_30
27. Ballis, A., Barricelli, M., Gloe, M.: Interaktive digitale 3-D-Zeugnisse und Holocaust Educa-tion – Entwicklung. Präsentation und Erforschung. Springer Fachmedien Wiesbaden (2019). https://doi.org/10.1007/978-3-658-24205-3_22
28. Ma, M., Coward, S., Walker, C.: Question-answering virtual humans based on pre-recorded testimonies for holocaust education. Serious Games Edutainment Appl. **II**, 391–409 (2017). https://doi.org/10.1007/978-3-319-51645-5_18
29. Artstein, R., Gainer, A., Georgila, K., Leuski, A., Shapiro, A., Traum, D.: New Dimensions in Testimony Demonstration. vol. 2016, pp. 32–36 (2016). https://doi.org/10.18653/v1/n16-3007
30. Lycan, B., Artstein, R.: Direct and mediated interaction with a holocaust survivor. Lect. Notes Electr. Eng. **510**, 161–167 (2019). https://doi.org/10.1007/978-3-319-92108-2_17
31. Artstein, R., Silver, K.: Ethics for a combined human-machine dialogue agent. AAAI Spring Symposium Series - Technical Report SS-16-01-, pp. 184–189 (2016)
32. Holocaust Encyclopedia: Anne Frank: Diary|The Holocaust Encyclopedia. https://encyclope dia.ushmm.org/content/en/article/anne-frank-diary. Accessed 12 Jan 2021
33. Davidson, S.: A hatchet job and the Holocaust. Institute of Public Affair, vol. 60 (2008)
34. Ong, W.J.: Orality and Literacy, the Technologizing of the Word. Routledge, London (1982)
35. Huberman, J.M.: The digital double burial: resurrecting Hertz in the digital age. Mortality **23**, 334–349 (2018). https://doi.org/10.1080/13576275.2017.1351937
36. Bassett, D.J.: Ctrl + Alt + Delete: the changing landscape of the uncanny valley and the fear of second loss. Curr. Psychol. (2018). https://doi.org/10.1007/s12144-018-0006-5

37. Engberg, M., Bolter, J.D.: The aesthetics of reality media. J. Vis. Cult. **19**, 81–95 (2020). https://doi.org/10.1177/1470412920906264
38. Murray, J.H.: Virtual/reality: how to tell the difference. J. Vis. Cult. **19**, 11–27 (2020). https://doi.org/10.1177/1470412920906253
39. Murray, J.: Hamlet on the Holodeck: The Future of Narrative in Cyberspace. The MIT Press (1998)
40. Dennett, D.: Conditions of Personhood
41. Savin-Baden, M., Burden, D., Taylor, H.: The ethics and impact of digital immortality. Knowl. Cult. **5**, 178–196 (2017). https://doi.org/10.22381/KC52201711
42. Fisher, J.A.: Empathic Actualities: Toward a Taxonomy of Empathy in Virtual Reality (2017). https://doi.org/10.1007/978-3-319-71027-3_19
43. Graham, C., Constable, M., Fernando, J.: Guest editors' introduction: the aesthetic of death and after-death in an Internet age. Vis. Stud. **30**, 32–36 (2015). https://doi.org/10.1080/1472586X.2015.996393
44. Films, B.: 116 Cameras. Op-Docs, USA (2017)
45. Foundation, S.: Introductory Film for Aaron Elster. Shoah Foundation, USA (2017)
46. Huberman, J.: Dearly departed: communicating with the dead in the digital age. Soc. Anal. **61**, 91–107 (2017). https://doi.org/10.3167/sa.2017.610306
47. Gaudenzi, S.: The Living Documentary: from representing reality to co-creating reality in digital interactive documentary, pp. 1–309 (2013)
48. Aston, J., Gaudenzi, S., Aston, J.: Studies in Documentary Film Interactive documentary : setting the field. vol. 3280, pp. 37–41 (2014). https://doi.org/10.1386/sdf.6.2.125
49. Holz, T., Campbell, A.G., Ohare, G.M.P., Stafford, J.W., Martin, A., Dragone, M.: MiRA-mixed reality agents. Int. J. Hum Comput Stud. **69**, 251–268 (2011). https://doi.org/10.1016/j.ijhcs.2010.10.001
50. Bolter, J.D., Grusin, R.: Introduction: The Double Logic of Remidiation. Remediat. Underst. New Media. vol. 2 (1999)
51. Hill, R.W.: Ethics of immersive technologies. In: Abbas, A.E.E. (ed.) Next-Generation Ethics: Engineering a Better Society. pp. 39–53. Cambridge University Press (2019). https://doi.org/10.1017/9781108616188.004
52. Sallnäs, E.-L.: Effects of communication mode on social presence, virtual presence, and performance in collaborative virtual environments. Presence Teleoper. Virtual Environ. **14**, 434–449 (2005). https://doi.org/10.1162/105474605774785253
53. Abramson, D.I., Johnson, J.: Creating a Conversational Chat Bot of a Specific Person, (2020)
54. Hogan, B.: The presentation of self in the age of social media: distinguishing performances and exhibitions online. Bull. Sci. Technol. Soc. **30**, 377–386 (2010). https://doi.org/10.1177/0270467610385893
55. Moncur, W., Kirk, D.: An emergent framework for digital memorials. In: Proceedings of the Conference on Designing Interactive Systems: Processes, Practices Methods, Techniques, DIS, pp. 965–974 (2014). https://doi.org/10.1145/2598510.2598516
56. Moncur, W., Bikker, J., Kasket, E., Troyer, J.: From death to final disposition: roles of technology in the post-mortem interval. In: Proceedings of the Conference on Human Factors in Computing Systems, pp. 531–540 (2012). https://doi.org/10.1145/2207676.2207750
57. Milgram, P., Kishino, F.: Taxonomy of mixed reality visual displays. IEICE Trans. Inf. Syst. **E77-D**, 1321–1329 (1994). https://doi.org/10.1.1.102.4646
58. Speicher, M., Hall, B.D., Nebeling, M.: What is mixed reality? In: Proceedings of the Conference on Human Factors in Computing Systems (2019). https://doi.org/10.1145/3290605.3300767
59. Schoen, S.W.: The rhetoric of evidence in recent documentary film and video. ProQuest Diss. Theses. 195 (2012)

60. Burke, K.: A Rhetoric of Motives. University of California Press, Berkeley (1969)
61. Facebook Finally Figured Out What to Do With Dead People. https://www.newsweek.com/facebook-legacy-death-306344. Accessed 12 Jan 2021
62. Brubaker, J.R., Callison-Burch, V.: Legacy contact: Designing and implementing post-mortem stewardship at Facebook. In: Proceedings of the Conference on Human Factors in Computing Systems, pp. 2908–2919 (2016). https://doi.org/10.1145/2858036.2858254
63. DeadSocial - Prepare for Death Digitally & Build Your Digital Legacy – About. https://deadsocial.org/about. Accessed 12 Jan 2021
64. LivesOn LLC.: LivesOn
65. Cheney-Lippold, J.: New algorithmic identity, soft biopolitics and the modulation of control. Theory Cult. Soc. **28**, 164–181 (2011)
66. Dre, Snoop D., Philip A., Dylan B., Digital Domain: Digital Domain Virtual Tupac, https://www.digitaldomain.com/work/virtual-tupac/. Accessed 15 Jan 2021

The Human Mind and Engineering Models

José J. Cañas(✉)

Mind, Brain, and Behaviour Research Centre, University of Granada,
18071 Granada, Granada, Spain
delagado@ugr.es

Abstract. The design of systems where people and machines interact is an area where engineers work together with psychologists, sociologists, anthropologists, and other social scientists who are experts in the structure and functioning of the cognitive system and the laws of human behaviour. Both groups of experts collaborate in designing the machines and the interaction between machines and human beings. In this collaborative work, several assumptions are made, among which one of the more important is that it is possible to model the human cognitive system and its behaviour independently of the context of the interaction because these are assumed to be relatively fixed and only modifiable by evolution and learning processes. Based on this assumption, a methodology is followed in which social scientists model the human cognitive system independently of the context and, based on this modelling, they bring human knowledge into the design process. However, there is evidence that the characteristics and functioning of the human cognitive system are not independent of conditions of interaction. Revisiting this assumption may have important consequences for how we design machines and how humans interact with them. Above all, if the assumption is reviewed, it would mean that it is not possible to expect that the human sciences can model the human cognitive system independently of the context of the interaction. As a consequence of this, cultural aspects of interaction must also be taken into account when modelling the functioning and characteristics of the human cognitive system.

Keywords: Human mind · Engineering models · Designing process

1 Introduction

Nowadays, engineers who design machines have a systemic view of design which implies that design must take into account that machines are part of a system that also includes the people who interact with those machines. Designers must therefore consider the design of both human and non-human components of the system and the interaction between them. For this purpose, many design models have been proposed. In these models, assumptions are made about what machines and human beings are like and how they should interact. Based on these assumptions, design procedures have been proposed and have been used quite successfully to design new technological systems. However, the assumptions inherent in these models and methods need to be rethought in order to extend this success into future designs.

© Springer Nature Switzerland AG 2021
M. Rauterberg (Ed.): HCII 2021, LNCS 12795, pp. 197–208, 2021.
https://doi.org/10.1007/978-3-030-77431-8_12

Engineers conceive the process of designing machines as depending on a thinking process that is limited by their own problem-solving abilities and the laws of physics that determine what the machines can and cannot do. However, in most engineering models, engineers see the human mind as a component that could not be designed but only modified by a learning process that could not be properly called a 'design process'. Somehow, in these models it is thought that the human mind has fixed characteristics that can be discovered by psychologists and other social scientists and communicated to engineers so that they can take them into account during the design process. The learning process could, within certain limits, modify these characteristics but it cannot affect the human mind's basic structure and functioning. Therefore, the task of psychology and other cognitive sciences is to provide engineers with information on these characteristics so that they can take them into account in the design process. For example, a typical question engineers will ask the psychologist is what the capacity of the short-term memory is. The psychologist is expected to answer with a number that may vary within a range (that depends on individual characteristics, for example) but will be relatively fixed. For decades, we have seen that engineers have been comfortable with an answer like 'the capacity of short-term memory is between 5 and 9 units of information'. This is the famous '7 ± 2' [1]. However, research has shown that short-term memory can use a chunking process, which ultimately depends on how the stimuli in the environment are organised, to overcome any limits of capacity that have been set [2]. Therefore, if a system designer asks a psychologist to tell them what the capacity of the short-term memory is, they will have to answer that it will depend on how the designer designs the stimuli of the task that the human being will have to memorise. This answer may seem circular because it means that instead of answering the engineer with a fixed number (within a range, of course), the psychologist is telling the engineer that this number will depend on what they do in the other components (machines) of the system, for example in the interface of the machine. Therefore, a psychologist's answer could be: 'I'll tell you the number you ask me if you tell me how you have designed the machine's interface'. This answer means that in order to define the characteristics of the human mind it is necessary to know the structures of the elements with which it interacts and how the context of interaction is constructed.

Of course, engineers recognise that there is more to complex systems than just the characteristics of individual components. For years, engineers, especially those who share the systemic view, have been talking about the 'emerging characteristics' that arise in complex systems during the interaction of their components [3]. However, it should be noted that in this systemic view these emerging characteristics are new, and they are added to the individual characteristics of the components but do not modify them. Thus, it is still assumed that in a complex system the characteristics of the machines will be those designed by the engineer, and the characteristics of the people will depend on the structure and function of the human cognitive system that will only change to a certain extent as a function of learning. The new emerging characteristics will be those that arise from the interaction of the human and artificial components of the system.

This way of considering the modelling of a complex system by asking psychology to provide a psychological model of the human being with fixed characteristics is widely assumed by psychologists, engineers, and specialists in Human Factors who work on the design of the interaction between humans and machines within complex systems. The simplest and most elegant way to present this idea is by considering Simon's famous 'Parable of the ant on the beach' [4]. Figure 1 shows the path followed by an ant on the beach to the point where it can find its food. According to Simon, if we try to explain the ant's path based solely on the ant's 'internal processes' we would be completely wrong. The trajectory also depends on the irregularities of the beach. The fundamental consequence of this idea is that providing the characteristics of the ant's internal system without considering its interaction with the environment will never explain the ant's behaviour. To explain the ant's behaviour, it is necessary to consider both the internal processes of the ant and the characteristics of the environment. However, in Simon's proposal it is still assumed that the ant's internal system can be modelled independently of the beach model. And also, of course, the beach could be modelled independently of the ant's internal processes. What Simon's proposal means is that the path of the ant on the beach cannot be modelled without considering both the ant's internal processes and the characteristics of the beach together. Simon's proposal refers to the ant's behaviour which has to be explained in terms of the interaction between the ant's internal processes and the characteristics of the beach. However, this proposal still assumes that the ant's internal processes, like those of the human mind, can be modelled independently.

Fig. 1. The Parable of the ant on the beach by Simon [4]. Image created by Mariano Sánchez.

Therefore, it is quite possible that the idea expressed as a parable by Simon is correct in one sense: if our intention is to explain the ant's behaviour, we need a model of the environment and a model of the ant's internal processes. However, this idea might be incorrect in another very important sense: it is assumed that it is possible that the modelling of the internal processes of the ant could not be done without considering its interaction with the environment. However, it is possible that the internal processes are dependent on the environment and cannot be modelled without considering the characteristics of the environment. It is not only that human behaviour depends on the internal states of the human being, the characteristics of the environment, the emerging characteristics of the complex system formed by the human being, and the other elements of the environment. It is also that the internal characteristics of the human being depend on the interaction with the environment. As research has repeatedly shown, the memory capacity of a skilled chess player depends on how the figures are placed on the chessboard

[5]. Thus, going back to the example of short-term capacity, we might say that the answer to the system engineers when they ask 'what is the capacity of short-term memory' must be that it depends on the design of the system in which the human being is interacting with machines and other human beings. In order to see how widespread this assumption expressed by Simon in his parabola is between among all participants in system design, we can consider a recent example in which this assumption underlies the researchers' approach to the problem they are studying.

In a recent study, Ferreira and Cañas [6] have modelled the behaviour of air traffic controllers (ATCo) in future scenarios when they have to interact with automatic systems. This work was carried out as part of the AUTOPACE[1] project. This project addressed the training of ATCo and the changes in contents, approaches, and requirements that will emerge from increased automation. The project methodology focussed mainly on the human participation in what were considered typical ATC situations. These typical situations reflect sequences of actions that would be carried out in order to fulfil ATC operational needs. To do this modelling the authors have used a methodology known as the Functional Resistance Analysis Method (FRAM) [7]. FRAM is a modelling tool that focusses on the interdependencies of systems, their dynamics, and complexity. This tool is based on the principles of resonance engineering by Hollnagel et al. [8] and in recent years has shown to provide innovative support to the understanding of complex operations and activities. FRAM is based on a description of the actual work (work as it is) as the functional elements of a socio-technical system (what needs to be done to achieve a given objective), which can then be used to produce various operational scenarios as model moments. It is also an instrument of 'abstraction' in the sense that it focusses on what must be carried out and what is needed (i.e. what resources are required) to achieve an operational objective. These characteristics of the framework were considered useful for the achievement of AUTOPACE's objectives, as it provided a basis for comparison between the different scenarios and events being studied.

The FRAM model is built on the basis of the description of functions. A system function is something of human, technological, or organisational nature, which transforms the state of the system towards the fulfilment of the operational objective of this system. This introduces a diversity of factors into the modelling, related to the dynamics of the system which are often not observed in models based on organisational structures or process flows, in particular those aspects related to the types and extent of operational variability. FRAM takes into account the non-linear nature of performance in complex systems, as opposed to the construction of cause–effect sequences of events over time.

The fundamental step in the use of this method is the identification and description of functions. Figure 2 illustrates the functional unit of a FRAM. Each function is defined by six descriptors (time, control, output, resource, precondition, and input).

Figure 3 shows the result of the application of FRAM methodology to model the interactions between system components in an average ATC automation scenario. The figure shows the set of functions that are carried out by the human operator in a scenario of medium automation. In such a scenario of 'medium automation', which is foreseen

[1] Facilitating the AUTOmation PACE—funded by the SESAR Joint Undertaking within the European Union's Horizon 2020 research and innovation programme under grant agreement No 699238 (autopace.eu).

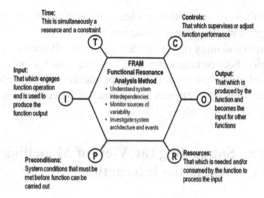

Fig. 2. Functional unit of FRAM

for the year 2035, the ATCo retains a considerable degree of traffic monitoring and decision-making responsibilities. The system will propose traffic solutions and prompt the ATCo for a decision on the most suitable one. In the figure, the functions carried out by the human operator are shown in blue and technological functions are shown in green.

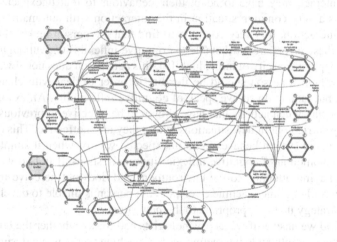

Fig. 3. FRAM model of ATC under scenario of medium automation

The important thing to understand from this methodology designed to analyse the interactions between human operators and machines is that the interaction is modelled according to the human and machine functions but it is assumed that the modelling of the human functions carried out by people has to be modelled independently from the functions carried out by machines, which are also modelled independently. What happens within a human function will depend on the input it receives, the time it has to act, the controls that oversee it, the preconditions that must be met before the function is carried out, and the resources available to it. However, the inner workings of the function are considered to be fixed by evolution and learning and can be studied independently of all these parameters that influence its functioning.

Thus, while this methodology represents a significant advance in our ability to model the dynamic interaction between elements of a system, it still assumes that human cognitive systems can and should be modelled independently of the context of interaction. In this sense, this methodology continues to assume the idea underlying Simon's parable of the ant on the beach.

2 Some Examples Supporting the View of Modelling the Human Mind 'in the Context of the Interaction'

However, let us now consider another example in which the possibility of independent modelling of the human cognitive system becomes difficult without considering the context of interaction. It has long been assumed that humans are adaptive and capable of adapting their behaviour to the conditions of the environment. This characteristic of the human cognitive system has been called cognitive flexibility. In the field of HMI, cognitive flexibility has been considered a very important characteristic of the human mind to explain how human beings adapt to changes in the environment of interaction. For example, when a person is faced with an unexpected action by the machine with which they interact, they have to adapt their behaviour to that unexpected machine action. This is a very common situation in the interaction with automatic systems. In this type of interaction, it is very common to find that the person makes mistakes. To some extent, these errors are attributable to cognitive inflexibility. Although flexibility could be an adaptive capacity of individuals [9], this adaptation does not always happen. In situations where a person should be flexible in order to deal with changes in the environment, but fails to do so, we speak of cognitive inflexibility. An example of this inflexibility occurs when actions that have shown to be effective in previous situations are insistently carried out in new situations where they are ineffective. This can happen when an automatic system behaves in an unexpected way or when it simply does not work. The phenomenon of cognitive inflexibility manifests itself in two ways: (1) the person stops paying attention to the environment and does not perceive the changes that have occurred (e.g. the machine error); (2) the person is unable to develop another behavioural strategy that is appropriate to the new situation.

What would we answer if we as psychologists had to say whether the human being would be flexible or inflexible interacting with a machine that is being designed? What factors would determine whether the person is flexible or inflexible? Cañas, Antoli, Fajardo, and Salmeron [10] had shown that the answer will depend on whether or not the machine with which the person has been interacting in the past has shown variability in its actions. If there has been variability in the machine's actions, attention will remain high with regard to possible changes in it and the person will try to have enough knowledge to be able to develop a new strategy to face this possible change in the machine's behaviour. If, on the contrary, the person has learned that the machine does not show any variability and its actions are constant, they will get used to this absence of variability and will not pay any more attention to the changes occurring in the machine and will stop acquiring knowledge to develop new interaction strategies. Therefore, to the question of whether the human cognitive system is flexible or not, we will have to answer another question about the history of interaction with a machine that has shown variability in its actions.

Therefore, if a feature of the inner workings of the human cognitive system depends on its history of interaction with a particular machine, in a particular context and under particular conditions, we cannot say that we can model those inner workings independently of that history of interaction. The reason for this is to be found in what is the most important characteristic of the functioning of the human mind, which is its capacity to simulate the world with which it interacts. Recognising this characteristic means that we must define the interaction between the human mind and the other elements of a system in terms of the human mind's capacity to simulate reality. But we must also recognise that this simulation is not possible without considering the elements with which the mind interacts.

This proposal can be explained by Cañas, Antolí, and Quesada's [11] definition of Mental Model. Many researchers in recent decades have proposed that in order to interact with a system it is necessary to possess a mental model of that system [12]. A mental model of a system is knowledge of the functioning and structure of that system. However, for a long time there was no agreement on what a mental model of a system is. For many researchers, a mental model was a representation stored in long-term memory [13]. However, given that it is a representation stored in long-term memory it does not help us to explain how it can be used to interact with the system. For this reason, Cañas, Antolí, and Quesada proposed that a Mental Model should be a dynamic representation created in working memory by combining information stored in long-term memory and characteristics extracted from the environment. The authors suggested that the information stored in long-term memory could be called the conceptual model of the system, and the term Mental Model should be used to name the simulation of the structure and the functioning of the system that is run in working memory by combining the permanent information (knowledge) stored in long-term memory and the information extracted from the environment through the perceptual processes.

The authors performed several experiments in which participants learned to operate a control panel device displayed on the computer screen. The device was a modified version of the one used by Kieras and Bovair [14] consisting of switches, push buttons, and indicator lights (See Fig. 4). They told the participants that it was a control panel of an electrical circuit. Their task consisted of making the current flow from panel S1 to panel S3. They were instructed on the three possible action sequences that allowed them to complete the task:

Route X: press button ON in panel S1 (light I1 turned on); switch toggle switch in panel S2 to X (light I2 turned on); press button B1 in panel S3 (light I3 turned on).
Route Y: press button ON in panel S1 (light I1 turned on) switch toggle switch in panel S2 to Y (light I2 remained off); press button B2 in panel S3 (light I3 turned on).
Route Z: press button ON in panel S1 (light I1 turned on); switch toggle switch in panel S2 to Z (lights I2 and I3 turned on).

This system was sufficiently simple so that the participants could learn it easily in a short period of time.

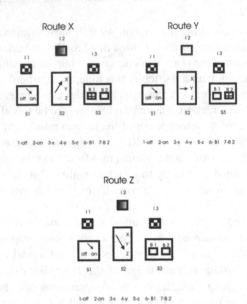

Fig. 4. Device set in the experiments by Cañas, Antoli, and Quesada [11]

Participants performed three tasks during the experimental session: (1) A Learning Task during which the participants learned and practised operating the system until they were capable of executing the three action sequences two times without making any mistakes. (2) A Declarative Task during which they answered ten questions on the operation of the interface. The purpose of this test was to have a measure of the declarative knowledge that participants had and to ensure that they had actually learned to interact with the interface. Thus, the authors could suppose that they had acquired the conceptual model of the system. All the participants that failed on one or more questions from the questionnaire were eliminated from the experiment. (3) An Elicitation Task where participants completed a relationship judgement task concerning 11 interface items. They were asked to assign ratings to pairs of items presented on the computer screen according to how related they thought the items were. The scale ranged from 1 to 6. A rating of one indicated that the items were unrelated, and a rating of six indicated a high degree of relatedness. The participants were asked to indicate their responses by pressing the numbers corresponding to their ratings on the keyboard. The instructions emphasised that they should work fast, basing their ratings on their first impression of relatedness.

In the elicitation task a group of participants rated the similarity of the interface items in the same sequence, and the computer generated a different random sequence for other groups of participants. The authors argued that if knowledge of the relationship between interface items was static and physical, it would have made no difference in judging the relationship between them whether the pairs of items appeared in the knowledge elicitation task in a fixed and equal manner or in a random and different sequence for each participant. However, the results showed that participants who judged the similarity of the items in a fixed and equal sequence for all made practically equal similarity judgements.

In contrast, participants who judged similarity in different and random sequences gave very different judgements. The authors concluded that these differences were due to the fact that during the task of judging the relationship between items, participants 'simulated the functioning of the system'. Thus, judging the relationship between a pair of items and simulating the relationship between those two items emphasised one dimension of that relationship. That dimension that had been emphasised remained in working memory when the relationship of another pair of items was to be judged. Thus, the judgement of one pair of items biased the judgement of the next pair of items. Thus, participants who judged the similarity of items in the same sequence of pairs made similar relatedness judgements, while participants who did so in different, random sequences made different relatedness judgements. The conclusion of these experiments was that when people are asked to use knowledge about the structure and functioning of a system, they do so by simulating interaction with this system. Therefore, it is not possible to consider the mental representation without taking into account the simulation of the interaction with the system.

A proposal along the same line of thought is made by Saariluoma [15] when he distinguished between perception and apperception. According to this author, mental representations are not 'extracted' from the stimulating environment but are constructed through the combination of information extracted from the environment and information already stored in the mind. The extraction of information from the environment is what we would call 'perception' and the process of combining this information with the information already stored is what we call 'apperception'.

The process of apperception is similar to the process of creating a mental model of a physical system proposed by Cañas, Antolí, and Quesada. The idea behind both proposals is that the human mind simulates reality as it interacts with the environment. Therefore, the interaction implies the simulation of reality and it is not possible to explain the functioning of this simulation process without taking into account what the environment is like.

Helfenstein and Saariluoma [16] performed several experiments to demonstrate that depending on priming information, people represent perceptually identical stimuli very differently, namely they ascribe different uses and meanings to objects, and they integrate them differently to compose distinct solutions. Thus, they demonstrated that people regularly rely on information, which is not, or cannot be perceived in principle. But also, this process of apperception implies that the information stored permanently in long-term memory serves to simulate reality and cannot be studied without taking into account this simulation, which also involves information about the particular system with which it interacts.

Also, in the same line of thought, we can also say that current research on emotions indicates that a fundamental characteristic of the human mind such as the emotional state is 'constructed' and cannot be studied independently of the context of its construction [17]. Attempts to develop a model of emotions that can be used during machine design have been unsuccessful. The fundamental reason for this could be that it has not been taken into account that emotions are possibly 'constructed'.

Finally, we must mention a characteristic of human beings that clearly affects their interaction with the environment. This characteristic is their belonging to a culture.

It is evident that culture is 'constructed' and changes during the interaction with the environment. Therefore, if we do not take into account that we have to study the role that culture plays during interaction, it is necessary to recognise that culture cannot be studied independently of the interaction of the human being with the environment. Culture is an instrument of interaction with the environment and is not independent of it. For example, scientists who are studying the effect of trust in interaction with automated systems are pointing out that trust in automation is dependent on culture and therefore we cannot understand trust without considering that culture is created during the interaction with the elements of the environment, which in this case are intelligent automated systems [18].

3 Conclusions

We will conclude by recognising that what we can answer when an engineer asks us what the human mind is like will depend on what the human mind is interacting with. To answer the question of how the human mind is we need to know how it has been or what it is interacting with. The fundamental implication of this view of the human mind is that research into its structure and functioning must be done 'during the design process' and not in isolation in a laboratory from which a fixed response is expected, independent of the context of the interaction. This view of the human mind coincides with the idea of adaptive machines [19]. But, also, this new view of the role of the human mind in the design process means that we have to revise our assumptions if we want to advance our understanding of the design process [20]. Just to take one final example, let us think about the definition of the concept of complexity. We have to recognise that complexity is not defined in the system, it is defined by the interaction between the system and the person. Similarly, the characteristics of the person are not defined in the person but in the interaction with the system. Thus, when we say that a trail is of high, medium, or low difficulty, the question is whether there is a measure of difficulty that is independent of the specific hiker who is going to walk it. Our proposal means that there is no such thing as an independent measure of difficulty that can be applied without considering the characteristics of the specific hiker. In the same way, we can't talk about a hiker's abilities without asking 'abilities for what? Two sitting hikers are not exactly the same.

There are two fundamental consequences of this new vision that we propose. First, it is now completely evident that the human being who will interact with the system being designed must be included from the very first moment in the design process. Although this has been said many times, it has not been done in the day-to-day reality of the design process. Rather, it has been the tradition that whenever engineers have had some doubt about how the user would think or act during the interaction with the system they are designing, they ask for an external report from some expert in human sciences about some characteristic of the human being that they believe will be important during the interaction. However, this report external to the design process is precisely what we are saying will not be what is required because it will imply that the knowledge about that characteristic will have been obtained in a context outside of the interaction with the system being designed (often a psychology lab).

If we accept that the human mind and human behaviour have to be studied in the context of the design of a particular system, the human sciences have to create appropriate methodologies to make this possible. The vast majority of methodologies that the human sciences currently use are appropriate for laboratory studies, however, they cannot be used during the design process. It is evident that it will be very difficult to create appropriate methodologies due to the characteristics of the design process that are very different from the characteristics of the traditional human sciences study. We have to be aware of the difficulties we will encounter in conducting research during the design process in which we want to measure neurological parameters. However, the first steps to develop such methodologies are already being taken, while acknowledging the difficulties involved, as Parasuraman and Rizzo did in their pioneering work on neuroergonomics [21].

References

1. Miller, G.A.: The magic number seven plus or minus two: some limits on our capacity for processing information. Psychol. Rev. **63**, 91–97 (1956)
2. Chase, W.G., Simon, H.A.: Perception in chess. Cogn. Psychol. **4**(1), 55–81 (1973)
3. Johnson, C.W.: What are emergent properties and how do they affect the engineering of complex systems? Reliab. Eng. Syst. Saf. **91**(12), 1475–1481 (2006)
4. Simon, H.: The Science of the Artificial. MIT Press, Cambridge, MA (1969)
5. Saariluoma, P.: Chess Players' Thinking: A Cognitive Psychological Approach. Psychology Press, New York. (1995)
6. Ferreira, P.N., Cañas, J.J.: Assessing operational impacts of automation using functional resonance analysis method. Cogn. Technol. Work **21**(3), 535–552 (2019)
7. Hollnagel E.: FRAM, The Functional Resonance Analysis Method: Modelling Complex Socio-technical Systems. Ashgate (2012)
8. Hollnagel E., Woods, D.D., Leveson, N. (eds.): Resilience Engineering—Concepts And Precepts. Ashgate, Farnham (2006)
9. Payne, J.W., Bettman, J.R., Johnson, E.J.: The Adaptive Decision Maker. Cambridge University Press, Cambridge (1993)
10. Cañas*, J.J., Antolí, A., Fajardo, I., Salmerón, L.: Cognitive inflexibility and the development and use of strategies for solving complex dynamic problems: effects of different types of training. Theor. Issues Ergon. Sci. **6**(1), 95–108 (2005)
11. Cañas, J.J., Antolí, A., Quesada, J.F.: The role of working memory on measuring mental models of physical systems. Psicológica **22**(1), 25–42 (2001)
12. Moran, T.P.: An applied psychology of the user. Comput. Surv. **13**, 1–11 (1981)
13. Gentner, D., Stevens, A.L.: Mental Models. LEA, Hillsdale, NJ (1983)
14. Kieras, D.E., Bovair, S.: The role of mental model in learning to operate a device. Cogn. Sci. **8**, 255–273 (1984)
15. Saariluoma, P.: Apperception and restructuring in chess players' problem solving. In: Gilhooly, K.J., Keane, M.T.G., Logie, R., Erdos, G. (eds.): Lines of Thinking: Reflections on the Psychology Of Thought, vol. 2. Skills, Emotion, Creative Processes, Individual Differences and Teaching Thinking, pp. 41–57. Wiley, Oxford (1990)
16. Helfenstein, S., Saariluoma, P.: Apperception in primed problem solving. Cogn. Process. **8**(4), 211–232 (2007)
17. Barrett, L. F. How Emotions are Made: The Secret Life of the Brain. Houghton Mifflin Harcourt. (2017)

18. Chien, S., Lewis, M., Sycara, K., Liu, J., Kumru, A.: The effect of culture on trust in automation. ACM Trans. Interact. Intell. Syst. **8**(4), 1–31 (2018). https://doi.org/10.1145/3230736

19. Ayne, J.W., Bettman, J.R., Johnson, E.J.: The Adaptive Decision Maker. Cambridge University Press, Cambridge (1993)

20. Saariluoma, P.: Foundational Analysis: Presuppositions in Experimental Psychology, vol. 2. Psychology Press, New York (1997)

21. Parasuraman, R., Rizzo, M. (eds.): Neuroergonomics: The Brain at Work. Oxford University Press, Oxford (2008)

Social Media Data for the Conservation of Historic Urban Landscapes: Prospects and Challenges

Manal Ginzarly[✉] [iD]

Lebanese American University, Beirut, Lebanon
manal.ginzarly@lau.edu.lb

Abstract. This study attempts to frame the contribution of social media data (SMD) to the conservation and management of historic urban landscapes with a focus on the dynamics of heritage co-production. It particularly addresses bottom-up digitally mediated heritage practices aside from institutional structures. To this end, it addresses two key issues: the co-construction of meanings of everyday landscape on social media and the heritage appropriation by online communities. The first employs SMD to study human-environment interactions and provides insights on individuals' encounters with the historic urban landscape. The second explores the contribution of online narratives to heritage conservation. The discussion focuses on the opportunities and challenges in analyzing big data on social media and the implications of knowledge gained for the scope of what is defined as heritage at the intersection of the heritage by appropriation and the authorized heritage discourse (AHD) as well as for sustainable heritage conservation and management.

Keywords: Social media · Historic urban landscape · Heritage co-production

1 Historic Urban Landscape, Digital Technologies, and Social Inclusion

The 2030 United Nations Agenda for Sustainable Development mentioned cultural heritage inter alia in goals 4, 8, 11, 16, and 17. The third and fourth points of goal 11 on sustainable cities and communities highlight the need "to protect and safeguard the world's cultural and natural heritage" to "make our cities inclusive, safe, resilient, and sustainable" [1]. The integration of policies and practices of cultural heritage conservation into the wider framework of sustainable urban development requires the application of an integrated landscape approach that responds to local cultural contexts and value systems and addresses policies and governance concerns at international and local levels [2]. A landscape approach to urban heritage addresses the city as a living heritage and as a multi-layering of meaning that changes across time and space. Within this approach, the historic urban landscape extends beyond the notion of historic centers and designated heritage to encompass the city as a whole [3] and recognize everyday

© Springer Nature Switzerland AG 2021
M. Rauterberg (Ed.): HCII 2021, LNCS 12795, pp. 209–223, 2021.
https://doi.org/10.1007/978-3-030-77431-8_13

landscapes that challenge heritage boundaries and dominant narratives of identity and collective memory. Central to this conceptualization is that cultural heritage is a socio-cultural construct subject to diverse interpretations and associations of meanings related to experiential values, personal perceptions, and knowledge [4, 5]. Nevertheless, capturing users' definition of heritage and the range of cultural values they ascribe to the historic urban landscape, and at the same time ensuring inclusion in the process, appears to be challenging and is often disregarded in practice [2, 6].

In the 21st century, the increased use of digital technologies, online applications, and social media have determined a rapid change in the production and consumption of cultural heritage and these changes have major implications on the conservation of cultural heritage. In the digital age, heritage activities are increasingly extending to online spaces and social media platforms are providing virtual public space for the co-production of heritage knowledge and the co-construction of meanings of everyday landscapes. Within this context, social media is providing a window to non-expert perceptions of heritage and alternative narratives to the "official" heritage discourse. Many cultural institutions have invested in crowdsourcing to increase audience engagement with heritage collections. In parallel, many digital grassroots initiatives have popped up to shape the dynamics of heritage production and foster inclusion and civic engagement [7]. In addition to active contributions, people passively engage in the co-construction of heritage by posting comments and sharing content on social media. In this context, the AHD is challenged as users engage as consumers and producers of heritage content.

Although the above-mentioned practices are often associated with participatory heritage praxis, some scholars argue that (1) digital platforms may reinforce hegemony depending on the mediated interaction between users and the platform [8, 9]; (2) the digital divide – the differential access and use of information and communication technologies – prevents some social and economic groups from contributing to collective expressions of identity [10]; and (3) the dependence of SMD retrieval and analysis on application programming interfaces (APIs) – the platform technical architecture that reflects the operational goals of a company – can exert significant influence on research design and outcome [11, 12].

In this article, I aim to frame the contribution of SMD to the conservation and management of historic urban landscapes. It is worth mentioning that this study is not an attempt to address top-down participatory heritage initiatives nor digital transformation in authorized cultural institutions, but to examine bottom-up digitally-mediated heritage practices aside from institutional structures. Within these processes, the public creates its own digital heritage landscapes, where sharing photos and narratives in the present leads to a collective interpretation of the past, and where communal views, experiences, and meanings evolve to construct what may be recognized as the cultural landscapes of tomorrow [13–16].

In this paper, I ask what are the opportunities and challenges in analyzing big data on social media and how can experts employ the knowledge gained to serve sustainable urban development and heritage conservation? Furthermore, what forms of grassroots heritage co-production are enabled by social media? Finally, what are their implications for the scope of what is defined as heritage at the intersection of the heritage by appropriation and the AHD?

To inspect these questions I carried out two investigations. The first reviews passive contributions to the interpretation of historic urban landscapes by looking at the application of SMD for extracting human-environment interactions. The second examines the various uses of social media in claiming heritage, building narratives about collective identity, and generating citizen heritage interpretation. In both investigations, I highlight the opportunities, challenges, and the way forward regarding the application of SMD in the conservation of historic urban landscapes.

2 Social Media and the Dynamics of Heritage Co-production

The extended use of smartphones and social media apps has changed many aspects of everyday practices as they have now become largely mediated by digital technology. Socio-cultural interactions and discussions about heritage are increasingly transferred to the digital sphere, whether in the form of discussion forums or the sharing of photos, videos, experiences, and opinions via social networks [17]. Social media apps provide analysts access to a wide range of shared data such as check-ins, geo-tagged images, tags, or reviews [18]. When people share content on social media, their online practices convey a collective image of landscapes and heritage values within the community realm [19]. The process of sharing affirms the online space as a socio-cultural space, creating a bridge between real and digital worlds and providing innovative tools to understand people's interests, preferences, motivations, and behavior [20–22]. As new knowledge about cultural heritage is co-created out of user-generated photos and folksonomies, virtual communities mediate the co-production of heritage knowledge. The following section provides insights into how we can harvest this knowledge and unveil everyday practices and cultural values from SMD.

2.1 Everyday Heritage on Social Media

The important role of social media for performing real-time analytics on people's interpretation of, and interaction with, the historic urban landscape is evidenced by the growing number of papers analyzing SMD. A Scopus search reveals that the number of heritage studies that use social media as a data source has grown exponentially from 5 in 2010 to 261 in 2020. Most of these studies explore the emerging role of social media in tourism and hospitality [18]. This field of research is very wide in scope and addresses visitors' experiences, behavior, visitation patterns, and spatial distribution. Moreover, some authors addressed online heritage practices outside the institutional domain, such as alternative narratives to heritage and the heritage-making form below [23, 24]. Within urban and environmental studies, scholars have also been exploring the use of SMD for landscape characterization, assessment of values ascribed to urban landscapes or cultural ecosystem services, landscape perception and preferences identification, and sustainable urban development. This field of research is growing gradually and publications increased from 4 in 2011 to 54 in 2020.

Given the wide scope of research and the increased number of papers, various systematic reviews were conducted to provide an overview of methods applied so far for the analysis of SMD and to identify knowledge gained from different social media platforms. For instance, Vassiliadis and Belenioti [25] reviewed 54 papers to present the opportunities of social media to museum experience and communication, its enhancement to museums' learning process as well as the problems and barriers associated with social media integration in museums. Whereas, Stock [26] analyzed 690 papers across 20 social media platforms, focusing particularly on the method used for the extraction of location information to discuss and compare extraction methods, and consider their accuracy and coverage. In tourism studies, Zeng and Gerritsen [27] reviewed and analyzed 279 papers focusing on social media in tourism, while Teles da Mota and Pickering [28] conducted a review of 48 publications that focused on the use of social media for the assessment of nature-based tourism.

In urban and environmental studies, Ilieva and McPhearson [29] reviewed 105 articles to address the emerging opportunities of using SMD in urban sustainability research. Bubalo et al. [30] reviewed more than 500 papers to assess the different crowdsourcing modes applied to collect geo-information on landscape perception and preferences and cultural ecosystem services. Calcagni et al. [31] conducted a systematic review of 29 publications to explore the extent to which relational cultural ecosystem services are inferable through social media. Toivonen et al. [32] reviewed 35 papers to present analytical approaches to mining and analyzing SMD for conservation science. Kong et al. [33] reviewed 224 papers amongst which 90 use SMD for urban sustainability research. These papers mainly address urban mobility, land use, environmental sustainability, social equity, and tourism. Zhang et al. [34] reviewed 58 articles using geolocated SMD to evaluate cultural ecosystem services, such as aesthetics, recreation, sense of place, and local identity. Liang et al. [35] reviewed 19 articles on digital community engagement to illustrate the contribution of social media in the process of cultural heritage management.

To provide a comprehensive reading on the application of social media to sustainable heritage conservation, I investigated the above mentioned systematic reviews and extracted the opportunities as well as methodological limitations and proposed solutions in the analysis of SMD. Table 1 presents the main findings. SMD are mostly derived from Twitter, Flickr, Facebook, Foursquare, Instagram, Sina Weibo, and Panoramio [18, 29].

This brief overview makes clear that methods that rely on the use of SMD can complement traditional survey methods to include a variety of data sources and groups of users to unveil the range of values attached to historic urban landscapes to inform decision-making. Moreover, it reveals that the analysis of SMD is a complex endeavor, which draws on a variety of technical-driven and data-driven challenges within the methodological workflow. The majority of heritage studies and urban environment studies deploy social media as a tool for analysis and/or community engagement. In doing so, they raise concerns related to the digital divide and representativeness issues among others, and draw on some solutions to overcome these limitations [19, 36–40]. Nevertheless, the discussion of these critical topics remains abstract and overly general [12]. I argue that rather than envisioning social media as a tool and focusing on what knowledge it might generate as its end product, we might approach it as a paradigm shift in the way the public engages with heritage. This approach requires us to consider the landscape of the digitally mediated heritage and the potential of digitally mediated interpretation, documentation, dissemination, and mobilization of heritage in actively contributing to the democratization of heritage values as well as in challenging regulatory and institutional systems.

There are different ways in which heritage is digitally mediated, from the digitization of tangible and intangible heritage attributes to audiences' contributions to heritage institutions and grassroots practices. Nevertheless, different forms of public outreach have been highly critiqued [41, 42]. Moreover, Taylor and Gibson [9] argue that even though the digital access to cultural heritage content makes the interpretation of heritage polyvocal and less dependent on experts, the decision of what is heritage and what is commissioned for digitization is not necessarily part of this democratization. Other scholars have argued that participation within official heritage websites is often manipulated and

Table 1. Summary of opportunities, challenges, and way forward in the application of SMD in Mapping aspects of the historic urban landscape and extracting human-environment interactions.

Methodological workflow	Opportunities	Challenges	Way forward
Data acquisition	Less costly and time-consuming	Ethics of data acquisition; The use of API might return only a subsample of the requested data; Uncertainty about future data availability; Some platforms, like Twitter and Instagram, have short time spam for available data	Use web crawling software, Secure data, and resolve ownership and IP issues
Data quality	Big data (spatial, temporal, textual, & visual); Real-time spatial resolution; Time-specific information	Noise level; The time resolution depends on the user's post frequency; Inadequate population representation; Absence of demographic information; The geographical data is not always accurate; The popularity of platforms change over time as well as their users; Data can be biased towards specific user groups; Spatial bias as a result of data gaps in places with poor data or poor reliability of geotags; Most studies use data from a single social media site	Combine data from multiple social media apps, Quantify biases by comparing results from different platforms and for time-separated datasets from the same platform; Employ different sources of data; Extract metadata from individuals' profile descriptions; Use text-based metadata to verify geotags; Separately analyze photos with upload location errors; Collapse photos taken by a single photographer within a given radius to a single arithmetically centered point

(continued)

Table 1. (*continued*)

Methodological workflow	Opportunities	Challenges	Way forward
Data processing	The scale of analysis; Real-time monitoring; First-hand observation; Social sensing	Difficult to pre-process textual data because of no standard spellings, abbreviations, creative language, Sarcasm and metaphors, and multiple languages; heterogeneity of data structure among different platforms; Cleaning and filtering the data; transforming the structure and format of the data. Photos classification and the coding of big textual data are challenging; Absence of a unified coding protocol; Most studies are based on the analysis of one data type-georeferenced data or photographs	Apply more sophisticated analysis methods and examine several elements of data together spatial, temporal, and visual; Apply methods from computer sciences and artificial intelligence that are marking progress with machine learning for analyzing visual and textual data; Develop domain-specific training data sets to assist in machine learning methods
Interpretation of results	Effective source for emotion analysis and personal opinion mining; Effective for environmental monitoring and characterization of land use and land cover; Credible for the assessment of visitation patterns; Analysis of hot and cold spots provide useful information to prioritize areas for conservation and cultural services management; Reveals perspectives that arise from directly experiencing and valuing the environment, Advantageous for retrieving relational values and a wide range of cultural values, including experiential, aesthetic, and spiritual symbolic; A window to people's preferences; Measures space attractiveness	Can't draw generalizations from results as they are representatives of the users of a specific social media platform; Researcher bias; Social media tends to broadcast the heritage value instead of strengthening the collaboration among stakeholders	Results should be compared with results from traditional data sources like surveys and questionnaires; Combine studies with other data sources, Carefully consider the biases; Move from results to action and work on the implication of data for social justice and sustainability; Interdisciplinary interpretation combining expertise in geography, social sciences, linguistics, and computer science

tends to reaffirm experts' values and the dominant heritage discourse and have questioned the contribution of digital technologies in enabling participative democracy [23, 43]. In this context, grassroots initiatives appear as a constructive mobilizing force that shapes the dynamics of heritage co-production, builds a further appropriation of local heritage values, fosters inclusion, and mediates conflicting interests in an urban context [44, 45]. The resulting broadened scope of what is defined as heritage complicates the process of conservation as it makes it difficult to mediate between diverse representations of history and urban experiences and reach consensus on 'what' to preserve and 'how', giving i) the diversity of values associated with the historic urban landscape, (ii) the conflicting interests among the different stakeholders, and (iii) the dynamic and continually changing character of the urban landscape and its associated values. Nevertheless, it is controversy that contributes to a more collaborative urban governance by providing an arena for grassroots initiatives [45]. Online grassroots communities and their digital exchange are highly localized and provide new prospects for digitally-enabled forms of social production of cultural values and non-experts perceptions of heritage [46–48].

2.2 Heritage Appropriation by Online Communities

Digital media far from being a tool for "holding" versions of the past, as it is not a passive "go-between", it mediates the construction of memory and past experiences and thereby "intrinsically shapes the way we build up and retain a sense of individuality and community, or identity and history" [49]. Users initiate and join Facebook groups, community pages, and hashtag communities driven by shared values and interests or a common cause [50]. Virtual communities provide a forum for narrating heritage and digitally exchanging memories and photos. Many scholars have addressed grassroots narrative practices on social media and have explored their contribution to heritage conservation. Table 2 provides an overview of these studies. It highlights their scope and opportunities for heritage conservation and, in some cases, challenges expressed by scholars and the way forward.

The different studies presented in Table 2 show how the analysis of the interactions within online communities enables bottom-up interpretations of everyday encounters with the historic urban landscape and provides insights into people's perceptions of heritage that defy the AHD and official conceptions of identity, history, and heritage values. Table 2 also shows that the most frequently used platform for the initiation of online communities is Facebook. People's narratives of identity and cultural heritage within online communities help to explain the processes of change and continuing identity, and these narratives can be identified as the foundation of conservation as the management of change [60]. While addressing grassroots online communities and their contribution to heritage conservation, it is important to differentiate between the digitization and digitalization of heritage.

Digitization and digitalization are often used interchangeably, but they are two different concepts that have different meanings. Digitization is the straightforward process of converting tangible or intangible heritage attribute to digital— like reproducing and representing heritage architecture digitally using the advancement of virtual reality technologies [61]. It is the process of moving from physical to digital— such as replacing the built physical heritage architecture with online 3D representation that acts as a digital

Table 2. Grassroots online communities and the role of social media in enabling inclusion in heritage conservation.

Publication	Scope	Role of Social media
Gregory [51]	Examined a Facebook group concerned with the loss of heritage assets	Opportunities Online communities enhance both awareness of and collective attachment to the past and help to generate the social capital needed to mobilize against the destruction of heritage buildings and places
Morgan and Pallascio [52]	Addressed engagement in digital heritage practices by examining purpose-built and community-created forums of difficult heritage on social media	Opportunities Unofficial virtual communities enable people to remember together and share stories, unfiltered personal testimonies, and unrestricted comments Challenges Authoritative voices are absent in unofficial online discussions of heritage and there is little connectivity apparent between academics, heritage interpreters, and the online stakeholder communities
Baker and Collins [53]	Examined a Facebook group to identify the challenges non-institutional community archives of popular music heritage face in achieving sustainability	Opportunities Generate prodigious amounts of archival content Challenges Minimal attention is paid to the durability of this content. Shared narratives may be lost when websites go offline because of a lack of resources. Arranged unsystematically the fact that challenges its interpretation by experts
Bennett and Strong [54]	Examined the capacity of *save the place* activists Facebook group to preserve aspects of the local popular music heritage	Opportunities Social media assists in giving a voice to competing discourses of cultural value and in broadening our understanding of the definition, nature, and function of heritage

(*continued*)

Table 2. (*continued*)

Publication	Scope	Role of Social media
Irimiás and Volo [55]	Investigated the knowledge-sharing process within virtual communities and compared user-generated content with destinations' official communication about heritage sites to identify, original and consumer-oriented narratives	Opportunities User-generated content narratives are emotionally engaging. UGC could improve institutional communication on heritage sites
Marinelli and Andò [56]	Analyzed the pragmatic use of Facebook by a social movement, *Cinema America Occupato*, as an expressive storytelling tool to collaboratively co-produce narratives about cultural heritage, and to reach and mobilize followers	Opportunities The strategic use of social media can establish a dialogue with different target stakeholders and promote social engagement and grassroots participation as well as urban action Way forward There is a necessity to fill in the theoretical gap between the political-sociological investigations of online and offline movements and the analysis of the symbolic and expressive needs that prompt "connected publics" to constantly rewrite participatory practices
Van der Hoeven [57]	Examined organizations participatory websites and non-institutional heritage-oriented Facebook groups, to discuss how social media contribute to urban heritage conservation through the online narrative practices of storytelling and mapping	Opportunities Online heritage practices (1) provide insight into the diverse narratives and values associated with a place; (2) they have more impact when they feed into wider media attention and combine different media types Way forward Grassroots online projects should consider collaborations with heritage institutions and vice versa Need a better understanding of how social media can be used in urban planning decisions

(*continued*)

Table 2. (*continued*)

Publication	Scope	Role of Social media
Ginzarly and Teller [58]	Explored the potential of social media as a framework for people-centered heritage. It examined 3 Facebook community groups to display their interpretation of heritage	Opportunities Provide knowledge on cultural values associated with the historic urban landscape by the users Could Mobilize users to take action against development projects that are considered a threat to cultural heritage Challenges Online activism does not always move beyond the virtual space. Decision-makers and experts do not engage in the discussion even if invited
Jeffrey et al. [59]	Drew on case studies from the ACCORD project, which involved ten community heritage groups, to discuss how community co-production of heritage records facilitate the production and negotiation of new forms of value and significance	Opportunities Digital recording offers a means of co-producing heritage content and capturing social values that challenge existing authorized regimes of significance Challenges Sometimes the focus on the potential future uses and techniques, such as 3D recording, distracts from the production process itself, as an engine for generating new forms of social value

surrogate to protect the loss of tangible and intangible data on the digital platform. Digitalization, on the other hand, is the on-going transformation of contemporary society and the restructuring of social life around digital communication and media infrastructures and encompasses many aspects of everyday practices [62, 63]. It refers to the use of digital technologies to create and harvest value in new ways [64]. In cultural heritage digitalization, digitized data is the basis of knowledge that can be used to take action and generate change. Whereas it is argued that the digitalization of cultural heritage has the potential to deconstruct power structures and existing practices of segregation in society, the process can result in reproduction instead of change. As the participation trends in digitalization within cultural institutions raise questions about the intersections of the authorized heritage discourse and power and the potential transformative character of digitalization [65], grassroots practices and a living heritage approach appear to be the answer to challenge the AHD and ensure co-production instead of re-production.

3 Conclusion

This article provided an overview of the application of SMD analysis to the study of human-environment interactions and perceived landscape character that identify people-centered heritage and collective identity. It showed that scholars from a range of disciplines have developed different methodological approaches to study social media platforms and the social phenomena they are entangled with. It also highlighted the use of social media by community groups to build online communities that promote engagement in heritage narratives and management. These two investigations pointed to a paradigm shift in the way the public engages with heritage. Digital engagement with heritage generates new processes of meaning-making. While the manifold expressions of heritage and the conflicting value systems among the different stakeholders often result in moments of conflict, social media provides a platform for the re-construction of cultural values and identity of place.

To ensure a just and inclusive representation, inter-governmental organizations like UNESCO and Council of Europe, as well as, expert networks like ICOMOS and ICCROM have recommended the application of a value-based living heritage approach that moves the focus of heritage from conservation to maintaining continuity and managing change [66, 67]. This approach also suggests the application of traditional and innovative participation tools, which constitute an integral part of urban governance dynamics, adapted to local contexts to enable cross-cultural dialogue between groups with conflicting interests to promote sustainable development [67]. In this light, cultural values become a means for bringing together diverse groups, experts, and citizens as well as locals and tourists, rather than being an end of heritage conservation and management [58]. However, in practice, the capacity of communities to influence decisions in processes of heritage identification, conservation, and management at the local and national levels is still questionable, especially in developing countries. In that connection, and in moments of controversy with the official heritage discourse, social media plays a major role as it empowers the community and helps to materialize and foster public engagement, especially when 'online' movements become influential and mobilize 'offline' (urban space) practices.

References

1. UN-HABITAT: Goal 11: Make cities inclusive, safe, resilient and sustainable. In: U. N. Sustain. Dev (2016). https://www.un.org/sustainabledevelopment/cities/. Accessed 29 Jan 2021
2. Ginzarly, M., Houbart, C., Teller, J.: The Historic Urban Landscape approach to urban management: a systematic review. Int. J. Herit. Stud. 1–21 (2018). https://doi.org/10.1080/135 27258.2018.1552615
3. Bandarin, F., van Oers, R.: The Historic Urban Landscape: Managing Heritage in an Urban Century. Wiley-Blackwell, Oxford, UK (2012)
4. Graham, P.B., Howard, P.P.: Heritage from below: class, social protest and resistance. In: The Ashgate Research Companion to Heritage and Identity, Ashgate Publishing, Ltd., pp. 143–158 (2012)

5. Taylor, K.: The Historic Urban Landscape paradigm and cities as cultural landscapes. Challenging orthodoxy in urban conservation. Landsc. Res. **41**, 471–480 (2016). https://doi.org/10.1080/01426397.2016.1156066
6. Jones, S.: Wrestling with the social value of heritage: problems, dilemmas and opportunities. J. Community Archaeol. Herit. **4**, 21–37 (2017). https://doi.org/10.1080/20518196.2016.1193996
7. Lewi, H., Smith, W., Murray, A., Cooke, S.: Visitor, contributor and conversationalist: multiple digital identities of the heritage citizen. Hist. Environ. **28**, 12 (2016)
8. Seltzer, E., Mahmoudi, D.: Citizen participation, open innovation, and crowdsourcing: challenges and opportunities for planning. J. Plan. Lit. **28**, 3–18 (2013). https://doi.org/10.1177/0885412212469112
9. Taylor, J., Gibson, L.K.: Digitisation, digital interaction and social media: embedded barriers to democratic heritage. Int. J. Herit. Stud. **23**, 408–420 (2017). https://doi.org/10.1080/13527258.2016.1171245
10. Pedrozo, S.: New media use in Brazil: digital inclusion or digital divide? Online J. Commun. Media Technol. **3** (2013). https://doi.org/10.29333/ojcmt/2415
11. Marres, N., Weltevrede, E.: Scraping the Social?: Issues in live social research. J. Cult. Econ. **6**, 313–335 (2013). https://doi.org/10.1080/17530350.2013.772070
12. Rieder, B., Abdulla, R., Poell, T., et al.: Data critique and analytical opportunities for very large Facebook Pages: lessons learned from exploring "We are all Khaled Said". Big Data Soc. **2**, 2053951715614980 (2015). https://doi.org/10.1177/2053951715614980
13. van Dijck, J.: Flickr and the culture of connectivity: sharing views, experiences, memories. Mem. Stud. **4**, 401–415 (2011). https://doi.org/10.1177/1750698010385215
14. Roe, M., Taylor, K.: New cultural landscapes: emerging issues, concepts, and themes. In: Roe, M., Taylor, K. (eds.) New Cultural Landscapes, pp. 1–23. Routledge, London, New York (2014)
15. Beel, D.E., Wallace, C.D., Webster, G., et al.: Cultural resilience: the production of rural community heritage, digital archives and the role of volunteers. J. Rural Stud. **54**, 459–468 (2017). https://doi.org/10.1016/j.jrurstud.2015.05.002
16. Prastyawan, A., Isbandono, P.: The Efforts of Joyoboyo Citizens in Preserving Traditional Children's Games Through Dolanan Village, pp. 378–381. Atlantis Press (2018)
17. Economou, M.: Heritage in the digital age. In: Logan, W., Craith, M.N., Kockel, U. (eds.) A Companion to Heritage Studies, pp. 215–228. John Wiley & Sons Inc, Hoboken, NJ (2015)
18. Owuor, I., Hochmair, H.H.: An overview of social media apps and their potential role in geospatial research. ISPRS Int. J. Geo-Inf. **9** (2020). https://doi.org/10.3390/ijgi9090526
19. Dunkel, A.: Visualizing the perceived environment using crowdsourced photo geodata. Landsc. Urban Plan. **142**, 173–186 (2015). https://doi.org/10.1016/j.landurbplan.2015.02.022
20. Munar, A.M., Gyimothy, S., Cai, L.: Tourism Social Media: Transformations in Identity, Community and Culture. Emerald Group Publishing (2013)
21. Bertacchini, F., Giglio, S., Gabriele, L., et al.: NEW Technologies for Improving Tourism Students Training, pp. 4155–4162. Palma, Spain (2018)
22. Giglio, S., Bertacchini, F., Bilotta, E., Pantano, P.: Using social media to identify tourism attractiveness in six Italian cities. Tour. Manag. **72**, 306–312 (2019). https://doi.org/10.1016/j.tourman.2018.12.007
23. Aigner, A.: Heritage-making from below: the politics of exhibiting architectural heritage on the Internet-a case study. Int. J. Herit. Stud. **22**, 181–199 (2016). https://doi.org/10.1080/13527258.2015.1107615
24. Carter-White, R.: Death camp heritage 'from below'? Instagram and the (re)mediation of Holocaust heritage. Herit (2018)
25. Vassiliadis, C.A., Belenioti, Z.-C.: Museums and cultural heritage via social media: an integrated literature review. Tourismos **12**, 97–132 (2017)

26. Stock, K.: Mining location from social media: a systematic review. Comput. Environ. Urban Syst. **71**, 209–240 (2018). https://doi.org/10.1016/j.compenvurbsys.2018.05.007
27. Zeng, B., Gerritsen, R.: What do we know about social media in tourism? A review. Tour. Manag. Perspect. **10**, 27–36 (2014). https://doi.org/10.1016/j.tmp.2014.01.001
28. Teles da Mota, V., Pickering, C.: Using social media to assess nature-based tourism: current research and future trends. J. Outdoor Recreat. Tour. **30**, (2020). https://doi.org/10.1016/j.jort.2020.100295
29. Ilieva, R.T., McPhearson, T.: Social-media data for urban sustainability. Nat. Sustain. **1**, 553–565 (2018). https://doi.org/10.1038/s41893-018-0153-6
30. Bubalo, M., van Zanten, B.T., Verburg, P.H.: Crowdsourcing geo-information on landscape perceptions and preferences: a review. Landsc. Urban Plan. **184**, 101–111 (2019). https://doi.org/10.1016/j.landurbplan.2019.01.001
31. Calcagni, F., Amorim Maia, A.T., Connolly, J.J.T., Langemeyer, J.: Digital co-construction of relational values: understanding the role of social media for sustainability. Sustain. Sci. **14**, 1309–1321 (2019). https://doi.org/10.1007/s11625-019-00672-1
32. Toivonen, T., Heikinheimo, V., Fink, C., et al.: Social media data for conservation science: a methodological overview. Biol. Conserv. **233**, 298–315 (2019). https://doi.org/10.1016/j.biocon.2019.01.023
33. Kong, L., Liu, Z., Wu, J.: A systematic review of big data-based urban sustainability research: state-of-the-science and future directions. J. Clean. Prod. **273** (2020). https://doi.org/10.1016/j.jclepro.2020.123142
34. Zhang, H., Huang, R., Zhang, Y., Buhalis, D.: Cultural ecosystem services evaluation using geolocated social media data: a review. Tour. Geogr. 1–23 (2020). https://doi.org/10.1080/14616688.2020.1801828
35. Liang, X., Lu, Y., Martin, J.: A review of the role of social media for the cultural heritage sustainability. Sustainability **13**, 1055 (2021). https://doi.org/10.3390/su13031055
36. Wood, S.A., Guerry, A.D., Silver, J.M., Lacayo, M.: Using social media to quantify nature-based tourism and recreation. Sci. Rep. **3**, 2976 (2013). https://doi.org/10.1038/srep02976
37. Kosinski, M., Matz, S.C., Gosling, S.D., et al.: Facebook as a research tool for the social sciences: opportunities, challenges, ethical considerations, and practical guidelines. Am. Psychol. **70**, 543–556 (2015). https://doi.org/10.1037/a0039210
38. Sloan, L., Morgan, J., Burnap, P., Williams, M.: Who tweets? Deriving the demographic characteristics of age, occupation and social class from twitter user meta-data. PLoS ONE **10**, (2015). https://doi.org/10.1371/journal.pone.0115545
39. Guerrero, P., Møller, M.S., Olafsson, A.S., Snizek, B.: Revealing cultural ecosystem services through instagram images: the potential of social media volunteered geographic information for urban green infrastructure planning and governance. Urban Plan. **1**, 1–17 (2016). https://doi.org/10.17645/up.v1i2.609
40. Jendryke, M., Balz, T., McClure, S.C., Liao, M.: Putting people in the picture: combining big location-based social media data and remote sensing imagery for enhanced contextual urban information in Shanghai. Comput. Environ. Urban Syst. **62**, 99–112 (2017). https://doi.org/10.1016/j.compenvurbsys.2016.10.004
41. Richardson, L.-J.: A Digital Public Archaeology? Pap. Inst. Archaeol. 23 (2013)
42. Walker, D.: Antisocial media in archaeology? Archaeol. Dialogues **21**, 217–235 (2014). https://doi.org/10.1017/S1380203814000221
43. Loader, B.D., Mercea, D.: Networking democracy?: Social media innovations and participatory politics. Inf. Commun. Soc. **14**, 757–769 (2011). https://doi.org/10.1080/1369118X.2011.592648
44. Beeksma, A., Cesari, C.D.: Participatory heritage in a gentrifying neighbourhood: amsterdam's Van Eesteren Museum as affective space of negotiations. Int. J. Herit. Stud. **25**, 974–991 (2019). https://doi.org/10.1080/13527258.2018.1509230

45. Ginzarly, M., Farah, J., Teller, J.: Claiming a role for controversies in the framing of local heritage values. Habitat. Int. **88** (2019). https://doi.org/10.1016/j.habitatint.2019.05.001
46. Giaccardi, E., Palen, L.: The social production of heritage through cross-media interaction: making place for place-making. Int. J. Herit. Stud. **14**, 281–297 (2008). https://doi.org/10.1080/13527250801953827
47. Caswell, M., Mallick, S.: Collecting the easily missed stories: digital participatory micro-history and the South Asian American Digital Archive. Arch. Manuscr. **42**, 73–86 (2014). https://doi.org/10.1080/01576895.2014.880931
48. Freeman, C.G.: The implications of online connectivity for world heritage in a digital platform society. Hist. Environ. **30**, 84 (2018)
49. van Dijck, J.: Flickr: Photo sharing sites between collective and connective memory. In: Shevchenko, O. (ed.) Double Exposure: Memory and Photography, pp. 211–231. Transaction Publishers (2014)
50. Vu, X.T., Abel, M.-H., Morizet-Mahoudeaux, P.: A user-centered and group-based approach for social data filtering and sharing. Comput. Hum. Behav. **51**, 1012–1023 (2015). https://doi.org/10.1016/j.chb.2014.11.079
51. Gregory, J.: Connecting with the past through social media: the beautiful buildings and cool places Perth has lost Facebook group. Int. J. Herit. Stud. **21**, 22–45 (2015). https://doi.org/10.1080/13527258.2014.884015
52. Morgan, C., Pallascio, P.M.: Digital media, participatory culture, and difficult heritage: Online remediation and the trans-atlantic slave trade. J. Afr. Diaspora Archaeol. Herit. **4**, 260–277 (2015). https://doi.org/10.1080/21619441.2015.1124594
53. Baker, S., Collins, J.: Popular music heritage, community archives and the challenge of sustainability. Int. J. Cult. Stud. **20**, 476–491 (2017). https://doi.org/10.1177/1367877916637150
54. Bennett, A., Strong, C.: Popular music heritage, grass-roots activism and web 2.0: the case of the 'Save The Palace' campaign. Cult. Sociol. **12**, 368–383 (2018). https://doi.org/10.1177/1749975518762569
55. Irimiás, A., Volo, S.: A netnography of war heritage sites' online narratives: user-generated content and destination marketing organizations communication at comparison. Int. J. Cult. Tour. Hosp. Res. **12**, 159–172 (2018). https://doi.org/10.1108/IJCTHR-07-2017-0079
56. Marinelli, A., Andò, R.: Collective action and affective publics: the "cinema America occupato" storytelling on facebook. Comun. Sociali. **2018**, 278–297 (2018)
57. van der Hoeven, A.: Valuing urban heritage through participatory heritage websites: citizen perceptions of historic urban landscapes. Space Cult. 1206331218797038 (2018). https://doi.org/10.1177/1206331218797038
58. Ginzarly, M., Teller, J.: Online communities and their contribution to local heritage knowledge. J. Cult. Herit. Manag. Sustain. Dev. (2020). https://doi.org/10.1108/JCHMSD-02-2020-0023
59. Jeffrey, S., Jones, S., Maxwell, M., et al.: 3D visualisation, communities and the production of significance. Int. J. Herit. Stud. **26**, 885–900 (2020). https://doi.org/10.1080/13527258.2020.1731703
60. Walter, N.: From values to narrative: a new foundation for the conservation of historic buildings. Int. J. Herit. Stud. **20**, 634–650 (2014). https://doi.org/10.1080/13527258.2013.828649
61. Roussou, M.: Virtual Heritage: From The Research Lab To The Broad Public. VAST Euroconference 2000, pp. 93–100. Arezzo, Italy (2002)
62. Brennen, J.S., Kreiss, D.: Digitalization. In: The International Encyclopedia of Communication Theory and Philosophy, pp. 1–11. American Cancer Society (2016)
63. Reis, J., Amorim, M., Melao, N., et al.: Digitalization: A Literature Review and Research Agenda, pp. 443–456 (2020)

64. Gobble, M.M.: Digitalization, digitization, and innovation. Res-Technol. Manag. **61**, 56–59 (2018). https://doi.org/10.1080/08956308.2018.1471280
65. Nyhlén, S., Gidlund, K.L.: 'Everything' disappears … reflexive design and norm-critical intervention in the digitalization of cultural heritage. Inf. Commun. Soc. **22**, 1361–1375 (2019). https://doi.org/10.1080/1369118X.2018.1424922
66. ICOMOS Australia: The Australia ICOMOS charter for the Conservation and Restoration of Places of Cultural Significance (1999)
67. UNESCO: The HUL Guidebook: Managing heritage in dynamic and constantly changing urban environments (2016)

Questions in Cognitive Mimetics

Antero Karvonen[✉]

University of Jyväskylä, Jyväskylä, Finland
anilkarv@jyu.fi

Abstract. Human thinking advances through questions and answers. Any field of human endeavor is permeated by the presence of questions, answers and pre-suppositions. Questions have a kind of universality, whereby one can place the question marks on anything, including questions themselves. The process of asking the right questions about the right things and in the right way are key for the explication of an approach. Recently, we have begun thinking about an approach to the design of intelligent technology: Cognitive mimetics. In brief, the idea is to take inspiration of empirical human thinking in specific contexts to develop AI solutions. The purpose of this article is to question this approach from various angles to take steps towards specifying it as a methodology. Some of the questions are like the chips a sculptor would make on a rough unfinished piece of marble. They and their answers uncover a particular shape immanent in the broad idea we have presented. Other questions are like the tools the sculptor needs to turn an idea into reality, these are the questions which will have permanent applicability within the methodology itself. Finally, some questions are promissory notes, they concern issues that will need to be responded to as the method construction proceeds further. The purpose is to establish a waypoint of where our thinking stands at the moment and an idea of where it may lead. The way we present and answer some of the questions may be of broader interest for researchers involved in fundamental and practical questions in AI design.

Keywords: Artificial intelligence · Design methods · AI design · Cognitive mimetics

1 Introduction

Poincare anticipated the frustration of an important group of would-be computer users when he said, "The question is not, 'What is the answer?' The question is, 'What is the question?'" —J. C. R. Licklider in Man-Computer Symbiosis (1960) [1].

The ability to ask questions is a basic feature of the human mind. The presence of questions permeates the sciences, as it is a necessary element in reasoning and argumentation. Indeed, some have called the interrogative method *the* theory of reasoning [2]. Questions and assumptions can be thought of as orienting systems for cognitive resources. A question, and how it is understood, sets the stage for a quest for an answer.

© Springer Nature Switzerland AG 2021
M. Rauterberg (Ed.): HCII 2021, LNCS 12795, pp. 224–239, 2021.
https://doi.org/10.1007/978-3-030-77431-8_14

This may lead to activities such as research and experiment in empirical science, thinking and discourse in philosophy, or the realization of a product in design. In all cases, it is the question plus assumptions that orient actors and communities in some way. Consequently, paradigms open up through questions and the refinement of assumptions.

Cognitive mimetics (CM) is about asking questions of expert performance in a selected domain and seeking to formulate the questions and answers in a way that can be translated or mapped into a computational form for the design of artificial intelligence. What does this mean? Questions can be seen as a way of focusing our mental lenses. If we ask a question like: When did it rain last time? or Why did it rain yesterday? Our mental resources are geared towards quite different sorts of answers. The question may entail a particular sort of answer that is admissible. In this article, we seek to state and answer some central methodological and practical questions that have emerged from the very idea of CM. Questions and assumptions orient the practice of mimetics: the kinds of questions we raise and the answers we expect influence activity in the field. Because CM straddles science, research, and design, we need to establish a harmony between the different orientations, in different phases of the mimetic process. CM can be understood in a "loose" and in a "tight" sense. A loose sense means simply taking inspiration from human thinking in solving AI problems or constructing solutions based on human thinking, without specifying further. A tight sense means explicating presuppositions and methodological questions in a more detailed manner. Here our plan is to take steps toward the latter, although still on a relatively high level. The idea is to ask the questions important for going forward to a more systematic description of the method.

1.1 Mapping Relations

As a preliminary, it will clarify the discussion to introduce the mapping relation in CM. The mimetic process (in general, including biomimetics) can be structured as a mapping ($\rightarrow$) relation between a source (S) and a target (T): $S \rightarrow T$. One way to differentiate mimetic design types is to evaluate what (and how) they are using as a source [3]. The broader field of biomimetics has traditionally been more focused on the functions, structures, and substances of biological entities. For CM, the source is the information content and processing of humans, and the target is, generally speaking, the software of a computer system. In terms of questions, we are asking how does the source do what it does and then asking how this can be implemented in the artificial system that is the target (AI) The $S \rightarrow T$ schema is useful for guiding broad questions in terms of what (in our case, who) is being used as a source, what is our target system, or what kind of a mapping relation could be constructed between them, among other questions. However, on the practical level, as research and design begins, the relation between the two is iterative. We must consult both poles of the equation—for example, as implementation reveals blank spots in research and research outlines directions for design. We may delineate this difference by replacing the mapping symbol ($\rightarrow$) with an iteration symbol ($\circlearrowleft$): $S \circlearrowleft T$. An important further point to note is that the iteration and mapping relation also involves a transformation, due to the differences between the source and the target. Perhaps most pressingly for us, these questions emerge with the construction of machine semantics based on human semantics. We give mental content a strong role in CM. Thus, the limits, problems, and possibilities of machine semantics define perhaps the most interesting frontier for CM to explore.

2 Fundamental Questions

The importance of questions and answers for human thinking can hardly be overstated. Even basic cognitive processes, such as the retrieval, inference, or generation of information, seem to loosely accommodate a question-answer structure. Whatever their types or other properties, all questions seem to relate to information. Information is, in different ways, in the background of the concept of questions and answers. However, the way information is generated or selected by questions is not completely straightforward. Answers provide information, and some question-answer processes create information. For example, in classic group game, binary yes-no answers divide (often recursively) the elements of the answer set until a single element is left or can be identified. This would be akin to the classic information-theoretic view of reduction in uncertainty [4]. A why-question, on the other hand, may involve the creation of new informational structures and contents, carving out aspects of reality before ill understood. This in turn is a very different notion of information: a far stronger one. This question type is often associated with science, broadly understood [5, 6]. Indeed, questions may be of many kinds [5, 7], and the same simple type of question can have quite different sorts of answers, depending on the approach and context. There is quite a bit of ambiguity in the difference between a why and a how question, even in scientific discourse. Put simply, a scientific answer seems to be an answer to a why question. But simply stating a why, without specifying a how, seems to yield an uninformative answer, as the classic blackness of ravens illustrates [8]. What ties them together, however, is their nature as an interrogative information process. Basic questions refer to general question types recognizable by all: binary yes-no questions and the so-called wh-questions (who, what, when, where, why, and how). Because basic questions are like functional operators employed across different contexts, care must be taken to explicate the presuppositions that influence how the question is understood and, indeed, what is supposed to count as answer. These are often understood in an intuitive fashion, which would benefit from explication [9]. As noted by Saariluoma, Canas, and Leikas [10], questions have a kind of permanence—owing to their status as operators—that answers do not. Thus, questions are a kind of universal tool for thinking. They can even be turned on themselves—or more precisely, on the presuppositions and contexts in which they are presented. In the following paper, we will address some of the fundamental questions of CM to bring to the surface and address some of our presuppositions. The motivation behind this broad discussion on fundamental issues is to show the specificities that get introduced to AI design when certain basic issues are combined with the S →T schema.

Let us begin at the beginning. What are the originary questions for computer science (CS) and AI? The origin of Turing Machines [11] was in seeking an answer to (a foundational mathematical) question proposed by Hilbert: the Entscheidungsproblem. The answer to the question was negative, but the by-product of the proof was something else: the Turing Machine (TM), which was the result of (conceptual) *design*. In other words, the TM is an *invention* [12]. By Turing's approach, thinking acquired a technological form. Later, Turing pioneered the emerging AI paradigm by presenting another question: "Can machines think?" [13]. His answer was that it was "too meaningless to deserve discussion." Instead, he replaced it with a new question, which was operationalized as a question-game: the imitation game, now commonly called the Turing test. This question explicitly turned attention to functional equivalence and provided room for AI and computer science to develop on their own terms—a significant precursor to the idea of multiple realizability (of intelligence). As an aside, note how Turing knew that understanding and answering (natural language) *questions* is a powerful indicator of intelligence.

Returning to the TM, what was Turing's question there? It was to answer in unambiguous terms what the computer (back then a human) was doing as an information processor. Turing based his model on his perception of mathematical thinking [14]. What Turing established was a mapping relation between (his idea of) human computation and an abstract technical system (the TM), such that the operations coincided completely with the operations of the machine. The question was, can human computation be so precisely and unambiguously described so that a machine can be made to do it, and by what architecture? In our thinking, Turing's work is an important and foundational example of what we have called CM [15, 16].

Turing's thinking was extremely influential. One can hear the echoes of Turing in the 1956 Dartmouth proposal [17], which was founded on the conjecture that "every aspect of learning or any other feature of intelligence can in principle be so precisely described that a machine can be made to simulate it." Note that if Turing [11] established that effective computation could be so precisely described, the question behind the 1956 proposal was whether all aspects of intelligence could be described as computation (broadly, as orderly symbol manipulation, transformation, storage, etc.). This in turn has bifurcated into the pragmatic questions of how intelligence can be created from this (computational) basis in AI and the philosophical-cognitive questions of whether the *human* is performing computations at some deeper level, even when not engaged in computation per se. The AI design question has been fruitful irrespective of its contested philosophical foundations [18, 19] because it is a design question rather than a purely theoretical one. The design question of AI is founded on the multiple realizability of (computational) information processes and the one-to-many qualities in design. This complex back-and-forth analogical mapping between computers and brains—or software and mind—has been a defining feature behind the spirit of past century [20, 21]. In passing, one might even note here that the theoretical successes of the cognitivist paradigm exemplified in Newell and Simon [22] have been tied to the success of the implemented computer models that perform the information processing task under investigation [23]—thus, tacitly to design.

Today, at least based on the highly popular AI textbook of Russell and Norvig [24], AI seems to have somewhat removed itself from a mimetic approach. They organize AI into four categories based on approach. The first they call the "acting humanly" approach, which is to make AI systems behave in more or less exactly the same way as humans. The second is the "thinking humanly" approach, which is the classical cognitive science method, to do with computational modeling of human information processing. The third they call the "thinking rationally" approach, which emphasizes pure logic and the making of correct inferences. The fourth (and the approach they advocate) is the "acting rationally" approach, which focuses more on achieving (by whatever pragmatic means) a rational outcome for the actions of the agent, taking into account the impossibility of perfect rationality in practice. While the borders are somewhat fuzzy between categories, let us attempt to see where CM might be placed on this map. To state the obvious, our approach is indeed rooted in the second, "thinking humanly" approach, but we take a more nuanced position. As already indicated, the mimetic approach starts from this position, but by adding the mapping relation plus basic assumptions about the difference between minds and machines, we accept it as necessary to approach machine intelligence on its own terms, be it the "rational approach" [24] or some other method. However, we believe that much of value to AI research and practice can be gleaned by starting from an analysis of an empirical source—the human expert. In all domains of sufficient complexity, intelligent behavior is a result of bounded rationality [25]. Thus, it seems that the rational approach [24], or limited rationality (a concept that came from Simon and the cognitive investigation of human limitations), is not possible to solve for all domains in the abstract. It is a useful concept and goal, but without understanding how experts in empirical settings *actually* make judgments and choices, it seems to require at least something *like* CM. Interestingly, Russell [26] may have noted this himself and expresses doubts as to whether the standard method of "building calculatively rational agents and then speeding them up" will "enable the AI community to discover all of the design features needed for general intelligence." CM is not primarily about artificial *general* intelligence, but even if it was, it seems like the rational place to look for its features would be human cognition. The conceptual benefit (and a goal) of CM is to make some of these issues clearer. The practical benefit is that the necessary bounds to rationality are not introduced tacitly or ad hoc by AI designers or programmers but are based on empirical research.

This leads to the important question of the goals of CM. Let us answer this by simply saying what it is not. CM is not about artificial general intelligence (AGI) [27] or the attempt to achieve strong AI. If it were, the route we have sketched would probably focus more on explaining general cognitive faculties in a different sense. Put simply, we would be more focused on theory and have followed the traditional terrain of cognitive science. Craver [28] presented a critical discussion of explanatory depth and what he called phenomenal and explanatory models in science. Anticipating this perspective, one might question whether CM only focuses on the phenomenal properties of its source, making sketches of it akin to Ptolemy's models. The answer however is no. On the level at which we focus our attention, we would say that it is precisely the mental contents that explain the actions (correct or incorrect). The explanatory ground for human action is in the mental contents, and the reasons and reasoning behind human action is our source. Of course, this is not the sole explanatory ground, but one that we feel is the most relevant, pragmatic, and in a way most interesting for AI design purposes. The difference is that we are not attempting to explain *the contents*, as such, in the source, in the abstract. We are seeking to explain *action* with respect to a context. It also tacitly opens up differences (between subjects), not on the level of general cognitive faculties, but on the level of the mental representations that they have. In researching many contexts, the common representation among actors will likely be saturated quite quickly, but the differences will be in the depth and variety of tacit knowledge, among other factors. The

CM perspective is not about uncovering abstract mechanisms behind mental phenomena, but about empirically exploring the context-specific mental contents, mental models, and other mental representations that, for us, are the most immediate explanatory ground for human intelligence in a domain. These are, of course, supported or based on a whole host of basic general abilities, but we start by abstracting these, rather than the contents.

Let us circle back to an issue that emerged earlier. From the classical cognitivist perspective, the computation metaphor and method was mapped onto the deepest explanatory levels of human cognition. CM does not, or does not need to, follow the idea that all facets of human mentality are somehow at base computational symbol manipulation. In fact, it seems more natural to say that the mind computes only when it computes and operates on symbolic structures only when it indeed does so [29]. However, that many mental processes can be described computationally is clear, as is the fact that significant parts of many mental processes seem to involve the creation and manipulation of symbolic constructs. What seems more likely, and certainly more useful for design thinking, is that there is a gradient of face-value applicability of the computation metaphor (or mode). For example, the applicability of TM operational logic to human (or a particular kind of) computation approximates 1:1. Note here we are speaking not even of similarity, but of applicability in the design context. Wells [30] noted how Turing's analysis was driven by the pursuit of the essential core in relation to the effective computation of a real number by the application of specified rules. In other words, there may be conative or affective mental states which are in effect in the real human in the process of calculation, but these are largely inessential in terms of the analysis Turing was seeking.

This question cannot be decided a priori, however, in the broader contexts where CM operates—and for CM the question is open until decided based on the task and the context of analysis. Obviously, the applicability of computation to emotion seems far more distant than for computation. Squaring this requires the forced mapping of a phenomenal event to something like a correspondence between inputs and outputs, or some other transformation into a symbolic abstract form. This is, of course, the classic functionalist move in cognitive science philosophy [31–33]. Now, discarding the identity of emotions as emotions in favor of a functional representation is a forced move owing to the computational cognition paradigm, which we do no need to make, philosophically. What we do need to accept from it, however, is that if and when an emotional state is important for the chosen action of a research subject, the mapping relation awaiting us in the mimetic part of the design will demand some kind of symbolic transformation. Practically, the emotion as such will need to be investigated in terms of its causes and effects. These will often reside in the tacit domain: subconscious intuitions and hunches or "bad feelings about that" are cases in point. Thus, whatever the ontological kind of the source mental phenomenon may be—tacit, emotional, intuitive, etc.—we know that to implement it on a machine, it needs to be explicated and mapped or converted to a symbolic form. Boldly put, for CM, the achievements of computational cognitive science become mimetic design methods for us—but not necessarily anything more. In fact, they become important precedents for how the mapping operation between the source and the target could proceed [34]. The end result of a CM design process would of course retain many features of the source and be a kind of model for it as an information-processing artifact. For us, however, it makes less difference whether it is plausible as a deep explanation of the behavior of the source as long as the artifact works. The criteria are simply different and come from the domain of design, rather than from (cognitive) science. It also distinguishes our work from work on cognitive modeling. These are not irrelevant and do inform our work, but to make the point crudely, it would seem senseless to imitate the limitations or fallibilities of human cognition in AI, as must be done in cognitive modeling.

Djikstra's [35] critique of mimetics illustrates this well. He stated that mimetic copying has the unfortunate connotation that one could not thereby improve limited and fallible human information processes. This is decisively not our intention. However, the danger here is that CM causes designers to fixate on sub-optimal strategies and solutions. This is something that we must guard against to see how it plays out empirically as the method construction proceeds further. Nevertheless, it is clear that AI is fundamentally about imitating—or at the very least replacing—human information processing. The problem is that this may proceed even more fallibly and in an ad hoc manner in specific contexts, if the source is not an actual expert but the imagination of a designer or programmer. Making this link explicit while managing presuppositions and allowing for freedom on the implementation level remains a valid path for AI.

Let us stress again, however, that our approach is not about foregoing explanatory depth. Indeed, to explain an action by referring to mental contents in any domain of expertise is at first glance an enormously complicated task, especially as common-sense knowledge begins to seep in from outside the specific domain. Which branches can be pruned and abstracted out is a question that can only be settled on a case-by-case basis. It is here that pragmatic design questions, the context of investigation, and the role of the designer using mimetics become important.

3 Design Questions

The importance of questions in design processes is obvious. Dym and Brown [36] illustrate this by the task of designing a "safe ladder." From the task immediate questions emerge. What is safety? For whom? What should the inclination of the ladder be? How much weight should the steps be able to bear? How can slipping be prevented? How can movability and stability be reconciled? What is the context of use? Each question may inspire further questions and, over the product design and development process, many more will be asked and answered [37]—either explicitly or tacitly. Each question is a step toward converging the many possible paths in design to some set of design problems to be solved, which of course inspires new questions. The goal is really to discover the right questions, as well as the right answers. The practical fact is that CM operates in the realm of (science-based) design, and the interdisciplinary nature of the work demands a kind of harmonization among perspectives. As noted in the introduction, CM can be understood in both a loose and a tight way. Following the loosest interpretation, CM offers an approach or perspective for AI design. A tighter formulation (which we are attempting here) begins to sharpen the idea towards a method or a collection of methods within an approach. CM is not there yet, but parts of it are taking shape. The importance of methodological work is clear [38, 39] and likely to be needed to gain the cognitive information in a form suitable for AI development. Along the way, there are many methodological, practical, and empirical questions to settle, some of which we will outline below.

Let us start by addressing a very basic question: what is CM's relation to theory or, more broadly, science? Gregor [40] provides a discussion of some of the background issues—although from a different perspective and in a different context. Gregor focuses on theory (in information systems, IS), which makes the details of the conceptualization ill-suited for our purposes. Nevertheless, with a different interpretation and context, the core concepts are quite useful. Gregor outlines a taxonomy of five types of theories:

1   analysis (says what is)
2. explanation (says what is, how, why, when, and where)
3. prediction (says what is and what will be)
4. explanation and prediction (says what is, how, why, when, where, and what will be)
5. design and action (says how to do something)

Is CM a theory? It is clearly not a *theory* but *a design approach*. Still, we can identify which of the above are most important for this approach. CM is about analysis (of the source). It is about explanation (of the source). Finally, it is about design and action (how to investigate and analyze the source and how to map it onto a target).

Naturally, our perspective is theory-laden [41] as we maintain certain presuppositions such as the very existence of information processing as an explanatory level of analysis, the centrality of mental contents in explanation of action, and the importance of explicating tacit knowledge. Here, they are in the first instance exploratory viewpoints or tools, whose value is measured in the extent to which the method or activity of CM leads to successful design outcomes. The key question is how this viewpoint is communicated across the mimetic process.

We have prioritized context-specific thinking over general cognitive faculties. First, this is due to the presupposition that the contents of particular minds explain their success in particular domains. General faculties are of course necessary, but we choose to keep this aspect secondary, because it allows for more freedom on the implementation level in computers. Thus, generic results (methodological or concrete) of CM may relate mostly to the possibility of machine semantics based on human semantics. The core question is really how to analyze the source in action and, in a faithful way, abstract the mental contents, and further, re-introduce those contents in a computational setting. This is where CM has the potential to place the question marks deeper for AI: what are the computational equivalents of mental contents? Such questions must be answered in practice, somehow. If among those answers emerge new ways of thinking about or solving this problem, CM will have in fact made a theoretical contribution to AI discourse. However, we choose to proceed via practice (i.e., the design approach way). In summary, CM is as a design method normative rather than theoretic. Technical artifacts—including the results of CM—are judged on normative grounds [42]. However currently, it is too early to specify the criteria by which the method or its' results should be evaluated. Simple performance may lead to guiding the method on the wrong path, and it is not yet clear where and how exactly the perspective will deliver most value. Two distinct starting points in computing history may illustrate this point.

One question, which relates to design goals, could be called the starting point of CM. The history of computing shows two related but subtly different starting points for the relationship between natural and artificial intelligence, which we can call the AI and symbiotic augmentation approaches. The history of computing and computer design has several mimetic or analogical mapping examples. Turing [11] is of course one on them, while Shannon's mapping of logic to circuitry provides another. It is not exactly CM, but on the other hand, logic is, despite whatever platonic qualities it may have, in the end a mental phenomenon. We have previously [15] called the McCulloch and Pitts [43] paper on neural nets an example of *bio*mimetics, which seems plausible on the one hand, given that it is focused on idealized versions of biological, physical neurons. However, the example is more complex, given that McCulloch and Pitts were mapping logic to these idealized neurons and in fact looking for and proving their equivalence (equipotentiality) with TMs. What we may call the AI-approach to computing seeks to match or surpass human information processing in some chosen domain. When considered carefully, one can see that even the most powerful or quasi-autonomous AI systems today are, in the final analysis, mappings from human thought to computational systems. It simply that the mapping here is from the thinking of the designer to the computer, rather than from the thinking of a domain-expert via a designer to the computer. Be it hard-coded or learning algorithms, it seems clear that all AI systems are in the final analysis actually *displacements* of human intelligence.

A related but noticeably different strand in the history of computers is what we might call *symbiotic augmentation* [1, 44, 45]. This is related more to the human-computer interaction side of AI design. The spirit of this branch is that, rather than replace, we should seek to expand and increase the power of human thinking by complementing it with the strengths of computers. Of course, sometimes to increase the power of human thought, parts of it should be replaced, so the difference between the AI and symbiotic augmentation approaches is not hard and fast.

The mimetic approach is, in principle, naturally suited to both *AI* and *symbiotic augmentation* perspectives. However, our answer to the question of which approach to explicate for the rest of this paper is the AI-approach. We start from the premise that in (cognitive) mimetics, there exists a source that can, by way of information processing, exhibit success in a task that we wish to implement on a computer. Our design goal is to construct a computational system that is equally successful in the task by the mimetic method of taking inspiration from human information processing. The scope of mimetics here is to develop autonomy for the digital artifact within the bounds of the task. In practice, however, the limitations of digital intelligence mean a co-habitation or co-working between artificial and natural information processing. One here notices the value of holding the *symbiotic* perspective in mind as well. It may be best to consider the symbiotic perspective in a way parallel to the AI-approach, but in terms of methodology, they are likely to be different, so for the sake of scope we will focus on the AI approach here.

3.1 Research

Let us next present the way we have approached the development of the method in terms of questions. Let us assume that we have already been presented with a task context:

operators of a paper machine. The company is seeking to find AI and/or automation potentials in the range of tasks that they perform in addition to ordinary work. This is on-going research, so we will discuss the findings on a rather broad level. On a general level, our first task is to identify a *system of regular actions* [10]. This is to be understood as a joint cognitive system [46], consisting of multiple actors interacting with technologies to complete overall tasks and goals. The natural question that follows is "who?" followed by "what?" and informed by a "where?" The who-question here refers to identification of those individuals who are involved and skilled in the tasks, giving us research subjects. The what-question refers to a description of the task: what they are doing, why, and how? The where-question is an approximation of contextual issues: where is the task to be done, by what means, and so on. Practically, it will be necessary to have someone with in-depth domain knowledge to facilitate translation and understanding between research subjects and researchers.

Next, we must ask the question of how and combine it with a distinct sense of the why. Essentially, having identified a system of regular actions and having sketched out some of its features, CM needs to penetrate deeper into the actions themselves. On a high level, action can be described by five structural elements: *goal, agent, artifact (tool), target,* and *context* [10]. Note that, in a particular sense, we have already answered these questions in our preliminary sketch of the research context, but the same elements can be used to probe more detailed questions with respect to very particular actions. For example, we could now begin to ask *why did the operator increase the RPM of the pump at time T?* We can see that the agent used a tool (a DCS in this case) to alter the state of a target (the pump RPM). To understand this action, we need to know what goal this action served to accomplish, what elements of the state of the system it affects, how those states relate to the operator's goals, and what the contextual issues that make this action reasonable at this stage are. These questions inspire further questions and begin to uncover the mental operations and contents that CM is seeking.

How can we gain information about mental contents for specific tasks and contexts? The answer must be empirical, so we have made use of observation and think-aloud protocols to gain research data. Here, and especially in follow-up interviews, questioning becomes a practical necessity. The idea is to probe and bring to the surface tacit knowledge concerning chosen actions. This is where depth of analysis is gained. This means that often the operators cannot provide an explanation for all of their behavior, although the behavior is correct and highly efficient. Thus, in research, we must triangulate between overt explanations from subjects, their behavior, verbal protocols, and contextual facts. The explanatory depth from CM emerges from discovering parsimonious content-level explanations for action. It is a content-based answer to a why-question.

3.2 Research Example

An example will illustrate this better. Let us observe that a human operator in a factory responds to an event by some series of actions. For convenience, let us say that the event is mapped to a meter reading, and the actions map to a set of remotely controlled pumps and valves. Cognitively, the meter reading is interpreted (mapped) as an event of some type by the operator. In fact, the operator is answering a tacit series of questions: what I am seeing, what does this mean, do I need to intervene, and by what operations can I do so—among others. The whole process is so efficient in an experienced operator that mere observation would likely only give us event-action pairs. The problem with expertise is that it seems to increase as a function of the degree to which to knowledge and skills become transparent (tacit) for the expert. Here is where iteration becomes important. Assuming we have observations of events and corresponding actions plus fragmented thoughts expressed in the protocols, to grasp the structure and the mental contents corresponding to action we need first to identify regularities and then to follow up with qualitative interviews. The purpose is to tune in to specific actions to discover their meaning. As stated, the operator's thinking seems to fit a kind of tacit self-questioning process, and thus questions like "why did you choose this action" or "why was this event significant" trigger outpourings of tacit knowledge. The operators can often answer these questions if asked.

The problem with researching actions in complex and dynamic settings is that it is difficult to establish a stable point of reference, such as is possible in many games like chess. Thus, discovering the "rules" and goals of the "game" is not definitively given beforehand, but must be discovered, and indeed is a major part of the results of the research. In practice, to establish a stable foundation we have searched for the following: goals, the space of possible measurements, and the space of possible actions. This triangulation provides one method of attack for the problems of relevance and action.

We have approached operator behavior in terms of goal seeking. This means that action and behavior can be explained in terms of reducing the distance between the current state of the system and a goal state. Events and observations are evaluated against deviations from this state or the path toward that state. This gives the behaviors of the operators an episodic structure: events occur and are dealt with if they violate the goals of the operator, which can be identified with a system state.

The state of the system maps onto measurements. For the measurements to make sense, the operator must have a mental model of the system, in which measurements map onto certain aspects of the system. On the face of it, the objective set of measurements is large and internally related. The cognitive answer to the question we are seeking is which measurements are relevant, which not, and when. The measurements simply map to facts about the system state, but how they relate to each other and to the state the operator is seeking is an open question before research. The goal is to discover relevance-based subsets of the measurements that can be explained by goals, mental models, and tacit knowledge.

It is often possible to compute the space of possible actions at least on the level of the interaction points between operator and machine. This could be thought of as the list of "moves" available to the operator. What we must seek to explain as a third part of the explanatory structure are the principles of the action selection. A goal or a goal-state maps onto the measurements. The moves, on the other hand, map onto system states and measurements. Thus, only subsets of moves (and their values) are either *relevant* for influencing the system state at some particular time, or *appropriate*. Again, we can foresee the problem of tacit knowledge here. The fact is that certain actions may have consequences beyond some small part of the system. Thus, the *path* towards the goal state chosen by the operator is likely constrained, or guided, by tacit knowledge of the interrelationships within the system and instantiated in a mental model of the system.

Triangulating and iterating between these perspectives is one method of uncovering the structure, properties, and contents of the cognitive system that currently keeps paper machines operational in our research context. Here we presented some viewpoints on how the method might be specified and some of the ways in which information can be gathered and classified. For us, this would *still* be a kind of initial sketch in terms of the explanation of actions. It provides a core framework in which to ask further questions. Some of those questions should come from design. The next stage is to establish a mapping relationship and step into the world of possible design solutions.

3.3 Implementation and Design

Next, we must ask the question of how—this time in a different sense, because we are now concerned with the mapping or implementation relation. So far, this part of the equation is speculative, as we have not engaged with AI designers or programmers. Let us assume that we have now established at least a direction for the idea of the tasks we wish to realize in AI. Our task going into the design phase would be to establish a principal solution, the key problems, and a set of conceptual design variations that answer those problems [39]. This is where the *problem* and *solution spaces* [38] should become informed by research. One may notice that we have already tried on, as it were, the designers' shoes by tacitly imagining a halfway abstraction between the source and the target. It seems almost impossible to think about these things without simultaneously imagining possible solution patterns [38]. This is not necessarily a problem, but something to be aware of, given Djikstra's [35] critique (for example) and the danger of fixating on sub-optimal solutions.

Our content-specific presupposition carries over to our presuppositions on design. Visser [47] summarized the problems with an oversystematic and formal approach to design. Design problems of creating paper machine AI are no less domain-specific than the paper machine operators' skills and knowledge themselves. Indeed, part of the whole point of cognitive mimetics is to understand the specificities that get introduced by the design context, the constraints of computational systems, and human thinking. Thus, the design process should not be too rigidly defined normatively, since actual design (or research, or any creative thinking) processes will not follow those patterns anyway. Too little specification on the other hand, and it becomes impossible to build the mimetic bridge and common understanding between different actors.

3.4 Design Problems and Representations

For Cross [38] a successful design process involves the skillful management of the *problem space* and the *solution space*. CM is intended to make contributions to both. We follow Visser [47] in noting that while design involves problem-solving, it not only problem-solving. Equally important are problem-finding, problem-specification, problem-structuring and re-structuring. Furthermore, some problems can be solved by routine methods, and this applies especially to AI and to software development more broadly. For instance, software patterns are a subfield of software development on solving recurring issues by applying known patterns [48]. Here is where intentional management of the problem space and the solution space becomes important. If a problem found in research has a known solution pattern in AI, there may be no need to invent something new by mimetic means. This is a likely scenario in many real-world settings. Nevertheless, it is fully possible that we may *want* to attempt to solve it by a new way for the sake of discovering a new pattern for solutions.

From another perspective, identifying and analyzing the *system of regular actions* [10] that is the source (and in a way the eventual target) of the mimetic process can uncover the structure of the problem space in many ways. First, we will by necessity uncover an expert-based understanding of the problem domain. It uncovers the real problems. This already scopes and ties the intended design to actual human action and a naturalistic picture of the domain. Second, by in-depth analysis, the empirical problem spaces (as they complete their tasks) *of the operators* become a direction towards possible technical solutions in AI. Just as there are patterns of software solutions [48], so there are (context-specific) patterns of solutions in human action. Typically, intelligence demanding tasks are such that they can be achieved in many different ways and the intelligent way is dictated partly by contextual issues. The variety of strategies for succeeding in tasks give direct inputs for possible technical solutions to the problems, which can be evaluated on normative *or* pragmatic grounds. One can even imagine collecting the patterns in human action to libraries for a kind of context-specific ontology of action which when abstracted (and connected to software solutions) could be employed across contexts.

Design processes, including problem and solution spaces, can be understood in terms of representations [47]. Namely, the design process is cognitively speaking a series of evolving representations (mental and concrete) that iteratively seek to specify the requirements, functions, objectives, and constraints for the artefact in an increasingly specific manner. This "arc" from abstract to concrete is, in mimetics, an arc from concrete to abstract and back to concrete, following a gradient from research subjects to design to embodiment in a computer system – and iterating over this arc as necessary. This "arc" presents some issues in terms of establishing shared and meaningful representations across the mimetic design process, which is in the end by necessity a joint venture among various fields of expertise, from human cognitive research to design and to programming.

Perhaps most clearly this danger will manifest if there is only a superficial understanding of what research is uncovering. There may be no silver bullet for this problem, as we do bring forth concepts from cognitive *science* that provide a framework for our thinking. But the thinking and the background of, for example, programmers, is different. Thus, it will be an interesting question to see how the mapping relation succeeds and what factors may cause or hinder success. The assumption is that the more deeply the programmer understands the source, more deep and interesting the solutions will be. For the broader development of AI, we can hope that the questions marks can be put deeper by this method. Put more pragmatically, there will be a "user" of the method, and in the very least, a user of the results of the research who is likely to come from a different field than cognitive science. Floridi [7, 49] has illustrated this by his idea of Level of Abstraction (LoA). It can be interpreted simply by saying that individuals with different backgrounds "see" different things when looking at the same object or phenomenon. In our case, it means that one LoA (of a LoA) is to be iteratively mapped onto another LoA. Put another way, there is the LoA that the source has (the operator in the paper mill), there is LoA which the mimetic research takes on the operators' LoA, which needs to be translated to the LoA of a programmer-designer who, in addition, creates a *machine*-LoA that structures the program. Establishing these translations and mappings is a key part of finding success with CM. Essentially, the method will fail if the mapping relation fails. Thus, it is important to consider, as a methodological design question, the kinds of mental activities that mimetics invokes (or should invoke) in practitioners, and the foremost is thinking by analogy [50, 51]. Indeed, CM can be thought of as a relative of *design by analogy* [52–54]. Moreno and colleagues' [54] study is promising, in terms of the benefits of analogical thinking on design results may have, but much more thinking will have to go into if and how this benefit can be realized in cognitive mimetics.

Finally, the question of multiple realizability and the possible ways in which cognitive processes can be implemented on machines remains an important theoretical issue for CM. Research, design, and practice have a common ground in this respect.

4 Conclusion and Future Directions

The impetus for this article was the need to specify and answer methodological questions in cognitive mimetics. One may read this as a report on a work in progress. The idea of the mapping relation seems to be an apt tool for surfacing major issues in the methodology. First, we discussed some historical antecedents and attempted to fence our idea with respect to some major ideas in cognitive research and AI. As noted, on the loosest interpretation, cognitive mimetics is simply about giving a name to an existing phenomenon, the fact that taking inspiration from human thinking has played a major role in AI and computer science history. From this simple premise, however, many questions emerge, and the purpose of this paper was to first state some of the questions and where possible answer them from our perspective. The point is that to that to make progress, these questions must be answered in some way. They provide compass points on an issue that involves enormous complexity if approached without the right questions. The way we have answered the questions shows the outline of a particular path towards AI solutions based on human cognition. This is not the only path – but it is a path we feel makes sense and gives a fresh perspective on the issues. It is also not necessarily the easiest path, indeed the specificities that are introduced by the mapping of human thinking to computational systems introduce a host of issues, the least of which is not the ability for different experts to achieve mutual understanding. Many of the questions are such that they can't be decided *a priori* by speculating on them in a reflective manner. Much work remains to tackle these issues and they can only be done by iteration in practice by combining research and design.

References

1. Licklider, J.C.: Man-computer symbiosis. IRE Trans. Hum. Factors Electron. **1**, 4–11 (1960)
2. Hintikka, J., Halonen, I., Mutanen, A.: Interrogative logic as a general theory of reasoning. Stud. Log. Pract. Reason. **1**, 295–337 (2002)
3. Karvonen, A., Kujala, T., Saariluoma, P.: Types of mimetics for the design of intelligent technologies. In: Ahram, T., Karwowski, W., Pickl, S., Taiar, R. (eds.) IHSED, pp. 40–46. Springer, Cham (2020). https://doi.org/10.1007/978-3-030-27928-8_7

4. Shannon, C.E.: A mathematical theory of communication. Bell Syst. Tech. J. **27**(3), 379–423 (1948)
5. Jaworski, W.: The logic of how-questions. Synthese **166**(1), 133–155 (2009)
6. Van Fraassen, B.C.: The Scientific Image. Oxford University Press, Oxford (1980)
7. Floridi, L.: What is a philosophical question? Metaphilosophy **44**(3), 195–221 (2013)
8. von Wright, G.H.: Explanation and Understanding. Cornell University Press, Ithaca (2004)
9. Saariluoma, P.: Foundational Analysis: Presuppositions in Experimental Psychology, vol. 2. Psychology Press, Hove (1997)
10. Saariluoma, P., Cañas, J.J., Leikas, J.: Designing for Life: A Human Perspective on Technology Development. Springer, Cham (2016). https://doi.org/10.1057/978-1-137-530 47-9
11. Turing, A.M.: On computable numbers, with an application to the Entscheidungsproblem. Proc. Lond. Math. Soc. **2**(1), 230–265 (1937)
12. Petzold, C.: The Annotated Turing: A Guided Tour Through Alan Turing's Historic Paper on Computability and the Turing Machine. Wiley Publishing, New York (2008)
13. Turing, A.M.: Computing machinery and intelligence. Mind **59**(236), 433–460 (1950)
14. Fortnow, L., Homer, S.: A short history of computational complexity. Bulletin EATCS **80**(01), 2003 (2003)
15. Kujala, T., Saariluoma, P.: Cognitive mimetics for designing intelligent technologies. Adv. Hum. Comput. Interact. **2018**, 9 p. (2018). Article ID 9215863. https://doi.org/10.1155/2018/9215863
16. Saariluoma, P., Kujala, T., Karvonen, A., Ahonen M.: Cognitive mimetics - main ideas. In: Proceedings on the International Conference on Artificial Intelligence (ICAI). The Steering Committee of the World Congress in Computer Science, Computer Engineering and Applied Computing (WorldComp), pp. 202–206 (2018)
17. McCarthy, J., Minsky, M.L., Rochester, N., Shannon, C.E.: A proposal for the Dartmouth summer research project on artificial intelligence, august 31, 1955. AI Mag. **27**(4), 12 (2003)
18. Haugeland, J. (ed.): Mind Design II: Philosophy, Psychology. Artificial Intelligence. MIT Press, Cambridge (1997)
19. Haugeland, J.: The nature and plausibility of cognitivism. Behav. Brain Sci. **1**(2), 215–226 (1978)
20. Thagard, P.: Mind: Introduction to Cognitive Science. MIT Press, Cambridge (2005)
21. Waldrop, M.M.: The Dream Machine: J.C.R. Licklider and the Revolution That Made Computing Personal. Viking Penguin, New York (2001)
22. Newell, A., Simon, H.A.: Human Problem Solving. Prentice-hall, Englewood Cliffs (1972)
23. Ohlsson, S.: The problems with problem solving: reflections on the rise, current status, and possible future of a cognitive research paradigm. J. Probl. Solving **5**(1), 7 (2012)
24. Russell, S.J., Norvig, P.: Artificial Intelligence: A Modern Approach. Pearson Education, London (2016)
25. Simon, H.A.: The Sciences of the Artificial. MIT Press, Cambridge (2019)
26. Russell, S.: Rationality and intelligence: a brief update. In: Müller, V.C. (ed.) Fundamental Issues of Artificial Intelligence, vol. 376, pp. 7–28. Springer, Cham (2016). https://doi.org/10.1007/978-3-319-26485-1_2
27. Schmidhuber, J., Thórisson, K.R., Looks, M. (eds.): AGI. LNCS, vol. 6830. Springer, Heidelberg (2011). https://doi.org/10.1007/978-3-642-22887-2
28. Craver, C.F.: When mechanistic models explain. Synthese **153**(3), 355–376 (2006)
29. Bunge, M.: Matter and Mind: A Philosophical Inquiry, vol. 287. Springer, Cham (2010). https://doi.org/10.1007/978-90-481-9225-0
30. Wells, A.J.: Turing's analysis of computation and theories of cognitive architecture. Cogn. Sci. **22**(3), 269–294 (1998)

31. Shagrir, O.: The rise and fall of computational functionalism. In: BenMenahem, Y. (ed.) Hilary Putnam, pp. 220–250. Cambridge University Press, Cambridge (2005)
32. Putnam, H.: Mind and machines. J. Symb. Log. **9**(1), 57–80 (1960)
33. Putnam, H.: The nature of mental states. In: Capitan, W.H., Merrill, D. (eds.) Art, Mind and Religion, pp. 1–223. Pittsburg University Press, Pittsburg (1967)
34. Polk, T.A., Seifert, C.M.: Cognitive Modeling. MIT Press, Cambridge (2002)
35. Dijkstra, E.W.: On the cruelty of really teaching computing science. Commun. ACM **32**(12), 1398–1404 (1989)
36. Dym, C.L., Brown, D.C.: Engineering Design: Representation and Reasoning. Cambridge University Press, Cambridge (2012)
37. Eppinger, S., Ulrich, K.: Product Design and Development. McGraw-Hill, Singapore (1995)
38. Cross, N.: Engineering Design Methods: Strategies for Product Design. Wiley, Hoboken (2021)
39. Pahl, G., Beitz, W.: Engineering Design: A Systematic Approach. Springer, Cham (2013). https://doi.org/10.1007/978-1-84628-319-2
40. Gregor, S.: The nature of theory in information systems. MIS Q. **30**(3), 611–642 (2006)
41. Hanson, N.R.: Patterns of Discovery: An Inquiry Into the Conceptual Foundations of Science. Cambridge University Press, New York (1981)
42. Franssen, M.: The normativity of artefacts. Stud. History Philo. Sci. Part A **37**(1), 42–57 (2006)
43. McCulloch, W.S., Pitts, W.: A logical calculus of the ideas immanent in nervous activity. Bull. Math. Biophys. **5**(4), 115–133 (1943)
44. Bush, V.: As we may think. Atl. Mon. **176**(1), 101–108 (1945)
45. Engelbart, D.C.: Augmenting Human Intellect: A Conceptual Framework. Air Force Office of Scientific Research, Washington, DC (1962)
46. Hollnagel, E., Woods, D.D.: Joint Cognitive Systems: Foundations of Cognitive Systems Engineering. CRC Press, Boca Raton (2005)
47. Visser, W.: Designing as construction of representations: a dynamic viewpoint in cognitive design research. Hum-Comput. Interact. **21**(1), 103–152 (2006)
48. Coplien, J.O.: Software design patterns: common questions and answers. In: Rising, L. (eds.) The Patterns Handbook: Techniques, Strategies, and Applications, vol. 13, p. 311. Cambridge University Press, Cambridge (1998)
49. Floridi, L.: The method of levels of abstraction. Minds Mach. **18**(3), 303–329 (2008)
50. Gentner, D., Holyoak, K.J., Kokinov, B.N. (eds.): The Analogical Mind: Perspectives from Cognitive Science. MIT Press, Cambridge (2001)
51. Gentner, D.: Structure-mapping: a theoretical framework for analogy. Cogn. Sci. **7**, 155–170 (1983). https://doi.org/10.1207/s15516709cog0702_3
52. Visser, W.: Two functions of analogical reasoning in design: a cognitive-psychology approach. Des. Stud. **17**(4), 417–434 (1996)
53. Qian, L., Gero, J.: Function-behavior-structure paths and their role in analogy-based design. AIEDAM **10**(4), 289–312 (1996)
54. Moreno, D.P., et al.: Fundamental studies in design-by-analogy: a focus on domain-knowledge experts and applications to transactional design problems. Des. Stud. **35**(3), 232–272 (2014)

Memory Modalities Opening-up Digital Heritage Infrastructures

Gertraud Koch(⊠) 🆔

University of Hamburg, Hamburg, Germany
gertraud.koch@uni-hamburg.de

Abstract. Memory is a double bind: on the one side, memory making is a basic individual and social practice of creating cultural traditions, and on the other side, it is a technical model in computer technology. Both concepts are entangled with each other. Since the introduction of computer technology and digital infrastructures, the means and modalities for making memories have changed enormously for professionals in Galleries, Libraries, Archives and Museums (GLAMs) and also people and groups in everyday life. HCI thus plays a crucial role for shaping these modalities of memory making, for creating connectivities between human and non-human memories as well as for opening up cultural memory making for participation by diverse stakeholders.

This chapter sets the stage for the inquiry into how HCI design may facilitate the opening-up of digital infrastructures for memory making to different people and groups in everyday life as well as to professional memory makers in GLAMs. It will highlight concepts which are used in both the realms of computer technology and socio-cultural theory, but still have specific meanings, such as memory making, accessibility, algorithm etc. A short description of memory making processes by individuals, groups and institutions will provide a basic understanding of memory making as a social practice. Furthermore, the relevance of media technologies for memory making processes will be sketched as a basis for shaping the modalities of digital memory making in respect to the experiences of people/users.

Keywords: Memory practices · Digital heritage · Participation · Infrastructure studies

1 Introduction

On the one side, making memory is the basic individual and social practice of creating cultural traditions, and on the other side, it is a technical model in computer science. While both concepts are entangled with each other, they still differ widely in the way they function. The interplay of both ideas of memory becomes most visible when computer technology and digital media infrastructures are introduced in the cultural sector. With computer and digital media infrastructures, means and modalities for making memories

---

The original version of this chapter was revised: an error in reference 33 has been corrected. The correction to this chapter is available at https://doi.org/10.1007/978-3-030-77431-8_31

have changed significantly for professionals in Galleries, Libraries, Archives and Museums (GLAMs), and also for people and groups in everyday life. The particular qualities of digital media technologies demand the transformation, re-interpretation or invention of memory making practices both in institutions as well as by people and groups.

HCI with its approaches to user experience (UX) design plays a crucial role in this process of re-inventing memory practices in the GLAMs and in everyday life. It can function as an intermediary between these different concepts of memory making in culture and in computer science. Creating connectivities between human and non-human memories requires more than a simple transfer of established mnemonic techniques and GLAM media systems into digital media infrastructures. With digitisation, the mnemonic techniques themselves undergo a fundamental change and thus provide the option to re-think memory making. The interactive potential of digital media infrastructures is fuelling the long established intention and need to open up the GLAMs to the participation of a broad spectrum of people and groups – beyond the established middle class and older audiences – by means of new inspiration and energy.

In this situation of using the digital media change for opening up memory making to people and groups of diverse backgrounds, and beyond the established approaches in digital heritage, there has been little collaboration with HCI design and memory studies. In order to trace the collaboration between the two fields of research, this contribution will highlight concepts which are used in both the realms of computer technology and socio-cultural theory, and which are simultaneously similar and different; memory, accessibility, and algorithm, for example, are among these common terms which are still used with particular meanings and emphasizes in both fields of research. Other terms are entirely unlike, such as the terms 'audiences' and 'users', with consequences for the idea of how interaction matters. Furthermore, I will provide an insight into the concept of memory making, as it is established in socio-cultural theory, and thus unfold some of the basic understanding that guides memory making in cultural heritage institutions and research. Finally, through the cultural lens, this contribution will provide a general understanding of how different media technologies matter in these processes of memory making for representing, storing, circulating, and transmitting knowledge. This cultural perspective on media facilitates the reflection of the changes emerging with the digital turn in memory making in respect to the experiences of people/users. These considerations set the stage for five contributions in this panel, which will outline entry points for HCI design approaches in digital memory making.[1]

---

[1] The idea for this panel stands in the context of the POEM ITN research network, which has received funding from the European Union's Horizon 2020 research and innovation programme under the Marie Skłodowska-Curie grant agreement No. 764859, cf. www.poem-horizon.eu. For the further outline of this idea, I owe much to the inspiring discussions and exchanges with the POEM researchers and supervisors in the network. The research focus in POEM is on how memory making can become participatory by building connectivities between people and groups, institutions, and digital media as modalities of memory. Moreover, I would like to thank Matthias Müller-Prove for his valuable comments on the concept of this panel and the abstracts of the three contributions of the four POEM fellows: Cassandra Kist & Quoc Tan Tran, Jennifer Krueckeberg, and Angeliki Tzouganatou. Matthias Müller-Prove comments through the lens of an HCI specialist was a great inspiration for the reflection of concepts and analytical approaches.

2 Making Memories

Memory making has both individual and collective dimensions since it refers to common experiences in a historical period and space with characteristic institutions, events and forms of living. Galleries, libraries, archives and museums are memory institutions which collect and curate collective memory and are thus memory making institutions. They are usually state financed and as such have both the responsibility and the authority to administer public memory. Through this act of recognition as relevant materials for public memory, the cultural expressions and objects they collect and curate become cultural heritage.[2] Individual and group memories may be part of public memory making, but this is not always the case, and it varies depending on the social situations and lifestyles of people and groups who, on the one side, have individual experiences, but on the other side also remember and commemorate collective events and forms of living. Their experiences are shaped through a personal standpoint in life and their membership in social groups in a larger population of a society. Collective memory provides a repertoire of how individual experiences can be told and expressed. Public, group, and individual memories are important sources of identification, and thus a meaningful concern in the organisation of social life [3, 14]. Community driven archives and museums, individual and group activities of people and groups on the internet, and decentral forms of commemoration in social media all represent the immense relevance of memory making [13].

2.1 Memory Making as Social and Cultural Process

Memory studies have been problematizing the changes in memory work emerging from the digital turn for a long time. While early voices feared a loss of relevant materials due to the short life span of content on the internet [2], today the discussion has broadened to more comprehensive perspectives on the immense changes of memory work at all levels, be they public, group or individual, because digital media infrastructures provide new sets of information and communication tools with specific mnemonic techniques and formats for the storage, retrieval and circulation of relevant content. Daily communication as well as individual and collective modes of remembrance are thus involved in a dynamic transformation in which people constantly enlarge their repertoires of memory making with individual digital text, photo, film and audio collections, offline and online, in clouds or shared on social media sites [11]. The ongoing change is obvious in the light of the manifold productions of digital materials that are more or less likely to become part of individual, group or public memory. What this change is about and which concepts are adequate for its analysis is a matter of scholarly debate, which seeks to grasp the transformation with terms such as "new memory ecologies" [9], "mediated memories" [35], "digital memories" [12] or "remediation of memory" [11] while the direction of this change is still in flux and debated.

---

[2] Memory studies and critical heritage studies are thus interrelated but still separate interdisciplinary research fields with different bodies of literature, journals for publication and scientific communities. Digital heritage constitutes a third research field which is relevant in the given context.

2.2   Institutional Memory Making

Another strand of the thread of reactions to the digitisation of media infrastructures emerges from the activities in the memory making GLAMs. By means of digitisation, they seek to keep track of their archived material and the aggregation of digital objects in digital libraries and repositories or exhibitions, and they are also introducing their audiences to digital communication formats. In this transformation process, they seek partnerships with non-governmental organisations such as Wikimedia or Open Knowledge Foundation, or with internet companies such as Google. The underlying motivation for these digitalization activities in memory institutions is to keep cultural material available for further usage for academic purposes, for creative industries and for attracting young people – the so-called digital natives with their high affinity to the use of digital media – to the GLAMs [29]. In particular for the smaller GLAMs, the trend towards digital heritage means enormous financial, organisational and personnel efforts, and these are only the prelude to a far-reaching reorganisation of institutional memory work in the course of the introduction of digital media infrastructures. At present, digitization projects are implemented in a rather hands-on manner, with little time for reflection in respect to the effects for memory making. In the future, the GLAMs will need to move towards new principles of memory making as consequence of the restructuring that goes along with the new digital media infrastructures. They will be guided by new regulations and process of negotiation about copyrights and open licenses, privacy issues, re-use of cultural materials and digital accessibility [23].

2.3   Memory Making of People and Groups

Aside from academic and institutional memory making, people and groups have individual practices of making memories - often not conceived of as such - when they communicate, share or post information on social media as part of their everyday communication with family, friends or peer groups. The archival character of social media sites for everyday life is intensely debated and heavily criticised as a rather tricky source for social research: incomplete, ambiguous and misleading when automated communication by bots cannot eliminated from the data set [28, 37, 38]. Nevertheless, the mass of posts on popular internet platforms documents the cultural productivity of media amateurs and of what they find worth showing, sharing and circulating. The activity of people and groups on social media sites demands answers to the question of why people and groups engage so actively in memory making there, but respond comparatively little to the offers for interaction and communication made by digital heritage libraries and museums. There seems to be a gap between the memory making practices of people and groups embedded in everyday communication on social media on the internet and in the GLAMs' institutional memory practices with digital media infrastructures. It is not likely that the social media use of people and groups can be paradigmatic for opening up digital memory making in GLAMs. Still, it raises the question of how the design of HCI can facilitate and motivate the ideas and social practices of people's and groups' memory making in their variety and diversity.

3   Shifting the Modalities for Memory Making: The Digital Turn

Memories are related to people, groups, and societies, and are thus embedded in social contexts and ways of life which need to be considered when digital media infrastructures for memory making are set up. When digital media infrastructures are implemented, the practices of memory making are affected [7]. Media (technologies) with their particular coverage and their repertoires for representing, storing, retrieving, and circulating knowledge shape the modalities of making memory, which form as assemblages of economic, institutional, organisational, legal, and technological elements which are all contributing to and crucial for memory making. Such assemblages are a highly flexible formation in situations of transformation; when the technologies develop, the relations to the various elements in the network may be affected, will be adapted, or new elements may become relevant in the network. There is no master plan for shifts; they emerge from the momentum of each element in the assemblage and possibly also from relevant factors outside of it [24, 25].

Shifts in media technology are most relevant for memory making. Media operate with systems of symbols (alphabets, number systems, images, etc.) and can be understood as a means for cultural production. Memory making depends on mediation through non-technological and technological media in various forms; oral cultures without a written language depend on story telling for memory making and the transmission of knowledge from generation to generation. The emergence of media technologies is closely connected to the social and cultural history of man [8]. In the 20th century, the growth of different types of media technologies was significant; with them, the forms, the amount and the distribution of cultural expressions grew enormously. Books, newspapers, photography, film, radio, television - representations of knowledge in media provide particular qualities and are conditional for its circulation, storage, preservation and transformation. With each media system, a remediation [6] of older media forms became necessary; with the internet, new options for creating and circulating information emerged, newspapers were challenged and needed to change to continue to exist. Every media (technological) change thus changes the basis for cultural articulation and memory making.

The discussions of what the digital turn means for memory making has not come to an end yet; how inclusive or dividing, how formative or fragmenting for social identity, how disruptive for social life digital media infrastructures based on the internet actually are is intensely debated [1, 9, 27, 34]. The ongoing discussions and diverging impressions are on the one side in accordance with the uncompleted dynamics of innovation of digital media infrastructures driven by controversial ideas of what digital media infrastructures should be. On the other side, a simple and consistent answer cannot to be expected. Meanings and effects of digital media technologies are diverging since they emerge in heterogeneous social contexts with a bundle of relational elements, each with its own momentum. In these heterogeneous memory making assemblages, causes and effects are a rather flexible multifactorial process which only comes to an end when constitutive elements and relations of this assemblage have stabilized. It is thus not the nature of the technology but an outcome of available technologies, regulations, norms, practices (usage) and design decisions if and how digital media infrastructures facilitate participatory memory practices. Design paradigms, approaches and decisions thus are the most crucial factors for opening up memory making to diverse people and groups. HCI plays an essential role in setting up such arrangements and in supporting the exploration and stabilization of connectivities between groups of people, memory institutions and digital media infrastructures as memory modalities for participatory memory practices.[3]

4 Opening up Memory Making in Digital Media Infrastructures

Openness is a characteristic value in contemporary European societies with their diverse populations; it is a noteworthy way of life in the cultural history of Europe, which in earlier times was determined by nationalism and wars before it turned towards cooperation across nations and established the EU as supra-national political institution. Openness has become an important value in European societies, driven by cultural exchange, peaceful coexistence, and the sustainability of democratic constitutions.

Openness cannot be taken for granted, as we learn from current nationalistic movements. Rather, it needs to be maintained and cared about. Culture is an important realm where openness can be and must be anchored. The concept of cultural citizenship refers to the importance of the presence of people and groups across ethnic and national identities as new inhabitants of Europe. In the context of cultural citizenship, we are observing the need to open up memory making to diverse people and groups.

4.1 Institutional Activities

GLAMs have established various strategies for opening up their collections for participatory memory making through digital media infrastructures. By now, considerable sums have been invested in digital heritage infrastructures, at least in the European GLAMs. Without claiming to be exhaustive, paradigmatic approaches to opening up cultural materials to new audiences include digital libraries and repositories, digital exhibitions, museum apps, hackathons, and social media communication [23]. Other ambitious projects such as chat bots [33] for explaining cultural heritage materials, augmented and virtual reality applications for experiencing ancient heritage sites, or website based applications such as the virtual exhibition website of the Deutsches Museum München are also gaining relevance in digital heritage infrastructures.[4] All these initiatives aim for FAIR cultural heritage data, i.e. free, accessible, interoperable and re-usable data.[5]

The most visible example of a digital heritage infrastructure may be the digital library Europeana, which comprises more than 51 million digital objects from more than 3700 European institutions. While the data are stored in the local repositories of the participating GLAMs, the Europeana makes them findable through a joint metadata standard and distributes them on the Europeana website. At the same time, Europeana initiates projects for engaging users with the cultural data provided through the digital library [5].

Another beacon project is the collaboration of the "Deutsches Museum" in Munich with Google Cultural Institute for digitizing their exhibitions and providing them online.

---

[3] www.poem-horizon.eu, last accessed 01.02.2021.

[4] See for example: https://mprove.de/chronolab/index.html.

[5] For a more detailed explanation, see the contribution by Angeliki Tzouganatou in this volume.

In a three-dimensional online environment, visitors can navigate through the rooms of the museum in the same manner as on Google Street View at the highest technological standard. The user rights of the digital exhibition of the cultural objects are held by both the "Deutsches Museum" and the private company Google.

On a smaller scale, apps are installed in a range of GLAMs to connect the collections in institutions to spaces outside and allow the retrieval of images and other information about cultural objects in situ during city walks, touristic activities or community projects. These apps have almost become a standard for GLAMs that think of themselves as relevant players in the cultural sector. Quite often, they are an outcome of initiatives for the so called "re-use" of cultural materials, initiated for example in cultural hackathons by Wikimedia and Open Knowledge Foundation in cooperation with GLAMs. These initiatives for opening up digitized cultural objects in GLAMs to the public seek to bring the "coder"-community and IT experts together with volunteers from different knowledge backgrounds for the purpose of creative collaborations and productions of new digital objects. The format "Coding da Vinci" established such initiatives for co-creation in the form of a competition, with prizes in different categories, to invent new usages for cultural materials and make it relevant again in today's life worlds.

While all these activities are undertaken with great commitment in the GLAMs, the outreach to people and groups does not turn out as expected, as can be gleaned from the user statistics of websites with digital heritage materials [10]. The catalogue of new criteria for measuring the impact of digital heritage websites speaks for itself in this respect [32]. While the digital heritage community celebrates the relevance and emphasizes the great need for the digitalisation of cultural materials in GLAMs [29], the questions in respect to impact, efficiency, and sustainability are becoming more critical [20, 23]. How open are open data in digital heritage infrastructures [19]?

4.2 Problems, Challenges, and Requirements for Opening up Memory Making

The provision of relevant cultural materials to a broad spectrum of people and groups is important for social and cultural life. Accessibility and free use of texts, images, photos, audios, videos and all other kinds of information in the GLAMs are relevant sources for learning, knowledge production and also for social processes of identity work. The aspiration to open up memory making to people and groups is thus met with a broad consensus in societies that understand themselves as democratic and open to diverse backgrounds. Still, a series of problems and paradoxes becomes visible when observing the strategies for opening up memory making through digital media infrastructures more closely.

Opening Up Memory Making To Whom? Current cultural materials in GLAMs are collected in the past, embedded in world views of that time, and thus biased in particular ways. Often, their collection was guided by bourgeois and colonial worldviews with a bourgeois impetus of education. A lot has been done already in the GLAMs to cope with the problematic biases inherent to the current collections, which is not an easy task. Still, the digitization of cultural materials in the GLAMs reproduces, repeats and further cements these biases. The promise of openness through digitalisation as a process of implementing digital technologies in particular contexts also reproduces these biases.

Digitized commons, as Jill Cousins, former Executive Director of Europeana, calls the aggregated cultural data of the Europeana, are commons with relevance only to particular populations; there is still aimed at a predominantly white, highly educated and middle class background.

Opening up GLAMS is thus not an automatic effect of the digitalization of cultural objects but needs further considerations and shifts for attracting these currently absent target groups of GLAMs in order to invite them to become users in the digital realm. The interest of young users, who are said to be "digital natives", in digital heritage did not come naturally either, as had initially been expected. The groups who are absent from GLAMs are heterogeneous in themselves; people from different countries use different languages and have different histories of migration; young people prefer different life styles, follow manifold interests and come from diverse social backgrounds; the spectrum of cultural capital of people with little formal education is manifold, and their life contexts are often complex.

The accessibility of digital heritage infrastructures is thus only partially a technological problem of a functioning system; it is also a question of how to connect the infrastructures to the social practices of people and groups with their specific competences, interests and motivations. It calls for an adjustment to the particular needs connected to living circumstances, media literacy, knowledge backgrounds as well as a range of other crucial factors. Through the lens of socio-cultural theory, accessibility is thus a multifaceted concept [18].

Sources for Opening Up. Increasing the accessibility of digital heritage for a broader spectrum of people to memory making is thus not primarily a problem of usability or technological accessibility, but a multidimensional challenge in setting up connectivities between the memory making practices of people and groups and public memory making in the GLAMS through the design of appropriate digital memory modalities. Digital/non-digital infrastructures may facilitate or hinder the modalities for building connectivities, depending on their design and implementation. HCI design thus plays a crucial role in shaping and implementing infrastructures that support memory making practices of diverse people and groups and at the same time allow the establishment of connectivities across social settings and contexts. To give an example from the analogue world: Stairs are not an infrastructure for wheel chair users [30]. Digital heritage infrastructures are thus not connective to everybody but need to refashioned, re-designed or newly set up for bottom-up memory making in communities and for people of diverse populations.

An important source for coping with the challenge is the ethnography of infrastructure and the idea of infrastructuring [31], which outlines a theoretical understanding for how material/technological elements of infrastructures and social practices of human actors relate to each other. Here, the entry points for shaping these relations are specified which can be used as reference for digital heritage infrastructures with its various approaches, the digital libraries, repositories, museums, re-use activities such as hackathons, and others that are currently implemented in the GLAMs. Moreover, it may be an inspiration for creating new forms that better connect to people's and groups' memory making practices by going beyond the proprietary and business driven social media platforms on the internet. Even though the internet and digital heritage infrastructures operate on a large scale, there is much to be gained from smaller-scale approaches and from studying particular modes of infrastructuring with their context specific elements. Opening up and shaping digital memory modalities for the use of diverse people and groups in specific social situations depends on customized solutions. From infrastructures studies as a theoretical perspective, we can also gain the idea of infrastructuring as a right [17]. By setting up infrastructures with politics and poetics [22] that facilitate people's and groups' requirements, these arrangements come close to people's everyday practices rather [4] than accomplish the predefined forms of social interaction run by internet companies on social media platforms or provided as state driven digital heritage infrastructures by GLAMs.

Requirements for Opening up Digital Heritage Infrastructures. Requirements are specific to the contexts in which digital heritage infrastructures are set up. Still, at a general level, some requirements emerge from the gaps that can be observed in the context of the current digital memory modalities provided by the GLAMs and on the internet. For the GLAM sector, major problems in opening up memory making through digital heritage infrastructures have already become visible in the situation described above. They constitute a starting point for the development of requirements which can be fundamentally described as the need to open up existing collections to new audiences with their specific motivations and practices of memory making. In the future, these new audiences will demand attention in advance when collections and exhibitions are planned and created. Furthermore, future activities that reach out to new audiences through digital heritage platforms will need to consider the general social issue of the digital divide [15, 26] and of diverging media literacies [21].

Other major concerns address internet platforms such as Twitter, Instagram, YouTube and others, which have become more or less informal infrastructures for the memory making practices of people and groups who share their materials on them. These platforms are mainly provided by internet companies with profit oriented business models in which individual users' data are exploited in manifold ways at the expense of privacy, data ownership and datafication of people's lives, i.e. the digital data driven representation and analysis of social life [36]. The loss of privacy as a concomitant of communication on free of charge internet platforms, paradoxes of being public on the internet, and further ethical issues in the broader context of intellectual property rights, ownership and cultural commons on the internet [39] add up to a complex mixture of problems for memory making practices of people and groups. Moreover, collective remembrance is threatened by fragmentation and disruptive forces on the internet [16].

At a general level, the requirements for opening up memory making to people and groups through digital media infrastructures are thus: a) business models for FAIR and open infrastructures, b) juxtapositions to the datafication of lives and c) the consideration of ethical issues in respect to privacy and different ways of being public. They demand specification in each social context where digital media infrastructures for participatory memory making are applied. All this is no easy feat, but calls for the development of context-sensitive solutions. At the moment, we are in a situation far beyond standardized solutions for these needs, but we may get to a point when enough explorations have been undertaken and experiences have been made in sufficient quality so that we can undertake the building of models of digital media infrastructures for opening up memory practices to diverse people and groups.

5 Digital Memory Modalities: Inquiring the Role of HCI

This panel presents five fresh perspectives on how the experiences of users contribute to opening up memory making to diverse people and groups. There is no silver bullet for how HCI, through the design of memory modalities, can facilitate this process. Still, in the past decade, there have been promising approaches to infrastructuring that point in the direction of how to make existing digital infrastructures more accessible how to open up existing digital heritage infrastructures and how to create new ones which better connect to people and groups' memory practices. Against the backdrop of these experiences, it is time now to open up memory making to the broad spectrum of memory practices of those people and groups who are not yet present in established digital heritage infrastructures. The papers of this panel will contribute to this intention in the following way:

Sanna Martilla and Andrea Botero will take up the rich body of HCI contributions that connect community based heritage making to digital heritage infrastructures. They explore how the creative reuse of digital heritage contributes to collective forms and practices of memory making, and they reflect how collective knowledge production in memory making refers to process of infrastructuring.

From the research undertaken by Cassandra Kist and Quoc-Tan Tran in two leading European Museums, the Glasgow Museum and the Swedish Historical Museum, the panel will gain insight on how the staff in GLAMs becomes a resource for opening up and creating connectivities through pushing the boundaries of infrastructures. Their research demonstrate how the accessibility of digital infrastructures for diverse people and groups emerges from "craft work" of museum staff. Moreover the shifts of sensory and emotional user engagement become visible as an issue which needs attention in HCI design.

Jennifer Krueckeberg focusses in her ethnographic research on the rarely studied practices of young people on online platforms. Her paper explores how young people attempt to circumvent or trick the algorithms on the social media platform Instagram when sharing photos. It provides important insights into how imaginaries shape the HCI on internet platforms, how the socio-material infrastructure of platforms influences memory making and thus repercussions on young people's lives.

Against the backdrop of her ethnographic research on open knowledge, Angeliki Tzouganatou critically discusses Application Programming Interfaces (API) as facilitators or hindrances for opening up knowledge in GLAMs to diverse people and groups. Furthermore, her contribution introduces the idea of a participatory API ecosystem as a future design approach. From this research we can learn that participatory design (PD) approaches may refer to single elements of the digital infrastructure, which is rarely focused on in PD as a holistic approach.

Kim Fortun and Mike Fortun present an alternative approach to making memories through community archiving with PECE, the Platform for collaborative ethnography, which is an open source platform, working independently from the digital heritage sector. Their paper will share an analytical framework to guide the design of civic community archives, drawing on cultural theory and practical experiences from large ethnographic projects. An emphasis will be put on how community archives can be designed to connect diverse users, analogue and digital, human and technological components, and complicated pasts to creative futures, in spite of various double binds of civic community archiving.

We can conclude from these distinguished papers in this session that memory modalities matter for opening up digital heritage infrastructures with its many facets and broad range of activities. These modalities are addressed by the participatory design approaches, which have made a start and provide a substantial and unique contribution to shape HCI. Against the backdrop of the findings presented in the papers of this session, further entry points for opening up digital heritage infrastructures are visible. Theoretically reflected design approaches guided by cultural theory mobilize professional capacity for communities and their concerns regarding memory making, as we observe in the making of the PECE platform, which is the issue of the working group of Kim and Mike Fortun. This scholarly approach anticipates problems of memory making and copes with the double binds in a professional way, thereby establishing by design a form of stewardship for the concerns of the communities. The crafting for access to digital heritage infrastructures is another crucial field of opening up through shaping digital memory modalities and HCI, as we can learn from the staff in the Glasgow Museum and the Swedish Historical Museum studied by Cassandra Kist and Quoc-Tan Tran. Their research shows that the operability of the infrastructures needs to be "translated" to the people's and groups' live worlds and daily practices. However the operability sets itself a frame for what memories can be made; the algorithms invisibly operating in the background need to be considered as an actor of memory making. Moreover, Jennifer Krueckeberg highlights in her ethnographic approach, in this invisibility they are a source of imaginations when young people use social media platforms on the internet. The operability of the digital infrastructure and the imagination of this infrastructure, both are relevant modalities for making digital memories. A suggestion for how to shape a tiny but crucial element of digital heritage infrastructures is made by Angeliki Tzouganatou based on an analysis of APIs in the GLAM sector. Even though just a small element of digital heritage infrastructures, they make a difference and thus become objects of participatory design approaches in a larger context of API ecologies of open knowledge.

Acknowledgements. I would like to thank all partners in the POEM Innovative Training Network for the inspiring collaboration and the European Commission for the funding. POEM studies Participatory Memory Practices, Concepts, strategies and media infrastructures for envisioning socially inclusive potential futures of European Societies through culture. This project has received funding from the European Union's Horizon 2020 research and innovation programme under the Marie Skłodowska-Curie grant agreement No. 764859.

References

1. Abend, P., Richterich, A., Fuchs, M., Reichert, R., Wenz, K. (eds.): Inequalities and divides in digital cultures. In: Digital Culture & Society (DCS), vol. 5, no. 1 (2019)
2. Assmann, A., Assmann, J.: Das Gestern im Heute. Medien und soziales Gedächtnis. In: Merten, K. (ed.) Die Wirklichkeit der Medien. Eine Einführung in die Kommunikationswissenschaft, pp. 114–130. Westdeutscher Verlag Opladen (1994)

3. Assmann, J., Czaplicka, J.: Collective memory and cultural identity. New Ger. Crit. **65**, 125–133 (1995)
4. Baker, K., et al.: What does infrastructuring look like in STS? When?: Workshop Report. In: Easst Review (2018)
5. Benardou, A., Dallas, C., Dunning, A.: From Europeana cloud to europeana research: the challenges of a community-driven platform exploiting Europeana content. In: Ioannides, M., Magnenat-Thalmann, N., Fink, E., Žarnić, R., Yen, A.-Y., Quak, E. (eds.) EuroMed 2014. LNCS, vol. 8740, pp. 802–810. Springer, Cham (2014). https://doi.org/10.1007/978-3-319-13695-0_82
6. Bolter, D.J., Grusin, R.: Understanding New Media. MIT Press, Cambridge (2000)
7. Bowker, G.C.: Memory Practices in the Sciences. MIT Press, Cambridge (2005)
8. Briggs, A., Burke, P.: A social History of the Media. From Gutenberg to the Internet, 3rd edn. Polity Press, Cambridge (2010)
9. Brown, S.D., Hoskins, A.: Terrorism in the new memory ecology: mediating and remembering the 2005 London bombings. Behav. Sci. Terrorism Polit. Aggress. **2**(2), 87–107 (2010)
10. Clough, P., Hill, T., Paramita, M.L., Goodale, P.: Europeana: what users search for and why. In: Kamps, J., Tsakonas, G., Manolopoulos, Y., Iliadis, L., Karydis, I. (eds.) TPDL 2017. LNCS, vol. 10450, pp. 207–219. Springer, Cham (2017). https://doi.org/10.1007/978-3-319-67008-9_17
11. Erll, A., Rigney, A. (eds.): Mediation, Remediation, and the Dynamics of Cultural Memory, 1st edn. De Gruyter, Berlin (2009)
12. Garde-Hansen, J., Hoskins, A., Reading, A.: Save as … Digital Memories. Palgrave Macmillan, Basingstoke (2009)
13. Hajek, A., Pentzold, C., Lohmeier, C., Davidson, G. (eds.): Memory in a Mediated World: Remembrance and Reconstruction. Palgrave Macmillan Limited, London (2015)
14. Halbwachs, M.: On Collective Memory. The Heritage of Sociology. University of Chicago Press, Chicago (1992)
15. Halford, S., Savage, M.: Reconceptualizing digital social inequality. Inf. Commun. Soc. **13**(7), 937–955 (2010)
16. Hoskins, A.: Memory of the multitude. In: Hoskins, A. (ed.) Digital Memory Studies. Media Pasts in Transition, pp. 85–109. Routledge, New York (2018)
17. Jiménez, A.C.: The right to infrastructure. A prototype for open source urbanism. Environ. Plann. D **32**(2), 342–362 (2014)
18. Jong, J. de, Rizvi, G.: The State of Access. Success and Failure of Democracies to Create Equal Opportunities. Brookings/Ash Center Series, Innovati. Brookings Institution Press, New York (2008)
19. Koch, G.: How open are open cultural data? Some critical remarks on an ongoing discussion. In: Lutz, S. (ed.) {DIGITAL HERITAGE}. Hamburger Journal für Kulturanthropologie, vol. 5, pp. 113–117, Hamburg (2017)
20. Lutz, S., Koch, G.: Sustainability, sustainable development, and culture: diverging concepts and practices in European heritage work. In: Albert, M.-T., Bandarin, F., Pereira Roders, A. (eds.) Going Beyond. HS, pp. 71–84. Springer, Cham (2017). https://doi.org/10.1007/978-3-319-57165-2_6
21. Koltay, T.: The media and the literacies: Media literacy, information literacy, digital literacy. Media Cult. Soc. **33**(2), 211–221 (2011)
22. Larkin, B.: The politics and poetics of infrastructure. Annu. Rev. Anthropol. **42**, 327–343 (2013)
23. Lutz, S.: {DIGITAL HERITAGE}. From cultural to digital heritage. Hamburger Journal für Kulturanthropologie (HJK) (7), pp. 3–23 (2017)
24. Marcus, G.E., Saka, E.: Assemblage. Theory Cult. Soci. **23**(2–3), 101–106 (2006)

25. Müller, M., Schurr, C.: Assemblage thinking and actor-network theory. Conjunctions, disjunctions, cross-fertilisations. Trans. Inst. Br. Geogr. **41**(3), 217–229 (2016)
26. Ragnedda, M., Muschert, G.W.: The Digital Divide: The Internet and Social Inequality in International Perspective. Routledge (2013)
27. Reichert, R.: Amateure im Netz: Selbstmanagement und Wissenstechnik im Web 2.0. Transcript Verlag (2015)
28. Risse, T., Peters, W., Senellart, P., Maynard, D.: Documenting contemporary society by preserving relevant information from Twitter. In: Weller, K., Bruns, A., Burgess, J., Mahrt, M., Puschmann, C. (eds.) Twitter and Society. Digital Formations, vol. 89, pp. 207–219. Lang, New York, NY [u.a.] (2014)
29. Sanderhoff, M.: Sharing is caring: openness and sharing in the cultural heritage sector. Statens Museum for Kunst (2014)
30. Star, S.L.: The ethnography of infrastructure. Am. Behav. Sci. **43**(3), 377–391 (1999)
31. Star, S.L., Bowker, G.C.: How to infrastructure. Handbook of new media: social shaping and social consequences of ICTs, pp. 230–245 (2006)
32. Tanner, S.: Measuring the Impact of Digital Resources. Measuring the Impact of Digital Resources. The Balanced Value Impact Model. King's College London (2012)
33. Tzouganatou, A.: Can heritage bots thrive? Toward future engagement in cultural heritage. Adv. Archaeol. Pract. **6**(4), 377–383 (2018). https://doi.org/10.1017/aap.2018.32
34. van Deursen, A., van Dijk, J.: The digital divide shifts to differences in usage. New Media Soc. **16**(3), 507–526 (2014)
35. van Dijck, J.: Mediated Memories in the Digital Age. Stanford University Press, Palo Alto (2007)
36. van Dijck, J.: The Culture of Connectivity. A Critical History of Social Media. Oxford University Press, Oxford (2013)
37. Weller, K.: The digital traces of user-generated content: how social media data may become the historical sources of the future. In: Foster, A., Rafferty, P. (eds.) Managing Digital Cultural Objects: Analysis, Discovery and Retrieval, pp. 61–86. Facet Publishing (2016)
38. Weller, K., Bruns, A., Burgess, J., Mahrt, M., Puschmann, C. (eds.): Twitter and Society. Digital Formations, vol. 89. Lang, New York, NY [u.a.] (2014)
39. Zimmer, M., Kinder-Kurlanda, K. (eds.): Internet Research Ethics for the Social Age: New Challenges, Cases, and Contexts. Peter Lang International Academic Publishers (2017)

Youth and Algorithmic Memory: Co-producing Personal Memory on Instagram

Jennifer Krueckeberg(✉) 🆔

University of Hamburg, Hamburg, Germany
jennifer.krueckeberg@uni-hamburg.de

Abstract. This paper discusses the impact of algorithms on young people's digital memory practices i.e. how memories are collected, shared and maintained. It takes the experiences of young people on Instagram to exemplify how young people's imaginaries of algorithms influence their choices of what to post and how. The paper further argues that the imaginary of algorithms is framing algorithms as actors who hinder young people's uses of Instagram and lead to the development of strategies to circumvent these gatekeepers. Using findings from ethnographic research into young people's memory practice it is demonstrated that the co-dependent relationship between algorithms and youth should gain a more prominent role in the study of digital memory making. Furthermore, the potential ramifications of commercial algorithmic feed recommendations on personal memory practices and collective remembering are being critically examined.

Keywords: Youth · Personal memory · Algorithms · Co-dependence · Imaginary

1 Introduction

Digital media has become a firmly established part of everyday life for a growing majority of people in the global north. Especially the youth relies on these technologies for entertainment, education, communication and their future work prospects. Although these 'new' technologies are no longer a novelty in people's day-to-day, digital technologies have a quickly changing nature that continues to drive shifts in how people collect, share and maintain their memories. Not only are all online activities automatically recorded, but social media platforms also use algorithms to sift through masses of data to rank the importance of information for individuals. Moreover, this algorithmic filtering reminds people of previously shared events and decides which content is displayed in people's feeds and which is not. For example, Facebook reminds individuals of event anniversaries by showing an image that was posted a year ago or curates slideshows that display one's 'friendship' with other people on the platform.

Algorithms are mathematical calculations that are used within computational operations to solve problems, process data or make decisions, establishing them as essential processes within a manifold of contemporary human-computer interactions. Nevertheless, this filtering is oftentimes programmed to work in favor of technology companies' goals and commercial interests [9]. Resulting from an increased dependency on digital

© Springer Nature Switzerland AG 2021
M. Rauterberg (Ed.): HCII 2021, LNCS 12795, pp. 253–264, 2021.
https://doi.org/10.1007/978-3-030-77431-8_16

media in ordinary people's lives and the application of machine learning and automated decision-making in services like law enforcement, credit scoring and the welfare state, algorithms are affecting culture and society in ever more significant ways, meaning that simplistic and practical definitions of algorithms no longer suffice. Consequently, these emerging issues have recently led a number of social science and humanities scholars to study algorithms concerning their social ramifications (see for example [1, 6, 13]).

While many of the wider societal implications have gained scholarly and public attention, the way ordinary people see algorithms in their everyday lives and what strategies they find to make them potentially useful for themselves has been less investigated. In this context, this paper explores how algorithms influence memory-making practices and young people's attempts to circumvent them on the photo sharing social media platform Instagram. It demonstrates that many young people do not think of algorithms as helpful aids, but rather annoying gatekeepers, which need to be bypassed to make the most of Instagram. The focus here does not lie within whether young people are actually successful in 'tricking' the algorithm, but emphasizes their experiences and ideas of what an algorithm is and how this understanding influences their online practices. These experiences and ideas are crucial for HCI design and improving algorithms to be more beneficial to individuals. Drawing on memory studies and anthropology, this paper suggests that imaginaries of algorithms should be a central part of studying digital memory, as they influence what young people share in their personal online archives and how future forms of memory are taking shaped.

2   Why Study Algorithmic Memory?

The question of how digital media influences memory has been of interest to scholars, since digital media arrived in people's homes and institutions. Memory is a term difficult to define as it transcends the cognitive ability of an individual to remember. Indeed, social influences can spark a neurological memory change within individuals and much of what we would like to remember is kept in material form [4]. Social and cultural influences are, thus, important within the study of memory and memory formations, which go beyond the individual. This type of memory, which is engrained within the culture of a social group, is referred to as collective memory. Depending on its scope, a collective memory can be narrowed down to a specific group or wider society and there are as many, often overlapping, collective memories as there are groups and institutions, e.g. national, generational, sub-culture or religious categorizations. How a specific collective memory looks like, therefore, depends on which criteria one uses to define an explicit group [10]. However, this neat distinction between a collective and personal memory cannot always be upheld, as collective memory is carried by individuals and individuals carry collective memory. From this perspective, not all knowledge of the past has to be personally experienced. Instead memory seems to always be derived from an already pre-existing knowledge that is applied to the circumstances and surrounding impressions of the present [16].

As mentioned before, in addition to social formations and close personal networks people also rely on mnemonic aids to keep their personal memory. This might manifest as objects like images, notes, narratives or sensorial experiences like smells or sounds.

The context of digital media is especially interesting, as people can simultaneously take on the role of producers and consumers of mass media; further blurring the distinction between personal and collective memory [17, 19]. Particularly, digital photography has taken on a central role in mediated memory practices on the internet. The focus behind these images often lies in making immediate connections to others based on sharing a moment someone is currently experiencing. For example sharing an image online while witnessing a concert. Yet, as José van Dijck points out despite its function as a means of immediate communication, photographs have not lost their importance as memory objects, since images are of high significance in terms of the emotional connection most people have to them [18]. Instagram serves as a fitting example for this argument as it is based on visual media in the form of images and videos that often reflect what a person is doing 'right now'. Nevertheless, it simultaneously functions as an archive of personal memory and memory is in various ways implicit in the design of this social media platform, even though the traditional timeline showing posts in a chronological order has been widely replaced by an algorithmically filtered feed [11].

Nonetheless, the effect of the platforms' algorithms on memory practices of individuals has been little researched, due to algorithms being notoriously hard to study. One of the biggest challenges is to understand why an algorithm works the way it does – an issue that is popularly dubbed as the 'black box problem'. Algorithms themselves do not have intentions and do not have an understanding of the content they run through. Yet, they are making decisions independently because humans do not know which exact information is being processed, meaning that people subsequently lose control over the produced results [5]. This elusiveness and lack of transparency often mystifies algorithms further and pushes into the background, that algorithms are programmed by human beings who often subconsciously integrate their own biases and value systems within them [15]. This view stresses the importance of algorithms as non-human actors who produce results that can, to differing degrees, deviate from their intended assignment.

While being invisible, silent and otherwise not sensorial perceivable, people become aware of the presence of algorithms in specific situations. As Tania Bucher [3, p. 32] mentions: "This implies that people do not necessarily need access to the precise instructions that tell the computer what to do in order to experience an algorithm". Bucher [3] stresses that algorithms are part of people's imaginary which in no way means that these experiences are not real, but that their realness lies within enacting material realities shaping social life. Accordingly, these abstract mathematical calculations are having an experiential effect on people's ordinary lives. This poses questions of how these algorithmic encounters influence people's personal memory practices and how these encounters are expressed within collective remembering. In his book "What Algorithms Want", Ed Finn further highlights that "The more we invest ourselves in these culture machines, the further we proceed down a path of collaboration. More than collaboration: a kind of co-identity. We are coming to define who we are through digital practice because virtual spaces are becoming more real to us than visceral ones" [7, p. 190]. Finn's remarks emphasize that human and non-human actors are collaboratively forming social realities of today. Memory practices represent expressions of the internalization of social norms within the individual [2], therefore, looking at the role of algorithms in such ordinary memory practices, provides an insight into one aspect of this human and non-human co-identity and how it affects culture.

For the purposes of this paper, it is thus helpful to reframe algorithms as culture, as proposed by anthropologist Nick Seaver who studied developers of music recommender systems, that algorithmically predict what a user might like to hear by ranking and filtering content. Instead of looking at what the exact configurations of an algorithm are at a certain moment, Seaver proposes to look at the cultural worlds that algorithms are part of, which can offer a profound insight in the relationship between human and non-human actors. In this view, algorithms are sociotechnical systems that are constituted by human practices [15]. This approach also supports researching and defining algorithms beyond black boxed software, because their entanglements with human culture, their heterogeneous and often diffused character are put into the foreground, which can be affectively studied. Adapting Seaver's framing of 'algorithms as culture', which makes algorithms part of broad patterns of meaning is beneficial in exploring how young people experience algorithms and how their presence affects their knowledge production on Instagram. It further aids in understanding how recommender systems capture people's attention and what these commercial interests mean for future memory.

3   Methodology

This paper is based on 12 months of ethnographic fieldwork working with young people aged between 19–27, living in London and several German cities. These youth are ordinary people forming a heterogeneous group representing different social, cultural, economic and educational backgrounds. I investigated how youth use digital media to collect, share and maintain personal memories as well as their relationship to digital technologies in their everyday lives. While having differing life experiences, the digital infrastructures that dominate young people's everyday lives are very similar if not identical, highlighting the dominance of a handful of technology firms like Facebook, Google, Apple, Microsoft and Samsung.

Using seventeen semi structured in-depth interviews and online participant observations, I additionally utilized photo elicitation to speak with participants about specific images on their Instagram accounts, complementing the visual analysis of their posts. Photo elicitation offered inside into the content as well as the practices, meanings and thoughts underlying memory practices of participants in the context of their everyday lives. Instagram will be used as an example of how algorithms influence young people's digital memory making, as it is the platform most used by this heterogeneous group of participants. The findings presented here are exemplary and show the relevance of further inquiry into how digital memory practices are shaped by the imaginary of algorithms.

4   Remembering Algorithmically

4.1   A Life of Digital Memories

All participants of this research grew up with digital media and, depending on their parents' approval, got their first social media account on Facebook, between the ages of

13–15. Many described their first experiences of Facebook as playful and rather naïve, as they posted without much concern for consequences or understanding what Facebook would do behind the scenes with their data. Most interactions were catered towards friends or classmates from school and, therefore, limited to people in their immediate social circle. Today, these images are part of their childhood memories that can be looked at in connection to comments and interaction with friends, making Facebook an archive of their juvenile selves. Accordingly, the majority of participants did not use Facebook actively anymore at the time of interviewing and left the platform to their parents, aunts, uncles and grandparents, who had discovered the platform for themselves. In addition, many felt that "Facebook is just ads now". Still Facebook-accounts were kept to preserve memories and to use the platform's events function, which they found useful to discover local activities.

This early experience with social media is important, as all participants have experienced a profound change in their usage of social media. Especially, the move to Instagram in their late teens and early twenties altered the playfulness of posting and chatting with friends to a careful and more calculated approach to social media. This adjustment of behavior was mainly described as a learning curve. Moreover, many described a growing awareness of their own online visibility and the commercial interests that lie behind Instagram.

When asking whether she posts often on Instagram, Anouké, 23, says: *"Not at all. I used to before. My Instagram account had loads of pictures, that I was mainly posting my charity events and stuff like that. I didn't really care about, when Instagram started, about how I look and stuff like that. But gradually when I started to see and exploring Instagram much more was all those beautiful pictures and for some reason I wanted to reduce or just archive."* For most participants, their relationship to Instagram is more ambiguous than it was with Facebook, as they perceive Instagram to have strong social norms they need to comply with.

On the one hand, Instagram is a vital tool in communicating with friends, family and acquaintances; notably during the Covid-19 pandemic where young people had to rely more on digital media to socialize. One of the practices I observed was the posting of images on the stories feature, which shows images or video clips of up to 15 s lengths that disappear again after 24h. Young people used this function to share images of what they did on the same day a year ago, which was labelled as "Memories" or the German equivalent of "Erinnerungen", expressing how much their lives had changed due to the pandemic. Moreover, these 'memory' stories were used to reach out to their friends, share common memories or to remind others that they were thinking of them. On the other hand, Instagram is seen as a superficial 'place', where people only show unrealistic or fake aspects of their lives. This shallowness made many feel like they could not be themselves and had to either conform to the platform or leave it. Some participants spoke about posting on Instagram as a means to get emotional support or to gain validation from others, but also described this desire negatively and almost with shame. Particularly, for female participants Instagram's superficiality and focus on idealized bodies and 'beautiful' faces made it an unaccommodating environment.

4.2 Algorithms as Singular Actors

Throughout fieldwork, many participants spoke about 'the algorithm' in connection to their experience of Instagram and described it as a factor in what made Instagram a 'crude' platform. While it is difficult to observe algorithms and their workings, as mentioned above, their effects are being felt and noticed by young people. Primarily a decreasing amount of likes on posts and an overall feeling of being less visible, less appreciated or even censored is what alerted several participants of the silent and invisible actor in the background. It is important to note, that for many young people, the algorithm is not only interfering with their self-expression, but can potentially also harm their income or activist work as private, professional and political uses are commonly intertwined.

Neele is 27 and used to be quite active on Instagram as she spent much of her free time with taking pictures with friends, editing images and putting a lot of thought in what content she would upload to make her feed interesting. Although not aiming at becoming an influencer, Neele spent several hours of her week with such activities and her account gained a rather large following of 3000 people. Nonetheless, her relationship with Instagram abruptly changed when she, like several other users, felt a shift in the visibility of her posts:

"[…]*before it [the account] clearly catered towards likes. To get recognition, to get comments and to, yes…I am very very glad I removed myself from this. Because in the end it's very toxic. Because at some point Instagram also got smarter and the algorithm got smarter. And at some point your picture, uhm, you had, you were used to always getting likes on your pictures and suddenly it decreased from getting three thousand likes to one thousand likes. Then you start questioning everything. You start to…or at least I started to take it personally straight away and thought "Oh god, what's wrong with this picture?" And I immediately removed it instead of questioning if it might be the algorithm, maybe my image didn't reach as many people as before. But no, I took it personally straight away.*" (Neele 27)[1].

While Neele was not able to follow or understand what exactly had happened or how algorithms acted differently in detail, she experienced these changes based on the decreased engagement with her posts, which resulted in changing her usual ways of posting. She tried to optimize her posts by guessing which aesthetics might be liked by the algorithm to pass by it. This example demonstrates that a vague understanding of algorithms and their effects exists amongst youth. 'The algorithm' is conceptualized as an invisible yet powerful actor who enforces Instagram's rules and values, controlling

---

[1] Translated from German: "[…] früher war es halt ganz klar nach Likes ausgerichtet. Nach Bestätigung, nach Kommentaren und ähm, ja ich bin sehr sehr froh, dass ich davon weggekommen bin. Weil es doch sehr toxisch ist. Weil an irgend'nem Punkt, Instagram hat ja auch dazu gelernt und der Algorithmus hat dazugelernt irgendwann…ja ja und irgendwann ist dein Bild ähm, du hattest, du warst voll daran gewohnt, dass deine Bilder immer mehr Likes bekommen und plötzlich bist du von dreitausend Likes runter auf eintausend. Dann hinterfragst du alles. Du nimmst das…oder ich hab das sofort persönlich genommen und hab gedacht 'Oh Gott, was ist mit diesem Bild los?'. Und ich hab's sofort runtergenommen anstatt zu hinterfragen vielleicht liegt es am Algorithmus, vielleicht haben jetzt gerade meine Bilder einfach nicht so viele Leute erreicht wie zuvor. Nee, ich hab es sofort persönlich genommen".

which content is appreciated and which is not. Moreover, it is capable of learning and seems to be always a step ahead.

Despite these obstacles posed by the algorithm, young people are trying to make sense of what this gatekeeper is doing and how to get around it. Seeing it as an actor means for some, that it can potentially be tricked in order to achieve personal aims on Instagram. The algorithm, therefore, represents a hindrance that is not benefiting the ordinary person, who struggles to get their content to be seen, but is an expression of the hierarchies within Instagram from which only celebrities and influencers seem to profit.

Ben is 26 and uses two separate Instagram accounts. One for his private interests with a limited number of friends following and a second public one for his work as an actor. Ben spends most of his time on Instagram with looking for inspirational and informative posts, but is also interested in sharing some of these insights with others. When it comes to his usage of the platform Ben experiments with different ways of engagement and images that he posts on his profile and in his stories. Additionally, he tries to optimize his own feed to see more posts that fit his interests. *"And you know, I really systematically, cracked the algorithm for myself."*[2] In Ben's descriptions, the algorithm is something that can be investigated and cracked like a riddle or a code. It is of course not probable to know exactly what signals the algorithm favors over others and which criteria it ignores. However, the idea that algorithms could be tricked into helping individuals instead of Instagram's inner workings remains a motivating factor.

Imagining complex algorithmic systems as a singular entity frames the algorithm as an opponent who can be beaten as long as one changes their own behavior accordingly. However, not knowing what the algorithm actually does and whether one's actions have an actual effect (apart from perceived changes in engagements and modifications of recommended content) allows algorithms to remain obscure [15]. The willful denial to provide access to a deeper knowledge of the algorithms, makes changing one's own behavior the only tangible way to counteract this mystical yet powerful actor.

As exemplified by Neele's and Ben's experiences, the adjustments to their posting practices were not an expression of rebellion against Instagram's norms. Instead, images posted to bypass the algorithm reiterated the credo of only sharing aesthetically pleasing images of the self, travel or food, while incorporating popular hashtags to gain traction. In fact, multiple online articles[3] exist which advice on how to 'trick', 'hack' or 'beat' the Instagram algorithm. However, the advice given here mainly focuses on how to market oneself better and to be more attractive to the algorithm, through focusing on frequent posting, using hashtags and posting to specific times during the day.

These adjustments made by young people are a response to their imaginary of algorithms, which is not only based on their experience, but also established through news and pop culture. Today, the role of technology monopolies in society is a more frequently discussed phenomenon as well as the existence and functions of algorithms - gradually integrating as part of common knowledge. These discussions are fueled by scandals like the 2018 Cambridge Analytica revelations that unearthed how Facebook

---

[2] Translated from German: "Und ich hab wirklich so, so mit System, die Algorithmen für mich genknackt".

[3] See for example Hamilton, Ruth (2019): How to hack the Instagram algorithm. Accessed on 19/12/2020: https://www.creativebloq.com/advice/how-to-hack-the-instagram-algorithm.

user data was used for the profiling of voters, which made many young people more aware of the importance of their data. Emily, 26, spoke about starting to think about these issues after watching a documentary: "*I always assumed that no one would be interested in my profile and social media, but then I realized they might be actually quite interested in who you are as a consumer and who you are as a voter and yeah, all of those things.*" Societal discourses feed into the imaginary of algorithms at least as much as own experiences and these also frame algorithms as entities that can be comprehended and maybe even circumvented. At the same time, the impression that a restructuring of the relationship with algorithms is up to individuals and their actions as opposed to being the responsibility of corporations is reproduced by such discourses, which rarely give tangible alternatives to the status quo.

4.3   What Does This Mean for Memory Making?

The ethnographic findings above illustrate the contemporary distribution of personal memory between private, institutional and corporate archives [8]. Using Instagram as an example, we can see how corporate interests and the needs for private uses are merged, yet repeatedly at odds with each other. While young people mainly want to access information, catch up with their friends, express themselves and, to varying degrees be seen by others, the platform owners are mainly interested in their attention and directing them towards commercial content to generate profits. So what does it mean for future memory when the sharing of images is motivated and formed by pleasing a proprietary algorithm, which only rewards certain types of content? One might say that this makes Instagram an unsuitable place for people's memories. Nevertheless, because people post over a prolonged period during their lives, they develop a certain attachment to the posts and express emotional responses when looking back at what they posted. In addition, the platforms archive function, with which individuals can move images from their profile to a storage where only they can see them, is becoming of greater importance as it allows people to not only keep the image, but also all the likes and comments a post has received. Whether intentional or not memory is still implicit in the personal practices surrounding Instagram.

The relationship between young people and 'the algorithm' shows that despite thinking to act against the algorithm memory is made *with it*. The imaginary of the algorithm being a single, while nebulous actor creates a fallacy in which people find themselves believing that their own behavior, when correctly adjusted can break through the norms imposed by it. However, calling young people naïve for doing so is unfair and beside the point. Youth had to navigate new technologies, which gained greater importance over the years, on their own without the guidance of previous generations, who themselves were still learning how to use and assess these technologies. Several participants wished that children today would learn how to use these platforms 'healthily', as they did not believe that digital media would disappear in the near future. While being content with their own learning curve, being taught how to use social media for example in school was voiced as a solution to prevent making mistakes like recklessly sharing personal information.

As Annette Markham [12] points out most people regardless of their age repeat existing ideologies and have problems to imagine alternative ways of how digital media could function. She argues that these challenges partly stem from the difficulty to comprehend, identify and critically reflect on the 'suprastructures' that are underlying to everyday digital activities. As she further expands: "Tech companies benefit from the "black boxing" of algorithms. Whether deliberate or not, the disqualification of the general public functions strategically to sustain the power of small groups of stakeholders in determining how our social interactions and streaming habits "should" work. But on an everyday level, this black boxing enables everyone to avoid thinking too much about the complicated infrastructures operating under the surface. The tasks of creating the infrastructure are left in the hands of the experts. This also removes agency from the situation, whereby the technologies themselves are unknowable." [12, p. 14].

Markham's remarks mirror my research findings. When asking participants what they would change to make Instagram a better place for their memories, if they could, most dismissed their own ideas for not being 'possible' as things were the way they are. Only when probing and encouraging them to share ideas even if they might seem 'utopic', participants responded with ideas mainly surrounding making Instagram a less hostile place 'to be themselves', while again focusing on other people's behaviors like leaving nasty comments or hate speech. Wanting to challenge corporate interests or fundamental infrastructures was expressed only occasionally.

While the dominance of monopolizing corporate actors and digital infrastructures creates a manifold of issues regarding surveillance, labor rights, copyrights, misinformation and questions of censorship, the dependency of ordinary people on them is also exposed. As Öhman and Aggarwal conclude, who use a thought experiment of what would happen if Facebook collapses, the disappearance of its, by now, central infrastructures, would have serious economic and political consequences [14]. Crucially for the context of this paper, the article also addresses the question of what would happen to the immense amount of personal data currently stored on the companies varies services, including Whatsapp and Instagram. Seeing Facebook as the first digital cultural artefact with a truly global reach, the authors highlight its significance as an archive for future generations. While the implications of a private company holding historical information of such significance when its business model relies on the selling of data needs to be questioned critically, this example also illustrates the dimensions to which memory is already entangled with the fate of such enterprises. Acknowledging this role is important to understand further how their infrastructures are co-producing memory and can point to a direction of developing alternatives.

As exemplified above young people are quite unhappy with the current state of social media platforms, particularly regarding the power structures and norms communicated through them. The idea that algorithms can be cracked through personal adjustments is thus rather an expression of this dislike than a feasible strategy for change. Hence, placing expectations on ordinary people to rebel against infrastructures they heavily depend on by changing their own behavior appear to be misplaced. For individuals using Instagram to create and keep their memories, a radical rethinking that challenges big tech companies and algorithmic decision making, therefore, needs to be complimented by attainable alternatives that are within reach for most.

Whether desired or not the current presence of proprietary algorithms shapes young people's memory making and, paradoxically, gaining awareness of them feeds into how people share images as memories. The adaptation of memory practices to these digital affordances are fundamentally molding mediated memory in its performances and its content. Moreover, personal memory is subconsciously being adapted to the norms of social media platforms although an overcoming of gatekeeping was initially desired. While we cannot look inside the algorithms or ask their makers what they do in detail, we can look at people's digital memory making as a co-production between them and algorithms, which frames personal memory as dependent on external factors. Going back to Halbwachs's [10] ideas of collective memory, algorithms are an addition to memories as social and cognitive processes, creating a collective memory that is based on social, cognitive and technological remembering - making memories an expression of human and computer interaction.

It is important to dismiss the conceptualization of algorithms as a neutral actor in this context as remembering on Instagram ultimately shows that these spaces are not neutral and have socio-cultural ripple effects. Even posts that have activist ambitions portraying charity work or political events follow a similar formula and popular aesthetics favored by algorithmic filtering. This does not necessarily mean that talking about once past online or using social media platforms as personal photo albums makes these expressions less genuine or meaningful to people. The expression of memories has always been shaped by social norms and material affordances. However, the adaptation to new norms, which are enforced through the actions of algorithms, requires new ways of examining its embodiments.

Since algorithmic filtering and recommending decides what is seen by people, they are not only influencing people's personal memory practices, but also directly affect what people will remember. When favored information gains more interaction and likes, while potentially equally important information is hidden, collective knowledge of the past is shaped by the priorities and norms embedded in algorithms, which creates a need to re-evaluate assumptions about digital memory and its meanings. When talking about how digital media allows individuals to become a public person more emphasis needs to be placed on the commercial dimensions of this as well as its effects on internet cultures in general. It is not enough to only look at the digital side and analyze online content, as it does not explain how people conceptualize and imagine the digital in their everyday lives. Nevertheless, assuming that people share their memories online only based on personal preferences and interests, ignores the influence the infrastructures have on them. Therefore, a more encompassing approach is needed that takes into account personal practices, algorithmic filtering, corporate interests and infrastructures.

5   Conclusion

Algorithms are important aspects in online practices and are thus crucial components of digital memory work. While invisible and hard to understand, they are accounted for as actors by the memory making practices of young people, ultimately affecting how people collect, create and share their memories as well as what is remembered. This shows that looking at digital memory objects as products of human remembering is not enough to understand digital memory fully, but requires more emphasis on the underlying human and non-human interactions. Although thinking of algorithms as actors embodying norms and goals of their creators can be challenging as they only follow instructions and do not understand the information they process, it is important to conceptualize them as actors because of their impact on human culture and society. In addition, they embody ideas and biases of developers and the companies who produce them.

As shown in this paper, algorithms are not viewed as benevolent or helpful by many young people, but as gatekeepers and enforcers of unpleasant norms, hindering individuals from expressing themselves and accordingly shaping what they will remember. While we cannot look inside algorithms, we can look at people's imaginaries and practices to understand better the role of algorithms in contemporary societies as well as how they affect future memory. What the consequences of the filtering and promoting of knowledge based on corporate interests is yet to be seen. However, the findings allude to the effects of a commercially driven memory and how the monopolization of digital memory, within a few companies, fails public needs.

Acknowledgements. This work is part of the POEM (Participatory Memory Practices) project and has received funding from the European Union's Horizon 2020 research and innovation program under the Marie Skłodowska-Curie grant agreement No. 764859. I would like to thank Prof. Dr. Gertraud Koch, Quoc-Tan Tran, Angeliki Tzouganatou and Cassandra Kist for their feedback on the initial drafts and insightful discussions that have influenced this work.

References

1. Ajunwa, I.: Hiring by algorithm. SSRN J. (2016). https://doi.org/10.2139/ssrn.2746078
2. Bourdieu, P.: Outline of a Theory of Practice. Cambridge Studies in Social Anthropology, vol. 16. Cambridge University Press, Cambridge (1977)
3. Bucher, T.: The algorithmic imaginary: exploring the ordinary affects of Facebook algorithms. Inf. Commun. Soc. **20**(1), 30–44 (2017). https://doi.org/10.1080/1369118X.2016.1154086
4. Dudai, Y., Edelson, M.G.: Personal memory: is it personal, is it memory? Mem. Stud. **9**(3), 275–283 (2016). https://doi.org/10.1177/1750698016645234
5. Esposito, E.: Algorithmic memory and the right to be forgotten on the web. Big Data Soc. **4**(1), 205395171770399 (2017). https://doi.org/10.1177/2053951717703996
6. Eubanks, V.: Automating Inequality. How High-Tech Tools Profile, Police, and Punish the Poor. Picador, New York (2019)
7. Finn, E.: What Algorithms Want. Imagination in the Age of Computing. MIT Press, Cumberland (2017)
8. Garde-Hansen, J.: Media and Memory. Media Topics. Edinburgh University Press, Edinburgh (2011)
9. Gillespie, T.: The relevance of algorithms. In: Gillespie, T., Boczkowski, P.J., Foot, K.A. (eds.) Media Technologies, pp. 167–194. The MIT Press (2014)
10. Halbwachs, M., Coser, L.A.: On Collective Memory. The Heritage of Sociology. University of Chicago Press, Chicago (1992)
11. Hoskins, A. (ed.): Digital Memory Studies. Media Pasts in Transition. Routledge, New York (2018)
12. Markham, A.: The limits of the imaginary: challenges to intervening in future speculations of memory, data, and algorithms. New Media Soc. 146144482092932 (2020). https://doi.org/10.1177/1461444820929322

13. Noble, S.U.: Algorithms of Oppression. How Search Engines Reinforce Racism. New York University Press, New York (2018)
14. Öhman, C., Aggarwal, N.: What if Facebook goes down? Ethical and legal considerations for the demise of big tech. Internet Policy Rev. 9(3) (2020). https://doi.org/10.14763/2020.3.1488
15. Seaver, N.: Algorithms as culture: some tactics for the ethnography of algorithmic systems. Big Data Soc. 4(2), 205395171773810 (2017). https://doi.org/10.1177/2053951717738104
16. Sebald, G., Döbler, M.-K. (eds.): (Digitale) Medien und soziale Gedächtnisse. Soziales Gedächtnis, Erinnern und Vergessen – Memory Studies. Springer, Wiesbaden (2018)
17. Sommer, V.: Mediatisierte Erinnerungen. Medienwissenschaftliche Perspektiven für eine Theoretisierung digitaler Erinnerungsprozesse. In: Sebald, G., Döbler, M.-K. (eds.) (Digitale) Medien und soziale Gedächtnisse. Soziales Gedächtnis, Erinnern und Vergessen – Memory Studies, pp. 53–79. Springer, Wiesbaden (2018). https://doi.org/10.1007/978-3-658-19513-7_3
18. van Dijck, J.: Digital photography: communication, identity, memory. Vis. Commun. 7(1), 57–76 (2008). https://doi.org/10.1177/1470357207084865
19. van Dijck, J.: Mediated Memories in the Digital Age. Cultural Memory in the Present. Stanford University Press, Stanford (2007)

Culture in the Post Pandemic Era

Apala Lahiri Chavan[✉]

Manipal Academy of Higher Education, Manipal, India
apala@humanfactors.com

Abstract. As we reflect upon the pandemic on the one hand and get increasingly situated in a digital world on the other hand, as a result of the restricted mobility being experienced at this point in time, the notion of culture is undergoing a sea change. The very notion of how culture is defined and manifests in the digital world is very different from the clear differentiation between the global and the local in our cultural experience of the physical world. Will the digital world and its design be based on more global values than before? OR will the rising voices discussing how to reclaim the local and be sensitive to the planet, in our digital environments, influence the future? Visualising the future, amidst these conflicting possibilities may be the most important activity for cross cultural researchers and designers.

Keywords: Cross cultural research · Cross cultural design · Speculative futuring

1 Introduction

With artificial intelligence, Big Data and Internet of Things becoming increasingly ubiquitous (and controversial), how do these technologies impact local cultures. Will these technologies create a global centralized culture that results from cultural templates that emerge from the coming together of these technologies? Will artificial intelligence imply algorithms being coded with biases that marginalize cultural diversity and privilege one dominant culture?

The transformational year of 2020 has seen some technology based narratives being challenged in different ways across the world. The future will see these emerging narratives unfold and it remains to be seen if the increasing rupture between the global north and global south in terms of rejecting homogenizing technologies in favour of indigenous ones will escalate or a middle path will be found.

Decolonising research methodologies in the area of cross cultural design has also found many advocates in 2020. Will that mean that the etic viewpoint will be totally discarded and new ways to describe local cultural dimensions and values will be foregrounded, leaving behind familiar cultural dimensions and values that have formed the bedrock of cross cultural research and design so far?

The pandemic has also brought much focus on the need to go beyond the Anthropocene, to not be 'human centred' in design BUT to be planet centred if we are to slow down the destruction of the natural habitat of the planet, thereby mitigating risks of

© Springer Nature Switzerland AG 2021
M. Rauterberg (Ed.): HCII 2021, LNCS 12795, pp. 265–273, 2021.
https://doi.org/10.1007/978-3-030-77431-8_17

future pandemics. What does a planet centred culture look like – is it based on universal value constructs that are arrived at by consulting all local cultures?

Or, will extreme personalization of lifestyles made possible by technology create a world where each individual represents a unique culture?

This paper will discuss these emergent perspectives and their implications on the question of cross cultural research and design in the future, by focusing on specific technologies.

If the future can be envisioned, perhaps that envisioning can help encourage discussions of our preferred/desired cultural future or futures and what needs to be done for our planet, to make those futures become reality.

2   Culture and AI

'Hey AI, Keep Culture Beautifully Weird!' (Ozenc 2018)

In an article by Kursat Ozenc (Ozenc 2018), the lack of cultural considerations in building AI is foregrounded with a discussion around the paper, Most People are not Weird (Henrich et al. 2010).The paper posits that much of the research based on which systems are built, privileges the cultures and values of people from the Western world. The article further cites that "96% of research participants in the scientific world are working with participants from the WEIRD world when they are only 12% of the world population." The implication is that the generalizations that influence systems are based on a minority of the world's population and hence the existence of cultural biases is a given. As Ozenc points out, "this is a not so glorious tradition of following the mistakes of modernism and orientalism, encoding and engraining the centuries-old biases to the emerging intelligent systems." If we don't create more inclusive frameworks which would act as the basis of AI systems, we enhance the danger of technology fueled conflicts arising due to the use of hegemonic cultural templates by AI algorithms (Fig. 1).

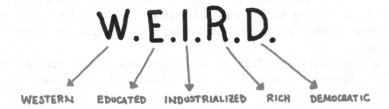

Fig. 1. Is it a W.E.I.R.D. world?

It is a heartening end note that Ozenc provides when he says "On a separate brainwave, culture is a beautifully weird thing. When we call something weird, especially that we are not necessarily familiar with, we are challenged by the unfamiliar and the new. As designers, we embrace this, weirdness and the quirkiness. It gives us paths to reach the new, and the unique and the beautiful."

How does culture influence our thinking and the resultant decisions we make every-day across a variety of situations? Kenneth Forbus points out, for example, that our moral decision making, according to psychological studies, is often influenced by "protected values (sometimes called sacred values), or cultural standards concerning what kinds of actions are not allowable (Forbus 2019)." As an AI researcher, he, therefore strongly puts forth the view that, "Creating AI systems that can take culturally influenced reasoning into account is crucial for creating accurate and effective computational supports for analysts, policymakers, consumers, and citizens." He also provides glimpses of a new paradigm to take culture into account when building AI systems.

Citing examples of how 'protected values' differ, Forbus describes the result of researcher Morteza Dehghani and his collaborators using stories with students of Tehran University and NorthWestern University to evaluate "whether participants of different cultural backgrounds reason by analogy to identify protected values in a situation (Dehghani 2009)." What they found was that based on familiar stories from their culture analogous to the ones that were presented to the students, the response to the question posed to them varied. Iranian students' internalisation of analogous stories from their culture made them respond very differently than the American students who were not familiar with analogous stories. Forbus writes, "This insight suggests that by using analogy in AI systems, such systems could more accurately capture the influence of culture on people's choices."

Dehghani has developed a computational model called MoralDM, based on the progress seen in cognitive science, in computational modelling of analogy (Dehghani 2009). MoralDM, as Forbus says, "takes a decision problem, stated in simple English, and works through what to do. It uses analogies with culturally specific stories and prior problems to make a decision. Its reasoning can be inspected, including the values identified and their source (Forbus 2019)." It is important to note that MoralDM's decisions change if the stories available to MoralDm that reflect cultural values (e.g., Iranian versus American) change.

This new computational model opens up the possibility of collecting cultural narratives and making them accessible to AI systems, thereby helping model various aspects of a culture. Enabling AI systems to be guided by cultural values and norms would enhance the probability of outcomes that are aligned with the cultures they operate in.

3 Decolonisation in Design and AI

"The ethos of the work I've been doing at OCAD [Ontario College of Art & Design University] is really decolonizing design to make it a space for our Black, indigenous, and people of color students and faculty to feel like they can bring their cultures of making into the institution so they can be seen—validated in some ways," says Dori Tunstall, dean of design at OCAD. "And by doing so, they can be confident about being a designer (Lorenzo 2020)."

Many voices are being raised, like Dori's, about the coloniality still experienced in technology and design. It may appear that science and technology is strictly objective and neutral and hence transcends coloniality but as Shakir Mohamed, a South African AI researcher says (Mohamed 2020) "as much as we aspire towards an ideal scientific-self—the scientist that is forward-looking, sceptical and inclusive—we often fall far from this ideal. At times, we replay a colonial-looking world view. We rely on inherited thinking and sets of unquestioned values; we reinforce selective histories; we fail to consider our technology's impacts and the possibility of alternative paths; we consider our work to be universally beneficial, needed and welcomed."

Diverse writing on Ai nationalism (Hogarth 2018), data imperialism and cyber colonisation is emerging even as the stranglehold of data on our lives increases every day. Different ways in which coloniality is manifested also makes for interesting reading (Hao 2020). In the paper on Decolonial AI (Mohamed et al. 2020), the authors write about the legacy of colonial practices on our current technology ecosystem and practices. They discuss issues such as **Algorithmic discrimination and oppression,** *Ghost work, Beta testing, AI governance and International Social Development to illustrate how coloniality perpetuates through modern means.*

On the very controversial topic of Algorithmic discrimination and oppression, the writers talk about the obvious link with colonial racism and how that leads to deep societal structures of racial inequality that are the products of history and politics. These structures are being replicated through algorithms "trained on data within a racially unjust society" (Hao 2020).

Ghosting, on the other hand, explain the writers (Mohamed et al. 2020), *is about "the invisible data labor required to support* innovation, neatly extends the historical economic relationship between colonizer and colonized. Many former US and UK colonies—the Philippines, Kenya, and India—have become ghost-working hubs for US and UK companies. The countries' cheap, English-speaking labor forces, which make them a natural fit for data work, exist because of their colonial histories."

Beta testing of new technologies (just as in the case of controversial drugs in the pharma industry) often happens in countries of the global south such as the beta testing of AI algorithms by Cambridge Analytica in Kenya and Nigeria during their general elections, thereby causing much disruption and conflict, especially in Kenya.

AI Governance – The uneven distribution of power that still persists as the residue of colonial rule can be seen in the area of AI governance. As the authors point out, the creation of AI ethics guidelines has unfortunately left out, countries from the global south, from the discussions. As a result, "developed countries continue to disproportionately benefit from global norms shaped for their advantage, while developing countries continue to fall further behind (Mohamed et al. 2020)."

International Social Development – The colonial thinking continues in the form of paternalistic programs such as 'AI for Good' which are often presented as initiatives to help developing countries. These initiatives force existing AI systems developed in countries of the global North to be used in the global South without giving these countries the opportunity to develop systems suited to their local ecosystems.

The writers note that making explicit the agenda to decolonize AI "enables us a new grammar and vocabulary to talk about both why these issues matter and what we are going to do to think about and address these issues over the long run (Mohamed et al. 2020)."

4 AI, Big Data and Personalisation

If there is one aspect that has caught the attention of corporations worldwide about emerging technologies, it is the lure of being able to provide hyper personalised recommendations to their customers. In other words, even what is known as the 'mass market' now suddenly seems to be ripe with the possibility of individualised attention, something that was possible to some extent so far, for the super affluent sections of the population.

This concept is not altogether new. In 'New Age of Innovation: Driving Cocreated Value Through Global Networks' published in 2008 late Professor C.K.Prahalad and Professor M.S.Krishnan laid out what looked like a cryptic formula, $N = 1$, $R = G$. What they meant by $N = 1$ was that "value is based on unique, personalized experiences of consumers." Hence even the largest corporations serving millions of customers would need to provide individualised experiences (Experientia blog 2008). $R = G$ completed what was a very out of the box concept at the time it was first published, the fact that to fulfil the varied needs and expectations of so many customers, companies would need to change their operating models. "All firms will access resources from a wide variety of other big and small firms—a global ecosystem," This, of course, is the global supply chain we see today.

CK Prahlad's favourite example was about Build a Bear workshop. An example that he used, to emphasise the importance of personalized customer experience for each individual customer. Prahalad described the co-creation that is the foundation of the workshops, or as he said, "product or service development that is collaboratively executed by developers and stakeholders together (Prahalad and Krishnan 2008)."

"Have you ever been at a Build a Bear store," asks Prahalad.

Build a Bear stores are the location of very unique experiences for their young customers. Buying a bear involves creating one's very own bear! This activity consists of selecting the empty fur shell, deciding on the voice, stuffing the bear, picking a heart,

Fig. 2. Build a bear

closing the shell with the selected items inside, naming the teddy, registering it and then getting the clothes and accessories (Experientia blog 2008). Voila! a one of its kind teddy!

"It takes you half an hour or more to make such a cuddly creature. And when you then go to the cash register, you have to pay 50 euro or more," says C.K. Prahalad. "But what are paying for actually? You are not buying a product, you are buying an experience, an experience that you will never forget anymore (Prahalad and Krishnan 2008)." (Fig. 2).

If the power of algorithms to 'learn' about each user of a digital channel is combined with flexibility and agility of global supply chains, it would be worth researching whether individual personality/behavioural attributes would become the area for cultural research and how would the still very controversial topic of 'universal' values play out in terms of defining a baseline of what culture consists of globally and how do individual values and preferences intersect and modify the universal value set.

5 Beyond Human Centredness

The pandemic has brought into sharp focus, than ever before, the disastrous consequences of the Anthropocene. The butterfly effect has been felt, of a virus that appeared in one corner of the world due to the increased destruction of our natural habitat, and the resulting increase in zoonotic diseases such as Covid 19. It is therefore, perhaps not surprising that books and research thesis such as the two examples below, have begun to appear on the radar more frequently than before.

Designs for the Pluriverse (Escobar 2018) - The blurb for Escobar's book says, "In *Designs for the Pluriverse* Arturo Escobar presents a new vision of design theory and practice aimed at channeling design's world-making capacity toward ways of being and doing that are deeply attuned to justice and the Earth."

Imagining Multispecies Worlds (Westerlaken 2020) – In this doctoral thesis published in 2020, Michelle Westerlaken writes, "In Chapter 1, I make use of the growing amount of literature in the field of Critical Animal Studies to problematize human exceptionalism, detail the notion of 'speciesism', and analyze the presence of speciesism in various aspects of contemporary societies. The goal here is to offer a comprehensive academic argument through which speciesist practices can be critiqued structurally and placed alongside other forms of oppression (such as racism and sexism). This critique grounds and motivates the search for a counter-concept to speciesism."

As Anab Jain, founder of Superflux Studio points out (Jain 2018), our collective buying into the neoliberal growth narrative has meant privileging certain narratives and associated symbols over others. The familiar graph showing ever upward movement of GDP is a symbol that has been privileged and presented as the dominant narrative of economic growth while what the graph excludes is deeply disturbing, such as that of species gone extinct during this same period of economic growth (Fig. 3).

Superflux, therefore created a speculative experience of the future called Mitigation of Shock "exploring one possible future where the Western world has moved from abundance to scarcity. We imagined living in a future city with repeated flooding, economic instability, periods with almost no food in supermarkets, and broken supply chains. What can we do to not just survive but prosper in such a world? What food can we eat?" (Jain

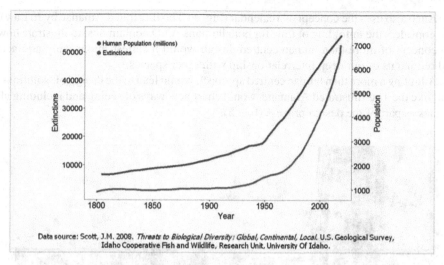

Fig. 3. The extinction curve

2018). The idea, says Anab, "is to start thinking of a more-than-human-centered approach where human beings are not at the center of the universe and are not at the center of everything."

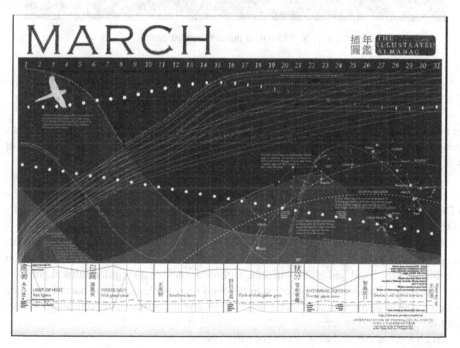

Fig. 4. The illustrated almanac of the illawarra and beyond

Anab also uses the concept of a calendar (Fig. 4 - The Illustrated Amanac by Jo Law), that considers the unfolding of time for both humans AND nonhumans, to illustrate how the concept of more than human centred design would manifest in our daily artefacts and remind us of our deep interrelationship with other species.

Adopting a more than human centred approach would lead to the design of 'solutions' that, like the The Illustrated Alamanc, would chart new ways of seeing and including all species as part of the design process (Fig. 5).

Think lightly of yourself and deeply of the world.
Miyamoto Musashi

Anab Jain / @anabjain / @superflux

Fig. 5. More than human centred design

6   Conclusion - Building a Cross Cultural Design System

In order for all of us to keep culture beautifully weird (Ozenc 2018), what if there was a design system meant to influence and inform the cultural foundation of any research or design that would impact the building of our digital world.

A design system is described as (Hacq 2018) - the single source of truth which groups all the elements that will allow the teams to design, realize and develop a product. So a Design System is not a deliverable, but a set of deliverables. It will evolve constantly with the product, the tools and the new technologies.

Imagine the existence of a Cross Cultural Design System that groups all the elements that will allow the teams to research, design, realize and develop experiences of products and services for local and global citizens, without imposing a singular cultural perspective. A system that would evolve constantly based on new elements and narratives being added to the system, with new technologies and new needs understood through a more than human centred process.

Such a cross cultural design system would consist of:

A computational model based on analogy that populates the cross cultural design system with cultural narratives collected from every culture across the world. These narratives would be accessible to the algorithms of the cross cultural design system, thereby helping model various aspects of different cultures.

Further, the cross cultural design system would have planetary information about seasons, flora, fauna, bio diversity, etc. from across the world. This information would also be available to the underlying algorithms of the cross cultural design system in the form of stories. These would add another layer to the cultural narratives to help combine local cultural perspectives with that of local and planetary natural ecosystems.

Lastly, the cross cultural design system would also have behavioural attributes based on various documented personality types from across the world. This would allow the final layer of personalization possibilities to be presented but ensconced within the relevant cultural and planetary models.

A cross cultural design system such as this would help researchers, designers and technologists who value this planet with its diversity of cultures and ecosystems, to enable their work to always be guided by the richness of local cultural nuances, individual behavioural attributes and planetary perspectives all combined into an integral whole and always speaking truth to coloniality.

References

Ozenc, K.: Culture meets Artificial Intelligence (2018). https://medium.com/ritual-design/culture-meets-artificial-intelligence-a2ad6dc82bb7. Accessed 21 Feb 2021

Henrich, J., Heine, S., Norenzayan, A.: Most people are not weird. Nature (2010)

Forbus, K.: Creating AI Systems That Take Culture into Account (2019). https://ai.shorensteinc enter.org/ideas/2019/1/14/creating-ai-systems-that-take-culture-into-account-aps9l. Accessed 18 Feb 2021

Dehghani, M.: A cognitive model of recognition-based moral decision making. Northwestern University dissertation (2009)

Lorenzo, D.: How OCAD's Dori Tunstall is rewriting the rules of design education (2020). https://www.fastcompany.com/90541079/how-ocad-us-dori-tunstall-is-rewriting-the-rules-of-design-education. Accessed 17 Feb 2021

Mohamed, S.: Decolonizing Artificial Intelligence (2020). http://blog.shakirm.com/2018/10/dec olonising-artificial-intelligence/. Accessed 20 Feb 2021

Hogarth, I.: AI Nationalism (2018). https://www.ianhogarth.com/blog/2018/6/13/ai-nationalism. Accessed 24 Feb 2021

Hao, K.: The problems AI has today go back centuries (2020). https://www.technologyreview. com/2020/07/31/1005824/decolonial-ai-for-everyone/. Accessed 20 Feb 2021

Mohamed, S., Png, M., Isaac, W.: Decolonial AI: decolonial theory as sociotechnical foresight in artificial intelligence. Philos. Technol. **33**, 659–684 (2020)

Prahalad, C.K., Krishnan, M.S.: New Age of Innovation: Driving Cocreated Value Through Global Networks. McGraw Hill (2008)

Management guru C.K. Prahalad and the experience of the teddy bear. https://blog.experientia. com/management-guru-ck-prahalad-and-the-experience-of-the-teddy-bear/. Accessed 21 Feb 2021

Escobar, A.: Designs for the Pluriverse. Duke University Press (2018)

Westerlaken, M.: Imagining Multispecies Worlds. Malmo University (2020)

Jain, A.: More than Human Centred Design. Interaction18 (2018)

Hacq, A.: Everything you need to know about Design Systems (2018). https://uxdesign.cc/everyt hing-you-need-to-know-about-design-systems-54b109851969. Accessed 13 Mar 2021

How to Access and Transform the Unconscious for Cultural Development

Matthias Rauterberg(✉) ⓘ

Eindhoven University of Technology, Eindhoven, The Netherlands
g.w.m.rauterberg@tue.nl

Abstract. For the future development of cultural technology, access to the cultural foundations of these culture carriers is necessary. One established theory of this cultural foundation is the collective unconsciousness with archetypes as building blocks. A methodological challenge is adequate access to these unconscious layers of the human mind. Recent research in neuroscience contributes in ways to determine the minimally conscious state. Combining these neuroscience results with the upcoming development of brain/body-computer interfaces enables us to envision new ways to establish interactions among culture carriers like humans and their cultural determinations. First, we present an overview of the known ways to get access to conscious layers, and then we discuss the potential of upcoming approaches. New technology enables us to develop new types of interfaces which are directly connected to brain/body processes. Next to direct brain connections, we introduce and discuss the possibilities of tapping into other physiological processes, especially processes of the autonomous nervous system. Finally, we are presenting and discussing the theoretical implications of the architecture of the human mind and the interfaces between all components of the conscious and unconscious parts. Potential access to the five unconscious layers of the human mind can enable new types of cultural developments.

Keywords: Archetype · Bio-signals · Brain/body computer interface ·
Collective unconsciousness · Consciousness · Culture · Interface technology

1 Introduction

The history of human-computer interaction (HCI) is rich and complex, and I have already summarized some of the major identified paradigms: (1) personal computing, (2) cooperative computing, (3) social computing, and now (4) cultural computing [1]. Originally HCI research was about ergonomics in man-machine interaction [2] and the emergence of the personal computing paradigm. In the 80s, HCI was investigating media-rich computing with the paradigm of networked computer-mediated interaction. Interactive multimedia was the focus of research and development. More recently, HCI was about the social computing paradigm with community-mediated interaction [3]. The HCI community investigated applications such as computer-supported cooperative work and the internet. With mobile, portable, and ubiquitous technology, HCI is looking at more personalized and intimate interaction with positive experiences [4].

© Springer Nature Switzerland AG 2021
M. Rauterberg (Ed.): HCII 2021, LNCS 12795, pp. 274–294, 2021.
https://doi.org/10.1007/978-3-030-77431-8_18

Several concepts have emerged in recent years for the future directions of HCI: ubiquitous, nomadic, mixed-reality computing, and so on. In general, all these new directions have some common properties: (1) the disappearing computer; (2) the ease of use and positive experience, and (3) the building of communities. Hence, I am exploring new ways for a novel direction in human-computer interaction named 'cultural computing', which aims to provide a new medium for cultural translation and unconscious metamorphosis [5].

In essence, cultural computing integrates verbal and nonverbal information, which proposes an emerging research area in "which computers can improve the exchange of cultural information by using cultural models" [6, p. 2]. This new field utilizes the behavior and lifestyles of humans in each culture to share common or peculiar aspects of different cultures. "At a more advanced level, culture could be viewed as an amalgamation of potentially related and relatively durable societal characteristics that describe an identifiable human population, such as a nation or ethnic group" [7, p. 17]. According to Minkov [7] all existing theories and concepts of culture can be categorized as follows: (C1) culture as mental programming or software of the mind (e.g. [8]); (C2) the sum of all created artifacts by individuals and residing outside them (e.g. art objects, clothing, work instruments, residential constructions, etc.); (C3) culture consists of all conventional patterns (i.e. all thoughts, activities, and artifacts passed on from generation to generation); (C4) culture as a set of shared meanings encoded into the norms that constitute them; (C5) culture as a collection of individual values, beliefs, attitudes, even aspects of personality, and aggregated to the societal level; and finally (C6) culture as a pure human construct completely bounded by the measurement methods. I can agree with all six categories because they just express the complexity by emphasizing different perspectives. I think these different views do not compete nor contradict but complement each other; different research communities have their specific preferences (computer scientists prefer C1, ethnographers C2, anthropologists C3 and/or C4, culturologists C5, and operationalists C6). To reduce this complexity and focus our research the interesting question is: Are there different aspects that all cultures have in common?

In sum, cultural constituents can be found on a personal, societal, and even universal layer. The universal aspects of culture are captured in the 'collective unconsciousness' (CU) as Jung defined [9, p. 42]: "The collective unconscious is a part of the psyche which can be negatively distinguished from a personal unconscious by the fact that it does not, like the latter, owe its existence to personal experience and consequently is not a personal acquisition. While the personal unconscious is made up essentially of contents which have at one time been conscious but which have disappeared from consciousness through having been forgotten or repressed, the contents of the collective unconscious have never been in consciousness, and therefore have never been individually acquired, but owe their existence exclusively to heredity. Whereas the personal unconscious consists for the most part of *complexes*, the content of the collective unconscious is made up essentially of *archetypes*." One of the central research questions is now how to get access to this CU and how to influence/transform it (if at all possible)? Before I can provide preliminary answers to these two questions, I have to discuss state of the art around 'consciousness'.

2 The Conscious-Non-conscious Dimension

Consciousness is *sentience* or *awareness* of internal and external existence. Despite millennia of analyses, definitions, explanations, and debates by philosophers and scientists, consciousness remains puzzling and controversial, being a very familiar but also a mysterious aspect of our life [10]. Perhaps the only widely agreed notion about the topic is the assumption that it exists [11]. Opinions differ about what exactly needs to be studied and explained as consciousness. Sometimes, it is synonymous with the mind, and at other times, an aspect of it. In the past, it was one's *inner life*, the world of introspection, of private thought, imagination, and volition [12]. Today, it often includes attention, cognition, experience, feeling, intuition, or perception [13]. It may be awareness, awareness of awareness, or self-awareness. There might be different levels or orders of consciousness, or different kinds of consciousness, or just one kind with different features [14]. Other questions include whether only humans are conscious, all animals, or even the whole universe. The disparate range of research, notions, and speculations raises doubts about whether the right questions are being asked [15].

Examples of the range of descriptions, definitions, or explanations are broad and diverse: (i) simple wakefulness, one's sense of selfhood or soul explored by introspectively *looking within*; (ii) being a metaphorical *stream* of contents, or being a mental state, mental event or mental process of the brain; (iii) having qualia and subjectivity; (iv) being the 'something that it is like' to 'have' or 'be' it; (v) being the *inner theatre* or the executive control system of the mind; and many more. As Crane put it: "The standard philosophical picture of the propositional attitudes [of the unconsciousness; added by author] is a mixture of important truths—the functionalist truisms about their dispositional profile, the ideas of direction of fit and representational content—and some unrealistic and misguided dogmas, such as relations to propositions, the pursuit of a compositional semantics for intentional states, or for sentences in a language of thought" [16, p. 20].

Plenty of evidence for unconscious processing has been accumulated in research areas of perceptual, affective, semantic, motor, and self-regulatory processes. "A variety of methods have been used, including subliminal priming, in which normal participants are presented with stimulus material for such short duration that it cannot be consciously perceived, and supraliminal manipulations, in which participants are aware of the stimulus material (e.g., scrambled sentences, hidden rules) but unaware of how it affects them. Evidence for unconscious processing is obtained if such manipulations reliably affect perception, feelings, judgments, or behavior in spite of participants' reported unawareness. Further evidence for unconscious processing comes from studies on patients with brain lesions… Some of these lesions appear to wipe out aspects of conscious processing while leaving intact lower-order unconscious processes of which patients are completely unaware" [17, p. 198].

2.1 Historical Approaches

At of the end of the 19th century when psychology emerged out of philosophy as a scientific discipline, most psychologists were interested in *consciousness*. They sought to examine the structure and elements of their thoughts and subjective experiences through introspective analysis. However, within a few decades, the introspective method was discredited, and introspective descriptions were rejected as scientific evidence. Psychology turned away from studies of individuals' descriptions of their thoughts and first-hand experiences and focused on observations of how other adults performed tasks in the laboratory [18].

The rejection of introspection made the study of thinking come to a virtual halt until the 1950s, when technological innovations such as the computer lead to the emergence of cognitive and information-processing theories of psychological phenomena [19]. In the new research approach to the study of thought processes, subjects were asked to *think aloud* (see also talk-aloud, teach-aloud, concurrent verbalization), leading to a new type of verbal reports of thinking that differed from the earlier introspective methods and became the core method of protocol analysis.

The cognitive revolution in the 1960s renewed interest in higher-level cognitive processes and the way how thinking allowed individuals to generate solutions to novel tasks. Cognitive theories described how individuals could apply acquired knowledge and procedures to novel problems, such as mental multiplication of any combination of two 2-digit numbers. Information processing theories proposed computational models that could reproduce the observable aspects of human performance on well-defined tasks through the application of explicit procedures.

2.2 Modern Approaches

The recent developments in cognitive science also support an information processing view of the brain and bodily processes [20]. Investigations of the function of consciousness in human information processing have focused mainly on two questions: (1) where consciousness enters the information processing sequence and (2) how conscious processing differs from pre-, sub-, and un-conscious processing. Input analysis is thought to be initially pre-conscious, pre-attentive, fast, involuntary, and automatic. This is followed by conscious, focal-attentive analysis, which is relatively slow, voluntary, and flexible [21]. It is argued that simple, familiar stimuli can be identified preconsciously, but conscious processing is needed to identify complex novel stimuli. Conscious processing has also been thought to be necessary for choice, learning and memory, and the organization of complex, novel responses, particularly those requiring planning, reflection, or creativity. Dijksterhuis and Nordgren presented a theory about human thought named the *unconscious-thought theory* [22]. This theory distinguishes between two modes of thought, conscious and unconscious, and is applicable to decision making, impression formation, attitude formation, and change, problem-solving, and creativity. Conscious and unconscious thoughts have different characteristics, and these different characteristics make each mode preferable under different circumstances. Contrary to popular belief, decisions about simple issues can be better tackled by conscious thought, whereas decisions about complex matters can be better approached with unconscious thought. This is a strong argument for the higher computational power of the unconscious than the conscious mode.

According to Sleigh, Warnaby, and Tracey [23], *selfhood* is linked to brain processes that enable the experience of a person as a distinct entity with being capable of agency. The presented framework incorporates a continuum of both non-conscious and conscious self-related information processing and includes a hierarchy of components, such as *awareness of existence* (core self), *embodied self* (sentience), *executive self* (agency/volition), and various other *higher-order cognitive processes*. Consciousness relates to *selfhood* but is not the same; understanding the processes required for selfhood can explain the partial consciousness states seen in anesthesia.

3 Approaches for Access to Mental Content

Two definitions have been the most prominent in the history of mind science called 'psychology' [18]. First, psychology is the *science of mind*: psychical processes are regarded as phenomena from which it is possible to infer the nature of an underlying metaphysical mind-substance. Second, psychology is the *science of inner experience*: "psychical processes are here looked upon as belonging to a specific form of experience, which is readily distinguished by the fact that its contents are known through 'introspection', or the 'inner sense' as it has been called to distinguish it from sense-perception through the outer senses" [24, p. 1]. Since Descartes from the seventeens century, we can assume to have guaranteed private access to our inner experience; "*I am thinking therefore I exist*, *was so secure and certain* that it could not be shaken by any of the most extravagant suppositions of the skeptics, I judged that I could accept it without scruple, as the first principle of the philosophy I was seeking" [25, p. 28]. This introspection was and still is the prime source of philosophical considerations. The emerging discipline of psychology [12, 24] tried to overcome this *exclusiveness* of introspection by objectifying the findings [18]: from *introspection* to *extrospection*!

Although I fully agree with Descartes' "cogito ergo sum", we must be very careful in accepting any introspective reports from a first-person perspective as a reliable and truthful source allowing to generalize the outcomes [26]. "On the one hand, thinking of mindfulness meditation as inner observation of a private mental realm feeds the internalist tendency in cognitive neuroscience to model mindfulness as a kind of mental activity instantiated in neural networks inside the head and visible through brain imaging tools such as electroencephalogram (EEG) and functional magnetic resonance imaging (fMRI). This approach runs the risk of confusing the biological conditions for mindfulness with mindfulness itself, which, as classically described, consists of the integrated exercise of a whole host of cognitive and bodily skills in situated and ethically directed action. On the other hand, thinking of meditation as the enactment of situated mind-body states and behaviors requires us to distinguish clearly between the causally enabling conditions for mindfulness, which include neural systems but are not limited to them, and the cognitive processes that constitute mindfulness as a meaningful form of human experience and that cannot be fully understood unless described phenomenologically. This is one way in which thinking through the enactive approach returns us to the phenomenology of lived experience as a necessary complement to scientific investigation" [27, pp. xxv–xxvi].

The question remains, can we really gain insight into the psyche and mind without whatever kind of introspection? In this respect, *radical behaviorism* [18] finally failed when the upcoming research in artificial intelligence demanded such kind of detailed insights into our minds [28]. Recognition of the growing significance of knowledge-based computing systems has put attention on processes of knowledge acquisition and transfer. Commercial application of expert systems was being impeded by the *knowledge-engineering bottleneck* and has led to the development of rapid prototyping tools [29]. After reviewing the historical arguments from the radical behaviorism against the use of introspection, Lieberman concluded "that most either is invalid or no longer possess their original force, so the benefits from a wider use of introspection now seem likely to outweigh the possible costs" [30, p. 319]. Although strict behaviorism declined in the 1960s and 1970s, "its main replacement, *cognitivist functionalism* (which treats functionally defined internal cognitive processes as central to psychological inquiry), generally continued to share behaviorism's disdain of introspective methods" [31, p. 24].

3.1 Introspection

Following Valsiner [32, p. 61], the move from Wundt's word association experiments to the change of accepting the validity of *inner observation* was the main contribution of the "Würzburg tradition" of Oswald Külpe, Karl Bühler, and others (1894 to the 1910s). Important method innovations were: (1) the *centrality* of the method of introspection of the "Würzburg School" of the early twentieth century, (2) the "Second Leipzig School's methods of *Aktualgenese* expanded into idiographic *microgenesis*, (3) the *thinking aloud* methods from Otto Selz and Karl Duncker to contemporary cognitive science, and (4) Frederic Bartlett's method of *repeated reproduction* with its contemporary extension into conversational repeated. Also, Piaget's *clinical method* in his study of children's reasoning processes belongs to the same group of methods which all sharing the notion that the person is an active constructor of one's psychological phenomena and has adequate but exclusive access to one's own inner constructions and complexes.

Introspection is used in contemporary research as a means of investigating one's own currently ongoing, or perhaps very recently past, mental states or processes. We can learn about our own mind in the same way we learn about others' minds, e.g., by asking good friends and family members for feedback about ourselves, by observing our own facial expressions (looking in a mirror), by examining readouts of brain activity through a clinical expert, by noting patterns of past behavior through diaries, by mindfulness/awareness meditation [27], etc. It's generally accepted that we can learn about our mind introspectively, in a private and exclusive way that no one else can. But what exactly is introspection? No simple definition is widely agreed upon beyond the fact of immediate, private, and conscious experience. Hofmann and Wilson [17, p. 204] "define introspection as a conscious mental activity by which attention is directed toward one's own phenomenal sensations and experiences in an attempt to form a self-referential proposition about these experiences with the use of inferential rules."

Introspection is a key concept in epistemology since introspective knowledge is often thought to be particularly secure, maybe even immune to skeptical doubt. Introspective knowledge is also often held to be more immediate or direct than sensory knowledge through extrospection. Both putative features of introspection have been cited in support of the idea that introspective knowledge can serve as a ground or foundation for other sorts of knowledge.

3.2 Extrospection

Extrospection is introspection turned outward—from the experiencer. Its process is thus like that of introspection, and it is constructive of the knowledge of the object of extrospection. The three techniques in extrospection are [32]: (1) interview, (2) questionnaire, and (3) experiment. However, all answers about internal states (e.g., emotions) from the investigated subjects – although externally observable through extrospection by the investigator – are finally based on introspective impressions. That was the main motivation to overcome the resistance against introspection and justify why these kinds of data are valid input for research. The milestone book of Ericsson and Simon on protocol analysis tried exactly this [33]. In this book, the authors argued that under certain conditions, verbal data based on introspective impressions could indeed be treated as reliable and valid data. Till today 'design cognition' "refers to the mental processes and representations involved in designing and has been a significant area of interest since the emergence of design research in the 1960s. The field now faces significant challenges moving into the future, with the major change required to overcome stagnation in research topics and methodologies" [34, p. 1].

Protocol analysis is a rigorous methodology for eliciting verbal reports of thought sequences as a valid source of data on thinking [33]. The central assumption of protocol analysis is that it is possible to instruct subjects to verbalize their thoughts in a manner that does not alter the sequence of thoughts mediating the completion of a task and can therefore be accepted as valid data on thinking. Based on their theoretical analysis, Ericsson and Simon [33] argued that the closest connection between thinking and verbal reports is found when subjects verbalize thoughts generated during task completion and problem-solving, resp. When subjects are asked to *think aloud*, some of their verbalizations seem to correspond to merely vocalizing 'inner speech,' which would otherwise have remained inaudible. Non-verbal thoughts can also be often given verbal expression by brief labels and referents.

Task analysis specifies the range of alternative procedures that people could use, considering their prior knowledge of facts and procedures, to generate correct answers to a task. The choice of alternative procedures participants use to generate the answer can be inferred by the time needed and verbal reports of their thoughts during problem-solving. In conclusion, the theoretical and methodological controversies about verbal reports have never cast doubt on people's ability to recall part of their thought sequences. The controversies have centered around efforts to go beyond the sequence of thoughts, to analyze their detailed structure through *introspection*, and infer the processes controlling the generation of new thoughts. In fact, all major theoretical frameworks concerned with thinking have advocated the use of verbally reported sequences of thoughts. However, it would be very useful to have an objective manner to describe and analyze problem-solving processes without the necessity of introspections.

Decades ago, I developed a theoretical framework to conceptualize a measure of behavior complexity (BC), system complexity (SC) and task complexity (TC) [35]. From this framework cognitive complexity (CC) is derived as $CC = SC + TC - BC$. In an empirical study to investigate different measures of cognitive complexity, six beginners and six experts solved four different tasks with a commercially available interactive database management software. Our special program the *automatic mental* *model evaluator* (AMME) was developed to analyze the empirically recorded logfile data during the interactive sessions [36]. I collected 48 (= (6 + 6)*4) complete logfiles which represented all task solving processes in an objective manner. The automatic analysis allowed me to analyze all these logfiles in a reasonable amount of time and run inferential statistics on the outcomes. Without such automatic support, it needs several days or even weeks to analyze just *one* logfile [37]. Four different approaches from the literature to measuring complexity in a quantitative way were considered and discussed to validate a measure of cognitive complexity based on observed behavioral data. The application of our four selected metrics was compared and statistically tested against the empirical results of the experiment. The complexity metric of McCabe proved to be the most effective and plausible measure for cognitive complexity. One of the astonishing results of my research approach was the discovery and measurement of the *knowledge about unsuccessful* behavior [38].

This kind of knowledge is not - or almost not - introspectively accessible but can now be indirectly measured through observed behavior. Also, Ericsson and Simon acknowledged that not every aspect of the mind can be investigated by introspection only: "Automation means that intermediate steps are carried out without being interpreted, and without their inputs and outputs using STM [Short Term Memory; added by the author]. The automation of performance is therefore quite analogous to executing a computer algorithm is compiled instead of interpretive mode. Automation (and compiling) have two important consequences. They greatly speed up the process (typically, by order of magnitude), and they make the intermediate products unavailable to STM, hence unavailable also for verbal reports" [33, p. 15].

3.3 Bio-signal Sensing

The automatic sensing of bio-signals (e.g., ECG, EEG, facial expression, NIRS, prosody, skin conductivity, step counter; see at [39]) opens the door to new applications and new types of feedback about the inner states of a person. Affective computing is the research area focusing on such topics [40]. Picard discovered that emotions play an essential role in decision making, perception, learning, and a variety of other cognitive functions and are not limited to art, entertainment, and social interaction. Hence, measuring emotions became an important research challenge. It is amazing how measuring *honest signals* can provide predictions about unconscious human decision-making. Using a specially developed *sociometer*, Pentland and his group have conducted many experiments relating human signaling and patterns of interaction to behavioral outcomes. They have found "that they can use the sociometer measurements to accurately predict outcomes in situations such as negotiations, dating, selling, bluffing, and other critical human activities" [41, p. 111]. Further on, I will only discuss in more detail two interesting and important topics: (1) pain measurement and (2) measuring archetypes.

Accurate pain measurement is a key for the management of chronic pain. Although in clinical practice, the *golden standards* of pain measurement are self-reported scales [42], the reliability and validity of such self-reports remain unclear. Unfortunately, "the reliability of these subjective methods could be easily affected by patients' physiological and psychological status, as well as the assessors' predispositions. Therefore, objective pain assessment has attracted substantial attention recently. Previous studies of functional magnetic resonance imaging (fMRI) revealed that certain cortices and subcortical areas are commonly activated in subjects suffering from pain. Dynamic pain connectome analysis also found various alterations of neural network connectivity that are correlated with the severity of clinical pain symptoms. Electroencephalograph (EEG) demonstrated suppressed spontaneous oscillations during pain experience. Spectral power and coherence analysis of EEG also identified signatures of different types of chronic pain. Furthermore, fMRI and EEG can visualize objective brain activities modulated by analgesics in a mechanism-based way, thus bridging the gaps between animal studies and clinical trials. Using fMRI and EEG, researchers are able to predict therapeutic efficacy and identify personalized optimal first-line regimens. In the future, the emergence of magnetic resonance spectroscopy and cell labeling in MRI would encourage the investigation on metabolic and cellular pain biomarkers. The incorporation of machine learning algorithms with neuroimaging or behavior analysis could further enhance the specificity and accuracy of objective pain assessments" [43, p. 1].

In the study of Ivonin et al. [44], conscious and unconscious traces related to archetypal experiences have been investigated. In their study with 36 subjects, they examined the effects of experiencing conglomerations of unconscious emotions associated with various archetypes on the participants' introspective reports and patterns of physiological activations. Their hypothesis for this experiment was that physiological data might predict archetypes more precisely than introspective reports due to the implicit nature of archetypal experiences. Introspective reports were collected using the Self-Assessment Manikin (SAM) technique. Physiological measures included cardiovascular, electrodermal, respiratory responses, and skin temperature of the subjects. The subjects were stimulated to feel four archetypal experiences and four explicit emotions by means of film clips. The data relating to the explicit emotions served as a reference in the analysis of archetypal experiences. Their findings indicated that while prediction models trained on the collected physiological data could recognize the archetypal experiences with an accuracy of 55 percent, similar models built based on the SAM data demonstrated performance of only 33 percent. Statistical tests enabled them to confirm that physiological observations are better suited for observation of implicit psychological constructs like archetypes than introspective reports.

4 Cognitive Architectures and Consciousness

In this chapter, I will discuss only two approaches to the cognitive architecture of the human's mind: for historical reasons, Freud's concept, and the most popular modern version of Kahneman. However, I am fully aware of all the many other famous concepts and established approaches, like ACT-R [45], Soar [46], and CLARION [47]; for a historical overview, see [48]. While ACT-R and Soar avoid addressing unconscious mental processes, CLARION has implemented this important distinction.

4.1 Freud's Cognitive Architecture

In response to the unstructured ambiguity and conflicting uses of the term 'the unconscious mind', Freud introduced the structured model of ego psychology (id, ego, superego) in the essay *Beyond the Pleasure Principle* (1920) and elaborated, refined, and made that model formal in the essay *The Ego and the Id* (1923). The main modules in Freud's cognitive architecture are (1) id, (2) ego, and (3) super-ego (see Fig. 1). These concepts are describing distinct, interacting 'agents' in the 'psychic apparatus'. These three agents are theoretical constructs that describe the activities and interactions of a person's mind. In this model of the psyche, the id is the set of uncoordinated instinctual desires; the super-ego plays the critical and moralizing role; and the ego is the organized, realistic agent that mediates, between the instinctual desires of the id and the critical super-ego; Freud explained that: "The functional importance of the ego is manifested in the fact that, normally, control over the approaches to motility devolves upon it. Thus, in its relation to the id, [the ego] is like a man on horseback, who has to hold in check the superior strength of the horse; with this difference, that the rider tries to do so with his own strength, while the ego uses borrowed forces. The analogy may be carried a little further. Often, a rider, if he is not to be parted from his horse, is obliged to guide [the horse] where it wants to go; so, in the same way, the ego is in the habit of transforming the id's will into action, as if it were its own." [49, p. 3960].

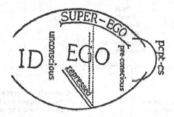

Fig. 1. High-level cognitive architecture according to Freud (adapted from [50, p. 111]) (remark: 'pcpt-cs' means 'perception – conscious')

The existence of the *super ego* is observable in how people experience norms and values such as guilty and bad, shameful and weak, and feel compelled to do certain things in a rightful manner. Freud described "the general character of harshness and cruelty exhibited by the [ego] ideal—its dictatorial 'Thou shalt'" [49, p. 3989]; hence, in the psychology of the ego, Freud hypothesized different levels of ego ideal or super-ego development with greater ideals: "… nor must it be forgotten that a child has a different estimate of his parents at different periods of his life. At the time at which the Oedipus complex gives place to the super-ego, they are something quite magnificent; but later, they lose much of this. Identifications then come about with these later parents as well, and indeed they regularly make important contributions to the formation of character; but in that case, they only affect the ego; they no longer influence the super-ego, which has been determined by the earliest parental images." [50, p. 64].

The earlier in the child's development, the greater the estimate of parental power; thus, when the child is in rivalry with the parental imago, the child then feels the dictatorial *Thou shalt*, which is the manifest power that the imago represents on four levels: (i) the auto-erotic, (ii) the narcissistic, (iii) the anal, and (iv) the phallic. Those different levels of mental development, and their relations to parental images, correspond to specific id forms of aggression and affection; thus, aggressive and destructive desires animate the myths in the fantasies and repressions of patients in all cultures.

4.2 Kahneman's Cognitive Architecture

The distinction between unconscious intuition and conscious reasoning has been a topic of intensive research in the past. In particular, the differences between the two modes of thought have been addressed in attempts to organize seemingly contradictory results in studies of the judgment under uncertainty. Today there is agreement on the characteristics that distinguish the two types of cognitive processes, which Kahneman [51] labeled system 1 (intuition) and system 2 (reasoning). The well-known scheme of Kahneman is a high-level cognitive architecture and summarizes these characteristics: (i) the operations of system 1 are fast, automatic, effortless, associative, and difficult to control or modify; (ii) the operations of system 2 are slower, serial, effortful, and deliberately controlled; they are relatively flexible and potentially rule-governed (see Fig. 2).

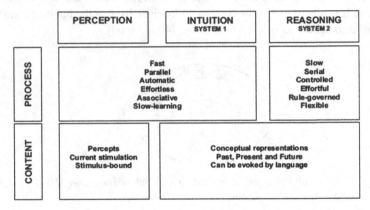

Fig. 2. High-level cognitive architecture according to Kahneman (adapted from [21, p. 451])

4.3 Communication Between Modules

We know that the non- and un-conscious mind do the largest part of the brain's work [52], but we do not know exactly how all of it gets done, and it is an active subject of study. For example, one major area of research is how emotions take shape in the unconscious [53]. Information is stored associatively in the brain, which is largely bundles of pathways of association and usually responsive to activation when needed [54]. A lot of concepts and frameworks about emotions are already available. In one of my papers, I argued for a new holistic view of the relation between the unconscious and the conscious information processing part of our brain [55]. And "there are reasons to believe that, psychologically, emotion is the collective outcome of operations throughout a cognitive system" [53, p. 6].

If we assume that emotions are perceived as important aspects in relation to other cognitive functions, then we could go so far as to conceptualize emotions as the appearance of the results of these unconscious cognitive processes to our consciousness. This is an internal perception loop about the own mental and bodily states. If we assume further that the information processing capacity of the unconscious is several magnitudes higher than the conscious, and both systems are somehow separate systems, we must answer the question of how these two systems communicate with each other. An elegant solution is that emotions can play this role as the 'voice of the unconscious' in telling the conscious the solutions found in a high dimensional non-, un-, and sub-conscious mind space. But these emotions are not only to inform the conscious internally, they also communicate to the social context around us. Our non-verbal body language is also part of the emotional expression space for the adjustment of social relations.

Hofmann and Wilson described a framework of a global workspace that leads to three different zones of consciousness [17, pp. 203–204]: The *first zone* (non-consciousness) includes the class of information that is forever impervious to consciousness because it is part of lower-order subroutines that cannot per se share their contents in the common communication protocol because of a lack of neural connectivity with the workspace. This first zone may be referred to as the realm of non-conscious processing in the strict sense. Even consciously not accessible, non-conscious modular processing can be the source of both processing outputs from the following zone-2 and of behavioral output.

The *second zone* (phenomenal consciousness) is given by the subclass of higher-order processing outputs from modular subsystems that has the potential to be recruited into the workspace but does not (currently) gain access to it, either because it is too weakly represented or because it does not receive top-down attentional amplification. The phenomenal consciousness of zone two may encompass a vast range of sensations and experiences, including perceptions, feelings, and other bodily sensations such as pain that people are having without being aware (in the sense of knowing) that they are having. Importantly, the information represented in this way may, under certain conditions (i.e., attentional amplification), become fully consciously accessible and gain the status of the third zone.

The *third zone* (full consciousness) is reserved for the elite information that has passed the gates of selective attention and, therefore, has become recruited into the global workspace. As part of the global workspace, it becomes accessible to a large range of different processing modules, including long-term memory, self-processing units, and speech production centers that translate the information into a propositional format. Experience has been tagged as such and becomes the object of higher-order thoughts directed at it. Access consciousness, therefore, refers to informational contents that people are aware of in the sense of knowing. These mental contents can be communicated in the form of propositional statements about oneself and the world.

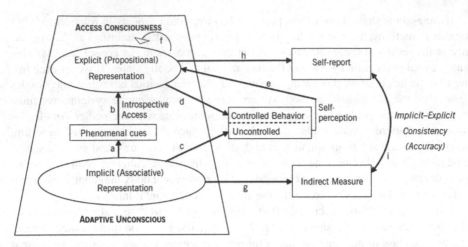

Fig. 3. A self-inference model for implicit–explicit consistency and accuracy (adapted from [17, p. 207])

According to the model of Hofmann and Wilson (see Fig. 3), "accurate explicit representations of implicit representations depend on whether valid phenomenal or behavioral cues are available (path a or path c, respectively) and whether these cues are detected (paths b and e, respectively). Furthermore, accuracy as assessed by implicit–explicit consistency (i) can be impaired by additional information integration or invalidation processes (arrow f) and by poor measurement (paths g and h)" [17, p. 207].

5   Influencing Consciousness

In specifying the general methods employed to produce *altered states of consciousness*, Ludwig [56] emphasized that there is some overlap among the various. For the sake of classification, Ludwig has categorized the various methods on the basis of certain variables or combinations of variables that appear to play a major role in the production of these altered states of consciousness: (1) Reduction of exteroceptive stimulation and/or motor activity; (2) increase of exteroceptive stimulation and/or motor activity and/ or emotion; (3) increased alertness or mental involvement; (4) decreased alertness or relaxation of critical faculties; and (5) presence of somato-psychological factors. All these five categories can be achieved, created or induced by different approaches: amnesia, anesthesia, brainwashing, coma, deprivation, dreaming, drugs, exercises, hypnosis, meditation, neurosis, pain, psychosis, rituals, sex, sleep, torture, trance, tribal ceremonies, etc. Most altered states of consciousness can be described and characterized as: (i) alterations in thinking, (ii) disturbed time sense, (iii) loss of control, (iv) change in emotional expression, (v) change of own body image, (vi) perceptual distortions, (vii) change in meaning or significance, (viii) sense of the ineffable, (ix) feelings of rejuvenation, and (x) hyper-suggestibility [56, pp. 15–18].

Anesthesia and Other Drugs: As an interesting example, anesthesia reversibly alters consciousness without shutting down the brain globally [57]. Depending on the anesthetic agent and dose, different consciousness states can be produced, including a complete absence of subjective experience (sub- or un-conscious states), a conscious experience without perception of the environment (called disconnected consciousness, e.g., during dreaming), or episodes of oriented consciousness with awareness of the environment (called connected consciousness). Each of these three consciousness states may potentially be followed by explicit or implicit memory reports of the patient after the anesthesia procedure. Many other drugs have a strong impact on mental states [58].

Hypnosis: Hypnosis can be defined as "a social interaction in which one person, designated the subject, responds to suggestions offered by another person, designated the hypnotist, for experiences involving alterations in perception, memory, and voluntary action. These experiences and their accompanying behaviors are associated with a subjective conviction bordering on delusion, and involuntariness bordering on compulsion" [59, p. 385]. The characteristics of a hypnotic state include (i) a redistribution of attention to an inward focus, (ii) a reduction of a critical judgment and reality check, (iii) a suspension of forward planning, (iv) an increased suggestibility, (v) heightened imagery or involvement in fantasy, and (vi) a hypnotic role behavior [60, pp. 3–4].

Priming: Priming is a phenomenon whereby exposure to one stimulus influences [positively or negatively] a response to a subsequent stimulus without conscious guidance or intention. The experiments of Bargh and Pietromonaco showed "that social categories can be primed passively by presenting the priming information *outside* of the subject's awareness" [61, p. 446]. E.g., the word *doctor* is recognized more quickly following the word *nurse* than following the word *bread*. priming can be affective, associative, conceptual, negative, perceptual, positive, repetitive, or semantic. Research has yet to firmly establish the duration of priming effects, yet their onset can be almost instantaneous. Priming works most effectively when the two stimuli are in the same perceptual modality. Priming also occurs between modalities or between semantically related words such as *doctor* and *nurse*. For further details, see [62] and [63].

Rituals: A ritual is a sequence of activities involving gestures, words, actions, or objects, performed in a sequestered place and according to a set sequence. Rituals can be prescribed by the traditions of a community, including a religious one. Rituals are characterized by invariance, formalism, performance, rule-governance, sacral symbolism, and traditionalism. Rituals are known for all human societies and cultures. They include not only the worship rites and sacraments of organized religions and cults but also rites of passage, atonement and purification rites, oaths of allegiance, dedication ceremonies, coronations and presidential inaugurations, marriages, funerals, and more [64]. Ritual studies provide several conflicting definitions of this concept. One is that a ritual is an outsider's category for a set of actions that seems irrational, non-contiguous, or illogical. The term *ritual* can also be used by an insider as an acknowledgment that this activity is such by the uninitiated onlooker. In psychology, the term *ritual* can be used in a technical sense for a repetitive behavior systematically used by a person to neutralize or prevent anxiety, bad luck, religious ceremonies, etc. Overall, rituals are highly automated cultural activities in a historically determined context of use.

6 Interface Technologies

Here I discuss only technical solutions that are based on sensors of inner states or contain cultural content to influence such inner states and might contribute to altered states of consciousness.

6.1 Feedback Systems

The design work of Neidlinger includes NeurotiQ as a brain animating fashion that illuminates and maps brain states with color. "The NeurotiQ Spa is an experiential journey for a group to embody their minds, be led in a mindful-yoga meditation class, and then receive a visualization of brain activity as a takeaway. SENSOREE™ therapeutic bio-media is technology to read the body and translate it to visual and tactile languages. We worked with the Muse™ Brain Sensing Headband to identify activity levels and brainwave frequency patterns from the user's mind. Then, we animated this information visually on the NeurotiQ headpiece" [65].

Among other feedback systems, Neidlinger designed a visualization for the feeling of awe. People in awe start to appreciate their sense of selfhood as less separate and more interrelated to the larger existence. "AWElectric is a novel wearable tactile interface that enhances the feeling of awe and shares the feeling with another. The biometric inflatable 3D print fabric amplifies the feeling of goosebumps by mimicking the ripple of skin, as well as the Audio Tactile fabric that creates a tickle to invoke the feeling of goosebumps." [66, p. 322].

6.2 Interactive Systems

To introduce the technical solutions, I focus on three projects: (i) bio-signals from our brain and (ii) two interactive installations based on cultural content. Cultural computing is not only integrating cultural aspects into the interaction with a product but also allowing the user to experience an interaction that is closely related to the core aspects of his/her own culture. As such, it is important to understand one's cultural determinants and how to render them during the interaction.

Brain-Computer Interface: "Brain–computer interfaces (BCIs) are systems that translate a measure of a user's brain activity into messages or commands for an interactive application. A typical example of a BCI is a system that enables a user to move a ball on a computer screen toward the left or toward the right by imagining left- or right-hand movement, respectively. The very term BCI was coined in the 1970s, and since then, interest and research efforts in BCIs have grown tremendously, with possibly hundreds of laboratories around the world studying this topic. This has resulted in a very large number of paradigms, methods, concepts, and applications of such technology" [67, p. 1]. Consumer-grade electroencephalogram and BCI systems, such as Neurosky (www.neurosky.com), Emotiv (www.emotiv.com), or other devices, are increasingly used. Many commercial BCI systems come with ready-to-use algorithms to detect mental states such as attention, emotions, or meditation [68]. The handbook from Nam, Nijholt, and Lotte provides an overview and tutorials of the multiple and rich facets of BCIs and their applications.

ZENetic Computer: The ZENetic computer from Tosa is an interactive tabletop installation as a means of cultural translation using scientific methods to represent essential aspects of Japanese culture based on Zen. "Using images—deriving from Buddhism and other Asian concepts, Sansui (landscape) paintings, poetry, and kimonos—that have not heretofore been the focus of computing, the authors project the style of communication developed by Zen schools over hundreds of years into an exotic computing world that users can explore. Through encounters with Zen koans and haiku, the user is constantly and sharply forced to confirm his or her self-awareness for the purposes of the story. There is no one right answer to be found anywhere" [69, p. 205].

ALICE Project: We addressed individually and collectively the cultural determinants of the Western culture in our ALICE project. Based on the narrative 'Alice Adventures in Wonderland', we have built a mixed reality installation to provide and investigate cultural user experiences. Alice's adventures happen in a world of paradox, the absurd, and the improbable. The key aspects of *Alice in Wonderland* are: (1) a nonlinear, nonconstant time flow, (2) a distortion of experience in space and with other characters, and (3) a counterintuitive, commonsense defying heuristics. The ALICE installation consisted of six consecutive stages, like a theme park attraction. The visitor moved individually and alone through them, one after the other [70].

In her quest, Alice had to go through surreal locations and events. The user in the role of Alice will go through an interactive experience and for example, at the very beginning getting bored in a park scene. Our investigation addressed the sequential arousal and interdependencies of two drives: boredom and curiosity. Based on the literature, we introduced general design guidelines for arousing boredom and explain how boredom can result in curiosity. We designed a park environment with the entrance to the rabbit hole. Effectively arousing boredom can be demonstrated in our experiment. Based on the experimental results, we redesigned the park environment. In a second experiment effectively, arousing curiosity was shown so that the sequence of events (e.g., the appearance of the 'White rabbit' robot) had a significant positive influence on the arousal of curiosity and on triggering and guiding intended user behavior [71]. Later the user meets a Caterpillar, who questions the participant's whereabouts of his/her *self-concept*. To determine the effect of this experience, we used a method that measures changes in a person's implicit self-concept. We predict that the experience will have an unconscious effect on individual metamorphosis. Using the 'implicit association test' (IAT), we could find a significant effect in the hypothesized direction [72].

7 Conclusion

Our brain, heart, and other organs are permanently active, even when we are asleep. The brain just changes the state of consciousness at different situations. In clinical practice, we can determine such levels; e.g., the *Rancho Los Amigos Scale* is an ordinal scale of recovery of function from traumatic brain injury and consists of eight ranks: (1) no response (coma); (2) generalized response (vegetative state); (3) localized response; (4)

confused-agitated; (5) confused, inappropriate, non-agitated; (6) confused-appropriate; (7) automatic-appropriate; (8) purposeful-appropriate [73]. Although this scale is one approach to measure levels of consciousness, it does not provide any deeper insight into the structure of consciousness. This scale is primarily based on observable behavioral response patterns. Unfortunately, more recent investigations do not provide useful additions [74].

Based on all the discussed literature above, I introduce the five-level model of consciousness (see Table 1). Level-0 describes all bodily activities which are not at all available through introspection (e.g., automated motoric behavior); level-1 is the unconscious part of our mind that needs special techniques (e.g. hypnosis) to get access to; level-2 is the sub-conscious part that we can access indirectly through free association or when we remember dreams, etc.; level-3 is the pre-conscious part that we can easily directly and indirectly control through our attention [75]; level-4 is our direct and immediate conscious experience. The difference between level-4 and level-3 can be described by an analogy: level-4 is like a torch and lights up the spot of our conscious, while level-3 is the whole 'dark' area where we can direct the torch beam to.

Table 1. The five different levels of consciousness.

Level	Description	Introspective access possible	External support required
0 - non-conscious	All bodily processes unavailable by any kind of introspective method	No, only by neuro-scientific methods	Yes, indirectly
1 - un-conscious	All indirectly available content and operations of the mind below the level of conscious awareness	No, e.g. by hypnosis	Yes, directly
2 - sub-conscious	All mental content to be only indirectly available	Yes, indirectly by free association	Partially
3 - pre-conscious	All mental content to be available by explicit attention allocation	Yes, by own extra effort	No but possible, e.g. priming
4 - conscious	Direct conscious experience	Yes, normal flow	No

Overall, our whole body, including our brain, is not only permanently active but also of huge information processing capacity. The cultural content is mainly embedded in level-1, if not also in level-0. It remains unclear where to place the collective unconscious of Jung exactly [76]. Emotions can be interpreted as messages from the unconsciousness to our consciousness.

Acknowledgment. I am very grateful for all the informative discussions I had with my dear colleagues over the last decades regarding aspects of this paper (alphabetically sorted): H. Aarts,

E. Barakova, HM. Chang, A. Dijksterhuis, J. Hu, C. Hummels, L. Ivonin, F. Kaiser, T. Kooijmans, BB. Li, R. Nakatsu, K. Overbeeke†, F. Ritter, P. Saariluoma, B. Salem, N. Tosa, M. Verkerk, S. Wensveen, D. Zhou.

References

1. Rauterberg, M.: From personal to cultural computing: how to assess a cultural experience. In: Kempter, G., Hellberg, P.V. (eds.) uDayIV–Information Nutzbar Machen, pp. 13–21. Pabst Science Publisher, Lengerich (2006)
2. Shackel, B.: Ergonomics for a computer. Design **120**(1), 36–39 (1959)
3. Casalegno, F.: Thought on the convergence of digital media, memory, and social and urban spaces. Space Cult. **7**(3), 313–326 (2004)
4. Saariluoma, P., Cañas, J.J., Leikas, J.: Designing for Life: A Human Perspective on Technology Development. Palgrave Macmillan, London (2016)
5. Nakatsu, R., Rauterberg, M., Salem, B.: Forms and theories of communication: from multimedia to Kansei mediation. Multimed. Syst. **11**(3), 304–312 (2006)
6. Tosa, N.: Cross-Cultural Computing: An Artist's Journey. Springer Series on Cultural Computing, Edited by. E. Edmonds. Springer, Heidelberg (2016)
7. Minkov, M.: Cross-Cultural Analysis: The Science and Art of Comparing the World's Modern Societies and Their Cultures. SAGE Publication, Los Angeles (2013)
8. Hofstede, G.H., Hofstede, G.J., Minkov, M.: Cultures and Organizations: Software of the Mind-Intercultural Cooperation and Its Importance for Survival. McGraw-Hill, New York (2005)
9. Jung, C.G.: The Collected Works: The Archetypes and the Collective Unconscious (1954). 2nd edn. Bollingen Series XX, Edited by H. Read, vol. 9, part 1. Princeton University Press, Princeton (1969)
10. Chalmers, D.: The hard problem of consciousness. In: Velmans, M., Schneider, S. (eds.) The Blackwell Companion to Consciousness, pp. 225–235. Blackwell Publishing, Malden (2007)
11. Dennett, D.C.: Consciousness Explained. Penguin Books, London (1993)
12. James, W.: The Principles of Psychology. American Science Series-Advanced Course, vol. 1. Henry Holt and Company, New York (1890)
13. Baars, B.J., Gage, N.M. (eds.): Cognition, Brain, and Consciousness: Introduction to Cognitive Neuroscience, 2nd edn. Academic Press, New York (2010)
14. Carruthers, P.: Higher-order theories of consciousness. In: Schneider, S., Velmans, M. (eds.) The Blackwell Companion to Consciousness, pp. 288–297. Wiley, Hoboken (2017)
15. Chalmers, D.J.: The Conscious Mind - In the Search of a Theory of Conscious Experience. Department of Philosophy, University of California, Santa Cruz, pp. 1–387 (1995)
16. Crane, T.: The unity of unconsciousness. Proc. Aristot. Soc. **117**(1), 4–20 (2017)
17. Hofmann, W., Wilson, T.D.: Consciousness, introspection, and the adaptive unconscious. In: Gawronski, B., Payne, B.K. (eds.) Handbook of Implicit Social Cognition: Measurement, Theory, and Applications, pp. 197–215. Guilford Press, New York (2010)
18. Skinner, B.F.: Science and Human Behavior (1953), Online edn. The B.F. Skinner Foundation, Cambridge (2005)
19. Newell, A., Simon, H.A.: Human Problem Solving. Prentice-Hall, Englewood Cliffs (1972)
20. Velmans, M.: Is human information processing conscious? Behav. Brain Sci. **14**(4), 651–726 (1991)
21. Kahneman, D.: Maps of bounded rationality: a perspective on intuitive judgment and choice. Nobel Prize Lecture **8**(1), 351–401 (2002)

22. Dijksterhuis, A., Nordgren, L.F.: A theory of unconscious thought. Perspect. Psychol. Sci. **1**(2), 95–109 (2006)
23. Sleigh, J., Warnaby, C., Tracey, I.: General anaesthesia as fragmentation of selfhood: insights from electroencephalography and neuroimaging. Br. J. Anaesth. **121**(1), 233–240 (2018)
24. Wundt, W.: Outlines of Psychology. Wilhelm Engelmann, Leipzig (1897)
25. Descartes, R.: A Discourse on the Method of Correctly Conducting One's Reason and Seeking Truth in the Sciences (1637). Oxfords World's Classics. Oxford University Press, Oxford (2006)
26. Schacter, D.L. (eds.): Memory Distortion: How Minds, Brains, and Societies Reconstruct the Past. Harvard University Press, Cambridge (1995)
27. Varela, F.J., Thompson, E., Rosch, E.: The Embodied Mind: Cognitive Sscience and Human Experience, Revised edn. MIT Press, Cambridge (2016)
28. Gaines, B.R.: Knowledge acquisition: past, present and future. Int. J. Hum Comput. Stud. **71**(2), 135–156 (2013)
29. Gaines, B.R.: An overview of knowledge-acquisition and transfer. Int. J. Man Mach. Stud. **26**(4), 453–472 (1987)
30. Lieberman, D.A.: Behaviorism and the mind: a (limited) call for a return to introspection. Am. Psychol. **34**(4), 319–333 (1979)
31. Schwitzgebel, E.: Introspection. In: Zalta, E.N. (eds.) The Stanford Encyclopedia of Philosophy. The Metaphysics Research Lab, Stanford, pp. 1–49 (2019)
32. Valsiner, J.: From Methodology to Methods in Human Psychology. SpringerBriefs in Theoretical Advances in Psychology, Edited by J. Valsiner. Springer, Cham (2017)
33. Ericsson, K.A., Simon, H.A.: Protocol Analysis: Verbal Reports as Data, Revised edn. MIT Press, Cambridge (1996)
34. Hay, L., Cash, P., McKilligan, S.: The future of design cognition analysis. Des. Sci. **6**(e20), 1–26 (2020)
35. Rauterberg, M.: A method of a quantitative measurement of cognitive complexity. In: van der Veer, G., et al. (eds.) Human-Computer Interaction: Tasks and Organisation, pp. 295–307. CUD Publication, Rome (1992)
36. Rauterberg, M.: AMME: an automatic mental model evaluation to analyse user behaviour traced in a finite, discrete state space. Ergonomics **36**(11), 1369–1380 (1993)
37. Ivory, M.Y., Hearst, M.A.: The state of the art in automating usability evaluation of user interfaces. ACM Comput. Surv. **33**(4), 470–516 (2001)
38. Rauterberg, M.: About faults, errors, and other dangerous things. In: Ntuen, C.A., Park, E.H. (eds.) Human Interaction with Complex Systems: Conceptual Principles and Design Practice, pp. 291–305. Springer, Heidelberg (1996). https://doi.org/10.1007/978-1-4613-1447-9_20
39. Da Silva, H.P., Fred, A., Martins, R.: Biosignals for everyone. IEEE Pervasive Comput. **13**(4), 64–71 (2014)
40. Picard, R.W.: Affective Computing. MIT Press, Cambridge (2000)
41. Pentland, A.: Honest Signals: How They Shape our World. MIT Press, Cambridge (2010)
42. Kang, Y., Demiris, G.: Self-report pain assessment tools for cognitively intact older adults: integrative review. Int. J. Older People Nurs. **13**(2 [e12170]), 1–29 (2018)
43. Xu, X., Huang, Y.: Objective pain assessment: a key for the management of chronic pain. F1000Research **9[F1000 Faculty Rev]**(35), 1–7 (2020)
44. Ivonin, L., et al.: Traces of unconscious mental processes in introspective reports and physiological responses. PloS One **10**(4, article e0124519), 1–31 (2015)
45. Anderson, J.R.: The Architecture of Cognition. Harvard University Press, Cambridge (1983)
46. Laird, J.E.: The Soar Cognitive Architecture. MIT Press, Cambridge (2012)
47. Sun, R.: Anatomy of the Mind: Exploring Psychological Mechanisms and Processes with the Clarion Cognitive Architecture. Oxford Series on Cognitive Models and Architectures, Edited by F.E. Ritter. Oxford University Press, New York (2016)

48. Kotseruba, I., Tsotsos, J.K.: 40 years of cognitive architectures: core cognitive abilities and practical applications. Artif. Intell. Rev. **53**(1), 17–94 (2018). https://doi.org/10.1007/s10462-018-9646-y

49. Freud, S.: The Standard Edition of the Complete Psychological Works of Sigmund Freud, vol. XIX-The Ego and the Id, and Other works. Hogarth Press, London (1975)

50. Freud, S.: New Introductory Lectures on Psychoanalysis. Carlton House, New York (1933)

51. Kahneman, D.: Thinking, Fast and Slow. 1st pbk. edn. Farrar, Straus and Giroux, New York (2013)

52. Tomasi, D., Wang, G.-J., Volkow, N.D.: Energetic cost of brain functional connectivity. Proc. Natl. Acad. Sci. **110**(33), 13642–13647 (2013)

53. Sun, R., Wilson, N., Lynch, M.: Emotion: a unified mechanistic interpretation from a cognitive architecture. Cogn. Comput. **8**(1), 1–14 (2016)

54. Libet, B.: How does conscious experience arise? The neural time factor. Brain Res. Bull. **50**(5–6), 339–340 (1999)

55. Rauterberg, M.: Emotions as a communication medium between the unconscious and the conscious. In: Nakatsu, R., Tosa, N., Naghdy, F., Wong, K.W., Codognet, P. (eds.) ECS 2010. IAICT, vol. 333, pp. 198–207. Springer, Heidelberg (2010). https://doi.org/10.1007/978-3-642-15214-6_20

56. Ludwig, A.M.: Altered states of consciousness. In: Tart, C.T. (ed.) Altered States of Consciousness, pp. 11–24. Anchor Books, New York (1972)

57. Bonhomme, V., et al.: General anesthesia: a probe to explore consciousness. Front. Syst. Neurosci. **13**(1), 36 (2019)

58. Pollan, M.: How to Change Your Mind: What the New Science of Psychedelics Teaches Us about Consciousness, Dying, Addiction, Depression, and Transcendence. Penguin Books, New York (2018)

59. Kihlstrom, J.F.: Hypnosis. Annu. Rev. Psychol. **36**(1), 385–418 (1985)

60. Burrows, G.D., Stanley, R.O.: Introduction to clinical hypnosis and the hypnotic phenomena. In: Burrows, G.D., Stanley, R.O., Bloom, P.B. (eds.) International Handbook of Clinical Hypnosis, pp. 3–17. Wiley, Chichester (2001)

61. Bargh, J.A., Pietromonaco, P.: Automatic information processing and social perception: the influence of trait information presented outside of conscious awareness on impression formation. J. Pers. Soc. Psychol. **43**(3), 437–449 (1982)

62. Dijksterhuis, A., Chartrand, T.L., Aarts, H.: Effects of priming and perception on social behavior and goal pursuit. In: Bargh, J.A. (ed.) Social Psychology and the Unconscious: The Automaticity of Higher Mental Processes, pp. 51–135. Psychology Press, New York (2007)

63. Lucini, F.A., et al.: How the brain transitions from conscious to subliminal perception. Neuroscience **411**(1), 280–290 (2019)

64. De Coppet, D. (ed.): Understanding Rituals. Routledge, New York (2002)

65. Neidlinger, K.: NeurotiQ Spa (2021). https://www.sensoree.com/artifacts/neurotiq-spa/

66. Neidlinger, K., et al.: AWElectric: that gave me goosebumps, did you feel it too? In: Peiris, R.L. (eds.) Proceedings of the Eleventh International Conference on Tangible, Embedded, and Embodied Interaction, pp. 315–324. ACM, New York (2017)

67. Nam, C.S., Nijholt, A., Lotte, F. (eds.): Brain–Computer Interfaces Handbook: Technological and Theoretical Advances. CRC Press, Boca Raton (2018)

68. Tan, L.-F., et al.: Effect of mindfulness meditation on brain–computer interface performance. Conscious. Cogn. **23**(1), 12–21 (2014)

69. Tosa, N., Matsuoka, S.: ZENetic computer: exploring Japanese culture. Leonardo **39**(3), 205–211 (2006)

70. Nakevska, M., et al.: Alice's adventures in an immersive mixed reality environment. In: IEEE International Symposium on Mixed and Augmented Reality (ISMAR), pp. 303–304. IEEE, Piscataway (2012)

71. van Aart, J., et al.: How to behave as Alice in Wonderland–about boredom and curiosity. Entertainment Comput. **1**(3–4), 125–137 (2010)
72. Kooijmans, T., Rauterberg, M.: Cultural computing and the self concept: towards unconscious metamorphosis. In: Ma, L., Rauterberg, M., Nakatsu, R. (eds.) ICEC 2007. LNCS, vol. 4740, pp. 171–181. Springer, Heidelberg (2007). https://doi.org/10.1007/978-3-540-74873-1_21
73. Whyte, J.: Rancho los amigos scale. In: Kreutzer, J.S., DeLuca, J., Caplan, B. (eds.) Encyclopedia of Clinical Neuropsychology, pp. 2110–2110. Springer, New York (2011). https://doi.org/10.1007/978-0-387-79948-3_67
74. Koch, C., et al.: Neural correlates of consciousness: progress and problems. Nat. Rev. Neurosci. **17**(5), 307–321 (2016)
75. DeCaro, M.S., Beilock, S.L.: The benefits and perils of attentional control. In: Bruya, B. (ed.) Effortless Attention: A New Perspective in the Cognitive Science of Attention and Action, pp. 51–73. MIT Press, Cambridge (2010)
76. Prinz, J.J.: Beyond Human Nature: How Culture and Experience Shape the Human Mind. WW Norton & Company, New York (2012)

Ethical Stance and Evolving Technosexual Culture – A Case for Human-Computer Interaction

Rebekah Rousi[✉] [ID]

Faculty of Information Technology, University of Jyväskylä, PO Box 35,
40014 Jyväskylä, Finland
rebekah.rousi@jyu.fi

Abstract. Issues relating to ethics and how moral principles evolve are imminently engrained in culture. Culture and technology cannot be separated from one another, as both are processes and reflections of social cognition and experience through action and practice. Technology is the embodiment of values and enabler of culture. As technology develops and human relationships to information technology (IT) become ever more intricate and intimate the cultural framework underpinning values and ethics also morphs. The Internet is everywhere and humans are reliant on it for everything from banking to maintaining family relationships. Anything an individual could possibly desire can be found within the masses of information and websites. The Internet has made access to domains that were either rare luxury or forbidden seemingly easy, convenient and free. What was once considered taboo and hedonic indulgence is now not only openly available, but widely accepted within popular Western culture. This paper concentrates on the topic of technosexuality, Internet facilitated sexual encounters, technologically enabled sex, and ideas around ethics and changing moral values. We refer to 'ethical stance' as a reflection of the socio-psychological positioning of humans in relation to their moral views and understandings. This is a theoretical paper that draws on contemporary examples from dating Apps and embodied technology (sex robots) in light of current discourse expressed in public online media.

Keywords: Ethics · Artificial intelligence · Social media · Sex robots · Culture

1 Introduction

The relationship between humans, sex and technology can be seen throughout human history. Whether it be to enhance sexual appeal, enhance sex, or compensate for sexual partners – either in a relationship or not – technology has been constantly present through the acts and creation of human beings. One historical example can be seen in the poet Publius Ovidius (Ovid) Naso's (43 BC- 17/18 AD) work *Metamorphoses* [1]. In the epic *Metamorphoses*, Ovid describes the story of Pygmalion, a single man and sensitive soul who was disheartened by witnessing the poor conditions of women. He chose to remain single for many years, during which time he carved a statue of a woman out of

© Springer Nature Switzerland AG 2021
M. Rauterberg (Ed.): HCII 2021, LNCS 12795, pp. 295–310, 2021.
https://doi.org/10.1007/978-3-030-77431-8_19

ivory. Pygmalion fell in love with the beauty of his ivory creation. He dressed the statue, whispered to it, kissed it and even felt that the statue had returned his kisses. Eventually after praying that she be his wife, the statue of perfection was transformed into flesh and blood.

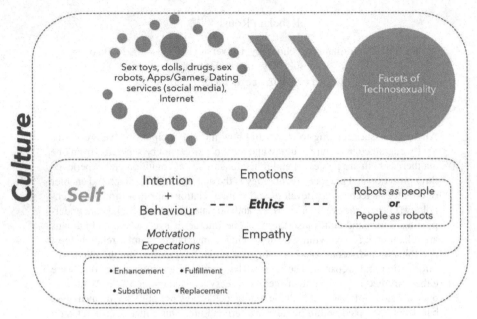

Fig. 1. Facets of Technosexuality in light of self and culture

The story characterizes two important points: 1) the fact that sex technology and objects used as human substitutes has a long history; and 2) that sex technology is not necessarily about human flesh and satisfaction through interaction with objects, but in fact human-to-human interactions and relations. The tale of Pygmalion indeed shows disillusionment between the reality of others (women, their behavior, being and conditions) and our expectations of what they should be - our ideals of others. This is known often times as the Pygmalion (or Rothendal) effect [2]. Yet, the Pygmalion effect concentrates on explaining the correlation between expectations of high performance and actual realization of high performance [3]. This matter cuts at the heart of traditional debate in sex technology, ethics and fields such as gender studies in the conflict between organic versus artificial, unconditional romantic (love) versus constituent, or confluent [4]. The following paper delves into ethical matters concerning technosexuality in light of self and culture (see Fig. 1). Technosexuality refers to engagement with sex-oriented technology and technology that facilitates sexual encounters. The focus in particular is on changing cultural conditions and ethical stance, and observing the varying types of ethical issues that are still arising given the evolving techno-cultural landscape.

2 Ethics, Moral Values and Ethical Stance

In this section, we describe what ethics are from the perspective of this paper, and explain our position on ethical stance. In the first place, 'ethics' is an area of philosophy that aims at examining and explaining the ways in which people evaluate phenomena in terms of 'good' and 'bad', or 'good' and 'evil' [5]. Ethics, are philosophical collections of moral principles that exist on differing levels in relation to each individual and their positioning in society [6], can be seen as culturally, socially and individually constructed [7]. They are used as a means by which people assess phenomena such as other people and their character traits, the way they behave and their associations (institutions, groups or ideologies they represent) [8], as well as things or systems, for instance technological systems such as Artificial Intelligence (AI), robotics and social media. Ethics is the term that explains sets of conditions that are thought to be designed to maximize benefits for as many people and parties possible [9]. Yet, they also are psychologically and socially present through immaterial values and frameworks through which we judge as to whether someone has behaved in an appropriate or 'good' way, or whether or not they have acted inappropriately with the wrong intentions in mind - the intention to act for personal benefit at the expense of others.

Moral principles, or ethics, guide the ways in which we understand what is morally right and morally wrong [8]. The subjects of these evaluations are not simply other people or e.g., technology, but also societal frameworks as a whole. For instance, do we always agree with the legislation and policies of our own countries? What about in regards to regimes and dictatorships? Just because we are told to act in a certain way, do we actually agree with these orders or the motives behind them? In other words, ethics is a complex philosophical and sociological field, in which the dynamics between individual, collective and society are analyzed from multiple perspectives and on varying levels, particularly when considering the types of ethics related subjects in question and why they exist [7].

2.1 Areas of Ethics

The field of ethics is said to be divided into three distinct areas: a) metaethics - this deals with what judgments mean, what they concern, whether or not there are multiple viewpoints to consider regarding particular subjects (i.e., is there really a true or false in relation to the matter in question, and if so, what is it?); b) normative ethics - looks at what these judgments comprise (the content and constructs of the judgments) - i.e., what parts of an action make it right or wrong, and in what ways can a good life be defined? [11]; and c) applied ethics - how ethics are played out in practice is relation to diverse issues such as animals rights, abortion, homosexuality, infanticide, war etc. [11] Moral principles or guidelines are translated to apply to the evaluation of contemporary life and society, this is achieved through focusing on isolating the properties of a just and fair society [10]. Lately, we can see this act of normative ethics being permeated through societal levels, particularly in discourse relating to design, technology and business. Sustainability in particular, is primarily concerned with operationalizing ethics - ascertaining what are the appropriate and correct ways of undertaking operations and considering design - in order to create and maintain structures, ecosystems and relations that will sustain in the long-term [11]. This also entails understandings of accountability and responsibility within action and interaction relationships [12].

Thus, within ethics, there are not only differing approaches but also differing scopes of promoting these understandings that entail i.e., moral theory or applied ethics. Moral theory aims to generate a systematic viewpoint on a wide range of disagreements and moral convictions and why these exist [13]. Applied ethics on the other hand, is seen in the above example of current trends in sustainability (environmental, social, economic etc.) and corporate responsibility in which ethical guidelines or moral principles are converted into action. Accountability could be said to be one of the grey areas in this ethical chain [12], and this is something that will be discussed more in relation to evolving ethical stance.

2.2 Ethical Stance and Moral Positioning

Ethical stance, or as some deem moral positioning, can be seen as the perspective from which an individual believes an action, matter or belief is correct and true [14, 15]. As John Seeley has aptly described, "An ethic is a morality become in its custom; it is self-willed, and the strength that makes possible that strenuous enactment lies in self-location, the appropriate placing of the self" (p. 382). This placing of the self, or positioning of oneself is either the active or passive choice to assume a stance. In other words, ethics exist and operate in relation to normified action (custom) and agency. People consciously on various levels decide what is right and wrong - locating themselves in relation to these criteria. As children humans are born within specific frameworks or social-cultural structures that define good and evil, yet as one grows older and social mechanisms become more explicit, people become more capable of locating themselves in relation to specific phenomena. This is what is meant here by ethical or moral stance. Seeley [16] goes on to outline the fact that ethical stance is taking a position in light of a dis-position - a position and posture that is acquired, indicated and held. Ethical stance is about making both explicit and implicit programmatic declarations. Intentionality, or intentions, can be viewed as sub-stances in relation to stance. Thus a stance, or when someone is taking a 'stand' (against or for) people are implying a status - the act (*motus* or movement) towards/against something.

Moral positioning can be seen as slightly different to ethical stance. In the case of moral positioning, the act of moralizing itself can be understood as a social phenomenon [13]. The theory of moral positioning aims to examine and discover patterns that aid in explicating social interaction during conflict. In turn, these patterns can be seen to be used by ordinary people on a daily basis during interaction with one another. Moral positioning is used to describe the process in which people attribute moral meaning and identity to objects and subjects. Where ethical stance can be seen in great respect as an introspective process of positioning the self, moral positioning can be seen as an interactive process in which people dialogically place themselves in a position according to a moral issue. This dialogical placement happens in social interaction. Unlike the deeper roots of ethical stance, moral positioning does not assume the handling of morality according to religion or philosophy, and is not concerned with framing phenomena as either good or evil. Rather, it is about how people apply morality in their everyday lives. Aström [17] focused on moral patterns either implicit or explicit, as well as moralizing processes. Sub-processes involved in this can be considered as moral gate-keeping, competitive moral positioning and moral position fixation.

We may consider ethical stance in particular, as not so much fixed, but gradually evolving over time. As people learn, experience and are exposed to different situations and viewpoints, their ethical stance evolves [18]. Where philosopher David Hume had argued that moral reason, or the way in which we ethically frame issues, is highly contingent on emotional reactions (this also links to further scholarship on evolutionary ethics for instance) [19]. Upon greater inspection this relationship between emotions and ethics is highly intricate [20]. Yet, as Bloom [18] states, "[e]motional responses alone cannot explain one of the most interesting aspects of human nature: that morals evolve." Research has actually shown for instance that people in general are more compassionate now than 100 years previously [21], but we are also more judgmental. The capacity of sympathy, and quite arguably, empathy has expanded, and people overall have greater understandings for social, racial, gender and sexuality-related issues than they had previously. This is owed greatly to the increase and accessibility of debate and rational deliberation that has increased awareness and information about not only how the issues exist on societal levels, but also how they impact on the individual lives that they affect.

2.3   Tight Link Between Technology and Ethical Stance

A substantial part of this information landscape through which people have access to data and broad, varying viewpoints is facilitated by the Internet and its supported and supporting technology. A tight link is apparent between the types of technology that are available, how easy they are to use and how closely it connects to our everyday lives, and what types of information and affordances (the things these technologies can do for us, see e.g., [22, 23]) the technology offers, in relation to what information people encounter, how they encounter it and how it fits in the schema of their lives. Fromm this perspective, we may consider that the Internet covers and applies to every area of any individual's life, from dishwashing to sex. Incidentally, one area of ethics that has been highly sensitive and vulnerable to debate is the matter of sex - also known as sexual ethics [24]. Sexual ethics can be understood in part as a sub-category of bioethics, in which scholars seek to explain the meaning of sexuality, as well as cause and effect relationships of sexual activities, orientations and attitudes. Sexual ethics additionally includes debate concerning disease and dysfunction, design versus obligation, justice versus purity. Here, emphasis is placed on establishing standards for intervention in physical processes, human rights and particularly self-determination, human growth ideals, and the critical role of social context on determining interpretation and regulation of sexual behavior.

Thus, the ethical layers posed by not only technology, its design and experience, but also by its use within other ethically challenging domains such as sex, forces researchers and developers alike to consider the diverse aspects that can influence and affect people's quality of life and societal health in general. Raising awareness of ethical questions relating to sex technology - sex robotics, toys and sexually-orientated social media (which additionally accrue further ethical questions, see, [25]). Yet, to understand the scope of these discussions, we need to see how sex-related technology has emerged and developed.

3 Evolution of Sex Tech - from Embodied to Social Media to Embodied Interactions

In this section we describe sex tech, what it means in the context of social media and embodied interactions and intelligent systems, and how its framing has evolved through the history of the Internet. Mark Davis [26] refers to the rise in sex tech consumption through the lens of technosexuality. Davis argues that the levels of technosexuality have risen along with the infiltration of the Internet, and the Internet's developmental history itself. In fact, the link between sex and the Internet is so strong that we may observe it through the French Minitel computer network in the 1980s [27]. During Minitel's early development even it was noted that the economic viability of the technology was held in its ability to facilitate distanced dating. Thus, through its very birth, the Internet has been strongly socially and economically connected to sex and sexuality. Sex and matchmaking has driven the technological development of the Internet and its associated industries [27]. The focus has evolved though from direct human to human communicational connections, to enveloping the spectrum of human sexual fantasies [28]. This matter is particularly important to remember when considering the connections between future technology vision and popular culture. For as seen in movie classics such as *The Lawnmower Man* (1992) and the more recent *WestWorld* (2016-onwards), there is an intricate link made between intelligent technology development, power through intelligence and desire, human-machine synthesis and moral grounding (ethics - ethical conduct) (see also, [29]). In other words, what does the desire for power, control and the sexual objectification of technology and through technology say about the core nature of humanity?

This matter has been taken up in the field of cultural studies, particularly in light of the troubled relationship between (sexed) human bodies and machines that represent great super power in popular culture [30]. In fact, the spectacle of cybernetic (organic-artificial) couplings of human flesh to technology is seen as a cultural, societal and arguably emotional reaction to transitional periods, especially those characterized by 'post' - the migration from industrialism to post-industrialism; reality to post-reality; modernity to post-modernity; human to post-humanity. We can also understand this cybernetic coupling through a different lens such as the history of sex toys, dolls and other technology. Thus, to broaden the scope we may see that technosexuality includes a wider range of technology, from biotechnology and drug manufacturing, to gadgets, toys and simulations. To begin with, sex technology itself as seen in sex dolls and other devices go back through human history [31]. Some examples in relatively modern history can be seen in the instances of cloth or sack effigies known as *dames de voyage* that were used by lonely sailors on their long voyages [32].

A dames de voyage in its simplicity may not have posed too much complexity in its need, design and use from perspectives such as ethics. A fairly simple, maybe decorated sack, hardly could have been mistaken for a human through its life-likeness. The physical, embodied sack was an intimate companion to sailors who were limited to the confines of the ship and the company of other sailors. From historical ethical stance, as well as religious and moral views towards homosexuality, for instance, the dames de voyage would have been the preferred option. Perhaps, the treatment of the dames de voyage may have generated a myriad of extra questions, and those are interesting for exploration in further papers. What is paramount here is not only the improvements to fidelity and quality of sex technology on offer - from dismembered and/or novel artificial body parts with multiple functions to sex robotics - but the ways in which these technological advancements, including the nature of intimate encounters through social (sex) media (e.g., Tinder) change the way in which we view sex. From an ethical standpoint, what is of particular concern is how the use and experience of these technologies change the ways in which we treat other people. From this vantage point then indeed we are delving into the field of how people understand and/or abide by moral principles - our ethical stance. Because it is through this ethical stance that we formulate a code of conduct via which we interact with, treat, experience and conceptualize other people in relation to ourselves [18]. For this reason, intentionality is pivotal in comprehending human consciousness and motivation, particularly when ascertaining how people position themselves in terms of ethical stance [33].

3.1 Intentionality, Ethical Stance and Technosexuality

To illustrate the role of intentionality within ethical stance and how people use technology for sexual purposes, we may observe that the historical dames de voyage may have been used as a tool to stand in for, or indeed substitute, one's marital partner. In the sailor's mind, the sack may have been the wife herself, and/or it was used as a tool to curve temptation in relation to engaging in a relationship outside of the marital institution. Likewise, sex toys could be seen as a means of substitution in the absence of intimate relationships, and/or enhancers for these relationships. Sex robots and their development have been discussed in great detail, particularly for this function - of substituting live partners [32, 34, 35] or curbing sexual deviance (i.e., pedophilia, see e.g., [36, 37]). Once again however, it may be questioned as to: a) whether or not sexual preditorism should be condoned through providing technologies that support this behavior; and b) how the use of technology in these ways further desensitizes the individual to the feelings and wellbeing of others. Where we continue this journey into deep murky waters, or the ethically unclear domain of 'healthy' or 'correct' human-sex robot relationships, has been when people begin to prefer being with a sex robot, and/or people who are already in relationships with human beings still engage in sex with robots [37].

This challenge does not simply belong to the domain of robotics, for the engagement of married humans with life-like sex dolls has also attracted the same types questions [34, 38]. Can engaging in intimate activities with technology be considered as adultery? Perhaps, in a similar way, while maybe not engaging directly in sexual activity per se, but extra-marital interactions between individuals on social media have also raised the same questions. Can flirtation or deep intimate discussion online with others outside the immediate marital/legal relationship be considered as adultery? What is acceptable in interaction - either directly with technology or other humans through technology - and what is not? How has the nature of social media, and particularly the development and popularity of Apps such as Tinder, Bumble and Match.com changed people's attitudes towards what is acceptable (socially and ethically) in online-offline interaction and what is not?

4 Sex Technology and Ethics

In fact, while sex toys and devices have played significant roles in our personal lives, there has been very little research specifically focusing on these technologies [32, 39]. The cousin domain of pornography has received considerable attention in recent times, yet, sex toys, dolls, robots and other sex-orientated technology have been relatively forgotten. With this said, the scarce research that is available, attempts to investigate the domain from the perspectives of sexual products, uses, users and outcomes. Döring and Pöschl [39] in particular, review research on sex technology through combining three distinct frameworks: 1) the positive sexuality framework [40]; 2) the positive technology framework [41]; and 3) the positive psychology approach [42]. Their argument was that sexual products could enable the improvement of sexual wellbeing in society. From the outset Döring and Pöschl's initiative can be seen as a practical move towards establishing an ethical code of conduct for sex technology, its use and experience.

Interestingly, while Döring and Pöschl focused on sex technology from a practical perspective of sexual wellbeing, several ethical issues automatically arose even without being labelled as such (see Fig. 2). Firstly, they mention that the consumption of female and even sex robots with child-like resemblances may lead to the objectification of real women and children by users [43, 44]. This links to observations made above whereby deviant sexual behavior may increase through high engagement in fetishes and paraphilias that can reduce inhibition [45]. Secondly, human loneliness and social anxieties may increase in connection to other human beings through people isolating themselves with sex technology and particularly sex robots [46]. Thirdly, quite fascinating is Döring and Pöschl's point on sex robots potentially reducing levels of prostitution, sex trafficking and indeed adultery [47]. The issue on sex trafficking is one matter that remains to be seen. Yet, the other two matters - prostitution and adultery - open the door to further debate. Firstly, focusing on adultery and as we query above - how do we define it? Is it simply the case of a partner being unfaithful to their spouse through engaging in relations with another human? Or can intimate engagement with a machine also be considered adultery? This is particularly if one's thoughts, actions and intentions become fixated on and directed to the machine and the ideals that the human holds regarding this technology. Secondly, would reduced consumption of prostitution generate outrage and concern for robotics taking over jobs as is heavily discussed in other industrial fields? Will sex robots replace prostitutes and render millions of human professionals without income?

On this note, and to step the 'robots will take our jobs' debate one more notch, we may consider, what at the end of the day is actually the most desirable sexual toy for humans - machines or real, organic human beings? Then, with this line of thought, and looking back towards the synthesis of humans and technology we may look at what dating (or instant sex) Apps are actually doing in practice. For, as with porn and the Internet enabling free access to pornographic material at any time of the day and anywhere, can we not see that Apps such as Tinder (and even Facebook) are doing the same thing to the field of prostitution. Why would people pay a prostitute for gratification, if they

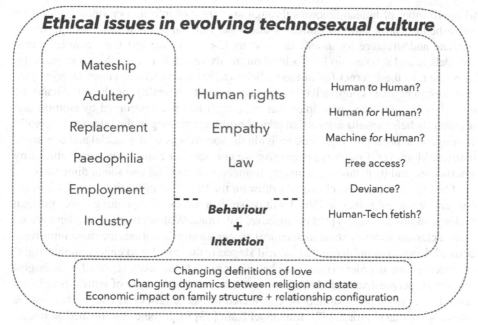

Fig. 2. Ethical complexity of technosexuality

can get the same service if not more for free through a dating App [38, 48]? Then, once more from the humanitarian perspective of ethics: do dating Apps simply reinforce the objectification of other human beings? This is particularly in light of the fact that in monogamous relationships, humans with either good ethical intention or deviant intentions usually need to devise social strategies for sustaining their relationships [49]. This may be through violence or manipulation, yet it also may be through good, fair and equal treatment and reciprocal relations with their partners. Especially empathy and the ability to feel the partner's emotions and concerns is critical for sustaining a healthy and meaningful relationship. In the case of sexual behavior existing in chains of fleeting intimate interactions that have been mediated by the Internet, what is the incentive for people to take the time to acknowledge and respect the dating App match in terms of the entire human being that they are? This is where concerns for empathy or the lack thereof relay human-to-human dating App interactions to the same category of human-robot sex interactions [50–53].

5   Evolving Sexual Technology and Ethical Stance

In understanding these dynamics, and particularly the prominence and popularity in modern Western societies of Apps such as Tinder, it is highly crucial to consider whether or not human beings' ethical stance has changed and in what ways. Would Tinder, and/or actions implicated in the contemporary use of dating Apps have been acceptable and as openly discussed maybe 15 to 25 years ago? Moreover, consideration needs to be made in regards to how the Internet, its social-cultural evolution and materialization (digitalization) of human fantasies through any times of information imaginable, have unleashed the *dark sides* of humanity and what religion and law have been trying to regulate and structure for thousands of years [54]. Over the last few centuries intensive debate and scholarship has focused on the dynamics between ethics and morality. In relation to the Internet for instance, Schultz [55] characterizes ethics as principles that seek to regulate cooperative burdens and benefits. Morality, on the other hand, he describes as comprising principles that are established and reinforced by cultural and religious beliefs. Schultz argues that ethical problems relating to the Internet are greatly contingent on principles regarding individuals, societies as well as social and economic matters. Moreover, from this perspective we can see that ethical concerns induced by Internet use and its nature are primarily founded in individual and social dimensions.

On a formal ethical level, we may draw on the traditions of *intuitionism, utilitarianism*, and *universal principle* [56]. Intuitionism is a means of explaining ethics through feelings and from Hume's [56] perspective, emotions. Within intuitionism, there are no formal classifications or standards, ethical processes and definitions are more intuitively derived. Regarding utilitarianism, ethical stance is the impulse to engage in the 'right' or correct action in order to maximize benefit or provide the greatest good for the largest number of people (parties). According to the universal principle of ethics, people act according to principles that may be considered universal law, or as could otherwise be known as 'social contract' [57]. Immanuel Kant [58] for instance established an understanding of universal ethical principles that may be seen as the foundations of society and civil means of behavior. One example can be seen in relation to credit. If people in general had no intention of paying credit card debts the entire credit system would not function. This relates to what Kant termed as 'Categorical Imperative' whereby people act according to principles that are somehow deemed as universal law. A more ancient example of this can be seen in the Golden Rule that dictates that people should treat others in the ways that they wish to be treated themselves [20].

The matter of Internet ethics is said to concern three main aspects - the individual, the social and the global [59]. Yet, through deeper understanding of the psycho-social composition of the individual, and indeed self, we may ascertain that the self is *always* social (this is how the self is defined - in relation to *others*) [59]. This self, through the Internet, is by default global on many levels. But this characteristic between the self and others - how the *I self*, the part of us that understands on some level how we are positioned and relate to society and the *Me self*, our self-image, self-concept, self-schemata (how we imagine and desire ourselves to be) [60] - is what drives our behavior and conscious awareness of the impacts of this behavior in online spaces. Business in particular, is driven by *self* desire. What generates interest and feeds this desire, is what makes money from the business perspective. Arguably, despite efforts regarding business ethics and current trends in ethical business (social responsibility etc.) deepseated desire through sexual fantasy that both gratifies the body and validates the self still is hard to resist from the business perspective. As has been observed, the Internet has radically changed not only human-human interactions, but also business models. What once required someone to reach into their pockets to extract money in exchange for services and encounters, not exists within the walls of Internet infrastructure and the surveillance economy - data as currency. This in turn, poses more ethical questions in the discussion of human-technosexual consumption.

From the perspective of sex and technology, research has revealed a tight link between technological advancement and sexual behavior [61]. Modes of courtship shifted from being facilitated by families to being more casual, individualistic and sexually oriented [62]. When looking historically at technological development, we may observe that cars and the entertainment industry were strong enablers in the liberalization of sex during the twentieth century [61]. This was afforded by transportation and spaces (drive-in practices, movie theatres and dance halls for instance) where youth and younger adults could escape the control of their parents. The innovation of the Internet, or world wide web (WWW) opened up physical boundaries to allow more people over vast distances to interact with one another [61]. Thus, many of these technology related questions have been about accessibility and opportunity. Interestingly, Daneback and colleagues [63] empirically studied this matter through examining the relationship between private Internet access versus public. Their study showed that people were more willing to engage in sexually related online material via private Internet access than they were through public Internet access. This seems logical, but what rests at the heart of this paper is the change of inhibition relating to sex that has emerged through human-technology interaction. Timmermans and Courtois' [61] Belgium-based study of Tinder users revealed that despite the critique that dating Apps such as Tinder had received particularly regarding casual sex, only relatively small amounts of online interactions had resulted in casual sex. In fact, their questionnaire of 1038 Tinder users demonstrated that only half of the online interactions resulted in offline meetings. Then, of these offline meetings, only one third of them resulted in casual sex. Interestingly, their study revealed that women were more likely to engaged in casual sex, which is contrary to a wealth of research that suggests otherwise (i.e., see [64–66]).

Moreover, in reference to the above description of ethical principles and particularly understandings of social contract and individual-social (self and other) contingencies, it can be seen that cultural conventions and framing play a major role in the interpretation and application of services such as Tinder [66]. Tinder was promoted as an effective hookup tool [66], and has then subsequently been adopted as a cultural object as such. This means that the object in itself attracts the attention of users who are seeking to engage in the technology for casual sexual purposes. It also means that the register of language and ways in which people interact with one another through these services have a slant and higher tolerance for interaction of a sexual nature. Maybe more than simply analyzing human interaction with sexual technology, or sexual interaction through technology, in terms of ethical stance, we may instead observe these developments through the lens of evolving understandings of human sexual relationships. During the past century alone there have been fragmentations and re-configurations of cultural frameworks defining love relationships. There was a move, for instance from 'romantic love' - lifelong commitment to one partner - to 'pure' or 'confluent love' [10]. In romantic love there is the search for the ideal partner, emphasizing monogamy for the rest of one's life, whereas in confluent love there is the aspect that people seek partners for perfect relationships in which both parties experience equality and satisfaction in all respects. In the confluent love scenario, mutual benefit needs to be sustained throughout the duration of the relationship. As soon as this benefit or satisfaction starts to dwindle, it is time to move on to seek the next ideal partner. In this model monogamy is still a trait of the relationship, yet the relationship is only as long as the satisfaction within it is sustained by both partners [10]. This mode of love is contingent upon a number of factors such as values, identities and interests [67].

The role of technology here can be seen on the micro-social level as influencing human-to-human interactions and experiences of other humans through design affordances [22, 23, 65]. The technical features, functions, materials, social and aesthetic properties, all play a part in facilitating interaction and experience. Where it is through the immediacy of online dating platforms, or through the realism and lack of objection from a sex doll or robot, the technology guides the ways in which we *can* interact with it and through it. A key design quality of Tinder for instance, is not only that it enables the arrangement of offline encounters, but it also facilitates multiple interactions simultaneously with many prospective sexual partners [68].

6 Conclusion

Just because an action is afforded by technology - be it available online content (pornography), social media or robotics - does it make it right? Once again we need to return to the questions of *what is the right action?* And, *how can we ensure the greatest benefit for the most parties?* Timmermans and Courtois [61] cite numerous studies in which particularly women benefit from casual sexual encounters such as those mediated by Tinder. In fact, a lot of research has also shown the benefits of pornography viewing [69]. Yet, the actional, interactional and experiential networks represented in the supply and consumption ecosystems of these products still need to be accounted for when taking an ethical stance. For instance, while pornography viewing experience can be beneficial on a number of social, psychological and sexual levels, how does it stand in relation to supply? When thinking of supply we are thinking of the lived conditions of the 'actors' shown within the content, how well they were paid, how safe and well looked after they are, and whether or not they actually have given full consent to the published content [70]. From this perspective there may indeed be inequalities from the viewpoint of human rights, and this also needs to be taken into account - not simply because of the immediate conditions of the 'actors', but also in terms of the social conditioning of the viewers and how they go on to treat *others* in subsequent interactions.

In the immediate instance of online-offline sexual encounters with other humans, it needs to be considered as to whether or not anyone will be hurt (physically, socially or psychologically), and how these encounters impact people and relationships surrounding the individuals engaging in the activity. There is then the subsequent 'ripple effect' of broken families for instance, mental health problems (depression, suicide, low self-worth), unemployment, substance abuse to name some. Then from a business and society perspective, if anyone does get hurt, there needs to be an understanding of who or what party should be held responsible. Since the Trump win of the 2016 United States elections, accountability and responsibility in tech business has been of major concern due to the role of fake news in influencing the elections. Thus, if responsibility and accountability is held by the corporate organizations facilitating the technology that enables these interactions, there should be clear ethical guidelines developed that seek to avoid and/or mitigate the problems arising from these interactions.

Then, there are the larger societal and economic considerations that were raised above relating to the roles of random partners in online-offline sexual interactions and sex robots and whether or not they can be seen as threats to the professional workforce and industry of prostitution. While these cultural configurations and re-configurations of sexual encounters and partnerships can be defined as cultural, within this viewpoint we can understand that ethics are structured by socio-cultural normative frames. There is a tight link between economics, technological development and use that sees people and culture evolve not only in behavior but also in thought and belief. In light of many of the issues raised in this paper, particularly in relation to the Pygmalion question - in the future, is what we are looking for really human-to-human relations through sex, or will we be happier when we are engaging with *Tinder playing sex robots*?

Acknowledgements. We would like to thank the University of Jyväskylä and Business Finland for funding this research, and particularly Professor Pekka Abrahamsson and his AI Ethics research group for supporting this work.

References

1. Ovidius (Ovid) Naso, P.: Pygmalion and the statue. In: More, B. (ed.) Metamorphoses. Cornhill Publishing, Boston (1922)
2. Mitchell, T., Daniels, D.: Motivation. In: Borman, W.C. Ilgen, D., Klimoski, R. (eds.) Handbook of Psychology, vol. 2, pp. 229–254. Wiley, Hoboken (2003)
3. Raudenbush, S.: Magnitude of teacher expectancy effects on pupil IQ as a function of the credibility of expectancy induction: a synthesis of findings from 18 experiments. J. Ed. Psych. **76**, 85–97 (1984)
4. Giddens, A.: The Transformation of Intimacy. Polity, Cambridge (1992)
5. Fieser, J.: Ethics. Internet Encyclopaedia of Philosophy (2020). https://iep.utm.edu/ethics/
6. Duncker, K.: Ethical relativity? (An enquiry into the psychology of ethics). Mind **48**, 39–57 (1939)
7. Moor, J.K.: Reason, relativity, and responsibility in computer ethics. ACM SIGCAS Comput. Soc. **28**, 14–21 (1998)
8. Lindebaum, D., Geddes, D., Gabriel, Y.: Moral emotions and ethics in organisations: introduction to the special issue. J. Bus. Ethics **141**(4), 645–656 (2017). https://doi.org/10.1007/s10551-016-3201-z
9. Svensson, G., Wood, G.: A model of business ethics. J. Bus. Ethics **77**(3), 303–322 (2007). https://doi.org/10.1007/s10551-007-9351-2
10. Gališanka, A.: Just society as a fair game: john rawls and game theory in the 1950s. J. Hist. Ideas **78**, 299–308 (2017)
11. Seay, S.: Sustainability is applied ethics. J. Leg. Eth. Reg. Is. **18**, 63–70 (2015)
12. Martin, K.: Ethical Implications and Accountability of Algorithms. J. Bus. Ethics **160**(4), 835–850 (2018). https://doi.org/10.1007/s10551-018-3921-3
13. Aström, T.: Moral Positioning: A Formal Theory. Ground. Theory Rev.: Int. J. **6**, 29–59 (2006)
14. IGI Global: Ethical Stance. Dictionary. https://www.igi-global.com/dictionary/ethical-stance/37711#:~:text=1.,to%20be%20right%20and%20true. Accessed 18 Jan 2021

15. Ryan, T.: Teaching and technology: issues, caution and concerns. In: Handbook of Research on New Media Literacy at the K-12 Level: Issues and Challenges (2009)

16. Seeley, J.: The making and taking of problems: toward an ethical stance. Soc. Probs. **14**, 382–389 (1966)

17. Aström, T.: In the force field of handicap. moral positioning and theory of social positioning. Doctoral Dissertation. University of Stockholm (2003)

18. Bloom, P.: How do morals change? Nature **464**, 490 (2010). https://doi.org/10.1038/464490a

19. Farber, P.: The Temptations of Evolutionary Ethics. Uni. of California, Berkeley (1994)

20. Saariluoma, P., Rousi, R.: Emotions and technoethics. In: Rousi, R., Leikas, J., Saariluoma, P. (eds.) Emotions in Technology Design: From Experience to Ethics. HIS, pp. 167–189. Springer, Cham (2020). https://doi.org/10.1007/978-3-030-53483-7_11

21. Haslam, N., McGrath, M., Wheeler, M.: Changing morals: we're more compassionate than 100 years ago, but more judgmental too. World Economic Forum. https://www.weforum.org/agenda/2019/03/changing-morals-we-re-more-compassionate-than-100-years-ago-but-more-judgmental-too/. Accessed 21 Jan 2021

22. Gibson, J.: The concept of affordances. Perceiving, acting, and knowing 1 (1977)

23. Norman, D.: The way I see IT signifiers, not affordances. Interactions **15**(6), 18–19 (2008)

24. Encyclopedia.com: Sexual ethics. https://www.encyclopedia.com/science/encyclopedias-almanacs-transcripts-and-maps/sexual-ethics. Accessed 18 Jan 2021

25. Condie, J., Lean, G., Wilcockson, B.: The trouble with Tinder: the ethical complexities of research location-aware social discovery apps. In: The Ethics of Online Research. Advances in Research Ethics and Integrity, vol. 2, pp. 135–158. Emerald Publishing, Bingley (2017)

26. Davis, M.: Sex, Technology and Public Health. Springer, Cham (2008). https://doi.org/10.1057/9780230228382

27. Castells, M.: The Rise of the Network Society, 2nd edn. Wiley-Blackwell, Hoboken (2009)

28. Paasonen, S.: Labors of love: netporn, Web 2.0 and the meanings of amateurism. New Media Soc. **12**(8), 1297–1312 (2010)

29. Rousi, R.: Me, my bot and his other (robot) woman? Keeping your robot satisfied in the age of artificial emotion. Robotics **7**(3), 44 (2018)

30. Botting, F.: Sex, Machines and Navels: Fiction, Fantasy and History in the Future Present. Manchester University Press, Manchester (1999)

31. Cheok, A.D., Zhang, E.Y.: Sex and a history of sex technologies. In: Cheok, A.D., Zhang, E.Y. (eds.) Human-Robot Intimate Relationships, pp. 23–32. Springer, Cham (2019). https://doi.org/10.1007/978-3-319-94730-3_2

32. Ferguson, A.: The Sex Doll: A History. Tangney & Fischer, McFarland (1995)

33. Ellsworth, P., Scherer, K.: Appraisal processes in emotion. Handbook of Affective Sciences 572, V595 (2003)

34. Döring, N., Mohseni, M.R., Walter, R.: Design, use, and effects of sex dolls and sex robots: scoping review. J. Med. Internet Res. **22**(7), e18551 (2020)

35. Levy, D.: Love and Sex with Robots: The Evolution of Human-Robot Relationships. HarperCollins, New York (2009)

36. Danaher, J.: Regulating child sex robots: restriction of experimentation? Med. Law Rev. **17**(4), 553–575 (2019)

37. Danaher, J., McArthur, N. (eds.): Robot Sex: Social and Ethical Implications. MIT Press, Cambridge (2017)

38. Kolivand, H., Ehsani Rad, A., Tully, D.: Virtual sex: good, bad or ugly? In: Cheok, A., Levy, D. (eds.) LSR 2017. LNCS (LNAI), vol. 10715, pp. 26–36. Springer, Cham (2018). https://doi.org/10.1007/978-3-319-76369-9_3

39. Döring, N., Pöschl, S.: Sex toys, sex dolls, sex robots: our under-researched bed-fellows. Sexologies **27**(3), e51–e55 (2018)

40. Williams, D.J., Thomas, J.N., Prior, E.R., Walters, W.: Introducing a multidisciplinary framework of positive sexuality. J. Positive Sex **1**, 6–11 (2015)
41. Riva, G., Banos, R.M., Botella, C., Wiederhold, B.K., Gaggioli, A.: Positive technology: using interactive technologies to promote positive functioning. Cyberpsychol. Behav. Soc. Netw. **15**(2), 69–77 (2012)
42. Seligman, M.E.P., Csikszentmihalyi, M.: Positive psychology: an introduction. Am. Psychol. **55**(1), 5–14 (2000)
43. Döring, N.: Vom Internetsex zum robotersex: forschungsstand und herausforderungen für die sexualwissenschaft [From Internet sex to robot sex: state of research and challenges for sexology] Z Sex-Forsch **30**(01) 35–57 (2017)
44. Richardson, K.: Sex robot matters: slavery, the prostituted, and the rights of machines. IEEE Tech. Soc. Mag. **35**(2), 46–53 (2016)
45. Sharkey, N., van Wynsberghe, A., Robbins, S., Hancock, E.: Our sexual future with robots - a foundation for responsible robotics consultation report (2017). Foundation for Responsible Robotics, The Hague. http://responsiblerobotics.org/wp-content/uploads/2017/07/FRR-Consultation-Report-Our-Sexual-Future-with-robots_Final.pdf. Accessed 21 Jan 2021
46. Sullins, J.P.: Robots, love, and sex: the ethics of building a love machine. IEEE Trans. Affect. Comput. **3**(4), 398–409 (2012)
47. Yeoman, I., Mars, M.: Robots, men and sex tourism. Futures **44**(4), 365–371 (2012)
48. White, N.: 'The industry is dying out': Madam claims dating apps like Tinder are taking away brothels 'bread and butter'. Daily Mail. https://www.dailymail.co.uk/news/article-4258556/Tinder-killing-brothels-taking-best-customers.html. Accessed 25 Jan 2021
49. Brunell, A-B., Campbell, W.K.: Narcissism and romantic relationships. In: The Handbook of Narcissistic Personality Disorders: Theoretical Approaches, Empirical Findings and Treatments, pp. 344–350. Wiley, Hoboken (2017)
50. Bhattacharya, S.: Swipe and burn. New Sci. **225**(3002), 30–33 (2015)
51. Hardey, M.: Mediated relationships . Inf. Commun. Soc. **7**(2), 207–222 (2004)
52. Landovitz, R.J., et al.: Epidemiology, sexual risk behavior, and HIV prevention practices of men who have sex with men using GRINDR in Los Angeles, California. J. Urb. Health **90**(4), 729–739 (2013)
53. Sales, N.J.: Tinder and the dawn of the 'Dating Appocalypse'. Vanity Fair (2015). http://www.vanityfair.com/culture/2015/08/tinder-hook-up-culture-end-of-dating. Accessed 18 Jan 2021
54. Rosenzweig, R.: Wizards, bureaucrats, warriors, and hackers: writing the history of the Internet. Am. Hist. Rev. **103**(5), 1530–1552 (1998)
55. Schultz, R.A.: Contemporary Issues in Ethics and Information Technology. IRM Press, Hershey (2005)
56. Hume, D.: An enquiry concerning the principles of morals. In: Schneedwind, J.B. (ed.) Moral philosophy from Montaigne to Kant. Cambridge University Press, Cambridge [1751] (2002)
57. Brownsey, P.F.: Human and the social contract. Philos. Quart. **28**(111), 132–148 (1978)
58. Kant, I.: Fundamental Principles of the Metaphysics of Ethics. Green and Co., London (1895). T. Kingsmill Abbott (trans.)
59. Neisser, U. (ed.): The Perceived Self: Ecological and Interpersonal Sources of Self Knowledge 5. Cambridge University Press, Cambridge (2006)
60. James, W.: The self. In: Baumeister, R.F. (ed.) Key Readings in Social Psychology. The Self in Social Psychology, pp. 68–77, Psychology Press, Hove (1999)
61. Timmersmans, E., Coutois, C.: From swiping to casual sex and/or committed relationships: exploring the experiences of Tinder users. Inf. Soc. **34**(2), 59–70 (2018)
62. Illouz, E.: Consuming the Romantic Utopia: Love and the Cultural Contradictions of Capitalism. University of California Press, California (1997)

63. Daneback, K., Månsson, S.A., Ross, M.W.: Technological advancements and Internet sexuality: does private access to the Internet influence online sexual behavior? Cyberpsychol. Behav. Soc. Netw. **15**(8), 386–390 (2012)
64. Grello, C.M., Welsh, D.P., Harper, M.S.: No strings attached: the nature of casual sex in college students. J. Sex Res. **43**(3), 255–267 (2006)
65. Hjarvard, S.: The Mediatization of Culture and Society. Routledge, Oxon (2013)
66. Duguay, S.: Dressing up Tinderella: interrogating authenticity claims on the mobile dating app Tinder. Inf. Commun. Soc. **20**(3), 351–367 (2017)
67. Gross, N., Simmons, S.: Intimacy as a double-edged phenomenon? An empirical test of Giddens. Soc. Forces **81**(2), 531–555 (2002)
68. LeFebvre, L.E.: Swiping me off my feet: explicating relationship initiation on Tinder. J. Soc. Pers. Relat. **35**, 1–17 (2017)
69. Rissel, C., Richters, J., De Visser, R.O., McKee, A., Yeung, A., Caruana, T.: A profile of pornography users in Australia: findings from the second Australian study of health and relationships. J. Sex Res. **54**(2), 227–240 (2017)
70. Albury, K., Crawford, K.: Sexting, consent and young people's ethics: beyond Megan's Story. Continuum **26**(3), 463–473 (2012)

AI Ethics - Critical Reflections on Embedding Ethical Frameworks in AI Technology

Henrikki Salo-Pöntinen[✉]

Cognitive Science, Faculty of Information Technology,
University of Jyväskylä, Jyväskylä, Finland
ponthebe@jyu.fi

Abstract. Embedding ethical frameworks in artificial intelligence (AI) technologies has been a popular topic for academic research for the past decade [1–7]. The approaches of the studies differ in how AI technology, ethics, role of technical artefacts and socio-technical aspects of AI are perceived. In addition, most studies define insufficiently what the connection between the process of embedding ethical frameworks to AI technology and the larger framework of AI ethics is. These deficiencies have caused that the concept of AI ethics and the construct of embedding ethical parameters into AI are used in an ambiguous, rather than in a complementary manner.

One reason for the ambiguity within this field of research is due to a lack of a comprehensive conceptual framework for AI ethics in general. I intend to fill this void by grounding AI ethics as a subfield of philosophy of technology and applied ethics and presenting its main issues of study by examining recognized spheres of activities through the method of levels of abstraction [8]. I put forward an initial hierarchical conceptual framework for AI ethics as an outcome. After this, I discuss the connection between the process of embedding ethical frameworks in AI and the larger AI ethics framework, leading to presenting basic requirements for the sphere of activity hereafter known as embedded ethics.

Keywords: AI ethics · Embedded ethics · Applied ethics · Human-technology interaction

1 Introduction

The need to design AI technology that embodies ethical frameworks has risen due to the ever-increasing role of AI in today's societies. It has been recognized that non-technical governance methods (e.g., legislation or guidelines) are in many cases insufficient in assuring that AI technologies function in a morally desirable manner [2–4]. Therefore, the sustainable development and deployment of AI systems require installing parameters into the AI systems themselves that guide their decision-making processes from a moral perspective.

However, it is not clear how this should be done. Some advocates propose to develop so called moral guards that are placed in the technical artifacts of AI to assess their outputs and authorize only those outputs that are morally acceptable [2, 5–7]. This leads

© Springer Nature Switzerland AG 2021
M. Rauterberg (Ed.): HCII 2021, LNCS 12795, pp. 311–329, 2021.
https://doi.org/10.1007/978-3-030-77431-8_20

to a dilemma of the kind of moral code the moral guards should follow and how would it be possible to develop the moral guards in an efficient way, since they would have to be able to authorize outputs that might not be possible to predict beforehand [2, 3]. In addition, it is seen as a decentralization of the moral responsibility of humans and by doing so obscuring the discourse of AI ethics [9].

Luciano Floridi and Mariarosaria Taddeo consider it to be misleading to treat ethical dilemmas as rising from the functioning of the technical artifacts, but to emerge from the myriad ways of processing and using data. And therefore, they should also be solved by analyzing forms of data used in AI and its further processing and by imposing codes of conducts, standards, and professional ethics to guide the discipline of data science so that its achievements will be morally acceptable [10]. In his proposition for systematizing the process of embedded ethics, Ibo van de Poel suggests that in addition to studying AI as technical artifacts, the sociotechnical aspects (as organizational institutions) of AI should be noted in the act of embedding ethical frameworks in the technology. Otherwise, AI is understood in a too narrow manner leading to imposing insufficient actions to successfully embed ethical frameworks in AI [3].

All forementioned views perceive the central information processing of AI as a technical process[1] and hence do not account for aspects related to human-technology interaction, which then again are perceived as pivotal in systems engineering [4, 11]. In addition, the view of Floridi and Taddeo[2] leads to a somewhat technocratic view of AI development and deployment, which is not durable [12, 13] considering AI's role as a central technology in the ongoing societal change towards intelligent societies [14, 15].

This scatteredness of views is partly result from looking at the issue from the perspective of single disciplines, partly due to the non-foundational approach of some of the views and mostly due to the yet unstructured multifaceted nature of AI ethics. We need to discover a comprehensive basis for the process of embedding ethical frameworks in AI technology, for it to be possible to produce complementary theories for it.

I agree with van de Poel in that there is a common ground to be found and I concentrate in two critical aspects to further the discourse in this paper. Firstly, I will clarify the general framework for AI ethics to facilitate more rigorous discourse. Secondly, I discuss the role of embedding ethical parameters to AI technology as part of the larger framework of AI ethics and evaluate what possibilities and boundaries its placing imposes for the ethical parameters that are to be instantiated in AI.

In the next section of this chapter, I provide a definition for AI and shortly discuss its further dimensions and connections with autonomous systems. The produced observations serve as an important part in the further chapters. In the second chapter I examine the multifaceted nature of AI ethics as to be revealed through spheres of activities recognized in earlier research related to the ethics of technology and AI ethics, but which has not yet been examined as forming a comprehensive whole. I use the method of levels of abstraction to further the examination and to illustrate the form of the AI ethics

---

[1] Even though Floridi and Taddeo focus on the information sphere, they examine it as phenomena emerging from the combination of data, algorithms and hardware and software applications [10].

[2] Floridi and Taddeo most likely understand this risk, since they propose that practices related to responsible research and innovation should be considered when examining important practices related to data ethics.

framework. In the third chapter I discuss the central sphere of activity for this paper, embedded ethics, as part of the larger framework of AI ethics and propose some basic requirements for a comprehensive theory of embedded ethics. In the conclusions I will discuss focal findings of this paper and suggest further research that would advance the discourse of embedded ethics and provide important information for the needs of AI development and deployment.

1.1 AI and Autonomous Systems

Providing a definition for AI is a fundamental, but notorious task within the field of AI ethics. For this paper, I use a definition that combines common features from definitions most used in AI research. Samoili et al. provide a comprehensive analysis of commonly used features to describe AI in their paper *Defining Artificial Intelligence* (2020). When comparing Samoili et al.'s analysis with Tony Gillespie's analysis of autonomous systems which he provides in his book *Systems Engineering for Ethical Autonomous Systems* (2019), I noticed the challenge of clarifying how AI and autonomous systems differ. Both refer to technological systems capable of autonomous goal attaining[3] through the means of observing their environment and adaption to changes in it. Therefore, it is not a surprise that much of research does not pursue for their distinction, but place AI as a heading which also accounts autonomous systems within it [17] or defines autonomous systems formally and AI informally, as is done in IEEE's global initiative on ethics of autonomous and intelligent systems *Ethically Aligned Design* (2019).

However, if we are to talk about AI ethics, we need to have a definition that is not too vague. When comparing the analysis of Samoili et al. and Gillespie, the most distinguishable difference between autonomous systems and AI seems to be in how the capability to process information is produced. For AI, the capability to process large masses of data is gained by algorithms that are formed through differing techniques (e.g., symbolic systems and machine learning) [16, 18]. The information processing of autonomous systems is then again produced by control systems (networks of nodes that react to fixed inputs) and feedback loops, which can be built to provide the system a capability to carry out very sophisticated functions [4].

From this observation I construct the following definition. In this paper artificial intelligence (AI) refers to technology that can achieve given goals through data collection (i.e., perception of its environment) and interpretation (reinforced by algorithm techniques) which enables it to perform tasks e.g. in the form of adapting its behavior to changes in the environment.

For further purposes it is important to acknowledge that AI and autonomous systems are parallel concepts and therefore research observations may benefit them both. In addition, AI is an umbrella concept which means that depending on the context of examination, further distinctions might be called for. Further distinctions may refer to the information processing techniques used (e.g., symbolic AI, guided machine learning, re-enforced machine learning, unguided machine learning and deep learning), [18, 19] levels of reflected intelligence (weak AI – strong AI/super artificial intelligence), or the

---

[3] The goals are always defined by human operators.

scope of tasks AI can manage autonomously (narrow AI - artificial general intelligence) [18, 20].

Due to the lack of explicit reference on the forementioned further definitions of examined AI, researchers may state their offset for a study as examining current or near future developments of AI but end up argumenting based on futuristic expectations.[4] Therefore, many discussions are done implicitly about AI that refers to AGI or super-intelligence, even though it might be that they are never reached [9, 18, 19, 21]. This kind of misleading argumentation produces alarmism[5], false expectations and obscures academic, as well as societal discourses of AI ethics.

For the sake of coherence, I consider it to be important to acknowledge the different information processing techniques and their differing influence on AI ethics. However, this paper considers the technical artifact of AI to be capable of reflecting only weak intelligence and narrow autonomy [4, 18, 19], which means that AI should not be perceived as to have a will of its own, but to always act on orders given by humans, its functional role in a process is and should be very precisely defined and limited [4] and AI should not be perceived as to hold moral agency [3, 9, 21].

2 Mapping the Conceptual Framework for AI Ethics

Applied ethics issues often rise from actors within or closely linked to the field in question noticing ethical dilemmas rising from status quo course of actions. This is one reason why studying manifestation of the dilemmas may take room from a more systematic analyzation of the whole sphere of activity related to the field – which is more likely to provide understanding about the roots that lead to the noticed problems [22, 23]. This is also evidential in the field of AI ethics, where most of the literature is concerned about describing key issues of accountability, explainability, fairness, privacy, safety and security [16]. While an important phase in acknowledging the need to take ethical aspects into consideration, perceiving the role of ethics as only detecting and describing evident issues recalls the analogy about looking for ways to get rid of smoke without detecting fire.

Another misleading way to understand applied ethics is to see it merely as applying some existing foundational moral theory (e.g., deontology, virtue ethics, utilitarianism, ubuntu, emotivism or eastern ethical traditions) to describe and solve observed dilemmas. While important in developing high dimensional viewpoints to issues [2], it is important to understand that foundational moral theories have strong underlying ontological and epistemological presumptions and are structured as universal theories, which may prevent from providing holistic conceptualizations that have context sensitive practical value for the issues at hand.

---

[4] This is the case for *Moral Machines* (2008), which I will elaborate in the third chapter of this paper.

[5] The research community has a responsibility to explicitly elaborate what their research considers. Not stating what the current development phase of technology is and not informing when one's paper considers theoretically possible, but unlikely scenarios, researchers legitimize pseudo problems, such as the closeness of singularity.

Understanding applied ethics broadly as outlining and systematizing issues and solutions to practical problems through the approaches and concepts known in the field of moral philosophy gives us a larger variety of tools to frame and analyze issues with case sensitivity and more flexibility to satisfy the need for practical solutions. It can be simplified, that the central study subject of moral philosophy is the connection of forms of human activities[6] and moral agency. Moral agency then again brings us to the concepts of good and bad (evaluative aspects of ethics) and right and wrong (normative aspects of ethics), which provide us with the possibility of framing standards upon which we measure the moral nature of our actions [24–27].

However, understanding the role of applied ethics in a broad manner is not sufficient as itself to produce a useful framework for AI ethics. It leaves too many questions open about how ethical argumentation can have a meaningful impact on development of AI. This void tends to lead to argumentation aiming to validate universal values or codes of principles that should guide actions within the studied field [3, 22]. Thus, also the field of AI ethics is abundant with lists of principles [28]. This type of argumentation leaves a similar gap between high-level principles and practical needs of the real world as the two first mentioned views of applied ethics [29].

I argue that we need to recognize focal spheres of activites related to AI ethics to avoid obscuring the connection between high level principles and practice. To do so, the spheres should account for different levels of abstractions and so distinguish study subjects that form a spectrum where one can move from high abstraction towards practical solutions. In this section I aim to provide such a framework by introducing spheres of activities as a key to understand focal observables for AI ethics and analyzing how the different spheres are positioned on different levels of abstractions.

2.1 Sphere of Activity

With the concept of sphere of activity, I refer to entities that reflect operational wholes and as such can be understood to be a focal subject of interest for applied ethics. However, distinct fields of applied ethics require analyzing what are the central spheres of activities for each of them separately. The most typical way of describing central activities related to AI ethics is design (including redesign) and development, implementation, deployment, and disposure [2]. This reflects the general idea of a product's lifecycle which helps to plan and impose for example design and management requirements on each phase.

I argue that to understand the multilayered role of ethics in AI, we need to recognize spheres of activities that support the needs of ethical contemplation and its operationalization towards practicality. One reason for this is that the lifecycle division recognizes only very practical phases, which inherently do not account for more abstract[7] phases necessary for AI ethics. To do this, we need to take a couple steps back from current discourses and look at the philosophical basis of AI ethics.

---

[6] Human activities always take place in social contexts, which are shaped by varying cultural, historical and political backgrounds [2, 24].

[7] The design phase is about bringing abstract ideas to exist in the real world, but to understand it only as a phase of a product's lifecycle is not enough for applied ethics.

AI Ethics. AI ethics is a subsection of ethics of technology – which in turn is a subfield of philosophy of technology. Therefore, to provide backdrop for understanding what the basis of AI ethics is, we need to understand what technology is and how this general understanding reflects on AI. In this paper, technology is understood as a combination of technical artefact(s)[8] and human action(s) to fulfill defined objectives. Furthermore, technology development – and AI development with it – is a practice for changing the world to what one sees as ought to be [31–33].

This leads us to the obvious but often implicit first sphere of activity that will be called (AI) deployment ethics. This sphere comprises from explicitly forming the abstract notions that are to guide what we want to accomplish through the deployment of AI technology. It is obvious for it is ever present in the development of technology, but often driven by tacit impressions, because technology is easily perceived as to develop as separated from other social development [13, 14].

In addition to the core definition of technology, it is important to acknowledge that technology is inevitably rooted in wider[9] sociotechnical contexts. In its narrow sense, the concept of sociotechnical refers to the institutions and organizations in which the technology is utilized in [3, 11] and its broader meaning refers also to the communities and societies where the technology's utilization takes place [12, 13, 32, 34].

For ethics of technology, it is pivotal to understand the concept of sociotechnical through its broader meaning. Otherwise, social impacts of technology are not taken into consideration and their steering becomes an ambiguous and reactive process [14, 28]. Additionally, it would lead to untenable power accumulation of influencing what kind of life should be pursued through technology development to the hands of few people[10] [12, 32, 34].

AI is distinct from many other technologies [12] in the sense that there is a wide consensus about the importance of considering the societal role and possible larger impacts of AI development and deployment. A reason for this may be that AI is seen as one of the central driving forces in the transition from information societies to intelligent societies, which will have large disruptive effects [14, 15].

Understanding the importance of sociotechnical aspects of technology and AI development requires us to add impact assessment and the process of enabling impactful societal discourse as central parts of deployment ethics [12, 26]. This means that the nature of deployment ethics requires balancing with the pursuance for good and prevention/reduction of harm.

Now we have the basis for the first sphere of activity of AI ethics. However, as is implied in the term AI ethics, we need to distinguish the (AI) deployment ethics

---

[8] Technical artifacts consist of the artifact (tangible or intangible) and its use-plan[30–31]. This definition shows how the artefacts are always a means to instantiate human intentions.

[9] By wider, I mean that the concept of sociotechnical stretches to refer to relations outside of mere user(s) - technical artefact(s) relation.

[10] Even in the situation that the few people have good intentions, the strong narrative that technology development is a morally neutral activity [13, 14], and the fact that a few people cannot in any shape perceive the needs and desires of large populations water down the possibility of accepting that kind of power to a small group of people [13, 23, 35]. Therefore, enabling meaningful societal discourse is one of the corner stones of (AI) deployment ethics [12, 32].

from technology ethics in general. Therefore, the next sphere of activity should be one that contemplates the ethical dimensions emerging from the nature of AI itself. As was noted in the introduction section of this article, AI and the varying forms of autonomous systems are distinguished by the data processing and refining capabilities invested in AI.

The field of data ethics [10] is committed to analyzing moral dimensions that are inherent in or emerge from the processes of deploying different types of data, their refinement, and the used information processing techniques (e.g., Symbolic systems and the various forms of machine learning) and contemplates their societal impacts. Therefore, data ethics is the second sphere of activity recognizable for AI ethics.

The reciprocal relation between deployment ethics and data ethics produces a cycle where high dimensional questions related to possibilities and risks of AI deployment is imposed on the sphere of data ethics and respectively viewpoints of data ethics provide flesh to the basis of deployment ethics, distinguishing its viewpoints from other fields of ethics of technology.

An example of how the reciprocal nature of deployment ethics and data ethics manifests is how the large volume of principles produced under AI ethics can be defined to originate from the five principles of beneficence, non-maleficence, justice, human autonomy and explicability, when they are understood through the lenses of data ethics [28]. For example, explicability should be understood as a principle that enables the attainment of the other principles, since many information processing techniques used in AI are inherently opaque [4, 28]. Additionally, explicability in AI includes two semantically distinct requirements – intelligibility and accountability. Intelligibility refers to being able to understand[11] and predict the behavior of used AI. Accountability then again refers to establishing mechanisms by which developers and deployers of AI technology can be held accountable for the technology's functioning even though the complexity of placing responsibility rises as the ecosystems responsible for the functioning of AI become more complicated [2, 28]. They both can be understood as components of justified trustworthiness of AI [36].

As we have distinguished two central spheres of activity for AI ethics – which provide the basis for ethical enquiry of AI and distinguishes AI ethics from other fields of ethics of technology – it is time to pursue further examination through the method of levels of abstraction for the reason of its illustrative power.

2.2 Levels of Abstraction in AI Ethics

Levels of abstraction is a well-known method in the field of computational sciences for modelling complex entities into more intelligible ones through distinguishing levels of knowledge representation of the observed subject matter. Luciano Floridi has clarified and refined the method in his paper *The Method of Levels of Abstraction* (2008) in which he demonstrates how the method can be used to elaborate empirical as well as purely

---

[11] It is important to notice that actors with different roles require different level of intelligibility [2, 28]. For example, operators of an AI system require understandable information explaining states relevant for the used basic functions, whereas engineers taking part in the AI systems redesign require explanations that reach the underlying phases of information processing behind the functions.

conceptual studies. According to Floridi, levels of abstraction should be understood as a method which elaborates the epistemological form of observed entities, since using it to distinguish ontological, or methodological levels of abstractions is on a more unstable basis.

The method consists of three main phases. Recognizing sets of observables that form distinct levels of abstractions (hereafter LoA's) in the studied subject, analyzing the relations between observables within a LoA to gain knowledge about the behavior of a single LoA, and finally analyzing relations between the recognized LoA's which gives understanding about the gradient of abstraction. The gradient of abstraction is a holistic illustration of how the LoA's are connected throughout the different abstraction levels starting from approximate LoA behavior description towards more comprehensive and detailed descriptions, "until the final LoA accounts for the desired behaviors" [8; 314].

Some additional definition of the concepts of observables and LoA behavior is required in addition to explaining what is meant by relations between LoA's. Floridi defines observables as "typed variables[12] together with a statement of what feature of the system under consideration they represent" [8; 306. footnote added]. For example, when forming basis of deployment ethics, one must consider variables such as *values* and *guiding principles* in addition to *risks* and *opportunities* that are to guide the formation of *goals* and *codes of conduct* for technology development. These variables form the observables of ethical argumentation.

LoA behavior reflects how the system of observables in a certain LoA is to behave in order to work properly. It is needed, since otherwise LoA's would consist merely of sets of observables that can take any value within their given set of values[13] [8]. In other words, by taking LoA behavior into account we avoid producing models with ambiguous functioning.

Floridi illustrates as an example of LoA behavior that in theory traffic lights (LoA) in a single crossroad could all hold the typed variable of showing green light (color as an observable) at the same moment of time, but that would not be a functional traffic light system. To avoid such dysfunctionality in a model, the LoA behavior should be described as exactly as possible. The description is provided in the form of a predicate, which reflects the connections and possible values that the observables may take in each LoA [8]. For a functional traffic light example, the describing predicate could be safety securing.

As I stated earlier, the perceived LoA's of a whole are to be connected to each other and their connections are illustrated as a gradient of abstraction (hereafter GoA). Floridi describes two types of connections that can be perceived between LoA's. Disjoint

---

[12] A typed variable is a variable that can hold only certain explicitly stated data. Data in this case can refer to either symbols of empirical perception or symbols related to purely conceptual theories [8].

[13] There are two types of information that are possible to depict by the levels of abstraction method: analogous and discrete. Analogous information refers to information used in natural sciences to depict the basis of natural phenomena. In analogous information the observables can take infinite number of values and their behavior is described with differential equations. The other type of information is discrete, meaning that the observables have a finite number of values they can take [8]. This research considers discrete information.

GoA describes a connection where the constituent observables differ between LoA's and nested GoA describes a connection where the constituent observables are common on each LoA [8]. To continue illustration through the traffic light example, a nested GoA for traffic light could consist of a first LoA in which the observable is color and the second LoA on a more concrete abstraction level where the observable would be wavelengths of color. A disjoint GoA for traffic light could consist of a LoA with the observable of color and another LoA where the observable would be the orientation of the lights. In the latter example, the LoA's can be perceived to be on the same level of abstraction from knowledge representation point of view but are complementary as they consider features of the same system.

These two types of relations between LoA's can be combined in a tree like form, in which the GoA contains hierarchical surjective[14] information about several perspectives of the observed issue [8]. The GoA of AI ethics as presented in Fig. 1 on the next page depicts a GoA with combined LoA relations.

AI Ethics Conceptual Mapping. For conceptual mapping of AI ethics, the method of levels of abstraction provides structure and the perceived spheres of activities provide content for distinct LoA's. In Fig. 1 I have placed central spheres of activities in the GoA of AI ethics to illustrate the conceptual mapping of AI ethics.

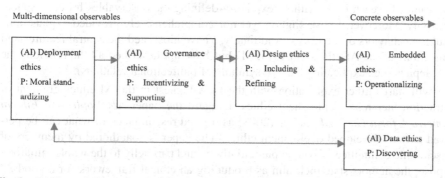

Fig. 1. Gradient of abstraction for AI ethics. The arrow on top illustrates the hierarchical relation of the GoA to go from LoA's consisting of multidimensional observables towards LoA's consisting of more concrete observables. Each level of abstraction (LoA) has a predicate (P) to describe its system behavior.

Figure 1 shows that I have added governance ethics, design ethics and embedded ethics as the remaining central spheres of activity for AI ethics. The reason for this is that they depict the line of activities required for integrating AI ethics into action. They are not arbitrarily chosen but relate to existing research on the topic.

---

[14] Surjective means that an abstract observation can be traced back to at least one concrete counterpart. Its strict meaning would allow only a single concrete counterpart per abstract observation but as Floridi points out, abstract information in the field of humanities is often traced back as a connection between several concrete counterparts.

As mentioned earlier, AI is always used and developed in social contexts (communities and organizations). Therefore, governance of the social is an inseparable part of how the high-level goals and concepts of the deployment ethics LoA disseminate into the technology [3, 14, 31]. The governance ethics LoA is currently the least developed sphere of activity related to AI ethics. Its importance is widely noticed for the purpose of incentivizing and supporting the integration of ethical frameworks to AI [2, 36], but so far studies have centered in describing issues, whilst providing little concrete recommendations [37, 38].

The sphere of design ethics is then again often regarded as the central sphere of activity for AI ethics since it is the stage where abstractions and real use cases are to be combined [2, 3, 32]. As for the sphere of activity illustrating the most concrete level of knowledge representation (together with data ethics), embedded ethics depicts the activity in which the operationalizations of high dimensional concepts and objectives described in deployment ethics are instantiated in the real world [2, 3].

Behaviors of the Spheres of Activity. As it is out of the scope of this – or any single article – to exhaustively uncover the sections of AI ethics described in Fig. 1, I shall pursue to depict their central functions and connections as parts of the gradient of abstraction of AI ethics.

As mentioned earlier, there are three main phases in the method of levels of abstraction. So far, I have illustrated spheres of activities as providing insight about the sets of observables for each LoA, without explicitly defining the observables for each sphere of activity. Moreover, I have slightly, yet not comprehensively provided explanations about the behaviors of the LoA's. And finally, I have illustrated the central features and connections of the AI ethics GoA (Fig. 1) but have not described all the relations the GoA depicts (i.e., explicating the two symbols of bidirectional relations).

I will start further explanation with the LoA highest in the AI ethics gradient of abstraction hierarchy, deployment ethics. I regard the paper *AI4People—An Ethical Framework for a Good AI Society* (2008) as a good resemblance of what can be perceived as well-developed deployment ethics. The paper is coauthored by members of the scientific committee of AI4people initiative[15] and parallelly to the whole initiatives purpose, the authors state their aim as producing an ethical framework for a good AI society. To do so, they analyze perceived opportunities[16] and risks that can emerge from pursuing human flourishment and promotion of human dignity by using AI. They suggest using the five principles of beneficence, non-maleficence, human autonomy, justice and explicability to successfully balance between the opportunities and risks while pursuing the forementioned goals of deploying AI.

From the example of AI4people, it would seem obvious to understand the high-level goals (e.g., human flourishment), opportunities, risks and moral principles as observables for deployment ethics. However, the real observables are the ethical arguments formed

---

[15] AI4people is an Atomium European Institution for Science, Media, and Democracy (EISMD) initiative which pursues to produce frameworks for a good AI society. For more information see https://www.eismd.eu/ai4people/.

[16] Opportunities can turn to missed opportunities if AI is underused for the sake of misleading argumentation.

by these variables. For the notion of ethical argumentation explains the role and meaning of the forementioned variables in the system of deployment ethics.

The AI4people working groups paper provides in addition a good example of the behavior of deployment ethics. In its last section, the working group announces 20 action points based on their ethical argumentation that are to guide governance and use of AI [28]. This can be perceived as the behavior of providing moral standards for the use of AI. Moral standardizing in this sense corresponds to the act of explicating guidance for what we want to achieve through AI development and describes the behavior of deployment ethics.

Next, I will further explain the LoA of (AI) data ethics as consisting of the observables of moral problems of data and moral problems of information processing. As forementioned, this section of AI ethics provides understanding of the ethical problems emerging from AI's nature as a technology based on data usage and its refining through information processing techniques.

In their paper *What is Data Ethics* (2016) Luciano Floridi and Mariarosaria Taddeo introduce data ethics as to represent a new focal level of abstraction in the continuum of information ethics. They describe data ethics as a paradigm shift which directs the disciplines focus to the invariant sphere of information formation, and as such, it recognizes moral dimensions that were earlier left unnoticed. This refers to acknowledging "even data that never translate directly into information but can be used to support actions or generate behaviors" [10; 1].

The moral problems related to data may emerge from the generation, recording, curation, processing, dissemination, sharing and use of data which makes them important variables for data ethics. In addition, Floridi and Taddeo consider algorithms (e.g., those used in symbolic systems and different machine learning techniques) and practices related to information processing (such as programming and hacking) as central variables for understanding the moral problems related to information processing [10]. The multifaceted observables of moral problems of data and information processing are used to discover moral dimensions that emerge from the basic nature of AI. Therefore, discovering is the behavior of (AI) data ethics.

To understand the central functions of (AI) governance ethics we need to distinguish ethical aspects of governance from judicial aspects related to AI as they are often implicitly dealt as analogous. Both, governance and judicial actions are normative forces that guide the development and deployment of AI. However, governance refers to establishing and implementing infrastructures and practices that support goal attaining of a given organization or government and judicial aspects of AI refer to the established institutionalized regulations that relate to AI, and their further processing [14, 39].

The regulative institutions are part of the larger frame of governance of a nation and regulations reciprocally set boundaries for governing actions in general. Therefore, it is understandable why they are sometimes misleadingly used in an analogous manner. Underlining their distinction is not to say that governance and judicial aspects would not be interrelated but to underpin that the LoA of governance ethics refers to all governance actions and not only to the judicial aspects of AI.[17]

Simply put, the LoA of governance ethics consists of the observables of infrastructures and processes that correspond to the further organizational dissemination of the moral standardization constructed in the LoA of deployment ethics. Management and success measurement, organizational structures, codes of conduct, standards, regulations, and auditing are examples of the typed variables forming the corresponding infrastructures and processes [2, 4, 14, 32]. The role of governance is not just to support but also to incentivize the forementioned dissemination and therefore the behavior of the governance ethics LoA is incentivizing and supporting [3, 14, 28].

Before clarifying the LoA of design ethics, I want to point out to the dissemination processes of the concepts and high-level goals adopted in the LoA of deployment ethics towards the lower abstraction levels starting from the LoA of governance ethics. The reciprocal relation between the LoA's of governance ethics and design ethics is important for illustrating differing disseminations. The reciprocal relation can be understood through an example of how certain values disseminate into technology through the social structure of design processes [13, 35] while others may be considered to result from an intentional implementation process [3] within the design phase. Consider for example the notion of non-discrimination[18], which has been acknowledged to be almost impossible to tackle without ensuring that the design teams developing AI are constructed as intercultural and gender balanced [35, 41]. This applies even though there are design tools to include multifaceted perspectives through user-inclusion to the design phase.

As governance actions are the ones which structure the social sphere of the organization, it is also the sphere of activity in which the values that disseminate through the social structure of design are to concretize [13]. Therefore, acknowledging the varied nature of how high-level goals disseminate to AI technology through the structure of the design phase as well as an intentional act of designers [3] requires us to understand the influencing relation of the LoA's of governance and design ethics to be inherently reciprocal. To put more simply, one must understand what kind of requirements value dissemination in the design phase imposes to governance actions to be able to construct impactful governance ethics frameworks. In Fig. 1 this is depicted with the bidirectional arrow.

The design ethics LoA illustrates the sphere of activity, in which the concrete use cases and abstract models and concepts for AI are integrated [2, 4, 30]. In this article, design is understood broadly as being inherently a science of problem solving [30–32]. Therefore, problem identification and definition is the starting point for a design process. In addition, the problem definition guides further design actions and thus must incorporate the ethical dimensions of deployment ethics for them to be realized in the developed technology [30, 32].

---

[17] Some aspects of the governance ethics LoA may be perceived to best serve its meaning if they were regulated nationally or by an intergovernmental covenant [40], but that is a whole other discourse and out of the scope of this article.

[18] It would be more accurate to talk about prejudice discrimination, since discrimination in its broad meaning refers to distinguishing groups of information from a mass of data. Therefore, discrimination in its broad meaning is a non-separational function of AI.

From the AI ethics point of view, the task for problem definition is to include the recognized ethical dimensions into the design process and refine them to suite the use case context. Thus, the design ethics LoA's behavior is including and refining. Design thinking and approaches must be suitable for this to be possible in such a way that the role of ethics is understood as part of the whole [32] instead of a compulsory, yet ineffective, checklist ticking [42] task within the design phase. Consequently, design thinking and approaches are the observables of the design ethics LoA and problem definitions are their typed variables. Problem definitions can be perceived as cognitive models that explicate how the moral abstractions and use cases can be – and ought to be – integrated [31, 32].

The GoA of AI Ethics. As Fig. 1 illustrates, the gradient of abstraction of AI ethics is a system describing hierarchical normative relations. It describes what is needed for the prescriptive information of the high dimensional LoA's to realize in the most concrete LoA. Therefore, it differs from GoA's describing phenomenal systemic wholes in how modifications in lower abstraction levels do not influence LoA's on a higher abstraction level but are caused by them. However, there are certain exceptions which have been described above and are depicted in Fig. 1 with bidirectional arrows.

The GoA depicts spheres of activities that are always relevant when AI ethics is considered. Therefore, it can be used to uncover necessary discourses within any context treating AI, be it a single team, organization or discipline, discourse of a single technology or a discourse about sector specific needs. Floridi describes in his paper considering the method of levels of abstraction that "specifying LoA's means clarifying from the outset the range of questions that a) can be meaningfully asked and b) are answerable in principle" [8; 315]. Due to the normative nature of ethics, I would add a third effect of the AI ethics clarification to be that it elaborates c) questions that ought to be asked.

In the next chapter, I will elaborate the LoA of embedded ethics and discuss how its relation to the other LoA's are to be taken into consideration when forming its conceptual understanding.

3 Embedded Ethics

As resembling the most concrete level of abstraction of AI ethics, embedded ethics should depict the concrete instantiations of the high-level goals and concepts of the higher abstractions. Therefore, the central questions for embedded ethics are what the ethically relevant parameters of AI technology are, and how can they be instantiated to AI. Existing research gives multiple distinct answers to these questions. I sum them as computational, norm-sensitive, information driven and systemic approaches.

The computational approaches emphasize the role of forming technical solutions to observed issues or high-level goal instantiations. I examine the concept of ethical governors as providing an example of a computational approach. The idea of ethical governors is laid down within a research field at present known as machine ethics. Its advocates bear concern for ethical implications of the increasing amount of highly complex automated systems in contemporary societies and especially in everyday social contexts. The concerns culminate to the question of how we can assure that the AI systems function in a morally desirable manner [5–7].

The introduction of ethical governors is based on understanding the problem of machine functioning to be first and foremost computational, which is why it is perceived that the means of providing an answer should also be computational [7]. The idea of ethical governors is that there should be formed technical subsystems that would assess the outputs of the AI system and only authorize functions that are morally acceptable according to moral codes that are encoded in them. This way, for example opaqueness of the systems functioning would not matter.

There are three ways in how the ethical governors could be built. Top-down refers to encoding specified moral codes as a symbolic system. Bottom-up refers to using machine learning techniques to provide the artifacts the ability to develop moral codes by observing their environment. These both are seen to have restrictions, as the top-down method requires the designers to code acceptable functions to all possible situations and the bottom-up method may lead to the system learning contradictory or unwanted action patterns. A hybrid approach is suggested to redeem the concept of ethical governors, as it would combine the adaptive features of machine learning with the predictive nature of symbolic systems as prescribing restrictions to what is learnt [2, 5–7].

The idea of ethical governors is tempting as it gives a promise of a carefree possibility to produce highly autonomous AI systems [7]. However, it appears superficial when considered through the AI ethics framework of this paper. It narrows technology as to focus on technical artefacts and the role of ethics as over-gluing action instructions to otherwise ready technology. This way it misses the larger ethical implications of technology development and its effects on societies. As the theories do not form proper understanding of how the aspects of deployment ethics relate to the encoded morality, they seem to concentrate on the how part of embedded ethics on the expense of what.

The approach to embedded ethics I refer to as norm-sensitive is from the IEEE document *Value Aligned Design* (2019). Its writers of the section concerning about embedding values into AI takes a step back from the technical aspects of AI and start the discourse with asking what are the parameters that ought to be embedded into AI. Its writers end up proposing social norms of communities as the instantiations of meaningful values [2]. This view focuses on the social interaction between humans and technology to form basis for the process of embedded ethics. Therefore, it differs from the computational approaches.

The writers of Value Aligned Design propose to use the same technical methods as is considered in ethical governors for the process of how to embed the recognized social norms. However, they add the requirement for redesign possibilities for actors of the community in which the AI systems are used [2]. This way the norm-sensitive approach supplements the computational approach by providing an answer to both questions, what and how, required in embedded ethics.

Nevertheless, when embedded ethics is examined as a continuum of the AI ethics framework, the embedding of social norms reflects merely a descriptive nature of AI ethics even though the other sections of the Value Aligned Design -document invoke normative measures to guide the development and deployment of AI systems. Therefore, it can be said that the deployment ethics LoA of Value Aligned Design and its LoA of embedded ethics are controversial, and that the embedded ethics of Value Aligned Design is too narrow. If the normative aspects of AI ethics are left to a higher abstraction level, there is a gap between values/codes and practical reality [29].

As another observation, both forementioned approaches of embedded ethics, computational and norm-sensitive, assume that AI systems are highly autonomous and have tangible appearances [2, 7]. Therefore, they leave out many AI systems such as decision aid systems that may not have complex tangible appearances, but will have major implications for future work, healthcare, exercise of justice and application processing within any sector just to name a few examples [43, 44].

The information approach refers to Floridi & Taddeo's introduction of data ethics as a response to the oversimplification of the multifaceted moral nature of data and information processing of theories that simply focus on the functioning level of AI [10]. Data ethics provides knowledge of concrete variables for how the nature of AI as an information processing system may cause the emergence of moral implications. It for example focuses on the differences of computational language and human intentionality as mediators of morally relevant information [3, 10]. This way it also provides good insight about how certain high-level goals such as fostering of privacy should be examined for it to be best instantiated in AI as computational means [10].

However, when observing AI ethics holistically, we need to acknowledge AI as forming from the interaction between humans and technical artefacts. And even though Floridi and Taddeo argue that the focus should be shifted to the lowest abstraction level of information formation, instead of the functioning of the technical artefacts, [10] they study information formation mostly through computational means and neglect human information processing as a component of technology.

The last approach towards embedded ethics that I examine is the one which I call the systemic approach. The theories of embedded ethics that I depict as part of this approach do not emphasize some aspect of AI as a pivotal area of embedded ethics but consider the process of successfully embedding ethical frameworks in AI as a sum of multiple factors. Ibo van de Poel represents this kind of approach in his article *Embedding Values in Artificial Intelligence (AI) Systems* (2020) where he sees the act of embedding values to AI to consist of perceiving organizational institutions as guiding the use of AI, users as intentional actors and the purpose of the use of the technical artefact and technical norms guiding the artefacts functioning. According to van de Poel, the combined effect of these parameters should be in place for the wanted value to be instantiated in AI.

Even though van de Poel brings many important aspects to the discourse, such as mental states of people and the need to count the immediate sociotechnical surrounding accordingly, he perceives human aspects of AI too narrowly. For example, he argues that the insufficiency of the operator in using the technical artefact in intended ways is in principle the user's fault [3]. The truth is that usability problems are often manifestations of not taking human factors into account in the design of the artifact [4, 32, 45]. Van de Poel perceives intentionality as the only important mental state of users, which causes him to neglect other aspects of human information processing, such as situational awareness or cognitive workload, which are vital in understanding human-technology interaction of AI systems [4, 43].

Van de Poel also builds his theory on grounds that all AI systems evolve during their use [3]. This is true only for certain machine learning techniques such as reinforced and unsupervised machine learning [18, 19]. The way an AI system adapts to its environment should be well limited in its design phase [4].

As a last example of embedded ethics, I examine approaches provided by systems engineering research, which also depict a systemic approach. To do so, I combine point of views from Tony Gillespie as the author of *Systems Engineering for Ethical Autonomous Systems* (2019) and Eric Hollnagel and David D. Woods as the authors of *Joint Cognitive Systems* (2005). The first significant perspective for embedded ethics stems from the fact that AI technology is always used to fill a functional task(s) in a given process [4, 11]. When embedded ethics is understood as a continuum of the design ethics LoA, process analyzation can be perceived as a lower abstraction level continuum for problem definitions. Accordingly, the process analyzation has a central role in combining abstractions with the use case.

For joint cognitive systems, the design process starts from accurately defining the process that is to be fulfilled. It is then examined as a continuous flow of events (continuous control process) required to follow through the process. This way actions and lines of actions related to the process are perceived as being part of the same flow of events, preventing from examining them as separate parts of the process. This type of understanding focuses on how the joint system of humans and technical artefacts can stay in control of a complex process[19]. It requires examining the human-technology interaction while not emphasizing the role of one or the other [11]. Tony Gillespie emphasizes that in addition to considering staying in control of the process, the functions included in the flow of events should be considered through a decide to delegate method, which seeks to ask if there are ethical implications of delegating functions for AI. As an example, Gillespie argues that on ethical grounds, an autonomous weapon system's control process can be automated at any stage, excluding the decide to act function, which is perceived as the point of making a possible human harming decision [4].

The systems engineering point of view provides us process definition as the observable for embedded ethics as it makes it possible to examine ethical aspects of the intended AI technology in the holistic manner that the AI ethics framework invokes. The typed variables for the process definition are the required flow of events for goal attaining and the decide to delegate examination. The flow of events can be further divided as functions carried out by the joint cognitive system of human (plural) actions and technical artefacts. In addition, the decide to delegate process can be divided to case sensitive ethical implications that connects the moral standardization of the deployment ethics phase and the use case context.

The exact nature of the ethical implications related to the decide to delegate examination must be contextually defined. For ethics has to do with the metalevels of action, meaning that there are no ethical actions per se, but the morality of an action is based on the context, agents, their roles, relations, and intentions [24]. For example, stabbing a burglar with a kitchen knife as self-defense versus stabbing someone in pursuance of robbery. Same action, different moral implications. For this reason, we should avoid about talking of general ethical actions or implications within embedded ethics but produce understanding about how to analyze the ethical aspects of the process and its context as in relation to the (AI) deployment ethics.

---

[19] Compare to the concept of meaningful human control as a HCI grand challenge [46].

4   Conclusions

The purpose of this paper was to put forward an initial conceptual framework for AI ethics that considers distinct levels of abstractions and discuss the connection between the process of embedding ethical frameworks to AI systems and the larger framework of AI ethics. Both objectives were fulfilled and the compiled conceptual framework consisting of (AI) deployment ethics, (AI) data ethics, (AI) governing ethics, (AI) design ethics and (AI) embedded ethics proved as an insightful tool for providing rigor to discussions about AI ethics and forming practical steps for ethical design of AI. The observations made in this article highlight the need for such discussions to form understanding of the landscape related to AI ethics and avoiding its oversimplifications as well as the oversimplifications of the process related to embedded ethics.

As the examination of existing approaches of embedded ethics pointed out, the deployment ethics stage and embedded ethics stage of AI ethics are often in contradiction even if they are considered in the same document. The conceptual framework can be used as a pragmatic tool to help form narratives about how to embed ethical frameworks to AI systems. It can also be used to study parts of AI ethics without rendering the whole as considering only questions related to that aspect, which is unfortunately common. The framework also makes it possible for researchers, policymakers, and organizational actors – who inevitably look at issues emphasizing the angle related to their position – to contemplate how their aspect is interrelated to the whole.

When perceived as part of the AI ethics framework, the process of embedded ethics must consider the basic features of technology and more precisely basic features of automated systems design as it being a parallel technology. This is often lost when embedded ethics is perceived as an extension of data ethics, or as the act of solving a single evident issue related to AI deployment. Other obscuring perceptions include that embedded ethics is often approached through a presumption of high-level autonomy for the AI system as well as it is presumed that the ethical or moral aspects of the systems decision making could be examined separately from the other system behavior.

As the behavior of the embedded ethics LoA is operationalizing the abstractions provided on the higher levels of AI ethics, its observable(s) should connect a systemic understanding of AI technology and use case sensitive ethical knowledge. As the problem definition provided in the design ethics phase should count for refining the goal of the automatable process to reflect the moral standardization, it is left for the embedded ethics phase to examine the functions within the process. Therefore, process analyzation and the decide to delegate examination are observables of embedded ethics.

This article concentrated in creating the frame for discourse about embedded ethics, and therefore further studies should pursue to refine details within it. It is not a simple task, for the complexity of the field necessitates interdisciplinary approaches, which combine engineering-, natural-, behavioral- and social sciences and humanities. It is not justifiable nor feasible to thrust this whole on engineering disciplines as is implicitly or explicitly often suggested in AI research and national AI strategies.

References

1. European Commission: Ethics guidelines for trustworthy AI. https://ec.europa.eu/digital-sin gle-market/en/news/ethics-guidelines-trustworthy-ai
2. The IEEE global initiative on ethics of autonomous and intelligent systems: ethically aligned design: a vision for prioritizing human well-being with autonomous and intelligent systems. First Edition. IEEE (2019)
3. van de Poel, I.: Embedding values in artificial intelligence (AI) systems. Mind. Mach. **30**(3), 385–409 (2020). https://doi.org/10.1007/s11023-020-09537-4
4. Gillespie, T.: Systems Engineering for Ethical Autonomous Systems. SciTech Publishing, London (2019). ISBN-13: 978-1-78561-372-2
5. Arkin R.: EMBEDDED ETHICS - "governing lethal behavior: embedding ethics in a hybrid deliberative/reactive robot architecture. In: Proceedings of the 2008 3rd ACM/IEEE International Conference on Human-Robot Interaction (HRI), Amsterdam, Netherlands, 12–15 March 2008, pp. 121–128. IEEE (2008)
6. Wallach, W., Allen, C.: Moral Machines: Teaching Robots Right from Wrong. Oxford University Press, New York (2008)
7. Anderson, M., Anderson, S.L. (eds.): Machine Ethics. Cambridge University Press, New York (2011)
8. Floridi, L.: The method of levels of abstraction. Mind. Mach. **18**, 303–329 (2008). https://doi.org/10.1007/s11023-008-9113-7
9. Johnson, D.G., Miller, K.W.: Un-making artificial moral agents. Ethics Inf. Technol. **10**(2), 123–133 (2008). https://doi.org/10.1007/s10676-008-9174-6
10. Floridi, L., Taddeo, M.: What is data ethics? Philos. Trans. R. Soc. A: Math. Phys. Eng. Sci. **374**(2083), 20160360 (2016). https://doi.org/10.1098/rsta.2016.0360
11. Hollnagel, E., Woods, D.D.: Joint Cognitive Systems – Foundations of Cognitive Systems Engineering. CRC Press/Taylor & Francis Group, London (2005). ISBN-13: 978-0-367-86420-0
12. Schomberg, R.V. (Ed.): Towards responsible research and innovation in the information and communication technologies and security technologies fields. Publication Office of the European Union, Luxembourg (2011). http://ec.europa.eu/research/science-society/document_lib rary/pdf_06/mep-rapport-2011_en.pdf
13. Jasanoff, S.: Future imperfect: science, technology and the imaginations of modernity. In: Jasanoff, S., Kim, S. (eds.): Dreamscapes of Modernity: Sociotechnical Imaginaries and the Fabrication of Power. The University of Chicago Press, London (2015)
14. Floridi, L.: Soft ethics and the governance of the digital. Philos. Technol. **31**(1), 1–8 (2018). https://doi.org/10.1007/s13347-018-0303-9
15. Cabinet Office of Japan: Society 5.0. https://www8.cao.go.jp/cstp/english/society5_0/index.html. Accessed 12 Mar 2021
16. Samoili, S., Lopez, C.M., Gomez, G.E., De Prato, G., Martinez-Plumed, F., Delipetrev, B.: AI WATCH. Defining Artificial Intelligence. EUR 30117 EN. Publications Office of the European Union, Luxembourg (2020). ISBN 978-92-76-17045-7. https://doi.org/10.2760/382730
17. Minsky, M.L.: Computation: Finite and Infinite Machines. Prentice-Hall, Englewood Cliffs (1967)
18. Norvig, P., Russel, S.: Artificial Intelligence – A Modern Approach, 3rd edn. Pearson, Boston (2010)
19. Pietikäinen M., Silven, O.: Tekoälyn haasteet: koneoppimisesta ja konenäöstä tunnetekoälyyn. Oulun Yliopisto, Oulu (2019). ISBN 978-952-62-2482-4
20. Bostrom, N., Yudkowsky E.: The ethics of artificial intelligence. In: Frankish, K., Ramsey, W. (eds.) The Cambridge Handbook of Artificial Intelligence, pp. 316–334. Cambridge University Press, Cambridge (2014). https://doi.org/10.1017/CBO9781139046855.020

21. Kostopoulos, L.: Decoupling Human Characteristics from Algorithmic Capabilities. The IEEE Standards Association (2014)
22. Beauchamp, T., Childress, J.: Principles of Biomedical Ethics, 7th edn. Oxford University Press, New York (2013)
23. Hansson, S.O.: Theories and methods for the ethics of technology. In: Hansson, S.O. (ed.) The Ethics of Technology. Rowman & Littlefield, London (2017). ISBN 978-1-7834-8658-8.
24. Hallamaa, J.: Yhdessä toimimisen etiikka [Ethics of acting together]. Gaudeamus, Helsinki (2017)
25. Westermarck, E.: The Origin and Development of the Moral Ideas, vol. 2. Macmillan, London (1908)
26. Habermas, J.: The theory of communicative action. In: Reason and the Rationalization of Society, vol. 1. Heinemann, London (1984)
27. Velasquez, M., Andre, C., Shanks, T., Meyer, M.: What is Ethics? Markkula center for Applied ethics (2019). https://www.scu.edu/ethics/ethics-resources/ethical-decision-making/what-is-ethics/. Accessed 12 Mar 2021
28. Floridi, L., et al.: AI4People—An ethical framework for a good ai society: opportunities, risks, principles, and recommendations. Mind. Mach. 28(4), 689–707 (2018). https://doi.org/10.1007/s11023-018-9482-5
29. Hallamaa, J., Snell, K.: Ethics in AI research – what and how? Finnish Center for Artificial Intelligence (2020). https://fcai.fi/eab-blog/2020/9/4/ethics-in-ai-research-what-and-how. Accessed 12 Mar 2021
30. Jones, D., Gregor, S.: The anatomy of a design theory. J. Assoc. Inf. Syst. 8(5), 312–335 (2007)
31. Simon, H.A.: The Sciences of the Artificial. MIT, Cambridge (1970)
32. Saariluoma, P., Cañas, J., Leikas, J.: Designing for Life. MacMillan, London (2016)
33. Franssen, M., Gert-Jan L., van de Poel, I.: Philosophy of technology. In: Zalta, E.N. (ed.) The Stanford Encyclopedia of Philosophy (Fall 2018 Edition) (2018). https://plato.stanford.edu/archives/fall2018/entries/technology/
34. Saariluoma, P., Oulasvirta, A.: User psychology: re-assessing the boundaries of a discipline. Sci. Res. 1(5), 317–328 (2010)
35. Homepage of Black in AI. https://blackinai.github.io/. Accessed 12 Mar 2021
36. European Commission: White Paper on Artificial Intelligence: a European approach to excellence and trust. Brussels (2020)
37. ETAIROS -project homepage. https://etairos.fi/en/front-page/. Accessed 12 Mar 2021
38. AIGA -project homepage. https://des.utu.fi/projects/aiga/. Accessed 12 Dec 2021
39. Canca, C.: AI & Global Governance: Human Rights and AI Ethics – Why Ethics Cannot be Replaced by the UDHR. United Nations University, Center for Policy Research (2019)
40. Ben-Israel, I., et al.: Towards regulation of AI systems. Council of Europe (2020)
41. Buolamwini, J., Gebru, T.: Gender shades: intersectional accuracy disparities in commercial gender classification. Proc. Mach. Learn. Res. 81, 1–15 (2018)
42. Vakkuri, V., Kemell, K.-K., Abrahamsson, P.: Implementing ethics in AI: initial results of an industrial multiple case study. In: Franch, X., Männistö, T., Martínez-Fernández, S. (eds.) PROFES 2019. LNCS, vol. 11915, pp. 331–338. Springer, Cham (2019). https://doi.org/10.1007/978-3-030-35333-9_24
43. Ruff, H., Narayanan, S., Draper, M.: Human interaction with levels of automation and decision-aid fidelity in the supervisory control of multiple simulated unmanned air vehicles. Pres. Teleoper. Virtual Environ. 11(4), 335–351 (2002)
44. Berk, R., Hyatt, J.: Machine learning forecasts of risk to inform sentencing decisions. Fed. Sentencing Report. 27(4), 222–228 (2015). https://doi.org/10.1525/fsr.2015.27.4.222
45. Norman, D.: The Design of Everyday Things, Revised and expanded edition. Basic Books (AZ) (2013). ISBN 9780262525671
46. Chairs, C.S., Salvendy, G., et al.: Seven HCI grand challenges. Int. J. Human-Comput. Interact. 35(14), 1229–1269 (2019). https://doi.org/10.1080/10447318.2019.1619259

Using Information Divergence to Differentiate Deep from Superficial Resemblances Among Discourses

Zachary K. Stine[1](✉) ⓘ, James E. Deitrick[2], and Nitin Agarwal[1] ⓘ

[1] University of Arkansas at Little Rock, Little Rock, AR 72204, USA
{zkstine,nxagarwal}@ualr.edu
[2] University of Central Arkansas, Conway, AR 72035, USA
deitrick@uca.edu

Abstract. In comparative analyses of discourses that reflect particular cultural identities, it is often necessary to differentiate superficial distinctions that arise primarily as cultural markers from deeper distinctions that arise from differences in cultural structures. In this paper, we build on previous work in order to operationalize this distinction between deep and superficial relationships between discourses using computational methods. To do so, we draw on the notion of divergence from information theory to measure the extent to which lexical items from a discourse act as signals of one cultural identity over another. We carry out a series of three types of comparisons between the discourses of fourteen English-language online discussion communities primarily focused on religion and spirituality. In the first type of comparison, discourses are compared at the level of individual words and their frequencies. In the second type, they are compared at the level of word-usage patterns learned from topic models. In the third, they are also compared at the level of word-usage patterns, but from topic models trained on their discourses after removing highly distinguishing terms that represent superficial distinctions between them. Our results indicate that, while some discourses share close resemblances both superficial and deep, others may appear to share close resemblances only superficially or may only share close resemblances after accounting for their superficial differences. These findings suggest that the approach we describe may be of use to researchers studying language in a variety of comparative contexts.

Keywords: Natural language processing · Cultural analytics · Information theory · Comparative religion · Digital religion

1 Introduction

A significant obstacle for comparative analyses of cultures is differentiating cultural expression that is only superficially distinct or similar between cultures being compared from cultural expression that is similar or distinct at a deeper level. In linguistic comparisons, distinctions between culturally specific lexical items may mask deeper cultural resemblances. For example, Prothero [1] argues that the adult religious life of Henry Steel

© Springer Nature Switzerland AG 2021
M. Rauterberg (Ed.): HCII 2021, LNCS 12795, pp. 330–347, 2021.
https://doi.org/10.1007/978-3-030-77431-8_21

Olcott—a well-known early American convert to Buddhism—was expressed through a Buddhist, South Asian cultural lexicon, but ultimately reflected American Protestant cultural structures at a deeper level. Another example of this distinction is used by Deitrick [2] in arguing that the social ethics of American Engaged Buddhism is structurally similar to a liberal, Protestant social ethics despite being expressed through a Buddhist lexicon.

In this paper, we are interested in using a quantitative approach to reduce the prominence of superficial distinctions between discourses in comparative analyses as a complement to existing qualitative approaches. We draw on concepts from distributional semantics and information theory to create representations of discourses that lack culturally specific lexical items while still retaining their underlying semantic structures.

This work builds on previous research that frames comparative cultural analysis as a meta-clustering problem wherein discourses are compared indirectly via their latent organizational schemes [3]. There, we saw that discourse around debates on vegetarianism within a Buddhist discussion community and abortion within a Christian discussion community, while distinct on a more superficial level, exhibited structural similarity as instances of ethically contentious debate. Here, we explore a different approach in which we do not compare the organizational schemes of each discourse, but rather compare discourses within a single organizational scheme reflecting all discourses under comparison and from which culturally specific terms have been removed.

The discourses we consider here are those of several online discussion communities from Reddit that are dedicated to discussions of religious and spiritual topics. This study thus contributes to ongoing scholarship concerning the relationship between social media and religion, often referred to as digital religion studies (see [4] for a recent overview of this scholarship).

We carry out a series of comparative analyses between the discourses of several online discussion communities from Reddit. Each pair of discourses undergoes three modes of comparison, which differ in how the discourses are represented. In the first, discourses are represented by probability distributions of words. In the second, discourses are represented within the latent semantic features derived from topic models trained on all of the discourses. Rather than probability distributions of words alone, the discourses are represented as probability distributions of "topics," the learned latent features. In the third, discourses are also represented as probability distributions of topics, but these topics are learned from a modified version of the corpus from which highly distinguishing terms have been removed.

We find that the resemblances and differences between discourses undergo substantial changes from one mode of comparison to another. Comparisons of word distributions may show a discourse closely resembling others, only for these resemblances to weaken at the topic-level and dissipate at the level of topics learned from the modified corpus. Conversely, we also find that a discourse may appear distinct from many of the others under both word-level and original corpus topic-level comparisons, but may have surprisingly strong resemblances to other discourses under the modified corpus topic-level comparisons. Finally, we find that the resemblances between discourses need not necessarily change between modes of comparisons. As we will show, three of the discourses we consider retain their close resemblances between each mode of comparison.

In the following sections, we provide background for our work, describe the data and methods used, report our results, and discuss them along with the limitations of the present study and our next steps.

2 Background

2.1 Religious and Spiritual Discourses on Reddit

The discussion communities of Reddit provide interesting sources for text data around a variety of topics including religion. These communities, called subreddits, allow users to author posts (or submissions) and to author comments on posts or other comments, resulting in discussion threads accompanying most posts. Scholarship on Reddit and religion include our previous work on comparative analyses of religious discourses [3], a study of the irreligious rhetoric of the subreddit, *r/atheism* [5], and an analysis of the influence of controversial religious news stories on *r/atheism*, *r/Christianity*, and *r/politics* [6].

Here, we focus our analysis on the following 14 subreddits: *r/Awakened*, *r/Bahai*, *r/Buddhism*, *r/Christianity*, *r/Hinduism*, *r/Islam*, *r/Judaism*, *r/Occult*, *r/Pagan*, *r/Philosophy*, *r/Psychonaut*, *r/Sikh*, *r/Spirituality*, and *r/Taoism*. These selections reflect general discussion communities around the so-called world religions (e.g., *r/Buddhism*, *r/Hinduism*, *r/Islam*), relatively newer religious movements (e.g., *r/Bahai*, *r/Pagan*), and several communities that resist easy categorization as religious or not.

The latter group comprises *r/Awakened, r/Occult, r/Psychonaut*, and *r/Spirituality*. These subreddits may draw on aspects of religion, but do not explicitly associate themselves with particular religious institutions. While the religiosity of these subreddits (or lack thereof) may be unclear, we can examine their resemblances to the other subreddits in order to gain a clearer picture of how their discourses are situated relative to the others. Despite their differences, each of these communities are marked by commitments to gaining wisdom, truth, insight, etc. outside the bounds of traditional religions. *r/Psychonaut* and *r/Occult* may be plausibly read as focused on certain technologies for insight, whether through the use of psychoactive substances in the former or magick in the latter, while *r/Spirituality* and *r/Awakened* are more general in their approaches. In particular, *r/Spirituality* presents an interesting case study given the emergence of the so-called spiritual-but-not-religious identity and the scholarship around it (e.g., [7–10]).

Finally, we include *r/Philosophy* to provide a point of contrast given that, while religious topics are certainly relevant in the community, we suspect that its discussions are motivated by distinct reasons from the other subreddits and that it is structurally quite dissimilar to the other subreddits we analyze.

A critical point to bear in mind is that these subreddits should not be viewed as samples of larger populations from which we can easily extrapolate conclusions; on the contrary, each subreddit should be viewed as its own population. In other words, there is little reason to suspect that conclusions about *r/Spirituality* will easily map onto spirituality writ large. Despite this, these subreddits constitute interesting cultures themselves that still offer insights into the landscape of popular English-language culture.

2.2 Latent Dirichlet Allocation

Latent Dirichlet allocation (LDA), a kind of topic model, provides a method for learning a set of latent features from a collection of text that reflect patterns of word-usage [11]. LDA has been used in various contexts to provide semantically richer representations of text including a comparative analysis of Confucian texts [12], a study of mind-body holism in medieval Chinese thought [13], and a comparative analysis of different natural language processing conferences' proceedings [14].

After training on a corpus, LDA provides these latent features, called "topics," in the form of probability distributions over the vocabulary of the corpus. Additionally, the trained LDA model can draw a distribution over the topics for each document. With both a document's distribution over topics and each topic as distribution over words, each token in a document can be probabilistically assigned to a topic. As discussed in [3], an LDA model trained on a discourse can be usefully thought of as representing a discourse's latent organizational or conceptual scheme.

The features learned by LDA—the probability distributions over the vocabulary—do not typically correspond to what we colloquially think of as "topics," and can be better thought of as contexts of language usage [15]. The number of topics to be learned, k, must be defined. While the selection of k may influence the resulting model, it likely acts as something like a dial on topic specificity [16]. Therefore, different selections of k may not be better or worse than others in any straightforward way, but may simply offer different yet equally plausible views into the corpus. For a thorough discussion of evaluating LDA models, see [17].

LDA is an unsupervised machine learning algorithm, meaning that it learns topics (or contexts) without them being pre-specified or other external guidance. The way LDA learns "meaningful" topics can be related to the notion of distributional semantics, the idea that something of a word's meaning can be glimpsed based on how the word is distributed among other words across documents. This notion is relevant for our work as we will be removing certain terms from the vocabulary while preserving the overall distributional semantic structure of the corpus. Previous research into a similar problem suggests that the semantic structures of a corpus are resilient to the removal or subsampling of certain terms [18].

2.3 Information Divergence and Comparative Analysis

To facilitate our comparisons of discourses, we use information divergence to measure the dissimilarity (and implicitly, the similarity) between representations of the discourses as probability distributions of linguistic features. From the divergences between discourses, we can also identify how strongly each feature of the discourse contributes to the discourse's overall dissimilarity from another.

We use two related measures of divergence, the Kullback-Leibler divergence (KLD) and the Jensen-Shannon divergence (JSD). While most measures of difference correspond to distance within some space (e.g., Euclidean, cosine), the KLD is better understood as an epistemic measure of surprise [19]. Given an expectation based on one probability distribution and a newly observed distribution, the KLD from the expectation to the newly observed distribution provides a measure of how surprising the observed distribution is relative to the expectation. It is an asymmetric measure—the KLD from Q to P is not necessarily the KLD from P to Q. Thus between any two distributions, there are two directions in which the KLD between them can be calculated. When the KLD from Q to P is larger than the KLD from P to Q, we can describe their relationship as one of enclosure wherein P encloses Q [19].

The JSD is a symmetrized form of the KLD such that the JSD between distributions P and Q is the mean of the KLD from M to P and the KLD from M to Q (where M is the mean distribution). The JSD is defined for the range [0, 1] and so it can be converted from a difference measure to a similarity measure by subtracting it from one.

Information divergences have been used in a variety of comparative contexts such as an analysis of what features characterize violent versus non-violent trials in a London court [20], an investigation of protestor and counter-protestor discourses [21], a comparison of two online discourses around China [22], and an analysis of language used by politicians of different parties [23]. In our comparative context, these divergences provide an important way of understanding one discourse through understanding how it relates to other discourses. By breaking down the divergences into the per-feature contributions, we can identify lexical markers that mark a discourse as belonging to one subreddit over another.

3   Methods and Data

In this section we describe the collected data and the steps taken in our analysis.[1]

3.1   Data and Preprocessing

We collect text data from 14 subreddits from their earliest submissions through the end of 2019. For each subreddit of interest, we collect all available submission IDs from the Pushshift Reddit database [24] and then use Reddit's API to collect the text for all available submissions. For each submission, we collect the text of the submission along with the text of all comments in the submission's comment threads. The collected text is primarily English-language. An overview of these data is provided in Table 1.

All collected text undergoes simple preprocessing. All text is tokenized into lower-case strings with a minimum length of three characters and with internal punctuation preserved. We remove a set of 78 highly frequent stopwords. For each subreddit, we additionally remove all words that occur in fewer than 50 submissions from that subreddit. Of the remaining terms from a subreddit, the ten thousand most frequent are kept as that subreddit's vocabulary. After doing this for each subreddit, the final vocabulary consists of the union of each subreddit-specific vocabulary, resulting in 22,742 total word types.

A single document comprises the submission text and all corresponding comment text. Documents with fewer than 35 post-processed tokens were excluded.

---

[1] The code used in this analysis is available at https://github.com/zacharykstine/cc21_discourse_resemblances.

Table 1. Overview of subreddit data ordered by the number of documents after preprocessing.

Subreddit	Date of earliest document	Documents collected	Documents after preprocessing
r/Christianity	2008-01-25	412,930	274,724
r/Islam	2008-03-05	205,914	83,907
r/Psychonaut	2008-12-08	110,012	73,657
r/Philosophy	2008-01-25	148,794	61,810
r/Buddhism	2008-03-25	87,792	61,339
r/Occult	2008-03-23	75,973	53,969
r/Judaism	2008-06-11	88,233	47,246
r/Spirituality	2008-03-23	41,475	20,510
r/Awakened	2012-06-17	23,021	16,411
r/Hinduism	2008-11-08	28,487	11,722
r/Sikh	2010-01-09	17,314	11,206
r/Pagan	2010-03-30	13,945	8,596
r/Taoism	2008-03-23	8,540	6,231
r/Bahai	2008-05-27	6,667	4,248

3.2 Word Distribution Comparisons

For each subreddit, we calculate the relative frequency of each word in the original unaltered corpus in order to compare subreddits with respect to the word distribution of each. We then calculate the Jensen-Shannon divergence (JSD) between each pair of subreddits' word distributions to measure the differences in word usage between subreddits. Additionally, we calculate the per-word contribution to the Kullback-Leibler divergence (KLD) between each word distribution for words where the KLD is defined (i.e., excluding words that do not occur in the subreddit from which the expectation distribution was formed).

3.3 Removal of Distinguishing Terms

While the JSD between each pair of subreddits reflects how different their word distributions are, the per-word KLD contributions measure how conspicuous a word is in one subreddit relative to another. Since the KLD is asymmetric, a single word type makes two KLD contributions when comparing one pair of subreddits: one for each subreddit's word distribution acting as the expectation distribution and then as the observed distribution. The larger a word's KLD contribution is, the more strongly it signals the observed distribution relative to the expectation distribution. Therefore, the larger a word's KLD contribution, the more it acts as a subreddit's distinct cultural lexicon by providing a stronger signal of that subreddit over the other.

In order to understand the relationships between the subreddits' discourses that persist after their more superficial differences are ignored, we create a second version of the corpus from which certain words are removed based on how strongly they act as signals of one subreddit over another based on per-word KLD contributions. Prior to this, we remove any words that do not occur at least once in each subreddit. This results in the removal of 7,400 words or almost a third of the original vocabulary.

Additional words are removed based on how well they distinguish one subreddit from another. To identify words for removal, we define a threshold for the per-word KLD contributions. If a word's KLD contribution is greater than this threshold within any pairwise comparison of the subreddits' word distributions, it is removed from the new corpus. After manually examining words removed based on different per-word KLD thresholds, we use a threshold of 0.001 bits. This results in an additional 1,473 words removed from the vocabulary of this new corpus. In addition to the previously removed words, this results in the modified corpus having 8,873 fewer words in its vocabulary than the original corpus, a reduction of 39%. A similar problem is explored in [18] within a different statistical framework.

3.4 Latent Dirichlet Allocation

We train topics models via latent Dirichlet allocation (LDA) in order to learn corpus features that are semantically richer than individual word types. Models are trained using the implementation of LDA in Gensim [25]. For each model that is trained, the relative frequencies of each topic in each subreddit are calculated by probabilistically assigning each token from the subreddit to a topic. We follow the method used in [18] for estimating each token's topic assignment for EM-based implementations of LDA.

Because the highest probability words in a topic are not often sufficient for interpreting the topic, we interpret topics of interest by reading a variety of exemplar documents for each topic in order to better understand how they relate to the topic's high-probability words.

Original Corpus Models. Fifteen models are trained on the original corpus. This includes all documents from each subreddit with the exception of *r/Christianity* and *r/Islam*. From these subreddits, 75,000 documents are sampled for model training in order to prevent them from dominating the model features. Five samples are drawn and combined with all documents from the remaining subreddits. For each of the five corpus samples, we train three models: one with 20 topics, one with 100 topics, and one with 250 topics.

Modified Corpus Models. We train fifteen additional models on the modified corpus. All documents from each subreddit that have at least 50 tokens are used for model training with the exception of *r/Christianity*, from which 75,000 documents are sampled due to it having many more documents even within the modified corpus. As was done for models trained on the original corpus, five samples are drawn with a 20-topic, 100-topic, and 250-topic model being trained on each sampled corpus.

3.5 Topic Distribution Comparisons

From the frequencies of token-topic assignments, the topic distributions of each subreddit are calculated and compared in a similar manner as the word distributions. Both the JSD and KLD are calculated between each pair of subreddits for all of the LDA models. Per-topic contributions to both the JSD and KLD are also calculated. For all models trained on the same version of the corpus, original or modified, and for the same number of topics, the mean JSD and KLD are calculated in order to summarize divergences across corpus samples.

Topics that are salient for a subreddit are identified as those with relatively large per-topic contributions to the KLD from others to that subreddit across comparisons.

4 Results

In this section, we describe our results and findings across the three modes of comparison: between word distributions, topic distributions from the original corpus, and topic distributions from the modified corpus from which words have been removed if they distinguish subreddits from each other. We illustrate each mode through examples from *r/Spirituality* and its relationship to the other subreddits. For brevity, we limit our results from topic distribution comparisons to models with 250 topics.

Importantly, we find that the relationships between subreddits have substantial differences between the different modes of comparison. The starkest change occurs between the word-level comparisons and the modified corpus topic-level comparisons. When comparing the similarity rank of each subreddit pair—such that the most similar pair of subreddits (excluding self-similarity) is ranked 1st and the least similar pair is ranked 91st—the sum of absolute rank differences across pairs from comparisons on word distributions to topic distributions from the modified corpus is 1,958, compared with 1,158 for word-level to topic-level comparisons in the original corpus, and 1,074 for original to modified corpus topic distributions.

4.1 Word Distribution Comparisons Results

Comparisons between the word distributions of each subreddit indicate how different or similar the proportion is of each word between subreddits. Of the 91 pairwise comparisons of the 14 subreddits (excluding self-comparisons), the smallest JSD between two subreddits' word distributions—0.02 bits—occurs between *r/Spirituality* and *r/Awakened*. The largest JSD—0.19 bits—is between *r/Psychonaut* and *r/Sikh*. Interestingly, the word distribution of *r/Sikh* appears to be something of an outlier relative to the other subreddits: the nine largest divergences among all comparisons involve *r/Sikh*. However, as we will see, this will not be the case within other modes of comparisons, suggesting that discussions in *r/Sikh* include many more highly distinguishing terms relative to the other subreddits.

r/Spirituality, *r/Awakened*, and *r/Psychonaut* all exhibit high similarity between word distributions, accounting for the three smallest divergences among all pairwise comparisons (see Fig. 1). As seen in the similarity network in Fig. 2, they form a

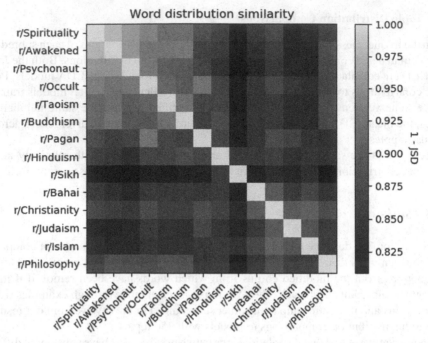

Fig. 1. Similarities between the word distributions of each subreddit where similarity is 1 − JSD.

densely-connected neighborhood along with *r/Occult*, *r/Buddhism*, and *r/Taoism*. These densely-connected nodes are bridged via *r/Philosophy* and *r/Pagan* to *r/Christianity*, which in turn, acts as the sole bridge to *r/Islam*, *r/Judaism*, and *r/Bahai*.

4.2 Topic Distribution Comparisons Results from the Original Corpus

Despite consisting of the same vocabulary, comparisons of topic distributions from the unaltered corpus produce relationships between subreddits that differ from those derived from word distributions in several ways. Both *r/Hinduism* and *r/Pagan* are more closely connected to the neighborhood of highly similar subreddits described above. However, *r/Christianity* and *r/Philosophy* now appear more dissimilar to several subreddits compared with their relationships under comparisons of the word distributions.

Several relationships persist at this mode of comparison from the word distribution comparisons. *r/Spirituality*, *r/Awakened*, and *r/Psychonaut* remain the three most similar subreddits, while the largest divergence now occurs between *r/Awakened* and *r/Islam*, a rank change from the 79th most similar pair to the 91st.

When comparing the magnitudes of change in rank of the most similar pairs of subreddits when comparing topics as opposed to word distributions, the nine largest drops in rank all involve *r/Philosophy* as one of the subreddits in the comparison. The biggest drop in rank occurs in the JSD between *r/Awakened* and *r/Philosophy*, dropping 44 places to the 67th most similar out of 91 pairs. This is reflected in the similarity network in which *r/Philosophy* is an isolated node, having no similarity score at or above the

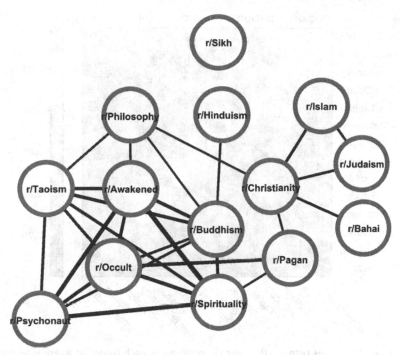

Fig. 2. The word distribution similarity network. Similarity is calculated as one minus the JSD between the word distributions of each subreddit. Edges indicate similarity scores at or above the 70th percentile (0.883). Edge thickness reflects similarity with thicker edges indicating greater similarity.

70th percentile (Fig. 4). Conversely, six of the seven largest increases in similarity rank involve *r/Sikh* with the largest rank increase between it and *r/Pagan*, which is the 49th most similar pair, up 36 places from the word distribution ranking.

4.3   Topic Distribution Comparisons Results from the Modified Corpus

70 of the 91 subreddit pairs (77%) undergo rank changes from word distributions to modified topic distributions that differ only in magnitude, but not in direction, i.e., positive or negative change. In other words, most subreddit pairs change rank in the same way that they did when going from word distributions to original corpus topic distributions. The primary difference between the changes seen in the modified corpus distributions versus the original topic distributions is due to the extent of the rank change: the absolute difference in rank is larger here, but positive changes are still mostly positive and negative rank changes are still mostly negative.

The relationships between subreddits are therefore not an extreme departure from the relationships between them under comparisons of topic distributions from the original corpus. The same group of highly similar subreddits continues to persist as a densely connected region of the similarity network (Fig. 6). *r/Hinduism* and *r/Pagan* continue

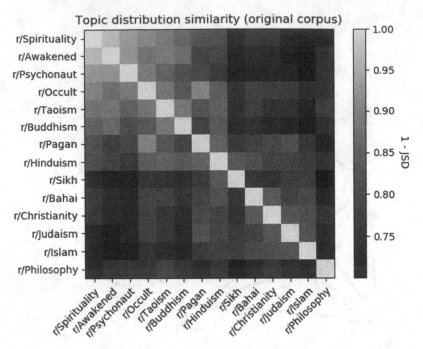

Fig. 3. Mean similarities between the topic distributions of each subreddit where similarity is 1 – JSD and calculated from the 250-topic models trained on the original corpus.

to act as bridges between network regions. *r/Philosophy* is still isolated from the others, but now joined by *r/Christianity* as another isolate.

The most notable change at this mode of comparison is the continued increase in similarity between *r/Sikh* and many of the other subreddits (see Fig. 5 and compare with Figs. 1 and 3). The five subreddit pairs with the largest positive changes in similarity rank from word-level to modified topic-level distributions all have *r/Sikh* as one of the subreddits in the pair. Of these, the most extreme case is *r/Sikh* and *r/Judaism*, which are ranked 80th most similar pair under word-level comparisons, but are ranked 4th most similar under modified topic-level distributions; a change of 76 places.

While *r/Spirituality* and *r/Awakened* remain the most similar pair, the 2nd through 6th most similar pairs are different than those in either the word-level or original topic-level comparisons. This is not because the subreddit pairs that previously occupied these rankings are necessarily more different, but because so many other subreddit pairs have become so much more similar under this mode of comparison with the lexical items that most differentiated them removed.

Of the ten largest negative changes in ranking from word-level to modified topic-level comparisons, eight include *r/Philosophy*. In the most extreme of these, *r/Philosophy* and *r/Awakened* move from the 23rd most similar pair under word-level comparisons down 64 places to the 87th most similar pair here.

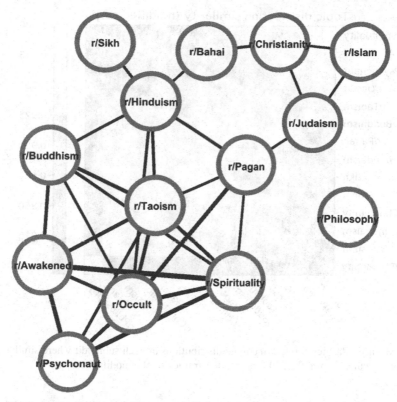

Fig. 4. The topic distribution similarity network from topic models trained on the original corpus with 250 topics. Edge weights are the mean similarity between subreddits where similarity is calculated as one minus the JSD between the topic distributions of each subreddit. Edges indicate similarity scores at or above the 70th percentile (0.825). Edge thickness reflects similarity with thicker edges indicating greater similarity.

4.4 Examples from *r/Spirituality*

A richer picture of the relationships between discourses can be uncovered through the exploration of which words and topics most differentiate a subreddit from another. Here, we summarize the words and topics which most differentiate *r/Spirituality* from other subreddits as a case study illustrating what linguistic features, both deep and superficial, characterize the discourse of the subreddit relative to the others.

Word-Level Comparisons. In comparisons of word distributions, the words from *r/Spirituality* which most distinguish it from the other subreddits include words like *spiritual, life, feel, love, spirituality, energy, yourself, ego, self, experience, mind, soul, consciousness, feeling,* and *meditation,* among others.

Notably, in most comparisons, the words which most distinguish *r/Spirituality* tend to make smaller per-word KLD contributions than the most distinguishing words of the subreddit to which *r/Spirituality* is being compared. In other words, the cultural lexicon of *r/Spirituality* is less distinct than the cultural lexicons of the other subreddits.

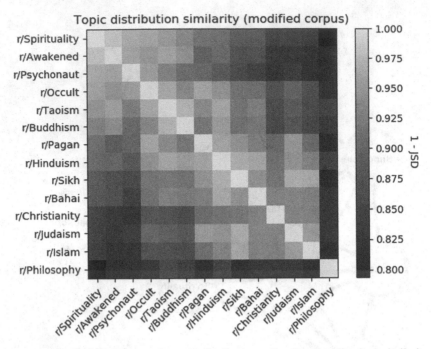

Fig. 5. Mean similarities between the topic distributions of each subreddit where similarity is 1 – JSD and calculated from the 250-topic models trained on the modified corpus.

For example, the word types which most differentiate *r/Buddhism* from *r/Spirituality* include *buddhism, buddha, buddhist, dharma, practice, dhamma, sutta, mahayana,* and *buddhists,* among others. These example words are much less likely to occur with high frequency in the other subreddits, compared with the less culturally specific terms that distinguish *r/Spirituality.*

Topic-Level Comparisons from the Original Corpus. In comparisons of topic distributions based on one of the 250-topic models trained on the original corpus, salient topics for *r/Spirituality* reflect life advice, personal stories and experiences, language about the nature of reality and fundamental truths, meditation, requests for help with difficult situations, the meaning and purpose of life, relationships, mental health, language about energy, vibrations, and auras, and others.

Similar to what was seen for word-level comparisons, *r/Spirituality* appears less distinct from the other subreddits as they do from it. More formally, in each comparison with another subreddit, the KLD from *r/Spirituality* to the comparison subreddit is always greater than the KLD from the comparison subreddit to *r/Spirituality.* In other words, observing *r/Spirituality* (as represented within the topic space) is less surprising relative to all other subreddits than the other subreddits are relative to *r/Spirituality.* The other subreddits are more distinct than *r/Spirituality* in each comparison.

Topic-Level Comparisons from the Modified Corpus. In comparisons of topic distributions based on one of the 250-topic models trained on the modified corpus with

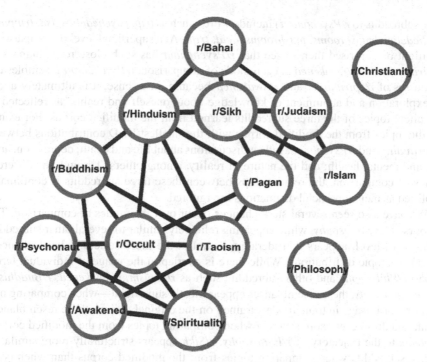

Fig. 6. The topic distribution similarity network from topic models trained on the modified corpus with 250 topics. Edge weights are the mean similarity between subreddits where similarity is calculated as one minus the JSD between the topic distributions of each subreddit. Edges indicate similarity scores at or above the 70th percentile (0.937). Edge thickness reflects similarity with thicker edges indicating greater similarity.

distinguishing terms removed, several of the salient topics for *r/Spirituality* share similarities with the topics discussed above learned from the original corpus. These include topics reflecting language around struggles, personal stories and experiences, the nature of reality, requests for help, and relationships. Additional salient topics reflect discussions on mental obstacles to personal growth, the nature of suffering, and loneliness.

As observed in the other two modes of comparison, the KLD from another subreddit to *r/Spirituality* is always less than the KLD from *r/Spirituality* to the other subreddit. Even after removing the terms which most distinguish each subreddit, the remaining features of *r/Spirituality* continue to be less distinct relative to the other subreddits.

5 Discussion

Through our results, we have described the changes undergone by the relationships between the subreddits' discourses across the three modes of comparisons. We have seen that some close resemblances persist across modes, most notably observed in the relationships between *r/Spirituality*, *r/Awakened*, and *r/Psychonaut*. The distinctive lexicon of *r/Psychonaut* (i.e., words that tend to make the largest contributions to the KLD from other subreddits to *r/Psychonaut*) include words such as *trip, psychedelics, lsd, tripping, psychedelic, dmt, shrooms, mushrooms, acid, trips.* At a superficial level of comparison, we might be surprised then to see that *r/Psychonaut* has such close resemblances to *r/Spirituality* and *r/Awakened* at each mode of comparison. *r/Psychonaut* resembles the discourses of *r/Spirituality* and *r/Awakened* because, in a sense, it is ultimately about the exploration and attainment of knowledge about oneself and reality, as reflected in the salient topics of the three subreddits learned from the modified corpus. For example, the topics from the modified corpus with the smallest KLD contributions between *r/Spirituality* and *r/Psychonaut* reflect discussions about life and death; depression, anxiety, and mental health; and the nature of reality, among others. Through the different modes of comparison, the relationships between these three subreddits is continually amplified as their superficial distinctions are ignored.

We have also seen several stark changes occur over the modes of comparison. The discourse of *r/Philosophy*, while appearing relatively similar to several other subreddits at the word level, appears considerably distant at the more structural level of modified corpus topic distributions. While there is overlap in the usage of individual terms among *r/Philosophy* and other subreddits such as *r/Taoism, r/Awakened, r/Buddhism,* and *r/Christianity*, these resemblances appear mostly superficial—when comparing patterns of word-usage in topic models trained on the original corpus, these resemblances shrink and do so even more severely when comparing topics from the modified corpus. Opposite to the trajectory of *r/Philosophy*, *r/Sikh* appears structurally more similar to several subreddits when comparing topics from the modified corpus than when comparing word distributions or even topics from the original corpus. Thus *r/Sikh* provides an example of a discourse whose relationships to other discourses are quite different between the two topic-level modes.

Given some of the similarities between the two modes of topic-level comparisons, it seems that simply comparing discourses within a topic space already results in more structural comparisons than is the case in the word-level comparisons. However, as noted above in the case of *r/Sikh*, it is not the case that the topic distributions from the modified corpus only provide an amplified (and therefore redundant) picture of the topic distributions from the original corpus. While the directions, positive or negative, of rank changes among 77% of the subreddit pairs are the same in both topic-level modes of comparison, the configuration of the subreddits is considerably different under the modified corpus topic comparisons. While the absolute divergence between subreddits is necessarily less overall under topics from the modified corpus compared to the original corpus, the characterizations we have provided have focused on the relative changes, such as the change in similarity rank or only including edges in the network visualizations for similarities at or above the 70th percentile.

Finally, we have also shown that *r/Spirituality* comprises less distinctive features in comparisons with the other subreddits. In the terminology of [19], we could say that *r/Spirituality* is "enclosed" by the other discourses—it is more general and is always less surprising relative to expectations set by the others. Interestingly, these enclosure relationships are unchanged, even at the deepest level of comparison between topics learned from the modified corpus. In other words, *r/Spirituality* is less distinctive even after forcing all other discourses to be less distinctive as well, implying that it is thematically broad, encompassing, or non-specific at a structural level by comparison.

The current study has several limitations. While we have chosen to investigate one per-word KLD threshold for removing distinguishing terms, a more thorough analysis of how the relationships between discourses change across a range of thresholds would yield more robust insights into the effects this threshold has. Additionally, while the distributional semantics underlying a corpus may remain relatively stable as words are removed, an open question remains to be answered about how much modification a corpus can undergo before its semantic structures become instable and incongruent with its original structure. These limitations will be explored in future work. Additionally, our next steps will include broadening this analysis to a larger set of subreddits to map out the larger religious landscape of Reddit.

6 Conclusion

We have presented an approach to comparative discourse analysis that removes superficial distinctions between discourses in order to facilitate comparisons of their deeper, structural aspects. Our findings suggest that both types of topic-level comparisons we explore offer fundamentally different views into the relationships between discourses compared to word-level comparisons. While similarities exist between comparisons of discourses within the space of LDA models trained on the original corpus and a modified corpus (from which highly distinguishing terms have been removed), the relationships between discourses within the modified corpus topics are substantially different. This suggests that the removal of highly distinguishing terms may uncover differences and similarities between discourses that would be otherwise hidden behind such superficial distinctions.

Acknowledgements. This research is funded in part by the U.S. National Science Foundation (OIA-1946391, OIA-1920920, IIS-1636933, ACI-1429160, and IIS-1110868), U.S. Office of Naval Research (N00014-10-1-0091, N00014-14-1-0489, N00014-15-P-1187, N00014-16-1-2016, N00014-16-1-2412, N00014-17-1-2675, N00014-17-1-2605, N68335-19-C-0359, N00014-19-1-2336, N68335-20-C-0540, N00014-21-1-2121), U.S. Air Force Research Lab, U.S. Army Research Office (W911NF-17-S-0002, W911NF-16-1-0189), U.S. Defense Advanced Research Projects Agency (W31P4Q-17-C-0059), Arkansas Research Alliance, the Jerry L. Maulden/Entergy Endowment at the University of Arkansas at Little Rock, and the Australian Department of Defense Strategic Policy Grants Program (SPGP) (award number: 2020-106-094) to the third co-author, Nitin Agarwal. Any opinions, findings, and conclusions or recommendations expressed in this material are those of the authors and do not necessarily reflect the views of the funding organizations. The researcher gratefully acknowledges the support.

References

1. Prothero, S.: The White Buddhist: The Asian Odyssey of Henry Steel Olcott, 1st edn. Indiana University Press, Indianapolis (1996)

2. Deitrick, J.E.: Engaged buddhist ethics: mistaking the boat for the shore. In: Queen, C., Prebish, C., Keown, D. (eds.) Action Dharma: New Studies in Engaged Buddhism, pp. 252–269, 1st edn. RoutledgeCurzon, New York (2003)
3. Stine, Z.K., Deitrick, J.E., Agarwal, N.: Comparative religion, topic models, and conceptualization: towards the characterization of structural relationships between online religious discourses. In: Karsdrop, F., McGillivray, B., Nerghes, A., Wevers, M. (eds.) Proceedings of the Workshop on Computational Humanities Research (CHR 2020). CEUR Workshop Proceedings. Amsterdam, Netherlands, vol. 2723, pp. 128–148 (2020)
4. Campbell, H.A., Evolvi, G.: Contextualizing current digital religion research on emerging technologies. Human Behav. Emerg. Technol. 2(1), 5–17 (2020). https://doi.org/10.1002/hbe 2.149
5. Lundmark, E., LeDrew, S.: Unorganized atheism and the secular movement: reddit as a site for studying "lived atheism." Social Compass 66(1), 112–129 (2019). https://doi.org/10.1177/0037768618816096
6. Sanders, W.S., Ferré, J.P.: Reader responses to religion news: discussions about ark encounter on reddit. J. Relig. Media Digit. Cult. 9(1), 107–130 (2020). https://doi.org/10.1163/21659214-bja10008
7. Fuller, R.C.: Spiritual, But Not Religious: Understanding Unchurched America, 1st edn. Oxford University Press, New York (2001)
8. Mercadante, L.A.: Belief without Borders: Inside the Minds of the Spiritual but not Religious, 1st edn. Oxford University Press, New York (2014)
9. Drescher, E.: Choosing Our Religion: The Spiritual Lives of America's Nones, 1st edn. Oxford University Press, New York (2016)
10. Jain, A.R.: Peace Love Yoga: The Politics of Global Spirituality, 1st edn. Oxford University Press, New York (2020)
11. Blei, D.M., Ng, A.Y., Jordan, M.I.: Latent Dirichlet allocation. J. Mach. Learn. Res. 3, 993–1022 (2003)
12. Nichols, R., Slingerland, E., Nielbo, K., Bergeton, U., Logan, C., Kleinman, S.: Modeling the contested relationship between Analects, Mencius, and Xunzi: preliminary evidence from a machine-learning approach. J. Asian Stud. 77(1), 19–57 (2018). https://doi.org/10.1017/S0021911817000973
13. Slingerland, E., Nichols, R., Neilbo, K., Logan, C.: The distant reading of religious texts: a "big data" approach to mind-body concepts in early China. J. Am. Acad. Relig. 85(4), 985–1016 (2017). https://doi.org/10.1093/jaarel/lfw090
14. Hall, D., Jurafsky, D., Manning, C.D.: Studying the history of ideas using topic models. In: Proceedings of the Conference on Empirical Methods in Natural Language Processing (EMNLP '08), pp. 363–371. Association for Computational Linguistics, USA (2008)
15. Allen, C., Murdock, J.: LDA topic modeling: contexts for the history & philosophy of science. In: 2020 Preprint of a Chapter to appear in Ramsey, G., De Block, A. (eds.) The Dynamics of Science: Computational Frontiers in History and Philosophy of Science. Pittsburgh University Press; Pittsburgh (2020, forthcoming)
16. Nguyen, D., Liakata, M., DeDeo, S., Eisenstein, J., Mimno, D., Tromble, R., Winters, J.: How we do things with words: analyzing text as social and cultural data. Front. Artif. Intell. 3 (2020). https://doi.org/10.3389/frai.2020.00062
17. Roberts, M.E., Stewart, B.M., Tingley, D.: Navigating the local modes of big data: the case of topic models. In: Alvarez, R.M. (ed.) Computational Social Science: Discovery and Prediction, pp. 51–97. 1st. ed., Cambridge University Press, New York (2016)
18. Thompson, L., Mimno, D.: Authorless topic models: biasing models away from known structure. In: Proceedings of the 27th International Conference on Computational Linguistics, pp. 3903–3914. Association for Computational Linguistics, Santa Fe (2018)

19. Chang, K.K., DeDeo, S.: Divergence and the complexity of differences in text and culture. J. Cult. Anal. **4**(11), 1–36 (2020). https://doi.org/10.22148/001c.17585
20. Klingenstein, S., Hitchcock, T., DeDeo, S.: The civilizing process in London's Old Bailey. PNAS **111**(26), 9419–9424 (2014). https://doi.org/10.1073/pnas.1405984111
21. Gallagher, R.J., Reagan, A.J., Danforth, C.M., Dodds, P.S.: Divergent discourse between protests and counter-protests: #BlackLivesMatter and #AllLivesMatter. PLoS ONE **13**(4), (2018). https://doi.org/10.1371/journal.pone.0195644
22. Stine, Z.K., Agarwal, N.: Comparative discourse analysis using topic models: contrasting perspectives on China from reddit. In: International Conference on Social Media and Society (SMSociety'20), pp. 73–84. Association for Computing Machinery, Toronto (2020). https://doi.org/10.1145/3400806.3400816
23. Sloman, S., Oppenheimer, D., DeDeo, S.: Can we detect conditioned variation in political speech? Two kinds of discussion and types of conversation. PLOS ONE **16**(2), e0246689 (2021). https://doi.org/10.1371/journal.pone.0246689
24. Baumgartner, J., Zannettou, S., Keegan, B., Squire, M., Blackburn, J.: The pushshift reddit dataset. In: Proceedings of the International AAAI Conference on Web and Social Media, vol. 14, pp. 830–839 (2020)
25. Řehůřek, R., Sojka, P.: Software framework for topic modelling with large corpora. In: Proceedings of LREC 2010 Workshop New Challenges for NLP Frameworks, pp. 46–50. University of Malta, Valletta (2010)

On Complexity of GLAMs' Digital Ecosystem: APIs as Change Makers for Opening up Knowledge

Angeliki Tzouganatou(✉) 📵

University of Hamburg, Hamburg, Germany
angeliki.tzouganatou@uni-hamburg.de

Abstract. This paper explores the role of Application Programming Interface, (API), in Galleries, Libraries, Archives and Museums (GLAM) sector, and reflects on its role for opening up cultural digital heritage for inclusive future memory making. It also discusses possibilities of a participatory API ecosystem, going beyond high quality metadata and data interoperability. APIs are often seen as facilitators for opening up knowledge, but when it comes to future memory making, little is known with regards to the power relations that are constructed within the digital ecosystem and how does this influence the interplay. The paper proposes a contribution towards this domain, critically exploring aspects that are facilitating or hindering people's participation for enabling future collective memory making.

Keywords: Digital heritage · Application programming interface · Digital ecosystem · Open knowledge

1   Introduction

The advent of new digital media technologies led to the expansion of the open knowledge movement. Initiatives ranging from a variety of fields (e.g. from Education to Government issues) started advocating for transparency, fairness, empowerment and inclusivity; Open Education, Open Government, Open Source, OpenGLAM (Galleries, Libraries, Archives and Museums), Open Data for Tax Justice etc. The advances of Web 2.0 brought up the potential of the Internet operating in a bidirectional way of communication, as a platform, creating, generating and sharing content by their users. The Internet was inundated with platforms promising to open up access to knowledge. However, there are still many open questions on how open, usable and accessible these platforms are in practice. Platforms are often discussed as driving forces of the digital economy, monopolizing knowledge while creating inequalities [23]. Yet, they should not be seen as solitary digital infrastructures, as their generated value does not come solely by their own activities, but rather, they are part of an ecosystem which is constantly emerging around them, adding value and influencing their activities [4, 10]. Using an ecological lens aid to vividly understand the interconnections, processes and complexities [7, 25] that are being conducted behind the scenes, thus are invisible, however they hold a pivotal position concerning

© Springer Nature Switzerland AG 2021
M. Rauterberg (Ed.): HCII 2021, LNCS 12795, pp. 348–359, 2021.
https://doi.org/10.1007/978-3-030-77431-8_22

knowledge production and ultimately how or what is going to be remembered, which influences thereafter the process of memory making. As infrastructures are both "relational and ecological" [24, p. 377], the sociotechnical elements necessary for their functionality interact in an iterative process [13]. In the digital condition, Application Programming Interfaces (APIs) infrastructures, are located at the center of content diffusion, therefore considered to be "gate-keepers", controlling data dissemination, while affecting future memory making. They are sociotechnical structures enabling software elements to interact to one another and share content, acting as "the underlying technological glue of the social web" [9, p. 4]. In addition, APIs are described as "a set of routines, protocols, and tools for building software applications" [15].

Building upon the growing literature on digital infrastructures and digital media ecologies, this paper will critically explore current API practices with respect to GLAMs, while envisioning emerging concepts towards participatory and inclusive future memory making. Cultural heritage institutions have been grappling for a long time now with digital media technologies for public engagement in an effort to attract and build new audiences [8, 12], nonetheless the discussions now focuses on how can GLAMs open up their collections online in a fair and participatory way. Digitizing artworks and make them available online is not enough anymore. The discussions have been centered around the openness of cultural data, and how it can be meaningfully re-used by the public. Recently adopted by GLAM institutions, Findable, Accessible, Interoperable and Reusable (FAIR) guiding principles [29] and also the Creative Commons licenses and Traditional Knowledge Labels, aim towards an open and fair data ecosystem. Yet, what are the key elements of the digital ecosystem that allowing this to be realized? API holds a prominent position in data access from third parties, allowing different services and applications to exchange information. Critically exploring infrastructural elements like the APIs' interoperability is pivotal in future memory making, as they act as intermediaries for data access between people and institutions.

2 State of the Art

2.1 Platform Ecosystem

During the past decades, GLAMs´ vision to digitize and open up their collections to the public has been at the core of their digital communications strategy. There have been initiatives by private and public aggregators, as well as social media that aided GLAMs in opening up their collections to the wider public. More recently, and particularly owing to the effects of the COVID-19 global pandemic, where the 'digital' has been increasingly interwoven with our everyday life, cultural heritage institutions are increasingly using social media platforms as a means to engage the public with their collections and activities while their premises are closed.

Platforms mediate social and economic interactions online [11], while facilitating multi-sided markets and are a newly predominant type of business model. Although the notion of platforms suggest that they are flat and everyone is equal, they are highly hierarchical structures (e.g. who designs them, who imposes the rules etc.). Today, digital media platforms have become critical infrastructures, as users become dependent on them. Van Dijck, Poell and De Waal [28] distinguishes two categories currently operating in the platform ecosystem; the infrastructural and the sectoral platforms. The first type refers to the platforms owned and operated by Google, Apple, Facebook, Amazon and Microsoft (GAFAM), providing the backbone for the second type; the sectoral [28]. Infrastructural platforms can acquire a lot of power as "all platforms outside of the Big Five constellation are dependent on the ecosystem's infrastructural information services." [28, p. 15]. To this end, the APIs connecting the ecosystem, while capable of facilitating new means of sharing access to data and participating, also provide a means for companies like Facebook to "achieve market dominance, as well as undermine privacy, data security, contextual integrity, user autonomy and freedom" [2] towards new regimes of sharing. By using social media platforms, we are using their APIs. Indisputably, in the often so-called attention economy [3], platforms such as social media networks, are monetizing users' data –actions, preferences, emotions [10]. The 'platformization of the Web' introduced by Anne Helmond, highlights the dominance of platforms as infrastructures and also their prevalent business model, putting APIs as a central point to this effect, and the transformation from social network sites to social media platforms [9].

Moreover, there have been discussions focusing around the current – more prevalent - model of GAFAM APIs that are in favor of the commodification of personal data and people's attention, creating platform monopolies and leading to surveillance capitalism [31]. This research paper takes this issue as a starting point in order to identify some pitfalls of the platform economy and extend this to the GLAM ecosystem, where other questions arise as well.

2.2 GLAM APIs

Considering the recent hype on GLAMs to develop publicly accessible APIs, it is topical to critically explore what are the processes for opening up knowledge in such a way, and how open and participatory this practice is indeed. Although there are different types of APIs concerning their architecture (e.g. REST, SOAP, RPC), the focus here will be in Representational state transfer (REST). In the cultural heritage sector, a REST web API provides "access to the metadata related to digitized cultural heritage objects available on the web" [30, p. 5].

Although APIs are not new, it is only during the last decade that this practice has been explored and adopted by cultural heritage institutions. There have been several initiatives by either GLAMs or cultural heritage aggregators to develop their own API and open up their collection through this emerging mode, bringing a potentiality for new modalities of participation from the audience. To name a few; Trove API [19], DigitalNZ API [5], Harvard Art Museum API [14], Rijksmuseum API [18], Europeana API [30], Finna [1] and a recent addition, that of the Smithsonian Institution API [22]. In February 2020, the Smithsonian Institution released 2.8 million high-resolution artworks from their collections into an open access platform, using their newly developed API.

Indisputably, making cultural digital heritage accessible through an API allow GLAMs to become more than just a portal to cultural heritage, by enabling people's participation [19]. For example, the Finna API, developed by the National Library of Finland and acting as the National Aggregator for Finland, has been used as a hub for innovative ideas created within the Finnish GLAM ecosystem, like the HelsinkiPhotos.fi.

(in Finnish: HelsinkiKuvia.fi[1]). HelsinkiPhotos.fi is a project initiated by the Helsinki City Museum, and is built on Finna API, the national infrastructure.

On the other hand, one of the challenges of a publicly available GLAM API is that it still cannot be actually used by the so-called public, unless they are developers or have coding skills. This means that even though the API is open and publicly available, it requires coding skills, and this is considered to be a hindrance and unlikely to be widely used. In that sense, rather than being socially inclusive, this practice actually excludes user participation, as coding requires specific knowledge and skills. To that respect, research has been conducted by the API expert Jolan Wuyts, as part of his MSc dissertation, on how to present open data and APIs to users with different needs with practical approaches and examples, emphasizing on the importance of API documentation [30]. It is extremely topical and crucial to explore new ways to "democratize" APIs accessibility and usability by a wider audience.

3 Methodology

The present research sought to explore the role of APIs in GLAMs for opening up knowledge. The project´s methodology has taken into account the fluidity of the emerging digital ecosystems, and has implemented qualitative research methods, combining Grounded Theory and Ethnographic approaches, in an effort to grasp and reflect this fluidity, comprising different methods to explore the field. The methodology used implemented qualitative means, including observations and interviews conducted during my fieldwork at the Finnish openGLAM chapter, part of Open Knowledge Finland (OKFI), and also beyond that period. In total, 21 expert interviews were conducted with 23 GLAM experts, social innovators, service designers, API experts and open knowledge activists. The participants were carefully selected for being experts at the intersection of GLAMs, digital technologies, social innovation and opening up knowledge towards fairer practices in the digital economy. The research used Grounded Theory approach, and after the transcription of the interviews, the stage of coding and data analysis took place. This systematic method made it possible to acquire a comprehensive understanding of emerging practices for opening up collections and more specifically, the importance of an API.

Therefore, in order to further explore this complex issue, and as derived from analyzing the data, I proposed a session dedicated on APIs at the Hack4OpenGLAM, part of the Creative Commons Summit 2020. The event titled "Accessing cultural heritage: Approaches from high to low" co-organized with my colleague Quoc-Tan Tran. On this event, GLAMs and cultural heritage aggregators were invited to discuss their own developed APIs, and also critically reflect on the smaller or under-resourced institutions that can't afford to build their own API, discussing ways that they can be part of a larger digital ecosystem. Moreover, more interviews were conducted after this event with a few participants.

---

[1] See the project here: https://www.helsinkikuvia.fi/. Accessed on 10.02.2021.

4 Findings

4.1 Loosen the Control of Cultural Data: Towards a Change of GLAMs Mind-Set

Cultural Heritage Institutions are often seen as reserved when it comes to opening up their collections freely online e.g. under Creative Commons licenses. This is because of two main reasons. GLAMs can have very hierarchal infrastructures, operating in well-established modes, and it is difficult to convince usually the decision makers of the institution, e.g. the board, for the benefits to open up their collections free of copyrights, advocating for the public domain, where possible of course. Indicative of this is the statement of Aki Pohjankyrö, Curator at Helsinki City Museum at the Picture Collections:

> *"I think it's the mind-set and the people. And kind of being able to communicate the benefits to the higher level people who actually make the decisions. I think that is one key thing. (...) the challenge was to communicate the benefits of opening the data to higher level people or like the museum director or the bosses of the departments in the museum."*

In addition to that, many GLAMs are still operating under a business model, which is benefiting and monetizing access to cultural data. This means that if a user wants to acquire a digital copy of an artwork, it is very likely that the GLAM will ask for a fee. Furthermore, another prevalent issue that was emerged during my fieldwork is that GLAMs are still reserved when it comes to opening up their collections online, considering the risks associated by losing control over data. GLAMs need to consider to loosen the control of cultural data, and in order to accomplish this, it requires a change in their mind-set on that. It is difficult for them to give up of the idea that someone might have an art work without any information and context (i.e. metadata), if this is attributed a CC-0 license for example. Indicative of this, is the statement of Hanna-Leena Paloposki, Senior Researcher at the Finnish National Gallery, and I quote:

> *"When you have a CC0 licence, you give free hands, people can do anything with them, without mentioning that is Akseli Gallen-Kallela's Lemminkäinen's Mother, or the original is here. (...) I think that the old-fashioned tradition, or whatever you call it in Museum work is that you have the metadata, and you have all these, and I think that is the idea of controlling, that people had it at first so difficult to think that you could just give out a picture, and someone could use it without knowing even that this is the Finnish painter Gallen-Kallela. (...) So I think there is a kind of controversy, between the traditional museum work and the way of thinking and then this openness. And that is why it takes a lot (of time), and then there has been some fears that somebody would in some way misuse the pictures."*

Indeed GLAMs, are afraid of losing the control over their cultural data, e.g. metadata that are very well curated by the research staff, as it is in their best interest to protect them as much as possible. Moreover, they fear that when opening up their collections online, fewer people will visit their premises. Change of mind-set takes time, especially for organizations such as GLAMs, where often norms of practice, concerns regarding authorship, control and organizational structures including institutional hierarchies persist and can perpetuate tensions with the digital. Mikael Seppälä, a Living Labs Specialist at Laurea University of Applied Sciences, connects the "new type of thinking" as a way to grasp the growing complexity and its relation to openness:

"You need very new type of thinking in order to be able to incorporate growing complexity and being open, because growing complexity requires even more openness than you would be able to deal with. (...) So we need to start creating ways by which we operate in decentralized manners."

Undoubtedly, GLAMs need to start opening-up to maintain relevancy but this will require challenging pre-existing structures, norms and ideas, which can include hierarchical structures and pre-conceptions regarding authorship and control as well [26]. This process necessitates a change of thinking and mind-set.

4.2 (In)Accessibility and Usability of APIs

A question that often comes up concerning the APIs is whom are they addressing, who is the end-user of this product? The current APIs are built by developers and are addressing developers (or at least people who have a solid understanding of coding and of course related advanced skills). Both the API service and its documentation are not made for the "creative users", meaning researchers, Masters' students and generally the often so-called "public". Jolan Wuyts, API expert, Collections Editor and Project Manager in the Collections Engagement team at Europeana, identifies this discrepancy as a crucial challenge:

"The biggest challenge has been to break through in that group of people (the API developers) *that are often also very, very defensive or protective about their product, because it's something that they find very important, that they use every day. (...) But it's a long road to opening that up and making it more accessible for different groups of people."*

The documentation of the service is usually written in a language that only developers would understand, although there have been efforts from GLAMs and aggregators, such as Europeana to "educate" the audience on how non-technical people can use these services, via tutorials and good documentation. Moreover, APIs can be seen as an additional approach to open up collections to "users" rather than "audiences", which at the same time demands further competences. Indisputably, there is a need for translating this knowledge in a more widely understandable language.

4.3 Reciprocity as a Future Opportunity

Reciprocity in terms of APIs, is potentially manifesting in terms of a bidirectional communication between the users and the service, and has been indeed a challenge for institutions. Most GLAMs are really interested in "getting to know" better their end-users and being able to communicate with them in more direct and creative ways, rather than just an email address, building in that sense social models as well, apart from business models. Currently institutions have no information about how their APIs are used for, what they are creating out of it, or if they need any help. Advances towards that direction are taking place as technologies are also moving forward. Susanna Eklund, Service Designer for the National Library of Finland, and particularly the Finna team, highlighted:

> *"It is our users, the API users, so it would be very interesting to hear from them and get to know that social scene as well, because (…) we put a lot of effort into knowing our content providers and that social scene, (…) so we have been trying to create a social model for reaching out and getting the information to go both ways, and give the content providers a feeling that we really are listening to what they need, and want from us. And also we need some kind of good way to reach out to them and get our information over to them."*

4.4 Collaboration Being an Act of Resilience

Another crucial issue that was raised at my fieldwork, is the significance of collaboration and partnerships within the GLAM ecosystem. As seen above, the current digital ecosystem in Europe is dominated by GAFAM [27], creating issues of power relations, and ultimately leading to platforms monopolies. GLAMs are no exception to that, either they actively use digital media platforms, or not, their audience does [17]. An ecological lens acknowledges both living and non-living elements in the nexus, their agency and affect, through complex "technocultural phenomena" [25, p. 8]. It is only through collaborations that the ecosystem can move towards digital sovereignty [6], but also be "open enough" at the same time. This is particularly evident when it comes to the APIs and their models. This point refers to twofold aspects; building and benefiting by a common API infrastructure, and also partnering with other (research) institutions to keep the infrastructure digital life cycle "healthy".

On the one hand, building common API infrastructures, either in a local or national level, provided possibly by aggregators so that even smaller institutions that are lacking resources to build their own API, can benefit from the shared infrastructure. This is evident in many cases, and particularly relevant for the sustainability of the ecosystem, as interested parties can gain from the shared resources that some parties have developed, build upon them and create more services that are open and potentially usable by another party. In that sense, more GLAMs can benefit by the same service, if being part of the same ecosystem. Among other participants, Aki Pohjankyrö, curator at Helsinki City Museum at the Picture Collections shared his opinion on this issue:

> *"Helsinki Photos it's built on Finna API. (..) when we did our own service HelsinkiKuvia.fi we didn't break from the national infrastructure. We actually built it on the national infrastructure. So we are a part of it. And we're in a dialogue with them because it would have been different if we would have just said that, we forget about Finna and we built this own service for our digital collections. (…) I think it was better to be on that common (infrastructure) (…) because we benefit from the dialogue and then maybe some other museums who are in Finna, they*

could take that Helsinki Kuvia source code. It's open source (...) and so basically, any Finna organization could make their own version of Helsinki Kuvia."

On the other hand, and along the same lines, collaboration could be seen from the side of partnerships, as an act of resilience for the sustainability of the API infrastructure, and if extending it- for the wider GLAM digital ecosystem as well. Many GLAMs have incorporated in their strategy evaluation methods to assess the impact of their API; who is using it, why they are using it and what are they developing with it, in an effort to improve the user experience and "get to know" their audience better. Cultural heritage institutions have been partnering up with research organisations, e.g. Universities or schools, to help them evaluate the experience and understand the end-users. In that respect for example, the Smithsonian Institution has collaborated with Parsons School of Design, The New School, to help evaluate their API-end users. Ryan King, Program Manager, Open Access Initiative Office, at the Smithsonian Institution mentioned:

"We've been fortunate to work with Parsons School of Design, and their Masters of Data Visualization program this year. And for all of their class projects, they've been using our API to dive in and pass through our collections from a variety of different lenses and perspectives and topics. And that feedback we received from them has been very informative and helpful. And in terms of, you know (...), the API is very just kind of version 1.0 right now. And so it's been nice to see and hear ways (in which) we can improve both the types of data that we're releasing and how they're kind of pulled together in buckets right now, both through the API and on GitHub."

5   Discussion

As this current research is part of the EU-funded Participatory Memory Practices (POEM) project, it is significant to share some critical reflections on the GLAM APIs through the lenses of the POEM goals, shedding light on how the project goals are aligned with what was discussed above, in the previous Findings section. POEM explores concepts, strategies and media infrastructures for envisioning socially inclusive potential futures of European societies through culture.

How do POEM research goals align with the proposed concept? At the heart of POEM lies openness, accessibility and social inclusion, which means the experimentation with fairer practices so that the digital ecosystem becomes more participatory.

5.1   Openness

APIs are indeed seen as change makers for the digital ecosystem interconnecting different parties involved while making it possible for new opportunities of sharing and participation to be realized. Openness is a quality that is linked with this type of infrastructure. While not inherently linked at first, in order to be able for the ecosystem to be sustainable and be maintained, while incorporating growing complexity, openness is necessary. Being open means also in organisational terms; the mode of sharing, collaborating, participating.

Furthermore, it refers to the openness of cultural heritage knowledge for the public. This is seen as an emerging way for opening up the collections online. The definition of open knowledge, provided by Open Knowledge International, is "any content, information or data that people are free to use, re-use and redistribute" [16]. The close link between open knowledge and open data is successfully explained as follows "open data are the building blocks of open knowledge. Open knowledge is what open data becomes when it's useful, usable and used" [16]. Therefore, being open should mean having the capability of being re-used and remixed as a central notion, that it is also possible to change; that is possible for someone else, to build upon, to pick up and carry on.

5.2 Accessibility

As discussed above, meaningful participation between the wider public and the GLAMs through the APIs can't be truly realized at the moment, at least at a large scale. People with no coding background are often intimidated to attempt accessing an API, as they consider lacking the necessary skills[2]. This is indeed most pertinent for cultural heritage practitioners, who usually have a Humanities research background and not (extensive) IT knowledge and skills. How could this gap be bridged? What does it require so that the APIs could be used directly by the public? Who is using the API, and who is often envision to be the end-user? In an effort for (possibly) any product or infrastructure to be able to meet the needs of their audience and be actually usable and useful for them, it needs to be created by design for them, tailored to their needs. Therefore, and as seen above, much work needs to be done in order for the API to be usable by the wider public, and hence be considered "a public infrastructure" in that sense. Incremental steps should be taken place with regards to a development of a framework for opening up APIs documentation for the wider public [30]. Moreover, it should be taken into consideration the need for shifting the target audience when designing an API, in an effort to start a dialogue for democratizing its potential use.

5.3 Social Inclusion

GLAMs have been striving to be inclusive and leaving behind the Ivory Tower to be open for the communities that are serving. However, when it comes to APIs there is still much room for improvement. How could APIs be more inclusive, and more participatory, enabling the creative participation from the audience? This directs towards two crucial points: the design practices and operational practices. The first aspect, the design practice and process, asks 'who designs the API?', whereas the operational practice asks 'who is using it?' As seen above, in both cases the answer is the developers. In this paper, I propose that the design practices need to be more inclusive towards people, and human-centered design for enabling meaningful participation. I advocate for the importance of all the GLAM's departments to work together to design the API. Then this is the way for altering the mind-set, collaboratively in a participatory sense, where all the stakeholders

---

[2] For more approaches on what access and accessibility mean, please see the contribution by Cassandra Kist and Quoc-Tan Tran on this volume, titled "Breaking boundaries, creating connectivities: Enabling access to digitized museum collections".

will be involved in an effort to co-design an infrastructure that would be potentially more open and inclusive.

Moreover, APIs are not only about the providers to generate value, but also what the users need and want. A human-centered design should lie at the heart of it, in an effort to be inclusive by design. Community or individual empowerment when it comes to memory work is critical. Decentralized forms of design practices that begin from grassroots, the communities, for collective memory making, need further exploration. It is with the combination of these tree qualities, openness, accessibility and social inclusion, that we could be able to envision a future collective memory.

Furthermore, another key concept which is linked to my PhD research, and with POEM goals in large, is the exploration of new economic and social models for the digital cultural heritage sector. An open API, by design socially inclusive, offers the opportunity for new apps to be developed and opportunities to be prospered linking open cultural data with the knowledge economy and to the creative industries as well, creating new streams of revenue and relevant engagement. Advocating also for reciprocity as a central point, so that the possibility of meaningful participation could be enabled. In that sense a meaningful bidirectional relationship between the digital infrastructures and their audiences [20] could be formed, in order to enable meaningful participation of non-professionals in heritage interpretation and process [21] towards digital infrastructures for the pubic engagement.

From an ecological perspective, it is crucial to move from hierarchical models, to fairer models that are human-centered, towards people and groups, in decentralized and distributed forms. In this respect, human-centered meaning both "public" centered, and also centered around the staff of an organization, their stakeholders, centered to their needs, empowering them, "protecting them" in a sense, encouraging them to be self-driven while fostering collaboration. The change of mind-set is at the core of this. Another point is that APIs are located at the center of content diffusion, and are controlling knowledge production while acting as an intermediary, or facilitator, for what or how something would be remembered. This is particularly relevant for memory modalities, a concept being developed by POEM that explores the different modalities for memory making in the digital memory ecosystem. Emerging models for a sustainable digital ecosystem enabling people's active and creative participation, in all the stages of this process.

On the other hand, digital media platforms are not neutral - API governance is of utmost importance to identify and secure related policies. Rather than a centralized API model, a distributed model, capable of incorporating adaptive governance is preferable. GLAMs should identify their API strategy and related policies to meet the needs of their organizations' mission and towards equitable practices.

It should be also highlighted that APIs need resources to be realized, built, developed and maintained. Not all GLAMs have this opportunity, as mentioned above, and there are many under-resourced cultural institutions that can't afford to actively develop and sustain an API. Such institutions could part of a larger ecosystem, where they could benefit by the resources shared there.

6 Conclusion

To conclude, APIs can be seen as change makers when it comes to opening up knowledge, while allowing new possibilities to be flourished; enhancing the creative reuse of cultural data, towards a participatory manner, e.g. innovative applications can be developed fostering the creative industries. Nonetheless, in order for this to be realized to their full potential, several improvements could be accomplished, as discussed above. APIs are complex sociotechnical interfaces acting as hubs between the audience and GLAMs, for data dissemination and abstracting complexity. Consequently, this affects knowledge production and ultimately what is going to be remembered, and also perhaps how. Indisputably, the potential of openness and open knowledge in the GLAM sector is immense, and indeed the APIs can become one way to manifest that by encouraging meaningful public participation and fostering synergies.

In addition, it is timely to address the call for a more equitable and fair model in the digital economy of big data. By envisioning beyond merely the current prevalent GAFAM API models, which are in favor of the commodification of data and attention, there is a need to explore models for social inclusion and public good. The "fight for digital sovereignty" [6, p. 371] is not a new issue, yet it is more than ever topical, particularly for the battle against power asymmetries, monopolies and control over the ownership of data. Therefore, new API models are needed, being capable of fostering meaningful participation, and be inclusive by design, integrating interested parties and relevant stakeholders in all the stages of design, development and evaluation. Building human-centered models by design, offering the capability of embracing more openness and the distribution of power, placing the human at the core of the ecosystem. In such a way, the potentiality of a social inclusive API ecosystem nurturing participation could finally be untapped apropos to social inclusion.

Acknowledgments. This work is part of the POEM (Participatory Memory Practices) project and has received funding from the European Union's Horizon 2020 research and innovation program under the Marie Skłodowska-Curie grant agreement No. 764859. I would like to thank Prof. Dr. Gertraud Koch, Cassandra Kist, Jennifer Krueckeberg and Quoc-Tan Tran for insightful conversations on drafts of this paper. Also, I would like to thank Sophia Mirashrafi for reviewing this paper.

References

1. Avoindata.fi: Finna. https://www.opendata.fi/data/en_GB/dataset/finna. Accessed 10 Feb 2021
2. Bodle, R.: Regimes of sharing. Inf. Commun. Soc. **14**(3), 320–337 (2011). https://doi.org/10.1080/1369118X.2010.542825
3. Celis Bueno, C.: The Attention Economy. Labour, Time and Power in Cognitive Capitalism. Critical Perspectives on Theory, Culture and Politics. Rowman & Littlefield International, New York (2017)
4. Cusumano, M.A., Gawer, A., Yoffie, D.B.: The Business of Platforms. Strategy in the Age of Digital Competition, Innovation, and Power. HarperCollins Publishers, New York (2019)
5. DigitalNZ: Developers. https://digitalnz.org/developers. Accessed 10 Feb 2021

6. Floridi, L.: The Fight for digital sovereignty: what it is, and why it matters, especially for the EU. Philos. Technol. **33**(3), 369–378 (2020). https://doi.org/10.1007/s13347-020-00423-6
7. Fuller, M.: Media Ecologies. Materialist Energies in Art and Technoculture. MIT Press, Cambridge, Leonardo (2005)
8. Giaccardi, E.: Heritage and Social Media. Understanding Heritage in a Participatory Culture, 1st edn. Routledge, New York (2012). Edited by Elisa Giaccardi
9. Helmond, A.: The platformization of the web: making web data platform ready. Soc. Med. + Soc. **1**(2), 205630511560308 (2015). https://doi.org/10.1177/2056305115603080
10. Jordan, T.: The Digital Economy. Polity, Cambridge, Medford (2020)
11. Kenney, M., Zysman, J.: The rise of the platform economy. Issues Sci. Technol. **32**(3), 61–69 (2016)
12. Kidd, J.: Enacting engagement online: framing social media use for the museum. Inf. Technol. People **24**(1), 64–77 (2011). https://doi.org/10.1108/09593841111109422
13. Koch, G.: Ethnography of digital infrastructures. In: Koch, G. (ed.) Koch, Gertraud 2017: Ethnography of Digital Infrastructures. Gertraud Digitisation: Theories and Concepts for Empirical Cultural Research, pp. 78–91. Routledge, London & New York (2017)
14. Ledesma, A.: How We Learned to Stop Worrying and Love Open Data: A Case Study in the Harvard Art Museums' API (2016). https://medium.com/@andrea_ledesma/how-we-lea rned-to-stop-worrying-and-love-open-data-a-case-study-in-the-harvard-art-museums-api-893c3f40ecb7. Accessed 23 Dec 2020
15. Norton, K.: API Definition & Meaning (2020). https://www.webopedia.com/definitions/api/. Accessed 23 Dec 2020
16. Open Knowledge Foundation: What is open? https://okfn.org/opendata/. Accessed 10 Feb 2021
17. Proctor, N.: Digital: museum as platform, curator as champion, in the age of social media. Curator: Museum J. **53**(1), 35–43 (2010). https://doi.org/10.1111/j.2151-6952.2009.00006.x
18. Rijksmuseum: RijksData (2021). https://data.rijksmuseum.nl/
19. Sherratt, T.: From portals to platforms: building new frameworks for user engagement (2013). https://www.nla.gov.au/our-publications/staff-papers/from-portal-to-platform#
20. Simon, N.: The participatory museum. Museum 2.0, Santa Cruz, California (2010)
21. Simon, N.: The art of relevance. Museum 2.0, Santa Cruz (California) (2016)
22. Smithsonian Institute: Open Access Developer Tools. https://www.si.edu/openaccess/dev tools. Accessed 10 Feb 2021
23. Srnicek, N.: Platform Capitalism. Theory Redux. Polity, Cambridge, Malden (2017)
24. Star, S.L.: The ethnography of infrastructure. Am. Behav. Sci. **43**(3), 377–391 (1999). https://doi.org/10.1177/00027649921955326
25. Taffel, S.: Digital Media Ecologies. Entanglements of Content, Code and Hardware. Bloomsbury Publishing, New York (2019)
26. Tan, L.: Museums and cultural memory in an age of networks. Int. J. Cult. Stud. **16**(4), 383–399 (2013). https://doi.org/10.1177/1367877912460615
27. van Dijck, J.: Governing digital societies: private platforms, public values. Comput. Law Secur. Rev. **36**, 105377 (2020). https://doi.org/10.1016/j.clsr.2019.105377
28. van Dijck, J., Poell, T., Waal, M. de: The Platform Society. Oxford University Press. Oxford Scholarship Online (2018). https://doi.org/10.1093/oso/9780190889760.001.0001
29. Wilkinson, M.D., et al.: The FAIR guiding principles for scientific data management and stewardship. Sci. Data **3**, 160018 (2016). https://doi.org/10.1038/sdata.2016.18
30. Wuyts, J.: Cultivating APIs in the cultural heritage sector. Master's dissertation, kU Leuven (2018)
31. Zuboff, S.: The Age of Surveillance Capitalism. The Fight for a Human Future at the New Frontier of Power. PublicAffairs, New York (2019)

Perspectives on Cultural Computing

Appropriation for Interdisciplinary Practice: The Case of Participatory Design in Brazilian Computer Science

Bernardo Alves Villarinho Lima$^{(\boxtimes)}$ ⓘ and Leonelo Dell Anhol Almeida ⓘ

Programa de Pós-Graduação em Tecnologia e Sociedade (PPGTE), Universidade
Tecnológica Federal do Paraná (UTFPR),
Av. Sete de Setembro, 3165, Curitiba, Paraná 80230-901, Brazil
berlim@alunos.utfpr.edu.br, leoneloalmeida@utfpr.edu.br

Abstract. Partner community participation in design enables the exploration of design spaces which could not be reached without partner knowledge and expertise, and also enables partner communities to exercise their personal power to influence technological change towards their own wants and needs. Participatory Design (PD) is an approach that since its inception seeks to build spaces of democratic technological change through practices with (rather than for) partner communities. From its origin in Scandinavia, the approach has been adopted by multiple academic communities around the world, and those adoptions have demanded changes to the underlying theories and methodologies to fit them into each different local reality, a process of appropriation which has transformed PD over the decades. As an example of a region which adopted and adapts PD, Latin America has specific epistemological and methodological challenges which emerge from historical and socioeconomic conditions, and in the context of the region, interdisciplinary practices have been discussed and applied in the context of partner participation in design. Considering the importance of academic communities for the advancement of PD towards meaningful changes to partner communities, this paper presents a systematic overview of PD in Brazilian Computer Science as an instance of such community. The study surveys articles from 2000 to 2020, seeking to expose how Brazilian PD operates in the region through the use of interdisciplinary referential. We expect that this contribution elucidates adaptation strategies of PD referential towards their appropriation by communities diverse from those the techniques were originally designed for, so that practitioners from other regions can discuss those strategies when adapting PD to the needs of their partners.

Keywords: Participatory design · Human-computer interaction · Interaction design · Latin American cultural studies.

This study was financed in part by the Coordenação de Aperfeiçoamento de Pessoal de Nível Superior - Brasil (CAPES) - Finance Code 001 and by the National Council for Scientific and Technological Development (CNPq). Project: 40106120191; Code: #141847/2020-4.

M. Rauterberg (Ed.): HCII 2021, LNCS 12795, pp. 363–386, 2021.
https://doi.org/10.1007/978-3-030-77431-8_23

1   Introduction

Since its origin in the 1970s, Participatory Design (PD) has been widely adopted by practitioners worldwide [76]. The approach was pioneered under the assumption that technology and technical change are inherently political [18], involving conflicts between groups who would be affected – benefited or threatened – from the introduction of new technology in work and living spaces and those who would not [31]. Early research on the approach presented goals of shifting technological change towards the needs of the people who would be most affected by it [54], enacting design processes that explicitly sided with its partner communities towards the improvement of their quality of life [79]. Over half a century of history, PD has sought to promote, among other agendas, empowerment and partner decision-making in design and action research [78].

However, as PD research and development communities changed their interests, the approach was also modified to enable the pursuit of diverse emergent agendas [78], including agendas which use participation for purposes other than Democratic Empowerment. An example of such agenda is the promotion of Functional Empowerment as discussed in the 1990s [25], which focuses on the development of artefacts with which users would be better at doing their jobs, rather than changing the power structures and spaces of work. Participation of persons who are not part of the design team, thus, has the potential of forwarding different agendas for different objectives, employing participant experience and creativity to enable design teams to achieve improvements none of the two parts could build alone [46]. State-of-the-art participatory design techniques and practices pursue the potential of exploring design spaces *other* than the ones designers are biased towards in different locations around the world, enabling rich discussions about how PD is transformed when used in each new location, with each new partner community [24, 27].

The epistemological and methodological debate of changes in participation and agendas is topical for PD academia. In 2020, the 16th Participatory Design Conference (PDC 2020) had *"Participations Otherwise"* as the theme for its call for papers [27]. The theme incentives the discussion of the role of alterities in participation, and opened a debate – in a historical opening of the conference to works in languages other than English, in order to enable Latin American communities to submit works – about how PD is practised differently in developing territories such as Latin America, and how the developing contexts present unique creative potentials for devising unique contributions in PD.

Researchers can plan for the appropriation of PD techniques in their local context, adapting them for a better fitting with their own agendas, issues and concerns. Strategies for appropriation relate to how participatory practices can be modified in their planning in order to create original spaces for participatory decision making with communities that may be different from the ones the practices were proposed for and with. Among academic communities that practice PD in Latin America, Brazilian Computer academia has a history of appropriating the approach and adapting participatory practices to diverse local contexts using multiple theoretical and methodological referential in novel ways [5, 73].

An Example of how processes of appropriation has occurred in Latin America is presented in outside Design and Computing, by Martín-Barbero's *appropriation strategies* [45] in technical communication, an interdisciplinary dialogue with Latin American Cultural Studies can be strategic for studying how the approach is transformed as it's applied in new locations.

This paper presents a systematic overview of PD in Brazilian Computer Science from 2000 to 2020, and exposes how Brazilian PD operates through the use of interdisciplinary referential (e.g. PD informed by Popular Education by Paulo Freire [35], and PD used in conjunction with Organisational Semiotics [65]). The overview aims to present original and characteristic constructions in the region towards solving local problems. This discussion also approaches how interdisciplinary theory and practice were appropriated by the Brazilian community along with Computer Science towards democratic dialogue spaces through participation in design. Based on the reviewed works we summarise actions to support researchers in setting project agendas and methodologies that have a fitting to partner communities in the Global South[1], and we expect that by presenting processes of appropriation towards democratic technologies, communities from other areas and regions considered "dependent" can critically adapt theoretical and methodological constructs from other regions.

This paper is organised as follows: Sect. 2 presents the method of the systematic study, including procedures for survey and analysis; Sect. 3 presents the findings of this study; Sect. 4 presents discussions regarding the appropriations of PD surveyed, including the perspectives of PD with visible designers, and the pursuit of digital and social inclusion among the findings and how those perspectives have the potential to change the practice towards political engagement and the mitigation of real social issues; Sect. 5 presents the conclusions of the study and opportunities for future work.

2   Method

The discussion of appropriation in Brazilian PD and its implications for academic work on the approach begins by systematically reviewing the community's scientific production in PD. Thus, as a starting point, we have conducted a systematic literature review (SLR), the method is structured as presented by Kitchenham [42] and draws from examples of instances by Brereton et al. [21] and by Kitchenham et al. [43]. The method presented herein differentiates from

---

[1] Considering the North/South divide presented by Santos and Meneses [67]. The Global south is a region of epistemic challenges related to the colonial and capitalist expansion which hampered its relation with the rest of the world. This conception of Global North-South partially overlaps with the notion of Geographic north and south, and considers as South only the regions that were submitted to European colonialism, and that did not achieve socioeconomic development levels comparable to developed countries in Europe and North America. The global south is, thus, separated from the North by a history of dependency relations, where the South is considered peripheries, and the North is considered the centre.

the SLR review due to its procedure of analysis, which has a qualitative focus. The SLR works we presented as examples respond to research questions by devising indicators for quality of the works, however, the metrics of quality of a PD article and project are unclear since each contribution has the potential to pursue a different agenda and has different community engagements and responses. In this study we survey peer reviewed articles so that the criteria of quality are based on the scientific community where each article was published. Considering the objectives of this study, the research questions which guide the methodology are:

Q1 How does Brazilian PD community in Computing define its approach?

   Q1.1 What materials are referenced by the community?

Q2 What issues and themes does the community approach with PD?

Q3 What are the PD techniques and practices employed by the community?

   Q3.1 Are the techniques adapted? How and why research groups adapt them to their contexts?

Q1 and Q1.1 can be answered by analysing each reviewed work's methodology. Through the referenced text, we can investigate whether the reviewed project's agenda is similar to or differs from the source of its methodology.

Q2 relates to each reviewed work's objectives and theoretical foundations, as they relate to research problems in PD history, such as disempowerment [19] or the need to design better computer artefacts [13,47].

Q3 and Q3.1 also relate to the reviewed works' methodology, but represent a differential of this review from other mappings of PD such as the one written by Muller et al. [47]. Beyond presenting community trends on applying techniques, this mapping also means to present the adaptations of the technique to local scenarios. Adaptations can be identified by comparing the reviewed work with the original proposal of the technique that was referenced in the text.

The review was meant to be exhaustive of published Brazilian PD practice in international libraries and scientific publications focused in Computing and HCI. The survey and review procedures were conducted in Digital Libraries: the ACM Digital Library[2]; IEEE Xplore[3]; and Springer Link[4]. The search procedure sought works of Brazilian affiliations which were about "Participatory design", "co-design", "codesign" or "contextual design", the Portuguese words for the two terms[5] were also added to search strings even though the three libraries are mostly indexed in English. The last automatic search was made for this study in October 20th, 2020. The search strings used for each of the three libraries are presented as follows:

– ACM:

```
"query": { Affiliation:(Brasil OR Brazil) AND AllField:
("participatory design" OR "co-design" OR "contextual design"
OR "codesign") } "filter": { ACM Content: DL }
```

---

[2] http://dl.acm.org.

[3] http://ieeexplore.ieee.org/.

[4] https://link.springer.com/.

[5] "Design Participativo" and "Design Contextual".

- IEEE:

```
((("Author Affiliations":Brazil) OR ("Author Affiliations":Brasil))
AND ("Participatory Design" OR "co-design" OR "codesign" OR
"Contextual Design"))
```

- Springer Link[6]:

```
("Participatory Design" OR "co-design" OR "codesign"
OR "Contextual Design") AND ("Brazil" OR "Brasil")
```

Additionally to the Digital Libraries, we have also reviewed relevant events for PD and for Brazilian Human-Computer Interaction (HCI): the Biannual International Conference on Participatory Design (PDC), surveyed separately in order to include early works not indexed as well as the plurilingual articles in the Volume 3 of the 2020 edition of PDC, which presents recently published research reports which are representative of Brazilian PD state-of-the-art – and are not indexed in the ACM Digital Library as of the writing of this study; and the Brazilian Symposium of Human Factors in Computing Systems (IHC), whose early editions were not indexed in the three surveyed digital libraries, though the IHC search did not provide any additional relevant results.

This study has the three following inclusion criteria: (i1) full works representing completed research, teaching and/or extension projects; (i2) published in peer reviewed academic Computer Science communications; and (i3) presenting research about PD where at least one author has Brazilian affiliation. This study also had two exclusion criteria: (e1) works not involving partner communities were excluded (e.g. texts about PD history, reviews such as this text, and proposals of techniques without case studies); and (e2) works not in Portuguese, English, or Spanish were not considered for analysis. The review selected and analysed 77 works, all of them were considered primary studies for the interest of surveying Brazilian PD, and there was no selection of secondary studies.

The extraction of the data involved reading of all the works. The research questions directed the analysis procedure towards qualitative analysis of the works, since each work presents an instance of a community appropriating PD referential, techniques and practices towards their own and their partner's goals. The analysis procedure is inspired by the *epistemological survey* presented by DiSalvo et al. [29], where for each primary study, the research team attempts to respond to every one of the research questions. The questions used for this surveying process are instantiated versions of Q1, Q2, Q3 and their sub-questions, and an overview of appropriations of PD in Brazilian Computer Science was constructed from instancing the research questions in every reviewed work. The data extracted from each article were: (1) title; (2) abstract; (3) keywords; (4) research questions and issues (for addressing Q1 and Q2); (5) PD techniques and

---

[6] This library did not feature an affiliation filter, works on that library were filtered manually for affiliation among the ones that had mentioned Brazil in any element of their text.

practices applied and adapted in the work (For addressing Q3 and Q3.1); and (6) references used in defining PD as an approach (for addressing Q1.1).

Discussion on the research questions of this study are aided by Martín-Barbero's category of *appropriation* [45]: through interpreting technical texts and re-contextualising them in their local realities, researchers from the Global South can advance theory and practice towards research issues that are relevant to their own local communities. This innovation can be divergent from advancements in global and international communities, since they are constructed upon localised ways of thinking and acting. The discussion in this studies seek to enumerate the appropriation strategies in the studied community, which direct the practice towards interdisciplinary methods for participation, through the use of referential in diverse disciplines.

3   Findings

The review's findings suggest that Brazilian PD in Computing community has a tendency towards agendas for accessibility, digital inclusion and social inclusion. This points to a difference in community goals when compared to the mapping of the PDC community by Halskov and Hansen [37]. Matters of accessibility extend towards making the practices themselves accessible to diverse partner communities [75] and affording informed and relevant decision-making about technologies in design [49,50]. Table 1 present the counts of works investigated in the systematic review, indicating that PD research is an emergent field in Brazilian Computing, with an increasing number of publications in peer-reviewed scientific sources.

Table 1. Survey *Corpus*: peer-reviewed scientific papers with PD practices in Computer Science with Brazilian affiliations, grouped by source and year of publication.

Library	Before 2005	2006–2010	2011–2015	2016–2020	Total
ACM	1	10	17	25	53
IEEE	0	0	6	5	11
Springer Link	0	1	5	1	7
PDC (before indexed events)	1	–	–	–	1
PDC 2020 (volume 3)	–	–	–	5	5
Total surveyed works	2	11	28	36	77

Methodologically, the proposition of original PD techniques presents itself as an important agenda. Out of 19 articles that propose new techniques for PD practice, more than half are motivated by the need to make the design process inclusive to people with low or no literacy (including digital literacy) and other factors that would hinder them from accessing and using computer technologies. Disability rarely relates to those adaptations (an example of practice idealised towards persons with disability in an example of finding in this study [20]). Participatory project *e-Cidadania* (also published as e-Citizenship in English-language publications) shows many examples of techniques for PD proposed towards participants with multiple levels of literacy and digital literacy [6]. The adaptations presented in this study have the potential to propose practices and agendas that are inclusive of diverse partner communities, and can be applied as strategies for the critical use of foreign referential from the North in Global Southern contexts, leading a discussion of strategies for appropriations for interdisciplinary PD in the community.

3.1   Addressing Q1: Foundations of PD in the Surveyed Works

This subsection exposes findings regarding the research question *(Q1)* on how Brazilian PD community define its approach, addressing the question through *(Q1.1)* theoretical ground presented in the surveyed works. Table 2 presents the texts cited in definitions of PD in the reviewed works. The works of Schuler and Namioka [70] (cited in 9 contributions) and Muller et al. (cited in 10 contributions) [47] are the most frequently adopted for defining the approach, however both texts are collections of different principles and design agendas. Schuler and Namioka [70] presented PD as an approach with many different meanings for many people, and Muller et al. [47] also consider that there is no consensus about what defines PD, however present principles which are characteristic of the approach (Democracy; Efficiency, Expertise and Quality; Participant Buy-In). Both texts reference literature from many locations (e.g. Scandinavia [14], United States [40] and Brazil, which is referenced in the field of politics [17]) in order to define the approach. Both works present PD as more than a means to develop better systems, and both present considerations about the importance of design *with* partner communities. Rocha and Baranauskas [62] are also cited as a theoretical foundation, the author's text is featured in a Brazilian textbook on HCI, and define PD through the use of both Schuler and Namioka [70] and Muller et al. [47].

The most cited text which presents a definition of PD as an approach is Muller's discussion of the approach as a means to explore *hybrid design domains*, which are not in the domain of any of the stakeholders – be they designers, domain experts, and other stakeholders [46]. The text does not prescribe techniques or political agendas that qualify contributions as being PD, except that they always intend to explore this space.

Baranauskas [12] proposes *Semio-Participatory Design*, an Interaction Design model which considers "interpretative, social and communicative" [12, p.38] aspects of HCI. The proposal of this approach includes agenda considerations that turn design towards a society designed *for all* [12, p.40]. This model builds on Organisational Semiotics as an epistemological referential and considers participatory practices as iterative and interactive, involving the production of meaning and interpretations by stakeholders in steps of design. *Semio-Participatory Design* practices are presented in the *e-Cidadania* project, which involved workshops during the development of an inclusive social network, presented in the survey in the following works: [4,6,38,51]. Bjerknes and Brat-

Table 2. Referenced texts in definitions of PD in the study.

Reference text	Occurrences
Works that present only references for techniques, not for PD as an approach	30
References cited once	21
Muller et al. [47]	10
Schuler and Namioka [70]	9
Muller [46]	5
Rocha and Baranauskas [62]	4
Baranauskas et al. [12]	3
Sanders [66]	3
Björgvinsson et al. [16]	2
Bjerknes and Bratteteig [15]	2
Simonsen and Robertson [76]	2

teteig [15] as well as Björgvinsson et al. [16] were also cited as foundations for the PD practices in the surveyed works.

3.2   Addressing Q2 and Q3: Themes and Practices in the Surveyed Works

This subsection reports findings relevant to discussing the research questions *(Q2)* regarding research problems and themes Brazilian Computing community approaches with PD and *(Q3)* regarding which PD techniques and practices the community employs, *(Q3.1)* including how and why are they adapted to fit into their local contexts. The surveyed works were classified based on their use and proposition of PD techniques. The classification is proposed based on a systematic review about collaborative systems evaluation by Santos et al. [68], in which the revision *corpus* presented contributions featuring new method proposals and also works which used existent and adapted methods. The contributions were classified as:

- **New techniques (27 contributions)**: the category includes contributions whose objective is specifically proposing new techniques for PD (e.g. [77] and [2]), works featuring the proposition of frameworks which prescribe participatory practices in any of its phases (e.g. [44] and [74]) are also included in this classification;
- **Adaptations and extensions of existing techniques (11 contributions)**: includes works that carry on participatory practices through adapted or extended techniques along with other Interaction Design methods (e.g. [39] and [75]). The extensions differentiate from propositions by the goals set by the authors of each work being analysed. If the objective of the work (as presented in its abstract and introduction section) is to present a novel

theoretical-methodological set, the work was classified as a new technique, otherwise it was classified as an extension;

- **Works which use or combine existing techniques (26 contributions)**: considers works which instance PD techniques without explicating whether alterations on procedures were carried over or not. Through this classification, we can identify tendencies of methodological referential use by the community;
- **Works that do not expose which techniques were used or referenced (13 contributions)**: includes works which only mention that PD was used, not presenting citation of texts defining the approach or precise definitions of which techniques were instantiated. Contributions in this classification were not considered for analysis since they provide insufficient information about how PD integrates their methodology.

Table 3 presents the contributions listed as *new techniques*. The works are presented in a taxonomy inspired by Muller et al. [47], presenting specifications of the technique in the terms: of the materials required by the practices; how many participants and recommended roles and profiles; expected results of the proposed technique; which phase of the development cycle this technique can be integrated. The tabulation of techniques also surveyed the motivations and justifications for proposing techniques presented in the contributions.

Out of all proposals presented in the study, we observe an increasing number of new techniques being proposed. Out of 36 works surveyed in the 2016–2020 period, 18 were proposals of new techniques for PD which involved partner communities during their development. This count represents an emerging trend of the Brazilian PD in Computing community towards identifying synergies of PD principles with local issues, without importing the principles as a closed methodological package. The community contributes with localised efforts towards promoting partner well-being in accordance to recent PD agendas presented in international publications by authors from the Global North (e.g. Participatory Design that Matters [11,18] and Participation in Design Things [32]).

Moreover, the findings do not reveal uncritical imports of those agendas. Contributions leverage referential that is locally researched, for instance, Popular Education (e.g. the use of Paulo Freire as a motivator for starting a PD project by Serpa et al. [72]) and Design Anthropology, which although has an origin in the Global North has been appropriated by Latin American scientific community through the use of concepts from Latin American Anthropology (e.g. Ibarra [41] presents a proposal of design towards correspondence using Arturo Escobar's work as a referential).

Considering the number of techniques presented in the survey, it was possible to also identify themes of accessibility and digital inclusion as motivators for proposing new techniques, however by appraising the date of publication of each paper in Table 3, two different movements emerge in the studied community. Proposals around the decades of 2000 and 2010 presented in this study show a tendency to focus on the universal access of knowledge through information and communication technologies [55].

Table 3. Techniques for participatory practice proposed in the surveyed works.

ID	Materials	Participants	Results	Phase	Why participate?
[81]	Pen, paper, stickers	16 experts	Visualising challenges, opportunities	Composing research agenda	PD is an emerging trend in Learning Analytics
[77]	Describes many activities (e.g. PICTIVE, forms)	Unspecified	Making games for therapeutic use	Whole life cycle	The design of therapeutic games require interdisciplinary understanding of player needs
[20]	Unspecified	One user, three health professionals, three designers	The design of customized systems for a specific user with motor disability	Whole life cycle	Participation is a diferential for the co-design of customised artifacts, promoting use according to specific needs of the partner
[73]	Unspecified	Unspecified	The design of serious games for health education	Requirements and prototyping	Popular education contributes to building a just society, as PD promotes empowerment
[8]	Cardboard, pictures of artefacts and work situations	6 health professionals	An artefact representing the workflow of every participant	Requirements	PD has the potential to assist the development of design patterns involving people who do not have experience with interface design
[9]	Three prototypes	Unspecified (Based in installations)	Guidelines for interfaces based in motion	Evaluation	PD can be used to overcome biases research teams may have towards developing WIMP interfaces
[52]	Describes many activities (includes pen, paper, crayons, tablet, programmable prototype)	Three groups of children aged 4 to 6	Constructing an interaction model based in Organisational Semiotics	Interaction modelling	Participation has the potential of adjusting existing technology towards empowerment and the democratisation of innovation
[65]	Many activities (Contextual Inquiry, Brainstorm, BrainDraw, Think Aloud)	45 children (Contextual Inquiry)	Creation and validation of prototypes with children	Whole life-cycle	In ubiquitous computing, PD can promote the construction of democratic and accessible designs

(*continued*)

Table 3. (*continued*)

ID	Materials	Participants	Results	Phase	Why participate?
[50]	Describes many activities (storytelling, Prototyping, Forum Theatre)	Elderly and older adults, different for each practice	An exploratory study investigating PD with the elderly	Study of viability of the practices	Participation is a method which potential end users act as members of the design team
[74]	Forms for requirements, scope, and non-requirements	20 students with knowledge in systems design	Requirements refining and prototyping for discussions about matters of privacy	Requirements	PD adds visions beyond the designers' in requirements specification for privacy
[49]	Four activities (two games, a calendar, and a diary)	12 elderly persons with diverse degrees of independence. 11 with advanced stages of dementia	Probing the executive and cognitive abilities of the partner community	Planning of Participatory Practices with the elderly	Enable people to develop realistic expectations about the design and improve democracy by enabling participants to make decisions about their lives and their work
[3]	Cards describing artefact features which other artefacts they can communicate with	4 persons with diverse profiles	Identifying the needs and preferences of users in ubiquitous computing environments	Interaction profiling	PD has the potential to deal with the unpredictability of user profiles
[4]	Describes two activities: (1) whiteboard and post-its; (2) one computer for each participant	(1) 12 partners, (2) 6 partners	(1) Requirements for instant messaging (2) Evaluation of an instant messaging system.	(1) Requirements e (2) Evaluation	PD promotes mutual learning through a greater understanding of the partners' lives
[6]	Interface elements print in paper	14 participant, active users of the evaluated system	Guidelines for system tailoring behaviour	Evaluation	PD is a means to promote universal and democratic access of information to local citizens
[64]	A web game for supporting distributed design	16 designers	A set of suggestions informed by specialists about what the system should be	Evaluation	Participation aids the production of universally designed artefacts
[30]	BrainDraw and electornic prototyping	5 participants	the inception of new installation-based prototypes	Prototyping	PD has the potential to bridge the gap between designers and users, audiences and artists

(*continued*)

Table 3. (*continued*)

ID	Materials	Participants	Results	Phase	Why participate?
[38]	Computers, paper and pen	Em 30 participantes with many different profiles	The creation of a help system for an inclusive social network	Requirements	PD promotes mutual learning between participants and designers
[44]	Paper, pen and sticky notes	3 participants	An evaluation of collaborative aspects of a prototype	Evaluation	PD is useful to evaluate collaborative systems, which are harder to evaluate than others
[10]	Singing and popular dances	Unspecified, open to public	Identifying what rights each participating part has in society that others do not	Composing research agenda and design framework	PD is permeated by differences in power and privilege between co-designers, a space that recognises those frictions is important for promoting PD that does not reduce persons to artefacts
[41]	Describes three activities (includes the creation of posters, t-shirts, music parodies, use of camera)	10 partners who organised the activities and could invite others	Collaborative measures for prevention of violent crimes in the partners' neighbourhood	Whole life cycle	PD and Design Anthropology can be used together to build collaborations where participants and designers can support each other on dealing with dangerous situations
[82]	A tablet computer for each participant	3 to 10 elderly persons with experience using smartphones	An evaluation of a tool's ability to enable self-expression	Summative evaluation	PD enables the discussion of means for the elderly to autonomously access and use web applications
[57]	Video camera and tools for traditional animation	Unspecified, every member of the partner community	Two animated short films about the community's religious practices	Whole life cycle	PD enables the communication of temporalities, spatialities and cultures other than hegemonic ones

(*continued*)

Table 3. (*continued*)

ID	Materials	Participants	Results	Phase	Why participate?
[53]	Canvas and pictures of work actions and situations	12 partners, 1 researcher	The design of tools and games for learning about the partner community's skills and achievements	Project and agenda planning	The synergy between Design and Anthropology has the potential to enable mutual learning between designers and partners in the making of a research and design agenda for women empowerment
[72]	Describes multiple activities (e.g. uses maps and timelines)	Unspecified	Four design experiments for discussing feminism, diversity and territoriality with students from peripheries	Composing research agenda	The works of Paulo Freire have synergy with PD in the Global South, and can serve as a theoretical framework for constructing plural and democratic spaces
[69]	Describes multiple activities (using analogue materials)	Unspecified, every member of the partner community	Establishing processes of mutual learning among designers and partners	Whole life cycle	Dialogue spaces for mutual learning can be established from collaborative practices where designers are at first taught by partners. Design can be a means to improve the living conditions of the partner community
[80]	Tabletop game with cards containing text and pictures	5 to 15 players	Creating and testing a game for political and research discussion	Design and evaluation	PD builds democratic processes that consider community interests and political disputes in a non-essentialist way
[28]	Pen and paper, cardboard	14 students, 3 teachers, the practices also involved interviewing other persons	An extracurricular teaching and learning process involving the design of an analogue game for discussing social issues with high school	Whole life cycle	Design activities can support the discussion of social issues in formal school environments, promoting communication between teachers and students

The second movement occurred in research between 2011 and 2020, proposals towards inclusion have a focus on political spaces – in a perspective resembling Ehn's [32] Design for Public Things perspective – and on broader aspects than promoting inclusion through inclusive access and use of technology, where the technology being introduced is only in support to spaces of dialogue and action which may work independently from the introduction or design of new artefacts, design activities are concerned (e.g. in findings: [10,53], and [72]). Many research issues emerged through the need of communities and groups that were historically excluded from the access of technology (e.g. [4,20,49]), and considering the need of accessible design, Brazilian PD community contributes to expanding the approach towards agendas of inclusion.

Table 4 presents adaptations of PD techniques presented in the survey, as well as the demands that justified the adaptations in the context of each contribution. Among adaptations, the survey shows that the Brazilian Computing community tends to adapt PD techniques towards access of the techniques by partner communities, motivated by the perspectives of inclusion in the articles (e.g. [75] and [33]). As with the articles with new technique proposals, works featuring adaptations present agendas towards digital and social inclusion. Moreover, contributions also present adaptations towards new domains and technologies (as termed in the survey presented by Halskov and Hansen [37]), such as adapting techniques for the co-design of products outside work environments [75] and artefacts beyond those considered conventional [22].

Table 4. PD techniques adapted in the investigated works.

ID	Adapted Technique	What was adapted?	Why was it adapted?
[36]	Contextual Inquiry	Add a design game to the procedure	In order to provide accessible means for discussing future products and services
[75]	CISP, Braindraw, Icon Design Game, HOOTD	CISP: adapted to be practised using assistive technologies for writing; Braindraw: the entire drawings were created individually, then in small groups, and then in the whole; Icon Design Game: the icons had been designed beforehand, the game was made for adjustment and choice of icons; HOOTD: use of analogue cards for representing the tool	Adjusting the technique to a partner community of elderly persons

(*continued*)

Table 4. (*continued*)

ID	Adapted Technique	What was adapted?	Why was it adapted?
[58]	SAC	Added an Organisational Semiotics artefact	The new artefact would enable articulating the development of technologies along with activities the partner community already practised in their daily lives
[39]	Storytelling Workshop	Extended to work with prototypes	Enable the study of multimodal interfaces
[22]	Braindraw	Unspecified	Enable the study of interactive TV applications
[23]	SAC	Added an Organisational Semiotics artefact	Adapt the practice artefacts to the partner community (experts in a corporate environment)
[34]	Future Workshop	Focus on discussing the reality of partners instead of fantastic futures	Evaluate the viability of PD practices in the domain
[59]	SPIDE	Changing the practice *ad hoc* based on partner choice	Adapting the practice to the public (blind and lower vision)
[33]	PD4CAT	Presents guidelines for executing and appropriating the technique	An increase of precision in customised assistive technology
[7]	Card Sorting	Cards changed to be similar to *wiki* articles	In order to make artefacts more adequate to the partner community (who had said that other low level prototypes had been *too abstract*)
[71]	Gallery of Hopes and Fears	Participants posed according to their expectations regarding the subject of the practice, not regarding the participatory workshop itself	Adapt the technique towards investigating partner expectations on centres for social assistance

4   Discussion

This article studies only part of the PD community in Brazil, considering that other areas besides Computing and HCI also use the approach [17], however it was possible to survey that the community has tendencies that differentiate it from other communities that research and practice PD, such as the international PD community presented by Halskov and Hansen [37] in their survey. This section presents discussions about the use of PD in Brazilian Computing, and presents suggestions towards the planning of practices for co-design.

The recent works published in the 2016–2020 period presented a large number of new proposals for PD practices. This has the potential to represent a maturing of the community towards use and application of foreign PD techniques towards the emergence of a community with research issues and theoretical referential to propose interdisciplinary advancements which put PD practices in dialogue with local scholarship, in a way that enables PD to be subjected to appropriation [45] strategies that enable it to contribute localised Democratic actions.

4.1 PD Agendas for Inclusion

The direction of Brazilian PD in Computing contributions towards accessibility and inclusion presents as a differential when comparing it to the direction of international communities represented by the PDC [37]. Moreover, works in the survey expose how participation requires communication between all stakeholders: effective and accessible communication is considered an essential need in order to to afford relevant and informed decisions regarding the designed artefacts and technologies [49,50,75].

This move towards inclusion is most commonly presented – in the surveyed works – through the *proposal of new techniques for PD workshops*, 14 out of 27 proposals presented in Table 3 present agendas related to the creation of techniques which afford decision-making of people in exclusionary situations, including digital exclusion. The proposal of techniques towards more inclusive participation, however, is rarely related to adapting workshop techniques towards access by people with disabilities e.g. as explored by Borges et al. [20]), and more commonly relate to research teams dealing with diversity of digital literacy in participatory practice. Practices proposed in the *e-Cidadania* project (e.g. [6]) are examples of proposals seeking co-design by people with diverse backgrounds involving different levels of literacy and experience with technology.

Adaptations in the perspective of inclusion occurred – in every instance surveyed except for the Gallery of Hopes and Fears practice [71] – through adaptations in the artefacts utilised during practices (e.g. [33,59]), instead of through alterations in individual steps of each technique. Contributions presented as adaptations show examples of how it is possible to modify PD techniques while keeping their intent to promote co-designer decision making and modify practice artefacts in order to nourish environments for democratic speech and action.

Another way the studied community deals with research issues of inclusion is the *use of techniques as proposed without adaptation* occurred in techniques already considered adequate to participants by research teams. An example is the PD4CAT method, presented by Borges et al. [20] as an approach for the design of customised assistive technologies [33]. Out of the 26 works which use PD techniques without adaptation, 9 present objectives related to accessibility and assistive technologies. Practices for design with people with disabilities had more occurrences than in the other two categories, with 5 out of 9 works (e.g. [56] e [26]). Although the surveyed works in this category do not explicitly expose adaptations in PD techniques, it is not possible to conclude that the uses of techniques as they were proposed were uncritical imports of foreign techniques, and that there were no processes of appropriations in which techniques were modified to attend to local demands. Akama and Light [1] discuss the unpredictability of the participatory practice space, considering that co-design is configured by practices, locals and structures in which practices occur, this way the values of each local communities emerge during design activities in the project.

4.2   Adapting and Proposing Appropriations for Interdisciplinary PD

Considering the surveyed PD techniques and practices of the Brazilian Computing community, it is possible to discuss approaches for adaptation, proposition and direction of agenda presented in the study, some of the actions can be categorised as follows:

1. *Adapting practices to a new domain*: the emergence of new groups which can benefit from computer artefacts and movements of communities – research and otherwise – towards inclusion presents opportunities to the expansion of PD to new domains [64]. The adaptation of preexisting and consolidated techniques from the literature to new domains is an appropriation strategy which considers the familiarity of design teams to the techniques [39] as well as the missing precedents in literature which occur due to the novelty of the domain [36,58];
2. *Proposing new techniques starting from community demands*: the proposal of new techniques can emerge from the necessity of partner communities to promote relevant changes to their situations [81]. The proposal of PD techniques in a participatory way – with the community also making meaningful choices about the structure of new practices – has the potential to assist with mitigating the risk of proposing techniques in a vacuum, the participation of the community since its inception can promote empirical validation to new proposals [44,49,50];
3. *Adapting Practices to technology*: as new artefacts become part of the daily lives of stakeholder communities, the space of research and design issues expands and opens opportunities for democratic participation in shaping of new technologies [18,22];
4. *Adapting Practices to a theoretical framing*: PD affords the expansion of design spaces towards a shared domain of the people involved in the co-design [48,60], and HCI historically presents interdisciplinary proposals [61,63]. The introduction of new theoretical referential for action research are contributions that emerged during the study (e.g. Semio-Participatory

Workshops [12], PD in Learning Analytics [81], PD for accessibility [77] and health [8]). The examples presented in Table 3 present means of how PD can be expanded through theoretical discussions with other theories and disciplines, thus presenting strategies of appropriation for PD that is informed by interdisciplinary referential, a growing trend within the studied as well as global communities.

5 Conclusions and Future Work

This study presented a systematic mapping of DP in Brazilian Computer Science scientific papers. As contributions of this research, we have reviewed proposals of PD techniques written by the studied community in peer-reviewed sources presented in digital libraries, the investigation and presentation of strategies for adaptation and appropriation of PD techniques by the community – including indicatives of how adaptation processes occurred and how each technique was adapted is also a contribution of this research.

The promotion of access to computer technology and initiatives for social inclusion through digital inclusion emerge as investigation topics with adhesion by the Brazilian Computing community which sets it apart from international PD communities, indicating that PD can be applied towards investigating local demands, which can differ from original propositions for the approaches and techniques.

The mapping has the potential to aid research teams in the choice of PD techniques for application in their own spaces. As opportunities for future works, we consider: the study on the *corpus* of this survey involving elements of PD beyond techniques and practices, such as the roles of designers, participants and other parts which shape design and practices; studies of the role of disciplines and theories such as Semiotics – which was evidently present both in proposals and adaptations – in Brazilian PD; and the mapping of PD contributions in Computing which did not involve partner communities, such as other surveys and theoretical proposals.

References

1. Akama, Y., Light, A.: Readiness for contingency: punctuation, poise, and co-design. CoDesign **16**(1), 17–28 (2020). https://doi.org/10.1080/15710882.2020.1722177
2. de Alencar, T.S., de Almeida Neris, V.P.: Sistemas ubíquos para todos: Conhecendo e mapeando os diferentes perfis de interação. In: Proceedings of the 12th Brazilian Symposium on Human Factors in Computing Systems, IHC 2013, pp. 178–187, Brazilian Computer Society, Porto Alegre, BRA (2013)
3. de Alencar, T.S., de Almeida Neris, V.P.: Sistemas ubíquos para todos: Conhecendo e mapeando os diferentes perfis de interação. In: Proceedings of the 12th Brazilian Symposium on Human Factors in Computing Systems, IHC 2013, pp. 178–187. Brazilian Computer Society, Porto Alegre (2013). http://dl.acm.org/citation.cfm?id=2577101.2577138

4. Almeida, L.D.A., Hayashi, E.C.S., Reis, J.C., Martins, M.C., Baranauskas, M.C.C.: Conversas online: a synchronous communication tool integrated to inclusive social networks. In: Proceedings of the IX Symposium on Human Factors in Computing Systems, IHC 2010, pp. 51–60. Brazilian Computer Society, Porto Alegre (2010). http://dl.acm.org/citation.cfm?id=1999593.1999600

5. Almeida, L.D.A., de Almeida Neris, V.P., de Miranda, L.C., Hayashi, E.C.S., Calani Baranauskas, M.C.: Designing inclusive social networks: a participatory approach. In: Ozok, A.A., Zaphiris, P. (eds.) OCSC 2009. LNCS, vol. 5621, pp. 653–662. Springer, Heidelberg (2009). https://doi.org/10.1007/978-3-642-02774-1_70

6. de Almeida Neris, V.P., Baranauskas, M.C.C.: Making interactive systems more flexible: an approach based on users' participation and norms. In: Proceedings of the IX Symposium on Human Factors in Computing Systems, pp. 101–110. Brazilian Computer Society, Porto Alegre (2010)

7. van Amstel, F.M.C.: Design participativo numa comunidade de software livre: O caso do website broffice.org. In: Proceedings of the VIII Brazilian Symposium on Human Factors in Computing Systems, IHC 2008, pp. 256–259. Sociedade Brasileira de Computação, BRA (2008)

8. Anacleto, J., Silvestre, R., Carlos Souza Filho, Santana, B., Fels, S.: Therapist-centred design of NUI based therapies in a neurological care hospital. In: 2012 IEEE International Conference on Systems, Man, and Cybernetics (SMC), pp. 2318–2323 (2012)

9. Anacleto, J., Fels, S.: Adoption and appropriation: a design process from HCI research at a Brazilian neurological hospital. In: Kotzé, P., Marsden, G., Lindgaard, G., Wesson, J., Winckler, M. (eds.) Human-Computer Interaction - INTERACT 2013, pp. 356–363. Springer, Berlin Heidelberg, Berlin, Heidelberg (2013)

10. Arruda, M., Haldrup, M., Samson, K.: Performing citizenship through design? In: Proceedings of the 16th Participatory Design Conference 2020 - Participation(s) Otherwise - Volume 2, PDC 2020, pp. 59–62. Association for Computing Machinery, New York (2020). https://doi.org/10.1145/3384772.3385139

11. Bannon, L., Bardzell, J., Bødker, S.: Introduction: reimagining participatory design - emerging voices. ACM Trans. Comput.-Hum. Interact. 25(1), 1:1–1:8 (2018). https://doi.org/10.1145/3177794

12. Baranauskas, M.C.C., Martins, M.C., Valente, J.A.: Codesign de Redes Digitais: tecnologia e educação a serviço da inclusão social. Penso Editora, Porto Alegre (2013)

13. Beyer, H., Holtzblatt, K.: Contextual Design: Defining Customer-Centered Systems. Morgan Kaufmann Publishers Inc., San Francisco (1998)

14. Bjerknes, G., Bratteteig, T.: Florence in wonderland: system development with nurses. In: Computers and Democracy: a Scandinavian Challenge. Institute of Informatics, University of Oslo, Oslo (1987)

15. Bjerknes, G., Bratteteig, T.: User participation and democracy: a discussion of scandinavian research on systems development. Scand. J. Inf. Syst. 7(1), 73–98 (1995). http://dl.acm.org/citation.cfm?id=211288.211293

16. Björgvinsson, E., Ehn, P., Hillgren, P.A.: Participatory design and democratizing innovation. In: Proceedings of the 11th Biennial Participatory Design Conference, PDC 2010, pp. 41–50. ACM, New York (2010). https://doi.org/10.1145/1900441.1900448

17. Boal, A.: Games for Actors and Non-Actors. Taylor & Francis (2005)

18. Bødker, S., Kyng, M.: Participatory design that matters - facing the big issues. ACM Trans. Comput.-Hum. Interact. 25(1), 4:1–4:31 (2018)

19. Bødker, S., Kyng, M., Ehn, P., Kammersgaard, J., Sundblad, Y.: A utopian experience: on design of powerful computer-based tools for skilled graphic workers. In: Bjerknes, G., Ehn, P., Kyng, M. (eds.) Computers and Democracy - a Scandinavian challenge, pp. 251–278. Gower Publishing, Farnham (1987)

20. Borges, L.C.L.D.F., Filgueiras, L., Maciel, C., Pereira, V.: A customized mobile application for a cerebral palsy user. In: Proceedings of the 31st ACM International Conference on Design of Communication, SIGDOC 2013, pp. 7–16. ACM, New York (2013). https://doi.org/10.1145/2507065.2507081

21. Brereton, P., Kitchenham, B.A., Budgen, D., Turner, M., Khalil, M.: Lessons from applying the systematic literature review process within the software engineering domain. J. Syst. Softw. **80**(4), 571–583 (2007)

22. Buchdid, S.B., Hornung, H.H., Pereira, R., Baranauskas, M.C.C.: Clarifying the situational context of a TV company towards the design of iDTV applications. In: Liu, K., Nakata, K., Li, W., Galarreta, D. (eds.) ICISO 2015. IAICT, vol. 449, pp. 70–79. Springer, Cham (2015). https://doi.org/10.1007/978-3-319-16274-4_8

23. Buchdid, S.B., Pereira, R., Baranauskas, M.C.C.: Creating an iDTV application from inside a TV company: a situated and participatory approach. In: Liu, K., Gulliver, S.R., Li, W., Yu, C. (eds.) ICISO 2014. IAICT, vol. 426, pp. 63–73. Springer, Heidelberg (2014). https://doi.org/10.1007/978-3-642-55355-4_7

24. Calderon Salazar, P., Huybrechts, L.: Pd otherwise will be pluriversal (or it won't be). In: Proceedings of the 16th Participatory Design Conference 2020 - Participation(s) Otherwise - Volume 1, PDC 2020, pp. 107–115. Association for Computing Machinery, New York (2020). https://doi.org/10.1145/3385010.3385027

25. Clement, A.: Computing at work: empowering action by low-level users. Commun. ACM **37**(1), 52-ff (1994). https://doi.org/10.1145/175222.175226

26. da Costa, S.E., Berkenbrock, C.D.M., Rosa de Freitas, L.E., Sell, F.F.S.: iLibras: using assistive and collaborative technology to support the communication of deaf people. IEEE Revista Iberoamericana de Tecnologias del Aprendizaje **14**(1), 11–21 (2019)

27. Del Gaudio, C. (ed.): PDC 2020: Proceedings of the 16th Participatory Design Conference 2020 - Participation(s) Otherwise -, vol. 1. Association for Computing Machinery, New York (2020)

28. Dias, C.M.E.A.: Olhares para o design de jogos analógicos em contextos formais de educação básica brasileira: Abordagens projetuais participativas na construção de situações de ensino-aprendizagem polifônicas. In: Proceedings of the 16th Biennial Participatory Design Conference, vol. 3. ACM, New York (2020)

29. DiSalvo, C., Sengers, P., Brynjarsdóttir, H.: Mapping the landscape of sustainable HCI. In: Proceedings of the SIGCHI Conference on Human Factors in Computing Systems, CHI 2010, pp. 1975–1984. ACM, New York (2010). https://doi.org/10.1145/1753326.1753625

30. Duarte, E.F., Gonçalves, F.M., Baranauskas, M.C.C.: InstInt: enacting a small-scale interactive installation through co-design. In: Proceedings of the 30th Australian Conference on Computer-Human Interaction, OzCHI 2018, pp. 338–348. ACM, New York (2018). https://doi.org/10.1145/3292147.3292158

31. Ehn, P.: Work-Oriented Design of Computer Artifacts. L. Erlbaum Associates Inc., Hillsdale (1990)

32. Ehn, P.: Participation in design things. In: Proceedings of the Tenth Anniversary Conference on Participatory Design 2008, PDC 2008, pp. 92–101. Indiana University, Indianapolis (2008). http://dl.acm.org/citation.cfm?id=1795234.1795248

33. de Faria Borges, L.C.L., Filgueiras, L.V.L., Maciel, C., Pereira, V.C.: Customizing a communication device for a child with cerebral palsy using participatory design practices: contributions towards the pd4cat method. In: Proceedings of the 11th Brazilian Symposium on Human Factors in Computing Systems, IHC 2012, pp. 57–66. Brazilian Computer Society, Porto Alegre, BRA (2012)

34. Faust Ramos, E., et al.: Designing for an ecological agricultural association-a PD case study. In: Participatory Design Conference Proceedings, vol. 23, p. 02 (2002)

35. Freire, P.: Pedagogia do oprimido. Paz e Terra, Rio de Janeiro (1970)

36. Geerts, D., van Beek, E., Miranda, F.C.: Viewers' visions of the future. In: Proceedings of the 2019 ACM International Conference on Interactive Experiences for TV and Online Video, TVX 2019, pp. 59–69. Association for Computing Machinery, New York (2019). https://doi.org/10.1145/3317697.3323356

37. Halskov, K., Hansen, N.B.: The diversity of participatory design research practice at PDC 2002–2012. Int. J. Hum.-Comput. Stud. **74**, 81–92 (2015). https://doi.org/10.1016/j.ijhcs.2014.09.003

38. Hayashi, E.C.S., Baranauskas, M.C.C.: Understanding meta-communication in an inclusive scenario. In: Proceedings of the 2010 ACM Symposium on Applied Computing, SAC 2010, pp. 1213–1218. ACM, New York (2010). https://doi.org/10.1145/1774088.1774343

39. Hayashi, E.C.S., Baranauskas, M.C.C.: Facing the digital divide in a participatory way – an exploratory study. In: Forbrig, P., Paternò, F., Pejtersen, A.M. (eds.) HCIS 2008. IIFIP, vol. 272, pp. 143–154. Springer, Boston, MA (2008). https://doi.org/10.1007/978-0-387-09678-0_13

40. Holtzblatt, K., Beyer, H.: Making customer-centered design work for teams. Commun. ACM **36**(10), 92–103 (1993). https://doi.org/10.1145/163430.164050

41. Ibarra, M.C.: Aproximaciones a un diseño participativo sentipensante: correspondencias con un colectivo de residentes en rio de janeiro. In: Proceedings of the 16th Biennial Participatory Design Conference, vol. 3. ACM, New York (2020)

42. Kitchenham, B.: Procedures for performing systematic reviews. Keele, UK, Keele University, vol. 33, pp. 1–26 (2004)

43. Kitchenham, B., Brereton, O.P., Budgen, D., Turner, M., Bailey, J., Linkman, S.: Systematic literature reviews in software engineering-a systematic literature review. Inf. Softw. Technol. **51**(1), 7–15 (2009)

44. Lima, B.A.V., Almeida, L.D.A.: A participatory method for multidimensional analysis and proposing improvements in collaborative systems. In: Proceedings of the 17th Brazilian Symposium on Human Factors in Computing Systems. IHC 2018. Association for Computing Machinery, New York (2018). https://doi.org/10.1145/3274192.3274194

45. Martín-Barbero, J.: Ofício de Cartógrafo. Edições Loyola, São Paulo (2004)

46. Muller, M.J.: Participatory design: the third space in HCI. In: Jacko, J.A., Sears, A. (eds.) The Human-Computer Interaction Handbook, pp. 1051–1068. L. Erlbaum Associates Inc., Hillsdale (2003). http://dl.acm.org/citation.cfm?id=772072.772138

47. Muller, M.J., Haslwanter, J.H., Dayton, T.: Participatory practices in the software lifecycle. In: Helander, M.G., Landauer, T.K., Prabhu, P.V. (eds.) Handbook of Human-Computer Interaction, pp. 256–300. North-Holland, Amsterdam (1997)

48. Muller, M.J., Kuhn, S.: Participatory design. Commun. ACM **36**(6), 24–28 (1993). https://doi.org/10.1145/153571.255960

49. Muriana, L.a.M., Hornung, H.: Who are you?: Getting to know and understanding older adults with dementia in participatory design at a nursing home. In:

Proceedings of the 15th Brazilian Symposium on Human Factors in Computing Systems, IHC 2016, pp. 16:1–16:10. ACM, New York (2016). https://doi.org/10.1145/3033701.3033717

50. Muriana, L.M., Hornung, H.H.: Including older adults into the design process: Challenges and lessons learned. In: Proceedings of the XVI Brazilian Symposium on Human Factors in Computing Systems, IHC 2017, pp. 30:1–30:10. ACM, New York, NY, USA (2017). https://doi.org/10.1145/3160504.3160535

51. Neris, V.P.D.A., Baranauskas, M.C.C.: Designing tailorable software systems with the users' participation. J. Brazilian Comput. Soc. 18(3), 213 (2012)

52. Neto, B.S., Neris, V.: Towards an interaction model for the programming of devices by children in the age of Internet of Things. In: Proceedings of the 17th Brazilian Symposium on Human Factors in Computing Systems, IHC 2018, pp. 53:1–53:5. ACM, New York (2018). https://doi.org/10.1145/3274192.3274245

53. Noronha, R., Aboud, C., Portela, R.: Design by means of anthropology towards participation practices: designers and craftswomen making things in maranhão (br). In: Proceedings of the 16th Participatory Design Conference 2020 - Participation(s) Otherwise - Volume 1, PDC 2020, pp. 203–211. Association for Computing Machinery, New York (2020). https://doi.org/10.1145/3385010.3385015

54. Nygaard, K., Bergo, O.T.: The trade unions-new users of research. Person. Rev. 4(2), 5–10 (1975)

55. de Oliveira Bueno, A., Ferreira, L.C., Ferreira, V., Anacleto, J.C.: Research trends in HCI in Brazil: an analysis in relation to the grandihc-br. In: Proceedings of the 15th Brazilian Symposium on Human Factors in Computer Systems, IHC 2016, pp. 22:1–22:10. ACM, New York (2016). https://doi.org/10.1145/3033701.3033723

56. Paim, P.D.S., Prietch, S.S.: Semiotic ladder artifact to design an assistive technology product for people who are deaf. In: Proceedings of the IX Latin American Conference on Human Computer Interaction, CLIHC 2019. Association for Computing Machinery, New York (2019). https://doi.org/10.1145/3358961.3358982

57. Paterman Brasil, I.: Dancing in fissures: embodied practices in animation to communicate a decolonial world. In: Proceedings of the 16th Participatory Design Conference 2020 - Participation(s) Otherwise - Volume 2, PDC 2020, pp. 55–58. Association for Computing Machinery, New York (2020). https://doi.org/10.1145/3384772.3385146

58. Piccolo, L.S., Pereira, R.: Culture-based artefacts to inform ICT design: foundations and practice. AI Soc. 34(3), 437–453 (2017)

59. Pita, G.L., Zabot, D., Rosa, J., Matos, E.: Adapting the SPIDe to include visually impaired users in interaction design. In: Proceedings of the XVI Brazilian Symposium on Human Factors in Computing Systems, pp. 53. ACM, New York (2017)

60. Posada, J.G., Baranauskas, M.C.C.: A socio-constructionist environment to create stories using tangible interfaces. In: Proceedings of the 14th Brazilian Symposium on Human Factors in Computing Systems (2015)

61. Preece, J., Rogers, Y., Sharp, H.: Interaction Design, 1st edn. John Wiley, New York (2002)

62. da Rocha, H., Baranauskas, M.: Design e avaliação de interfaces humano-computador. Unicamp, Campinas (2003)

63. Rogers, Y.: HCI Theory: Classical, Modern, and Contemporary. Synthesis Lectures on Human-Centered Informatics. Morgan & Claypool Publishers, San Rafael (2012). https://doi.org/10.2200/S00418ED1V01Y201205HCI014

64. Romani, R., Baranauskas, C.: Helping designers in making choices through games. In: Proceedings of the 11th Brazilian Symposium on Human Factors in Computing Systems, pp. 229–238. Brazilian Computer Society, Porto Alegre (2012)

65. Rosa, J., Matos, E.: Semio-participatory framework for interaction design of educational software. In: Proceedings of the 15th Brazilian Symposium on Human Factors in Computing Systems, pp. 33. ACM, New York (2016)

66. Sanders, E.: From user-centered to participatory design approaches. Des. Soc. Sci.: Making Connections 1(8), 1 (2002)

67. Santos, B.d.S., Meneses, M.P.: Epistemologias do sul. Cortez Editora, São Paulo (2014)

68. Santos, N.S., Ferreira, L.S., Prates, R.O.: An overview of evaluation methods for collaborative systems. In: 2012 Brazilian Symposium on Collaborative Systems, pp. 127–135. SBC, Porto Alegre (2012)

69. Santos, T., Noronha, R.G.: Design anthropology como práticas colaborativas: correspondências entre artesãs, designers e sementes no maracanã-são luís - ma. In: Proceedings of the 16th Biennial Participatory Design Conference, vol. 3. ACM, New York (2020)

70. Schuler, D., Namioka, A. (eds.): Participatory Design: Principles and Practices. L. Erlbaum Associates Inc., Hillsdale (1993)

71. Schultz, E., Garcia, L.S., Fernandes, L.A., Paixão, M.R., Kawasaki, F., Pereira, R.: Cultivating creative coexistence(s): towards a critical education for creativity praxis to construct fairer human coexistences. In: Proceedings of the 16th Participatory Design Conference 2020 - Participation(s) Otherwise - Volume 1, PDC 2020, pp. 33–43. Association for Computing Machinery, New York (2020). https://doi.org/10.1145/3385010.3385019

72. Serpa, B., Portela, I., Costard, M., Batista, S.: Political-pedagogical contributions to participatory design from paulo freire. In: Proceedings of the 16th Participatory Design Conference 2020 - Participation(s) Otherwise - Volume 2, PDC 2020, pp. 170–174. Association for Computing Machinery, New York (2020). https://doi.org/10.1145/3384772.3385149

73. da Silva, C.C., de Alcantara, B.G.M., Olimpio, J.C.S., de Gusmao, C.M., da Silva Filho, A.G., dos Santos, W.P.: Ilera-aiye: a virtual world for the development of serious games for health education and promotion in the northeastern Brazilian countryside. In: 2014 IEEE 3nd International Conference on Serious Games and Applications for Health (SeGAH), pp. 1–8. IEEE, Washington, DC (2014)

74. Silva, D.P., de Souza, P.C., de Jesus Gonçalves, T.A.: Early privacy: Approximating mental models in the definition of privacy requirements in systems design. In: Proceedings of the 17th Brazilian Symposium on Human Factors in Computing Systems. IHC 2018. Association for Computing Machinery, New York (2018). https://doi.org/10.1145/3274192.3274211

75. Silva, N.C.D.D., Valle, A.M.D., Kawashita, I.M.S.: Participatory design with the elderly in software development: a case study. In: Proceedings of the 18th Brazilian Symposium on Human Factors in Computing Systems, IHC 2019. Association for Computing Machinery, New York (2019). https://doi.org/10.1145/3357155.3358486

76. Simonsen, J., Robertson, T.: Routledge International Handbook of Participatory Design. Routledge, Abingdon (2012)

77. de Souza, P.M., Rodrigues, K.R.D.H., de Almeida Neris, V.P.: Semth: an approach to the design of therapeutic digital games. In: Proceedings of the 18th Brazilian Symposium on Human Factors in Computing Systems, IHC 2019. Association

for Computing Machinery, New York (2019). https://doi.org/10.1145/3357155. 3358440

78. Spinuzzi, C.: A Scandinavian challenge, a us response: methodological assumptions in Scandinavian and us prototyping approaches. In: Proceedings of the 20th Annual International Conference on Computer Documentation, SIGDOC 2002, pp. 208–215. ACM, New York (2002). https://doi.org/10.1145/584955.584986

79. Sundblad, Y.: UTOPIA: participatory design from Scandinavia to the world. In: Impagliazzo, J., Lundin, P., Wangler, B. (eds.) HiNC 2010. IAICT, vol. 350, pp. 176–186. Springer, Heidelberg (2011). https://doi.org/10.1007/978-3-642-23315-9_20

80. Szaniecki, B.: Jogos como dispositivos de conversação: investigando modos de participação e design. In: Proceedings of the 16th Biennial Participatory Design Conference, vol. 3. ACM, New York (2020)

81. Verbert, K., Ochoa, X., De Croon, R., Dourado, R.A., De Laet, T.: Learning analytics dashboards: the past, the present and the future. In: Proceedings of the Tenth International Conference on Learning Analytics and Knowledge, LAK 2020, pp. 35–40. Association for Computing Machinery, New York (2020). https://doi.org/10.1145/3375462.3375504

82. Viel, C.C., Rodrigues, K.R.H., Cunha, B.C.R., Pimentel, M.G.C.: Elderly vloggers: authoring and sharing stories with mobile media and DTV using the the ghostwriter service. In: Proceedings of the 25th Brazillian Symposium on Multimedia and the Web, WebMedia 2019, pp. 185–192. Association for Computing Machinery, New York (2019). https://doi.org/10.1145/3323503.3360303

Towards a Generic Framework for Intercultural User Interface Design to Evoke Positive Cross-Cultural UX

Rüdiger Heimgärtner(✉)

Intercultural User Interface Consulting (IUIC), Berlin, Germany
ruediger.heimgaertner@iuic.de

Abstract. So far, there are more plausible than reliable intercultural user interface design recommendations. Furthermore, there is a lack of plausible and model-based explanations of which sustainable and use-case-crossing products might apply. The goal of the considerations presented in this paper is to find a way to use results from empirical studies to be able to generate sustainable rules for UI design for cultural contexts in general to generate cross-cultural user experience. This is done through an explanatory approach by extending the existing IUID approach in a way that elementary explanatory design guidelines for intercultural UI design based on human factors should emerge. Based on a hybrid approach covering cultural contexts in human–computer interaction (HCI) design using a model of culturally influenced HCI, the IUID method-mix is extended by the concepts of user needs, interaction principles and task complexity to obtain a generic framework for intercultural user interface design (IUID) as condition of possibility for positive cross-cultural user experience.

Keywords: Chinese human factors · Generic framework · IUID · Culture · Task complexity · Human factors · UX · Positive UX · User experience · Usability engineering · Intercultural user interface design · Cross-cultural design · Toolbox · Cultural dimensions · HCI dimensions · HCI indicators · Cultural HCI indicators · Culture dependent HCI model · Model · IUID · HCI · HMI · User needs · Emotion · Cognition · Values · Beliefs · Attitudes · Identity · Motives · Preferences · Interaction principles · Generic IUID framework

1 Intercultural User Interface Design as a Prerequisite for Cross-Cultural UX

[1] pointed out the difference between the terms "intercultural" and "cross-cultural" design as early as 2000. The differences in the meanings have to do with the perspectives we take when interacting with people from other cultures. The term "cross-cultural" is often used for comparing or contrasting cultures whereas "intercultural" implicates a deep understanding and respect for cultures. Intercultural communication focuses on the mutual exchange of ideas and cultural norms and the development of deep relationships in contrast to cross-cultural communication. Cross-cultural design considers the

© Springer Nature Switzerland AG 2021
M. Rauterberg (Ed.): HCII 2021, LNCS 12795, pp. 387–406, 2021.
https://doi.org/10.1007/978-3-030-77431-8_24

cultural differences across the cultures in designing user interfaces (UI). In addition, intercultural user interface design (IUID) tries to integrate the inherent insights between the desired cultures (cf. [2]). "Intercultural" is used for research and the development of user interfaces in design phases, "cross-cultural" is used for the application of user interfaces at runtime across cultures. User experience (UX) cannot be designed in the "design phase", but it is created "at runtime". Hence, there is no "intercultural UX", but "cross-cultural UX" because of designing good user interfaces by IUID. In this sense, UX can only and should exist *across* cultures. To do this, you first must know what is necessary cross-culturally, i.e., it is to be examined interculturally what is necessary to design UIs in such a way that a cross-cultural user experience is created. UX cannot be designed, only UIs can be designed that lead to a user experience. "UX design" thus is a contradiction in terms. As a designer, you cannot design (or even define) the user experience at design time, but only design the UI in such a way that the most positive UX possible can result from it. UX is generated by the perceptions and reactions of a user resulting from the use and/or the expected use of an interactive system. UX occurs before, during, and after the user's interaction with an interactive system. For example, when applying for the device before using it, the user acquires a user experience that shapes the user toward using the device. If the user looks forward to using the sand-blasted device with good appearance, the user obtains a positive attitude about using it. If using the device turns out to be good to use as well, this maintains the positive user experience already acquired. For example, the web page on which the product is advertised can be designed well. If the user finds his way around it and gets a positive impression of the device, this also maintains the state of the positive user experience. That is, the user has a positive user experience even before buying the device. If, due to good customer service, this remains the case also after the device has been used, e.g., in the event of a repair, then this also has the effect of a positive user experience. But you need user interface design to design the sales website, device, and service to create a positive user experience. Hence, UI design is the condition of the possibility of positive user experience. And for generating positive user experience in cultural contexts, this condition of possibility is IUID. IUID is a prerequisite for improving the intercultural usability of software, which in turn is a prerequisite for cross-cultural UX and, hence, global sales opportunities.

Using methods of intercultural usability engineering, further design guidelines for IUID can be iteratively derived from the results of the tests and the feedback of potential users from all over the world. Hence, the perception and consideration of the customs and requirements of other cultures by the developers of intercultural user interfaces is one of the main tasks within intercultural user interface design. Based on feedback from tutorials and workshops on IUID and the revised summary of the state of research on IUID [2], the author reviewed the synopsis of well the documented IUID method-mix (cultural dimensions, intercultural variables, user interface characteristics and human computer interaction (HCI) dimensions) for intercultural user interface design (IUID) [3] to come to a reasonable toolbox for IUID [4] that will be extended in this paper towards a generic framework for IUID to cover arbitrary cultural contexts taking into account additional concepts such as user needs, interaction principles and task complexity.

2 Background and Related Work

Differences between cultures can be found by analyzing critical interaction situations between people [5]. [1] made this method available for cultural differences in Human-Machine Interaction (HMI): critical interaction situations that arise due to problematic functionality of user interfaces must be analyzed. [6] found that e.g., Hofstedes "Individualism Index" [7] is related to user satisfaction and usability of the product and has a significant influence on intercultural usability. [8] proposed the "Method for Culture-Oriented Design" (MCD), which integrates the factors of new concepts of culture-oriented HCI design and the knowledge of cultural differences into existing concepts of HCI design. Relevant cultural variables for intercultural HCI design must be determined analytically based on literature and requirement studies. Their values represent culture-dependent variations that occur at all levels of HCI localization (surface, functionality, interaction) and that can be used for IUID. Similarly, for culture-oriented design, [9] considered a simplified version a culture-centered HCI design process while focusing on social and cultural aspects to cover the value of the user's cultural context. Further methods are applying user interface characteristics [10] or cultural markers [11]. To make cultural dimensions available for user interface design, [10] developed characteristic factors for user interfaces and gave examples that can influence user interface design (such as different colors or behaviors). Cultural markers have been determined by empirical studies (e.g., [11–13]), which are specific for a certain culture and which are preferably used within this certain culture (such as flags). Other approaches, e.g., [14] or [15], are based on semiotic theory. In semiotic engineering, HCI is seen "as a two-tiered communicative process: one is the designer-to-user communication and the other is the user-system interaction. [..] HCI can only be achieved if both levels of communication are successfully achieved." [16]: 55.

One of the most promising methods to preserve cultural differences in HCI is the observation and analysis of user interaction with the system (cf. [17]). The results of observations of cultural variables and their manifestations serve as a basis for:

- guidelines for IUID (e.g., cultural interaction indicators (cf. [18]),
- cultural adaptive user interfaces (cf. [19]),
- cultural adaptive frameworks for user interfaces (cf. [20]),
- intercultural interaction analysis tool (cf. [21]),
- profound cultural empirical studies (cf. [22]),
- culture dependent HCI models (cf. [23]),
- culturally aware systems (cf. [24]),
- IUID method mix (cf. [3]),
- IUID toolbox (cf. [4]),
- generic framework for IUID.

3 Path to a Generic Framework for IUID

The path to an initial version of a generic framework for IUID is described as follows: First, necessary concepts for the generic IUID framework are presented. Second the integration of the combined use of the concepts within a hybrid approach is explained. Third, the application of the IUID method-mix as the main functionality provider for the generic IUID framework is exemplified. The most relevant aspects and important constituents driving recommendations for IUID are subsequentially elucidated. Together with the application of the enhanced systematic procedure for the generic IUID framework, consisting of steps of how to reasonably use the properly arranged methods and concepts, the way to a generic framework for IUID is paved.

3.1 IUID Method Mix

The IUID toolbox uses a hybrid approach integrating a combined use of the following concepts ("IUID Method-Mix" for short) to derive cultural HCI indicators relevant for the derivation of recommendations for IUID:

- HCI dimensions,
- Cultural dimensions,
- Intercultural variables,
- User interface characteristics,
- The culture dependent HCI model,
- The method of culture-oriented design.

HCI dimensions represent classes of HCI variables useful for HCI design describing the behavior of a user (HCI style) with an interactive information processing system [23]. HCI dimensions are expressed by information science variables such as information density or interaction frequency at the interaction level [22]. To measure the parameters, the characteristics of the HCI dimensions must be very precise and concrete. Therefore, the HCI dimensions are operationalized in many quantitative variables (HCI indicators) to obtain a basic HCI metrics. There must be at least one HCI indicator as a measurement variable to represent the character of an HCI dimension. For real use, however, several empirically proven HCI indicators should be used.

Cultural standards (i.e., orientation systems according to [5]) and cultural dimensions (e.g., individualism vs. collectivism, uncertainty avoidance, long term orientation and masculinity vs. femininity from [7] or action chain orientation, network density and context orientation from [25]) serve to describe and compare cultural systems. The characteristics of cultural dimensions influence the user experience and provide orientation for the usability engineering process. Differences between cultures can be found by analyzing critical interaction situations between people []. The mental model of the user about the system depends on the culture of the user, his expectations about the characteristics of the system and his experience of interaction with the system. The cultural aspects and their manifestations can be empirically determined using qualitative and quantitative methods.

Cultural dimensions are too rough for intercultural user interface design. For this reason, additional cultural variables are necessary which – in relation to user interface design – divide the cultural aspects into smaller units (cf. [8]). Intercultural variables describe the differences in HCI design with respect to the preferences of users from different cultures. Direct intercultural variables are most important because they have a direct and essential influence on the HCI design. "Visible" intercultural variables are immediately perceptible at a certain time (font, color, window size, navigation, etc.). In contrast, "invisible" (or "hidden") intercultural variables are only recognizable over a certain period (such as interaction speed, information display duration, dialogue display frequency, use of the navigation bar).

The user interface characteristics "Metaphor", "Mental Model", "Navigation", "Interaction" and "Presentation" can be linked to Hofstedes cultural dimensions (cf. [7, 8, 10]). User interface characteristics can be used in conjunction with empirical surveys on their characteristics for the corresponding cultural target context to derive recommendations for the development of intercultural user interfaces.

Cultural models and cultural HCI indicators, which have been generated by the analysis of user interaction, can be used to describe the needs of the user in terms of the HCI depending on his culture as well as to develop an explanatory model for culturally influenced HCI and to improve the methods of intercultural usability engineering. With the help of a culture dependent HCI model, examples of different culturally conditioned behavior of users can be explained with interactive systems. For this purpose, the explanatory models must be determined based on analytical considerations and verified using empirical data and statistical methods. A successful explanatory model can be applied to new examples or application cases and thus verified, which in turn allows predictive design recommendations to be generated.

The "Method for Culture-Oriented Design" (MCD) integrates the factors of culture-oriented HMI design and the knowledge of cultural differences into existing concepts of HMI design [8] (cf. Fig. 1).

However, some more concepts must be considered in addition to the IUID method mix in order achieve an enhanced explanatory and therefore, generic, IUID framework. These concepts are presented in the following.

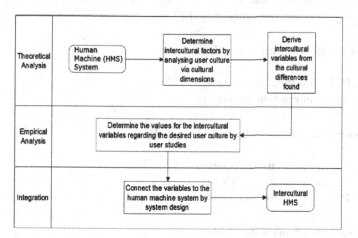

Fig. 1. Simplified version of the method of culture-oriented design (Source: [22]: 66).

3.2 Connecting HCI to Culture

Figure 2 shows the content of the culture dependent HCI model representing the hypothetical relationships between cultural and HCI dimensions [23].

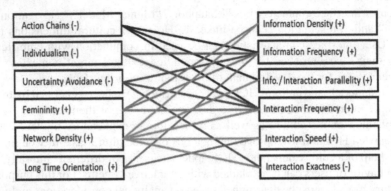

Fig. 2. Hypothetical relationship between cultural and HCI dimensions [23].

The model contains the following rules expressing the connection between the values of the cultural dimensions and the values of the HCI dimensions, thereby determining the denotation level for culture and HCI (for details refer to [23]):

1) The lower action chain orientation:

   a) the higher information frequency (IN-F).
   b) the higher information parallelism (IN-P) and interaction parallelism (INT-P).
   c) the higher interaction frequency (INT-F).

2) The lower individualism index (IDV):

   a) the higher information frequency.
   b) the higher interaction frequency.

3) The lower uncertainty avoidance index (UAI):

   a) the higher information frequency.
   b) the higher interaction frequency.
   c) the lower interaction exactness (INT-E).

4) The lower masculinity index (MAS):

   a) the higher information density (IN-D).
   b) the higher information frequency.
   c) the higher interaction frequency.

5) The higher network density and context orientation:

   a) the higher information density.
   b) the higher information and interaction parallelism.
   c) the higher interaction frequency.
   d) the higher interaction-speed (INT-S).
   e) the lower interaction exactness.

6) The higher long-term orientation index (LTO):

   a) the higher information frequency.
   b) the higher interaction-speed.

7) And vice versa for all six rules (i.e., for Rule 1: the higher action chain orientation, the lower information/interaction frequency and parallelism).

According to the changed values of the cultural dimensions on the left side of the model (antecedences in the production rules in Fig. 2), the values of the HCI dimensions change on the right side of the model (consequences in the production rules in Fig. 2). Therefore, this model does not depend on nations or countries but can be used to cover every cultural group (with at least 20 members, if using Hofstede's Values Survey Module (VSM) (cf. [7] to determine the cultural characteristics of the group).

3.3 Task Complexity

[26] elaborated a measurement methodology for the classification of task complexity added as requirement to the process steps. The basics of this measurement methodology for the classification of the task complexity are as follows:

"low complexity" when there are 0–5 variable steps ($n \leq 5$) in the process execution with more than 50% process steps at the user-SW interface,

"medium complexity" when there are 6–8 variable steps ($5 < n < 9$) in the process execution with more than 50% process steps at the user-SW interface,

"high complexity" when there are 9 and more variable steps ($n \geq 9$) in the process execution with more than 50% process steps at the user SW interface.

As an example, take the task "Sending a text message via SMS". This task can be decomposed into the following subtasks:

(1) Open the text messenger (US)
(2) Define the addressee (U)
(3) Select the addressee (US)
(4) Think about the text message (U)
(5) Enter the text message (US)
(6) Initiate sending the message (US)
(7) Close the text messenger (US)

We have 7 tasks, 2 of them are user related (U), 5 relates to the interface between user and system (US), i.e., 5 of 7 process steps is a share of 71%. (1) and (7) are start and end nodes, (2)–(6) represent task related nodes, i.e., there are 5 task related process steps, which means a medium complexity because the share of (US) is greater than 50%. For medium complexity, [26] recommends employing online help, semantic system evaluation, database-based support, and navigation aids. Keyboard input and mouse control should be extended by touch/multi-touch operation, display devices as well as expected and foresighted assistance. These aspects affect many of the presented concepts presented for the IUID method mix as well as for human factors as shown in Sect. 3.5.

3.4 Interaction Principles

ISO 9241-110 "[..] deals with the ergonomic design of interactive systems and describes dialogue principles which are generally independent of any specific dialogue technique and which are applicable in the analysis, design and evaluation of interactive systems." (cf. English version of DIN EN ISO 9241-110:2008-09, [27]: 4). Even if part 110 of ISO 9241 relates to all kinds of interactive systems, it does not cover the specifics of all contexts of use such as safety critical systems or collaborative work. Another special context of use is the intercultural context that must be considered to apply the dialog principles of ISO 9241-110 correctly in intercultural contexts: questions concerning the interaction level, the mind, and the cognition as well as the behavior of users in applying the dialogue principles in cultural contexts are either not answered or only partly so until now (cf. [28]). How can or must we use the dialogue principles (e.g., "controllability") in the intercultural context correctly to evaluate how different cultures interfere and affect navigation within applications? How are other dialogue principles such as "suitability for individualization" involved or how can they be involved in the intercultural context? Are there significant improvements when comparing an application without considering intercultural differences with the adapted version of the application? Can users from different cultures have different experiences when interacting with applications from their own or other cultures? This question concerns the whole user experience (UX) affecting all dialogue principles. Such questions in relation to the framework of applying dialogue principles, the dialogue requirements and the dialogue techniques must be answered by research to provide useful hints for designers and developers of user interfaces to apply the dialogue principles correctly in intercultural contexts. Many such questions need to be answered regarding the compatibility of the dialogue principles in intercultural contexts. If ISO 9241-110 claims to be valid internationally as an international standard, then it must be possible to apply the content of ISO 9241-110 across nations independently at least from their cultural contexts on national level. However, the analysis of the use of the dialogue principle "suitability for the task" in the intercultural context using cultural dimensions at national level indicated that the existing dialogue principles defined in ISO 9241-110 should be used with care to be successfully applied in intercultural contexts (cf. [28]). The dialogue should present the user with information related to the successful completion of the task. However, presentation of information as well as the requirements to complete the task and even the task itself can be culture specific (cf. [29]). If the needs of the task are culture specific, the required quality, quantity, and type of information to be presented is also culture specific. Automatic default setting for typical input values according to the task seems to be culturally independent at the first sight. However, for this purpose, it can be necessary for the system to identify the user to provide reasonable default data. This in turn can be problematic in cultures with high uncertainty avoidance or power distance (cf. [7]), which has effects on the user's information needs as mentioned above and on the willingness of the user to provide personal information for identification purposes to the system (such as email address or passwords). Another general goal of this dialog principle for the design of dialogues is the following: "The steps required by the dialogue should be appropriate to the completion of the task, i.e., necessary steps should be included, and unnecessary steps should be avoided." (English version of DIN EN ISO 9241-110:2008-09, [27]: 8). The steps required by the dialogue to complete the task depend on the culturally influenced concepts "task" and "required steps". According to mono-causal or multi-causal thinking, the user expects more or fewer steps to complete the task (cf. [30]). Again, the dialogue principle "conformity with user expectances" is strongly involved here. Also, the channels for inputs and outputs offered by the dialogue system can vary here and can be differently loaded according to the cultural imprint of the users (cf. users showing holistic or analytic perception, cf. [31]). These are just some aspects that should be considered in using the dialog principle "suitability for the task" in intercultural contexts. Furthermore, all of these and more aspects must be analyzed in more depth to derive recommendations about how to apply this dialogue principle correctly in intercultural contexts.

3.5 Human Factors

Human factors are the applications of psychological and physiological principles to the engineering and design of products, processes, and systems [32] to make people use systems or machines efficiently, safely, and comfortably. It involves human cognition, emotion, and behavior patterns [33] as well as physiological and biomechanical characteristics related to physical activities [34]. Cognition includes consciousness, imagination, perception, thinking, judgement, language, and memory. To determine relevant human factors for HCI, human information processing models such as [35] can be used because they involve context-sensitive mechanisms such as mental and cognition models that can cover the implications of cultural dimensions in cultural contexts. Values, attitudes, beliefs, cognition style and communication style are influenced by culture [36] which in turn influence needs and motivation. The mental model in cognition influences interaction of a user with a system. The communication style, language and behavioral patterns influence the human's output. Cultural contexts affect cognitive style, sensation, perception, memory, and conceptual network, i.e., human factors are influenced by culture. Figure 3 shows the circle of the influence of culture on human factors: after perceiving the world, in and via cognition, the motives, preferences, beliefs, values, attitudes and identity are built up and form the needs which in turn trigger emotion, behavior and language. The cultural environment imposes new feedback to the perception to form the cognition and the circle starts again.

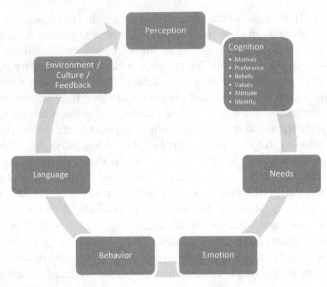

Fig. 3. Cultural influence on human factors.

Motivation and preference belong to the same basic level. Motivation is willingness of action or behavior including need-based motivation [37] and reward-based motivation that is related to emotion [38]. Human preferences regarding a thing or object expresses the desires caused by needs which are in contrast essentially necessary. Values are enduring beliefs which are influenced by culture. Meaning in life or purpose is related to values and motivations (cf. [39]) that can overlap (cf. [40]). In contrast to needs that are basic, dynamic, and contextual, values are long-term oriented. Values consciously serve to priorities the needs and are related to action and behavior (cf. [41]). Identity represents the sum of the knowledge and understanding of oneself including self-identity expressed by self-image and social identity shown by one's social role. Self-image is the view we have of ourselves (cf. [42]). Self-image and social roles are a powerful driver of cognition and behavior (cf. [43]). Cognition is a term referring to the mental processes involved in gaining knowledge and comprehension. It contains attention, perception, memory, thinking, decision-making, learning and language (cf. [44]). The theory of cognitive dissonance (cf. [45]) proposes that people have a motivational drive to reduce dissonance by changing their attitudes, beliefs, and behaviors, or by justifying or rationalizing their attitudes, beliefs, and behaviors. Language describes abstract thoughts, situations, objects, and sounds and is related to cognition (cf. [46]) and serves as a communication tool, which transmits cultural knowledge and influences social behavior (cf. [47]). Emotion is a conscious and unconscious mental reaction subjectively experienced as strong feeling usually directed toward a specific object, thing or person and is typically accompanied by physiological and behavioral changes in the body. It is associated with thoughts, feelings, and behavioral responses across the whole process ranging from motivation to behavior and mutual interaction with the whole process.

Example: Chinese Human Factors. Chinese human factors are the Chinese aspects of or preferences for the following dimensions: motivation [48], perception, thinking, action, selection (communication, attribution, trust, and acceptance), memory, language (Chinese and mandarin or dialects), emotion, behavior patterns or habits, anthropometry, and biomechanics. For example, [7] and [49] found that Chinese and German have significant scores on power distance and individualism. Chinese are more likely to think themselves as interdependently self. Social roles are how they see themselves in society, which affects what they think they should do in a particular role, and the things that they consider to be important. So, the common values, attitudes and beliefs in China have an influence on the individual's identity. [50] stated the unique Chinese emotion, such as hyper-cognition of shame. [51] wrote a handbook of Chinese psychology, which mentions Chinese beliefs, values, well-being, emotion, and thinking styles. Taking the user needs "competence" and "autonomy" as an example, self-determination theory has relations to the needs of autonomy, competence, and relatedness. The theory states that individuals who grow in environments that provide optimal challenges, support for autonomy, competence feedback, and a secure relational base tend to develop a strong autonomy orientation, i.e., a tendency to experience choice and freedom in activities, to interpret the environment as informational, and to seek out opportunities for autonomy. Optimal challenges are those that stretch slightly beyond one's skill. But it is different across individuals (cf. [52]). Some individuals optimize experience in more adventurous, exploratory conditions (i.e., if challenges are greater than skills), whereas others optimize experience in less adventurous, more mastery-practice conditions (i.e., if skills are greater than challenges). Culture moderates the optimal challenges [48]. Moneta's study measured both Chinese and US college students' intrinsic motivation by work preference inventory and found that the optimal challenge/skill ratio is biased toward skills for both US and Chinese participants. But the bias is greater for Chinese participants, which means Chinese are likely to participate in the more mastery-practice condition as they are interdependent self-construal (collectivism). Therefore, the task for Chinese should be easier a little bit within the range of their mastered skills. Table 1 shows some examples regarding possible relationship between user needs and the values of the culture dimensions for Chinese people.

Example: Politeness in Germany and China. Behavior is 'polite' when it is displayed because otherwise another person might feel personally affected when we use it to "consider the effect of our words on others" (cf. [54]: 42). The orientation of behavior towards a concrete counterpart makes a difference between etiquette rules and 'politeness'. Politeness and etiquette fulfil a similar function: they serve as social lubricants; they reduce friction between individuals in social contact through preventive measures. They are rules of self-restraint, of putting one's own interest aside to prevent a conflict of interests and to maintain harmony, social peace, without the need for violent enforcement. However, there is a difference regarding the application of politeness in China and in Germany (cf. [55]). In China, "Politeness refers to concrete expressions of the moral norms that regulate interpersonal interaction in our social life and coexistence. Politeness serves to bring more harmony to our social life and to avoid many unnecessary conflicts. The core content of politeness is mutual respect and letting each other come first. It is not without reason that the Li begins with the words 'show respect'. This

Table 1. Possible relationship between user needs according to [53] and the values of culture dimensions for China.

User Needs	Explanation	Culture dimension for China
Relatedness	Being close to people: romance, intimacy, family	Collectivism
Popularity	Inspiring others: acknowledgment, influence, helping	Collectivism and high-power distance: interdependent self-construal's and face saving
Autonomy	Acting according to my values: independence, freedom, ideals	Power distance: face saving
Stimulation	Discovering new and interesting things: curiosity, mystery, gaming	Low uncertainty avoidance
Security	Feeling safe and in control: order, rest, habits	Low uncertainty avoidance: risk perception
Physicality	Being bodily active: nature, health, agility	Low uncertainty avoidance, high-power distance, long-term orientation
Competence	Successfully handling difficult tasks: performance, influence, control	Collectivism: achievement is low

classic goes on to say: 'Those who wish to behave politely should humble themselves and show respect to others'. Mutual respect and mutual humiliation should be sincere and come from the heart. Politeness is not synonymous with nice-sounding words and a friendly face. Politeness is based on sincerity of heart." quoted from the translation by [56]: 77.

4 First Approach to a Generic Framework for IUID

The idea is to extend the IUID method mix by the concepts of user needs, interaction principles and task complexity. Furthermore, the system approach for an IUID toolbox must be extended by enhancing the procedure of using the IUID method mix. Finally, the derived hypothetical IUID recommendations must be empirically verified by further research in the wild. The cultural differences can be transferred thereby by observing the behavior in different cultures, making implicit rules explicit, explain observed difference in the cultures, recognize the relationship between culture and HCI style, compare them empirically, derive rules for intercultural HCI design and integrate the results into the product and build models for the future to derive IUID recommendations in a generalized way.

4.1 Procedure of a Generic Framework for IUID

One important goal for intercultural HCI designers and intercultural usability experts is to consider fundamental cultural differences when dealing with members of cultures interacting with machines. Hence, the most important step is to bridge the gap between cultural aspects (e.g., derived from cultural dimensions) and HCI design by determining relevant cultural parameters for IUID using analytical research tools and doing evaluation by empirical studies. The aim is to find the actual connection between the interaction indicators and their (postulated cultural) causes represented by the relationship between cultural and HCI dimensions (and their variables respectively). The connections between cultural, information-related, and interaction-related dimensions were modelled using the cultural interaction indicators. Results found applying this approach [23] led to the conviction that it is justified and useful to use cultural interaction indicators for intercultural HCI research to obtain a reasonable explanatory model for culturally influenced HCI [23]. The explanatory model is based on some of the best-classifying cultural interaction indicators, indicating that the expressions of the HCI dimensions depend on the cultural imprint of the users, which can be described by the expressions of cultural dimensions: the higher the relationship orientation (collectivism), the higher the information density, information speed, information frequency, interaction frequency and interaction speed (and vice versa).

The procedure in the IUID framework applied a combined use of cultural dimensions, intercultural variables, user interface characteristics, HCI dimensions and the model of culture dependent HCI as well as the relationship to user needs from human factors, interaction principles and task complexity in a systematic way to derive generic IUID recommendations for arbitrary cultural contexts.

4.2 Systematic Procedure for Deriving IUID Recommendations

The hybrid approach integrating all the mentioned concepts above by a systematic procedure to analytically derive design recommendations for IUID is described in detail in [3] and [4]. The procedure to derive IUID recommendations is as follows: First, the application, main uses cases and the desired target cultures are chosen. In this context, the relevant user needs derived from the human factors according to the cultural background and to the desired use case are identified. Depending on the use case, the respective UI elements (e.g., layout, buttons, text fields) must be determined and mapped to the category of the cultural variables (direct, indirect, visible, hidden) as well as to the user interface characteristics (presentation, interaction, navigation, mental model, and metaphor). In addition, the task complexity is evaluated and from this the cultural requirements to the user interface elements and to the interaction principles are determined. Using this information, the time and space related HCI dimensions must be identified (such as information density or interaction frequency). Via the rules of the explanatory model of culture dependent HCI, the related HCI dimensions must be connected to the cultural dimensions to obtain relevant cultural HCI indicators. Having the cultural HCI indicators in hand, recommendations for IUID can be drawn according to the designated culture of the user.

4.3 Exemplifying the Procedure

Table 2 shows the output of using the IUID toolbox [4] (i.e., the results obtained by systematically applying the IUID method-mix [3]).

Table 2. Results by using the IUID toolbox [4].

Application(s)	Word processor on a mobile phone
Use Case(s)	Sending a text message via SMS
Task Complexity	Medium
User Need(s)	Autonomy, Competence, Stimulation, Security
Politeness	Superfluous, utterance, role based versus from heart, showing respect, honesty
Cultural Dimension(s)	Power distance, individualism, uncertainty avoidance
User Interface Characteristic(s)	Presentation: text, character, character set, layout, skin, edit field, send button, receiver list box
Interaction Principle(s)	Suitability for the task
Intercultural Variable(s)	Direct, visible, surface (language, color, layout, skin)
HCI Indicator(s)	Number of pieces of information per space, number of SMS per day, number of saved contacts
HCI Dimension(s)	Information density, interaction frequency and speed, information and interaction parallelism, interaction exactness
Culture Dependent HCI Model	China (IDV low ➔ IN-F high, INT-F high; UAI low ➔ IN-F high, INT-F high, INT-E low), Germany (IDV high ➔ IN-F low, INT-F low; UAI high ➔ IN-F low, INT-F low, INT-E high)
Cultural HCI Indicator(s)	Number of pieces of information per space, number of SMS per day and number of saved contacts vary from low to high
IUID Implication(s) / Recommendation(s)	Adapt system memory; choose appropriate input method editor (IME) and sorting algorithms; allow customization of the number of entries in lists

Assume, a UI designer wants to identify design recommendation for IUID for users from China or Germany regarding an application with the use case "sending a short text message via SMS on a mobile phone".

The first step is to identify the cultural dimensions representing the highest cultural distance between the target cultures. The value of the cultural dimensions can be looked up in the literature of culture experts (such as [7] or [57]). According to Hofstede's cultural compass, these are the power distance index (PDV), the individualism index (IDV) and the uncertainty avoidance index (UAI) (cf. [7]). Then, the user needs can be related to the cultural dimensions as indicated in Table 1 in Sect. 3.5 before.

The next step is to identify the UI elements (e.g., text, characters, character set, layout, skin, send button, receiver list box) that are concerned in the use case and to relate them to the user interface characteristics (e.g., presentation). Having the localization levels (surface, interaction, functionality) and the intercultural variables in mind, corresponding HCI indicators (operationalized quantitative variables) can be identified. Consequently, similar HCI indicators can then be grouped to the fitting HCI dimension. Now, the mapping of the UI characteristics to the intercultural variables. Presentation concerns direct, visible cultural variables on the surface of the user interface (such as language, color, layout, skin). The effort for this mapping depends significantly on the computed task complexity.

The relationship between cultural dimensions and HCI dimensions comes into play by following the rules of the explanatory model expressing the connection between the values of the cultural dimensions and the values of the HCI dimensions (cf. Fig. 1). For instance, IDV is related to information and interaction frequency and UAI is related to information and interaction frequency as well as to interaction exactness. If individualism in a culture is low (e.g. for China in contrast to Germany according to [7], then information frequency and interaction frequency tends to be high (e.g. for China in contrast to Germany according to [23]). Furthermore, HCI dimensions are also related to UI characteristics. For example, information density is affected by the cultural presentation requirements (cf. culturally different communication patterns, [58]). This different communication behavior can be expressed using adequate cultural HCI indicators such as number of pieces of information per space, number of SMS sent per day or number of contacts.

This in turn leads to the following requirements for system design and recommendation for IUID: The HCI system at hand needs to have enough memory for storing contacts and sent short messages. Furthermore, it needs an input method editor for the different character sets in China and Germany to quickly choose and select the desired receiver name from an adequately sorted list. Moreover, the user interface should be customizable to the number of presented pieces of information, e.g., the number of entries in lists or menus (cf. hierarchical versus flat menu structure [59]).

The entire model consists of more than 300, mainly quantitative, potential parameters that are relevant for intercultural HCI design and, depending on the culture, have been analytically established by literature research (cf. for details [22]) and can be used to support analytic processing. These reflections can also be used for culturally adaptive systems [19] that can automatically change the user interface characteristics according to the cultural needs of the user because they are already aware of them by design or becoming aware of them by learning over time [24].

5   Discussion

In the following, considerations applying the culture dependent HCI model and evidence for the proper application of the generic IUID framework are discussed elucidating why and how cultural aspects play a role in HCI design and usability/UX engineering thereby showing the strengths and weaknesses and possible alternatives regarding the approach, usefulness, and limitations of the IUID framework.

5.1   Strength of the Scientific Basis

The results so far serve to reveal a basis and some proven facts that are useful for the acquisition of general recommendations for trends in intercultural HCI design (cf. [22]) and culturally adaptive systems (cf. [24]). The "Intercultural Interaction Analysis Tool (IIA-Tool)" [21] served to record and analyze the user's interaction with the system to identify culture dependent variables such as color, positioning, information density, and interaction speed as well as their values, which enabled the verification of parts of the culture-dependent model of HCI as well as preliminary design rules for intercultural HCI design [22]. With the right combination of cultural HCI indicators it is possible to get HCI differences that are purely culturally imprinted [22]. This means that the analysis (recognition and classification) of cultural HCI patterns representing the cultural differences in HCI and the derived cultural HCI indicators are sufficiently statistically discriminating to detect them and to relate the users to a certain cultural imprint (cf. [22]).

5.2 Usefulness of the IUID Framework

The results so far led the author to the concept of intercultural HCI style scores, which can be computed for the designated cultural group from Hofstede's indices to estimate the development expense for new IUID projects. The intercultural HCI style score expresses the average degree of information density and frequency as well as interaction frequency and speed the members in the designated cultural group expect according to the culture dependent HCI model [23]. From Hofstede's data, one can infer, for example, that the cultural distance between China and Germany is high in contrast to Austria and Germany, which is also reflected in the HCI style score and therefore in the behavior of the user interaction with the system. Although cultures are constantly changing, at least for a product life cycle of a few years, trends can thereby be determined, and for special cases of application even selective parameters can be determined, which serve IUID.

5.3 Limitations of the Approach Today

Many aspects must be considered simultaneously to obtain possible cultural explanations for their effect on HCI. One cannot predict how the single parts of the cultural puzzle will fit together (cf. [25]). This has implications for the methods used in intercultural HCI design and in intercultural usability engineering (cf. [60]). Parallel to extensive research literature, empirical investigations regarding intercultural user interface characteristics are necessary, more specifically by comparing several systems of different cultures (benchmark tests) as well as usability evaluation (usability testing). Until the assumed connections between cultural dimensions and HCI dimensions are not completely empirically verified, the presented approach is not very resilient. Therefore, much research effort is still necessary because of the number and complexity of the relationships in HCI determined by culture. A possible reduction of the evaluation effort of the culture dependent HCI model, the revised principle of culturally adaptive HMI (cf. [22]) could be applied abstaining from cultural categorization as already required by [61]. This principle suggests instead to use cultural dimensions to detect the HCI style of the user and adapt the HCI accordingly.

6   Conclusion and Outlook

The IUID framework represents a hybrid approach integrating several cultural methods and applying them systematically. Using the hybrid IUID method-mix and the toolbox is a reasonable approach towards an IUID framework integrating the methods and the explanatory model of culture dependent HCI. Areas such as intercultural usability engineering and intercultural user interface design (IUID) can benefit to the extent that the model is further developed and empirically validated to be successfully applied to new applications, use cases and products allowing predictive design recommendations in conjunction with the user needs as a condition for the possibility of evoking positive cross-cultural user experience.

Not all aspects of the approach to the generic IUID framework and the resulting IUID recommendations have been empirically proven yet. Therefore, it is very reasonable (or even necessary to have first hypotheses) for further development and research to consider some rules of thumb as provisional that should be still treated with the greatest possible care. However, the final version of the generic IUID framework should enable the derivation of IUID recommendations based on the current state of research in IUID and the requested user needs according to the relevant cultural context to evoke positive cross-cultural user experience.

Acknowledgements. I thank all persons who supported me in working on the topics presented - especially Prof. Pei-Luen Patrick Rau and Miss Zhi Guo for their valuable input regarding Chinese human factors.

References

1. Honold, P.: Interkulturelles usability engineering: Eine Untersuchung zu kulturellen Einflüssen auf die Gestaltung und Nutzung technischer Produkte (Als Ms. gedr. ed. Vol. 647). Düsseldorf: VDI Verl. (2000)
2. Heimgärtner, R.: Intercultural user interface design. In: Blashki, K., Isaias, P. (eds.) Emerging Research and Trends in Interactivity and the Human-Computer Interface (2014)
3. Heimgärtner, R.: IUID method-mix: towards a systematic approach for intercultural user interface design (IUID). J. Comput. Commun. 07, 162–194 (2019). https://doi.org/10.4236/jcc.2019.77015
4. Heimgärtner, R.: Towards a toolbox for intercultural user interface design. In: CHIRA 2019 (2019). https://doi.org/10.5220/0008345201560163
5. Thomas, A., Kinast, E.-U., Schroll-Machl, S.: Handbook of Intercultural Communication and Cooperation. Basics and Areas of Application. Vandenhoeck & Ruprecht, Göttingen (2010)
6. Vöhringer-Kuhnt, T.: The Influence of Culture on Usability. (M.A. master thesis), Freie Universität Berlin (2002)
7. Hofstede, G.H., Hofstede, G.J., Minkov, M.: Cultures and Organizations: Software of the Mind, 3rd edn. McGraw-Hill, Maidenhead (2010)
8. Röse, K: 3. The development of culture-oriented human machine systems: specification, analysis and integration of relevant intercultural variables. In Michael, K. (ed.) Cultural Ergonomics, vol. 4, pp. 61–103. Emerald Group Publishing Limited (2004)
9. Shen, S.-T., Woolley, M., Prior, S.: Towards culture-centred design. Interact. Comput. 18(4), 820–852 (2006). https://doi.org/10.1016/j.intcom.2005.11.014
10. Marcus, A.: Cross-cultural user-experience design. In: Barker-Plummer, D., Cox, R., Swoboda, N. (eds.) Diagrams 2006. LNCS (LNAI), vol. 4045, pp. 16–24. Springer, Heidelberg (2006). https://doi.org/10.1007/11783183_4
11. Badre, A., Barber, W.: Culturabilty: the merging of culture and usabilty. In: Proceedings of the 4th Conference on Human Factors and the Web. Basking Ridge, NJ, USA (1998)
12. Dormann, C.: Cultural representations in web design: differences in emotions and values. In: McEwan, T., Benyon, D., Gulliksen, J. (eds.) People and Computers XIX - The Bigger Picture, London, pp. 285–299 (2006)

13. Sun, H.: Building a culturally competent corporate web site: an exploratory study of cultural markers in multilingual web design. Paper presented at the Proceedings of SIGDOC, New York (2001)
14. Castro, S., Luciana, C., Leitão, C., Souza, C.: Semiotic engineering and culture. In: A Journey Through Cultures, pp. 19–42. Springer, London (2013)
15. Pereira, R., Baranauskas, M.C.C., Liu, K.: The value of values for HCI: an informed discussion beyond philosophy. Paper presented at the Proceedings of the 14th Brazilian Symposium on Human Factors in Computing Systems, Salvador, Brazil (2015)
16. Souza, C.S.D., Barbosa, S.D.J., Prates, R.O.: A semiotic engineering approach to HCI. Paper presented at the CHI 2001 Extended Abstracts on Human Factors in Computing Systems, Seattle, Washington (2001)
17. Heimgärtner, R.: Research in progress: towards cross-cultural adaptive human-machine-interaction in automotive navigation systems. In: Day, D.L., Evers, V., del Galdo, E. (eds.) Designing for Global Markets 7: bridging cultural differences. Proceedings of the Seventh International Workshop on Internationalization of Products and Systems, IWIPS 2005, Amsterdam, The Netherlands, 7–9 July, pp. 97–111. Grafisch Centrum, Amsterdam,The Netherlands (2005)
18. Heimgärtner, R.: Measuring cultural differences in human computer interaction as preparatory work for cross-cultural adaptivity in navigation systems: results from a survey. In: Useware 2006: Nutzergerechte Gestaltung technischer Systeme, Düsseldorf, Germany, VDI-Bericht 1946, pp. 301–314. Düsseldorf: VDI (2006)
19. Heimgärtner, R., Holzinger, A. Adams, R.: From cultural to individual adaptive end-user interfaces: helping people with special needs. In: Miesenberger, K., et al. (eds.) Proceedings of 11th International Conference on Computers Helping Peolpe with Special Needs, Linz, Austria, July 2008. LNCS 5105, pp. 82–89. Springer, Heidelberg (2008)
20. Heimgärtner, R.: Towards a generic adaptability framework for automotive HMI. In: Lucke, U., Kindsmüller, M.C., Fischer, S., Herczeg, M., Seehusen, S. (Hrsg.) Workshop Proceedings der Tagungen Mensch & Computer 2008, DeLFI 2008 und Cognitive Design 2008. "Viel Mehr Ideen", Proceedings of AUIIA 08, 7–10 September, Lübec (2008)
21. Heimgärtner, R.: A tool for getting cultural differences in HCI. In: Asai, K. (ed.) Human Computer Interaction: New Developments, pp. 343–368. InTech, Rijeka (2008)
22. Heimgärtner, R.: Cultural Differences in Human Computer Interaction - Towards Culturally Adaptive Human Machine Interaction. Dissertation. Lehrstuhl für Informationswissenschaft. Universität Regensburg. Oldenbourg Verlag (2012)
23. Heimgärtner, R.: Reflections on a model of culturally influenced human computer interaction to cover cultural contexts in HCI design. Int. J. Hum.-Comput. Interact. (2013)
24. Heimgärtner, R.: Culturally-Aware HCI systems. In: Faucher, C. (ed.) Advances in Culturally-aware Intelligent Systems and in Cross-Cultural Psychological Studies. ISRL, vol. 134, pp. 11–37. Springer, Cham (2018). https://doi.org/10.1007/978-3-319-67024-9_2
25. Hall, E.T., Hall, M.R.: Understanding Cultural Differences: Germans, French and Americans. Intercultural Press, Boston, Mass (2009)
26. Lange, O.: Methodik zur Gestaltung und Evaluierung der Software-Gebrauchstauglichkeit bei der ersten oder bei seltener Anwendung. Fraunhofer Verlag, Stuttgart (2019)
27. DIN: DIN EN ISO 9241–110 Ergonomics of humans-system interaction Part 110: Dialogue principles: Beuth (2006)
28. Heimgärtner, R.: Human factors of ISO 9241–110 in the intercultural context. Adv. Ergon. Des. Usability Special Popul.: Part 3, 18 (2014)
29. Windl, H., Heimgärtner, R.: Intercultural design for use – extending usage-centered design by cultural aspects. In: HCII 2013 Proceedings. Springer, Las Vegas (2013)

30. Röse, K., Zühlke, D., Liu, L.: Similarities and dissimilarities of German and Chinese users. In: Johannsen, G. (Hrsg.) Preprints of 8th IFAC/IFIP/IFORS/IEA Symposium on Analysis, Design, and Evaluation of Human-Machine Systems (S. 24–29), Kassel (2001)
31. Nisbett, R.E., Miyamoto, Y.: The influence of culture: Holistic versus analytic perception. Trends Cogn. Sci. **9**(10), 467–473 (2005)
32. Wickens, C.D., Gordon, S.E., Liu, Y.: An introduction to human factors engineering (1998)
33. Gerrig, R.J., Zimbardo, P.G.: Psychology and Life, vol. 20. Pearson, Boston (2010)
34. International ergonomics association. Human Factors/Ergonomics (HF/E) (2020). https://iea.cc/what-is-ergonomics/
35. Card, S.K., Moran, T.P., Newell, A.: The psychology of human-computer interaction (1983)
36. Choong, Y.Y., Plocher, T., Rau, P.L.P.: Cross-cultural web design. In: Proctor, R. (ed.) The Handbook of Human Factors in Web Design. Lawrence Erlbaum Associates, NJ (2004)
37. Maslow, A.H.: Motivation and Personality. Prabhat Prakashan (1981)
38. Reeve, J., Lee, W.: Motivational neuroscience. In: The Oxford Handbook of Human Motivation, pp. 355–371 (2019)
39. Siwek, Z., Oleszkowicz, A., Słowińska, A.: Values realized in personal strivings and motivation and meaning in life in polish university students. J. Happiness Stud. **18**(2), 549–573 (2017)
40. Breitsprecher & Breitlinks: Values, Needs, Wants (2016)
41. Devoe, D.: Viktor Frankl's logotherapy: The search for purpose and meaning. Inquiries J. **4**(07) (2012)
42. Swann, W.B., Jr., Jetten, J., Gómez, Á., Whitehouse, H., Bastian, B.: When group membership gets personal: a theory of identity fusion. Psychol. Rev. **119**(3), 441 (2012)
43. Lynch, K.D.: Modeling role enactment: linking role theory and social cognition. J. Theory Soc. Behav. **37**(4), 379–399 (2007)
44. Solso, R.L., MacLin, M.K., MacLin, O.H.: Cognitive Psychology. Pearson Education, New Zealand (2005)
45. Festinger, L.: A Theory of Cognitive Dissonance, vol. 2. Stanford university press (1957)
46. Perlovsky, L.: Language and cognition interaction neural mechanisms. Comput. Intell. Neurosci. 2011 (2011).
47. Krauss, R.M., Chiu, C.Y.: Language and social behavior. In: Gilbert, D., Fiske, S., Lindsey, G. (eds.) Handbook of Social Psychology, vol. 2, 4th edn., pp. 41–88. McGraw-Hill, Boston (1998)
48. Moneta, G.B.: The flow model of intrinsic motivation in Chinese: cultural and personal moderators. J. Happiness Stud. **5**(2), 181–217 (2004)
49. Cyr, D.: Modeling web site design across cultures: relationships to trust, satisfaction, and e-loyalty. J. Manag. Inf. Syst. **24**(4), 47–72 (2008)
50. Yik, M.: How unique is Chinese emotion. In: The Oxford Handbook of Chinese Psychology, pp. 205–220 (2010)
51. Bond, M.H. (ed.): The Handbook of Chinese Psychology, pp. 208–226. Oxford University Press, Hong Kong (1996)
52. Moneta, G.B., Csikszentmihalyi, M.: Models of concentration in natural environments: a comparative approach based on streams of experiential data. Soc. Behav. Personal. Int. J. **27**(6), 603–637 (1999)
53. Hassenzahl, M., Diefenbach, S., Göritz, A.: Needs, affect, and interactive products – facets of user experience. Interact. Comput. **22**(5), 353–362 (2010). https://doi.org/10.1016/j.intcom.2010.04.002
54. Tannen, D.: Das hab' ich nicht gesagt! Kommunikationsprobleme im Alltag. Kabel Verlag, Hamburg (1992)

55. Gillessen, M.: Wie aus Höflichkeiten Irritationen werden - ein chinesisch-deutscher Normvergleich. In: Sozialwissenschaftlicher Fachinformationsdienst soFid, pp. 9–48. DEU (2003).
56. Liang, Y.: Höflichkeit im Chinesischen. München (1998)
57. Schwartz, S.H.: Mapping and interpreting cultural differences around the world. In H. Vinken, J., Ester, S.P. (eds.) Comparing Cultures, Dimensions of Culture in a Comparative Perspective, pp. 43–73. Brill, Leiden, The Netherlands (2004)
58. Lewis, R.D.: Handbuch internationale Kompetenz: Mehr Erfolg durch den richtigen Umgang mit Geschäftspartner weltweit. Frankfurt/Main: Campus-Verl (2000)
59. Gould, E.W., Marcus, A., Chavan, A.L.: International usability evaluation SIG: issues and strategies. Paper presented at the CHI 2006 Extended Abstracts on Human Factors in Computing Systems, Montreal, Quebec, Canada (2006)
60. Nielsen, J., Bødker, M., Vatrapu, R.: Culture and (i)literacy as challenges to scandinavian cooperative design. Paper presented at the Proceedings of the 3rd International Conference on Intercultural Collaboration, Copenhagen, Denmark (2010)
61. Rathje, S.: Ist wenig kulturelles Verständnis besser als gar keins? - Problematik der Verwendung von Dimensionsmodellen zur Kulturbeschreibung. Interculture-Online, 05 August 2003. http://www.interculture-journal.com/index.php/icj/article/view/12/14. Access 30 July 2019

Transformation of Landscape into Artistic and Cultural Video Using AI for Future Car

Mai Cong Hung[1], Mai Xuan Trang[2], Naoko Tosa[1], and Ryohei Nakatsu[1(✉)]

[1] Kyoto University, Kyoto 606-8501, Japan
tosa.naoko.5c@kyoto-u.ac.jp, ryohei.nakatsu@design.kyoto-u.ac.jp
[2] Faculty of Computer Science, Phenikaa University, Hanoi 12116, Vietnam
trang.maixuan@phenikaa-uni.edu.vn

Abstract. When autonomous driving comes to reality in near future, a space in a car would become a special space where people can enjoy various kinds of entertainment. This paper proposes one such entertainment in which the outside landscape is to be changed into moving art. Firstly, the outside landscape is captured by a camera set near to a driver's head. Then each frame of the captured landscape video is transformed into an artistic image by utilizing the image transformation capability of CycleGAN, one of the recent AI technologies. And the converted video is projected on the windshield. Landscape seen from side windows can be changed into artistic moving images in the same way. In this way, passengers, as well as a driver of a future car, can enjoy artistic moving images that are converted from outside landscape into art video with any art style.

Keywords: CycleGAN · Art style · Transformation of landscape · Autonomous driving

1 Introduction

What would be an interior space of a future car that will adopt autonomous driving capability? If autonomous driving becomes possible, the interior space of a car will not be a simple space where passengers have to stay during their traveling time, but space where the time during driving can be spent for entertainment [1–3]. At that time, the windshield and side glass will be transformed into a screen for entertainment.

What kind of content would be appropriate to be shown on that screen? Of course, showing a movie is an idea. Another idea is to use the scenery outside the car as a material for entertainment. At present, viewing the scenery outside the vehicle is what we experience while traveling by car. Driving while enjoying the beautiful scenery is a great pleasure when traveling by car. However, when the same landscape continues for a long time, or when driving in a trashed urban space, it is tiring to see the scenery outside the vehicle.

In such a case, is it possible to transform the scenery outside the car into something else? Art is a good object to convert. Art has the power to deeply appeal to people by

© Springer Nature Switzerland AG 2021
M. Rauterberg (Ed.): HCII 2021, LNCS 12795, pp. 407–417, 2021.
https://doi.org/10.1007/978-3-030-77431-8_25

relaxing and sometimes straining their hearts. Is it possible to use this power of art to transform the mobile space into an art space?

In this paper, we propose a method to meet such demands by using the latest AI technology, show the concrete method, and show several examples of converting the landscape into art. Section 2 proposes the concept of our proposal including its merit and problem. Section 3 briefly describes CycleGAN, which is one of recent AI technologies called GANs and which play an important role to convert scenery into artistic videos. Section 4 describes our experiment to convert scenery videos shot while driving into artistic videos including several target artworks we have selected. Section 5 shows some of the results we have obtained and describes some discussions. As there are several problems with the obtained results, Sect. 6 proposes an improvement of our method described in Sect. 4 and describes the improved results. Finally, Sect. 7 concludes the paper.

2 Concept

The basic method proposed in this paper is to transform the scenery outside the car into an art-like video in real-time. GANs (Generative Adversarial Networks), which is an AI technology that has been attracting attention recently, is used to convert landscapes into art videos. The details of the method will be described later.

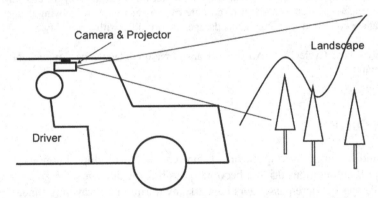

Fig. 1. System structure.

There are levels 1 to 5 for autonomous driving [1–3]. Level 5 is for fully autonomous driving, but it takes a considerable amount of time to realize it. For the moment, the realization of levels 2 and 3, in which autonomous driving is restricted in a free-way, etc., is being tried. In this case, a person in charge of driving will be called a driver, because the person needs to intervene in driving if necessary. Figure 1 shows a system structure that can convert a driver's visible landscape into an art video. This can be applied not only to level 5 which is completely autonomous driving but also to levels 3 and 4 where the driver needs to intervene in driving. However, applying this system to levels 3 and 4 need revision of the Road Traffic Law, so we are currently proposing the system as a concept.

As shown in Fig. 1, a camera and a projector are installed in the vehicle near the driver's head. The video captured by the camera is converted into an art video, which is projected on the windshield by the projector. The windshield is transparent and at the same time has the capability that images can be projected with a projector [4]. The projection on the windshield in this way is an art video of the outside scenery seen from the driver's viewpoint. The features of this method are as follows.

1. A scenery outside a car that a driver sees during driving is converted into an art video. The driver not only appreciates it as an art but also can drive the car in the space expressed in the art video. The driver and other passengers can feel as if they are moving in the art space.
2. Except for the driver, the passengers do not see the converted landscape from their viewpoint. But it is considered that there is a little problem because the difference in viewpoint is not so large.
3. It is possible to select any art style for converting an actual landscape into an art video. For example, it is possible to change the natural scenery outside the car into a Monet style or Cezanne style art video. On the other hand, what kind of effect can be obtained for drivers and passengers by making the outside scenery into an abstract art style, and what kind of abstract art style is suitable for this system are interesting research issues.
4. Further, it is possible to gradually convert the actual landscape into the art video by blending them. In current cars, it is possible to change the air conditioning temperature and air volume at several levels. It is possible to select the blending level, in the same way, depending on the driver or passenger's preference.

3 CycleGAN for Art Style Transfer

The task of converting scenery outside the car into an art video is connected to style transfer topics in AI. There are numerous methods in Deep Learning/Machine Learning [5] dealing with the problem of art style transfer. In this research, we use the celebrated method named CycleGAN, a variation of GANs.

GANs (Generative Adversarial Networks) is a Deep Learning structure including both generative models and discriminative models in a deep neural network [6]. The name "generative" and "discriminative" came from the fact that generative models can generate new data instances while discriminative models can discriminate between different categories of data. In art style transfer, we would expect a generative model to transfer a photo or video frame into a specific style. The advantage of GANs is their efficiency while not requiring large amounts of training data.

The architecture of GANs is represented in Fig. 2. In GANs, generator G learns to generate data from random noise while discriminator network D tries to identify the generated data whether it is real or fake. The training process can be interpreted as a zero-sum game between G and D. The training process on G tries to maximize the probability of the generated data to lie on the distribution of target sets and the training process on D tries to minimize it. This minimax mechanism helps the networks to converge even with a relatively small number of training data. By modifying the basic configuration, a large number of GANs variation has been developed.

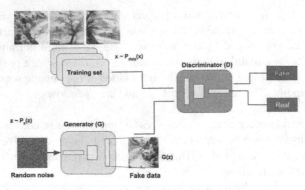

Fig. 2. The basic configuration of GANs

Among the variations of GANs, CycleGAN is an elegant method to study the style-to-style level of image transformation [7]. We consider the generative models on CycleGAN as the main tool to transfer landscape into artworks. The architecture of a CycleGAN network is illustrated in Fig. 3. We add an inverse transformation G_{BA} of the generator network G_{AB}, which has the data of domain A as input to transform them into elements of domain B. We also use two discriminators D_A and D_B for the domains A and B, respectively. We would measure the difference between A and $\hat{A}$ (the reconstruction data in A by applying G_{AB} then G_{BA}) and the error caused by the difference between B and the domain given by applying G_{AB} to A. The training process would minimize the sum of these two errors. The data generated by G_{AB} and G_{BA} provides the mutual transformation between the two domains.

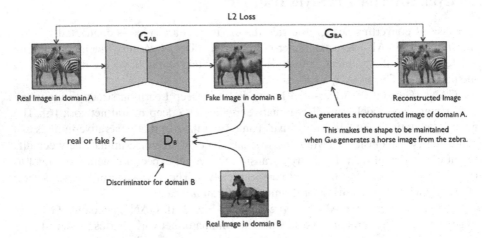

Fig. 3. The basic configuration of CycleGAN [6]

The most important difference between generators of GANs and CycleGAN is that GANs learn to generate data to fit in a target set while CycleGAN learns the set-to-set level of transformation. Because of this, CycleGAN could be used to establish mutual

Zebras ⟳ Horses

Fig. 4. Horses-Zebras transfer (Image source [7])

conversion between these two groups of images - the key point to do the task of style transfer. Figure 4 shows how horses are converted into zebras and vice versa. The development of CycleGAN has opened a new way to transform regular images into artworks that have specific art styles, because of the set-to-set level of style transfer instead of image-to-image level transfer. Therefore, we can perform flexible transformations when the outside scenery changes at high speed.

4 Experiment

We used the datasets shown below and make experiments of mutual transformation via CycleGAN between A and B1, B2, B3, B4 respectively. After finishing the training phase, we applied the generator of each experiment to convert landscape video taken in a driving car in real-time (frame by frame).

Dataset A: Road-scene photos mixed by self-taken data and Nuscenes Dataset from APTIV (partly).
Dataset B1: Kandinsky abstract artworks in Wiki Art [8].
Dataset B2: Naoko Tosa's Sound of Ikebana [9, 10].
Dataset B3: Sansui artworks in CS231N project "Chinese Painting Generation Using Generative Adversarial Networks" at Stanford University [11].
Dataset B4: Ikebana photos in Flickr.

We choose these datasets to transfer the outside scenery into Western abstract art (A-B1), Japanese abstract art (A-B2), traditional Oriental arts (A-B3, A-B4). Figure 5 shows several of the Kandinsky artworks. Figure 6 shows several images of the Sound

Fig. 5. Examples of Kandinsky artworks.

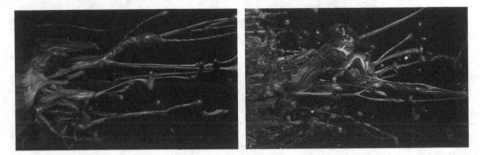

Fig. 6. Examples of Sound of Ikebana images.

Fig. 7. Examples of Sansui Artworks.

of Ikebana. Figure 7 shows several Sansui artworks. Figure 8 shows several Ikebana photos.

The Sound of Ikebana was created by Naoko Tosa, one of the authors. It is a video artwork that was created by giving sound vibration to color paints, letting them jump up, and shooting the created form by a high-speed camera. She was inspired by watching various fluid dynamics based phenomena such as "milk crown" and after various experiments succeeded in creating beautiful forms. Although created forms are abstract, many

Fig. 8. Examples of Ikebana photos.

people indicated that they feel Japanese beauty in these abstract forms [9]. Therefore, we think that the Sound of Ikebana would be a good representation of Japanese abstract art.

5   Results and Discussion

After applying the style transfer functions generated by CycleGAN, we get the transformation as shown in Fig. 9. For the original scenes, two different types of scenes were selected; one is a countryside scene, and another is a cityscape scene.

In our eye-checked evaluation, the transformation A-B1 and A-B2 give the most qualified results in the cityscape scenes while A-B3 and A-B4 give the best results in the countryside scenes. We consider the reason as abstract art is suitable to represent artificial objects such as buildings, traffic lights, etc., and Oriental traditional art was inspired by a natural landscape.

The A to B1, B2, B3, B4 transformation opened a new way to create original video art. CycleGAN is used to work with images of relatively similar sizes, themes, and categories such as horses and zebras, Monet paintings and landscape photos, winter scenes, and summer scenes. But if we perform some "unusual transformation" between relatively different domains of objects (for example between cityscapes and flowers), we could create original art of a high-abstract level.

In the next research, we would improve some limits of the current work. Firstly, the direction of the original training data is vertical or horizontal on a 2D frame but the direction of the front scene while driving is in the last dimension of the 3D frame. Another problem is that sometimes the transition between frames is not smooth enough, we present an improvement for this problem in the next section.

Fig. 9. Transformation of actual scenes into art style scenes (From top to bottom: original scene (A), Kandinsky style (B1), Sound of Ikebana style (B2), Sansui style (B3), Ikebana style (B4))

6   DriveGAN: Improvement of the Method

To obtain smooth transitions between frames in the generated video, we try to include frame loss into the total loss of the CycleGAN. The goal is to minimize the difference between the frame transitions in the real video and the generated video. In our experiment, a video captured by a car's camera is extracted to frames that form the source image set (*A*). The target art image set (*B*) is described in Sect. 4.

In the original CycleGAN, the full objective function is defined as follows:

$$
\begin{aligned}
\mathcal{L}(G_{AB}, G_{BA}, D_A, D_B) = {} & \mathcal{L}_{GAN}(G_{AB}, D_B, A, B) \\
& + \mathcal{L}_{GAN}(G_{BA}, D_A, B, A) \\
& + \lambda \mathcal{L}_{cyc}(G_{AB}, G_{BA})
\end{aligned}
\tag{1}
$$

where $\mathcal{L}_{GAN}(G_{AB}, D_B, A, B)$ is the adversarial loss for the mapping function (the generator) $G_{AB} : A \rightarrow B$ and its discriminator D_B. $\mathcal{L}_{GAN}(G_{BA}, D_A, B, A)$ is the adversarial loss for the mapping function (the generator) $G_{BA} : B \rightarrow A$ and its discriminator D_A. $\mathcal{L}_{cyc}(G_{AB}, G_{BA})$ is the cycle consistency loss that captures the forward and backward cycle consistencies: $a \rightarrow G_{AB}(a) \rightarrow G_{BA}(G_{AB}(a)) \approx a$ and $b \rightarrow G_{BA}(b) \rightarrow G_{AB}(G_{BA}(b)) \approx b$.

To define the frame loss, we denote the input frame sequence (or source image set) as $A = \{f_{m+it}\}_{i=0}^{N-1}$ where m is the index of the first frame that we want to include in the source images, t is the frame step. t is also a hyperparameter to tune when training our GAN. The frame loss between two sequences of frames is defined as follows:

$$\mathcal{L}_{FRAME}(G_{AB}, G_{BA}) = \mathbb{E}_{a \sim p_A(a)}\left[\left\| \begin{array}{c} (G_{BA}(G_{AB}(f_{m+(i+1)t})) - G_{BA}(G_{AB}(f_{m+it}))) \\ -(f_{m+(i+1)t} - f_{m+it}) \end{array} \right\|_1\right]$$

We add this frame loss to the Eq. (1), the full objective function of our proposed DriveGAN becomes:

$$\begin{aligned} \mathcal{L}(G_{AB}, G_{BA}, D_A, D_B) &= \mathcal{L}_{GAN}(G_{AB}, D_B, A, B) \\ &+ \mathcal{L}_{GAN}(G_{BA}, D_A, B, A) \\ &+ \lambda \mathcal{L}_{cyc}(G_{AB}, G_{BA}) \\ &+ \gamma \mathcal{L}_{FRAME}(G_{AB}, G_{BA}) \end{aligned} \tag{2}$$

where γ control the relative importance of the frame loss. The training process would also try to minimize the frame loss to ensure the differences between consecutive frames after transforming would be small if the difference of consecutive frames in the original scenes is small. We replace the training data of A by a collection of video taken by camera to generate sequences of consecutive frames.

Figure 10 shows the result of the transformation of several continuous landscape images into Kandinsky style images and Sound of Ikebana style images. Based on eye-checked evaluation, the created videos look smooth and could be used as contents that is a transformation of outside landscape into artistic videos.

Fig. 10. Transformation of continuous frame images into art style images (From top to bottom: original scene (A), Kandinsky style (B1), Sound of Ikebana style (B2)

7 Conclusion

A method of transforming outside sceneries seen from the inside of a car into artistic video is proposed. For the transformation, we adopted CycleGAN to transform a set of landscape images into a set of art images, as CycleGAN, one of the latest AI technologies, has the capability of mutual transformation between two image sets.

For source images, we collected various road images (A). As target art images we selected four types of art images; Kandinsky art images (B1), Sound of Ikebana art images created by one of the authors, Naoko Tosa (B2), Sansui art images (B3), and Ikebana photos (B4). By using these training sets and CycleGAN the transformation functions from A to B1, B2, B3, B4 were achieved. Then each frame of several videos taken from a driving car was transformed into each of B1, B2, B3, and B4 styles. And some discussions were carried out regarding the obtained results.

As a next step, we tried to improve the original CycleGAN to delete a flicker observed in the generated video. By including frame loss into the total loss function and by minimizing the frame loss during the training process, we succeeded in obtaining a smooth transition between frames in the generated video.

For future research, we will carry out a user study to evaluate the feasibility of the proposed method. Also, transformation into several other art styles including anime-style [12] will be carried out.

References

1. Self-Driving Car. https://en.wikipedia.org/wiki/Self-driving_car. Accessed 10 Jan 2021
2. Levinson, J., et al.: Towards fully autonomous driving: systems and algorithms. In: 2011 IEEE Intelligent Vehicles Symposiums, pp. 163–168 (2011)

3. Garcia Cuenca, L., et al.: Machine learning techniques for undertaking roundabouts in autonomous driving. MDPI Sens. **19**, 2286 (2019)
4. Glass on Web. https://www.glassonweb.com/news/agc-releases-infoverretm-mirror-enabling-unique-information-display-mirror. Accessed 10 Jan 2021
5. Kelleher, J.D.: Deep Learning. MIT Press, Cambridge (2019)
6. Creswell, A., et al.: Generative adversarial networks: an overview. IEEE Sig. Process. Mag. **35**(1), 53–65 (2018)
7. Zhu, J.-Y., Park, T., Isola, P., Efros, A.A.: Unpaired image-to-image translation using cycle-consistent adversarial networks. In: The IEEE International Conference on Computer Vision (ICCV), pp.223–2232 (2017)
8. Wikiart: Wassily Kandinsky. https://www.wikiart.org/en/wassily-kandinsky. Accessed 10 Jan 2021
9. Tosa, N., Pang, Y., Yang, Q., Nakatsu, R.: Pursuit and expression of Japanese beauty using technology, Special Issue "The Machine as Artist (for the 21st Century)". Arts J. MDPI **8**(1), 38 (2019)
10. Tosa, N., Yunian, P., Zhao, L., Nakatsu, R.: Genesis: new media art created as a visualization of fluid dynamics. In: Munekata, N., Kunita, I., Hoshino, J. (eds.) ICEC 2017. LNCS, vol. 10507, pp. 3–13. Springer, Cham (2017). https://doi.org/10.1007/978-3-319-66715-7_1
11. Wang, G., Chen, Y., Chen, Y.: Chinese Painting Generation Using Generative Adversarial Networks. http://cs231n.stanford.edu/reports/2017/pdfs/311.pdf
12. Chen, Y., Lai, Y., Liu, Y.: CartoonGAN: generative adversarial networks for photo cartoonization. In: 2018 IEEE/CVF Conference on Computer Vision and Pattern Recognition, pp. 9465–9474 (2018)

The Collection Method of Heterogeneous Smart Farm Data Based on Model Transformation Technique for Human Computer Friendly Learning

Woo Sung Jang, Jang Hwan Kim, Chae Yun Seo, and R. Young Chul Kim[✉]

SE Laboratory, Department of Software and Communication Engineering, Hongik University, Seoul, Korea
{jang,janghwan}@selab.hongik.ac.kr, {chaeyun,bob}@hongik.ac.kr

Abstract. Recently, smart farm technology is in the spotlight as the solution of existing agricultural problems as spreading ICT convergence technology. For assisting expert farmers or guiding non-farmers, there is a need for a predicting method of growing and benefiting of crops as well as cultivating them through the cultivating method on AI/Big data approach. To do this, we absolutely need to collect a large amount of the right data to predict the growth of good or bad crops, and then consider how to gather the collected learning data. Therefore, we propose a data collection method based on metamodeling of Model Driven Architecture, which transforms heterogeneous data into a uniform learning data with model transformation rule. With this approach, we apply for easily customizing any prediction, and expect for even non-farmers to use any smart farm cultivation.

Keywords: Smart farm · Meta model · Model transformation · Heterogeneous data collection

1 Introduction

Recently, smart farm technology is in the spotlight as the solution of existing agricultural problems as spreading ICT convergence technology [1]. Additionally, there is a need for a predicting method of growing and benefiting of crops as well as cultivating them through the cultivating method on AI/Big data approach. To do this, we absolutely need to collect a large amount of the right data to predict the growth of crops. So, we are also considering how to gather the collected learning data.

We prepare first to build a smart farm environment to collect the learning data with the big data, and second to collect big data provided by external organizations such as *Korea Agriculture, Forestry and Fisheries Food Education Cultural Information Institute* [2] and *Korea Public Data Portal* [3] for their growth data of the cultivated crop. They provide their data through Open API to the public with each different format. To use their data, we need to transform their data with a data processing algorithm.

© Springer Nature Switzerland AG 2021
M. Rauterberg (Ed.): HCII 2021, LNCS 12795, pp. 418–431, 2021.
https://doi.org/10.1007/978-3-030-77431-8_26

We propose a data collection method based on metamodeling of Model Driven Architecture for heterogeneous data to transform a uniform learning data with model transformation rule. This provides very intuitive information presentation and model management [4]. More important thing is continuing adding other farm data formats without changing the program algorithm. We may apply for the integrated collection of heterogeneous big data.

2 Related Works

2.1 Meta Model-Based Model Transformation Method

Model to Model (M2M) transformation is a method of generating a target model from a source model using model transformation language. The components of this method are composed of Model, Meta-model, Transformation language, and Transformation engine as shown in Fig. 1 [5]. To perform M2M of Transformation Engine, the Meta-model of Source model and Meta-model of Target model must be defined. Meta-model is a schema that can read model information. Next, the Transformation Language should be defined. Transformation language refers to the meta-model and describes the rules for transforming the source model into the target model. The transformation language consists of information on adding, deleting, and modifying models. Transformation engine transforms the source model to the target model by executing the transformation language.

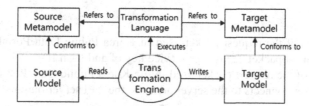

Fig. 1. Model to model translation mechanism

Eclipse Modeling Framework (EMF) [6] provides ecore model that can define meta-model. Model transformation can be performed using either a model transformation language (ATL [7], ETL [8], QVT-O [9], etc.). Since the metamodel complies with the OMG standard data file, XMI [10], optimal model transformation can be performed.

2.2 Big Data Collection Process for General Korean Smart Farm

A general Korean smart farm big data center provides big data through an API server. Users create a data collection server, and request and receive data from each center's API server through the data collection server. The detailed structure is shown in Fig. 2 below. Figure 2 shows the process of requesting and receiving data from two centers that provide smart farm big data in Korea.

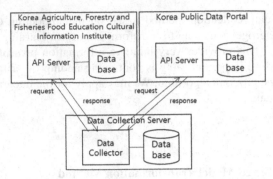

Fig. 2. Flow of obtaining data from smart farm big data server

Table 1. Structure of request packet used by Korea Public Data Portal

Category	Size	Sample	Description
serviceKey	100	%ED%95%9C%EA%B8%80	Authentication key
pageSize	15	10	Result count per page
pageNo	15	1	Number of pages
searchFrmhsCode	50	Testfarm01	Farm ID
searchMeasDt	10	2019010100	Information search date
returnType	10	xml	Response specific type

The structure of the request packet used in Korea Public Data Portal is shown in Table 1. The request packet needs user service key of and farm ID.

The sample of the request packet used in the Korea Public Data Portal is shown in Table 2. If the user connects to the server address, the API server outputs XML data.

Table 2. Sample of request packet used by Kore Public Data Portal

http://apis.data.go.kr/1390000/SmartFarmdata/envdatarqst?ser-
viceKey=%ED%95%9C%EA%B8%80&searchFrmhsCode=TestFarm01&searchMeasDt=2
019010100&returnType=xml

The part of the response packet used in Korea Public Data Portal is shown in Table 3.

Table 3. Part of response packet used by Kore Public Data Portal

Category	Size	Sample	Description
resultCode	2	00	Result code
[...] (omission)			
inTp	15	24.5	Internal temperature ('C)
outTp	15	10.5	External temperature ('C)
inHd	15	78.9	Internal humidity (%)
inCo2	15	434.0	Internal CO_2 (ppm)

The part of response packet sample used in Korea Public Data Portal is shown in Table 4.

Table 4. Part of response packet sample used by Kore Public Data Portal

```
<?xml version="1.0" encoding="UTF-8" standalone="true"?>
-<response>
-<items>
-<item>
<inTp>24.5</inTp>
<inHd>78.9</inHd>
<inCo2>434.0</inCo2>
                                        [...] (omission)
</item>
</items>
<numOfRows>10</numOfRows>
</response>
```

3 The Collection Method of Heterogeneous Smart Farm Data Based on Meta-model

We show our design of a smart farm system. In Fig. 3, we consist of smart farm data integration server, client server, and external organization. The integration server gathers sensor data from the client and external organizations trains the collected data and predicts crop production using the training data.

We propose the design of a Data Collector based on Meta-model (DCM) for Plant Growth Prediction System in the integration server. The DCM requests crop data to API Servers in heterogeneous external organizations and stores the received data in a database.

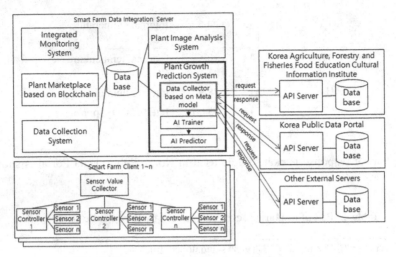

Fig. 3. The overall structure of a smart farm system

The DCM automatically generates a request and response model and the packet data from each model for each organization.

Figure 4 shows the automatic generation process of data request packet for heterogeneous external organizations. The DCM generates an integrated request model as a file. The transformation engine reads the integrated request model file, and automatically generates a data request model file for the Korea Public Data Portal. The structure of the model file is generated using information from the metamodel. Packet information of the automatically generated model is transmitted to the Korea Public Data Portal.

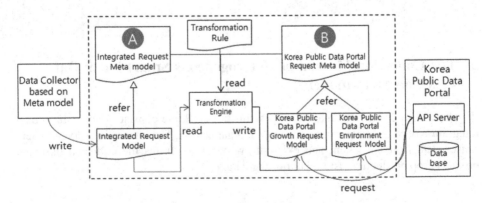

Fig. 4. Automatic request packet generation process with model transformation technique

Figure 5 shows the structure of the Integrated Request Meta-model. It consists of the address of the API server, environment request information, and growth request information. Environment and Growth present information using Request Data.

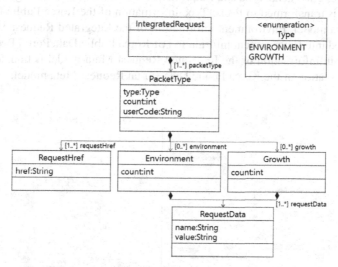

Fig. 5. Structure of Integrated Request Meta model (A)

Figure 6 shows the structure of the Korea Public Data Portal Request Meta model. The meta-model consists of the API server address of Korea Public Data Portal, environment request information for Korea Public Data Portal, and growth request information for Korea Public Data Portal.

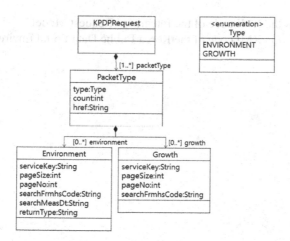

Fig. 6. Structure of Korea Public Data Portal Request Meta model (B)

Figure 7 is the transformation process between meta models using the transformation engine. Figure 7-(a) is the structure of the Integrated Request Meta-model. Figure 7-(b) is the structure of the Korea Public Data Portal Meta-model. Each model are expressed in the XMI code. The PacketType and RequestHref information of the Integrated Request Meta model is transformed to PacketType information of the Korea Public Data Portal Request Meta model. Environment information of the Integrated Request Meta-model is transformed into Environment information of Korea Public Data Portal Request Meta model. Growth information of the Integrated Request Meta-model is transformed into Growth information of the Korea Public Data Portal Request Meta model.

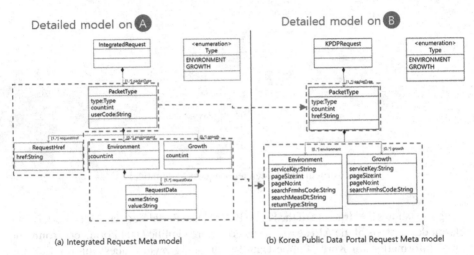

(a) Integrated Request Meta model   (b) Korea Public Data Portal Request Meta model

Fig. 7. The transformation rule between meta model A and B

Table 5 shows the XMI code of the Integrated Request Model.

Table 6 shows the XMI code of the Korea Public Data Portal Environment Request Model.

Table 5. XMI code of the Integrated Request Model

```
<?xml version="1.0" encoding="UTF-8"?>
<ir:IntegratedRequest xmi:version="2.0" xmlns:xmi="http://www.omg.org/XMI"
xmlns:xsi="http://www.w3.org/2001/XMLSchema-instance" xmlns:sed="http://integrat-
edrequest/1.0" name="Model">
   <PacketType type="ENVIRONMENT" count="1" us-
erCode="%ED%95%9C%EA%B8%80">
      <RequestHref href="http://apis.data.go.kr/1390000/SmartFarmdata"/>
      <Environment count="7">
         <RequestData name="hrefFolder" value="envdatarqst" />
         <RequestData name="serviceKey" value="%ED%95%9C%EA%B8%80" />
         <RequestData name="pageSize" value="" />
         <RequestData name="pageNo" value="" />
         <RequestData name="searchFrmhsCode" value="TestFarm01" />
         <RequestData name="searchMeasDt" value="2019010100" />
         <RequestData name="returnType" value="xml" />
      </Environment>
   </PacketType>
</ir:IntegratedRequest>
```

Table 6. XMI code of the Korea Public Data Portal Environment Request Model

```
<?xml version="1.0" encoding="UTF-8"?>
<req:KPDPRequest xmi:version="2.0" xmlns:xmi="http://www.omg.org/XMI"
xmlns:xsi="http://www.w3.org/2001/XMLSchema-instance" xmlns:sed="http://kpdpre-
quest/1.0" name="Model">
   <PacketType type="ENVIRONMENT" count="1"
href="http://apis.data.go.kr/1390000/SmartFarmdata/envdatarqst">
      <Envoronment
         serviceKey="%ED%95%9C%EA%B8%80"
         pageSize=""
         pageNo=""
         searchFrmhsCode="TestFarm01"
         searchMeasDt="2019010100"
         returnType="xml"
      />
   </PacketType>
</req:KPDPRequest>
```

Table 7 is a request packet generated from the Korea Public Data Portal Model. To receive public smart farm data, we transmit this request packet to Korea public data portal.

Table 7. The request packet generated from the Korea Public Data Portal Environment Request Model

http://apis.data.go.kr/1390000/SmartFarmdata/envdatarqst?serviceKey=%ED%95%9C%EA%B8%80&searchFrmhsCode=TestFarm01&searchMeasDt=2019010100&returnType=xml

If a new organization (new big data center) is added, the transformation rule file and the meta-model file for this new organization can be added as shown in Fig. 8.

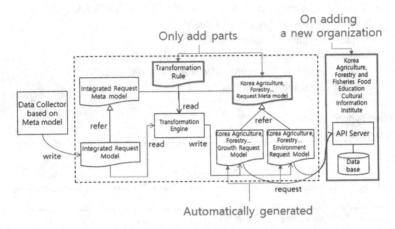

Fig. 8. The added files for adding new organization

Figure 9 shows the process of automatically transforming response packets received from heterogeneous external organizations into integrated response packets. The received packet is created as a response model file. The transformation engine reads the response model file of Korea Public Data Portal and automatically transforms the response model into an integrated response model file. The structure of the model file is

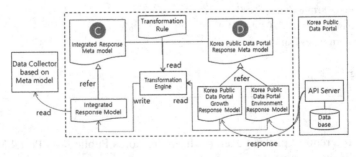

Fig. 9. Automatic response packet generation process with model transformation technique

created using information from the meta-model. The automatically generated integrated response model information is stored in the database.

Figure 10 shows the structure of the Integrated Response Meta model. Meta model consists the farm ID (userCode), environment response information, and growth response information. Environment and Growth presents information using ResponseData.

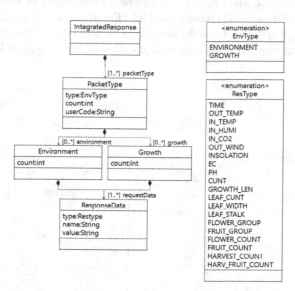

Fig. 10. Structure of Integrated Response Meta model (C)

Figure 11 shows the structure of the Korea Public Data Portal Response Meta model. The meta-model consists of the farm ID of Korea Public Data Portal, environment response information for Korea Public Data Portal, and growth response information for Korea Public Data Portal.

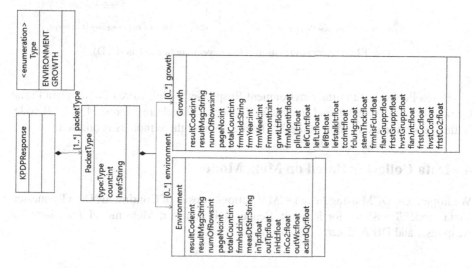

Fig. 11. Structure of Korea Public Data Portal Response Meta model (D)

Figure 12 is the transformation process between meta-models using the transformation engine. Figure 12-(c) is the structure of the Integrated Response Meta model. Figure 12-(d) is the structure of the Korea Public Data Portal Response Meta model. Each meta models are expressed in XMI code. The PacketType information of Korea Public Data Portal Response Meta model is transformed to PacketType information of the Integrated Response Meta model. Environment information of Korea Public Data Portal Response Meta model is transformed into Environment information of the Integrated Response Meta model. Growth information of Korea Public Data Portal Response Meta model is transformed into Growth information of the Integrated Response Meta model.

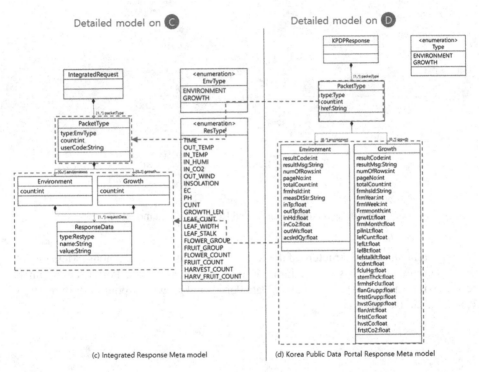

Fig. 12. The transformation rule between meta models (C, D)

Korea Public Data Portal Environment Response Model, Korea Public Data Portal Growth Response Model, and Integrated Response Model are expressed in XMI code. In this paper, the expression of the XMI code of these three models is omitted.

4   Data Collector Based on Meta Model

We implement DCM using Java. DCM functions consist of Continuous Data Requester, Meta model Translator for Request, Sender, DB Adapter, Meta model Translator for Response, and DB Adapter.

The detailed structure of DCM is shown in Fig. 13. Continuous Data Requester creates an Integrated Request Model to request the latest data every day and delivers it to the Meta model Translator for Request. Meta-model Translator for Request automatically transforms the received Integrated Request Model into a heterogeneous Request Model and delivers a transformed model to the Sender. Meta model Translator for Request includes Transformation Rule and Meta model for Korea Public Data Portal Model Transformation, Transformation Rule, and Meta model for Korea Agriculture, Forestry and Fisheries Food Education Cultural Information Institute. Sender automatically transforms heterogeneous Request Models into packets and delivers them to API Server. The receiver automatically transforms heterogeneous response packets received from API Server into heterogeneous Response Models and delivers them to Meta-model Translator for Response. Meta-model Translator for Response automatically transforms the received heterogeneous Response Model into Integrated Response Model and delivers transformed model to DB Adapter. Meta model Translator for Response includes Transformation Rule and Meta model for Korea Public Data Portal Model Transformation, Transformation Rule and Meta model for Korea Agriculture, Forestry, and Fisheries Food Education Cultural Information Institute. The DB Adapter stores the information of the received model to the MySQL.

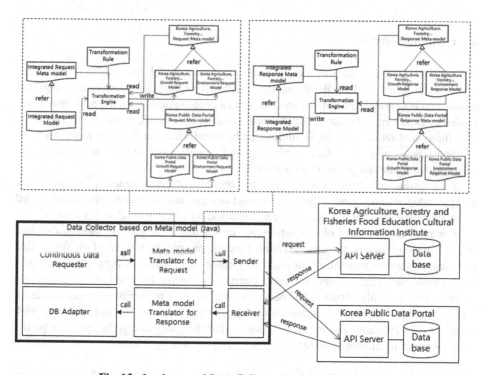

Fig. 13. Implemented Data Collector based on Meta model

5 Experiment Result

We use the implemented DCM to collect big data from two organizations. We correctly collect 403,920 data from the Korea Public Data Portal, and 2,694,936 data from Korea Agriculture, Forestry, and Fisheries Food Education Cultural Information Institute (Table 8).

Table 8. Number of data saved by Data Collector based on Meta model

	Korea Public Data Portal	Korea Agriculture, Forestry and Fisheries Food Education Cultural Information Institute
Number of normally stored data	403,920	2,694,936
Number of abnormally stored data	0	0

6 Conclusions

We propose a data collection method based on meta-model for collecting heterogeneous smart farm big data. We define the integrated request metamodel, the integrated response meta-model, the request meta-model of each organization, the response meta-model of each organization, and the transformation rule between those meta-models. The integrated request model is automatically transformed to the data request model of each organization. The data response model of each organization is automatically transformed to the integrated response model.

As a result, we automatically collect the big data of heterogeneous organizations, and provide for easily adding packets of other organizations. This method can be used as an automatic AI training data collection method for smart farm data prediction.

For mid-level farmers of domestic scale competing with global markets, the data collection technique we propose can contribute to enhance the system of the farm. This also suggests a new possibility for multiple farmers with different data systems to join forces with the social role and inclusive elements of technology to help local farmers survive. This not only serves as the basis for local farmers to survive competition from global markets, but it also suggests a new possibility to unite multiple farmers with different data systems. Therefore, it is hoped that this proposed technique can be the basis of major technologies in the future society as a new paradigm.

Acknowledgement. This research was supported by Basic Science Research Program through the National Research Foundation of Korea (NRF) funded by the Ministry of Education (2020R1I1A1A01072928).

References

1. Ahn, M.H., Heo, C.-M.: A study on the effect of perceived usefulness factors of smart farm on the rural entrepreneurial intention. Asia-Pac. J. Bus. Ventur. Entrepreneursh. **15**(4), 161–173 (2020)
2. Korea Agriculture, Forestry and Fisheries Food Education Cultural Information Institute. https://www.smartfarmkorea.net
3. Korea Public Data Portal. https://www.data.go.kr
4. Jang, W.S., Kim, R.Y.C.: A case study of cost reduction for maintenance of photovoltaic energy monitoring system based on model driven architecture. In: KCSE, vol. 21, no. 1, pp.159–161 (2019)
5. Czarnecki, K., Helsen, S.: Feature-based survey of model transformation approaches. IBM Syst. J. **45**(3), 621–645 (2006)
6. Budinsky, F., Merks, E., Steinberg, D.: EMF: Eclipse Modeling Framework. Addison-Wesley, Boston (2009)
7. Wikipedia, ATL. https://en.wikipedia.org/wiki/ATLAS_Transformation_language. Accessed 10 Feb 2021
8. ETL. https://www.eclipse.org/epsilon/doc/etl/. Accessed 10 Feb 2021
9. QVT-O. https://projects.eclipse.org/projects/modeling.mmt.qvt-oml. Accessed 10 Feb 2021
10. OMG, XML Metadata Interchange (XMI) Specification Version 2.5.1, OMG Document Number: Formal/2015-06-07

Quick Buttons on Map-Based Human Machine Interface in Vehicles is Better or Not: A Cross-Cultural Comparative Study Between Chinese and Germans

Johannes Mehler[1,2], Zhi Guo[1], Andong Zhang[1], and Pei-Luen Patrick Rau[1(✉)]

[1] Tsinghua University, Beijing, People's Republic of China
rpl@mail.tsinghua.edu.cn
[2] RWTH Aachen University, Aachen, Germany

Abstract. Map navigation is the main task and the main page of human-machine interface (HMI) in vehicles. The design of map page is paramount to improve user experience of automotive HMI. The present study was to examine whether the design of quick buttons or icons on map page has an influence on Chinese and German driver's preference and experience during using car console infotainment system. Firstly, a Chinese HMI and a German HMI was designed according to Hofstede's culture model and cross-cultural design elements. The two interfaces have the same functions, and the main difference is whether there are quick buttons on map page or not. Secondly, sixteen Chinese drivers and sixteen German drivers were recruited to use and evaluate two interfaces by user experience scale and interview in a simple driving simulator: one is with the design of quick buttons on map page, the other is without this design. Participants were asked to finish four tasks when using HMI in vehicles, respectively navigation, phone call, play music, and the return to main page. The results indicated that Chinese driver prefer to use the HMI with quick buttons on map page, but German prefer to use simple and clear HMI without quick buttons on map page.

Keywords: Cultural data analytics · In-vehicle HMI · Cross-cultural study

1 Introduction

The Chinese car market is a fast-growing and important market for car manufacturers, such as BMW, Daimler, and Volkswagen. The market share of German car manufacturers in the Chinese car market from 2009 to 2016 is shown in Fig. 1 [1]. Since 2013, the Chinese market was growing more rapidly than the sales figures of the German brands, which means German companies were losing market share at this time.

Thus, we want to figure out which reasons lead to this decline and why German car manufacturers are struggling to keep up with the Chinese market growth pace. One reason is that the German human-computer interface in the car is not adapted to the Chinese market. Heimgärtner [2] stated that the communication between human and

© Springer Nature Switzerland AG 2021
M. Rauterberg (Ed.): HCII 2021, LNCS 12795, pp. 432–449, 2021.
https://doi.org/10.1007/978-3-030-77431-8_27

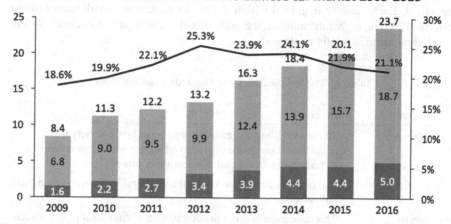

Fig. 1. Development of the market share of German car manufacturers in the Chinese car market 2009–2016

machine is similar to that of human and human as the system is designed by human according to their understanding, therefore the human-machine interface is influenced by culture. Map navigation is the main task and the main page of the human-machine interface (HMI) in vehicles. The design of the map page is paramount to improve the user experience of automotive HMI. But there are significant differences in designing the top mobile apps about the map in Western countries and China. For example, there are more quick buttons about other functions in Chinese map apps. Rössger and Peissner [3] state that HMI in vehicles needs to be adapted to cultural differences. Heimgartner established a model of culturally adaptive HMI, and got some insights into general findings about information identity and interaction habits by empirical studies [2].

This study focuses on the cross-cultural design of map page of the in-vehicle console infotainment system in China and Germany. Two questions are raised: 1) what makes up a culturally fitting HMI in the vehicle, and 2) how to design a culturally adapted HCI focusing more on map page for Chinese and Germans. Within the present study, HMI design elements and cultural models are combined to build up culturally adapted HCIs. These HCIs are tested and evaluated to see whether culturally adapted HMIs are developed with the proposed method. Second, two culturally adapted human-machine interfaces are designed according to the guidelines and findings in the literature. Furthermore, it is examined if these guidelines lead to a culturally fitting HMI for Chinese and Germans.

2 Literature Review

2.1 Hofstede's Cultural Model

Hofstede's model is considered the most influential cultural framework [4]. It has a certain degree of analytical flexibility, which is valuable in assigning values to cultures

[5]. The cultural model of Hofstede [6, 7] consists of in total five elements. These are power distance, individualism, masculinity, uncertainty avoidance, and long-term orientation. Each country is graded within these five dimensions with values ranging from 0 to 100. The higher the number, the more this element is part of a culture. In Table 1, each dimension is briefly explained.

Table 1. The five dimensions of Hofstede's cultural model

Dimensions	Description
Power distance	The power distance dimension represents how a society treats inequality. It shows the degree to which the weaker members of a culture accept an unequal distribution of power
Individualism	The individualism score values the relationship between groups and individuals
Masculinity	This dimension is about the distribution of emotional roles between genders. If a country scores high in masculinity, the society prefers heroism, achievement, competition, material rewards for success, and assertiveness. The opposite of masculinity is femininity. It focuses on cooperation, caring for the weak, relationships, as well as quality of life
Uncertainty avoidance	This dimension expresses how a society feels about unknown situations, uncertainty, and ambiguity. If a country scores high in this dimension, the members of the society do not feel well exposed to uncertainty
Long-term orientation	This dimension shows the extent to which a society is willing to accept delayed gratification of social and emotional needs as well as of material

Also, the values for both Germany and China in the five dimensions are compared. First, China's power distance value is very high while the one of Germany is relatively low. The opposite is true for individualism and uncertainty avoidance, in which Germany scores high and China low [8]. In the last two dimensions of masculinity and long-term orientation, these two countries' values are nearly the same. Therefore, it is assumed that only three of the five dimensions need to be taken into account more consciously when studying the differences between Chinese and German preferences regarding human-machine interfaces in vehicles (Fig. 2).

2.2 Cross-Cultural HMI Design

To study the cultural influence on in-vehicle HMI, we need to determine the design elements of interfaces. Russo and Boor [9] divide the user interface into six elements: text, number & date, images, symbols, flow, and functionality, which need to be considered when designing an interface for local use. Cyr and Trevor-Smith [10] suggest that the user interface consists of seven elements: language, layout, symbols, content and

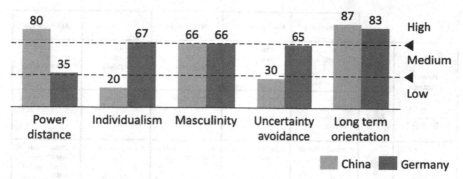

Fig. 2. The scores of China and Germany in the five dimensions of Hofstede's cultural model (data input from Hofstede Insights [8])

structure, navigation, multi-media, and color. Marcus [11, 12] states that UI consists of five elements: metaphors, mental models, navigation, interaction, and appearance. Marcus [12] also links these elements' arrangement to the cultural model of Hofstede and provides a guideline on how to consider the different cultural values when designing an HMI. These principles are used to build up the experimental human-machine interfaces, which are tested with Chinese and German users. Figure 3 shows the guidelines of Aaron Marcus.

When it comes to HMI Chinese and German preference towards in-vehicle HMI design, two main differences were summarized. First of all, the rating of uncertainty avoidance is different. As China is rated low in this category, it is assumed that Chinese users like complex organized interfaces and prefer high parallel processing. In contrast to that, Germans are high uncertainty avoidance and like low parallel processing. Heimgartner found Chinese has higher number of parallel tasks in task bar than German does [2]. German like simple, organized interfaces. Second, the rating difference of the individualism dimension influences the HMI design. Chinese culture is seen as a rather collective one. Thus, the design should be very contextual. In opposition to that, Germans are rated as an individualistic culture. The design in Germany should be task-oriented and having low context. Heimgartner found Chinese have higher information density and higher interaction number per time unit than German have; he also found Chinese has higher number of point of interest per area in the map display than German does [2].

Therefore, when it comes to HMI design, we assume that Chinese users prefer additional quick buttons on the navigation map to provide context-oriented service. In summary, a culturally-adapted HMI for Chinese users should be more complex-organized and have more quick links, while a German one should be simple-organized and with no quick links.

2.3   Usability Analysis of Cross-Cultural HMI

To test our assumptions on culturally adapted HMI design, we measure user experience towards different cultures' HMI design. In general, usability measures fall into two dimensions: usefulness and ease of use. Usefulness refers to the extent to which a product meets the users' functional needs. In contrast, ease of use refers to how easy and intuitive

		Metaphors	Mental models	Navigation	Interaction	Appearance
Power distance	↑	• Clear hierarchies	• Complex, organized	• Restricted access • Passwords	• Severe error messages • Guides lead usage	• Images of leaders • National/corp./govern. themes • Formal speech
	↓	• Informal • Emphasize equality & options	• Simple • Informally organized	• Open access • Multiple options	• Supportive error messages • User-driven options	• Popular themes • Informal speech
Individualism	↑	• Action-oriented • Tool-oriented	• Product- or task-oriented	• Individual paths • Customizable	• Customizable	• Customizable • Low context • Direct & active verbs
	↓	• Relationship-oriented • Content-oriented	• Role-oriented	• Group-oriented • Official choices	• Limited	• High context • Passive verbs
Masculinity	↑	• Competition-oriented	• Goal-oriented • High level views	• Limited choices • Synchronic	• Individual-oriented • Mastery-oriented	• "Masculine" colors, shapes, sounds
Uncertainty avoidance	↑	• Familiar, stable • Representation	• Simple, clear • Limited choices	• Clear organized options • Fine tuning controls	• Precise • Detailed input and feedback	• Simple & clear
	↓	• Novel • Abstraction	• Implicit • Tolerance for ambiguity	• Tolerance for simple searches, redundant options	• General • Ambiguous input and feedback	• Less-consistent • More varied
Long term orientation	↑	• Stable family references • Concrete metaphors	• Responsibility • Support	• Tolerance for long paths • Context-oriented	• Harmony • Personalized messages	• Cultural markers • Soft focus

Fig. 3. Marcus' design guidelines for the cultural values of interest

the use of a product is, including learnability, interaction, and interface design. The concepts of usefulness and ease of use are initially distinguished in Technology Acceptance Model [13]. These concepts are widely used in usability testing. Besides, many scholars develop the concept of usability based on their own experience and research. They add some new elements according to the practical situation. In the System User Satisfaction Scale (SUS), James Lewis [14] finds two dimensions of satisfaction: learnability and availability.

In regards to the Usability Metric for User Experience scale, short UMUX, Finstad [15] argues that in addition to effectiveness and efficiency, usability also includes dimensions of user subjective satisfaction, where utility corresponds to usefulness and efficiency corresponds to ease of use. Harrison, Flood, and Duce [16] argue that availability also needs to include the system's fault tolerance and the cognitive load of the user. More specifically, Lee and Koubek [17] highlight the impact of product aesthetics in usability testing. They also believe that users' perceptions of product availability vary before and after actual use and that more information is kept in separate measurements.

Therefore, research question and hypotheses are presented.

RQ1. What are the differences in user behaviors (using time, number of clicks) between Chinese and German drivers?

H1. Chinese drivers and German drivers get along better with the correspondingly-designed map-based HMI in vehicles.

H1a. Chinese drivers prefer complex-structured map-based HMI with quick buttons in vehicles.

H1b. German drivers prefer simple-structured map-based HMI without quick buttons in vehicles.

3   User Study

3.1   Materials

Two different human-machine interfaces were designed according to the principles of Aaron Marcus [11, 12]. The interfaces are built up using different levels of depths. The first clusters represent the first options to choose from when starting the interface. The six main clusters identified are navigation, multimedia, telephone, connectivity, settings, and status (see Fig. 4). Based on these clusters, different detailed levels are integrated to enable the needed functions. Table 2 gives an overview of the main clusters and related functionalities, including screenshots of the German HMI. The functionalities stay the same between the Chinese and the German UI.

Fig. 4. Main menu of German HMI

As shown in screenshots, the interface consists of three parts: the header bar, the main body, and the navigation bar. The primary click buttons are located in the main body, and the content changes from slide to slide. In contrast to that, the header bar and the navigation bar are visible on every page. There are the main menu buttons and a return

Table 2. Overview of main functional clusters and further functionalities

Main cluster	Further functionalities		Screenshots of German HMI
Navigation	Enter address Points of interest Map Settings	Last destinations Address book Stored trips	
Multimedia	Actual music CD USB	Radio Bluetooth Setting	
Telephone	Dial Email Emergency	Message Contacts Settings	
Connectivity	Bluetooth WIFI Cloud	USB Network Settings	
Settings	Navigation Telephone Status	Multimedia Connectivity Other settings	
Status	Maintenance Fill level Engine Settings	Latest notifications Air-condition Tyres	

button in the navigation bar. Users are directed to the corresponding main cluster by clicking these buttons. Through the orange coloring, users can identify in which cluster he is now, even though he is on one of the subclusters.

The human machine interfaces are designed to be culturally adapted according to Hofstede's cultural model and Aaron Marcus design guidelines [12]. According to literature review, a culturally-adapted HMI for Chinese users should be more complex-organized and have more quick links, while a German one should be simple-organized and with no quick links.

First, the Chinese version is built up of more layers. An extra layer is used in the main menu and in the contacts, which leads to the fact that starting a function within the Chinese HMI consists of more steps. Exemplary, starting the navigation to a saved address is compared in Fig. 5 and Fig. 6. As mentioned, the Chinese version consists of two extra layers. Therefore, starting the navigation to a saved address needs at least five steps within the Chinese interface. In contrast, doing the same within the German one only takes three steps. Both processes are starting from the main menu.

Second, As depicted in Fig. 7, six quick buttons are included in the Chinese version. They are linked to subclusters of the main clusters. Thus, they lead to "Dial," "Message," and "Email" of the main cluster telephone, as well as to "Actual music", "Radio", and "CD" of multimedia. In the German version, these six buttons do not exist because Germans are less context-oriented.

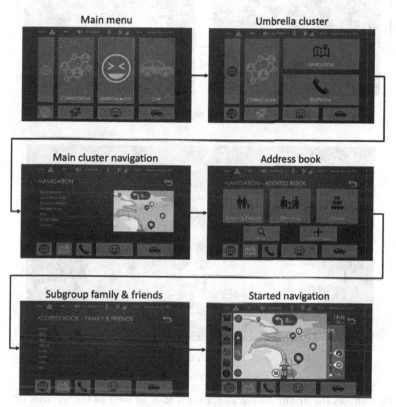

Fig. 5. Starting navigation to a saved address using the Chinese HMI

These two diversities also go in line with the rating difference in the uncertainty avoidance dimension. German culture is rated high in this category, so the design should be clear, simple, straightforward, and have limited choices. In contrast, the Chinese culture rating for uncertainty avoidance is low, leading to less structured designs and redundant options. These aspects are seen in the mentioned aspects. Additionally, the German version only uses limited colors, mainly orange and grey, whereas the Chinese one is more colorful with green, yellow, and blue.

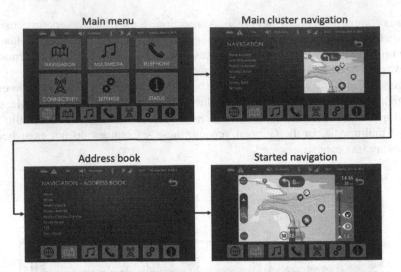

Fig. 6. Starting navigation to a saved address using the German HMI

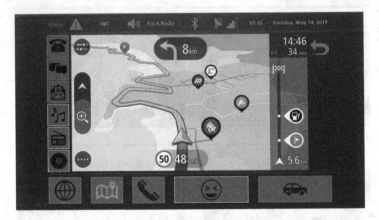

Fig. 7. Implementation of high context aspect

Table 3 shows the minimum clicks for each task as well as the number of possible ways. These further possible ways are also straightforward without any mislead-ing clicks or errors. They are other possibilities to resolve the task. However, users might need a lot more clicks if they get confused and misled. For the German HMI, the click amount stays the same for each of the other possible ways. In contrast, with-in the Chinese version, the numbers of clicks differ from option to option. Another way might add two additional clicks before fulfilling the task. In most of the tasks, the German version requires a less or equal number of clicks. However, the Chinese version is more efficient for changing the radio station as it has quick buttons next to the map, which can lead directly to the radio slide. However, as mentioned, this is just one of the possible ways. Another one might require more clicks. Thus, considering this analysis, the German adapted interface is more direct and more explicit, as it requires fewer clicks most of the time and offers less redundant ways.

Table 3. Task analysis using the two different HMIs

Task	Minimum clicks		Possible ways	
HMI	Chinese	German	Chinese	German
Start navigation to saved address	5	3	1	1
Call saved contact	3	3	3	2
Return to navigation map	2	2	2	2
Change the radio station	3	4	3	2

3.2 Measures

According to the literature review on usability measurements in 2.3, the UMUX scale is adopted to measure the usability of culturally-adapted HMIs. Lewis [18], Berkman and Karahoca [19] have proven the UMUX scale's reliability in their studies. The UMUX scale consists of four questions. Each of them addresses one of the elements of usability. The fourth one points towards the general aspect of usability (see Table 4). Each of the questions is answered using a seven-step Likert scale whereby 1 represents "Strongly disagree" and 7 "Strongly agree" [15]. Among them, "Effectiveness" and "Efficiency" are scored in reverse, which means the lower the score, the better the performance.

Table 4. Usability components and corresponding questions

Usability component	UMUX question
Effectiveness	[This system's] capabilities meet my requirements
Satisfaction	Using [this system] is a frustrating experience
Overall	[This system] is easy to use
Efficiency	I have to spend too much time correcting things with [this system]

3.3 Experiment Procedure

The experiment is divided into six steps (see Fig. 8). First of all, the test users are asked to fill in a pre-experiment survey, providing their background information. Questions are asked regarding their gender, age, occupation, nationality, driving experience, and driving frequency.

After filling out the first part of the survey, the users need to perform the four mentioned tasks with two culturally-adapted HMI. While performing, the time is measured to fulfill each of the tasks. Moreover, the number of clicks is counted as well. These two measures are used as indicators of how easy or intuitive the design of the interface is. As a learning effect is expected, half of each group starts with the German and half with the Chinese version to eliminate the learning effects. After each run, the test persons need to rate the experience regarding the usability of the system.

At the end of the experiment, participants are interviewed in an unstructured way. They are asked to discuss how they feel using the different interfaces, what they prefer or not. Furthermore, they are asked which differences they perceive between the two interfaces.

During the experiment, the human-computer interface is shown on a touchscreen. A steering wheel is put next to it to make the participants feel more like in a car. As Germans and Chinese drive on the left side of the street, the steering wheel is put on the left side of the interface, as it would be in real cars in China and Germany (see Fig. 9). The test users are seated in front of the interface and asked to perform the tasks.

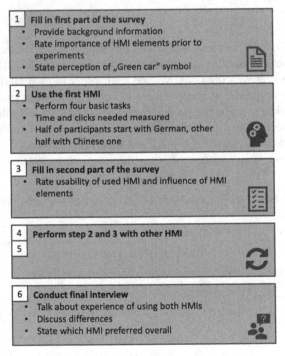

Fig. 8. The six steps of the experiment

3.4 Participants

The participants are recruited from the university. In total, 32 persons participate in the experiments. Fifty percent of them are Chinese, the other half German. Of these, 5 Chinese and 3 German are female. Overall, the mean value of the Chinese is 22.25 years

Fig. 9. Experiment setup

with a standard deviation of 2.96 years. For the German participants, the mean value is 23.75 and the standard deviation 1.53 years. Thus, the Germans are slightly older but less distributed in regards to their age.

Figure 10 shows the driving experience of the test participants. As a reference, the time since getting the driver's license is chosen. The Chinese participants are more distributed than the Germans, with four test users who have never driven at all.

Finally, the difference in the experience driving cars manufactured of companies from several countries is compared. One basic assumption is that the manufacturers use not culturally adapted interfaces and build them according to their own culture. Seven countries are selected based on data about the registration of cars and the sales figures of the different brands in Germany and China [20, 21]. They are Germany, China, Japan, South Korea, the United States of America, Italy, and France.

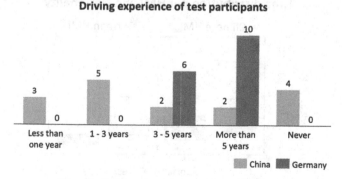

Fig. 10. Driving experience of test participants

As depicted in Fig. 11, the Germans are generally used to more different brands. However, none of the German has ever driven a Chinese car, whereas five of the 16 Chinese have. Another interesting point is that 69% of the Germans have driven a French car, whereas none of the Chinese did. To summarize, it is concluded that the Germans are used to a wider variety of cars. Therefore, it might be easier for them to adapt to different interfaces, as they already used several of them.

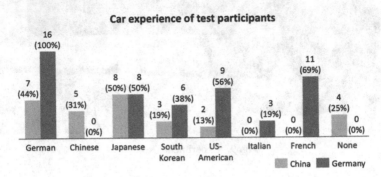

Fig. 11. Car experience of test participants

4   Results

4.1   Time Analysis

The time users take to finish required tasks using two interfaces is analyzed. This data is visualized in Fig. 12, distinguishing between Chinese and German users. The result points out that using the Chinese HMI cost generally longer time. A t-test proves this with a p-value of 0.0016 (H0: $\mu ChineseHMI \leq \mu GermanHMI$, Ha: $\mu ChineseHMI >$

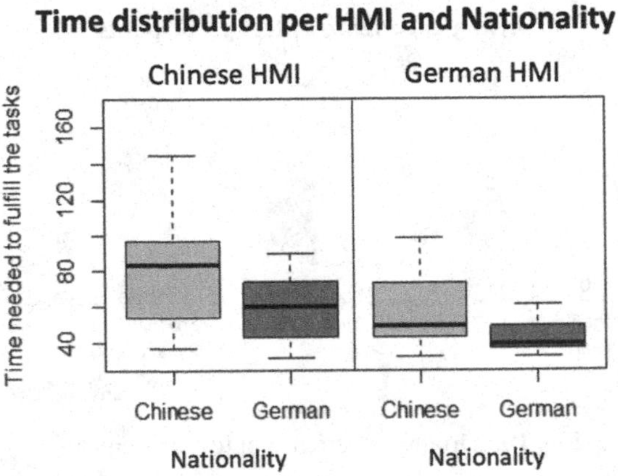

Fig. 12. Time distribution of Chinese and German HMI differentiating nationality

$\mu GermanHMI$). Furthermore, Fig. 12 also indicates that Chinese users need longer than Germans on average, no matter which interface they use. T-tests prove these hypotheses with p-values of 0.0189 and 0.0044. The correlation between the time needed to fulfill the four tasks and other factors is calculated as well. The factorial ANOVA indicates that only the nationality and the used HMI significantly influence the time needed to do the four tasks.

4.2 Click Analysis

After examining the time needed to accomplish the tasks, the amount of clicks for the same results is assessed. Before calculating ANOVA tables, the overall click distribution is evaluated. It is assessed whether there is any significant difference in the number of clicks required to finish the two interfaces' tasks. This data is depicted in Fig. 13, differentiating between Chinese and German users. The data points out that using the Chinese HMI needs more clicks in general. The t-test with H0: $\mu ChineseHMI \leq \mu GermanHMI$ rejects the null hypothesis with a p-value of 0.0017. In addition to that, Fig. 13 indicates that Chinese, on average, need more clicks than Germans, no matter which interface they use. T-tests prove these hypotheses with p-values of 0.0478 and 0.0009. Based on that analysis, the correlation of the number of clicks needed to fulfill the four tasks and other factors is examined. The factorial ANOVA shows a significant influence of nationality, used HMI, the interaction of these two factors, and the interaction of used and preferred HMI on the number of clicks to significance level 0.05.

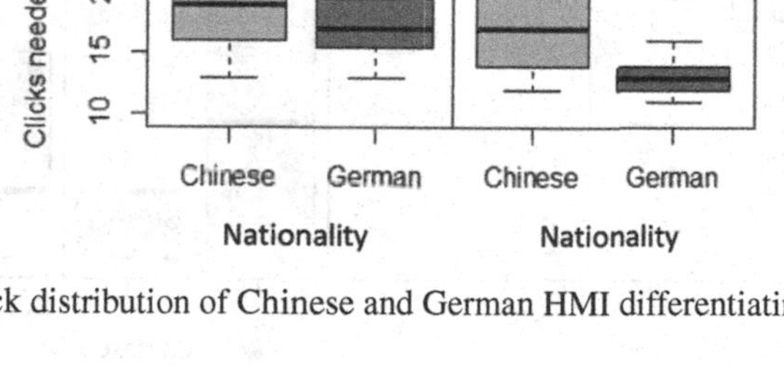

Fig. 13. Click distribution of Chinese and German HMI differentiating nationality

4.3 Usability Analysis Based on Nationality

After experience two interfaces, the test persons are asked to state which of the interfaces they prefer. Figure 14 gives an overview of the results. 12 of 16 Chinese prefer the Chinese HMI, while 13 of the 16 German participants like the German HMI more. Computing

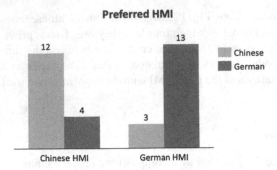

Fig. 14. Overview of preferred HMI of Chinese and German test users

two-proportions z-test shows that the proportions of persons preferring one HMI are significantly different (p = 0.0046).

Also, an analysis based on the two human-computer interfaces differentiating the two nationalities is conducted. There is no significance between Chinese users' UMUX ratings on German and Chinese HMI (ps > 0.05).

Compared to the ratings by Chinese test users, the one by Germans appears differently. Significant differences are found in all of the four categories of UMUX (see Fig. 15). The corresponding t-tests support this perception (see Table 5). Each of the four null hypotheses is rejected. Therefore, the Germans rate the German HMI better in UMUX as "Effectiveness" and "Efficiency" are scored in reverse (Fig. 16).

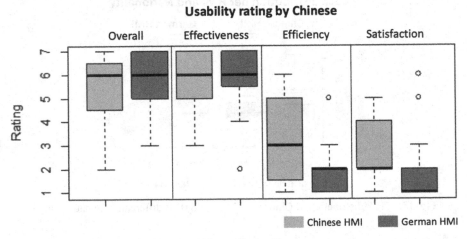

Fig. 15. Usability rating by German users

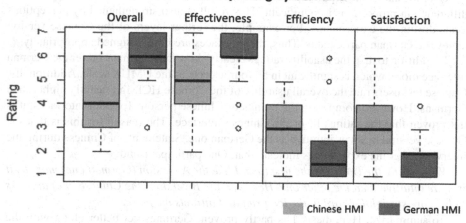

Fig. 16. Usability rating by Chinese users

Table 5. Usability ratings by Chinese and German users

	Chinese HMI		German HMI		t-test
	Mean	SD	Mean	SD	p-value
Overall	4.38	1.63	6.06	1.12	0.0010
Effectiveness (Reverse)	4.94	1.48	6	1.15	0.0158
Efficiency (Reverse)	3.19	1.33	2.06	1.53	0.0170
Satisfaction	3.12	1.54	1.81	0.911	0.0036

5 Discussion

Overall, the time and clicks' measures needed to fulfill the tasks using the Chinese HMI are significantly higher. The reason for this is the design of the interface. As stated in Sect. 3.2, the Chinese version consists of more layers compared to the German one. Therefore, more time and clicks are needed automatically. So, it is not helpful to compare these two performance measures based on one nationality. Comparing the users of different nationalities towards one HMI, we find significant differences between Chinese and German participants. Chinese need more time and clicks when using the interfaces, which is proven significantly for the Chinese and the German HMI. Therefore, it is concluded that the Germans get along better with their culturally adapted HMI and the Chinese version, compared with the Chinese users' performance. The reasons might be Germans are used to more car brands, so they are getting along more effortlessly with a new HCI. Another reason for this result is the different approach to a new interface. During the experiment, it is perceived that the Chinese feel pressured to do the right thing. If it does not work directly, they are more likely to get stressed and to click wildly on the screen.

Overall, the Chinese participants like the Chinese HMI more, and vice versa. The difference in proportions is significant. This result is also strengthened by perceptions made during the experiments. For example, the further layers of the Chinese version annoy the German participants. Thus, the interfaces are both designed appropriately.

In addition to that, the usability ratings clearly show that Germans prefer the German interface more, which is significant in all four aspects of the UMUX scale. Additionally, Chinese test users rate the overall usability of the Chinese HCI significantly higher than Germans. However, comparing the ratings of Chinese persons for both interfaces, it is not proven that the ratings favor the Chinese interface. The reason for this is that the Chinese version is not as intuitive as the German one. Statements of Chinese during the interview after the experiments indicate that. One participant said:

When using the HMIs for the first time, I like the A version (German one) more as it is more intuitive than the other one. However, the B version (the Chinese one) appears to be more straightforward in the long run and attracts me more.

To summarize, Hypothesis 1 is partly proven. Germans get better along with the German interface. Only slight proof that the Chinese perceive their interface better is found.

6   Conclusions

As globalization shapes the way how companies operate, they sell their products world-wide. In every part of the world, cultural differences exist. Thus, the issue of culturally-adapted design arises. In this thesis, a method to design culturally-adapted interfaces for vehicles is introduced and assessed. It builds upon existing frameworks and combines them. Using the method interfaces for Chinese and Germans are designed and tested with Chinese and German users. The results indicate that Chinese drivers prefer to use the HMI with quick buttons on the map page, but German prefer to use simple and straightforward HMI without quick buttons on the map page. The interview also found that Chinese perceive better user experience than German when using the HMI with quick buttons. As Chinese is a collectivist and polychronic culture, Chinese drivers emphasize the relationship of tasks and prefer to do multitask at once. Therefore, when Chinese drivers use the car console infotainment system, they prefer to use quick buttons on the map page.

The design method for culture-adapted in-vehicle HMIs is a practical approach when designing interfaces for different cultures. It is based on design guidelines that are linked to Hofstede's cultural models. The cultural values of many countries are available online. Thus, it is easy to detect the functional design characteristics.

References

1. Fuss, P.: Der Pkw-Absatzmarkt China 2009 bis 2016: Analyse der Bedeutung Chinas für die deutsche Automobilindustrie (2017). https://www.ey.com/Publication/vwLUAssets/ey-auto-absatzmarkt-china-2017/$FILE/ey-auto-absatzmarkt-china-2017.pdf
2. Heimgärtner, R.: Cultural differences in human-computer interaction: towards culturally adaptive human-machine interaction. Walter de Gruyter (2012)

3. Roessger, P., Peissner, M.: Interkulturelle Unterschiede der Mensch-Maschine-Schnittstelle von Fahrer-Informations-Systemen/Cross cultural differences in human machine interfaces of driver-information-systems. Vdi Berichte (2002)
4. Steenkamp, J.B.E.M.: The role of national culture in international marketing research. Int. Mark. Rev. 18(1), 30–44 (2001)
5. Pollay, R.: Measuring the cultural values manifest in advertising. Curr. Issues Res. Advert. 6, 71–92 (2012)
6. Hofstede, G.H.: Culture's consequences: comparing values, behaviors, institutions and organizations across nations. Behav. Res. Ther. 41(7) (2001)
7. Hofstede, G., Hofstede, G.J., Minkov, M.: Cultures and organizations, software of the mind. Intercultural cooperation and its importance for survival. South. Med. J. 13(3), S219–S222 (2010)
8. Hofstede Insights: Country comparison (2018). https://www.hofstede-insights.com/country-comparison/
9. Russo, P., Boor, S.: How fluent is your interface? In: Conference on Human factors in Computing Systems, INTERACT 1993, CHI 1993 (1993)
10. Dianne et al.: Localization of web design: an empirical comparison of German, Japanese, and United States web site characteristics. J. Am. Soc. Inf. Sci. Technol. (2007)
11. Marcus, A., et al.: Cross-cultural user-interface design. In: CHI 2001 Extended (2001)
12. Marcus, A.: Icons, symbols, and signs: visible languages to facilitate communication. Interactions 10, 37–43 (2003)
13. Davis, F.D., Warshaw, B.P.R.: User acceptance of computer-technology - a comparison of 2 theoretical-models. Manag. Sci. 35(8), 982–1003 (1989)
14. Lewis, J.R.: IBM computer usability satisfaction questionnaires: Psychometric evaluation and instructions for use. Int. J. Hum. Comput. Interact. 7(1), 57–78 (1995)
15. Finstad, K.: The usability metric for user experience. Interact. Comput. 22(5), 323–327 (2010)
16. Harrison, R., Flood, D., Duce, D.: Usability of mobile applications: literature review and rationale for a new usability model. J. Interact. Sci. 1(1), 1–16 (2013). https://doi.org/10.1186/2194-0827-1-1
17. Lee, S., Koubek, R.J.: Understanding user preferences based on usability and aesthetics before and after actual use. Interact. Comput. 22(6), 530–543 (2010)
18. Lewis, J., Utesch, B., Maher, D.: UMUX-LITE: when there's no time for the SUS, pp. 2099–2102 (2013)
19. Berkman, M.I., Karahoca, D.: Re-assessing the Usability Metric for User Experience (UMUX) scale. J. Usability Stud. 11, 89–109 (2016)
20. Demandt, B.: China car sales analysis 2018 – brands (2019). https://carsalesbase.com/china-car-sales-analysis-2018-brands/
21. Kraftfahrt-Bundesamt: Neuzulassungen von Personenkraftwagen nach Marken und Modellreihen (2019). https://www.kba.de/DE/Statistik/Produktkatalog/produkte/Fahrzeuge/fz10/fz10_gentab.html

Culturally Aware Intelligent Learning Environments for Resource-Poor Countries

Phaedra S. Mohammed[1(✉)] and André Coy[2]

[1] Department of Computing and Information Technology, The University of the West Indies,
St. Augustine Campus, St. Augustine, Trinidad and Tobago
phaedra.mohammed@sta.uwi.edu
[2] Department of Physics, The University of the West Indies, Mona Campus, Kingston, Jamaica
andre.coy02@uwimona.edu.jm

Abstract. This paper presents current work being done on the development of a speech and language technology (SLT) based intelligent tutoring system for coaching young learners from a Caribbean context in developing literacy skills. The system uses speech recognition, socio-cultural modelling and educational technology techniques that aim to enable two-way, dynamic communication between a young reader and the synthetic SLT tutor. Two goals of the research are to firstly model a reader computationally from instructional and socio-cultural perspectives, and secondly to create speech models that capture the unique linguistic variations and pronunciations expressed by young readers in Trinidad and Jamaica in particular.

Keywords: Intelligent tutoring system · Literacy · Speech · Cultural awareness

1 Introduction

Intelligent Learning Environments (ILEs), such as Intelligent Tutoring Systems, have a long track record of resulting in improved learning outcomes for students, almost as effective as a human tutor [60]. The majority of these ILEs however originate from research based in western, industrialised, rich nations [8]. Prior to the COVID-19 pandemic of 2020, there was growing interest in extending the reach of these systems using culturally aware intelligent features applicable to developing world contexts [6, 46]. Compelling connections between culture and learning quietly propelled the research into culturally-aware information technology since culture has been shown to influence students' learning styles [24], impact on teachers' instructional strategies [59], stimulate motivation, and promote affective learning [44]. Many theoretical models exist in the literature that describe approaches and techniques for enculturating educational systems and instructional activities. However, few of these propose clear steps towards computationally viable approaches. Consequently, limited practical systems are in use and those that have been developed are limited to narrowly-focused pilot studies [43]. Intelligent systems and software tutors also do not perform as well, or as expected in learning environments that differ culturally from the original context of use [51]. Factor in the advent of machine learning techniques, such as recurrent neural networks, transformers

© Springer Nature Switzerland AG 2021
M. Rauterberg (Ed.): HCII 2021, LNCS 12795, pp. 450–460, 2021.
https://doi.org/10.1007/978-3-030-77431-8_28

and attention models that rely on human sources of data, and this cultural bias becomes more prominent as the source of the data changes. For instance, in [15], classroom audio data was used to detect features of teaching events, such as questions and answers, that may be beneficial to student learning. The risk with using such data in these ways is that the models are trained to detect patterns that are dictated by the data. When data comes from a particular source, naturally those patterns will be skewed towards the environmental conditions of the source environment, and actors and models may or may work well in alternate cultural conditions [55].

Across the Caribbean, there have been increasing calls to improve literacy rates, as too often young people complete their schooling without adequate literacy skills. This is due to a variety of problems including teachers' inability to give individual attention to students in large classes, students' inability to respond to traditional approaches and the lack of customised software tools for the Caribbean context to assist with further learning. There is significant evidence of an educational attainment gap between Caribbean children of differing socio-economic backgrounds and gender [13]. With the advent of the COVID-19 pandemic, there is a risk that this gap will be significantly widened [16]. This is an urgent problem that requires immediate, creative interventions to address the slide in attainment of the most vulnerable children in the region. It is therefore critical to help at-risk children to develop their reading and literacy skills, before they become marginalised, at-risk adults, given the overwhelming evidence that the majority of students that fail to grasp basic literacy concepts at an early age are never able to catch up [27, 39]. An autonomous reading tutor that listens to a reader and provides useful, real-time feedback has been shown to replicate the experience of having a one-to-one session with a literacy specialist [1, 5, 48, 60, 63]. These are some of the motivating factors driving this research.

The rest of the paper is organised as follows: Sect. 2 describes related work with examples of culturally-aware ILEs and reading systems from research and commercial settings. Sections 3 and 4 present the architecture, components and implementation rationale of the SLT-based Literacy Tutoring System. The paper concludes in Sect. 5 with future work and the road ahead.

2 Related Work

Culturally-aware ILEs can be broadly categorized as either adaptation-oriented or acquisition-oriented [7]. Both types of systems aim to interpret, model and use cultural backgrounds and influences of either individuals or social groups but for different purposes. Adaptation-oriented systems aim to change system appearance, behaviour and content to suit individual learners whereas acquisition oriented systems aim to teach an individual about a particular social group or how to acquire skills for interacting with them. In both cases the use and generation of cultural contexts can be preset or manually loaded, partially automated or fully automated. Within adaptation-oriented culturally-aware systems, the work described in [45, 66] demonstrate how premade localised content can be used successfully to produce significant learning gains or how Wizard of Oz approach can be used to simulate cultural behaviour [19]. The adaptive and intelligent systems described in [23, 40, 43] along with the encultured conversational agents (ECAs) in [4, 17, 53] provide examples of semi-automated and fully automated approaches within the same grouping. Within acquisition-oriented culTEL, practical systems are commonly used for developing intercultural communication skills in the form of virtual learning environments and serious games such as in [32]. The Tactical Language and Culture Training System (TLCTS) [30] was the first of its kind to pioneer these kinds of culturally-aware systems. Since then many commercial grade examples are produced by Alelo which uses avatar-based AI solutions to deliver cultural awareness training.

Several reading tutors have been developed over the years - see [63] for a systematic review of modern reading tutors. Early systems, such as Watch me Read! [62], Project Listen [49], the Colorado Literacy Tutor - COLIT - [26] and STAR [56], were developed at a time when ITSs were relatively new and did not employ a constructivist approach to learning, preferring to employ specific reading strategies. More recently, the majority of reading tutors have adopted a constructivist method, almost as default. [63] highlighted a number of these systems, including: Alphie's Alley [11], conText [34], iStart [38], ITSS [41] and Summary Street [21].

A unique aspect of the SLT tutor presented in this research paper is catering for Caribbean-accented speech [61] as opposed to the more common-place American or British pronunciations using dynamic models that automatically produced customised content. The aim is to leverage and adapt the existing technological approaches and best practices described in the research and examples highlighted in this section to the individual needs of these target readers while considering the real challenges that exist in a developing world context. The resulting tutor is therefore intended to be used to diagnose specific literacy challenges inherent in the Caribbean, track students' progress over time, and prescribe targeted culturally-appropriate interventions as readers grow in confidence and skill.

3 Architecture

ILEs are difficult to transfer to other cultural contexts due to complex designs, hard-coded instructional strategies, dependencies on specific types of platform technologies (devices, hardware, software), and heavy reliance on prebuilt custom content. Adaptation of situated educational content into culturally appropriate forms is a significant aspect of the localisation process, and the large majority of these localisations so far are done manually [50].

The architecture of the SLT system, shown in Fig. 1, employs a layered theory-driven and data-driven approach to mitigate some of these challenges. The layers separate the standard components of intelligent tutoring systems (views, expert, domain, student and instructional models) and promote a modular component-based design. The aim is to produce a lightweight robust solution that is capable of scaling and which supports incremental development and testing. Theory-driven approaches are critical for effective instructional design, logically scaffolding learners through activities, modelling foundational aspects of student behaviour, backgrounds and expectations. Data-driven approaches facilitate discovery of realistic usage patterns, enable evidence-based interventions and targeted customisations and promote fine-grained decision making. To balance the bias risks inherent in each approach, as described in [36], the SLT system combines both strategies and techniques from both approaches.

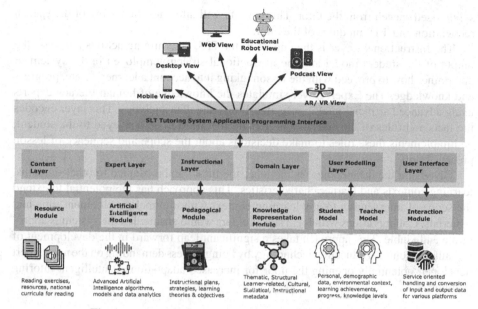

Fig. 1. Architecture of the SLT-based literacy tutoring system

The User Interface Layer communicates with the learner, ideally through interactive dialogue; this is the means by which the SLT-based literacy tutor receives and presents information to the user. The inputs and outputs are handled through standard services which allow diverse interface views and multimodal content delivery. This allows students to access content from different platforms and devices.

The User Modelling Layer tracks and models a learner's educational progress, academic achievements and shortfalls, affective states and overall learning goals using a computational student model. Within this layer, teachers may also be modelled in a similar fashion. These profiles are used to select effective instructional strategies, diagnose a learner's psychological and motivational states, and offer corrective feedback to the learner. By creating a profile of the learner, the literacy tutor is able to learn about and adapt to a learner's specific needs. Using knowledge representation techniques, the aim is to capture important details, qualities and characteristics about the reader's core identity, reading behaviour and skill, and above all learning goals, preferences and progress.

The Domain Layer contains details of what is to be learned by the user of the system. This consists of complex representations of symbolically represented knowledge that can be presented in a hierarchical fashion, in order to foster incremental learning. It is within this model that common misconceptions are encoded. The Content Layer incorporates culturally appropriate material with the purpose of engaging the reader with material that is more familiar to them and may more readily stimulate their interest. Reading exercises and passages, audio files, image files, instruction lists, hierarchical hints and corrective feedback baselines are stored in this layer. The most important interactions between the learner and tutor will take place using natural speech from the user and synthesised speech from the tutor. This activity will allow for the testing of the speech recognition and TTS modules of the tutor.

The Instructional Layer is the engine of the ITS, determining actions based on the output of the student model and the instructional strategy employed in the system. It determines how to proceed with the lesson taking into account a learner's state, progress and knowledge. The Expert Layer simulates the knowledge of human literacy experts using advanced artificial intelligence algorithms and data analytics. This layer encodes the facts and rules of the educational domain that need to be conveyed to the student, and implements these rules to make decisions about the scope and sequence of lesson presentation.

Given that the development is modular, the tutor can be adapted to other domains, learning contexts and learner characteristics. This approach has the potential to extend the scope of intervention to any learning context with minimal development time and materials. Collaborations with local stakeholders would ensure that the system is appropriate and viable. This approach takes a significant leap forward in the development of modular systems for education technology by being far less demanding on the non-expert developer, potentially opening the door for increased adaptation of intelligent tutoring systems.

4   Implementation Methodology

This section sets out the approach to the system development and gives the rationale for the design choices. Each of the modules represents an active area of research, with a wide body of research that informs the decisions. The state-of-the-art techniques will be adopted initially, based on the anticipated outcome. However, it is anticipated that adaptations will be made for some of the layers as suggestions from stakeholder consultations are considered.

4.1   User Interface Layer

A Model-View-Controller approach will be used for modular development overall in conjunction with design patterns [20, 37]. Specifically an observer design pattern will be used to decouple the backend of the tutor with a generic API. This will facilitate different but consistent-looking frontends (views) which can be switched in and out according to the mode of delivery that is appropriate for a user. General UI principles such as easy navigation, consistent design, provision of visual cues and system status indicators will be followed throughout the design in alignment with a multicultural approach [54]. Communication between the tutor and the user will be facilitated by ASR and TTS. State-of-the-art techniques for low-resource languages, such as teacher-student and transfer learning, will be used to improve existing speech models of Jamaican accented voices and to create models of Trinidadian accented voices [25, 61, 65]. End-to-end synthesis techniques will be employed to model Jamaican and Trinidadian voices [22, 64].

4.2 User Modelling Layer

Three major techniques are at the forefront of the user models in the SLT tutor: skill modelling [14], open learner models [10], and cultural modelling [47]. These will be used to analyse learner actions through model tracing. For the reading tutor, probabilistic methods and constraint based modelling will be combined with ontological representations. This follows common approaches in the ITS field so that the learning style or academic ability of learner and the level of difficulty of a learning activity (both modelled using ontologies) are compared such that the knowledge imparted by the tutor during an instructional resource can be adjusted to suit using data analytics [52, 57]. The organisation of this data further allows for the possibility of an open cultural learner model which may allow more accurate predictions by reducing cultural misconceptions about learners through data analytics. Using knowledge representation techniques, the aim is to capture important details, qualities and characteristics about the reader's core identity, reading behaviour and skill, and above all learning goals, preferences and progress.

4.3 Domain Layer

The domain layer creates the architecture that organises semantics of low level data in the content layer (reading exercises, files, images). Ontological engineering techniques [31] will be used to construct light-weight ontologies and knowledge graphs [18] based on the work of [41]. The implicit meanings, semantic representations and context of use surrounding the instructional content are encoded in machine readable formats (OWL, XML) which sets the stage for dynamic content creation. Rule-based techniques and description logics are then used to analyse the data and make recommendations for content that is appropriate for the learner when there are many options available (e.g. more than one reading exercise).

4.4 Expert Layer

The core of the expert layer is a rule-based, cognitive model, which aims to solve problems in the same way that users of the tutor are being taught to do [2, 3]. Pedagogical agents have been shown to be effective with the types of young students targeted by this research project [29]. Theory from closed multi-agent systems [28] will be incorporated in this layer. Agent communication languages, declarative rules and belief/intent schemas are examples of the technologies that will be used for coordination and communication.

4.5 Instructional Layer

The DISTAR method, also known as Direct Instructional System for Teaching and Remediation will be used by the pedagogical agent to conduct the tutoring. This method is highly structured and well suited for implementation in a computer-based tutoring system. The focus is on strengthening the following five basic skills: phonemic awareness, phonics, fluency, vocabulary, and comprehension [58].

4.6 Content Layer

Custom educational content for the tutor will be created for the DISTAR method mentioned earlier. The content will be first produced manually by experts in alignment with the schemas from the domain layer. Gradually, new comprehension content will be generated dynamically using lexical [35] and cultural semantics [47], and techniques from adaptive hypermedia [9].

5 Future Work and Conclusion

There is no more important undertaking than to contribute to the education of a child; this process begins with learning to read. Engagement with the process is more likely to occur with reluctant or struggling readers when said readers feel that their specific needs are being catered for. This paper has provided details of ongoing work that aims to develop a reading tutor that so closely models the reader that every user feels as if the tutor was developed just for them.

The novel socio-cultural modelling proposed opens the door to an, under used aspect of user engagement - rapport. When the reader hears the tutor speak in a familiar accent, her interest will be piqued. However, when the tutor understands what she says, then the process of learning can begin on another level, as the user will identify with the tutor in a way that might not occur with a tutor whose prosody and cadence are less familiar.

The approach, as outlined here, builds upon the literature on tutor enculturation in such a way as to avoid the pitfalls of previously developed systems. Given the practical need for a viable, culturally aware reading tutor in the countries targeted, this work has the potential to move beyond a scientific exploration to become an educational lifeline for underserved, vulnerable communities.

The most pressing work now is the development of a representative corpus of Trinidadian-accented speech to be used for modelling speech recognition and speech synthesis systems. Testing these systems on the target population will provide insight into the range of acceptability of these systems among potential users of the tutor.

References

1. Adams, M.J.: The promise of automatic speech recognition for fostering literacy growth in children and adults. Handb. Lit. Technol. **2**, 109–12 (2005)
2. Aleven, V.: Rule-based cognitive modeling for intelligent tutoring systems. In: Nkambou, R., Bourdeau, J., Mizoguchi, R. (eds.) Advances in Intelligent Tutoring Systems, vol. 308, pp. 33–62. Springer, Heidelberg (2010). https://doi.org/10.1007/978-3-642-14363-2_3
3. Anderson, J.R., Corbett, A.T., Koedinger, K.R., Pelletier, R.: Cognitive tutors: lessons learned. J. Learn. Sci. **4**(2), 167–207 (1995)
4. Aylett, R., Paiva, A., Vannini, N., et al.: But that was in another country: agents and intercultural empathy. In: Decker, K.S., Sichman, J.S., Sierra, C., et al. (eds.) Proceedings of 8th International Conference on Autonomous Agents and Multi Agent Systems, pp. 329–336. Richland, SC: International Foundation for Autonomous Agents and Multiagent Systems, Budapest, Hungary (2009)

5. Banerjee, S., Beck, J.E., Mostow, J.: Evaluating the effect of predicting oral reading miscues. In: Eighth European Conference on Speech Communication and Technology, pp.3165–3168. Eurospeech, Geneva (2003)
6. Blanchard, E.G., Allard, D.: The Handbook of Research on Culturally-Aware Information Technology: Perspectives and Models. Information Science Publishing, Hershey (2011). https://doi.org/10.4018/978-1-61520-883-8
7. Blanchard, E.G., Ogan, A.: Infusing cultural awareness into intelligent tutoring systems for a globalized world. In: Nkambou, R., Mizoguchi, R., Bourdeau, J. (eds.) Advances in Intelligent Tutoring Systems. Studies in Computer Sciences, vol. 308, pp. 485–505. Springer, Berlin Heidelberg (2010). https://doi.org/10.1007/978-3-642-14363-2_24
8. Blanchard, E.: Socio-cultural imbalances in AIED research: investigations, implications and opportunities. Int. J. Artif. Intell. Educ. 25(2), 204–228 (2014). https://doi.org/10.1007/s40 593-014-0027-7
9. Brusilovsky, P.: Methods and techniques of adaptive hypermedia. User Model. User-Adapt. Interact. 6(2), 87–129 (1996). https://doi.org/10.1007/BF00143964
10. Bull, S., Kay, J.: Open learner models. In: Nkambou, R., Bourdeau, J., Mizoguchi, R. (eds.) Advances in Intelligent Tutoring Systems. Studies in Computational Intelligence, vol. 308, pp. 301–322. Springer, Heidelberg (2010). https://doi.org/10.1007/978-3-642-14363-2_15
11. Chambers, B., et al.: Computer-assisted tutoring in success for all: reading outcomes for first graders. J. Res. Educ. Effect. 1(2), 120–137 (2008)
12. De Jong, M., Warmelink, H.: OASISTAN: an intercultural role-playing simulation game to recognize cultural dimensions. Simul. Gaming 48(2), 178–198 (2017)
13. De Lisle, J.: Insights on the marginalization of poor children in the education system of Trinidad and Tobago. In: Blackman, Stacey N J., Conrad, Dennis A., Brown, Launcelot I. (eds.) Achieving Inclusive Education in the Caribbean and Beyond, pp. 89–119. Springer, Cham (2019). https://doi.org/10.1007/978-3-030-15769-2_6
14. Desmarais, M.C., Baker, R.S.J.D.: A Review of recent advances in learner and skill modeling in intelligent learning environments. User Model. User-Adapt. Interact. 22(1), 9–38 (2012). https://doi.org/10.1007/s11257-011-9106-8
15. Donnelly, P.J., Blanchard, N., Samei, B., et al.: Automatic teacher modeling from live classroom audio. In: Proceedings of 24th ACM International Conference on User modeling, Adaptation, and Personalization (UMAP), pp. 45–53. ACM, New York (2016). https://doi.org/10.1145/2930238.2930250
16. Education Endowment Foundation. Impact of school closures on the attainment gap. Rapid Evidence Assessment, London: Education Endowment Foundation (2020)
17. Endrass, B., André, E., Rehm, M., Nakano, Y.: Investigating culture-related aspects of behavior for virtual characters. Autonom. Agents Multi-Agent Syst. 27(2), 77–304 (2013)
18. Fensel, D., et al.: Knowledge Graphs: Methodology, Tools and Selected Use Cases, 1st edn. Springer, Heidelberg (2020). https://doi.org/10.1007/978-3-030-37439-6
19. Finkelstein, S., Yarzebinski, E., Vaughn, C., Ogan, A., Cassell, J.: The effects of culturally congruent educational technologies on student achievement. In: Lane, H.C., Yacef, K., Mostow, J., Pavlik, P. (eds.) AIED 2013. LNCS (LNAI), vol. 7926, pp. 493–502. Springer, Heidelberg (2013). https://doi.org/10.1007/978-3-642-39112-5_50
20. Fowler, M., Beck, K.: Refactoring: Improving the Design of Existing Code. 2nd edn. Addison-Wesley Signature Series (2018)
21. Franzke, M., Kintsch, E., Caccamise, D., Johnson, N., Dooley, S.: Summary Street®: computer support for comprehension and writing. J. Educ. Comput. Res. 33(1), 53–80 (2005)
22. Fu, R., Tao, J., Wen, Z., Yi, J., Wang, T.: Focusing on attention: prosody transfer and adaptative optimization strategy for multi-speaker end-to-end speech synthesis. In: IEEE International Conference on Acoustics, Speech and Signal Processing (ICASSP), Barcelona, Spain, pp. 6709–6713 (2020). https://doi.org/10.1109/ICASSP40776.2020.9054319

23. Gasparini, I., Pimenta, M.S., Moreira de Oliveira, J.P.: How to apply context awareness in an adaptive e-learning environment to improve personalization capabilities? In: Acuña, G., Baier, J.A. (eds.) Proceedings of 30th International Conference of the Chilean Computer Society, SCCC, Curico, Chile, 9–11 November 2011, pp. 161–170. IEEE Computer Society, Washington, DC (2011)

24. Gilbert, J.E., et al.: Teaching algebra using culturally relevant virtual instructors. Int. J. Virtual Reality 7(1), 21–30 (2008)

25. Giollo, M., Gunceler, D., Liu, Y., Willett, D.: Bootstrap an end-to-end ASR system by multilingual training, transfer learning, text-to-text mapping and synthetic audio. arXiv preprint (2020). arXiv-2011.12696

26. Hagen, A., Pellom, B., Cole, R.: Children's speech recognition with application to interactive books and tutors. In: IEEE Workshop on Automatic Speech Recognition and Understanding (IEEE Cat. No.03EX721), St Thomas, VI, USA, pp. 186–191 (2003). https://doi.org/10.1109/ASRU.2003.1318426

27. Heckman, J.J.: Skill formation and the economics of investing in disadvantaged children. Science 312, 1900–1902 (2006). https://doi.org/10.1126/science.1128898

28. Huhns, M.N., Stephen, L.M.: Multiagent systems and societies of agents. Multiagent Syst.: Mod. Approach Distrib. Artif. Intell. 1, 79–114 (1999)

29. Johnson, W., Lester, J.: Face-to-face interaction with pedagogical agents, twenty years later. Int. J. Artif. Intell. Educ. 26(1), 25–36 (2015). https://doi.org/10.1007/s40593-015-0065-9

30. Johnson, W.L., et al.: Tactical language training system: an interim report. In: Lester, J.C., Vicari, R.M., Paraguaçu, F. (eds.) ITS 2004. LNCS, vol. 3220, pp. 336–345. Springer, Heidelberg (2004). https://doi.org/10.1007/978-3-540-30139-4_32

31. Kendall, E.F., McGuiness D.: Ontology Engineering. Morgan & Claypool Publishers (2019)

32. Kim, J., et al.: BiLAT: a game-based environment for practicing negotiation in a cultural context. Int. J. Artif. Intell. Educ. 19, 289–308 (2009)

33. Kumar, K., et al.: Generative adversarial networks for conditional waveform synthesis. Adv. Neural Inf. Process. Syst. 32, 14910–14921 (2019)

34. Lenhard, W., Baier, H., Endlich, D., Schneider, W., Hoffmann, J.: Rethinking strategy instruction: direct reading strategy instruction versus computer-based guided practice. J. Res. Read. 36(2), 223–240 (2013)

35. Lin, H.: Syntactic and lexical approaches to reading comprehension. In: Proceedings of 5th Workshop on Natural Language Processing Techniques for Educational Applications, Melbourne, Australia, pp. 11–19 (2018)

36. Lugren, B., Frommel, J., Andre, E.: Combining a data-driven and theory-based approach to generate culture-dependent behaviours for virtual characters. In: Faucher, C. (ed.) Advances in Culturally-Aware Intelligent Systems and in Cross-Cultural Psychological Studies. Intelligent Systems Reference Library, vol. 134, pp. 111–14. Springer, Cham (2018). https://doi.org/10.1007/978-3-319-67024-9_6

37. Martin, R.: Clean Architecture: A Craftsman's Guide to Software Structure and Design. 1st edn. Pearson (2017)

38. McCarthy, K.S., Soto, C.M., de Blume, A.P., Palma, D., González, J.I., McNamara, D.S.: Improving reading comprehension in Spanish using iSTART-E: a pilot study. Int. J. Comput.-Assist. Lang. Learn. Teach. 10(4), 66–82 (2020)

39. McCracken, M., Murray, S.: The economic benefits of literacy: evidence and implications for public policy. Canadian Language and Literacy Research Network, London, Ontario, Canada (2009)

40. Melis, E., Goguadze, G., Libbrecht, P., et al.: Culturally-aware mathematics education technology. In: Blanchard, E.G., Allard, D. (eds.) The Handbook of Research on Culturally-Aware Information Technology: Perspectives and Models, pp. 543–557. IGI Global, Hershey (2011)

41. Meyer, B.J., Wijekumar, K.: A web-based tutoring system for the structure strategy: theoretical background, design, and findings. In: Reading Comprehension Strategies: Theories, Interventions, and Technologies, pp. 347–375 (2007)

42. Mohammed, P., Mohan, P.: Contextualising learning objects using ontologies. Comput. Intell. **23**(3), 339–355 (2007)

43. Mohammed, P., Mohan, P.: Dynamic cultural contextualisation of educational content in intelligent learning environments using ICON. Int. J. Artif. Intell. Educ. **25**(2), 249–270 (2015)

44. Mohammed, P., Mohan, P.: Integrating culture into digital learning environments: studies using cultural educational games. Caribbean Teach. Scholar **1**(1), 21–335 (2011)

45. Mohammed, P., Mohan, P.: The design and implementation of an enculturated web-based intelligent tutoring system for computer science education. In: Proceedings of 11th IEEE International Conference on Advanced Learning Technologies (ICALT), pp. 501–505 (2011)

46. Mohammed, P.S., Watson, E.N.: Towards inclusive education in the age of artificial intelligence: perspectives, challenges, and opportunities. In: Knox, J., Wang, Y., Gallagher, M. (eds.) Artificial Intelligence and Inclusive Education. Perspectives on Rethinking and Reforming Education, pp. 17–37. Springer, Singapore (2019). https://doi.org/10.1007/978-981-13-816 1-4_2

47. Mohammed, P.S.: Ontological support for the cultural contextualisation of intelligent learning environments for inclusive education. In: Proceedings of International Workshop on Context and Culture in Intelligent Tutoring Systems at Intelligent Tutoring Systems 2018, 12 June 2018, Montreal, Canada (2018)

48. Mostow, J., Aist, G., Burkhead, P., Corbett, A., Cuneo, S., et al.: Evaluation of an automated reading tutor that listens: comparison to human tutoring and classroom instruction. J. Educ. Comput. Res. **29**, 61–117 (2003)

49. Mostow, J., Roth, S.P., Hauptmann, A.G., Kane, M.: A prototype reading coach that listens. In: Proceedings of the Twelfth National Conference on Artificial Intelligence (AAAI-94), Seattle, WA (1994)

50. Nye, B.D.: Intelligent tutoring systems by and for the developing world: a review of trends and approaches for educational technology in a global context. Int. J. Artif. Intell. Educ. **25**(2), 177–203 (2015)

51. Ogan, A., Yarzebinski, E., Fernández, P., Casas, I.: Cognitive tutor use in chile: understanding classroom and lab culture. In: Conati, C., Heffernan, N., Mitrovic, A., Verdejo, MFelisa (eds.) AIED 2015. LNCS (LNAI), vol. 9112, pp. 318–327. Springer, Cham (2015). https://doi.org/10.1007/978-3-319-19773-9_32

52. Panagiotopoulos, I., Kalou, A., Pierrakeas, C., Kameas, A.: An ontology-based model for student representation in intelligent tutoring systems for distance learning. In: Iliadis, L., Maglogiannis, I., Papadopoulos, H. (eds.) AIAI 2012. IAICT, vol. 381, pp. 296–305. Springer, Heidelberg (2012). https://doi.org/10.1007/978-3-642-33409-2_31

53. Rehm, M., Andre, E., Nakano, Y., et al: The CUBE-G approach - coaching culture-specific nonverbal behavior by virtual agents. In: Mayer, I., Mastik, H. (eds.) ISAGA 2007: organizing and learning through gaming and simulation (2007)

54. Reinecke, K., Bernstein, A.: Knowing what a user likes: a design science approach to interfaces that automatically adapt to culture. MIS Q. **37**(2), 427–453 (2013)

55. Rudovic, O., Utsumi, Y., Lee, J., et al.: CultureNet: a deep learning approach for engagement intensity estimation from face images of children with autism. In: IEEE/RSJ International Conference on Intelligent Robots and Systems, Madrid, Spain, 1–5 October 2018. IEEE Xplore (2018)

56. Russel, M., Series, R.W., Wallace, J.L., Brown, C., Skilling, A.: The STAR system: an interactive pronunciation tutor for young children. Comput. Speech Lang. **14**, 161–175 (2000)

57. Sergis, S., Sampson, D.: An analysis of open learner models for supporting learning analytics. In: Sampson, D., Spector, J.M., Ifenthaler, D., Isaías, P., Sergis, S. (eds.) Learning Technologies for Transforming Large-Scale Teaching, Learning, and Assessment, pp. 155–190. Springer, Cham (2019). https://doi.org/10.1007/978-3-030-15130-0_9

58. Sexton, C.W.: Effectiveness of the DISTAR reading i program in developing first graders' language skills. J. Educ. Res. **82**(5), 289–293 (1989). www.jstor.org/stable/27540356

59. Uchidiuno, J, Yarzebinski, E., Madaio, M., et al.: Designing appropriate learning technologies for school vs home settings in Tanzanian rural villages. In: Proceedings of 1st ACM SIGCAS Conference on Computing and Sustainable Societies, Menlo Park and San Jose, CA, USA, 20–22 June 2018. ACM, New York (2018)

60. VanLehn, K.: The relative effectiveness of human tutoring, intelligent tutoring systems, and other tutoring systems. Educ. Psychol. **46**(4), 197–221 (2011)

61. Watson, S., Coy, A.: JAMLIT: a corpus of Jamaican standard English for automatic speech recognition of children's speech. In: SLTU, pp. 243–247 (2018)

62. Williams, S.M., Nix, D., Fairweather, P.: Using speech recognition technology to enhance literacy instruction for emerging readers. In: Fishman, B., O'Connor-Divelbiss, S. (eds.) 4th International Conference of the Learning Sciences, New Jersey, Mahwah, N.J., pp. 115–120 (2000)

63. Xu, Z., Wijekumar, K., Ramirez, G., Hu, X., Irey, R.: The effectiveness of intelligent tutoring systems on K-12 students' reading comprehension: a meta-analysis. Br. J. Educ. Technol. **50**(6), 3119–3137 (2019)

64. Zhang, H., Lin, Y.: Unsupervised learning for sequence-to-sequence text-to-speech for low-resource languages. In: Proceedings of Interspeech 2020 (2020). https://arxiv.org/abs/2008.04549

65. Zhang, Z.Q., Song, Y., Zhang, J.S., McLoughlin, I., Dai, L.R.: Semi-supervised end-to-end ASR via teacher-student learning with conditional posterior distribution. In: Proceedings of Interspeech 2020, pp 3580–3584 (2020)

66. Zualkernan, I.A., Karim, A.: Using a traveling van to deliver blended learning in a developing country. In: Proceedings of 13th IEEE International Conference on Advanced Learning Technologies (ICALT), July 2013, Beijing (2013)

A Stranger in the Classroom: Pre-service Teachers' Anxiety and Negative Attitudes Toward Humanoid Social Robots

Violeta Rosanda[1]($\boxtimes$) (iD) and Andreja Istenič[1,2,3] (iD)

[1] Faculty of Education, University of Primorska, Koper, Slovenia
[2] Faculty of Civil and Geodetic Engineering, University of Ljubljana, Ljubljana, Slovenia
[3] Institute of Education and Psychology, Kazan Federal University, Kazan, Russia

Abstract. While exploring a pre-service teacher population, which is not willing to accept social robots in their future classroom, we find a low level of robot anxiety, slightly negative general attitudes toward social robots in education and a strong positive correlation between anxiety and negative attitudes in general. Our findings put in evidence also a strong positive correlation between anxiety and negative attitudes toward interactions with robot, which we interpret with Anxiety/uncertainty management theory. In human relations the communication with a stranger of another culture results in the managment of uncertainty and in some associated anxiety and can lead to communication avoidance with strangers.

The participants of our research were exposed to videos showing NAO robot performing a pedagogical role in the classroom environment and did not have direct interactions with the robot.

Keywords: Pre-service teachers · Negative attitudes toward social robots · Anxiety

1 Introduction

Social robots are attempting to transition from the controlled environment of laboratory experimentations into the "wild" classroom environment [1–4 - Sect. 1.4]. At this stage the aim is more often HRI research rather than the implementation of robots in the regular school curricula [5]. The important challenge for their regular teaching process implementation is represented by their acceptance by their intended users [6]. In education the aspect of intended user involves at least teachers and students, at lower educational levels also parental acceptance might be important. The acceptance of robots in the educational environment is in a wider sense an issue that affects society as a whole [7].

We define technology integration in this context, based on Redmann and Kotrlik [8], as employing various technologies available in instruction to support, enhance, inspire and create learning. Classroom implementation of novel technologies and their real effective and efficient usage largely depend on teacher's individual decisions. Berliner [9] explains teaching doesnt' have many observers, there is hence little pressure on teacher's

© Springer Nature Switzerland AG 2021
M. Rauterberg (Ed.): HCII 2021, LNCS 12795, pp. 461–473, 2021.
https://doi.org/10.1007/978-3-030-77431-8_29

to follow the research findings. The disconnect between educational research and practice [9] will, due to the fast-paced development of education technology, not be limited by the gap between the practice and the science of teaching/learning, but rather it will be limited by ever more complex technology. Holzmann, Schwarz and Audretsch's [10] findings also evidence teachers as being "indifferent to important other peoples' thoughts and opinions" [pp. 271], which means less possibilities for social influence.

Humanoid social robots are "physically embodied autonomous robotic technology, equipped with artificial intelligence and social skills, developed to become equal partners in social relations, capable of human-like situational and role appropriate interaction" [11]. This high-level novel technology with human appearance mimics human social skills and behaviors. It is hence being designed to build relationships with its human users. As we expect that humanoid social robots will be deployed in some very delicate domains, as for example the up-bringing of future generations, it will be natural that acceptance resistance will be encountered [7]. The exploration of acceptance and influencing factors becomes crucial [12].

Novel technology adoption in education has been poorly explored until now, especially the adoption of technologies with a high novelty level [10]. We also know relatively little about attitudes towards social robots in education [12]. The goal of this paper is to give a limited empirical contribution, by exploring anxiety and attitudes toward humanoid social robots use as expressed by pre-service teachers. These two factors significantly impact novel technology adoption [10 pp. 271].

2 Anxiety and Attitudes Toward Robots

Acceptance studies regarding social robot technology in education frequently use Unified Theory of Acceptance and Use of Technology (UTAUT). UTAUT is based on the theory of planned behavior which explains that the usage of technology is preceded by behavioral intention [13] which is determined also by attitude [10].

Few studies have however focused on the education specialists' attitudes and on the anxiety measured with Negative Attitudes Towards Robots Scale (NARS) and Robot Anxiety Scale (RAS) both developed by Nomura, Kanda, Suzuki and Kato [14]. Studies which assessed attitudes and anxiety with Heerink, Krose, Evers and Wielinga [15] toolkits and models based on UTAUT report generally positive attitudes and low or no anxiety [16–18]. The studies that utilize NARS and RAS scales come to a different conclusion.

When it comes to the construct and more specifically on how the methodologies focus on attitude and anxiety there is a significant difference between the UTAUT and the NARS and RAS scales. Compared to the UTAUT anxiety construct the RAS scale is focused on different anxiety aspects; i.e. on anxiety evoked by users toward robot with social skills situated in the social context. It measures the anxiety toward communication with robots, toward behavior characteristics of robots and toward discourse with robots. It does not focus on the problematics of the practical utilization of the robot and its inherent consequences. This is more typical of the UTAUT model anxiety. Also the definitions are different. Heerink et al. [15 pp. 2] define anxiety as "Evoking anxious or emotional reactions when using the system". RAS authors instead define it as "a feeling of mingled dread and apprehension about the future without a specific cause for the fear, a chronic fear of mild degree, strong overwhelming fear, a secondary drive involving an acquired avoidance response, or the inability to predict the future or to resolve problems". They further explain it comprises of state (individuals' stable characteristic) and trait anxiety (transiently evoked in specific situations, changing depending on the situation and time) [14, 19].

Moreover also the definitions of attitude are different. Heerink et al. [15 pp. 2] define attitude construct as "Positive or negative feelings about the appliance of the technology." NARS authors define it as "a relatively stable and enduring predisposition to behave or react in a certain way toward persons, objects, institutions, or issues" [14 pp. 442]. For the purpose of our study we use the modified Venkatesh, Morris, Davis and Davis's [13] definition: attitude is the overall affective reaction of pre-service teachers to using the technology. Reich-Stiebert and Eyssel [20] observe that the anxiety and the attitudes toward social robots are poorly explored from the education specialists' standpoint. The research was focused mostly on students attitudes towards social robots even though Xia and LeTendre [2] mention studies which suggest that teachers' initial attitudes towards robots are one of the important factors which influence their willingness to use social robots in classrooms. As Nomura et al. [14] explain concrete behavior toward robots is associated with anxiety and negative attitudes and able to lead education specialists to avoid communicating with social robots. As explained by Redmann et al. [8] "As teachers' technology anxiety [...] increases, their experimentation scale scores decrease". Experimentation in this context defines the initial phase during which they begin to use technology.

In addition, Conti, Commodari and Buono [21] clarify the importance of understanding the teacher's attitudes as a precondition for a successful teacher training for the introduction of robots in education.

2.1 NARS Assessed Negative Attitudes

Kim and Lee (2015) as quoted in [20] assessed 140 elementary school teachers' attitudes in Korea using NARS scale. Their findings show negative attitudes.

Reich-Stiebert et al. [20] explored German teachers' attitudes toward teaching and learning with education robots. For this purpose they developed a new scale which encompasses also NARS scale statements. Their findings put in evidence the elementary, secondary and vocational schoolteachers' negative attitudes toward teaching and learning with education robots. They also highlight significant differences between teachers at different school types and levels. Elementary school teachers expressed a less positive attitude compared to higher education levels teachers. Elementary teachers' concerns regarded children's wellbeing in robot-based education. Their concerns are similar to this pre-service teachers' sample [11].

Hence we build the following hypothesis:

H 1: NARS scale will put in evidence our pre-service teachers' negative attitudes toward social robots in education.

2.2 Anxiety

Holzmann et al.'s [10] findings evidence anxiety as one of the significant predictors of an individual's intention to use novel technology. In their study anxiety was assessed with the UTAUT model.

Redmann et al. [8] deal with the concept of technology anxiety in the pedagogical environment. They connect anxiety with teachers' technology utilization during instruction and report that anxiety may influence the integration of technology. The utilization of technology in a classroom environment without proper teacher training and curriculum alignment increases the teachers' anxiety relative to the implementation of said technology.

Current attempts for social robot integration are not preceded with teacher training. The use of robots is rarely aligned with the curriculum and curricular activities. Hence we can hypothesize:

H 2: RAS scale will evidence our pre-service teachers' anxiety toward social robots in education.

Furthermore Erebak and Turgut [22] suggest that anxiety is in general negatively related with a positive attitude. We formulate the following hypothesis:

H 3: Pre-service teachers' anxiety toward robots is related to negative attitudes toward robots in education.

Nomura, Suzuki, Kanda and Kato's [19] findings show a significant moderate correlation between negative attitudes toward interaction with robot and state and trait anxiety. Therefore we hypothesize:

H 4: Pre-service teachers' negative attitudes toward interaction with robot in education are correlated with anxiety.

3 Research Goal, Material and Methods

In this paper we investigate one pre-service teachers' population anxiety and negative attitudes toward social robots with pedagogical roles used in an educational environment.

3.1 Participants

The intervention involved 121 teacher candidates (90.1% women, age mean of 19.47; SD, 1.45) attending the Educational technology course at the Faculty of education of Koper in the academic year 2019/2020. Preliminarily they were informed about the study, the voluntariness of participation and that their participation/non-participation would not affect their grades. They provided free consent.

3.2 Study Setting, Procedure and Instruments

Participants were shown 3 videos: Robots For Early Childhood Education (https://www.youtube.com/watch?v=NLaDE4OsjQI); The iPal Robot goes to Kindergarten (https://www.youtube.com/watch?v=qGR4G91y5dQ); Social robot helps teaching toddlers a second language (https://www.youtube.com/watch?v=vlmjvKgWtmU).

Since the videos were the starting material for the questionnaire, they showed humanoid social robots acting with pedagogical roles in a real classroom context.

In this study we analyze the following questionnaire sections:

a) *Demographic questions*

b) *Participants negative attitudes toward humanoid social robots* measured with Negative Attitudes Towards Robots Scale (NARS). Krägeloh, Bharatharaj, Sasthan Kutty, Nirmala and Huang [12] report that NARS is the most highly cited psychometrically validated scale used to investigate social acceptability of robots. It was developed by Nomura et al. [14] to assess human attitudes towards social robots, measuring the opinions people usually have about robots [23]. The scale has 14 items classified into three subscales: S1- Negative Attitude toward Interaction with Robots; S2- Negative Attitude toward the Social Influence of Robots; and S3- Negative Attitude toward Emotional Interactions with Robots. For the scale items overview see Nomura et al. [14 pp. 444]. We used 5-point Likert scale ranging from 1 (strongly disagree) to 5 (strongly agree). A higher NARS score shows a more negative attitude toward robots reflecting NARS's focus on exclusively negative attitudes towards robots. Items 12, 13, and 14 need to be reverse coded (marked *). We removed the statement I feel comforted by being with robots that have emotions because our participants did not directly interact with robot.

We examined the structure of the scale by conducting exploratory factor analyses on the questionnaire scores, to check for the possibility that the items from the questionnaire load onto different factors compared to the original subscales items. We conducted the Principal axis factoring (PAF) with a Direct Oblimin rotation. We selected an oblique rotation as factors were expected to be interrelated. PAF yielded a two-factor solution (NARI) with slightly different item allocation and some deleted items. Factor Negative attitude toward Interaction with Robots (NARINT) maintains the original items: I would feel very nervous just standing in front of a robot; I would feel uneasy if I was given a job where I had to use robots; I would feel paranoic talking with a robot; and I would feel nervous operating a robot in front of other people. The second factor groups two items: If robots had emotions I would be able to make friends with them* (in the original NARS scale in the construct Negative Attitude toward Emotional Interactions with Robots) and I would hate the idea that robots or AI were making judgements about things (in the original scale in the Negative Attitude toward Interaction with Robots construct). We named the second factor Negative attitudes towards the robots' emotions and judgements (NAREJ). The two factor solution explains 63.51% of the variance.

c) *Participants' anxiety measured with robot anxiety scale* (RAS). RAS was developed by Nomura et al. [14] to measure human anxiety induced by robots in real and imaginary interactions with humans. RAS consists of three subscales: Anxiety toward Communication with Robots, Anxiety toward Behavior Characteristics of Robots and Anxiety toward Communication with Robots. For the scale items overview see Nomura et al. [14 pp. 444]. We collected the responses with the same 5-point Likert scale used for NARS.

Based on the results of PAF we concluded that a one factor solution with all four items, see Table 3 in Results section, of the original Anxiety Behavior toward Behavioral Characteristics of Robots subscale was the most appropriate. The one factor solution (RAI) explains 70.63% of the variance.

The reliability of the factors was established by calculating Cronbach's alpha.

3.3 Data Analyses

- *Descriptive statistics* for attitude and anxiety factor solution and factor scores (mean, min, max, SD)
- A *single statement analysis for negative attitude and anxiety factor solution* was used to identify the most relevant aspects. Consistent with Conti, Di Nuovo, Buono, Di Nuovo [24] descriptive statistics (minimum and maximum scores, mean and SD), the percentage of positive (POS), negative (NEG) and neutral (NEU) perceptions were calculated. The percentage of positive responses indicates values on Likert scale greater than 3 indicating more negative attitudes and more anxiety, since these scale items express negative attitudes and anxiety. The percentage of negative answers indicates average score lower than 3 and less or no negative attitudes and anxiety. Value 3 indicates a neutral perception.
- *Correlations* between the factors of NARI factor solution scores, between NARI and RAI and between single factors of NARI and RAI factor solution were calculated.

4   Results

4.1   Demographics

121 pre-service teachers (90% female) aged between 18 and 33 years ($M = 19.47$, SD $= 1.46$) have filled the survey. The most populous group (59.5%) was 19 years old, followed by 20 years old (25,6%).

4.2   Descriptive Statistics and Cronbach's α

Table 1. Cronbach's α and descriptive statistics for NARI and RAI factor solution and scores.

	Alpha	Min	Max	Mean	SD
NARI	.751	1.17	5.0	3.24	.77
NARINT	.762	1.00	5.00	2.92	.88
NAREJ	.608	1.00	5.00	3,90	.97
RAI	.861	1.00	5.00	3.17	1.01

In one item, the reliability was α > 0.60. The decision was made based on Conti et al. [24], who according to Kline [25] considered the items acceptable if the score α > 0.60, while solid factors have an alpha of at least .700.

High factor mean value means strong negative attitude or high anxiety level.

4.3 Anxiety and Negative Attitudes Towards Social Robots (H1, H2)

a) Descriptive statistics: Descriptive statistics results (Table 1) confirm our H1 and H2. Our participants expressed a low level of anxiety (M = 3.17) and low level of general negative attitudes toward robots (M = 3.24). They hold strong negative attitudes toward Robots' emotions and judgements (M = 3.90) but not toward the interaction with the robot (M = 2.92).

To get a better insight into their anxiety and negative attitudes we report also the levels of negative attitudes or anxiety for single items (Table 2).

Table 2. Negative attitudes towards robots: single answers analysis

Factors	Items	Mean	Min	Max	SD	NEG (%)	POS (%)	NEU (%)
Negative Attitude toward Interaction with Robots (NARINT)	I would feel uneasy if I was given a job where I had to use robots	3.13	1.00	5.00	1.26	34	36	30
	I would feel nervous operating a robot in front of other people	3.22	1.00	5.00	1.11	25	40	35
	I would feel very nervous just standing in front of a robot	2.58	1.00	5.00	1.19	50	18	32
	I would feel paranoic talking with a robot	2.72	1.00	5.00	1.08	42	20	38
Negative Attitudes towards Robots' Emotions and Judgements (NAREJ)	If robots had emotions I would be able to make friends with them* (reverse)	3.91	1.00	5.00	1.14	11	65	25
	I would hate the idea that robots or AI were making judgements about things	3.89	1.00	5.00	1.15	12	67	21

The highest mean have the two items, which are directly focusing on the emotional and cognitive capacities of the robots. I would hate the idea that robots or AI were making judgements about things has one of the highest means of all items (M = 3.89); 67% of participants agrees with this statement. It is followed by: If robots had emotions I would be able to make friends with them (M = 3.91). As this is a reversed item 65% participants expressed that if robots had emotions they would not be able to make friends with them.

Also toward the statements: I would feel nervous operating a robot in front of other people (M = 3.22) and I would feel uneasy if I was given a job where I had to use robots (M = 3.12) the participants express slightly negative attitudes.

Table 3. Single statement descriptive statistics for robot anxiety factor solution

Item	Mean	Min	Max	SD	NEG (%)	POS (%)	NEU (%)
What kind of movements the robot will make	2.92	1.00	5.00	1.23	39	32	29
What the robot is going to do	3.39	1.00	5.00	1.18	24	52	24
How strong the robot is	3.57	1.00	5.00	1.16	18	57	25
How fast the robot will move	2.80	1.00	5.00	1.26	45	30	25

The single statement descriptive statistics for robot anxiety factor solution shows significant uncertainties. Approximately a quarter of all participants is neutral with respect to all the anxiety items. On average they are however neutral with regards to: What kind of movements the robot will make (M = 2.92) and How fast the robot will move (M = 2.80). The highest two means, that diverge from the neutral value of 3 are seen in connection with the items: How strong the robot is (M = 3.57), this worries 57% of participants and What the robot is going to do (M = 3.39), this worries 52% of participants.

b) Correlations
We have explored the relationships among negative attitudes and anxiety as well as between the two factors of negative attitude factor solution.

Table 4. Correlations between NARI factors and between NARI and RAI factor solution and scores.

Negative attitudes	Anxiety	Pearson correlation	Sig. (2-tailed)
NARI	RAI	.681	.000**
NARINT	RAI	.740	.000**
NAREJ	RAI	.249	.006**
NARINT	NAREJ	.350	.000**

All the correlations in Table 4 are significant and positive, confirming our H3 and H4. There is a strong positive correlation between anxiety and negative attitudes factor solution (.681) as well as between anxiety and negative attitudes toward interaction with robot (.740). The correlation between anxiety and negative attitudes towards robots' emotions and judgements is mild (.249) and mild is also the correlation between NARINT and NAREJ (.350).

5 Discussion and Conclusions

This study is a part of a mixed methods research design study through which we also investigated the acceptability and concerns towards robots of one pre-service teacher population from one faculty in Slovenia. Previous findings show that they are not willing to accept the idea to use social robots in their classrooms, their problematic perception of the robots' social dimension [4] and their concerns for the pupil's wellbeing in social robot-based instruction [11].

In this paper we explored their negative attitudes and anxiety toward social robots. In the planning and design of social robot integration and training it is necessary to know the attitudes and anxieties of the target group of in- and pre-service teachers.

Our results have confirmed all our hypothesis. Participants hold slightly negative general attitudes toward social robots in education (H1). This is consistent with the findings of other studies which assessed negative attitudes with NARS or scales which encompass NARS items: Kim et al. (2015) qtd. in Reich-Stiebert et al. [20] and Reich-Stiebert et al. [20]. Interestingly studies which explored acceptance of in- and/or pre-service teachers with Heerink et al.'s [15, 26] UTAUT based toolkits report more positive attitudes. The reason could be in the different statement focus of anxiety construct: in UTAUT more on the general and positive attitudes, in NARS on the specific negative aspects, which include the social aspects of classroom dynamics. It is our opinion that we should be careful in just simply comparing the attitude results obtained from these two different scales. The insight into two negative attitude factors statements shows that more than 60% of participants hold strong negative attitudes toward the robots' emotions, judgements, and possibility of friendly relation with robots (M = 3.91) and toward robots or AI forming judgements (M = 3.89). This finding shows, in our opinion, that they are not willing to accept social robot as a human equivalent social entity. In Istenič, Bratko and Rosanda [11] we identified the underlying reasons as the belief in human uniqueness and the opinion that children have to be educated and socialized by teachers.

Humanoid social robot in an education environment evoked in our participants a low level of anxiety (H2 confirmed) regarding what the robot is going to do in the classroom and with respect to the robots' power. In the education context special attention should be paid to assess the technology anxiety, i.e. how much anxiety do education specialists feel when they think about using technology in their instruction [8]. It would be ideal to inform and train about the robot implementation anxiety, which might stem from a lack of professional training (teacher preparation), lack of appropriate curriculum and learning material for teachers [5].

We found a strong positive correlation between anxiety and negative attitudes in general (H3 confirmed), which is consistent with Erebak et al. [22]; as well as between anxiety and negative attitudes toward interaction with robot, consistent with Nomura et al. [19] (H4 confirmed). As the participants have been directed to reflect on the performance of the robot in a pedagogical role within the classroom environment, they analyzed the presence of the social robots in the classroom at professional level. It hence could be that the negative attitudes toward the interaction with the associated anxiety reflect the participants' uncertainty regarding the educational process and class management. According to Anxiety/uncertainty management theory managing the uncertainty and anxiety in interpersonal and intergroup communications is crucial as they affect our communication with strangers. In this context the anxiety and uncertainty experienced when we communicate with others are associated and furthermore related with communication avoidance with strangers of a different culture. Currently in the classroom environment humanoid robot represents a stranger.

We assume that, during the initial encounters, the interaction processes identified by Duronto, Nishida and Nakayama [27] in the communication between strangers of a different culture take place: positively related anxiety and uncertainty and communication avoidance behavior. For the children is, at least initially, the presence of robots in the classroom exciting [28]. This is however not true for the adults, who need to introduce and accept the robot in the wider environment, determine the role of the robot and its duties and finally delegate responsibilities to the robot. This can clearly result in high levels of anxiety. "The placement of technology into classrooms without teacher preparation and curriculum considerations [has produced] may produce high levels of anxiety among teachers" [8].

The school environment is a comprehensive, well determined, structured system. It is governed by detailed rules defining the roles, tasks and responsibilities of all participants. The entrance of the robot in this environment represents for the participants a situation similar to the one that occurs in interhuman relations with the arrival of a stranger. It brings uncertainty about its behavioral patterns and roles. It leads to the change of settled and predictable interaction patterns between the adult participants and learners. It therefore follows that any study and conceptualization of the interaction in the school environment cannot be limited to the child-robot interaction or teacher-robot interaction, but it is necessary to introduce the concept of a triangular interaction between learner(s), teacher and robot.

The correlation between anxiety and negative attitudes towards the robots' emotions and judgements is mild (.249). Future research will have to explore the causal relationship and also more precisely for whom do the participants interpret the mimicking of emotions as inappropriate and anxious; is that for themselves or for their students? Similarly it is important to explore the participants' view of AI's judgements.

In this paper we present one pre-service teachers' population anxiety and negative attitudes towards social robots performing pedagogical roles in classroom. The findings of other studies which measured education specialists' anxiety and negative attitudes toward social robots with NARS and RAS scales report similar results to ours, i.e. education specialists hold negative attitudes toward robots [20]. These studies are rare and we found no study reporting about education specialists' absence of anxiety and negative attitudes when measured with NARS and RAS scales. As we mentioned in Sect. 2 when anxiety and attitude are measured with other instruments the studies may show different results [16–18]. As we have not encountered any attitudes and/or anxiety study, which would thoroughly investigate the education specialists using both qualitative and quantitative data analyses we are unable to compare this part of the research to existing literature. The results from our quantitative study [4] support this paper and Istenic, Bratko and Rosanda's [11] qualitative study results. Many studies productively examine robot's interaction with children in innovative ways and study teachers' attitudes and perceptions. Arroyo, Guo, Shidujaman, and Fernandes [29] recently explored robot's interaction with children in distance learning identifying teachers' inclination towards robotic educational technology.

Similarly to Reich-Stiebert et al. [20] our participants did not have a direct interaction with the robot. In the intervention they were exposed to videos showing Nao performing the pedagogical role in classroom. According to Li [30], robots which are physically embodied and physically present in the user's space are more persuasive, receive attention and are perceived positively. In [4, 11] we thoroughly analyse our participants' rejection of social robots in classrooms and the underlying reasons. We are therefore of the opinion that the results would not have been significantly different even if the participants were directly exposed to the interaction with the robot.

In addition, our findings reveal that the development of robotics and artificial intelligence requires from teachers to reflect on their role in the classroom [31].

6 Limitations

Our intervention presented social robotic affordances and usage in the classroom context without a specifical focus on the limitations of AI. Future research should explore the impact of these limitations on in- and pre-service teachers' negative attitudes and anxiety.

Our participants were not randomly sampled therefore our findings cannot be generalized.

Acknowledgments. Both researchers have equally participated to the study. The work of Andreja Istenič was financially supported by Slovenian Research Agency (P2-0210).

References

1. Belpaeme, T.: Advice to new human-robot interaction researchers. In: Jost, C., et al. (eds.) Human-Robot Interaction. SSBN, vol. 12, pp. 355–369. Springer, Cham (2020). https://doi.org/10.1007/978-3-030-42307-0_14

2. Xia, Y., LeTendre, G.: Robots for future classrooms: a cross-cultural validation study of "negative attitudes toward robots scale" in the US context. Int. J. Soc. Robot. 1-12 (2020). https://doi.org/10.1007/s12369-020-00669-2

3. Rosanda, V., Istenič, A.: A review of social robots in classrooms: emerging educational technology and teacher education. Educ. Self Dev. **14**(3), 1–20 (2019). https://doi.org/10.26907/esd14.3.09

4. Istenič, A., Bratko, I., Rosanda, V.: Are pre-service teachers disinclined to utilise embodied humanoid social robots in the classroom? (2021, in press)

5. Mubin, O., Stevens, C.J., Shahid, S., Mahmud, A.A., Dong, J.J.: A review of the applicability of robots in education. Technol. Educ. Learn. **1**, 1–7 (2013). https://doi.org/10.2316/Journal.209.2013.1.209-0015

6. Dillon, A.: User acceptance of information technology. In: Karwowski, W. (ed). Encyclopedia of Human Factors and Ergonomics, pp. 1–10. Taylor and Francis, London (2001). https://hdl. handle.net/10150/105880

7. Eurobarometer, S.: Public attitudes towards robots. European Commission. Special Eurobarometer 382/Wave EB77.1 – TNS Opinion & Social, pp. 1–18 (2012)

8. Redmann, D.H., Kotrlik, J.W.: Analysis of technology integration in the teaching-learning process in selected career and technical education programs. J. Vocat. Educ. Res. **29**(1), 3–25 (2004). https://doi.org/10.5328/JVER29.1.3

9. Berliner, D.C.: Research, policy, and practice: the great disconnect. In: Lapan, S.D., Quartaroli, M.T. (eds). Research Essentials: An Introduction to Designs and Practices, pp. 295–326 (2009)

10. Holzmann, P., Schwarz, E., Audretsch, D.: Understanding the determinants of novel technology adoption among teachers: the case of 3D printing. J. Technol. Transf. **45**(1), 259–275 (2018). https://doi.org/10.1007/s10961-018-9693-1

11. Istenič, A., Bratko, I., Rosanda, V.: Pre-service teachers' concerns about social robots in the classroom: a model for development. Educ. Self Dev. **16**(2) (2021, in press). https://doi.org/10.26907/esd.16.2.05

12. Krägeloh, C.U., Bharatharaj, J., Sasthan Kutty, S.K., Nirmala, P.R., Huang, L.: Questionnaires to measure acceptability of social robots: a critical review. Robotics **8**(4), 88, 1–14 (2019). https://doi.org/10.3390/robotics8040088

13. Venkatesh, V., Morris, M.G., Davis, G.B., Davis, F.D.: User acceptance of information technology: toward a unified view. MIS Q. **27**(3), 425–478 (2003). https://www.jstor.org/stable/30036540?seq=1#metadata_info_tab_contents

14. Nomura, T., Kanda, T., Suzuki, T., Kato, K.: Prediction of human behavior in human - robot interaction using psychological scales for anxiety and negative attitudes toward robots. IEEE Trans. Robot. **24**(2), 442–451 (2008). https://doi.org/10.1109/TRO.2007.914004

15. Heerink, M., Krose, B., Evers, V., Wielinga, B.: Measuring acceptance of an assistive social robot: a suggested toolkit. In: RO-MAN 2009-The 18th IEEE International Symposium on Robot and Human Interactive Communication, pp. 528–533. IEEE (2009). https://ieeexplore.ieee.org/abstract/document/5326320

16. Fridin, M., Belokopytov, M.: Acceptance of socially assistive humanoid robot by preschool and elementary school teachers. Comput. Hum. Behav. **33**, 23–31 (2014). https://doi.org/10.1016/j.chb.2013.12.016

17. Conti, D., Cattani, A., Di Nuovo, S., Di Nuovo, A.: A cross-cultural study of acceptance and use of robotics by future psychology practitioners. In: 24th IEEE International Symposium on Robot and Human Interactive Communication (RO-MAN), pp. 555–560 (2015). https://doi.org/10.1109/ROMAN.2015.7333601

18. Conti, D., Cattani, A., Di Nuovo, S., Di Nuovo, A.: Are future psychologists willing to accept and use a humanoid robot in their practice? Italian and English students' perspective. Front. Psychol. 1–13 (2019). https://doi.org/10.3389/fpsyg.2019.02138

19. Nomura, T., Suzuki, T., Kanda, T., Kato, K.: Altered attitudes of people toward robots: investigation through the negative attitudes toward robots scale. In: Proceedings of AAAI-06 Workshop on Human Implications of Human-Robot Interaction, pp. 29–35 (2006)

20. Reich-Stiebert, N., Eyssel, F.: Robots in the classroom: what teachers think about teaching and learning with education robots. In: Agah, A., Cabibihan, J.-J., Howard, A.M., Salichs, M.A., He, H. (eds.) ICSR 2016. LNCS (LNAI), vol. 9979, pp. 671–680. Springer, Cham (2016). https://doi.org/10.1007/978-3-319-47437-3_66

21. Conti, D., Commodari, E., Buono, S.: Personality factors and acceptability of socially assistive robotics in teachers with and without specialized training for children with disability. Life Span Disabil. **20**(2), 251–272 (2017). https://shura.shu.ac.uk/id/eprint/18254

22. Erebak, S., Turgut, T.: The mediator role of robot anxiety on the relationship between social anxiety and the attitude toward interaction with robots. AI Soc. 1–8 (2020). https://doi.org/10.1007/s00146-019-00933-8
23. Nomura, T., Shintani, T., Fujii, K., Hokabe, K.: Experimental investigation of relationships between anxiety, negative attitudes, and allowable distance of robots. In: Proceedings of the 2nd IASTED International Conference on Human Computer Interaction, pp. 13–18. ACTA Press, Chamonix (2007)
24. Conti, D., Di Nuovo, S., Buono, S., Di Nuovo, A.: Robots in education and care of children with developmental disabilities: a study on acceptance by experienced and future professionals. Int. J. Soc. Robot. 9(1), 51–62 (2016). https://doi.org/10.1007/s12369-016-0359-6
25. Kline, P.: The Handbook of Psychological Testing, 2nd edn. Routledge, New York (2000)
26. Heerink, M., Kröse, B., Evers, V., Wielinga, B.: Assessing acceptance of assistive social agent technology by older adults: the almere model. Int. J. Soc. Robot. 2, 361–375 (2010). https://doi.org/10.1007/s12369-010-0068-5
27. Duronto, P.M., Nishida, T., Nakayama, S.I.: Uncertainty, anxiety, and avoidance in communication with strangers. Int. J. Intercult. Relat. 29(5), 549–560 (2005). https://doi.org/10.1016/j.ijintrel.2005.08.003
28. Kanda, T., Sato, R., Saiwaki, N., Ishiguro, H.: A two-month field trial in an elementary school for long-term human–robot interaction. IEEE Trans. Robot. 23(5), 962–971 (2007). https://doi.org/10.1109/TRO.2007.904904
29. Arroyo, D., Guo, Y., Yu, M., Shidujaman, M., Fernandes, R.: Towards the design of a robot for supporting children's attention during long distance learning. In: Wagner, A.R., et al. (eds.) ICSR 2020. LNCS (LNAI), vol. 12483, pp. 332–343. Springer, Cham (2020). https://doi.org/10.1007/978-3-030-62056-1_28
30. Li, J.: The benefit of being physically present: A survey of experimental works comparing copresent robots, telepresent robots and virtual agents. Int. J. Hum.-Comput. Stud. 77, 23–37 (2015). https://doi.org/10.1016/j.ijhcs.2015.01.001
31. Istenič Starčič, A.: Human learning and learning analytics in the age of artificial intelligence, pp. 2974–2976 (2019). https://doi.org/10.1111/bjet.12879

Bie-Modernism and Cultural Computing

Jianjiang Wang[✉] and Haiguang Chen

Shanghai Normal University, Shanghai 200234, People's Republic of China

Abstract. Civilization is the parasitic host of barbarism. Pseudo-modernity has lodged in modern civilization through high technology including computer technology and artificial intelligence technology, and has formed a threat to human modern civilization. Bie-modernism is a doctrine that expresses the idea of distinguishing the true modernity or true world from the pseudo modernity or the false world. Bie-modernist Culture Computing (BCC) is a kind of cultural computing guided by Bie-modernism, so as to defend the legitimate interests of people. It includes two parts, one is Visual Identification System, which combined with the background of the times and the humanistic environment, we can build a supporting platform for calculating the characteristics of the characters, and combine big data and NLP and other computer technologies to identify the real and pseudo characters. Another is Digital Identification System, which is from the perspective of cultural value, the feature model library of real and pseudo identification system is built to form a new foundation of digital global identification system. For paper regulation here we just introduce one of them.

Keywords: Bie-modernism · Pseudo modernity · Distinguish · Culture computing · Bie-modernist culture computing · Visual identification system · Algorithm model

1 Civilization is the Parasitic Host of Barbarism and Pseudo-modernity is the Enemy of Human Civilization

The global pandemic of COVID19 has brought unprecedented disaster to human beings. More than one hundred million people have been infected with the virus and more than two millions died, and the spread of this infection has not weakened so far, and has greatly harmed the safety of human life and property.

Epidemics are often associated with modern civilization, the modern civilization is based on the high tech. progress, especially nowadays based on computer calculation. Therefore, the theme of modern civilization and cultural computing is an important topic.

Human civilization is closely connected with the social forms and temporal developments which constitute pre-modern, modern and post-modern civilization. However, in some countries and regions, the three forms of society or civilization do not develop linearly in stages, but are mixed together to form the spatialization of time or the hybridity of civilization. I call this civilization Bie-modern [1]. In the Bie-modern state, modernity accounts for a small proportion, while pre-modernity accounts for a large proportion.

© Springer Nature Switzerland AG 2021
M. Rauterberg (Ed.): HCII 2021, LNCS 12795, pp. 474–489, 2021.
https://doi.org/10.1007/978-3-030-77431-8_30

Moreover, with the interests of the rulers and their hobbies, the direction of the development of the whole society is full of uncertainty and randomness. Moreover, with the disappearance of imperial colonies after World War II, the concept of world civilization has been generally accepted, which leads to the prevalence of pseudo modernity and pseudo civilization in countries with insufficient modernity. They often engage in pre-modern activities under the guise of universal value and universal civilization, thus hindering the further development of human civilization [2].

This so-called "modernity" is a concept with a historical development moving from material wealth to institutional facilities to ideology, which is the symbol of modern civilization. Material wealth provides people with the foundation for peaceful development, and avoids the low-end jungle competition for survival caused by poverty, such as the lack of clothing and food, leading to the exchange of children for food. Freedom, democracy and rule of law in the system provide legal guarantees for the healthy development of the society. Ideological freedom, independence, fairness and justice provide each individual with a spiritual space for free survival and creation. Modernity, sprouted in the Renaissance, formed in the age of Enlightenment, matured after World War II, has become a modern civilization shared by all humanity. This kind of modern civilization is often manifested in the conventions of peaceful development by which humanity abides.

The once brilliant ancient civilization will shine again on the stage of modern civilization when true modernity has been attained, but it is impossible to revive independently of modern civilization, let alone replace modern civilization and restore the old system.

In the face of true modernity, savagery and barbarism can no longer be openly swaggered through the market, but they often rely on a false modern civilization to return, and pretend to be modern with pseudo modernity.

After human beings enter the stage of civilization, we must clearly realize that a fundamental human truth, in spite of standardizing people's words and deeds, civilization is still the host of parasitic barbarism, and barbarism devours civilization through civilization itself. This is because, with the development of advanced civilization, the primitive tribes in the primitive forest, including a few other cannibal tribes, have been patronized by modern human civilization. Instead of being a primitive barbaric state, they are the mirror image of modern civilization, the research object of anthropology and ethnography, reflecting the progress of modern civilization. By contrast, the primitive barbarism drawn from human nature being unable to travel freely and openly, is placed in and attached to the civilized society in the guise of civilization. Thus, civilization becomes the host of barbarism, and barbarism devours civilization by virtue of civilization. The two world wars in the last century were the wars which were first launched by the so-called civilized countries and quickly spread all over the world. Among them, the mass massacre of Jews by the German Nazis, the Nanjing Massacre by Japanese aggressors and the secret massacre of Polish prisoners by the Soviet Red Army are the chief evils. Moreover, civilization can never get rid of the entanglement of barbarism, which will show up in war or in peace, anytime and anywhere, bringing terror and disaster to humanity. Of course, the premeditated suppression and massacre of people organized with the slogans of scientific and technological progress, cultural progress, cultural revolution, fairness and justice, in which the planners themselves do not directly kill people, but the consequences are far greater than those conducted by the planners themselves. Therefore, the seemingly absurd statement that civilization is the host of barbarism just reveals the hidden evil within civilization. Therefore, the question is not whether barbarism will attach itself to civilization and devour civilization, but how and to what extent.

The more advanced the civilization is, the more barbarism wants to feed upon it. This is because the greater the distance between civilization and barbarism, the easier barbarism can be identified and eliminated. Therefore, barbarism must disguise itself and exist with the help of civilization. By contrast, if the distance is smaller and the boundary is blurred, the possibility of being identified and cleared will be reduced. Therefore, the necessity of savagery to disguise itself will be reduced. If the crime under the sun can go smoothly, then why should the crime under the camera mind? Because of this, with the rapid development of human civilization, barbarism will gain unprecedented opportunity by virtue of pseudo modernity. The success of Musk's Neuralink in artificial intelligence has made technical preparations for the accelerated development of humanity, of human criminality, and even the destruction of human civilization itself. Once it is monopolized by dictators or exploited by inhumane people, the resulting evil and destruction is unimaginable in its scale and degree.

However, the frequency and intensity of barbarism are different between advanced and underdeveloped civilizations. This can be illustrated by comparing the cases of white police killing black people in the United States during the pandemic and the genocide in Rwanda in 1994, which killed millions of people. In democratic countries or countries of advanced civilization, the low frequency and intensity of barbaric incidents lies in the fact that democratic countries or advanced civilizations have the functions of self-organization, self-control and self-regulation, which limit the scale and frequency of barbaric incidents, and limit social problems, national and ethnic conflicts within the scope of the rule of law, and do not allow them to spread into disaster. In addition, people in advanced civilized countries usually have high moral standards, and can consciously resolve ethnic, national and social conflicts in folk ways. Although the white American police killed George Floyd by kneeling on him, it has caused a wave of protest throughout the United States, and even triggered global protest movements. These protest movements are often accompanied by a certain degree of violence, but they do not cause instability in the country, let alone global chaos. On the contrary, this kind of protest shows the righteous act of human beings, that is, how the goodness of human nature in advanced civilization can resolve contradictions and conflicts. The army and police knelt down to the protesters to ask for reconciliation and stability. The white people washed the black people's feet to show their repentance and understanding. All these show that although civilization is the host of barbarism, barbarism relies on civilization and devours civilization, but this host has a magic weapon to conquer and overcome barbarism. This magic weapon is nothing else but the system of civilization itself - rule of law rather than rule of man; It lies in the trust between people and their belief in freedom, dignity, human rights and fraternity. It also lies in the self-confidence and self-discipline established by breaking away from the crisis of survival caused by material poverty. By contrast, the barbaric conflicts which frequently break out in some underdeveloped countries, the mechanism of self-regulation, self-control and self-resolution has not been formed, so they have to let the incidents continue to deteriorate and escalate abruptly, resulting in the large-scale casualties of innocent people. When the crime under the camera still has the possibility of not being known, the killing in the sun is reckless, so the killed will be millions rather than two or three individuals.

Although civilization is the parasitic host of barbarism, barbarism always appears in the guise of civilization and devours civilization, the function of autonomy in human civilization limits the freedom of barbarism. The Geneva Conventions, International Human Rights Law and International Civilization Conventions will require all countries to abide by them and restrict, stop and punish the countries that violate them by virtue of an international intervention, so as to make barbarism lose its reason for existing in the face of law and morality. However this also creates a good international environment for the barbarism, although it devours civilization, but civilization could restrain barbarism.

Although, in light of the historical trend towards common human progress, open barbarism has lost its reason for existence, barbarism often remains the extreme expression of selfish desire. As the desire to conquer and to rule, disguised barbarism will appear on the stage and swagger through the market even when open barbarism is controlled. This kind of disguised barbarism is called pseudo modernity in modern society.

There are a number ways of expressing pseudo modernity, which are summarized as follows:

1. Pseudo modernity, in the name of modernity, especially using modern scientific and technological achievements, inherits and promotes the malpractices and evils of the pre-modern and the primitive accumulation of capitalism. With the help of modern scientific and technological means and material conditions, it is common for people to violate human rights and neglect human life, and corruption is prevalent.
2. Speaking of universal value, some countries in fact exhibit the inhumaneness of extreme egoism and nationalism. They use modern scientific and technological achievements, fight against generality and universality with individuality and particularity, oppose the universal value of human beings, hinder the promotion of the universal value of human beings, and even dare to conquer other nations and destroy humanity by launching wars and nuclear wars.
3. Speaking of the state, some countries use modern scientific and technological achievements, practice autocratic rule, depriving individual rights with state power, violating law and discipline in the name of law, suppressing the people in the name of the people, while dreaming of restoring the feudal monarchy.
4. Speaking of honesty and integrity, some countries are permeated by counterfeit goods disguised by modern high-tech reproduction technology and hidden rules which lead to the collapse of the integrity of the social system, and a large number of unjust and false cases.
5. Speaking of freedom of speech and democracy, some countries use modern high-tech reproduction technology to restrict civil liberties, suppressing speech, and preventing the exposure of hypocrisy and evil.
6. Pseudo aesthetics, represented by plastic surgery and the infusion of poisonous "chicken soup" into the soul, conspire together with the beauty industry by means of hypocrisy, disguise and seduction, to endorse falsehood, emptiness, evil and ugliness.
7. The most typical pseudo-modernity in cultural computing is a fake world brought about by the wide application of deep fake technology.

The most typical pseudo-modernity in cultural computing is a fake world brought about by the wide application of deep fake technology.

The most typical pseudo-modern culture is widely used in the calculation of the pseudo-deep (deep fake) technology has brought a fake world. This kind of fake world does not exist in pre-modern society. This kind of deep pseudo-technology puts the cloak of civilization on barbarism and is more dangerous than barbarism.

In short, as people are familiar with, the pseudo-modern will use modern technological advances, including cultural calculations, to disguise itself, and use the "post-truth era" as an excuse to conceal the truth, forge products, hide the truth, reverse right and wrong, confuse black and white, and raise modern the scientific and technological achievements are transformed into anti-civilization methods. Therefore, it can be said that the modern civilization of mankind is being shrouded by the pseudo-modernity supported by high-tech, and human beings live in a world where the true and the false are confused.

The harm of pseudo modernity to modern civilization lies in the following aspects:

First, in the name of modernity, it conducts the practice of pre-modernity and the primitive accumulation of capitalism, which has greatly enlarged the disadvantages and evils of the pre-modern accumulation of capitalism. Human rights violations and corruption are unprecedented and become the enemy of modernization.

Second, it confuses the boundaries between modern and non-modern, barbarism and non-barbarism, desecrates the universal value of human beings, forms a distorted view of civilization, provides a hotbed for barbarism to live in and devour civilization, and hinders the normal development of human civilization.

Third, a pseudo culture is formed with contempt for and violation of the laws and regulations with the implementation of hidden rules resulting in the prevalence of crimes and illegal cases, promoting barbarism and unjust trials while compliance with laws and regulations will be punished.

Fourth, lying and deception are commonly seen to cover evils and crimes so that the ugly and barbaric acts are uninhibited, poisoning the social atmosphere, polluting people's spiritual realm and lowering the level of human civilization.

Finally, disguised barbarism is more awful than blatant barbarism because the former paralyzes people and makes them neglect prevention and causes greater harm, while the latter can reduce the harm to the minimum degree by early prevention and early avoidance.

The purpose of Bie-modernism is to distinguish true modernity from false modernity, to establish real modernity, and to establish a real world. In other words, it not only maintains modern civilization, but also protects national culture, promotes modern civilization and avoids barbarism. However, the foundation for protecting national culture is to have real modernity and integrate it into modern civilization rather than to oppose modern civilization by protecting national culture or adhering to nationalism. Therefore, the overall promotion of modern human civilization is to distinguish the true and false modernity, improve the ability of human beings to identify true and false modernity, wake up from the confusing right and wrong, and liberate themselves from being fooled.

2   How to Realize Bie-Modernism in Cultural Computing?

2.1   What is Bie-Modern and Bie-Modernism?

Bie-modernism is a doctrine that has attracted the attention of the international academic and artistic communities in recent years. Borrowing the origin from the oracle bone inscription of Chinese character Bie which means the separation of flesh and bones, Bie-modernism expresses the idea of distinguishing the true modernity or true world from the pseudo modernity or the false word (Fig. 1).

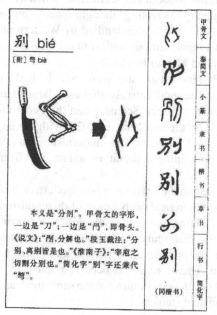

Fig. 1. The Chinese character of "Bie"(别), one of the ancient Chinese hieroglyphics with a history of over 3,000 years, originally means the separation of flesh and bones by knife.

In 2014, the theory of Bie-modernism was put forward by Jianjiang Wang, a well-known international scholar, the leader of Literature and Art major of Shanghai Normal University, the director of the Institute of Aesthetics and Aesthetic Education, the national highest level professor of Arts, the director of the Chinese Aesthetic Society, the director of the Chinese Literature and Art theory society, and the board member of the 9th International Cultural Computing Conference in 2021. It has been widely impacted at home and abroad. In recent years, more than 100 academic papers have been published in Chinese, English, Italian and Serbian, including nearly 30 groups of Chinese and English column articles. Many of them have been reprinted by the National People's University, University Arts and Social Sciences Degist, Xinhua Degist and Social Sciences Degist. Four Bie-modern series books in Chinese and English have been published, covering the fields of philosophy, aesthetics, literature, art, artistic creation, writing, linguistics, law, economics, tourism, psychology, sociology, artificial intelligence, etc.

Famous and well-known scholars at home and abroad, such as Aleš Erjavec, Keaton Wynn, Ernest Zenko, Yuneng Zhang, Bohai Chen, Zhongyi Xia, Xuan Wu, etc., participated in the discussion. Many powerful artists consciously create Bie- modernism art. There have been several doctoral dissertations from universities outside Shanghai to study Bie-modernism theories. Six international academic conferences and international art touring exhibitions have been held on the theme of Bie-modern theories. Two universities in the United States and Europe have set up CCBMS/CBMS one after another, and Italy has established Bie-modernism Website (www.biemodernism.org), Wikipedia has a special introduction, Baidu search "Bie-modernism" word, network click through rate of more than 100 million. Bie-modernism has been regarded by the international famous scholars as the covering theory of creating "thought space" "philosophical moment" and "philosophical quadrilateral". It has been studied by Western philosophers in comparison with the theories of French famous philosophers such as Jacques Rancière, Alain Badiou, Jacques Derrida and Michel Foucault.

At the same time, Professor Jianjiang Wang was invited to give nearly one hundred academic lectures on Bie-modernist Aesthetics in famous universities at home and abroad, domestic Academy of Social Sciences and the Federation of Social Sciences, which were well received by the audience. In 2020, with the approval of the Graduate School of Shanghai Normal University, Bie-modernist aesthetics is set as the direction of doctoral enrollment and training in literature and art, and from 2021, it is opening to the whole country.

Bie-modernism is based on the analysis of Bie-modern (a doubtful modernity) social form. It puts forward the theoretical proposition of distinguishing real modernity from pseudo modernity and realizing real modernity, which conforms to the historical trend that human beings need to distinguish real from pseudo in order to protect their own rights and interests with the prevalence of pseudo modernity in the era of mechanical civilization reproduction. Therefore, it has been responded by the social elites of less developed countries and developed countries at the same time, and has gradually become an international distinguished studies.

2.2 Bie-Modernist Culture Computing

Culture Computing

Human computer interaction (HCI) is the main cultural mode for human beings to enter the information age, which has a decisive impact on design, production, control, feedback and communication. Entertainment computing is a new mode of application of computer artificial intelligence technology in life, games and artistic creation since the beginning of this century. It has a growing impact on quality life, happy games, immersive experience and artistic imitation. Its practice mode and practice path are causing a revolutionary change in artistic creation and aesthetic form. However, entertainment computing, a new model in the ascendant, is being overtaken by Naoko Tosa in Inter-Culture Computing: ZENetic Computer, 2004, and developed by Rauterberg M.'s team, which will be introduced into the proposed new base. This is the cultural computing model, an effort to sublimate the attributes of computer tools into cultural attributes in comparison with ZENetic computing model in the East, especially in Japan.The impact of this effort on culture and art lies in the computational regeneration of classical art images, which leads to new ideas such as Rauterberg M's "Cultural computing" [3] "Reality determination through action" [4]. These ideas have direct positive significance for the development of human science and cultural creation. With the emergence of culture computing, the global cultural industry model of technology + art is being replaced by a new model of technology + Art + philosophy.

Bie-Modernist Cultural Computing

Bie-modernist Culture Computing (BCC) is a kind of cultural calculation guided by the concept of Bie-modernism. It focuses on the difference between the real and pseudo modernity or the true world and false world, the difference between the fake and inferior cultures and their products in different countries, nationalities and cultures due to mechanical reproduction, so as to defend the legitimate interests from individuals to countries and then to the whole world, remove the pseudo modernity and the false world and establish the real modernity and the true world.

Cultural computing should first form a self-restraint mechanism and consciously resist pseudo-modernism, and then set up a system for distinguishing the real from the pseudo in Bie-modernist cultural computing.

Visual Identification System

Visual Identification System of Bie-modernist focuses on the identification and shaping of real and pseudo images under the theme of distinguishing real modernity or the true world and the pseudo modernity or the false world, explores the famous images in Chinese classical novels, and embodies the spirit of seeking truth of Bie- modernism: for example, the identification of real and pseudo Sun Wukong/Monkey King in Chinese classical novel Journey to the West, the identification of real and pseudo Li Kui in Outlaws of the Marsh, and the identification of male and female in ancient poem Hua Mulan discrimination and its shaping. From here, we can deduce some works of art with culture computing support and rich flavor of the times and aesthetic heritage, excavate and establish the most essential characteristics of the characters. At the same time, combined with the background of the times and the humanistic environment, we can build a supporting platform for calculating the characteristics of the characters, and combine big data and NLP and other computer technologies to identify the real and pseudo characters.

Digital Identification System

At present, in the global scope, the problem of real and pseudo artifacts has become increasingly prominent, and its intensity has reached or even exceeded the real and pseudo duel in Chinese classical novels. China is the only country that has set up "March 15 Cracking Down on Counterfeit Goods" festival in the world, which also shows that the project not only has cultural value, but also has practical significance. The technology of real and pseudo identification has a wide application prospect in reality. From the perspective of cultural value, the feature model library of real and pseudo identification system is built to form a new foundation of digital global identification system.

3 The Necessity and Significance of Distinguishing the Real from the Pseudo in Bie-Modernist Culture Computing

3.1 Necessity

It is urgent for us to distinguish the real from the pseudo. Taking the U.S. presidential election as an example, the phenomenon of fraud will also appear in the machine voting, which shows the rampancy of pseudo modernity in the world and the necessity and urgency of establishing a global digital identification system.

3.2 Significance

The purpose of establishing the global Bie-modernist cultural computing authenticity identification system is to protect everyone's rights from infringement, protect everyone's conscience and dignity from pollution, remove the fake and shoddy, and safeguard the synchronous and healthy development of human spiritual civilization and material civilization.

3.3 Technical Support

The technical support for the establishment of global Bie-modernist cultural computing authenticity identification system comes from digital image identification technology, quantum computing technology and holographic energy system technology. These three technologies can form a whole rapid recognition from the dimension of holography and the ability of light speed calculation, from image to connotation.

3.4 A Proposal for a Global Bie-Modernist Cultural Computing System to Identify the Real and Pseudo

The establishment of a global Bie-modernist cultural computing authenticity identification system will be included in the main topic of this conference, which will be discussed in the plenary session.

Global cooperation is carried out around the global Bie-modernist cultural computing authenticity identification system, including technology equity, capital integration, cooperative experiment, joint development, joint use, etc.

4 Examples of Bie-Modernist Visual Identification Systems

Relate Work

This section will mainly discuss the deep learning method of character identification based on text information, analyze the advantages and disadvantages of some algorithms, and finally explain the reasons why this algorithm is suitable for this research.

4.1 Document Classification Algorithm

Document classification is one of the most common applications in natural language processing. It aims to solve the problem of how to accurately classify a document or a piece of text given it. Document categorization often requires a combination of traditional text processing techniques and machine learning or deep learning algorithms to accomplish tasks such as "categorizing" documents.

The main ideas of document classification algorithm are document annotation, document format conversion, dictionary generation, word weight calculation, topic modeling, training classification model, prediction and so on. In the process of training classification model, machine learning model, such as support vector machine, logistic regression model, etc., can be applied, or the method of constructing neural network classifier based on deep learning, which is popular in recent years, can be applied for document classification task.

This paper focuses on the research of character identification task, which is also a classification task based on text information. From the input level, the document classification task and the character identification character studied in this topic are both text information. In the output level, document classification algorithm mainly focused on the multiple classification problems, which is in the limited class number on the document's exact algorithm to estimate the category, and the purpose of this paper is to target detection, namely, through the characters' words and deeds, appearance, wear, surface characteristics, such as into the character's personality, background of the characters and the characters' behavior to better deeper characteristics, such as a character identification. Because the character identification task is not a simple classification problem.

In addition to the algorithm idea, the character identification task studied in this paper can use the document classification algorithm for reference; At the same time, part of the implementation steps of document classification algorithm can also be used for reference. Input text information, generate part of the dictionary information, and finally generate deep character characteristics for character identification.

4.2 Word Segmentation Algorithm

For most current models of natural language processing algorithms, word segmentation is the most basic work. The so-called word segmentation is the process of regrouping successive word sequences through certain norms. Because the difference between Chinese and English is that there are Spaces between English words, it is easy to distinguish each word, while Chinese only has punctuation marks between sentences, and there is no way to divide between words, so the word segmentation of Chinese text is more complex than the word segmentation task of English text.

At present, Chinese word segmentation algorithms can be roughly divided into three categories. The first type is based on string matching. This method mainly scans the string and matches if the substring of the string is found to be the same as the word in the dictionary. The second category is a word segmentation method based on statistics and machine learning, which primarily based on the artificial marking of parts of speech and statistical characteristics of the Chinese model, namely according to annotating corpus information training of model parameter, in the segmentation stage through model to compute the probability of each word appears, will be the biggest probability segmentation results as the final result. At present, common sequence labeling models include HMM [1] and CRF [2]. The core idea of the third type of Chinese word segmentation algorithm is to make the computer simulate human's understanding of the sentence and then produce the result of word segmentation. Although this kind of algorithm has not been applied specifically yet, it is also the main direction of future research.

For the deep learning character identification based on text information studied in this paper, the N-gram [3] model based on statistics and machine learning is adopted. The model is based on the assumption that the occurrence of the Nth word is only related to the first n-1 words and not to any other words, and that the probability of the whole sentence is the product of the occurrence probabilities of each word. In this paper, n is set as 3 and the Trigram model [4] is adopted, because the high-order n-gram is sensitive to more context, but the data has more sparseness, while the low-order n-gram considers very limited context information, but has stronger robustness. Therefore, the Trigram model is chosen based on comprehensive considerations.

Similarly, this paper also adopts the classic Jieba participle [5]. Jieba, the most commonly used Chinese word segmentation tool today, comes with a dictionary called "dict.txt", which contains more than 20,000 words, including the number of entries and part of speech. These more than 20,000 words are put into a TRIE tree for word map scanning. TRIE tree is a well-known prefix tree, that is to say, if the first few words of a word are the same, they have the same prefix, and can be stored using TRIE tree, which has the advantage of fast search speed.

4.3 Word2Vec Algorithm

Since the parameters of the Ngram model [6] will increase explosively with N, the value of N is generally no more than 3. In addition, the Ngram model only considers the foreword of each predicted word, but ignores the internal relations and similarities among words. As the Ngram model treats words as isolated units, for each word, it corresponds to a one-hot vector. In the Ngram model, the length of the vector corresponding to each word is the size of the lexicon. If there are thousands of words in the corpus, then the problem of the dimension explosion of the word vector is faced.

In order to solve the problem of Ngram model, Bengio et al. [7] proposed the concept of word embedding in 2003, which mainly solved the two major problems of conditional probability calculation in statistical language model and expression of word vector in vector space model. However, there are still some limitations in the language model. At present, the main bottleneck is that the model is still difficult to deal with the variable length sequence and the slow training speed. In order to solve this problem, Mikolov et al. [8] proposed a Word2vec method. Word2vec is mainly divided into two models: CBOW [9] and Skip gram [10]. The former predicts the central word according to the context of the central word, and the latter, on the contrary, uses the central word to predict the context. At the same time, there are two optimization algorithms in Word2vec: Hierarchical Softmax and Negative Sampling. The former decomposes the complex normalized probability into a series of conditional probabilities and uses Huffman tree to improve the training efficiency, while the latter is mainly to transform the likelihood function of the model to solve the problem of parameter estimation of the probability model that cannot be normalized.

In view of the subject studied in this paper, the main function of Word2Vec is to vectorize the input text, specifically, it is to vectorize the "word" of the input text to get the densely-word vector that can represent the semantics, so as to do a good job of the basic work for the subsequent steps of the algorithm.

4.4 DOC2Vec Algorithm

After each word vector of the text is obtained by Word2vec algorithm, it is how to associate the word vector with the document vector of the input text, that is, how to generate the document vector with the acquired word vector, and keep the semantic richness and high quality of Word2vec word vector.

In order to solve this problem, Doc2Vec [11] algorithm was put forward in 2014. It is an unsupervised learning algorithm, which can obtain the vector representation of sentences, paragraphs and documents, which is an extension of Word2Vec. Doc2vec is to add the document vector as an additional input when the word vector is entered in the input layer, which will be mapped to the projection layer together with other word vectors for cascading or averaging.

In view of the content studied in this paper, Doc2vec model is used to directly obtain the document topic vector representation, that is, each text for each character can use Doc2vec algorithm to obtain the character's text feature vector set as the input vector set for training.

4.5 Convolutional Neural Network

Convolutional Neural Network (CNN) [12] is a neural network model developed in recent years and widely used on a large scale. At present, it is mainly used in the field of image processing, but some scholars have gradually introduced CNN into the field of natural language processing.

Convolutional neural network is mainly composed of convolutional layer, pooling layer and full connection layer. The convolution layer is mainly composed of filters and activation functions. The pooling layer is used to set the pooling mode of the network model. The full-connection layer is a row of fully connected neurons used in the neural network.

And in this paper, based on the characters of text information identification mainly is to use the network to handle or word document matrix vector matrix spliced into the document, using the network can reduce model complexity, extract the key features in the document, improve training efficiency and generalization ability of the model, by CNN, can obtain a lower dimension, higher would be the document vector.

4.6 Personal Character Algorithm

In this paper, we study person's character identification task, so we need according-ing to the surface characteristics of a given character (including demeanor, wearing, appearance), etc., this paper USES the data set is in the story of journey to the west, about the depiction of the characters, mainly to extract the Sun wukong, Zhubajie, Tangseng, Shaseng character's dialogue, get the character's personality traits, and other characteristics of deeper.

The quantitative methods of personality have been studied for more than 100 years, and the Big Five Theory of Personality [13] has been widely used in the research of personality algorithms. The personality descriptions in the Big Five Personality Theory were mainly covered by five traits – Openness, Conscientiousness, Extroversion, Agreeableness and Neuroticism. Openness mainly reflects the degree to which individuals accept new things. People who score high in openness tend to be more willing to explore the unknown field and keep an open attitude to knowledge or life state that they have never touched. People who score lower tend to be conformist, conservative and traditional. The sense of responsibility mainly reflects the degree of self-control of individuals. People with high sense of responsibility are usually reliable and trustworthy. People who score low tend to have low self-control. Extroversion, on the other hand, mainly reflects the ability to have fun with others. People who score high on extroversion tend to be more sociable, while those who score low on extroversion tend to be more cautious and introverted. Agreeableness mainly reflects the individual's attitude towards other individuals. High scores of agreeableness are usually attributed to those who are sympathetic and easy to trust others. People who score low on agreeableness tend to be scheming and ruthless. Neuroticism is the performance of the character's individual emotional regulation, mainly reflects the emotional instability. People who score high on neuroticism tend to have more intense expression of external stimuli, while those who score low on neuroticism have better emotional management.

Algorithm

4.7 Overall Introduction to the Algorithm

In this paper, Word2vec model + CNN algorithm model is adopted at first. First adopted Jieba segmentation method to statistical occurrences of names in "the journey to the west", and the "Xingzhe", "Bajie", "Shifu", "Meihouwang", "sanzang", "tang seng", "shaseng", and "heshang" add custom thesaurus, through Jieba participle tool loading custom key library to improve the effect of word segmentation.

4.8 Word2vec and Parameter Settings

Then the results of word segmentation are vectorized by Word2vec model. The parameters for Word2Vec are set to min_count = 1, size = 50, window = 5, workers = −1. Min_count can truncate the dictionary, and words whose word frequency is less than the number of min_count will be discarded. Here, it is set to 1, indicating that no word will be given up when training the document vector. Window = 5 represents the window size, indicating the maximum distance that the current word can predict the word in a sentence. Workers indicate how many CPUs are currently in use for training, depending on how many cores the CPU has, and Workers = −1 indicates that all of the current CPUs are used for training the task.

After the word vectors are obtained using word2vec, all the word vectors are stitched together into a document matrix for each description of the person.

Subsequently, the convolutional neural network is required for processing. The convolutional processing is carried out through 300 convolutional kernels with a height of 2, 3 and 4, and then the results obtained are pooled to the maximum to obtain a 300-dimensional feature document vector.

The flow chart of the whole algorithm is shown as follows (Fig. 2):

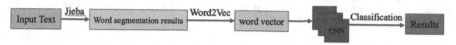

Fig. 2. The flow of the algorithm

4.9 Experimental Demonstration

Data Preparation
For the character identification task studied in this paper, it is mainly based on the "static text" data to get the deeper character characteristics, and at the same time, combined with the background, history and other factors of the character, to accurately identify the character. At the same time, the algorithm used in this paper has a certain universality.

In the selection of input text, Journey to the West is selected as the main analysis text. Journey to the West is one of the four great masterpieces of China. Although the length of the characters is not very long, each character in the novel is very distinct under the description of the author Wu Cheng 'en, so it has a certain representative significance for research. At the same time, the use of Journey to the West as the analysis of characters in this paper has a certain authority, and has a certain practical and reference significance in the related issues of natural language processing.

Display of Analysis Results
Based on the static text information in Journey to the West and the character analysis algorithm, the characters in Journey to the West are deeply characterized. The final result is as follows (Table 1):

The prediction results reflect the five major personality scores of the characters, and show the orientation of the characters in each dimension, which can be used as the polarization analysis of the characters. At the same time, it is proved that when the surface features are obtained, the deep features of the characters can be obtained through the above algorithm model, and finally the function of character identification can be realized.

Experimental Summary
In particular, this paper chose the "Journey to the West" 58, the true and false Sun Wukong/Monkey King chapters in the back will be compared with the characteristics of the six ears rhesus monkey Sun Wukong found according to the text and dialogue

Table 1. The character analysis algorithm in Journey to the West

Name	Sunwukong/Monkey King	Tangseng/Master	Zhubajie/Second elder brother	Shaseng/Youngest brother
Agreeableness	64.13	82.12	78.23	85.48
Conscientiousness	73.12	93.42	63.21	92.13
Extroversion	93.16	68.93	87.16	64.27
Openness	82.97	78.32	88.74	59.48
Neuroticism	85.31	56.43	73.28	43.25

information (i.e., the characteristics of the surface), are the two basic characteristics of deep (features) is similar, but the combination of factors such as the background of the characters, it is known that six ears macaques and Sun Wukong/Monkey King for different historical background, thus can identify true and false Sun Wukong characters. Thus, the work of character identification studied in this paper is realized.

References

1. Wikipedia "Bie-modernism". www.biemodernism.org, biemodern.net, website home page
2. Wang, J.: Bie-Modern: Space Encounter and Time Span, Preface. China Social Sciences Press (2017)
3. Rauterberg, M., Hu, J., Langereis, G.: Cultural computing – how to investigate a form of unconscious user experiences in mixed realities. In: Nakatsu, R., Tosa, N., Naghdy, F., Wong, K.W., Codognet, P. (eds.) ECS 2010. IAICT, vol. 333, pp. 190–197. Springer, Heidelberg (2010). https://doi.org/10.1007/978-3-642-15214-6_19
4. Rauterberg, M.: Reality determination through action. In: Proceedings of IEEE International Conference on Culture and Computing - C&C, pp. 24–29. IEEE, Piscataway (2017)
5. Mikolov, T., Sutskever, I., Chen, K., et al.: Distributed representations of words and phrases and their compositionality. In: Neural Information Processing Systems, pp. 3111–3119 (2013)
6. Yin, Z.Y., Jiang, Y., He, J.: Analysis of mobile internet multi-context user preference. Adv. Eng. Res. (AER) **130**, 1175–1180 (2017). https://doi.org/10.2991/fmsmt-17.2017.232
7. Levy, O., Goldberg, Y.: Dependency-based word embeddings. In: Proceedings of the 52nd Annual Meeting of the Association for Computational Linguistics (Volume 2: Short Papers), vol. 2, pp. 302–308 (2014)
8. Pennington, J., Socher, R., Manning, C.: GloVe: global vectors for word representation. In: Proceedings of the 2014 Conference on Empirical Methods in Natural Language Processing (EMNLP), pp. 1532–1543 (2014)
9. De Marneffe, M.C., Manning, C.D.: Stanford typed dependencies manual. Technical report, Stanford University (2008)
10. Bamman, D., Popat, S., Shen, S.: An annotated dataset of literary entities. In: Proceedings of the 2019 Conference of the North American Chapter of the Association for Computational Linguistics: Human Language Technologies, Volume 1 (Long and Short Papers), pp. 2138–2144 (2019)
11. Qiu, L., Zhang, Y.: Word segmentation for Chinese novels. In: Twenty-Ninth AAAI Conference on Artificial Intelligence (2015)

12. Frermann, L., Szarvas, G.: Inducing semantic micro-clusters from deep multi-view representations of novels. In: Proceedings of the 2017 Conference on Empirical Methods in Natural Language Processing, pp. 1873–1883 (2017)
13. Massey, P., Xia, P., Bamman, D., et al.: Annotating character relationships in literary texts. arXiv preprint arXiv:1512.00728 (2015)
14. Bamman, D., O'Connor, B., Smith, N.A.: Learning latent personas of film characters. In: Proceedings of the 51st Annual Meeting of the Association for Computational Linguistics (Volume 1: Long Papers), vol. 1, pp. 352–361 (2013)
15. Neal, T., Sundararajan, K., Fatima, A., et al.: Surveying stylometry techniques and applications. ACM Comput. Surv. (CSUR) **50**(6), 86 (2018)
16. Hammond, A., Brooke, J., Hirst, G.: A tale of two cultures: bringing literary analysis and computational linguistics together. In: Proceedings of the Workshop on Computational Linguistics for Literature, pp. 1–8 (2013)
17. Elson, D.K., Dames, N., McKeown, K.R.: Extracting social networks from literary fiction. In: Proceedings of the 48th Annual Meeting of the Association for Computational Linguistics, pp. 138–147. Association for Computational Linguistics (2010)

Correction to: Memory Modalities Opening-up Digital Heritage Infrastructures

Gertraud Koch

Correction to:
Chapter "Memory Modalities Opening-up Digital Heritage Infrastructures" in: M. Rauterberg (Ed.):
Culture and Computing, **LNCS 12795,**
https://doi.org/10.1007/978-3-030-77431-8_15

In the originally published version of chapter 15, reference 33 contained an error in the DOI. This has now been corrected.

The updated version of this chapter can be found at
https://doi.org/10.1007/978-3-030-77431-8_15

Author Index

Printed in the United States
by Baker & Taylor Publisher Services